PMP®
Project Management
Professional Study Guide
Fifth Edition

ABOUT THE AUTHORS

Joseph Phillips, PMP, PMI-ACP, ITIL, Project+, CTT+, is the Director of Education for Instructing.com, LLC. He has managed and consulted on projects for industries including technical, pharmaceutical, manufacturing, and architectural, among others. Joseph has served as a project management consultant for organizations creating project offices, maturity models, and best-practice standardization.

As a leader in adult education, Joseph has taught organizations how to successfully implement project management methodologies, adaptive project management, information technology project management, risk management, and other courses. He has taught at Columbia College, University of Chicago, Ball State University, and for corporate clients like IU Health, the State of Indiana, and Berkeley Laboratories. A Certified Technical Trainer, Joseph has taught more than 50,000 professionals and has contributed as an author or editor to more than 35 books on technology, careers, and project management.

Joseph is a member of the Project Management Institute and is active in local project management chapters. He has spoken on project management, project management certifications, and project methodologies at numerous trade shows, PMI chapter meetings, and employee conferences in the United States and in Europe. When not writing, teaching, or consulting, Joseph can be found behind a camera or on the working end of a fly rod. You can contact him through www.instructing.com.

About the Technical Editor

Todd C. Williams is a consultant, author, expert witness, and educator who helps companies build a comprehensive strategic foundation coupled with execution excellence to help them thrive. He has published two books. *Filling Execution Gaps: How Executives And Project Managers Turn Corporate Strategy Into Successful Projects* (De Gruyter, 2017) describes how to fill six critical gaps that prevent organizations from turning strategy into successful projects—common understanding, executive sponsorship, effective governance, change management, corporate goal to project alignment, and leadership. *Rescue the Problem Project: A Complete Guide to Identifying, Preventing, and Recovering from Project Failure* (AMACOM, 2011) defines a project audit and recovery process for rescuing red projects that focuses on root-cause correction and prevention.

He also writes for *The CEO Magazine, American Management Association*, and his own *Back From Red* blog, and he contributes to numerous other publications, including *Fortune/ CNN Money, CIO Magazine, CIO Update, ZDNet, Enterprising CIO*, and *IT Business Edge*. He is also an internationally acclaimed speaker and educator who makes more than 40 presentations a year throughout the United States, Canada, United Kingdom, and European Union.

PMP®
Project Management
Professional Study Guide
Fifth Edition

Joseph Phillips

New York   Chicago   San Francisco   Athens
London   Madrid   Mexico City   Milan
New Delhi   Singapore   Sydney   Toronto

Library of Congress Cataloging-in-Publication Data

Names: Phillips, Joseph, author.
Title: PMP : project management professional study guide / Joseph Phillips.
Description: Fifth edition. | New York : McGraw-Hill Education, [2018] |
    Includes index.
Identifiers: LCCN 2017054917 | ISBN 9781259861987 (alk. paper)
Subjects: LCSH: Project management—Examinations—Study guides.
Classification: LCC HD69.P75 P4946 2018 | DDC 658.4/04—dc23 LC record available at
https://lccn.loc.gov/2017054917

McGraw-Hill Education books are available at special quantity discounts to use as premiums and sales promotions, or for use in corporate training programs. To contact a representative, please visit the Contact Us pages at www.mhprofessional.com.

PMP® Project Management Professional Study Guide, Fifth Edition

3 4 5 6 7 8 9   LCR   21 20

ISBN: Book p/n 978-1-259-86195-6, CD p/n 978-1-259-86196-3, and insert p/n 978-1-259-86199-4
of set 978-1-259-86198-7

MHID: Book p/n 1-259-86195-3, CD p/n 1-259-86196-1, and insert p/n 978-1-259-86199-6
of set 1-259-86198-8

Sponsoring Editor *Wendy Rinaldi*	**Technical Editor** *Todd Williams*	**Composition** *Cenveo Publisher Services*
Editorial Supervisor *Jody McKenzie*	**Copy Editor** *Lisa Theobald*	**Illustration** *Cenveo Publisher Services*
Project Manager *Jyotsna Ojha,* *Cenveo® Publisher Services*	**Proofreaders** *Richard Camp*	**Art Director, Cover** *Jeff Weeks*
Acquisitions Coordinator *Claire Yee*	**Indexer** *Jack Lewis*	**Cover Designer** *Peter Grame*
	Production Supervisor *James Kussow*	

*For the love of my life, Natalie...thank you for the encouragement,
laughs, friendship, and time to write.*

CONTENTS AT A GLANCE

Part I
Project Initiation

1   Introducing Project Management 3

2   Managing Projects in Different Environments 63

3   Serving as a Project Manager 103

Part II
PMP Exam Essentials: Knowledge Areas

4   Implementing Project Integration Management 147

5   Managing the Project Scope 225

6   Introducing Project Schedule Management 279

7   Introducing Project Cost Management 355

8   Introducing Project Quality Management 409

9   Introducing Project Resource Management 459

10 Introducing Project Communications Management 515

11 Introducing Project Risk Management 555

12 Introducing Project Procurement Management 623

13 Introducing Project Stakeholder Management 675

14 The PMI Code of Ethics and Professional Conduct 719

Part III
Appendices

A   Critical Exam Information 745

B   About the CD-ROM 761

     Glossary 765

     Index 807

CONTENTS

Preface .... *xxv*

Acknowledgments .... *xxix*

Introduction .... *xxxi*

Exam Readiness Checklist .... *xxxii*

Part I
Project Initiation

1 Introducing Project Management **3**

The *PMBOK Guide*, This Book, and the PMP Exam 4

    All About the *PMBOK Guide* 4

    All About This Book 5

    All About the PMP Exam 6

    Code of Ethics and Professional Conduct 10

Defining What a Project Is—and Is Not 10

    Projects Create Unique Products, Services, or Results 11

    Projects Are Temporary 11

    Projects Change Things and Environments 12

    Projects Create Business Value 13

    Consider the Project Initiation Context 13

Defining Project Management 13

    Tailoring the Project Process 18

Examining Related Areas of Project Management 19

    Exploring Program Management 19

    Consider Project Portfolio Management 20

    Implementing Subprojects 22

    Projects vs. Operations 23

    Projects and Business Value 25

Revving Through the Project Life Cycle 25

    Working with a Project Life Cycle 26

    Project Phase Deliverables 33

Defining Project Management Data and Information 38

    Understanding Data and Information 38

    Reviewing a Project Business Case 39

    Creating a Project Benefits Management Plan 40

Certification Summary 40

    Key Terms 41

  ✓ Two-Minute Drill 45

Q&A Self Test 48

    Self Test Answers 53

2   Managing Projects in Different Environments 63

Utilizing Enterprise Environmental Factors 64

    Reviewing Internal Enterprise Environmental Factors 64

    Reviewing External Enterprise Environmental Factors 65

Leveraging Organizational Process Assets 66

    Recognizing Common Organizational Process Assets 67

    Utilizing Organizational Knowledge Repositories 68

Working with Organizational Systems 68

    Examine Organizational Governance Frameworks 69

    Consider Portfolio, Programs, and Project Governance 70

    Relying on General Management Skills 70

    Considering Organizational Culture 72

Completing Projects in Different Organizational Structures 73

    Working in an Organic, or a Simple, Structure 74

    Managing Projects in Functional Organizations 74

    Dealing with Multidivisional Structures 75

    Managing in Matrix Structures 76

    Serving in a Virtual Organization 77

    Managing Projects in Hybrid Organizations 78

    Operating Under Project Management Offices 78

Certification Summary 82

    Key Terms 82

  ✓ Two-Minute Drill 86

Q&A Self Test 88

    Self Test Answers 93

3   Serving as a Project Manager 103

Defining the Project Management Role 104

    Leading the Project Team 105

    Communicating Project Information 105

    Negotiating Project Terms and Conditions 107

    Active Problem Solving 107

Exploring the Project Manager Influence 108

    Influencing the Project 110

    Influencing the Organization 111

Managing Social, Economic,
and Environmental Project Influences 111
Considering International Influences 112
Reviewing Cultural and Industry Influences 112
Building the Project Management Competencies 113
Considering Your Skills and Competencies 113
Exploring the PMI Talent Triangle 114
Recognizing Politics in Project Management 116
Leading and Managing the Project 118
Exploring Leadership Styles 118
Applying a Leadership Personality 119
Performing Project Integration 121
Examining Process-Level Integration 121
Examining Cognitive-Level Integration 122
Examining Context-Level Integration 123
Certification Summary 123
Key Terms 124
✓ Two-Minute Drill 127
Q&A Self Test 129
Self Test Answers 135

Part II
PMP Exam Essentials: Knowledge Areas

4 **Implementing Project Integration Management** **147**

Exploring Project Integration Management 149
Considering Trends for Project Integration Management 150
Tailoring Project Integration Management 151
Considering Project Integration Management
in Agile Environments 152
Developing the Project Charter 153
Creating the Project Charter 154
Examining Benefit Measurement Methods 158
Examining Constrained Optimization Methods 162
Developing the Project Management Plan 163
Understanding the Project Plan's Purpose 164
Preparing to Develop the Project Plan 164
Applying Tools and Techniques for
Project Plan Development 165
Examining the Typical Project Plan 167

Directing and Managing the Project Work 173
    Applying Corrective Action 174
    Considering Preventive Actions 174
    Managing Defect Repair 174
    Managing Change Requests 174
    Implementing Tools and Techniques for Project Execution 175
    Examining the Outputs of Project Plan Execution 176
Managing Project Knowledge 179
    Preparing to Manage Knowledge 180
    Reviewing Knowledge Management Tools and Techniques 181
    Reviewing the Results of Knowledge Management 182
Monitoring and Controlling the Project Work 183
    Preparing for Monitoring and Controlling Processes 183
    Creating Work Performance Information 184
    Reviewing the Final Inputs for Monitoring and Controlling 184
    Using Monitoring and Controlling Tools and Techniques 185
    Examining the Results of Project Work 187
Performing Integrated Change Control 188
    Implementing Tools and Techniques
      for Integrated Change Control 190
    Deciding on Project Changes 193
    Revisiting Planning Processes 193
    Evaluating the Outputs of Integrated Change Control 194
Closing the Project or Phase 194
    Preparing to Close the Project or Phase 194
    Closing the Project or Phase 196
    Reviewing the Results of Project Closure 197
Certification Summary 198
    Key Terms 200
   ✓ Two-Minute Drill 207
Q&A Self Test 209
    Self Test Answers 215

5 Managing the Project Scope **225**

Exploring Project Scope Management 226
    Tailoring Project Scope Management 227
Planning Project Scope Management 228
    Project Scope vs. Product Scope 229
    Creating the Scope Management Plan 230

Using Scope Planning Tools and Techniques 230
Creating the Scope Management Plan 231
Collecting and Eliciting Requirements 232
Interview the Stakeholders 234
Leading a Focus Group 234
Relying on Surveys 234
Leveraging Data Analysis 235
Making Group Decisions on Requirements 235
Using Group Decisions 237
Hosting a Requirements Workshop 238
Utilizing a Context Diagram 238
Creating Prototypes 239
Observing Stakeholders 239
Benchmarking the Requirements 240
Managing the Requirements 240
Defining the Project Scope 241
Examining the Inputs to Scope Definition 242
Consulting with Experts 242
Finding Alternatives 243
Facilitating Meetings and Workshops 243
Using Product Analysis 243
Examining the Project Scope Statement 244
Reviewing the Project Document Updates 245
Creating the Work Breakdown Structure 246
Using a Work Breakdown Structure Template 247
Decomposing the Project Deliverables 248
Defining the Scope Baseline 249
Validating the Scope 250
Examining the Inputs to Scope Validation 251
Inspecting the Project Work 251
Formally Accepting the Project Deliverables 252
Controlling the Scope 252
Examining the Inputs to Scope Control 253
Considering the Results of Controlling Scope 255
Certification Summary 257
Key Terms 257
✓   Two-Minute Drill 261
Q&A   Self Test 263
Self Test Answers 269

6 Introducing Project Schedule Management **279**

Exploring Project Schedule Management 280
    Tailoring Project Schedule Management 281
    Considerations for Agile and Adaptive Environments 281
Creating the Schedule Management Plan 283
    Building the Schedule Management Plan 283
    Exploring the Schedule Management Plan 284
Defining the Activities 285
    Getting to Work: Defining the Activities 286
    Relying on Templates 287
    Decomposing the Project Work Packages 287
    Using Rolling Wave Planning 287
    Using Planning Components 288
    Compiling the Activity List 288
    Documenting the Activity Attributes 289
    Finalizing Activity Definition 290
Sequencing Activities 291
    Considering the Inputs to Activity Sequencing 292
    Creating Network Diagrams 292
    Using the Precedence Diagramming Method 292
    Determining the Activity Dependencies 294
    Considering Leads and Lags 295
    Utilizing Network Templates 296
    Examining the Sequencing Outputs 296
    Using a Project Network Diagram 297
    Updating the Project Documents 297
Estimating Activity Durations 298
    Considering the Activity Duration Estimates Inputs 298
    Estimating the Project Work Considerations 300
    Considering Resource Availability 301
    Considering the Calendars 302
    Creating a Resource Breakdown Structure 302
    Updating the Activity List 303
    Applying Expert Judgment 303
    Creating an Analogy 304
    Applying Parametric Estimates 304
    Creating a Three-Point Estimate 305
    Creating a Bottom-Up Estimate 306
    Using the Delphi Technique 306

Using the Fist-to-Five Approach 307
Factoring in Reserve Time 307
Evaluating the Estimates 308
Developing the Schedule 310
Revisiting the Project Network Diagram 310
Relying on Activity Duration Estimates 311
Evaluating the Project Constraints 311
Reevaluating the Assumptions 313
Evaluating the Risk Management Register 313
Examining the Activity Attributes 313
Defining the Project Timeline 313
Performing Schedule Network Analysis 314
Calculating Float in a PND 315
Encountering Scheduling on the PMP Exam 318
Optimizing Resource Utilization 318
Applying Duration Compression 320
Using a Project Simulation 321
Using Project Management Software 322
Relying on a Project Coding Structure 322
Examining the Project Schedule 323
Utilizing the Schedule Management Plan 324
Updating the Resource Requirements 324
Planning the Schedule in Agile Environments 324
Reviewing the Results of Developing the Schedule 324
Controlling the Schedule 325
Managing the Inputs to Schedule Control 326
Measuring Project Performance 327
Examining the Schedule Variance 327
Updating the Project Schedule 328
Applying Corrective Action 328
Writing the Lessons Learned 328
Certification Summary 329
Key Terms 330
✓ Two-Minute Drill 334
Q&A Self Test 337
Self Test Answers 343

7   Introducing Project Cost Management 355
Exploring Project Cost Management 356
Tailoring the Project Cost Management Approach 356

Planning the Project Costs 357
    Considering the Cost Planning Inputs 358
    Creating the Cost Management Plan 358
Estimating the Project Costs 359
    Considering the Cost Estimating Inputs 360
    Estimating Project Costs 364
    Using Analogous Estimating 365
    Using Parametric Estimating 365
    Using Bottom-Up Estimating 367
    Creating a Three-Point Cost Estimate 367
    Analyzing Data for Cost Estimating 368
    Using Computer Software 369
    Making Decisions in Cost Estimating 369
    Analyzing Cost Estimating Results 369
    Refining the Cost Estimates 370
    Considering the Supporting Detail 370
Creating a Project Budget 371
    Developing the Project Budget 372
    Creating the Cost Baseline 373
    Establishing Project Funding Requirements 373
Implementing Cost Control 374
    Considering Cost Control Inputs 375
    Managing Changes to Costs 375
Measuring Project Performance 376
    Finding the Variances 377
    Calculating the Cost Performance Index 378
    Finding the Schedule Performance Index 378
    Preparing for the Estimate at Completion 378
    Calculating the To-Complete Performance Index 380
    Finding the Estimate to Complete 380
    Finding the Variance at Completion 382
    The Five EVM Formula Rules 382
    Additional Planning 383
    Using Computers 384
    Considering the Cost Control Results 384
    Creating Change Requests 384
    Updating Lessons Learned 385
Certification Summary 386
    Key Terms 387

✓   Two-Minute Drill 391
Q&A   Self Test 394
       Self Test Answers 400

8   Introducing Project Quality Management 409

Looking at the Big Quality Picture 410
    Accepting the Quality Management Approach 410
    Quality vs. Grade 411
    Implementing Quality Project Management 412
    Tailoring Quality in Project Management 413
    Considering Quality in Agile Environments 413
Preparing for Quality 414
    Determining the Quality Policy 415
    Reviewing the Scope Baseline 415
    Consider Schedule and Costs 416
    Reviewing the Standards and Regulations 417
Planning for Quality Management 417
    Applying Benchmarking Practices 418
    Brainstorming and Interviews 419
    Using a Benefit/Cost Analysis 419
    Considering the Cost of Quality 420
    Utilizing Multicriteria Decision Analysis Tools 420
    Representing Data in Quality Management Planning 421
    Planning for Testing and Inspection 421
    Creating the Quality Management Plan 421
    Identifying the Quality Metrics 422
Managing Quality 422
    Preparing to Manage Quality 423
    Managing Quality for a Project 423
    Completing a Quality Audit 424
    Utilizing the Design for X Approach 425
    Implementing Problem-Solving Techniques 425
    Reviewing the Results of Managing Quality 425
Implementing Control Quality 426
    Preparing for Quality Control 427
    Inspecting Results 427
    Data Representation Tools 428
    Creating a Control Chart 430
    Creating Pareto Diagrams 432

Creating a Histogram 432
Creating a Run Chart 433
Creating a Scatter Diagram 434
Completing a Statistical Sampling 434
Revisiting Flowcharting 434
Applying Trend Analysis 434
The Results of Quality Control 435
Certification Summary 436
Key Terms 437
✓ Two-Minute Drill 440
Q&A Self Test 442
Self Test Answers 448

9 Introducing Project Resource Management **459**

Exploring Project Resource Management 460
Reviewing Project Resource Management Foundations 461
Exploring Trends in Managing Resources 462
Preparing for Resource Planning 463
Identifying the Resource Requirements 464
Completing Organizational Planning 465
Charting the Project Resources 465
Creating the Role and Responsibility Assignments 466
Relying on Templates 466
Applying Resource Practices 467
Relating to Organizational Theories 467
Creating a Resource Management Plan 471
Creating a Team Charter 472
Estimating Project Activity Resources 473
Preparing to Estimate Activity Resources 474
Estimating the Resources for Activities 474
Reviewing the Results of Estimating Activity Resources 475
Acquiring the Project Resources 475
Preparing to Acquire Project Resources 476
Acquiring the Resources 476
Negotiating for Resources 477
Recruiting Project Team Members 477
Working with Preassigned Staff 478
Acquiring Human Resources 478
Working with Virtual Teams 478
Reviewing the Outputs of Acquiring Resources 479

Developing the Project Team 480
    Preparing to Develop the Project Team 480
    Dealing with Team Locales 481
    Creating Team-Building Activities 481
    Naturally Developing Project Teams 482
    Relying on General Management Skills 482
    Rewarding the Project Team 483
    Training the Project Team 483
    Completing Project Performance Appraisals 483
    Examining the Results of Team Development 484
Managing the Project Team 484
    Dealing with Team Disagreements 485
Controlling Resources 488
    Preparing to Control Resources 489
    Reviewing the Tools and Techniques to Control Resources 489
    Reviewing the Results of Controlling Resources 490
Certification Summary 491
    Key Terms 492
  ✓ Two-Minute Drill 496
Q&A Self Test 498
    Self Test Answers 504

10 Introducing Project Communications Management **515**
Communicating in Projects 516
    Consider Communication Activities 517
    Tailoring Communications in Project Management 518
    Communicating in Agile Environments 519
Planning Communications 519
    Considering the Project Management Plan and Charter 520
    Leveraging Enterprise Environmental Factors 521
    Identifying Communication Requirements 522
    Exploring Communication Technologies 523
    Examining Communication Skills 524
    Creating Successful Communications 525
    Creating the Communications Management Plan 526
Managing Project Communications 527
    Exploring Communication Technology and Methods 528
    Distributing Information 529
    Examining the Results of Communication Management 530

Monitoring Project Communications 530
    Preparing for Communications Monitoring 531
    Reviewing the Monitoring Communications
        Tools and Techniques 532
Reporting Project Performance 532
    Reviewing Project Performance 533
    Completing Trend Analysis 533
    Examining the Results of Performance Reporting 533
Certification Summary 535
    Key Terms 536
  ✓ Two-Minute Drill 538
Q&A Self Test 539
    Self Test Answers 545

11 Introducing Project Risk Management **555**
Building a Strong Risk Understanding 556
    Reviewing Project Risk Considerations 557
    Tailoring Risk Management in Projects 558
Planning for Risk Management 559
    Examining Stakeholder Tolerance 559
    Relying on Risk Management Policies 561
    Creating the Risk Management Plan 561
    Examining the Risk Management Plan 562
    Creating Risk Categories 564
    Using a Risk Management Plan Template 564
Identifying Risks 565
    Preparing for Risk Identification 565
    Identifying the Project Risks 566
    Reviewing Project Documents 567
    Testing the Assumptions 567
    Brainstorming the Project 567
    Using Checklists 568
    Identifying Risks Through Interviews 568
    Analyzing SWOT 569
    Utilizing Diagramming Techniques 569
    Using Prompt Lists 570
    Creating a Risk Register 570
    Creating a Risk Report 571
Using Qualitative Risk Analysis 572
    Preparing for Qualitative Risk Analysis 572
    Completing Qualitative Analysis 573

Applying Probability and Impact 575
Creating a Probability-Impact Matrix 575
Building a Hierarchical Chart 577
Examining the Results of Qualitative Risk Analysis 577
Preparing for Quantitative Risk Analysis 578
Considering the Inputs for Quantitative Analysis 579
Interviewing Stakeholders and Experts 580
Applying Sensitivity Analysis 581
Finding the Expected Monetary Value 581
Using a Decision Tree 582
Using a Project Simulation 583
Examining the Results of Quantitative Risk Analysis 583
Planning for Risk Responses 584
Preparing for Risk Response 584
Creating Risk Responses 585
Escalating the Risk Event 585
Avoiding the Negative Risk and Threats 586
Transferring the Negative Risk 586
Mitigating the Negative Risk 586
Managing the Positive Risks and Opportunities 588
Accepting a Risk 589
Creating a Project Contingency Response 589
Examining the Results of Risk Response Planning 590
Working with Residual Risks 591
Accounting for Secondary Risks 591
Creating Contracts for Risk Response 591
Justifying Risk Reduction 592
Updating the Project Plan 592
Implementing Risk Responses 593
Preparing to Implement Risk Responses 593
Reviewing the Tools and Techniques
  for Implementing Risk Responses 593
Examining the Results of Implementing Risk Responses 594
Monitoring Risks 594
Preparing for Risk Monitoring 595
Completing Risk Monitoring 595
Completing Risk Response Audits 595
Completing Periodic Risk Reviews 596
Using Earned Value Analysis 596
Measuring Technical Performance 596
Completing Additional Risk Planning 596
Examining the Results of Risk Monitoring 597

Certification Summary 598
    Key Terms 598
    ✓ Two-Minute Drill 602
Q&A Self Test 605
    Self Test Answers 611

12 Introducing Project Procurement Management 623

Building the Project Procurement Foundation 624
    Considering Procurement Practices for Projects 625
    Tailoring the Procurement Processes 626
Planning for Purchases 627
    Evaluating the Market Conditions 628
    Referring to the Scope Baseline 628
    Relying on the Project Management Plan 629
    Teaming with Other Organizations 629
    Planning for the Project Requirements 630
    Completing Procurement Planning 630
    Determining to Make or Buy 630
    Using Expert Judgment 632
    Determining the Contract Type 632
    Summary of Contract Types 636
    Using the Statement of Work 636
    Determining the Source Selection Criteria 638
    Reviewing the Procurement Management Plan 639
    Creating the Procurement Documents 640
Conducting Procurements 641
    Procuring Goods and Services 642
    Examining the Results of Contracting 642
    Selecting the Seller 643
    Preparing for Source Selection 643
    Completing the Seller Selection Process 644
    Examining the Results of Conducting Procurement 645
Controlling Procurements 647
    Preparing for Contract Administration 647
    Completing Contract Administration 650
    Inspecting and Auditing the Procurement Process 651
    Reviewing the Results of Procurement Control 651
Certification Summary 652
    Key Terms 653

✓	Two-Minute Drill	657
Q&A	Self Test	658
	Self Test Answers	664

13 Introducing Project Stakeholder Management 675

Building a Strong Stakeholder Management Foundation	676
Leading Stakeholder Management	677
Tailoring the Stakeholder Management Processes	677
Identifying the Project Stakeholders	678
Preparing for Stakeholder Identification	679
Performing Stakeholder Identification	680
Visualizing Stakeholder Influence	681
Reviewing the Results of Stakeholder Identification	682
Planning for Stakeholder Management	683
Organizing the Planning	684
Analyzing Stakeholder Engagement	685
Building the Stakeholder Management Plan	686
Managing Stakeholder Engagement	687
Engaging Stakeholders	688
Examining Results of Stakeholder Engagement	690
Monitoring Stakeholder Engagement	690
Taking Action for Stakeholder Engagement	691
Completing Stakeholder Engagement Monitoring	693
Reviewing the Results of Monitoring Stakeholder Engagement	694
Certification Summary	695
Key Terms	696
✓ Two-Minute Drill	698
Q&A Self Test	700
Self Test Answers	706

14 The PMI Code of Ethics and Professional Conduct 719

Responsibilities to the Profession	720
Complying with Rules and Policies	720
Applying Honesty to the Profession	721
Advancing the Profession	721
Responsibilities to the Customer and to the Public	722
Enforcing Project Management Truth and Honesty	723
Eliminating Inappropriate Actions	723
Respecting Others	724

Certification Summary 724
    Key Terms 724
   ✓ Two-Minute Drill 725
  Q&A Self Test 726
    Self Test Answers 732

Part III
Appendices

A   **Critical Exam Information** **745**

Exam Test-Passing Tips 745
    Days Before the Exam 746
    Practice the Testing Process 746
    Testing Tips 746
    Answer Every Question—Once 747
    Use the Process of Elimination 748
Everything You Must Know 748
    The 49 Project Management Processes 748
    Magic PMP Formulas 750
    Earned Value Management Formulas 750
    Quick PMP Facts 750

B   **About the CD-ROM** **761**

System Requirements 761
Total Tester Premium Practice Exam Software 762
Installing and Running Total Tester
    Premium Practice Exam Software 762
Video Training from the Author 763
Secure PDF Copy of the Book 763
Technical Support 763
    Total Seminars Technical Support 763
    McGraw-Hill Education Content Support 764

    Glossary **765**

    Index **807**

T his book is organized in such a way as to serve as an in-depth review for the PMP Project Management Professional exam for those with a strong foundation in project management, as well as for those who are new PMP candidates. Each chapter covers a major aspect of the exam, with an emphasis on the "why" as well as the "how to" of project management.

Digital Content

For more information regarding the digital content and how to access it, see Appendix B.

■ **Author videos**, provided by the Joseph Phillips, give you in-depth instruction to supplement the book. Be sure to watch the videos when you see the video icon in the book's margin. The video instruction aligns with the content of the chapter in which it appears.

■ **Worksheets and exercises** are available in Excel and PDF formats. The Time Value of Money and Earned Value worksheets help you double-check your math when calculating these formulas. The PDF Float Exercises provide additional practice to help you calculate Project Float in Chapter 6.

Exam Readiness Checklist

At the end of the "Introduction" section coming up, you will find an Exam Readiness Checklist. This table has been constructed to enable you to cross-reference the official exam objectives with the objectives as they are presented and covered in this book. Use the checklist to gauge your level of expertise on each objective at the outset of your studies. Then check your progress and make sure you spend the time you need on more difficult or unfamiliar sections. References have been provided for the objective exactly as the Project Management Institute presents it and related chapter references.

In Every Chapter

We've created a set of chapter components that call your attention to important items, reinforce important points, and provide helpful exam-taking hints. Take a look at what you'll find in every chapter:

- Every chapter begins with **Certification Objectives**—what you need to know to pass the section on the exam dealing with the chapter topic. The objective headings identify the objectives within the chapter, so you'll always know an objective when you see it!

- **Exam Watch** notes call attention to information about, and potential pitfalls in, the exam. These helpful hints are written by the author, who has taken the exams and received his certification—who better to tell you what to worry about? He knows what you're about to go through!

Don't forget that resources are more than just people. Equipment, facilities, and materials are resources, and these can affect the project duration, too.

- **On the Job** notes describe the issues that come up most often in real-world settings. They provide a valuable perspective on certification and product-related topics. They point out common mistakes and address questions that have arisen from on-the-job discussions and experience.

- **Inside the Exam** sidebars highlight some of the most common and confusing problems that students encounter when taking a live exam. Designed to anticipate what the exam will emphasize, getting inside the exam will help you make sure that you know what you need to know to pass it. You can get a leg up on how to respond to those difficult-to-understand questions by focusing extra attention on these sidebars.

- The **PMP Coach** is there to encourage you. It's the author's way of saying, "Keep going and don't give up!"

- The **Certification Summary** is a succinct review of the chapter and a restatement of salient points regarding the exam.

- The **Key Terms** you will need to know for the exam, as well as their definitions, are listed after each Certification Summary.

✓
- The **Two-Minute Drill** at the end of every chapter is a checklist of the main points of the chapter. It can be used for last-minute review.

Q&A
- The **Self Test** offers questions similar to those found on the certification exams. The answers to these questions, as well as explanations of the answers, can be found at the end of each chapter. By taking the Self Test after reading each chapter, you'll reinforce what you've learned from that chapter while becoming familiar with the structure of the exam questions.

Some Pointers

Once you've finished reading this book, set aside some time to do a thorough review. You might want to return to the book several times and make use of all the methods it offers for reviewing the material.

Reread all the Two-Minute Drills, or have someone quiz you. You also can use the drills as a way to do a quick cram before the exam. You might want to make some flashcards out of 3×5 index cards that have the Two-Minute Drill material on them.

Reread all the Exam Watch notes and Inside the Exam elements. Remember that these notes are written by authors who have taken the exam and passed. They know what you should expect—and what you should be on the lookout for.

Retake the Self Tests. Taking the tests right after you've read the chapter is a good idea, because the questions help reinforce what you've just learned. However, it's an even better idea to also go back later and run through all the questions in the book in one sitting. Pretend that you're taking the live exam. When you work through the questions, mark your answers on a separate piece of paper. That way, you can run through the questions as many times as you need to until you feel comfortable with the material.

Study Appendix A: Critical Exam Information. Appendix A should become your best friend. It contains everything you must know to pass the PMP. We've taken the absolutely critical information from the book and condensed it down to just one chunk of information. Appendix A doesn't really explain the concepts (that's what the chapters are for), but it does zoom in on just the most important elements of the entire book.

ACKNOWLEDGMENTS

Books, like projects, are never done alone.

Thank you to Wendy Rinaldi for all of your help, great conversations, and guidance on this book and others. Thank you, Claire Yee, for your management and organization of this book—you are fantastic. Thank you to Jody McKenzie for your keen eye, attention to detail, and for all your hours and help. Lisa Theobald, thank you for helping me be a better writer. Thank you to Production Supervisor Jim Kussow for his work on this book. Thanks also to the production teams at McGraw-Hill Professional and Cenveo Publisher Services for your hard work in making this book a success.

I would also like to thank the hundreds of folks who have attended my PMP Boot Camps over the past couple of years. Your questions, conversations, and recommendations have helped me write a better book. A big thank you to my friends Greg and Mary Huebner, Jonathan Acosta, Brett and Julie Barnett, Don "Just Publish It Already" Kuhnle, Greg Kirkland, Beatrice Best, my Sarasota pals, Monica Morgan, and all my clients. Thank you also to my friends and in-laws Bernie and Alice Morgan. Finally, thanks to my parents, Don and Virginia Phillips, and my old, old brothers, Steve, Mark, Sam, and Ben.

INTRODUCTION

This book is divided into two major parts. Part I, which consists of Chapters 1, 2, and 3, discusses the broad overview of project management and how it pertains to the PMP examination. Part II contains Chapters 4 through 14, which detail each of the ten knowledge areas and the PMI Code of Ethics and Professional Conduct.

If you are just beginning your PMP quest, you should read Part I immediately, because it'll help you build a strong foundation for the PMP exam. If you find, however, that you already have a strong foundation in project management and need specific information on the knowledge areas, move on to Part II. PMP candidates who have years of project management experience can move on to Part II.

The book is designed so that you can read the chapters in any order you'd like. However, if you examine *A Guide to the Project Management Body of Knowledge*, you'll notice that the order of information presented there is the same as the order of information presented in this book. In other words, you can read a chapter of the *PMBOK Guide* and then read a more detailed explanation in this book. This book is a guide to the guide. In addition, practically every question in this book stems directly from the *PMBOK Guide*—so it's a good idea to have the *PMBOK Guide* handy as you read.

The following Exam Readiness Checklist includes all of the exam domains and tasks a project manager will do in each domain. This information is current as of this book's print date. However, it's always a good idea to visit www.pmi.org to see if PMI has made any changes to these exam objectives. Chances are, if history is any indicator, PMI will reorder these topics.

Exam Readiness Checklist

Exam Domain and Exam Percentage	Chapter No.	Beginner	Intermediate	Expert
Initiating the Project......13%				
Conduct project selection methods	1, 3, 4, 13			
Define scope	1, 3, 4, 5, 13, 14			
Document project risks, assumptions, and constraints	1, 3, 5, 11, 14			
Identify and perform stakeholder analysis	1, 2, 3, 4, 5, 10, 13			
Develop project charter	1, 3, 4, 13, 14			
Obtain project charter approval	1, 3, 4, 13			
Planning the Project......24%				
Define and record requirements, constraints, and assumptions	1, 2, 3, 5, 6, 7, 13			
Identify project team and define roles and responsibilities	1, 3, 9, 13, 14			
Create the WBS	1, 5			
Develop change management plan	5			
Identify risks and define risk strategies	11, 14			
Obtain plan approval	1, 4, 13			
Conduct kick-off meeting	4, 5			
Executing the Project......31%				
Execute tasks defined in project plan	1, 4, 5, 6, 7, 14			
Ensure common understanding and set expectations	1, 4, 5, 8, 13			
Implement the procurement of project resources	1, 4, 5, 6, 7, 12, 14			
Manage resource allocation	5, 6, 7, 9, 12, 13, 14			
Implement quality management plan	4, 5, 8			
Implement approved changes	4, 5, 6, 7, 8, 10, 11, 12			
Implement approved actions and workarounds	4, 5, 6, 7, 8, 11			
Improve team performance	4, 9, 13			

Exam Readiness Checklist

Exam Domain and Exam Percentage	Chapter No.	Beginner	Intermediate	Expert
Monitoring and Controlling the Project......25%				
Measure project performance	5, 6, 7, 8, 10, 11			
Verify and manage changes to the project	4, 5, 6, 7, 8, 9, 10, 11, 12, 13			
Ensure project deliverables conform to quality standards	4, 5, 8			
Monitor all risks	4, 5, 11, 14			
Closing the Project......7%				
Obtain final acceptance for the project	4, 5, 10, 13			
Obtain financial, legal, and administrative closure	4, 5, 7, 10, 13			
Release project resources	3, 4, 5, 9, 13, 14			
Identify, document, and communicate lessons learned	4, 5, 6, 7, 8, 9, 10			
Create and distribute final project report	4, 5, 10			
Archive and retain project records	10, 13			
Measure customer satisfaction	1, 3, 4, 8, 9, 10, 13, 14			

Part I

Project Initiation

CHAPTERS

1   Introducing Project Management
2   Managing Projects in Different Environments
3   Serving as a Project Manager

For the most part, if you follow the *PMBOK Guide*, you'll increase your odds of project success. That means you'll be more likely to complete the project scope, reach the cost objectives of your project's budget, and achieve those schedule commitments to which your project must adhere. But there's no guarantee.

PMP
Coach **Throughout this book, you'll see little tips like this one. These tips are here to cheer you on, get you moving, and remind you that you can do this. Create a strategy to study this book and the *PMBOK Guide*, and keep working toward your goal of earning the PMP.**

The *PMBOK Guide* readily admits that not everything in it should be applied to every conceivable project. That just wouldn't make sense. Consider a small project to swap out all of the workstation lights in an office building versus a project to build a skyscraper. Guess which one needs more detail and will likely implement more of the practices the *PMBOK Guide* defines? The skyscraper project, of course.

In the *PMBOK Guide*, sixth edition, PMI tells us that the *PMBOK Guide* is based on *The Standard for Project Management*, another PMI publication that walks through the five process groups of project management (Initiating, Planning, Executing, Monitoring and Controlling, and Closing). In the *PMBOK Guide*, sixth edition, you'll see that *The Standard for Project Management* is now included as part of the *PMBOK Guide*—something new in this edition of the *PMBOK Guide*.

So, what's the difference between the *PMBOK Guide* and *The Standard for Project Management*? There is much overlap between the two publications, but the *PMBOK Guide* offers much more detail on project management concepts, trends, tailoring the processes, and insight to the tools and techniques of project management. *The Standard for Project Management* is a foundational publication that describes, not prescribes, the most common, best practices of project management. This book, and your PMP exam, will focus on the contents of the *PMBOK Guide*, not *The Standard for Project Management*.

All About This Book

Your PMP examination is based largely on the *PMBOK Guide*. As mentioned, the *PMBOK Guide* is not a study guide; this book is. The following explains what this book will do for you:

- Cover all of the objectives as set by PMI for the PMP examination
- Focus only on exam objectives
- Prep you to pass the PMP exam, not just take it
- Encapsulate exam essentials for each exam objective

- Offer 950 PMP total practice questions
- Serve as a handy project management reference guide
- Not be boring

Every chapter in this book correlates to a chapter in the *PMBOK Guide*. If you have a copy of the *PMBOK Guide*, blow the dust off it and flip through its 13 chapters. Now flip through this book, and you'll see that it covers the same 13 chapters in the same order. And there's a magical Chapter 14. Okay, it's not magical, but it explains in detail the Code of Ethics and Professional Conduct, which is a major exam objective. Chapter 14 covers leadership, motivation, and how to balance stakeholder interests. Chapter 14 also introduces the concept of project priorities and dealing with cultural issues.

Each chapter is full of exciting, action-packed, and riveting information. Well, that's true if you find the PMP exam exciting, action-packed, and riveting. Anyway, each chapter covers a specific topic relevant to the PMP exam. The first 3 chapters of this book offer a big-picture view of project management, while the remaining 11 chapters are most specific to the PMP exam.

In each chapter, you'll find an "Inside the Exam" sidebar. This is what I consider to be the most important message from the chapter. At the end of the chapter, you'll find a quick summary, key terms, and a two-minute drill that recaps all the major points of the chapter. Then you'll be given a 25-question exam that's specific to that chapter.

e x a m

ⓌＡＴｃｈ The questions in this book will give you some idea of what to expect on the actual PMP exam. Though not the actual exam questions, the questions in this book are styled similarly to what you'll eventually run into. Focus on understanding why your answer to a question was right or wrong. The questions are part of the learning process. The questions in this book and on its accompanying CD are tricky, pesky questions. If you can make it through these questions, you should be able to get through the PMP, too.

All About the PMP Exam

Not everyone can take the PMP exam—you have to qualify to take it. And this is good. The project management community should want the PMP exam to be tough, the application process to be rigorous, and the audits to be thorough. All of this will help elevate the status of the PMP and ensure that it doesn't fall prey to the "paper certifications" other professions have seen.

There are two paths to earn the PMP: with a degree or without a degree, as shown in Figure 1-1. With a degree, you'll need 36 non-overlapping months of project management

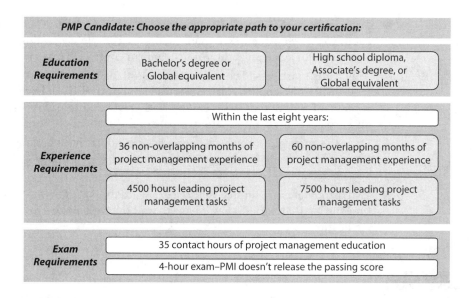

FIGURE 1-1

There are two
paths to qualify
for the PMP
examination.

experience and 4500 hours leading project management tasks within the last eight years.
Without a degree, you'll need 60 non-overlapping months of project management experience
and 7500 hours of project management tasks within the last eight years. Note that non-
overlapping months of project management experience means that if you're managing
two projects at the same time for 6 months, that's just 6 months of project management
experience—not 12 months of experience.

In addition to these requirements, you'll need 35 contact hours of project management
education. (My company, Instructing.com, is a PMI Registered Education Provider, and
I teach a qualified PMP Exam Prep course online that's accepted by PMI. Check out the
course at www.instructing.com.) Finally, you'll have to pass the 4-hour exam and then
maintain your PMP credential with ongoing education.

Here are the major details of the 2018 PMP examination as of this writing. Always check
on PMI's web site to confirm the exam particulars:

- PMI doesn't tell us what the passing score is for the exam—it's a secret—but the
  longstanding traditional score is 61 percent. The exam has 200 multiple-choice
  questions, 25 of which don't actually count toward your passing score. These
  25 questions are scattered throughout your exam and are used to collect statistics
  regarding student responses to see if they should be incorporated into future
  examinations. So this means you'll actually have to answer 106 correct questions
  out of 175 live questions.

- Clear and factual evidence of project management experience must be shown in each
  process group. On your PMP exam application, you'll have to provide specifics on tasks
  you've completed in a process group. (See Table 1-1 for specific examples from PMI.)

- Each application is given an extended review period. If your application needs an audit, you'll be notified via e-mail. Audits are completely random, and there's nothing you can do to avoid an audit. Audits confirm your work experience and education.
- Applicants must provide contact information for supervisors on all projects listed on their PMP exam application. In the past, applicants did not have to provide project contact information unless their application was audited. Now each applicant must give project contact information as part of the exam application.
- Once the application has been approved, candidates have one year to pass the exam. If you procrastinate in taking the exam by more than a year, you'll have to start the process over.
- PMP candidates are limited to three exam attempts within one year. If they fail each time during that period, they'll have to wait one year before resubmitting their exam application.

TABLE 1-1   The Five Domains of Experience Needed to Pass the PMP Exam *(Continued)*

Exam Domain	Domain Tasks	Percentage of Exam
Initiating the Project		**13 percent**
	Conduct project selection methods	
	Define the scope	
	Document project risks, assumptions, and constraints	
	Identify and perform stakeholder analysis	
	Develop the project charter	
	Obtain project charter approval	
Planning the Project		**24 percent**
	Define and record requirements, constraints, and assumptions	
	Create the Work Breakdown Structure (WBS)	
	Create a budget plan	
	Develop the project schedule and timeline	
	Create the human resource management plan	
	Create the communications plan	
	Develop the project's procurement management plan	
	Establish the project's quality management plan	

| **TABLE 1-1** | The Five Domains of Experience Needed to Pass the PMP Exam |

Exam Domain	Domain Tasks	Percentage of Exam
	Define the change management plan	
	Create the project risk management plan	
	Present the project management plan to the key stakeholders	
	Host the project kickoff meeting	
Executing the Project		**30 percent**
	Manage project resources for project execution	
	Enforce the quality management plan	
	Implement approved changes as directed by the change management plan	
	Execute the risk management plan to manage and respond to risk events	
	Develop the project team through mentoring, coach, and motivation	
Monitoring and Controlling the Project		**25 percent**
	Measure project performance	
	Verify and manage changes to the project	
	Ensure project deliverables conform to quality standards	
	Monitor all risks and update the risk register	
	Review corrective actions and assess issues	
	Manage project communications to ensure stakeholder engagement	
Closing the Project		**8 percent**
	Obtain final acceptance for the project	
	Perform operational transfer of the project deliverables	
	Ensure financial, legal, and administrative project closure	
	Create and distribute the final project report	
	Archive and retain project records	
	Measure customer satisfaction	
TOTAL		**100 percent**

Always check the exam details on PMI's web site: www.pmi.org. They can change this information whenever they like. You can, and should, download the *PMP Handbook* from www.pmi.org to confirm your study efforts.

The PMP exam will test you on your experience and knowledge in five different areas, as Table 1-1 shows. You'll have to provide specifics on tasks completed in each knowledge area of your PMP examination application. The preceding domain specifics and their related exam percentages are taken directly from PMI's web site regarding the PMP examination. Although this information is correct as of this writing, always hop out to www.pmi.org and check the site for any updates as you prepare to pass the PMP exam.

Code of Ethics and Professional Conduct

Right at the beginning of the *PMBOK Guide* we're introduced to the Code of Ethics and Professional Conduct. This code is something that you must read and agree to adhere to when submitting your PMP exam application. The Code of Ethics and Professional Conduct address the values project managers should possess and address—responsibility, respect, fairness, and honesty.

The Code of Ethics and Professional Conduct offers aspirational standards and mandatory standards for all PMI members, volunteers, certificate applicants, and certificate holders, not just PMPs. As a PMP candidate, the code will affect you in your exam application, in your career as a project manager, and in your dealings with vendors, stakeholders, and other project managers. You will encounter ethical questions on the PMP exam, and you'll always have to choose the best answer, even if you don't like the choices presented. I've included an entire chapter in this book to walk through the particulars of the Code of Ethics and Professional Conduct.

CERTIFICATION OBJECTIVE 1.02

Defining What a Project Is—and Is Not

Projects are endeavors. Projects are temporary. A project creates something, provides a service, or brings about a result. I know, I know, it sounds like some marriages.

To define a project, you can simply think of some work that has a deadline associated with it, that involves resources, that has a budget to satisfy the scope of the project work, and for which you can state what the end result of the project should be. So, projects are temporary work assignments with a budget, that require some amount of resources (people, equipment, tools, and so on), that require some amount of time to complete, and that create a definite deliverable—a service, result, or product.

Let's look at project characteristics in more detail.

Projects Create Unique Products, Services, or Results

This one isn't tough to figure out. Projects have to create a thing, invent a service, or change an environment. The deliverable of the project—a successful project, that is—satisfies the scope that was created way, way back when the project got started. Projects create the following deliverables:

- **Products** Projects can create tangible products such as a skyscrapers or a design for piece of electronics, which is the end of the project. Or projects can create components that contribute to other tangible products, such as a project to design and build a specialized engine for a ship or custom electronics for a prototype device.
- **Services** A project creating a service could establish a new call center, an order fulfillment process, or a faster way to complete inventory audits.
- **Results** Projects can be research driven. Consider a research-and-development project with a pharmaceutical company to find a cure for the common cold.
- **Combination** And, yes, projects can even be a combination of products, services, and results. There's no rule that your project can create a product and a service; for example, you might be leading a project to develop a new drug. Developing the drug is the tangible product, creating a lab test that you run for a doctor to diagnose the illness is a service, and the clinical trials to get FDA certification are results.

Projects are unique. This means that every project you ever do is different from all the other projects you've done in the past. Even if it's the same basic approach to get to the same end result, there are unique factors within each project, such as the time it takes, the stakeholders involved, the environment in which the project takes place, and on and on. All projects are unique, even if your company does the same type of project repeatedly. Lucky you.

Projects Are Temporary

Regardless of what some projects may seem like, they must be temporary. If the work is not temporary, it is operations. Like a good story, projects have a beginning, a middle, and an end. Projects end when the scope of the project has been met—usually. Sometimes projects end when the project runs out of time or cash or when it becomes clear that the project won't be able to complete the project objectives, so it's scrapped. You might also experience the end of the project when it becomes clear that the project is no longer needed, such as when a new technology supersedes the project you're managing.

The goal of a project will vary based on what the project's deliverable is, but typically, the result is to create something that'll be around longer than the process it took to create it. For example, if you're managing a project to build a skyscraper, you expect the skyscraper to be around much longer than the time it took to build it.

So *temporary* means that the *project* is temporary, and the deliverable *may or may not* be temporary. You can have a project to host a giant picnic for your entire organization and its customers. The project's logistics, invitations, and coordination of chefs may take months to complete, but the picnic will last only a few hours. However, you could argue that although the picnic event was temporary, the memories and goodwill your picnic created could last a lifetime. (That had better be one good picnic!)

Sometimes *temporary* describes the market window. We've all seen fads come and go over the past years: pet rocks, the dot.com boom, streaking, and more. Projects can often be created that capitalize on fads, which means projects have to deliver fast before the fad fades away and the next craze begins. Fads and opportunities are temporary; projects that feed off these are temporary as well.

When's the last time you managed a project in which the entire project team stuck with the project through the entire duration? It probably doesn't happen often. Project teams are often more temporary than the project itself, but, typically, project teams last only as long as the project does. Once the project is complete, the team disbands and the project team members move on to other projects within the organization.

PMP
Coach   **Project teams don't have to be big groups of people to complete a project. In fact, the *PMBOK Guide* advises that projects can be completed by even a single person.**

Projects Change Things and Environments

When you think about a project—any project—it's all about change. Any project you've ever worked on changed something. You added a server to your work environment? Change. You created a new product for your customers? Change. You led a project to develop a new product? Change again. All projects drive change. In the business world, your projects move the organization from its current state to a desired future state, and projects facilitate that change from now to then. As a general rule, projects can be mapped to a MACD description:

- **Move**   A project moves something. You centralized all of your company's data centers into one location. That's a move project.
- **Add**   A project adds something to the current environment. You lead a project to build a new bridge in your city. That's adding to the current city's environment.
- **Change**   Projects can change the environment. You upgrade your workstations to the latest and greatest operating systems. That's a change project.
- **Delete**   Projects can remove things and services from the current environment. You lead an effort to demolish derelict or abandoned houses as part of urban revitalization program. That's a delete project.

Projects Create Business Value

Projects need to provide business value. Business value is the sum of the benefits that an organization can quantify. Benefits can usually be defined in financial terms, but they may also be intangible benefits, such as goodwill, brand recognition, benefits to the public, strategic alignment, and even your organization's reputation. Time savings, a common business value, can be quantified. You're looking for benefits for stakeholders in the form of monetary assets, equity, utility, fixtures, tools, and market share.

Business value is almost always quantified in financial terms—something that helps set the objectives of the project. You might be asked to predict the profitability of a project to justify the organization's investment in the project. As you know, projects cost money and time, and you'll have to justify that investment of resources up front. This is where we'll get into project selection, return on investment, and whether your project—or any project—should move forward or not.

Consider the Project Initiation Context

In alignment with business value is the discussion of project initiation: Why choose a project at all? For most project managers, this question is out of their scope of responsibilities, but they may get called upon to contribute to the project selection and initiation conversation. As a general practice, there are four reasons why projects get initiated:

- Satisfy stakeholder requests, needs, and opportunities
- Meet regulatory requirements, legal requirements, or social requirements
- Change business and/or technological strategies in the organization
- Improve upon existing products, processes, or services or add new products, processes, and services

CERTIFICATION OBJECTIVE 1.03

Defining Project Management

Project management is the supervision and control of the work required to complete the project vision. The project team carries out the work needed to complete the project, while the project manager schedules, monitors, and controls the various project tasks. Project management requires that you apply your knowledge, skills, tools, and techniques, and do whatever it takes, generally speaking, to achieve the project objectives. Project management is about getting things done.

Projects, being the temporary and unique things that they are, require the project manager to be actively involved with the project implementation. Projects are not self-propelled. Project management is accomplished by using the correct project management processes at the right time, to the correct depth, and with the correct technique. These processes, which you'll learn throughout this book, are logically organized in five process groups:

■ Initiating
■ Planning
■ Executing
■ Monitoring and controlling
■ Closing

Although the information covered in this chapter is important, it is more of an umbrella of the ten knowledge areas that you'll want to focus on for your PMP exam. You'll see all of the 49 project management processes in detail in the upcoming chapters. At the beginning of each chapter, we'll highlight the processes that the knowledge area deals with. Here's a breakdown of the 49 processes that you'll learn about throughout this book.

Initiating the Project

There are just two processes to know for project initiation:

■ Develop the project charter.
■ Identify project stakeholders.

Planning the Project

There are 24 processes to know for project planning:

■ Develop the project management plan.
■ Plan scope management.
■ Collect project requirements.
■ Define the project scope.
■ Create the work breakdown structure.
■ Plan schedule management.
■ Define the project activities.
■ Sequence the project activities.
■ Estimate the activity duration.
■ Develop the project schedule.
■ Plan cost management.

- Estimate the project costs.
- Establish the project budget.
- Plan quality management.
- Plan resource management.
- Estimate activity resources
- Plan communications management.
- Plan risk management.
- Identify the project risks.
- Perform qualitative risk analysis.
- Perform quantitative risk analysis.
- Plan risk responses.
- Plan procurement management.
- Plan stakeholder engagement.

Executing the Project

There are ten executing processes:

- Direct and manage project work.
- Manage project knowledge.
- Manage quality.
- Acquire resources.
- Perform team development.
- Manage the team.
- Manage communications.
- Implement risk responses.
- Conduct procurements.
- Manage stakeholder engagement.

Monitoring and Controlling the Project

There are 12 monitoring and controlling processes:

- Monitor and control the project work.
- Perform integrated change control.
- Complete scope validation.
- Control the scope.

- Perform schedule control.
- Perform cost control.
- Administer quality control.
- Control resources.
- Monitor communications.
- Monitor risks.
- Control procurements.
- Monitor stakeholder engagements.

Closing the Project

There is only one closing process:

- Close out the project or the project phase.

Process Group Interactions

As a project manager you'll move between these five processes groups as appropriate in the project. Most projects begin with an identification of a business or societal need. Business needs generally focus on improving or maintaining profits, and societal needs include improving living conditions with new roads or cleaner water. This process may include some high-level requirements, costs, value statements, and timelines—what it'll take for the project to be complete and to be considered successful. Your ongoing concern is to keep the stakeholders satisfied on the project's progress by communicating the status of the project, showing evidence of progression toward project completion, and keeping the project constraints in balance. A *constraint* is any factor that limits the parameters of the project. The most common constraints in any project are time, cost, and scope, but you should also consider quality, resources (people, equipment, tools, and the like), and risks. Projects that are poorly managed are plagued by missed deadlines, blown budgets, quality issues, rework, scope expansion, stakeholder turmoil, and overall failure in achieving the project goals. Keep the following in mind:

- Process groups are collections of project processes to bring about a specific result.
- Process groups are not project phases. The project may follow a workflow through the process groups, but the phases of the project are specific to the actual project work.

Process groups are iterative. You can use the sequence of processes throughout the entire project, in each phase of the project, or both. I'll discuss these points throughout the book, but for now this is a good foundation to understand why we all need effective, controlled project management. We achieve that goal through the five process groups and the project management processes. A project will also typically use ten project management knowledge areas. What you do in one knowledge area has a direct effect on the other knowledge areas. Chapters 4 through 13 will explore the following knowledge areas in detail:

- **Project integration management**   This knowledge area focuses on creating the project charter, the project scope statement, and a viable project plan. Once the project is in motion, project integration management is all about monitoring and controlling the work. If changes happen—and they will—you have to determine how that change may affect all of the other knowledge areas.

- **Project scope management**   This knowledge area deals with the planning, creation, protection, and fulfillment of the project scope. One of the most important activities in all of project management happens in this knowledge area: creation of the work breakdown structure. Oh, joy!

- **Project schedule management**   Schedule management is crucial to project success. This knowledge area covers activities, their characteristics, and how they fit into the project schedule. This is where you and the project team will define the activities, plot out their sequence, and calculate how long the project will actually take.

- **Project cost management**   Cost is always a constraint in project management. This knowledge area is concerned with planning, estimating, budgeting, and controlling costs. Cost management is tied to time and quality management—screw up either of these and the project costs will increase.

- **Project quality management**   What good is a project that's done on time if the scope isn't complete, the work is faulty, or the deliverable is horrible? Well, it's no good. This knowledge area centers on quality planning, assurance, and control.

- **Project resource management**   This knowledge area focuses on organizational planning, staff acquisition, and team development. You have to acquire your project team, develop this team, and then lead the team to the project results.

- **Project communications management**   The majority of a project manager's time is spent communicating. This knowledge area details how communication happens, outlines stakeholder management, and shows how to plan for communications within any project.

- **Project risk management**   Every project has risks. This knowledge area focuses on risk planning, analysis, monitoring, and control. You'll have to complete qualitative analysis and then quantitative analysis to prepare adequately for project risks. Once the project moves forward, you'll need to monitor and react to identified risks as planned.

■ **Project stakeholder management**   Stakeholders are the all people who are affected positively or negatively, or perceived to be, by your project. They can influence your project's success, because a subset of them defines the projects goals. This knowledge area requires that you and the project team

  ■ identify stakeholders,
  ■ plan how you'll manage their concerns and requirements in the project,
  ■ plan how you'll manage and control their engagement in the project, and
  ■ balance the needs, wants, threats, and concerns that stakeholders introduce to the project with the identified project requirements.

■ **Project procurement management**   Projects often need to procure products, services, and results purchased from outside vendors in order to reach closing. This knowledge area covers the business of project procurement, the processes to acquire and select vendors, and contract negotiation. The contract between the vendor and the project manager's organization will guide all interaction between the project manager and the vendor.

e x a m

ⓦ a t c h   You will learn about each of these knowledge areas in detail throughout the book. What happens in one knowledge area affects what happens in other knowledge areas. Project integration management is the coordination of these events.

Tailoring the Project Process

Chances are that you follow a prescribed methodology to manage projects where you work. Your work environment uses names for some of these processes that differ slightly from those presented here and in the *PMBOK Guide*, and that's perfectly fine. The methodology that your organization uses to manage projects is just that—a method. The *PMBOK Guide* is not a methodology, but a guide to the best practices of project management.

The flexibility of the *PMBOK Guide* and project management is beautiful, when you think about it. Okay, maybe "beautiful" isn't the best word, but the flexibility is important. The processes and approaches that you utilize in your project management approach involves tailoring of the processes, and that's what's needed in every project. Tailoring enables you to choose what processes should be used on a project and to what depth the processes should be used.

You do not use every process on every project. The larger the project, the more processes you will likely use. Consider a low-level project to swap out keyboards in an organization. Contrast that to a high-level project to construct a new headquarters for your company. The construction project has more uncertainties and will require more project management processes—and more tailoring of the processes to fit the uniqueness of the project.

CERTIFICATION OBJECTIVE 1.04

Examining Related Areas of Project Management

Project management is the administration of activities to change the current state of an organization into a desired future state. It manages a complex relationship between decision-making, planning, implementation, control, and documentation of the experience from start to finish. In addition to traditional project management, you may encounter, have encountered, or are actively participating in related areas. These related aspects often are superior to individual project management, are part of project management, or equate to less than the management of any given project.

Organizational project management (OPM) is an organizational approach to coordinate, manage, and control projects, programs, and portfolio management in a uniform, consistent effort. The philosophy of OPM is that by doing all work within projects, programs, and portfolio management with the same type of processes, actions, and techniques, the organization will consistently deliver better results than it would if the processes and approach were independent of one another. While project, program, and portfolio each have different skill sets, there is overlap in their approach, and these endeavors may utilize the same resources—including you, the project manager—to accomplish their objectives.

This section dissects the related areas of project management to see how they tie together to change a current state to a desired future state.

Exploring Program Management

Program management is the management of multiple projects all working in unison toward a common goal. Programs achieve benefits by managing projects collectively, rather than independently. Projects within a program can better share resources, improve communications, manage interdependencies, resolve issues quickly, leverage resources, and provide more benefits for the organization than they would if each project were not managed collectively under a program. Projects within a program still have project managers, but the project managers work with, and often report to, the program manager.

Consider all of the work that goes into building a skyscraper, for example. Within the overall work, several projects may lead to the result. You could have a project for the planning and design of the building. Another project could manage the legal, regulatory, and project inspections that would be required for the work to continue. Another project could be the physical construction of the building, and other projects might entail electrical wiring, elevators, plumbing, interior design, and more. Could one project manager effectively manage all of these areas of expertise? Possibly, but probably not.

A better solution could be to create a program that comprises multiple projects. Project managers would manage each of the projects within the program and report to the program manager. The program manager would ensure that all of the integrated projects work together on schedule, on budget, and ultimately toward the completion of the program.

Another example is a program within NASA. NASA could create a program within the organization to explore space, and it comprises individual projects within that program. Each project included in the program has its own goals, initiatives, and objectives that are in alignment with the overall mission of the space program. Programs are a collection of individual projects working in alignment toward a common end.

Basically, programs have much larger scopes than projects do. Project plans and program plans differ in that project plans are often detail-oriented, while program plans are often at a higher level, with the details left to the project teams within the program. Although project managers are usually resistant to change, program managers expect change to happen within the program. Because programs are made up of projects, project managers can expect the program manager to interact regularly with their projects to monitor and control the success of each project. Programs are deemed successful, just like projects, based on their abilities to meet requirements, meet performance objectives, and benefit delivery.

Consider Project Portfolio Management

Portfolios include projects, programs, and even operations that are managed and coordinated and should link to the strategic objectives for the organization, as demonstrated in Figure 1-2. Portfolios are created and controlled by upper-level management and executives and include financial considerations of the investment, return on investment, and distribution of risks for the programs, projects, and operations included in the portfolio. A portfolio describes the collection of investments in the form of projects and programs in which the organization invests capital. Project managers and, if applicable, program managers report to a portfolio review board on the performance of the projects and programs. The portfolio review board may also direct the selection of projects and programs.

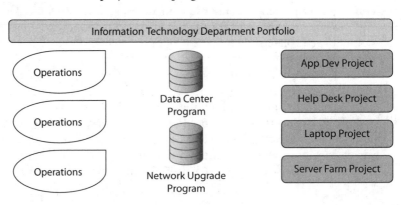

FIGURE 1-2

Portfolios can contain operations, programs, and projects.

Information Technology Department Portfolio

Operations

Operations

Operations

Data Center Program

Network Upgrade Program

App Dev Project

Help Desk Project

Laptop Project

Server Farm Project

The portfolio review board—or even the direct management of the organization—also has a scope of projects and programs they'd like to invest in. This scope, however, is at a higher level than the scope of projects and programs, because the endeavors selected by the portfolio review board must fall within the strategic objectives of the company. Investments are made in projects and programs when there is a viable, strategic opportunity. Portfolio managers oversee the portfolio and monitor the organizational and marketplace environments to ensure that the components of the portfolio make sense to continue and to support the organizational objectives.

Consider these elements that may cause an organization to invest in a project or program as part of its portfolio:

- Legal requirement
- Compliance needs
- Advancement in technology
- Change in the market demand
- Efficiency improvements, business need, or productivity analysis
- Changes in operational capability
- Environmental opportunity
- Social need

The investments the company makes in projects and programs should have, of course, a positive return. These investments are monitored by the portfolio review board and portfolio manager through communications with the program managers and the project managers. The organization wants to see a return on investment through profits, social or performance improvements, reduction in waste, or other key performance indicators established at the selection of the projects and program investment.

While the focus of this book, the *PMBOK Guide*, and your PMP exam is on project management, it's nearly impossible to avoid having a discussion on operations. Operations are the day-to-day activities that move a business forward. Projects are unique and temporary, while operations are not. Operations, programs, and projects overlap and work with one another, not opposed to one another. For your exam, you won't need to know much about operations, other than that operations are ongoing. Portfolios can include, to be clear, operational activities, but our focus will be on the projects and programs within the portfolios.

Portfolio projects could be interdependent, but they don't have to be. A portfolio is not the same as a program; it is a collection of projects, programs, and operations. The projects in a portfolio could be within one line of business, could be based on the strategies within an organization, or could follow the guidance of one director within an organization. There is a balance of risk in the selection of projects and programs. It's not unusual to have some low-risk, high-risk, and moderate-risk selections to distribute the risk exposure across the components.

Project selections may pass through a project selection committee or a project steering committee, where executives will look at the return on investment, the value of the project, risks associated with taking on the project, and other attributes of the project. This is all part of project portfolio management.

Portfolios, programs, and projects obviously interact, but they each have a different purpose. A term you might occasionally see is *organizational project management (OPM)*. OPM is the ideal model an organization uses when coordinating the efforts, goals, strategies, and investments of time and resources into portfolios, programs, and projects. An organizational strategic plan defines what investments should be made where, the expected return on investment, the risk distribution of each investment, and how each investment (the portfolio, program, or project) will contribute to the project's achievement of benefits.

Implementing Subprojects

Subprojects are an alternative to programs. Some projects may not be wieldy enough to require the creation of a full-blown program, yet they may be large enough that some of the work can be delegated to a subproject. A subproject exists under the parent project, but it follows its own schedule for completing one or more deliverables. Subprojects may be outsourced, assigned to other project managers, or managed by the parent project manager but with a different project team. The following illustration shows a project containing multiple subprojects.

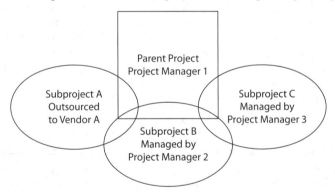

Subprojects are often areas of a project that are outsourced to vendors. For example, if you were managing a project to create a new sound system for home theaters, a subproject could be the development of the user manual included with the sound system. You would thus hire writers and graphic designers to work with your project team. The writers and designers would learn all about the sound system and then retreat to their own spaces to create the user manual according to their project methodology. The deliverable of their subproject would be included in your overall project plan, but the actual work done to complete the manual would not be in your plan. You'd simply allot the funds and time required by the writers and graphic designers to create the manual.

Subprojects do, however, follow the same quality guidelines and expectations of the overall project. The project manager has to work with the subproject team regarding supplying any needed materials, scheduling, value, and cost to ensure the deliverables and activities of the subproject integrate smoothly with the "master" project.

Projects vs. Operations

Meet Jane. Jane is a project manager for her organization. Vice presidents, directors, and managers with requests to investigate or to launch potential projects approach her daily— or so it seems to Jane. Just this morning, the sales manager met with Jane because he wants to implement a new direct-mail campaign to all of the customers in the sales database. He wants this direct-mail campaign to invite customers to visit the company web site to see the new line of products. Part of the project also requires that the company web site be updated so that it's in sync with the mailing. Sounds like a project, but is it really? Could this actually be just a facet of an ongoing operation?

In some organizations, everything is a project. In other organizations, projects are rare exercises in change. There's a fine line between projects and operations, and often these separate entities overlap in function. Consider the following points shared by projects and operations:

- Both involve employees.
- Both typically have limited resources: people, money, or both.
- Both are hopefully designed, executed, and managed by someone in charge.

Jane has been asked to manage a direct-mail campaign to all of the customers in the sales database. Could this be a project? Sure—if this company has never completed a similar task and there are no internal departments that do this type of work as part of their regular activities. Often, projects are confused with general business duties: marketing, sales, manufacturing, and so on. The tell-tale sign of a project is that it has an end date and that it's unique from other activities within the organization. Here are some examples of projects:

- Designing a new product or service
- Converting from one computer application to another
- Building a new warehouse
- Moving from one building to another
- Organizing a political campaign
- Designing and certifying a new airplane

The end results of projects can result in operations. For example, imagine a company creating a new airplane. This new airplane will be a small personal plane that would enable people to fly to different destinations with the same freedom they use in driving their cars. The project team will have to design an airplane from scratch that would be similar to a car, so that consumers could easily adapt and fly to Sheboygan at a moment's notice. The project to create a personal plane is temporary, but not necessarily short-term. It may take years to go from concept to completion—but the project does have an end date. A project of this magnitude may require hundreds of prototypes and years of certification before a working model is ready for the marketplace. In addition, there are countless regulations, safety issues, and quality control concerns that must be pacified before completion.

Once the initial plane is designed, built, and approved, the end result of the project is business operations. As the company creates a new vehicle, they would follow through with the design by manufacturing, marketing, selling, supporting, and improving the product. The initial design of the airplane is the project—the business of manufacturing it, supporting sold units, and marketing the product constitutes the ongoing operations part of business.

In the creation of the plane, before the manufacturing of the actual plane begins, the project manager would have to involve the operational stakeholders in the project. The project manager needs the expertise of the people who'll be doing the day-to-day operations of the plane manufacturing. Although operations and projects are different, they are also reliant on one another in most projects. The project deliverables often have a direct impact on the day-to-day operations of the organization. Communication and coordinated planning is needed between the project manager and the operational stakeholders.

Operations are the day-to-day work that goes on in the organization. A manufacturer manufactures things, scientists complete research and development, and businesses provide goods and services. Operations are the heart of organizations. Projects, on the other hand, are short-term endeavors that fall outside of the normal day-to-day operations an organization offers.

on the **Job** Let's be realistic. In some companies, nearly everything's a project. This is probably true if you work in an organization that completes projects for other companies. That's fine and acceptable, however, since you're participating in management by projects. There are still many operational activities that exist in these companies, such as accounting, payroll and HR, sales, marketing, and the like.

exam

Watch The customer is the most important person in any project. The project is created for and to suit the customer.

Once the project is complete, the project team moves along to other projects and activities. The people who are actually building the airplanes on the assembly line, however, have no end date in sight and will continue to create airplanes as long as there's a demand for the product.

Projects and Business Value

Projects must support the corporate vision, mission, and objectives or they don't bring value to the organization. Business value is simply what the organization is worth; it is the sum of the tangible and intangible components of an organization. Tangible elements are easy to identify: cash, assets, equipment, real estate, and so on. Intangible elements are things like reputation, the company brand, and trademarks. Projects must contribute to the business value or they likely don't fit within the strategic goals of the company.

CERTIFICATION OBJECTIVE 1.05

Revving Through the Project Life Cycle

Consider any project, and you'll also have to consider any *phases* within the project. Construction projects have definite phases. IT projects have definite phases. Marketing, sales, and internal projects all have definite phases. Projects—all projects—comprise phases. Phases make up the project life cycle, and they are unique to each project. Furthermore, organizations, project managers, and even project frameworks such as Agile or Scrum can define phases within a project life cycle. Just know this: The sum of a project's phases equates to the project's life cycle.

watch
Phases are unique to each project. Phases are not the same as initiating, planning, executing, monitoring and controlling, and closing. These are the process groups and are universal to all projects.

In regard to the PMP exam, it's rather tough for the PMI to ask questions about specific project life cycles. Why? Because every organization may identify different phases within all the different projects that exist. Bob may come from a construction background and Susan from IT, each one being familiar with totally different disciplines and totally different life cycles within their projects. However, all PMP candidates should recognize that every project has a life cycle—and all life cycles comprise phases.

Because every project life cycle is made up of phases, it's safe to assume that each phase has a specific type of work that enables the project to move toward to the next phase in the project. When we talk in high-level terms about a project, we might say that a project is launched, planned, executed, and finally closed, but it's the type of work, the activities the project team is completing, that more clearly define the project phases. In a simple construction example, this is easy to see:

- Phase 1: Planning and prebuild
- Phase 2: Permits and filings

- Phase 3: Prep and excavation
- Phase 4: Basement and foundation
- Phase 5: Framing
- Phase 6: Interior
- Phase 7: Exterior

Typically, one phase is completed before the next phase begins; this relationship between phases is called a *sequential relationship*. The phases follow a sequence to reach project completion—one phase after another. Sometimes project managers allow phases to overlap because of time constraints, cost savings, and smarter work. When time's an issue and a project manager allows one phase to begin before the last phase is completed, it's called an *overlapping, or parallel, relationship* because the phases overlap. You might also know this approach as *fast tracking*. Fast tracking, as handy as it is, increases the risk within a project.

A project is an uncertain business—the larger the project, the more uncertainty. It's for this reason, among others, that projects are broken down into smaller, more manageable phases. A project phase allows a project manager to see the project as a whole and yet still focus on completing the project one phase at a time. You can also think of the financial distribution and the effort required in the form of a project life cycle. Generally, labor and expenses are lowest at the start of the project, because you're planning and preparing for the work. You'll spend the bulk of the project's budget on labor, materials, and resources during project execution, and then costs will taper off as your project eases into its closing.

Working with a Project Life Cycle

Projects are like snowflakes: No two are alike. Sure, sure, some may be similar, but when you get down to it, each project has its own unique attributes, activities, and requirements from stakeholders. One attribute that typically varies from project to project is the project life cycle. As the name implies, the project life cycle determines not only the start of the project, but also when the project should be completed. All that stuff packed in between starting and ending? Those are the different phases of the project.

In other words, the launch, a series of phases, and project completion make up the project life cycle. Each project will have similar project management activities, but the characteristics of the project life cycle will vary from project to project.

Completing a Project Feasibility Study

The project's feasibility is part of the initiating process. Once the need has been identified, a feasibility study is introduced into the plan to determine if the need can realistically be met.

on the
Job

Project feasibility studies can be a separate project.

So how does a project get to be a project? In some organizations, it's pure luck. In most organizations, however, projects may begin with a feasibility study. Feasibility studies can be, and often are, part of the initiation process of a project. In some instances, however, a feasibility study may be treated as a stand-alone project.

Let's assume that the feasibility of Project ABC is part of the project initiation phase. The outcome of the feasibility study may tell management several things:

- Whether the concept should be mapped into a project
- If the project's concept will deliver the anticipated value
- The expected cost and time needed to complete the concept
- The benefits and costs to implement the project concept
- A report on the needs of the organization and how the project concept can satisfy these needs

PMP
Coach

There is a difference between a feasibility study and a business case. A feasibility study examines the potential project to see if it's feasible to do the project work. A business case examines the financial aspect of the project to see if the project's product, service, or result can be profitable, what the profit margin may be, what the financial risk exposure may be, and what the true costs of the project may be. Some projects can generate profit directly. A construction company running a project to build a new strip mall will hopefully net a profit when the project is done. The investment firm, say, who hired the contractor to build the strip mall as part of a larger development project will not see a profit until leasing operations start generating income.

Examining the Project Life Cycle

By now, you're more than familiar with the concept of a project life cycle. You also know that each project is different and that some attributes are common across all project life cycles. For example, the concept of breaking the project apart into manageable phases to move toward completion is typical across most projects.

As we've discussed, at the completion of a project phase, an inspection or audit is usually completed. This inspection confirms that the project is in alignment with the requirements and expectations of the customer. If the results of the audit or inspection are not in alignment, rework can happen, new expectations may be formulated, or the project may be killed.

Exploring Different Project Life Cycles

As more and more projects are technology-centric, it makes perfect sense for the *PMBOK Guide* to acknowledge the life cycles that exist within technology projects. Even if you don't work in a technology project, it behooves you to understand the terminology associated with these different life cycles for the PMP examination. You should know about five technology-based life cycles:

- Predictive life cycles
- Iterative life cycles
- Incremental life cycles
- Adaptive life cycles
- Hybrid life cycles

Predictive Life Cycles   The predictive approach requires the project scope, the project time, and project costs to be defined early in the project timeline. Predictive life cycles have predefined phases, in which each phase completes a specific type of work and usually overlaps other phases in the project. You might also see predictive life cycles described as *plan-driven* or *waterfall* methodologies, because the project phases "cascade" into the subsequent phases and the Gantt chart looks like a waterfall.

Iterative Life Cycles   This approach requires that the project scope be defined at a high level at the beginning of the project, but the costs and schedules are developed through iterations of planning as the project deliverable is more fully understood. The project moves through iterations of planning and definition based on discoveries during the project execution. The project team focuses on iterations of deliverables that can be released while continuing to develop and create the final project deliverable.

Incremental Life Cycles   Incremental life cycles create the final product deliverable through a series of increment. Each increment of the project will add more and more functionality. Like the iterative life cycle, increments are a predetermined set amount of time, such as two or four weeks, for example. Before each increment, the team and a specific stakeholder determine what can be created within each increment, and then the increments begins and the team tackles the defined objectives. The project is done when the final increment creates a deliverable with sufficient capability as determined by the stakeholders.

Adaptive Life Cycles   Adaptive life cycles are either agile, iterative, or incremental. Adaptive life cycles follow a defined methodology such as Scrum or eXtreme Programming (XP). Change is highly probable, and the project team will be working closely with the project stakeholders. You might also know this approach as *agile* or *change-driven*, because the team must be able to move or change quickly and the project scope and requirements are likely to change throughout the project. This approach also includes iterations of project work, but the iterations are fast sessions of planning and execution that usually last about two weeks. At the start of each phase, or iteration, of project work, the project manager, project team, and stakeholders will determine what requirements will be worked on next, based on the set of project requirements and what has been completed in the project.

Hybrid Life Cycles   The hybrid life cycle is a combination of predictive and adaptive life cycles. Parts of the project can follow the predictive life cycle, such as project requirements and the budget, yet still utilize the flexibility and iterations that the adaptive life cycle offers. Hybrid life cycles can be, well, a bit messy, because there may be debates over what's established and what's being flexible. The project team and the project manager need a clear understanding of the "must haves" in the project and what components provide flexibility.

See the video "Project Life Cycle."

Working Through a Project Life Cycle

Most projects phases move the project along. They allow a project manager to answer the following questions about the project:

- What work will be completed in each phase of the project?
- What resources, people, equipment, and facilities will be needed within each phase?
- What are the expected deliverables of each phase?
- What is the expected cost to complete a project phase?
- Which phases pose the highest amount of risk?
- What must be true in order for the phase to be considered complete?

Armed with the appropriate information for each project phase, the project manager can plan for cost, schedules, resource availability, risk management, and other project management activities to ensure that the project progresses successfully.

Although projects differ, other traits are common from project to project. Here are a few examples:

- Phases are generally sequential, as the completion of one phase enables the next phase to begin.
- Cost and resource requirements are lower at the beginning of a project but grow as the project progresses. In a project, the bulk of the budget and the most resources are used during the executing process. Once the project moves into the final closing process, costs and resource requirements taper off dramatically.

- Projects fail at the beginning, not at the end. In other words, the odds of completing are low at launch and high near completion. This means that decisions made at the beginning of a project live with the project throughout its life cycle, and a poor decision in the early phases can cause failure in the later phases.

- The further the project is from completing, the higher the risk and uncertainty. Risk and uncertainty decrease as the project moves closer to fulfilling the project scope.

- Changes are easier and more likely at the early phases of the project life cycle than near completion. Stakeholders can have a greater influence on the outcome of the project deliverables in the early phases, but in the final phases of the project life cycle, their influence on change diminishes. Thankfully, changes at the beginning of the project generally cost less and have lower risk than changes at the end of a project.

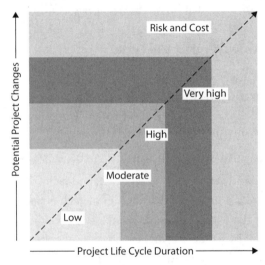

Your projects probably already follow a phasing structure that's unique to the development, construction, or industry that you're involved in. Typical phases of a project can include the following:

- Concept
- Feasibility study creation
- Requirements gathering
- Solution development
- Design and prototype creation
- Build or execution
- Testing

- Operational transfer or transition
- Commissioning
- Reviewing
- Lessons learned documentation

Project Life Cycle vs. Product Life Cycle

There is some distinction between the project life cycle and the product life cycle. We've covered the project life cycle, the accumulation of phases from start to completion within a project, but what is a product life cycle?

In a project delivering products, a product life cycle is the parent of projects. Consider a company that wants to sell a new type of lemon soft drink. One of the projects the company may undertake to sell its new lemon soft drink is to create television commercials showing how tasty the beverage is. The creation of the television commercial may be considered one project in support of the product creation.

Many other projects may fall under the creation of the lemon soft drink: research, creation and testing, packaging, and more. Each project, however, needs to support the ultimate product: the tasty lemon soft drink. The product life cycle, though, also includes the ongoing operations of manufacturing, marketing, selling, distributing, and potentially end-of-life decommissioning of the product. Decommissioning of the product may involve a series of projects, but the other items are not projects—they are operations. Thus, the product life cycle oversees the smaller projects within the process and operations.

As a general rule, the product life cycle is the cradle-to-grave ongoing work of the product. Projects affecting the product are just blips on the radar screen of the whole product life cycle. Consider all of the projects that may happen to a home. The home is the product, while all the projects are things that make the product better or that sustain the existing product.

The Project Life Cycle in Action

Suppose you're the project manager for HollyWorks Productions. Your company would like to create a new video camera that allows consumers to make video productions that can be transferred to different media types, such as VHS, DVD, and PCs. The video camera must be small, light, and affordable. This project life cycle has several phases from concept to completion (see Figure 1-3). Remember that the project life cycle is unique to each project, so don't assume the phases within this sample will automatically map to any project you may be undertaking.

1. **Proof-of-concept** In this phase, you'll work with business analysts, electrical engineers, customers, and manufacturing experts to confirm that such a camera is feasible to make. You'll examine the projected costs and resources required to make the camera. If things go well, management may even front you some cash to build a prototype.

FIGURE 1-3

The project life
cycle for Project
HollyWorks

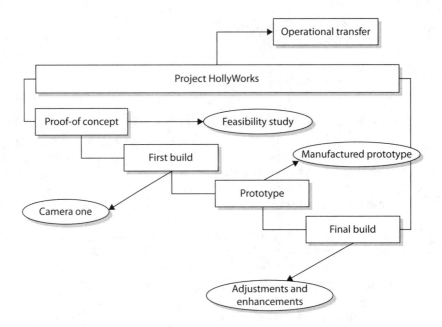

2. **First build** Management loves the positive information you've discovered in the proof-of-concept phase—they've set a budget for your project to continue into development. Now you'll lead your project team through the process of designing and building a video camera according to the specifications from the stakeholders and management. Once the camera is built, your team will test, document, and adjust your camera for usability and feature-support.

3. **Prototype manufacturing** Things are going remarkably well with your video camera project. The project stakeholders loved the first build and have made some refinements to the design. Your project team builds a working model, thereby moving into prototyping the video camera's manufacture and testing its cost-effectiveness and ease of mass production. The vision of the project is becoming a reality.

4. **Final build** The prototype of the camera went fairly well. The project team has documented flaws, and adjustments are being made. The project team is also working with the manufacturer to complete the requirements for materials and packaging. The project is nearing completion.

5. **Operational transfer** The project is complete. Your team has successfully designed, built, and moved into production a wonderful, affordable video camera. Each phase of the project allowed the camera to move toward completion. As the project came closer and closer to moving into operations, risk and project fluctuation waned.

Project Phase Deliverables

Every phase has deliverables. It's one of the main points to having phases. For example, your manager gives you an unwieldy project that will require four years to complete and has a hefty budget of $16 million. Do you think management is going to say, "Have fun—see you in four years"?

Oh, if only they would, right?

Of course, in most organizations, that's not going to happen. Management wants to see proof of progress, evidence of work completed, and good news about how well the project is moving. Phases are an ideal method of keeping management informed of the project progression. The following illustration depicts a project moving from conception to completion. At the end of each phase, there is some deliverable that the project manager can show to management and customers.

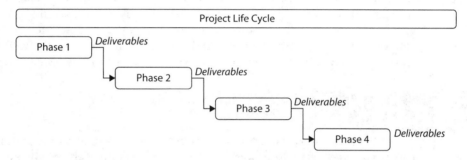

Project Advancement

Once a phase concludes, how does the project manager know it's safe to continue? Based on the size and type of the project, some form of scope verification must take place. Management and customers will want to see if the deliverable you have completed to date is in alignment with what they expected.

Project governance defines the rules for a project, and it's up to the project manager to enforce the project governance to ensure the project's ability to reach its objectives. The project management plan defines the project governance and how the project manager, the project team, and the organization will all follow the rules and policies within the project. Project governance can be seen as a constraint, but it really defines the project's boundaries and expectations.

Let's go back to that juicy project with the $16 million budget. We know management is not going to set us loose for four years. They'll want a schedule of when we'll be spending their money and what they'll be getting in return. And when will this fun happen? At the end of a project phase. The project manager will be accountable for several things at the end of a project phase:

- The performance of the project to date
- The performance of the project team to date
- Proof of deliverables in the project phase
- Verification of deliverables in alignment with the project scope

The verification of the performance and the project deliverables are key to management determining whether the project (cross your fingers) should continue or not. Imagine that your project with a $16 million budget has produced a lousy deliverable that is outside of the project scope, and you've blown a few hundred thousand *more* than you said it would take to get to this point in the project. Hmmm.... Do you think the project will continue? An analysis by management will determine whether the project should be killed or allowed to go on. The idea of killing a project at phases is why phase completion is also called a kill point. (Uh, kill point for the project, not the project manager—hopefully.) Who's to blame or why the project should be killed can be debated on a scenario-by-scenario basis.

e x a m

ⓦ a t c h   Monies already spent on a project are called *sunk costs* and should not be taken into consideration when determining whether a project should continue. Instead, the cost of the work to complete is one of the elements that should be taken into consideration when deciding whether to kill a project.

Usually, one phase completes before the next phase begins—it's a sequential relationship between phases. Each phase of a project relies on the phase before it. However, if you've ever driven past a large construction project, you may have seen something different at work. For example, we lived in Indianapolis during the construction of the new stadium for the Indianapolis Colts. During construction, we could see the foundation for one side of the stadium well underway and loads of construction happening. On the other side of the stadium, it was muddy and construction was just barely starting on the foundation.

The construction company chose to allow phases of the construction to overlap as it worked. Rather than completing all of the foundation for this giant stadium first, the next phase of the project was started as soon as possible—even if not all of the first phase was completed. Smart, huh? This approach to scheduling is called an *overlapping relationship*, and you might also know it as *fast tracking*. Fast tracking allows phases to overlap in order to compress the schedule and finish the job faster. Fast tracking does, however, add some risk to the project, as errors that go undetected in the prior phases could affect the current phase of the project work.

Finally, project managers can use an iterative relationship to manage project phases. Iterative relationships are great for projects such as research and software development. The idea is that the next phase of the project is not completely planned until the current phase of the project is underway. The direction of the project can change based on the current work in the project, the market conditions, or the discovery of more information.

Stage Gates

Project phase completions are also known as *stage gates*. Stage gates are used often in manufacturing and product development; they enable a project to continue after a performance and deliverable review against a set of predefined metrics. If the deliverables of the phase, or stage, meet the predefined metrics, the project is allowed to continue. Should the deliverables not meet the metrics, the project may not be allowed to pass through the gate to move forward. In this unfortunate case, the project may be terminated or sent through revisions to meet the predetermined metrics. The following illustration shows the advancement of the project through phases.

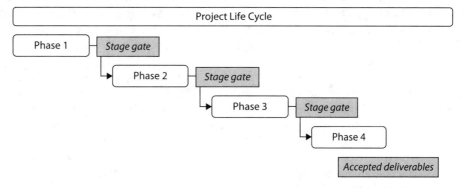

on the **Job**

As a project manager, you should identify the requirements and all of the stakeholders as close to the project launch as possible. With the expectations and requirements, the project manager can know what the exit criteria for a phase may be and can plan accordingly. There are few things more frustrating than getting to the end of a project phase only to learn the exit criteria you had in mind is different from what the customer is expecting.

The completion of a phase may also be known as a *phase exit*. A phase exit requires that the project deliverables meet some predetermined exit criteria. Exit criteria are typically inspection-specific and are scheduled events in the project schedule. Exit criteria can include many different activities, such as the following:

- Sign-offs from the customer
- Regulatory inspections and audits
- Quality metrics
- Performance metrics
- Security audits
- The end of a project phase

exam

ⓦatch   **Your company might call this end-of-phase review a stage gate, phase review, phase gate, or just a milestone. If the project isn't going as expected, this creates an opportunity to cancel the project; this is called a kill point. A phase gate, at the end of a phase, enables the project manager and stakeholders to compare the actual results against the project documentation to see how well the project is fairing.**

Of course, not all organizations are profit-driven; consider your favorite charities. These not-for-profit entities, however, still have a strategic vision and they use business philosophies to increase the value of their organization. The value of their organization can help them grow their presence, bring more donors to their cause, and promote awareness of their vision. Projects within these companies must also bring business value or they are a detriment to the organization. Projects—all projects—in for-profit or not-for-profit organizations must support the strategic objectives of the organization or they are a waste of resources.

Business value planning is an executive-level goal, but it is accomplished through upper management, portfolio managers, operations, program managers, and project managers within the company. The actions of the people within each organizational component have a direct influence on the business value. Errors, wasted materials, delays in the project, cost overruns, and other negative aspects of a project directly affect the profitability of the project, the success of the organization, and the overall business value of the organization.

INSIDE THE EXAM

The PMP exam is not for rookies. The application process alone can filter out the unqualified and the merely curious. You're reading this book to find more information on how to pass the exam, what the exam entails, and to prep for your exam—a wise decision. Now make another wise decision: Begin completing your PMP exam application. The application process can be lengthy, since you'll have to track down past information relating to projects you've completed.

By starting sooner rather than later in completing your exam application, you'll be focusing more on completing your exam studies than on completing the exam application. In addition, response time from the Project Management Institute (PMI) to accept and approve your application usually takes up to ten days. Start now and you'll be on your way.

PMI's PMP exam will present you with scenario-based questions that will test your project management abilities. The chapter exams and the exams on the CD for this book have been written to be tricky and tough, and to make you think. Practice these exams repeatedly, and they'll help you prepare to pass your PMP exam.

In addition to answering practice questions, you'll want to focus on how the project manager should react in different scenarios. Specifically, you'll need to know how the project manager works through the project processes. You should

be familiar with the project management process groups, what a project deliverable is, and the requirements of a project scope.

All projects are bound by the Triple Constraints of Project Management: time, cost, and scope. Quality is affected by the balance of these three components. The Triple Constraints model is also known as the Iron Triangle, as shown in the following illustration. If any side of the triangle changes, the other two sides should change as well—if not, quality will suffer.

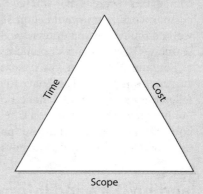

Know that the project moves through phases to reach completion. The project manager oversees the project work as it moves through phases, but the project customer must approve the work. Specifically, the results of phases must pass through scope verification, which is the formal acceptance of the project work.

Defining Project Management Data and Information

A core responsibility for a project manager is writing about the project. You'll be writing about the intent for the project, what's actually occurred in the project, what your plans are for when things go awry in the project (rarely does any project execute as planned), and loads more. Few people enjoy writing about project work, creating project plans, communicating via reports and e-mails, but it's something that's required of every successful project manager.

Here's some good news: Although documenting the project is important, you don't always have to start from scratch. You can reuse plans, reports, and documentation from a previous project, if you have one, as templates for your current project. Use what's been done in the past to help you better communicate and manage your current project. Of course, this assumes that you have access to past project records on which to base your current work. These could come from similar projects you or others in the company have worked on. And if you don't have documents to use as a starting point, a quick Internet search will reveal many documents you can adapt to fit your current project.

For your PMP exam, you'll be asked to adapt past project records as templates for your current project. You'll still have lots of documents to create, but go with the idea that you're following a standard documentation approach in the organization, even if in real life that's not how it works for you. You'll be introduced to lots of documentation throughout the book and in preparation of your passing the PMP, but in this section we'll look at some of the most important project documents.

Understanding Data and Information

Before we get too deep into documentation, however, let's nail down some terms that relate to project management data and information. In a project, lots of data and information will be created, added to your project management information system (PMIS), compiled into reports, distributed, communicated, and sometimes even ignored. You'll need to have good project knowledge to access the needed data and information quickly to communicate what's happening in your project and determine why things are going the way they are.

You need to know three specific concepts that you'll see throughout this book and that describe data and information:

- **Work performance data** This is the raw data and facts about your project work. As your team completes assignments and works on assignments, they'll report their status. The status can be communicated as a percent complete, as in progress, using start and finish dates, and in a number of different formats. You will likely also track the cost of the activities, number of change requests, defects, durations, and more. This business is all about the raw data—good to have, but not actually very useful until you analyze the data.

■ **Work performance information**   Once you've collected the raw data—that is, the work performance data—you'll analyze the data to make sense of it all. This analysis gives you useable information to help you better understand how well your project is actually performing. Work performance information can include the status of deliverables, status of change requests, and project forecasting on time and cost. It's useable information, not just raw data.

■ **Work performance reports**   Ah, reports—the love of every project manager I know. Well, maybe not, but the reports enable you to format and formalize the work performance information and communicate the information to management and stakeholders, and to create a record of where you've been and where you're going in the project. You likely know work performance reports as status reports, memos, dashboards, or project updates. Work performance reports help to communicate project status, but they're also used to help stakeholders make decisions about events and issues within the project.

Reviewing a Project Business Case

Projects that are large in scope will likely be preceded by a *business case*, an analysis of the financial feasibility and validity of the proposed project. The business case will walk through the proposed project, include a sense of how much the project will likely cost, calculate the return on investment for the project, and offer reasons why the project should, or should not, be initiated. The business case can help decision-makers (the project sponsors or the project steering committee) make a go/no-go decision to proceed with the project.

The business case will present details of a needs assessment, or why the project is needed. It will map out the current need or opportunity the project will resolve and the stakeholders affected by the project, and it may rough out the project scope. This document will help identify how the proposed project meshes with the organizational goals and strategies. Business cases provide an analysis of the current state, insight into the risks and opportunities the project presents, and often include a recommendation regarding how the organization should, or should not, deal with the proposed project.

Business cases often begin with the analysis of the need and define the root cause of the project. Also included will be any known risks associated with the proposed project, success factors for the project, and decision criteria for the project, such as required, desired, and optional. A business case might also present options for the project, such as do nothing and maintain business as usual, do the minimum work needed to address the problem or opportunity, or do more than a minimum amount of work and seize the project opportunity.

Creating a Project Benefits Management Plan

When a project is initiated, it sets about to accomplish something, to create something, and, most importantly, to achieve business value for the organization. The project will create a result, and that result is all about benefits. *Benefits* are the results and outcomes of project actions. Consider a construction company, for example: When it constructs a building for a client, there are obvious benefits to the client and community, but there are also benefits for the construction company. The company will generate income, create opportunities to market itself based on the project success, maintain employees, provide educational opportunities with the team, and obtain other benefits as a result of the project work.

A benefits management plan defines the project benefits and typically addresses at least seven components:

- **Target benefits** The tangible and intangible values the project will create. Benefits include the *net present value* of the project, which shows the value of longer projects with intermittent benefits realized during the project.
- **Strategic alignment** How the benefits of the project align with the organizational business strategies.
- **Benefits realization timeline** Defines when the benefits will be realized and useable.
- **Benefits owner** The individual accountable to monitor, record, and provide status of the benefits throughout the project.
- **Metrics** Measurements to show performance on benefits realization.
- **Assumptions** Anything that is believed to be true, but that hasn't actually been proven to be true.
- **Risks** Opportunities or threats for the realization of business. Risks aren't always negative; positive risks are called *opportunities*.

Like most plan development in project management, the development of the benefits management plan is an ongoing, iterative activity. As more information becomes available, things shift in the project, or the organizational goals change, the benefits management plan may need to be updated to reflect the changing environment within the organization.

CERTIFICATION SUMMARY

This chapter covered the fundamentals of project management and the expectations for the PMP examination. The *PMBOK Guide* is an excellent book that documents the ideal processes and procedures for project management. The PMP exam is based on the *PMBOK Guide,* and this book (the one you're reading now) focuses on the key exam essentials to help you pass your PMP exam.

We discussed what a project is and is not. Projects are temporary endeavors to create a unique thing, product, or service. An operation, on the other hand, is a series of activities that go on and on, such as manufacturing a car, writing a newspaper column, or running a business. Many businesses have a business model of completing projects for other people or organizations.

The PMP exam will focus on the function of the project manager, which covers the ten knowledge areas of project management: integration management, time, cost, scope, quality, human resources, communications, risk, procurement, and stakeholder management. Each of these knowledge areas will be discussed in detail in Chapters 4–13 in this book. In this chapter we also discussed the project life cycle and the project management life cycles. The PMP Code of Ethics and Professional Conduct is also discussed in Chapter 14.

Finally, we discussed project documentation. Even before a project begins, documentation is created through business cases and feasibility studies. Business cases examine the financial aspect of completing a project, while feasibility studies examine the feasibility of the organization taking on the project work. If a project is launched, the project documentation abounds. Project documentation can be based on historical information from past projects. Project documentation stems first from the raw data—the work performance data. Once the work performance data is analyzed, it becomes work performance information—information that you can use to make decisions and forecast project performance. Work performance information is then compiled and communicated through work performance reports, such as status reports, memos, or dashboards.

KEY TERMS

To pass the PMP exam, you will need to memorize the following terms and their definitions. For maximum value, create your own flashcards based on these definitions and review them daily.

adaptive life cycle   Adaptive life cycles can be either agile, iterative or incremental. Change is highly probable, and the project team will work closely with the stakeholders regarding any changes in the project. You might also know this approach as *agile* or *change-driven.*

application areas   The areas of discipline that a project may be based on. Consider technology, law, sales, marketing, and construction, among many others.

business value   The total value of the tangible and intangible elements of an organization. Consider liquid assets, real estate, equipment, reputation, brand recognition, and trademarks.

Code of Ethics and Professional Conduct   Addresses the values project managers should possess and addresses integrity, respect, fairness, and honesty.

deliverable   A product, service, or result that a project creates; projects generally create many deliverables as part of the project work.

hybrid life cycle   A combination of predictive and adaptive life cycles. Parts of the project can follow the predictive life cycle, such as project requirements and the budget, yet still utilize the flexibility and iterations that the adaptive life cycle offers.

incremental life cycle   Incremental life cycles create the final product deliverable through a series of increments. Each increment of the project will add more and more functionality. Increments are a predetermined by a set amount of time, such as two or four weeks, for example.

Iron Triangle   A term used to describe the three constraints of every project: time, cost, and scope. The sides of the Iron Triangle must be kept in balance or the quality of the project will suffer. Also known as the Triple Constraints model.

iterative life cycle   This approach requires that the project scope be defined at a high level at the beginning of the project, but the costs and schedules are developed through iterations of planning as the project deliverable is more fully understood. The project moves through iterations of planning and definition based on discoveries during the project execution.

operations   A generic term used to describe the activities that support the core functions of a business entity; the ongoing work of the business.

organizational project management (OPM)   An organizational approach to coordinate, manage, and control projects, programs, and portfolio management in a uniform, consistent effort.

PMBOK Guide   The abbreviated definition for PMI's *A Guide to the Project Management Body of Knowledge.*

PMP   Your goal. A PMP is certified by the Project Management Institute as a Project Management Professional.

portfolio   A collection of projects and programs that have been selected by the organization based on factors such as risk, profitability, business value, business need, market demand, and other components.

predictive life cycle   An approach that requires that the project scope, the project time, and project costs be defined early in the project timeline. Predictive life cycles have predefined phases, where each phase completes a specific type of work and usually overlaps other phases in the project.

programs   A collection of projects working in unison to realize benefits that could not be achieved by managing each project independently of the others.

progressive elaboration   The process of starting with a large idea and, through incremental analysis, actions, and planning, making the idea more and more specific. Progressive elaboration is the generally accepted planning process for project management, wherein the project management team starts with a broad scope and works toward a specific, detailed plan.

project   An undertaking outside of normal operations to create a unique product, service, or result. Projects are temporary, while operations are ongoing.

project communications management   One of the ten project management knowledge areas; it is the planning and management of communication among project stakeholders. (See Chapter 10 for more information on this topic.)

project cost management   One of the ten project management knowledge areas; it is the estimating, budgeting, and controlling of the project expenses. (See Chapter 7.)

project feasibility study   A study that examines the potential project to determine whether it is feasible to do the project work.

project human resource management   One of the ten project management knowledge areas; projects are completed by people, and the project manager generally oversees the management of the human resources on the project team. (See Chapter 9.)

project integration management   One of the ten project management knowledge areas; this knowledge area coordinates the activities and completeness of the other nine knowledge areas. (See Chapter 4.)

project life cycle   The phases of a project as it moves from its launch to completion. Project life cycles are unique to each project and are not universal.

project management   The management of the projects within an organization. It is the initiation, planning, executing, monitoring and controlling, and closing of the temporary endeavor of the project.

project management life cycle   Universal to all projects, this life cycle comprises the project management process groups of initiating, planning, executing, monitoring and controlling, and closing. The process groups are not phases, but collections of processes.

project manager   The individual who manages the project's activities for an organization.

project portfolio management   A management process to select the projects that should be invested in. Specifically, it is the selection process based on the need, profitability, and affordability of the proposed projects.

project procurement management   One of the ten project management knowledge areas; this knowledge area oversees the purchasing and contract administration for a project. (See Chapter 12.)

project quality management   One of the ten project management knowledge areas; this knowledge area defines quality assurance, quality control, and the quality policy for the project. (See Chapter 8.)

project risk management   One of the ten project management knowledge areas; project risk management defines the risk identification, analysis, responses, and control of risk events. (See Chapter 11.)

project schedule management   One of the ten project management knowledge areas; this knowledge area defines the approach to time estimating, scheduling, and control of the project activities. (See Chapter 6.)

project scope management   One of the ten project management knowledge areas; this knowledge area defines the project requirements, scope creation, and control. (See Chapter 5.)

stage gates   Also known as project phase completions, these allow a project to continue after a performance and deliverable review against a set of predefined metrics. If the deliverables of the phase, or stage, meet the predefined metrics, the project is allowed to continue.

subprojects   Exists under a parent project, but follows its own schedule to completion. Subprojects may be outsourced, assigned to other project managers, or managed by the parent project manager but with a different project team.

The Standard for Project Management   A foundational publication, included in the *PMBOK Guide*, sixth edition, that describes, not prescribes, the most common best practices of project management.

work breakdown structure   The visual decomposition of the project scope that represents all of the deliverables the project promises to create.

TWO-MINUTE DRILL

The *PMBOK Guide*, This Book, and the PMP Exam

- ❑ The PMP exam is based on your experience and the sixth edition of PMI's book *A Guide to the Project Management Body of Knowledge.*
- ❑ This book, the one you're reading now, explains project management in plain language and helps you prepare to pass the PMP exam.
- ❑ Not everyone can take the PMP exam—you have to qualify for the test first.

Defining What a Project Is—and Is Not

- ❑ Projects are temporary, unique, and create a product, result, or service.
- ❑ Projects move from concept to completion through progressive elaboration.
- ❑ Not all projects get selected. The reasons for choosing one project over another may vary from organization to organization. The selection of projects to be initiated and invested in is part of project portfolio management.
- ❑ Projects have a definite beginning, middle, and ending; operations do not.
- ❑ Programs are a collection of projects working in unison to realize benefits that would not be available if the projects were managed independently of one another.

Defining Project Management

❑ Within the project management framework are ten knowledge areas that span the project management life cycle.

❑ The focus of project integration management is managing all of the interactions of project components, processes, and knowledge areas.

❑ The focus of project scope management is on protecting, fulfilling, and achieving the project objectives and benefits.

❑ The focus of project schedule management is on scheduling activities, monitoring the project schedule, and working with the project team and stakeholders to ensure that the project completes on time.

❑ The focus of project cost management is on estimating and maintaining project costs.

❑ The focus of project quality management is on setting the quality expectations and then delivering the project product with the expected level of quality.

❑ The focus of project human resources management is on developing the project team to work together to deliver the project as expected.

❑ The focus of project communications management is on delivering needed information to the correct parties at the correct time. Much of project communications involves keeping the stakeholder informed of the project issues, risk, progress, and overall performance.

❑ The focus of project risk management is on identifying and managing project threats and opportunities.

❑ The focus of project procurement management is communicating with, selecting, and managing vendors to complete project work, deliver a project subcomponent, or supply project materials.

❑ The focus of project stakeholder management is identifying project stakeholders, planning the management of the stakeholders, and then managing and controlling the stakeholder engagement throughout the project.

Examining Related Areas of Project Management

❑ Projects often operate under the auspices of a program. A program is a collection of projects working together for a common goal. By orchestrating the management of the projects, benefits are realized that may not have been achieved if the projects were managed independently of one another.

❑ A project manager must have multiple skills to be successful, including the ability to organize, solve problems, communicate, manage a budget, negotiate, and provide leadership for the project.

❑ Project managers in different sectors of business, government, and nonprofit entities will encounter situations unique to their area of expertise. For example, a project manager of a construction project will have issues and concerns that differ from those of a project manager of a manufacturing project.

Revving Through the Project Life Cycle

❑ Predictive life cycles predict the work that will happen with the project. Predictive life cycles are known as waterfall projects or plan-driven projects.

❑ Iterative life cycles plan the scope at a high level at the beginning of the project, but project costs and schedules are developed through iterations of planning as the deliverables of the project are more clearly defined.

❑ Incremental life cycles create the final product deliverable through a series of increments. Each increment of the project will add more and more functionality. Like the iterative life cycle, increments are a predetermined set amount of time, such as two or four weeks.

❑ Adaptive life cycles are either agile, iterative, or incremental. Adaptive life cycles follow a defined methodology such as Scrum or eXtreme Programming (XP). Change is highly probable, and the project team will be working closely with the project stakeholders.

❑ Hybrid life cycle is a combination of predictive and adaptive life cycles. Parts of the project can follow the predictive life cycle, such as project requirements and the budget, yet still utilize the flexibility and iterations that the adaptive life cycle offers.

Defining Project Management Data and Information

❑ Work performance data is the raw data and facts about the project work. Work performance data are items likes percent of activities completed, start and finish dates, number of change requests, and actual duration of tasks.

❑ Work performance information is the processed, useable analysis of work performance data. Work performance data is analyzed and then becomes work performance information—useable information to make project decisions.

❑ Work performance reports are communications about project performance, such as status reports or variance reports. Work performance reports take the work performance information and formats and publish the information to communicate what's happening within the project.

SELF TEST

1. As a PMP candidate, you must have a firm grasp on what constitutes a project. Which one of the following is *not* an attribute of a project?
    A. Has a definite starting date
    B. Has no definite end date
    C. Creates a product, service, or result
    D. Requires resources

2. You are a project manager for Johnson Keyboards, Inc. Your organization has adapted the *PMBOK Guide* as a standard tool for how projects should operate, and you are involved in shaping the standardization for all future projects. In light of this information, what is the recommended course of action for the processes and procedures in the *PMBOK Guide*?
    A. Not all processes and procedures in the *PMBOK Guide* are actually required on all projects.
    B. All processes and procedures are to be followed as defined in the *PMBOK Guide*.
    C. Not all processes and procedures are needed, unless the *PMBOK Guide* states the process or procedure is a requirement for the project type.
    D. All processes and procedures are to be followed as identified in the *PMBOK Guide*; otherwise, the PMP is in violation of the PMP Code of Ethics and Professional Conduct.

3. Your organization is considering launching a new project. Robert, the CEO, wants to know what business value the proposed project will contribute. Which one of the following is *not* an example of business value consideration for a new project?
    A. Return on investment
    B. New equipment
    C. Skills obtained by doing the project
    D. Risk assessments within the project

4. You are explaining to a junior engineer the difference between a project and operations. Which one of the following is true only of operations?
    A. They are performed by people.
    B. They are constrained by limited resources.
    C. They are ongoing.
    D. They are planned, executed, and controlled.

5. You are the project manager for your company, Mark Manufacturers. Your company has a large client that has requested that a special component be created for one of its test engines. Your

organization agrees and creates a standard contract with the customer, and your manager assigns you to manage this project. The project was launched because of which one of the following?

    A. A customer request

    B. A change in the technology your customer is creating

    C. A legal requirement (contractual)

    D. An organizational need

6. Project managers are not responsible for which one of the following in most organizations?

    A. Identifying the project requirements

    B. Selecting the projects to be initiated

    C. Balancing demands for time, cost, scope, and quality

    D. Establishing clear and achievable project objectives

7. You and William, a project stakeholder, are discussing risks within your project. Which one of the following best describes risk?

    A. Any event that can cause your project to fail

    B. Any event that may have a positive or negative effect on your project's team

    C. An uncertain event that may have a positive or negative effect on your project

    D. An event that will cause time and cost constraints to be broken

8. You are the project manager for a large software development project. You have concerns that one of the components of the Iron Triangle is slipping. Your project sponsor, Jim Bob, is not familiar with the Iron Triangle, so you explain the concept to him. What will be affected if any angle of the Iron Triangle is not kept in balance?

    A. Cost

    B. Quality

    C. Time

    D. Scope

9. Which knowledge area includes the creation of the project charter?

    A. Project scope management

    B. Project cost management

    C. Project integration management

    D. Project communications management

10. Beth is a project manager and she's working with Karen, the program manager. There is some disagreement about the project management methodology Karen is requiring all project managers to operate by. Who has authority over this decision in this scenario?

    A. Project sponsor

    B. Karen, as she is the program manager

    C. Beth, as she is the project manager

    D. Beth, as each project manager can select the appropriate project management methodology regardless of the program

11. You are working on a construction project that proceeds through the following sequential steps: planning and prebuild, permits and filings, site prep and excavation, build basement and foundation, framing, interior, and exterior. Each needs to be executed to the highest quality. Which one of the following is an example of a project life cycle phase?

    A. Framing

    B. Phase gate review

    C. Project quality management

    D. Executing

12. Smith Construction has won a contract to build a 77-story condominium building in downtown Chicago. The building will have 650 condos, a parking garage, indoor and outdoor pools, two floors for retail, two floors of offices, and several shared community rooms. Mary Anne Kedzie has elected to create a program for the creation of the building. Which one of the following best describes a program?

    A. A standardized approach to project management within an organization

    B. A standardized approach to project management with multiple projects coordinated together

    C. A collection of related projects managed in coordination to gain control that would not necessarily be available if the projects were managed independently

    D. A collection of related projects all contributing to one deliverable

13. Which one of the following statements best defines the difference between a program and a portfolio in regard to scope?

    A. Programs do not have scopes, because they are made up of projects. Portfolios have an organizational scope.

    B. Programs have larger scopes than projects. Portfolios have an organizational scope.

    C. Programs have larger scopes than projects. Portfolios don't have scopes because they are a financial investment.

    D. Programs and portfolios can share the same scope because a portfolio may have two or more programs.

14. Who is usually responsible for portfolio management within an organization?

    A. Project managers

    B. Project sponsors

    C. Stakeholders

    D. Senior management

15. You are the project manager of a large project to install 1900 kiosks throughout college campuses in North America. The kiosks will collect applications for credit cards, phone services, and other services marketable to college students. The bulk of your project is focused on information technology integration, the wide area network (WAN) connections from each kiosk, security of the data transferred, and the database of the information gathered. For ease of management, you have hired local contractors to install the kiosks that you will ship to each campus. The contractors

on each campus will be responsible for the WAN connection, the electrical connection, the security of the kiosk, and all testing. The local contracted work could be called what?

A. Risk mitigation

B. Operations

C. Subprojects

D. Management by projects

16. You'll need to know and be familiar with several different project life cycle approaches for your PMP exam. Which life cycle approach defines the project scope, timeline, and project costs early in the project?

A. Predictive

B. Iterative

C. Incremental

D. Adaptive

17. Which of the following is likely to be part of an operation?

A. Providing electricity to a community

B. Designing an electrical grid for a new community

C. Building a new dam as a source for electricity

D. Informing the public about changes at the electrical company

18. Of the following, which one is *not* part of project integration management?

A. The creation of the project plan

B. The interaction between project teams

C. The execution of the project plan

D. The documentation of changes to the project plan

19. You are the project manager for the Fixture Installation Project in your organization. You've just completed the second of three phases. What event will happen next?

A. Phase gate review

B. Initiating of the third phase

C. Project quality management activities

D. Phase closure

20. You are a new project manager in a company that uses a project management office. A new technology has been released in the marketplace that will supersede the technology your project is implementing. There are doubts that the project should continue. Martin, a member of the project management office, is considering the amount of funds already invested in the project. What term is given to the monies you've already spent in the project?

A. Capital losses

B. Return on investment

C. Sunk costs

D. In the red

21. What term best describes the raw data of a project, such as number of change requests and actual duration?
    A. Project data outcomes
    B. Work performance information
    C. Work performance data
    D. Work performance reports

22. The project manager typically devotes the most amount of time to which of the following tasks?
    A. Communications
    B. Budget management
    C. Project organization
    D. Management of team negotiations

23. You have an excellent idea for a new project that can increase productivity by 20 percent in your organization. Management, however, declines to approve the proposed project because too many resources are already devoted to other projects. You have just experienced what?
    A. Parametric modeling
    B. Management by exception
    C. Project portfolio management
    D. Management reserve

24. Which one of the following documents is an analysis of the financial feasibility of a proposed project?
    A. Feasibility study
    B. Business case
    C. Feasibility case
    D. Portfolio analysis review

25. Of the following, which is the most important stakeholder involved with a project?
    A. The project manager
    B. The project sponsor
    C. The chief executive officer (CEO)
    D. The customer

SELF TEST ANSWERS

1. As a PMP candidate, you must have a firm grasp on what constitutes a project. Which one of the following is *not* an attribute of a project?
   A. Has a definite starting date
   B. Has no definite end date
   C. Creates a product, service, or result
   D. Requires resources

   ☑ **B.** A project does have a definite end date; operations do not.
   ☒ **A, C,** and **D** are incorrect. Projects do have a definite starting date; they do create a unique product, service, or result; and all projects require resources.

2. You are a project manager for Johnson Keyboards, Inc. Your organization has adapted the *PMBOK Guide* as a standard tool for how projects should operate, and you are involved in shaping the standardization for all future projects. In light of this information, what is the recommended course of action for the processes and procedures in the *PMBOK Guide*?
   A. Not all processes and procedures in the *PMBOK Guide* are actually required on all projects.
   B. All processes and procedures are to be followed as defined in the *PMBOK Guide*.
   C. Not all processes and procedures are needed, unless the *PMBOK Guide* states the process or procedure is a requirement for the project type.
   D. All processes and procedures are to be followed as identified in the *PMBOK Guide*; otherwise, the PMP is in violation of the PMP Code of Ethics and Professional Conduct.

   ☑ **A.** Not all information in the *PMBOK Guide* should be applied uniformly to all projects. It is the responsibility of the project management team to determine what practices are appropriate for each project.
   ☒ **B, C,** and **D** are incorrect. They are all false statements regarding the implementation of the *PMBOK Guide*.

3. Your organization is considering launching a new project. Robert, the CEO, wants to know what business value the proposed project will contribute. Which one of the following is *not* an example of business value consideration for a new project?
   A. Return on investment
   B. New equipment
   C. Skills obtained by doing the project
   D. Risk assessments within the project

☑   **D.** A risk assessment within the project is not a business value, but a project management activity. Risks can be positive or negative, but the assessment of a risk is not a business value element. Business value means that the project is contributing something positive for the organization.

☒   **A, B,** and **C** are incorrect. **A** is incorrect because return on investment is an example of business value. **B,** new equipment, can be a business value consideration because the equipment will be owned as an asset by the organization and can be used in other endeavors. **C,** skills obtained by doing the project, is a business value. By doing the project, the project team members may learn skills that can enable the organization to grow on future projects and in operations.

4. You are explaining to a junior engineer the difference between a project and operations. Which one of the following is true only of operations?
    A.   They are performed by people.
    B.   They are constrained by limited resources.
    C.   They are ongoing.
    D.   They are planned, executed, and controlled.

☑   **C.** Operations are ongoing and can last for as long as the organization is in business. Projects are temporary; they do not go on forever.

☒   **A, B,** and **D** are incorrect. Projects and operations are performed by people, are constrained by limited resources, and are planned, executed, and controlled.

5. You are the project manager for your company, Mark Manufacturers. Your company has a large client that has requested that a special component be created for one of its test engines. Your organization agrees and creates a standard contract with the customer, and your manager assigns you to manage this project. The project was launched because of which one of the following?
    A.   A customer request
    B.   A change in the technology your customer is creating
    C.   A legal requirement (contractual)
    D.   An organizational need

☑   **A.** This project was launched because the customer requested the new component.

☒   **B, C,** and **D** are incorrect. **B** is incorrect because the project is not a response to a change in technology, but a customer request. **C,** a legal requirement, is incorrect because this actually refers to a law or mandated regulation that has been created. **D,** an organizational need, typically refers to a project to improve the performance of the organization.

6. Project managers are not responsible for which one of the following in most organizations?
    A.   Identifying the project requirements
    B.   Selecting the projects to be initiated
    C.   Balancing demands for time, cost, scope, and quality
    D.   Establishing clear and achievable project objectives

☑ **B.** Project managers typically do not select which projects are to be initiated. The project selection committee, customers, or project sponsors are typically responsible for this.

☒ **A, C,** and **D** are incorrect. The project manager is responsible for these activities.

7. You and William, a project stakeholder, are discussing risks within your project. Which one of the following best describes risk?

A. Any event that can cause your project to fail

B. Any event that may have a positive or negative effect on your project's team

C. An uncertain event that may have a positive or negative effect on your project

D. An event that will cause time and cost constraints to be broken

☑ **C.** Risk is an uncertain event that can have a positive or negative effect on your project.

☒ **A, B,** and **D** are incorrect. These are all characteristics of risk, but the best choice is **C** because risk is uncertain and may have a positive or negative effect on the project.

8. You are the project manager for a large software development project. You have concerns that one of the components of the Iron Triangle is slipping. Your project sponsor, Jim Bob, is not familiar with the Iron Triangle, so you explain the concept to him. What will be affected if any angle of the Iron Triangle is not kept in balance?

A. Cost

B. Quality

C. Time

D. Scope

☑ **B.** If any angle of the Iron Triangle is changed, the quality of the project will suffer.

☒ **A, C,** and **D** are incorrect. Cost, time, and scope are the three sides of the Iron Triangle. These three sides must be kept in balance or quality will suffer.

9. Which knowledge area includes the creation of the project charter?

A. Project scope management

B. Project cost management

C. Project integration management

D. Project communications management

☑ **C.** Project integration management, which focuses on the coordination of all components of project management, includes the development of the project charter.

☒ **A, B,** and **D** are incorrect. **A** is incorrect because project scope management focuses on the creation and control of the project scope. **B,** project cost management, is incorrect because its role is to manage, control, and respond to the financial concerns within the project. **D,** project communications management, focuses on who needs what information, when is it needed, and in what modality.

10. Beth is a project manager and she's working with Karen, the program manager. There is some disagreement about the project management methodology Karen is requiring all project managers to operate by. Who has authority over this decision in this scenario?

    A. Project sponsor

    B. Karen, as she is the program manager

    C. Beth, as she is the project manager

    D. Beth, as each project manager can select the appropriate project management methodology regardless of the program

    ☑   **B.** Karen, the program manager, oversees the project managers and the approach they'll take in managing their individual projects.

    ☒   **A, C,** and **D** are incorrect. A is incorrect because the project sponsor would defer to the program manager, as this decision fits within Karen's roles and responsibilities. **C** is incorrect; Beth may be the project manager, but she must follow Karen's directives for project management within the program. **D** is also incorrect, because each project manager doesn't choose her project management methodology, but defers to a common approach for projects within the program.

11. You are working on a construction project that proceeds through the following sequential steps: planning and prebuild, permits and filings, site prep and excavation, build basement and foundation, framing, interior, and exterior. Each needs to be executed to the highest quality. Which one of the following is an example of a project life cycle phase?

    A. Framing

    B. Phase gate review

    C. Project quality management

    D. Executing

    ☑   **A.** Of all the choices presented, only framing is a project life cycle phase. A life cycle phase is unique to a project and shows the type of work and expected deliverables achieved within that phase.

    ☒   **B, C,** and **D** are incorrect. These are not project phases. **B,** the phase gate review, happens at the end of a phase. **C,** project quality management, is a knowledge area, not a phase. **D,** executing, is a process group.

12. Smith Construction has won a contract to build a 77-story condominium building in downtown Chicago. The building will have 650 condos, a parking garage, indoor and outdoor pools, two floors for retail, two floors of offices, and several shared community rooms. Mary Anne Kedzie

has elected to create a program for the creation of the building. Which one of the following best describes a program?

A. A standardized approach to project management within an organization

B. A standardized approach to project management with multiple projects coordinated together

C. A collection of related projects managed in coordination to gain control that would not necessarily be available if the projects were managed independently

D. A collection of related projects, all contributing to one deliverable

> ☑ **C.** A program is a collection of related projects managed and coordinated together to gain a higher level of control.
> ☒ **A, B,** and **D** are incorrect. These do not accurately describe a program. **D** is not the best answer, because programs typically create many deliverables and benefits—rarely just one deliverable.

13. Which one of the following statements best defines the difference between a program and a portfolio in regard to scope?

A. Programs do not have scopes, because they are made up of projects. Portfolios have an organizational scope.

B. Programs have larger scopes than projects. Portfolios have an organizational scope.

C. Programs have larger scopes than projects. Portfolios don't have scopes because they are a financial investment.

D. Programs and portfolios can share the same scope because a portfolio may have two or more programs.

> ☑ **B.** Portfolios have an organizational scope that reflects the strategic goals of the organization. Programs have larger scopes than projects and may be part of portfolios.
> ☒ **A, C,** and **D** are incorrect. **A** is incorrect because programs do have scopes. **C** is incorrect because portfolios do have organizational scopes and are not financial investments. **D** is incorrect because programs and portfolios won't have the same scope. Programs may be part of a portfolio, but portfolios have an organizational scope.

14. Who is usually responsible for portfolio management within an organization?

A. Project managers

B. Project sponsors

C. Stakeholders

D. Senior management

> ☑ **D.** Senior management is responsible for portfolio management.
> ☒ **A, B,** and **C** are incorrect. **A** is incorrect because project managers are responsible for a project's success, but they are not responsible for the portfolio. **B,** project sponsors, authorize projects. **C,** stakeholders, is incorrect because stakeholders is too vague to be an acceptable answer.

15. You are the project manager of a large project to install 1900 kiosks throughout college campuses in North America. The kiosks will collect applications for credit cards, phone services, and other services marketable to college students. The bulk of your project is focused on information technology integration, the wide area network (WAN) connections from each kiosk, security of the data transferred, and the database of the information gathered. For ease of management, you have hired local contractors to install the kiosks that you will ship to each campus. The contractors on each campus will be responsible for the WAN connection, the electrical connection, the security of the kiosk, and all testing. The local contracted work could be called what?
    A. Risk mitigation
    B. Operations
    C. Subprojects
    D. Management by projects

    ☑ **C.** This is the best answer because work that is subcontracted out for ease of management, as in this situation, becomes a subproject.
    ☒ **A, B,** and **D** are incorrect. **A** is incorrect because risk mitigation describes the measures a project manager takes to reduce or eliminate risks. The scenario did not provide enough information to determine what risks would have been mitigated. **B,** operations, is incorrect because it does not describe this scenario at all. **D,** management by projects, is incorrect because this term describes a company that operates through projects. There is no indication that this is true of the scenario presented.

16. You'll need to know and be familiar with several different project life cycle approaches for your PMP exam. Which life cycle approach defines the project scope, timeline, and project costs early in the project?
    A. Predictive
    B. Iterative
    C. Incremental
    D. Adaptive

    ☑ **A.** The predictive approach requires the project scope, the project timeline, and project costs to be defined early in the project timeline. Predictive life cycles have predefined phases, where each phase completes a specific type of work and usually overlaps other phases in the project.
    ☒ **B, C,** and **D** are incorrect. These life cycles do not plan the project scope, the project timeline, and the project costs early in the project.

17. Which of the following is likely to be part of an operation?
   A.   Providing electricity to a community
   B.   Designing an electrical grid for a new community
   C.   Building a new dam as a source for electricity
   D.   Informing the public about changes at the electrical company

☑   **A.** An electrical company's primary operation is to provide electricity; it is ongoing and there is no end to its operation.
☒   **B, C,** and **D** are incorrect. **B** and **C** are projects, not operations. Although **D,** providing information, could potentially be part of an ongoing operation, **A** is still the best answer presented.

18. Of the following, which one is *not* part of project integration management?
   A.   The creation of the project plan
   B.   The interaction between project teams
   C.   The execution of the project plan
   D.   The documentation of changes to the project plan

☑   **B.** Project integration management focuses on the project plan and its implementation, not the interaction between project teams. Although this answer could, in some instances, be considered part of integration management if the project plan had some interaction with other project teams, that assumption cannot be made in this question.
☒   **A, C,** and **D** are incorrect. These are all part of project integration management, so they are not valid answers.

19. You are the project manager for the Fixture Installation Project in your organization. You've just completed the second of three phases. What event will happen next?
   A.   Phase gate review
   B.   Initiating of the third phase
   C.   Project quality management activities
   D.   Phase closure

☑   **A.** Phase gate reviews happen at the end of each project phase and before the next phase begins. These are an opportunity to review the project work so far and to confirm that the project can and should move forward.
☒   **B, C,** and **D** are incorrect. **B** is incorrect, because the third phase of the project will commence after the phase gate review. **C,** project quality management activities, will happen throughout the project, not just at the end of a phase. **D** isn't a valid project management term.

20. You are a new project manager in a company that uses a project management office. A new technology has been released in the marketplace that will supersede the technology your project is implementing. There are doubts that the project should continue. Martin, a member of the project management office, is considering the amount of funds already invested in the project. What term is given to the monies you've already spent in the project?
    A. Capital losses
    B. Return on investment
    C. Sunk costs
    D. In the red

    ☑   **C.** Sunk costs describe the funds already "sunk" into a project, and they should not be considered when determining whether a project should move forward or not.
    ☒   **A, B,** and **D** are incorrect. **A** is incorrect because capital losses describe the money that is lost, never to be recouped. **B** is incorrect because return on investment is the money earned after the project is completed and as a result of the investment made in the project endeavor. **D,** in the red, is a term used to describe a project that is losing money. *In the red* is a financial slang for an endeavor that is not profitable (*in the black*, on the other hand, means that your project is profitable).

21. What term best describes the raw data of a project, such as number of change requests and actual duration?
    A. Project data outcomes
    B. Work performance information
    C. Work performance data
    D. Work performance reports

    ☑   **C.** Work performance data is the raw data and facts about the project work.
    ☒   **A, B,** and **D** are incorrect. **A,** project data outcomes, is not a viable project management term. **B** is incorrect because work performance information is the result of analyzed data, not raw data. **D,** work performance reports, are documents that communicate information about the project.

22. The project manager typically devotes the most amount of time to which of the following tasks?
    A. Communications
    B. Budget management
    C. Project organization
    D. Management of team negotiations

    ☑   **A.** It's been said that project managers spend 90 percent of their time communicating.
    ☒   **B, C,** and **D** are incorrect. The project manager does not devote most of his time to these tasks.

23. You have an excellent idea for a new project that can increase productivity by 20 percent in your organization. Management, however, declines to approve the proposed project because too many resources are already devoted to other projects. You have just experienced what?

A. Parametric modeling

B. Management by exception

C. Project portfolio management

D. Management reserve

☑ **C.** Project portfolio management is the process of choosing and prioritizing projects within an organization. An excellent project idea can still be denied if there aren't enough resources to complete the project work.

☒ **A, B,** and **D** are incorrect. **A** is incorrect because parametric modeling is used to estimate costs, such as cost per ton or cost per hour. **B** is incorrect because this is a management theory to manage people and problems. **D** is incorrect because management reserve is an amount of time and money reserved for projects running late or over budget.

24. Which one of the following documents is an analysis of the financial feasibility of a proposed project?

A. Feasibility study

B. Business case

C. Feasibility case

D. Portfolio analysis review

☑ **B.** Projects that are large in scope will likely be preceded by a business case. A business case is an analysis of the financial feasibility and validity of a proposed project.

☒ **A, C,** and **D** are incorrect. **A,** feasibility study, is a study of whether the organization has the capabilities to undertake the proposed project or whether some aspect needed for the project can do what it is supposed to do (for instance, can the technology perform as specified?). This could be a phase of a project. **C** and **D** are incorrect because these are not valid project management terms.

25. Of the following, which is the most important stakeholder involved with a project?

A. The project manager

B. The project sponsor

C. The CEO

D. The customer

☑ **D.** Customers, internal or external, are the most important stakeholders in a project.

☒ **A, B,** and **C** are incorrect. **A** is incorrect because the project manager manages the project for the customer. **B** is incorrect because the project sponsor authorizes the project. **C** is incorrect because the CEO may not even know about the project—and even so, she would be interested in the success of the project for the customer.

Chapter 2

Managing Projects in Different Environments

CERTIFICATION OBJECTIVES

2.01	Utilizing Enterprise Environmental Factors	2.04	Completing Projects in Different Organizational Structures
2.02	Leveraging Organizational Process Assets	✓	Two-Minute Drill
2.03	Working with Organizational Systems	Q&A	Self Test

Where you work as a project manager is likely different from where other readers of this book work. Just as every project is unique, so, too, is the environment in which a project exists. Consider software development projects, construction projects, IT infrastructure projects, learning and development projects, and many other different types of projects. Each of these projects operates in a distinct environment. The environment is a factor of influence in these projects and in your projects.

The environment in which a project exists can influence the expectations of the project manager, how you manage the project, how stakeholders contribute to the project, and a myriad of other concerns. Understanding the environment and what's expected of the project manager as far as formalities, processes, rules, and regulations—and even simpler things like templates and forms—are all part of the project environment.

Often when we discuss the project environment, we think of things like the tangible attributes of where the project takes place: construction sites, offices, hospital settings, and more. Although these are certainly part of the environment, there's also the political landscape, the reputation of the project manager and stakeholders, and the industry influence in which the project is operating. The environment includes all characteristics of where the project exists—all the moving parts, the seen and unseen, and the expectations of management regarding the project manager; these are all parts of the project environment.

CERTIFICATION OBJECTIVE 2.01

Utilizing Enterprise Environmental Factors

Enterprise environmental factors are the elements that directly or indirectly influence the management of the project, but the project manager has no direct control over these elements. For example, your organization may have particular rules for bringing a project team member onto your project. This rule is outside of your control, and you must abide by it. This rule might sometimes hinder you from zipping along in project execution, but it also helps bring order and control to the projects within the organization. Just as organizational process assets are inputs to many project management processes, so, too, are enterprise environmental factors.

Every organization has unique enterprise environmental factors. For the PMP exam, you'll need to recognize that enterprise environmental factors are things that the project manager must abide by but has very little control over. Enterprise environmental factors are basically rules and policies, but they could also include regulations that directly influence how the project manager manages the project. You'll see enterprise environmental factors often through this book, the *PMBOK Guide*, and likely your PMP exam.

Reviewing Internal Enterprise Environmental Factors

There are internal and external enterprise environmental factors that you'll have to work with—and know for your exam. Internal enterprise environmental factors are the factors unique to your organization. To be clear, there's sometimes a negative connotation about enterprise environmental factors, because you're required to use them and abide by them. Sure, some enterprise environmental factors may be a pain to deal with and work through, but they're designed to create structure and framework, and to establish a common approach to all projects within your organization.

Here are some common internal enterprise environmental factors:

- **Organizational culture, structure, and governance** Probably the most obvious internal enterprise environmental factor is the makeup of your organization. Consider the leadership, vision, beliefs, hierarchy of management, ethics, and organizational code of conduct expectations.
- **Physical location of resources and facilities** In a large organization, facilities and resources may be dispersed around the globe. The physical location of resources and worksites can directly influence how you manage your project. Challenges can include communications, risks, and sharing and accessing resources.
- **Infrastructure of your organization** Consider the equipment, facilities, tools, communication channels, technology, and the availability and capabilities of these resources.
- **IT software** Most project managers utilize software for scheduling, configuration management, online systems, and work authorization systems. This software, often required to be used, is a great example of an enterprise environmental factor.
- **Resource availability** Resources aren't just people and could also include tools, equipment, facilities, and materials. The internal processes the project manager must follow to obtain resources, such as procurement, contracting, and subcontractors, can all influence the project management approach.
- **Employee capability** You must also examine the capabilities of the employees involved in the project. You'll need to consider their expertise, skillsets, competencies, and any specialized knowledge. You're looking for those with skills as well as those who need training.

These are just some of the more common internal enterprise environmental factors. Other factors in your organization may cause the project management approach to be limited in other ways. For your PMP exam, however, these are the most common ones to recognize.

Reviewing External Enterprise Environmental Factors

External enterprise environmental factors are conditions, regulations, and other influences that affect how you manage your project. Not all projects will, of course, have the exact same external enterprise environmental factors, because many factors are industry specific. For example, a healthcare organization won't have the same enterprise environmental factors as a banking organization. External factors are somewhat broad, and your industry will likely have more specific factors because of the nature of your work. For your exam, you should be familiar with the following external enterprise environmental factors:

- **Marketplace conditions** The marketplace you operate within is an enterprise environmental factor. Consider your competition, market share, organizational brand, trademarks, and the economic makeup of your industry.

- **Cultural influences and issues** How your industry is perceived is an external enterprise environmental factor. The political climate, customer perceptions, and news within your industry all are cultural influences and issues that make up the unique external enterprise environmental factors. For example, consider the cultural factors surrounding the weapons industry and how they affect these organizations' operations.

- **Laws and regulations** Laws and regulations are external enterprise environmental factors that directly affect the management of projects.

- **Commercial databases** Databases that organization purchase to help predict cost and schedule estimating, risk studies, and benchmarking directly affect how a project is estimated and managed.

- **Academic research** Some organizations rely on information from academic studies, white papers, and other publications to guide their efforts and projects.

- **Government and industry standards** Organizations can adhere to government and industry standards for production, environmental considerations, expectations of quality, and the products or services they provide.

- **Financial** Organizations that span countries will likely consider currency exchange rates and tariffs. Longer projects may consider inflation and interest rates.

- **Physical enterprise environmental factors** There's little you can do about the weather, and that's a great example of a physical factor that can affect a project. The environment where the project is taking place is also a physical enterprise environmental factor.

See the video "Enterprise Environmental Factors and Organizational Process Assets."

CERTIFICATION OBJECTIVE 2.02

Leveraging Organizational Process Assets

"Organizational process assets" is a nice way of referring to all the resources within an organization that can be used, leveraged, researched, or interviewed to make a project successful. This means past projects, subject matter experts within your organization, risk databases, procedures, plans, processes, stakeholder knowledge, and methods of operations.

As a project manager, your goal is to get things done—that's what project management is all about. Too many project managers get stuck in planning for too long and don't get into execution. I'm not saying you don't need to plan—you do, but you don't need to start from zero every time. When you consider the projects that you manage, chances are there's some similarity between the projects. You're doing the same type of projects over and over, because you're working in a specific industry where the nature of the projects you manage all support the organizational vision and strategies.

You have knowledge that is relevant to your projects types, and you likely have lots of information from past projects to call upon. Past projects can provide information for current projects. Lessons learned, records, and past project files can be leveraged to manage the current project and usher along the planning processes. Sure, there will be some specific things that take time to plan, but you can rely on past projects to speed up portions of the existing projects. This is one of the most valuable concepts of organizational process assets: the past helps the present.

Recognizing Common Organizational Process Assets

Of course, organizational assets will vary from industry to industry, but for the PMP exam, consider all the following:

- Standards, policies, and organizational procedures
- Standardized guidelines and performance measurements
- Templates for project documents such as contracts, work breakdown structures, project network diagrams, and status reports
- Guidelines for adapting project management processes to the current project— remember that not every process needs to be completed on every project
- Financial controls for purchasing, accounting codes, and procurement processes
- Communication requirements within your organization, such as standard forms, procedures, and reports that you must use as a project manager in your organization
- Processes for project activities, such as change control, closing, communications, financial controls, and risk control procedures
- Project closing procedures for acceptance, product validation, and evaluations

Throughout this book, you'll see the term "organizational process assets" used for different processes and inputs for processes. It simply means that you'll rely on information that has been created to help you, the project manager, complete your current job. Organizational process assets are templates, software, and historical information that you can use on your current project. A template, by the way, doesn't always mean a shell of a document, as you might use in Microsoft Word. Templates in project management can be past project plans, scope statements, and just about any other document that you adapt for your current project. There is no reason to reinvent the wheel—project management is tedious enough.

Utilizing Organizational Knowledge Repositories

Ideally, your organization has a method for cataloging, archiving, and retrieving information from past projects and work. The PMBOK calls these the "knowledge repositories." This is most likely an electronic data storage and retrieval system, or it might just be a hallway closet full of past project files. Things the corporate knowledge base should provide include the following:

- Project files from past projects—specifically good records on schedule, cost, risk information, stakeholders, calendars, and overall project measurements
- Historical information and lessons learned about past project decisions, successes and failures, and the outcomes of risk management
- Issue and defect databases that document what issues, defects, or errors were discovered and how they were managed and resolved
- Configuration management databases for versioning software and hardware
- Financial databases with information on project costs, labor costs, cost overages, and other financial concerns

CERTIFICATION OBJECTIVE 2.03

Working with Organizational Systems

A system is a way of doing things. When I wash the dishes, I have a system for how I load the dishwasher that's completely different from my wife's approach. Or when I make purchases, track receipts, and do my company's bookkeeping, I have a system that's orderly and reasonable. Organizations, big and small, need a system that provides structure for how projects and operations complete the assigned work, strategies, and vision of the organization. The organizational system is unique to that company and may have been planned from the start or evolved over time through trial and error.

For your PMP exam, you should know that organizational systems provide structure and governance for how the project manager leads the project team and manages the work of project management. Your organization may have a clearly defined system, or it could be a loose collection of rules and policies that you operate within. In either case, there are management elements, such as permissions, work authorization, and employee discipline, that you abide by. A large organization, or even a small organization managing a large project, may have governance that acts as boundaries and rules for the project manager and stakeholders.

Systems aren't defined by the project manager, but typically by the management and leadership of the organization. The entities, people, departments, and forms and processes within the system are the components of the system. *System dynamics* is a way of describing the relationship between the components, such as the relationship between the IT department and the accounting department. The project manager can find herself mired in office politics, bureaucracy, rules, policies, governance, and other components all while trying to achieve the project goals successfully and get the project done. Understanding how to navigate the system, its components, and governance takes time and finesse, but it's the understanding of the formal and informal organizational systems that will help the project manager better influence the organization for the good of the project.

You'll need to be familiar with the concept of organizational systems—and it's not a tough concept to grasp—for your PMP exam. You won't need to be proficient in organizational systems and theories, but you should recognize that the organizational systems in which a project manager must operate directly affect her amount of power and control over the projects.

Examine Organizational Governance Frameworks

Governance defines what you can and cannot do within an organization. It includes the rules, policies, procedures, and boundaries that you and your colleagues operate within. Governance describes how you operate within a system: the cultural norms, relationships, and organizational processes used to get things done. Consider purchasing, for example: Your organization likely has a process regarding how you contact vendors, move through contracting, sign off on the contracted work, and pay the vendor. This process is all part of the organizational governance framework specifically for your organization. Your framework is likely completely different from that of your competitors, a company in a different industry, and other businesses.

A *framework* is just a way of describing the structure you operate within. Frameworks can be packaged as the boundaries, swim lanes, or ways of doing business for the project manager. Every role, from project manager to manager, operates within the organization's framework. The roles and responsibilities of each person fit into the framework, and the governance of the organization ensures that everyone is following the framework. Yes, governance and frameworks go together—they provide the structure and the rules. For your PMP, know that project governance and frameworks are the boundaries, rules, and space in which to operate for the project manager.

Consider Portfolio, Programs, and Project Governance

A project manager will deal with governance on several different levels. *Portfolios* are the collection of projects and programs that the organization invests in. *Programs* are a collection of projects working toward a common goal. In a program, projects are managed uniformly to achieve benefits that you likely wouldn't get if each project were managed independently of the others. And *projects*, of course, are the temporary endeavors to create a unique product, service, condition, and result. For each of these items, a project governance defines the rules and policies that affect the project manager.

A project manager will have to address four project governance domains: alignment to corporate vision and strategy, risk, project performance, and communications. These four governance domains begin with portfolio management and are implemented into the programs and projects. That's one of the key reasons why projects and programs must first align with the corporate vision and strategy, and contribute to business value in an organization.

What kind of an organization are you in? Does your organization complete projects for other entities? Does your organization treat every process of an operation as an operation? Or does your organization not know what to do with people like you: project managers?

exam

ⓦatch **The portfolio management review board is made up of the organization's decision-makers, who will review, approve, or decline proposed projects and programs.**

Relying on General Management Skills

Management elements are the functions of a manager, including to some extent project managers. Through the governance framework, managers are expected to utilize varying levels of management skills. As a project manager, you'll likely have some, if not all, of the following management elements as part of your role of a project manager:

- Delegation of project work to the project team
- Authority to assign resources to project work
- Expectations of respect for others, authority, and organizational rules
- Unity of command (one person is in charge)
- Unity of direction (one plan driven by one person)
- Clear communication channels
- Provision of materials to people as needed
- Fair and equal treatment of people on the project team and stakeholders
- Positive, optimistic personality

You cannot be an effective project manager without having some abilities as a manager. Makes sense, right? Get this: Management is focused on results. So to get your project team, vendors, and stakeholders to create project results, you should rely on the following:

- Planning for project strategy, tactics to achieve objectives, and operational planning
- Accounting and cash flow management
- Sales and marketing (within your organization and to stakeholders outside of the project)
- Procurement processes, including contracting procedures
- Logistics for travel, schedule, supply chain, and order fulfillment
- Human resource practices and procedures, including working within organizational structures; managing team personnel, compensation, and benefits; and helping project team members reach their career goals
- Industry-specific health and safety practices
- Working with information technology

It's also beneficial to understand how and why your company undertakes projects. Some projects may be internal, others external. When it comes to project management, organizations fall into one or more of three models that affect the management elements of the project manager:

- **Completing projects for others**   These entities swoop into other organizations and complete the project work based on specifications, details, and specification documents. Classical examples of these types of organizations include consultants, architectural firms, technology integration companies, and advertising agencies.

- **Completing projects internally through a system**   These entities have adopted Management by Projects. Management by Projects means that every endeavor in the organization is a project. Organizations using Management by Projects have accounting, time, and management systems in place to account for the cost, time, and worth of each project.

- **Completing projects as needed**   These non-project-centric entities can complete projects successfully but may not have the project systems in place to support projects efficiently. The lack of a project support system can cause the project to succumb to additional risks, lack of organization, and reporting difficulties. Some organizations may have special internal business units to support the projects in motion that are separate from the accounting, time, and management systems used by the rest of the organization.

Considering Organizational Culture

Imagine what it would be like to work as a project manager within a bank in downtown London, versus working as a project manager in a web development company in Las Vegas. Can you picture a clear difference in the expected cultures within these two entities? The organizational culture of an entity will have a direct influence on the success of a project. Organizational culture includes the following:

- Policies and procedures for managing projects in the organization
- Industry regulations, policies, rules, and methods for doing the work
- Values, beliefs, and expectations
- Views of authority, management, labor, and workers
- Work ethic
- Expectations on hours worked and contributions made
- Views toward organizational leadership

As you can imagine, projects with more risk (and expected reward) may be welcome in an organization that readily accepts entrepreneurial ventures rather than in an organization that is less willing to accept chance and risk. Project formality is typically in alignment with the culture of an organization.

Another influence on the progress of a project is the management style of an organization. A project manager who is autocratic in nature will face challenges and opposition in organizations that allow and encourage self-led teams. A project manager must take cues from management as to how the management style of a project should operate. In other words, a project manager emulates the management style of the operating organization.

exam watch

The unique style and culture within each organization is called the *cultural norm*. It's just a way to describe the expectations of behavior within an organization. You won't find the same cultural norm in my company, a small and limber management consulting and training firm, as you would in a Wall Street–based international investment firm. You should also know that the cultural norm in an organization is also an enterprise environmental factor for the project manager.

As a rule, the larger the project, the more people will be involved. More people, as you might anticipate, means you've got more communications work to do as the project manager. Projects that span across the globe have additional challenges for communications: languages, time zones, technological barriers, and cultural differences. We'll talk more about communications management in Chapter 10, but for now you'll need to be aware that expectations for communications, available technologies to communicate, and the culture of the people involved in the communications are all part of the organization's influence on the project's success.

CERTIFICATION OBJECTIVE 2.04

Completing Projects in Different Organizational Structures

Organizations are structured into one of ten models, each with an organizational structure that will affect the project in some aspect. The organizational structure will set the level of authority, the level of autonomy, and the reporting structure that the project manager can expect to have within the project. Figure 2-1 shows the level of authority in each of the organizational structures for the project manager and the functional manager.

I'll discuss the following organizational structures:

- Organic or simple
- Functional (centralized)
- Multidivisional
- Weak matrix
- Balanced matrix
- Strong matrix
- Project-oriented (composite, hybrid)
- Virtual
- Hybrid
- PMO structure

on the **Job**

Being able to recognize your organizational structure regarding project management will enable you to leverage and position your role effectively as a project manager.

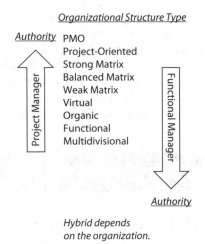

FIGURE 2-1

The organizational
structure affects
the project
manager's
authority.

Organizational Structure Type

Authority   PMO
Project-Oriented
Strong Matrix
Balanced Matrix
Weak Matrix
Virtual
Organic
Functional
Multidivisional

Project Manager

Functional Manager

Authority

*Hybrid depends
on the organization.*

Working in an Organic, or a Simple, Structure

In an organic, or a simple, organizational structure, the work groups within the organization
are flexible. People work alongside one another regardless of their roles in the organization,
and the project manager may have little to no authority over the project resources. The
resources dedicated to the project are low, as the people working on the project will
oscillate between their day-to-day work and the project work. The owner of the organization
will be the individual in charge of the budget. In this structure, it's also unlikely that the
there'll be any administrative staff to help the project manager.

Managing Projects in Functional Organizations

Functional organizations, sometimes called centralized organizations, are entities that have
a clear division regarding business units and their associated responsibilities. For example,
a functional organization may have an accounting department, a manufacturing department,
a research and development department, a marketing department, and so on. Each department
works as a separate entity within the organization, and each employee works in a separate
department. In these centralized organizations, there is a clear distinction between an
employee and a specific functional manager.

Functional organizations do complete projects, but the projects are specific to the function
of the department the project falls into. For example, the IT department could implement
new software for the finance department. The role of the IT department is separate from the
role of the finance department, but the coordination between the two functional departments
would be evident. Communication between departments flows through functional managers

down to the project team. Figure 2-2 depicts the relationships between business departments and the flow of communication between projects and departments.

Project managers in functional organizations have the following attributes:

- Little authority
- Little autonomy
- Report directly to a functional manager
- May be known as project coordinators or team leaders
- Have a part-time role (the project team will also be part time as a result)
- May have little or no administrative staff to expedite the project management activities
- Not in control of the project budget (the functional manager manages the project budget)

Dealing with Multidivisional Structures

In this organization, there'll likely be replication of functions for each division. For example, accounting may have its own IT staff, rather than following the centralized model of a pure functional organization. This structure is similar to the functional organization within each division. The project manager will have little authority and could be called a project coordinator rather than a project manager. The resources for the project will also be part time, though there could a part-time administrative staff to help the project manager. In this structure, the functional manager will also manage the project budget.

FIGURE 2-2

Projects in functional organizations route communications through the functional managers.

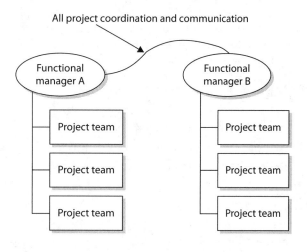

Managing in Matrix Structures

Matrix structures are organizations that utilize employees who perform a blend of departmental and project duties. This type of structure allows for project team members to be from multiple departments, yet all work toward the project completion. In these instances, the project team members have more than one boss. Depending on the number of projects a team member is participating in, he may have to report to multiple project managers as well as to his functional manager.

Weak Matrix

Weak matrix structures map closely to a functional organization. The project team may come from different departments, but the project manager reports directly to a specific functional manager. In weak matrix organizations, the project manager has the following attributes:

- Limited authority
- Management of a part-time project team
- Project manager's role is part time
- May be known as a project coordinator or team leader
- May have part-time administrative staff to help expedite the project
- Not in control of the project budget (the functional manager manages the project budget)

Balanced Matrix

A balanced matrix structure has many of the same attributes as a weak matrix, but the project manager has more time and power with regard to the project. A balanced matrix still has time-accountability issues for all the project team members, since their functional managers will want reports on their time spent on the project. Attributes of a project manager in a balanced matrix include the following:

- Low to moderate amount of authority
- Management of a part-time project team
- Part-time role as a project manager
- May have part-time administrative staff to help expedite the project
- Project manager and functional manager share management of the project budget

Strong Matrix

A strong matrix equates to a strong project manager. In a strong matrix organization, many of the same attributes for the project team exist, but the project manager gains power and time when it comes to project work. The project team may also have more time available for the project even though they may come from multiple departments within the organization. Attributes of a project manager in a strong matrix include the following:

- Moderate to high level of power
- Management of a part-time to nearly full-time project team
- Full-time role as a project manager
- Full-time administrative staff to help expedite the project
- Manage the project budget

Project-Oriented

A project-oriented organizational structure groups employees, collocated or not, by activities on a project. The project manager in a project-oriented structure may have complete, or very close to complete, power over the project team. Project managers in a project-oriented structure enjoy a high level of autonomy over their projects, but they also have a higher level of responsibility regarding the project's success. Sometimes, project-oriented structures are created in a composite or hybrid structure; this means although the organization is typically a functional structure, for example, for a project, the organization will create a project-oriented project manager and team.

Project managers in a project-oriented structure have the following attributes:

- High to complete authority over the project team
- Work full-time on the project with their team (though there may be some slight variation)
- A full-time administrative staff to help expedite the project
- Manage the budget

Serving in a Virtual Organization

A virtual organization utilizes a network structure within the organization. Points of contact represent the different departments or lines of business within the organization. Communication can be a challenge in a virtual organization, as messages are filtered through the point of contact for each department or stakeholder group. The project manager has low authority over the project team and shares authority over the project budget with the functional manager. The project manager could be full time or part time, and the project team members are likely to be working part time on the project. Administrative staff for the project could also be part time or full time—it depends on the organization.

Managing Projects in Hybrid Organizations

On paper, these organizational structures look great. In reality, there are very few companies that map only to one of these structures all the time. For example, a company using the functional model may create a special project consisting of talent from many different departments. Such a project team reports directly to a project manager and will work on a high-priority project for its duration. These entities are a composite, called *hybrid organizations*, in that they may be a blend of multiple organizational types. Figure 2-3 shows a sample of a hybrid structure. Although the AQQ Organization in the figure operates as a traditional functional structure, they've created a special project-oriented project in which each department has contributed resources to the project team.

Because hybrid structures are unique to each organization, it's impossible to define the level or authority and the project manager's role in a project. In some organizations using a hybrid model, the project manager may have total control over the team and the project budget, while other organizations may allocate the project manager authority over the team, but keep the budget management for the functional manager.

Operating Under Project Management Offices

A project management office (PMO) organizes and manages control over all projects within an organization. A PMO is also known as a program management office, project office, or sometimes, the program office. (And I'm sure some project managers have other names for them that won't be on the PMP exam.)

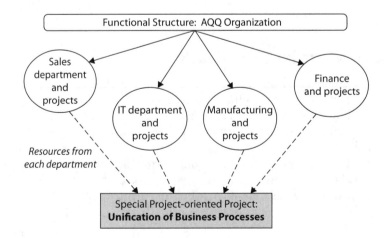

FIGURE 2-3

Hybrid structures are a blend of traditional organizational structures.

PMOs usually coordinate all aspects, methodology, and nomenclature for project processes, templates, software, and resource assignment. Ideally, a PMO creates a uniform approach within an organization so that all projects, regardless of their discipline, technology, or purpose, are managed with the same approach. The PMO can help project managers share resources (people, facilities, and equipment) across projects, offer coaching and communication, help with change control and stakeholder management, and help resolve issues.

Besides creating a uniform approach to project management within an organization, a PMO provides support to the project managers. The support the PMO gives will vary, of course, from organization to organization. Typically, project managers who act within a PMO can expect training, software, templates, standardized project management approaches, and mentoring.

You should be familiar with three general types of PMOs for your exam:

- **Directive PMO** Manages and controls all projects within the organization. The PMO control is considered high.
- **Controlling PMO** Defines project governance through project management frameworks, templates, forms, project management activities, and communications. The PMO control is considered moderate.
- **Supportive PMO** Acts as a consultative role by offering advice, best practices, lessons learned, forms and software, and project information from similar projects. The PMO control is low.

PMOs have an advantage over decentralized project management: risk and communication centralization. All projects have risks, and a PMO can centrally track and monitor all risks within all projects and take advantage and prepare for risks that may, or may not, come to fruition. Thus, a PMO can create a risk database to track pending and past risks and plan accordingly.

On the communications front, a PMO can centralize communication among project managers, project sponsors, managers, and other stakeholders. A centralized communication center can alleviate the demand on project managers to communicate with stakeholders, as all communications can flow through the PMO rather than the individual project manager.

Table 2-1 outlines the benefits and drawbacks of various organizational types.

exam

ⓦatch **The functional manager controls the project's budget in the functional, weak matrix, and to some extent in the balanced matrix. The project manager gains budget control in the strong matrix and project-oriented organizations.**

TABLE 2-1   Benefits and Drawbacks of Various Organizational Types

Organizational Type	Pros	Cons
Organic or simple	People are flexible and work together to do whatever it takes to get the project work done.	People may feel overwhelmed with their day-to-day duties and the added tasks of the project.
Functional	Ideal for organizations with recurring projects, such as manufacturing. Everyone on the project knows who is in charge: the functional manager.	The project manager has little, if any, project authority and may be known as a project expeditor.
Multidivisional	There are clear lines of communication and authority.	There may be duplication of project efforts between departments.
Project-oriented	The project manager has autonomy of control of the project decisions. Improves communication as teams focus on current project work.	Project teams may compete for or stockpile resources. The project team may also lose focus near the end of the project as they are uncertain about their next assignment.
Strong matrix	Project team may be assigned to a project for 50–90 percent of its duration. The project manager has a high level of authority. This model also provides good communication.	Competition over resources still exists. Overall costs may also increase due to redundant administrative staff among projects.
Balanced matrix	The project manager has balanced project authority with management. This model allows efficient use of functional resources.	The functional manager and the project manager may battle for project team members' time. The project team may feel they are reporting to multiple bosses.
Weak matrix	The project manager has little project authority and acts as a project coordinator.	The project is more a part of the functional department operations than a separate activity. Project team resources may be divided among too many projects at once.
Virtual	Resources and departments are segmented and there's a single point of contact for each group represented in the project.	Communication can be a challenge as bottlenecks could exist in the project, based on the availability of the single point of contact for each project group represented in the project.
Project management office	Centralized and standard approach to project management for the entire organization or department.	Can feel stifling or disconnected from the project manager, project team, and stakeholders.

INSIDE THE EXAM

Enterprise environmental factors are the rules that you must work with and abide by on your project in your organization. The industry that you operate in, from construction to healthcare, will have its own set of enterprise environmental factors. Internal environmental factors describe the governance framework and the common approach for getting things done in an organization. External enterprise environmental factors describe the things outside of the organization's control, such as laws and regulations, that also affect how the project manager leads the project.

Projects don't last forever. Though projects may sometimes seem to last forever, they fortunately do not. Operations, however, go on and on. Projects pass through logical phases to reach their completion, while operations may be influenced, or even created, by the outcome of a project.

Along with enterprise environmental factors, you'll also rely on organizational process assets. Organizational process assets are the items that have been created for you to help manage the current project. Organizational process assets can be things like templates and forms, but they can also include historical information. Past projects that are similar

to your current project can hold a trove of information, plans, and resources that you can review and adapt to your current project. This saves time, creates more reliable estimates, and helps to avoid past mistakes and risks that earlier projects may have succumbed to.

Your organization should also have knowledge repositories that are electronic data storage and retrieval systems (though it could be just a filing cabinet of information). Knowledge repositories can be past project files, historical information, lessons learned, issue and defect databases, configuration management databases, and financial databases. The knowledge repositories are supporting details for project decisions, estimates, and actions you'll take on the current project.

You'll see these three items—enterprise environmental factors, organizational process assets, and knowledge repositories—over and over throughout the *PMBOK Guide* and in this book. These are the foundations of good project planning, management, and execution. You'll also want to keep good records of your current project, because what you do today will be tomorrow's historical information. What you do now, and the records you keep, can affect future projects in your organization.

CERTIFICATION SUMMARY

This chapter detailed the enterprise environmental factors, organizational process assets, knowledge repositories you'll utilize, and different organizational structures project managers operate within. The combination of these things controls the amount of authority the project manager has over project resources, the decisions you'll make in the project, and what you're allowed, or not allowed, to do as a project manager.

Projects must operate within the organizational structure. Organizational structures control how the project manager can obtain resources, the level of authority the project manager can expect, and the participation of the project team. There are ten organizational structures:

- Organic or simple
- Functional (centralized)
- Multidivisional
- Weak matrix
- Balanced matrix
- Strong matrix
- Project-oriented (composite, hybrid)
- Virtual
- Hybrid
- PMO structure

You'll need to recognize the characteristics of these ten different organizational structures for the PMP exam. Questions could be based on scenarios in which you're operating in a specific type of structure that would affect the best answer. This can prove challenging for some PMP candidates as they might be tempted to choose how they'd solve the question based on where they work—not a good idea for the PMP exam. Understand the structure to answer the question best based on the structure type, not on your organization.

KEY TERMS

To pass the PMP exam, you will need to memorize these terms and their definitions. For maximum value, create your own flashcards based on these definitions and review them daily.

controlling PMO   Defines project governance through project management frameworks, templates, forms, project management activities, and communications. The PMO control is considered moderate.

cultural norm   The accepted practices, culture, ideas, vision, and nature of an organization.

dedicated project team   This project team works full time on the project for the duration of the project.

directive PMO   Manages and controls all projects within the organization. The PMO control is considered high.

enterprise environmental factors   Elements that create the boundaries for the project manager. These may help or hinder the project manager's ability to navigate within the project. Examples include rules, regulations, industry standards, and organizational procedures the project manager is obliged to follow, and the project team has no control over them.

external enterprise environmental factors   Factors that are outside of the organization's control but confine the decision for the project manager and the project. For example, laws and regulations are external enterprise environmental factors that directly affect the project manager.

functional managers   The managers of the permanent staff in each organizational department, line of business, or function such as sales, finance, and technology. Project managers and functional managers interact on project decisions that affect functions, projects, and operations.

functional organizations   Entities that have a clear division regarding business units and their associated responsibilities. Project managers in functional organizations have little power and report to the functional managers. This organization groups staff according to their expertise—for example, sales, marketing, finance, and information technology. Project managers in functional structures report to functional managers, and the project team exists within one department.

hybrid organizational structure   The organization utilizes a mix of other project structures to create a project structure for a specific project. For example, an organization could be a weak matrix, but for one high-priority project, it shifts to a project-centric environment.

internal enterprise environmental factors   Factors unique to an organization that confine the project decisions for the project manager and the project team.

matrix structure   An organization that groups staff by function but openly shares resources on project teams throughout the organization. Project managers in a matrix structure share the power with functional management. Three types of matrix structures—weak, balanced, and strong—describe the amount of authority granted to the project manager.

multidivisional structure   Replication of functions for each division. This structure is similar to the functional organization within each division. The project manager will have little authority and could be called a project coordinator rather than a project manager.

operations manager   Deal directly with the income-generating products or services the company provides. Projects often affect the core business, so these managers are stakeholders in the project.

organic organization structure   Sometimes called a simple organization structure. The work groups within the organization are flexible. People work alongside one another regardless of their roles in the organization, and the project manager may have little to no authority over the project resources.

organization knowledge repositories   Databases of past project files, historical information, lessons learned, issue and defect databases, financial databases, and other knowledge that can be quickly accessed for the current project.

organizational governance frameworks   The structure and approach to managing a project within your organization. Governance framework describes how you operate within a system: the cultural norms, relationships, and organizational processes to get things done.

organizational process assets   Resources that have been created to assist the project manager in better managing the project. Examples include historical information, forms, project approaches, defined procedures, and templates.

organizational systems   Provide structure and governance for how the project manager leads the project team and manages the work of project management.

part-time project team   The project team works on the project for a percentage of their scheduled work time. The project team may work on core operations and other projects in addition to the current project.

portfolio management review board   A collection of organizational decision-makers, usually executives, who review proposed projects and programs for their value and return on investment for the organization.

product life cycle   The unique life, duration, and support of the thing a project creates. A product life cycle is separate from the project life cycle.

program manager   Coordinates the efforts of multiple projects working together in the program. Programs comprise projects, so it makes sense that the program manager would be a stakeholder in each of the projects within the program.

project governance   Defines the rules for a project; it's up to the project manager to enforce the project governance to ensure that the project reaches its objectives. The project management plan defines the project governance and how the project manager, project team, and organization will follow the rules and policies within the project.

project management office (PMO)   A stakeholder of the project, because it supports the project manager and is responsible for the project's success. PMOs typically provide administrative support, training for the project manager, resource management for the project team and project staffing, and centralized communication.

project management team   A group of people who are involved with managing the project.

project manager   The person accountable for managing the project and guiding the team through the project phases to completion.

project-oriented structure   Grouping employees, collocated or not, by activities on a particular project. The project manager in a project-oriented structure may have complete, or very close to complete, power over the project team.

project sponsor   A person or group that authorizes the project and ensures that the project manager has the necessary resources, including monies, to get the work done. The project sponsor is within the performing organization and has the power to authorize and sanction the project work; this person is ultimately accountable for the project's success.

project team   The collection of individuals who will work together to ensure the success of the project. The project manager works with the project team to guide, schedule, and oversee the project. The project team completes the project work.

supportive PMO   Acts as a consultative role by offering advice, best practices, lessons learned, forms and software, and project information from similar projects. The PMO control is low.

virtual organizational structure   The organization uses a network structure with points of contact for each group represented in the project. The project manager may have low to moderate authority over the project resources and share authority over the project budget with the functional manager.

TWO-MINUTE DRILL

Utilizing Enterprise Environmental Factors

❑ Enterprise environmental factors directly or indirectly influence how the project manager is allowed to manage the project.

❑ Internal enterprise environmental factors are factors that the organization has established, such as boundaries and policies.

❑ External enterprise environmental factors are factors outside the organization's control, such as laws and regulations, that affect how the project manager will manage the project.

Leveraging Organizational Process Assets

❑ Organizational process assets are items that have been created prior to the current project that the project manager can utilize to manage the current project better.

❑ Past project files, forms, and templates are common examples of organizational process assets.

❑ Knowledge repositories are databases of past financial information, errors and issues, lessons learned, and configuration management.

Working with Organizational Systems

❑ Organizational systems define how work is completed within an organization. It's the system in place to authorize work, complete organization processes, and provides structure within the organization.

❑ The project manager's authority over the project team is determined by the enterprise environmental factors and the organizational structure. Project-oriented organizations allow the project manager the most authority, while functional organizations give the authority to the functional manager. The strong, balanced, and weak matrix structures describe the anticipated amount of authority the project manager has over the project team.

❑ Systems aren't defined by the project manager, but typically by the management and leadership of the organization. The entities, people, departments, and forms and processes within the system are the components of the system. System dynamics is a way of describing the relationship between the components.

❑ Governance defines what the project manager can and cannot do within an organization. It is the rules, policies, procedures, and boundaries that the organizational employees operate within. Governance describes how you operate within a system: the cultural norms, relationships, and organizational processes used to get things done.

Completing Projects in Different Organizational Structures

❑ Organizational structures have direct influence over the project. Organizational structures determine the procedures that the project manager must follow and the amount of authority the project manager possesses. A project management office may oversee project management activities and provide additional support in any of the organizational structures. The organizational types and the level of authority a project manager can expect are shown in the following table:

Organizational Structure	Level of Project Manager Power
Organic or simple	Low to none
Functional	Low to none
Multidivisional	Low to none
Weak matrix	Low
Balanced matrix	Low to moderate
Strong matrix	Moderate to high
Project-oriented	High to complete
Virtual	Low to moderate
Hybrid	Mixed
PMO	High to complete

❑ Beyond the concept of completing the work, project managers must also consider the social, political, economic, and environmental influences that may sway a project. Specifically, the project manager must evaluate the project to determine its social, political, economic, and environmental impacts—as well as note the project's surroundings. The project manager may have some external guidance in these areas in the form of standards and regulations.

❑ Standards are guidelines that are generally followed but not enforced or mandated. Regulations come in the form of laws and industry demands that are enforced by various governing bodies.

SELF TEST

1. You are the project manager for the application deployment project. This project will deploy software to 450 sites throughout North America and in Europe. Because this project will span multiple countries, you must consider the limitations imposed by communications, accessing resources, and other concerns. These international concerns that limit your choices in the project are known as which of the following?
   A. Internal enterprise environmental factors
   B. External enterprise environmental factors
   C. Cultural norms
   D. Organizational process assets

2. You are the project manager for your organization and you're planning a project in consideration of some regulations in your industry. These regulations are also known as which of the following?
   A. Constraints
   B. External enterprise environmental factors
   C. Internal enterprise environmental factors
   D. Industry organizational process assets

3. You are the project manager of the NHQ Project. Your project team consists of experts from different departments within your organization. What type of organizational structure is this?
   A. Virtual
   B. Weak matrix
   C. Noncollocated
   D. Dedicated

4. Beth is a new project manager for her company, and she's working with her project team to develop the project management plan. Beth knows that she must rely on several different skills to make her first project successful. Of the following management skills, which will she use most?
   A. Leading
   B. Communicating
   C. Influencing the organization
   D. Negotiating

5. Harold is the manager of the manufacturing unit for your company, and he'll be a key stakeholder on your upcoming project. To get to know Harold better, you're having lunch with him and discussing some of the goals of the upcoming project. Harold doesn't quite understand what you

do as a project manager, so you explain the concept to him. Managing a project is best described as which one of the following?

A. Establishing direction

B. Functionally controlling the project team and stakeholders

C. Consistently producing key results expected by stakeholders

D. Motivating and inspiring the project team to produce results that are expected by project stakeholders

6. You are the project manager of the Server Deployment Project for your company. You're meeting with the key stakeholders to gather the requirements and review the intent of the project. You know that you'll have to meet with the stakeholders throughout the project and their influence can help or hinder the project's success. You'd like to create a solid communications management plan for the project. Where can you access another communications management plan to use as a template?

A. Internal enterprise environmental factors

B. External enterprise environmental factors

C. Organizational process assets

D. Other current projects in the organization

7. Which one of the following is an example of a physical enterprise environmental factor that could affect a project?

A. Weather

B. Regulations

C. PMO

D. Past project files

8. You are the project manager for your organization. Influencing your organization requires which of the following?

A. An understanding of the organizational budget

B. Research and documentation of proven business cases

C. An understanding of formal and informal organizational systems

D. Positional power

9. Management has asked you, the project manager, to create a method to store your project information electronically. Your project records will help future project teams to make better decisions and can also be used to support the product that your project is creating. What does management want to create for your project?

A. Organizational process assets

B. Organizational knowledge repository

C. Project database

D. Project management plan

10. What does an organizational system accomplish for projects within any organizational structure?
    A. Defines the roles and responsibilities of each project team member
    B. Provides structure and governance for the project manager
    C. Identifies regulations and standards that the project manager must adhere to
    D. Provides accountability for the project manager, the project team, and project stakeholders

11. You are the project manager of the JHK Project and working with the IT department and the accounting department on some project requirements. There is a relationship and dynamic between IT and accounting that is likely to affect the project requirements. What is this relationship between these two components called?
    A. Business links
    B. Matrix
    C. System dynamics
    D. Functional structuring

12. An organization has created a program for a new endeavor. The program manager is establishing all the rules, policies, and approved approaches for project management within the program. What term best describes the rules, policies, and approved project management approaches that the program manager is creating?
    A. Framework
    B. Program governance
    C. Constraints
    D. Program threshold management

13. You are the project manager for the ERP Project. Your organization uses a PMO. The primary purpose of a project office is to do which of the following?
    A. Support the project manager
    B. Support the project sponsor
    C. Support the project team
    D. Identify the stakeholder objectives

14. An organization has multiple departments, and within each department is an IT structure that supports only that department. IT projects are launched within one department and not all departments in the organization as the whole. What type of organizational structure is this?
    A. Multidivisional structure
    B. Functional structure
    C. Hybrid structure
    D. Strong matrix structure

15. You are the project manager of a project. The project is nearing its completion and the project team is experiencing some anxiety as to what their next project will be. What type of organizational structure are you operating in?
    A. Matrix
    B. Project-oriented
    C. Functional
    D. Multidivisional

16. What type of project management office manages and controls all projects within the organization?
    A. Controlling project management office
    B. Supportive project management office
    C. Directive project management office
    D. Functional project management office

17. Beth is a project manager in small startup company. The project team is loosely organized and people chip in to help however they can, based on their skills and the work that needs to be completed. The organization owner, Sarah, has control over the project resources. What structure is Beth likely operating in?
    A. Organic
    B. Functional
    C. Weak matrix
    D. Strong matrix

18. An organization that typically operates as a weak matrix has decided that for a high-priority project, the team will work on the project full time. In addition, the project manager will manage just this one project full time. What type of organization structure is this?
    A. Simple
    B. Project-oriented
    C. Strong matrix
    D. Hybrid

19. Henry, the project manager of the MHB Project, is operating within a multidivisional organizational structure. Who will make decisions about the project budget?
    A. Henry
    B. Functional manager
    C. Program manager
    D. Portfolio manager

20. A company has hired you as a project manager to lead a new software development project. You have an assigned budget and several milestones in the project. The project sponsor has asked you to wait on launching the project execution a month or two because of some unsettling news in the marketplace. The marketplace conditions are best described as which one of the following?
    A. High costs and high demand for resources
    B. External organizational process assets
    C. Internal enterprise environmental factors
    D. External enterprise environmental factors

21. All of the following are organizational process assets that can be used within a project except for which one?
    A. Templates for project documents
    B. Historical information
    C. Regulations
    D. Performance measurements

22. Tracey is the project manager of the KHG Project. Her organization is a classic functional environment. Her level of authority as a project manager can be best described as which of the following?
    A. Low
    B. Moderate
    C. Balanced
    D. High

23. Project team members are most likely to work full time on a project in which of the following organizational structures?
    A. Functional
    B. Weak matrix
    C. Organizational
    D. Project-oriented

24. A project manager is operating in a weak matrix. She has asked management for information from a past project that is similar to her project. Where is the best place for the project manager to find this information?
    A. Organizational knowledge repository
    B. Organizational process assets
    C. Internal enterprise environmental factors
    D. From the project manager of the past project

25. Stacey is the project manager of the GBN Project for her company. She'll be using several templates for a project, but she's not certain where these templates should originate. Where can a project manager usually expect to receive templates?
    A. Commercial databases
    B. The project management office
    C. The project sponsor
    D. PMIS

SELF TEST ANSWERS

1. You are the project manager for the application deployment project. This project will deploy software to 450 sites throughout North America and in Europe. Because this project will span multiple countries, you must consider the limitations imposed by communications, accessing resources, and other concerns. These international concerns that limit your choices in the project are known as which of the following?
    A. Internal enterprise environmental factors
    B. External enterprise environmental factors
    C. Cultural norms
    D. Organizational process assets

    ☑   **A.** These are internal enterprise environmental factors, because the factors are internal to the organization, but they do restrict options for the project.
    ☒   **B, C,** and **D** are incorrect. **B** is incorrect because external enterprise environmental factors are factors outside of the organization's control. **C** is incorrect because cultural norms are factors of the organization culture, attitude toward work, and accepted practices within the organization. **D,** organizational process assets, are things that have been created prior to the current project that the project manager can leverage to manage the current project.

2. You are the project manager for your organization and you're planning a project in consideration of some regulations in your industry. These regulations are also known as which of the following?

A. Constraints
B. External enterprise environmental factors
C. Internal enterprise environmental factors
D. Industry organizational process assets

☑ **B.** Laws and regulations are external enterprise environmental factors.
☒ **A, C,** and **D** are incorrect. **A,** constraints, are anything that limit your options, such as predefined budget or deadline. Although regulations could be considered a constraint, this isn't the best answer for the question. **C** is incorrect because internal enterprise environmental factors are factors that affect the project decisions within the organization's control. **D,** industry organizational process assets, is not a valid project management term, so this choice is incorrect.

3. You are the project manager of the NHQ Project. Your project team consists of experts from different departments within your organization. What type of organizational structure is this?

A. Virtual
B. Weak matrix
C. Noncollocated
D. Dedicated

☑ **B.** This is an example of a matrix structure. Although the question doesn't define whether the matrix is truly strong, weak, or balanced, weak matrix is the best answer presented.
☒ **A, C,** and **D** are incorrect. **A** is incorrect because a virtual team describes an organizational network approach, with a point of contact within each group represented in the project. **C** is incorrect because this isn't a valid organizational structure type. "Noncollocated" can be used to describe a virtual project team, but this isn't the best answer. **D** is also incorrect, because there's no evidence that the people on this project team will be working only on this project; neither is it a valid organizational structure type.

4. Beth is a new project manager for her company, and she's working with her project team to develop the project management plan. Beth knows that she must rely on several different skills to make her first project successful. Of the following management skills, which will she use most?

A. Leading
B. Communicating
C. Influencing the organization
D. Negotiating

☑ **B.** Communication is the key general management skill a project manager will use the most.
☒ **A, C,** and **D** are incorrect. They are necessary, but communication accounts for the majority of a project manager's time.

5. Harold is the manager of the manufacturing unit for your company, and he'll be a key stakeholder on your upcoming project. To get to know Harold better, you're having lunch with him and discussing some of the goals of the upcoming project. Harold doesn't quite understand what you do as a project manager, so you explain the concept to him. Managing a project is best described as which one of the following?
   A. Establishing direction
   B. Functionally controlling the project team and stakeholders
   C. Consistently producing key results expected by stakeholders
   D. Motivating and inspiring the project team to produce results that are expected by project stakeholders

☑ **C.** Managing has to do with consistently producing key results that are expected by stakeholders.
☒ **A, B,** and **D** are incorrect. **A** and **D** describe the leadership qualities a project manager must possess, but they are do not best describe the concept. **B** is incorrect because it describes the functional management position over project team members.

6. You are the project manager of the Server Deployment Project for your company. You're meeting with the key stakeholders to gather the requirements and review the intent of the project. You know that you'll have to meet with the stakeholders throughout the project and their influence can help or hinder the project's success. You'd like to create a solid communications management plan for the project. Where you can access another communications management plan to use as a template?
   A. Internal enterprise environmental factors
   B. External enterprise environmental factors
   C. Organizational process assets
   D. Other current projects in the organization

☑ **C.** Of all the choices presented, this answer is best. Organizational process assets include past project records. You can adapt a previous project's communications management plan to fit the current project.
☒ **A, B,** and **D** are incorrect. Internal and external enterprise environmental factors and other current projects are not the best locations for communications management plans.

7. Which one of the following is an example of a physical enterprise environmental factor that could affect a project?
   A. Weather
   B. Regulations
   C. PMO
   D. Past project files

   ☑ **A.** Weather is an example of a physical enterprise environmental factor. The environment in which the project is taking place is a physical enterprise environmental factor.
   ☒ **B, C,** and **D** are incorrect. **B** and **C** are incorrect because regulations and PMOs are not physical enterprise environmental factors. **D** is incorrect because past project files are an example of an organizational process asset.

8. You are the project manager for your organization. Influencing your organization requires which of the following?
   A. An understanding of the organizational budget
   B. Research and documentation of proven business cases
   C. An understanding of formal and informal organizational systems
   D. Positional power

   ☑ **C.** To influence an organization (to get things done), a project manager must understand the explicit and implied organizational system.
   ☒ **A, B,** and **D** are incorrect. **A** is incorrect because the project manager may not even have access to an organizational budget. **B** is incorrect because a proven business case may not map to every scenario when influencing an organization. **D** is incorrect because positional power may relate only to a small portion of an organization, not to multiple facets of influence.

9. Management has asked you, the project manager, to create a method to store your project information electronically. Your project records will help future project teams to make better decisions and can also be used to support the product that your project is creating. What does management want to create for your project?
   A. Organizational process assets
   B. Organizational knowledge repository
   C. Project database
   D. Project management plan

   ☑ **B.** Management wants you to create an organizational knowledge repository. Ideally, this would already exist in an organization, but the organization must start somewhere.
   ☒ **A, C,** and **D** are incorrect. **A** is incorrect because organizational process assets are things that have already been created, such as forms and templates. **C** is incorrect because a project database is only one form of knowledge repository. **D** may be a tempting answer, but project management plan isn't the best choice because this is needed for every project and won't necessarily be an electronic database of information that can be accessed by others projects.

10. What does an organizational system accomplish for projects within any organizational structure?
   A. Defines the roles and responsibilities of each project team member.
   B. Provides structure and governance for the project manager.
   C. Identifies regulations and standards that the project manager must adhere to.
   D. Provides accountability for the project manager, the project team, and project stakeholders.

   ☑ **B.** Of all the choices presented, **B** is the best answer because organizational systems do provide structure and governance for the project manager and how the project manager leads and manages the project team and project work.
   ☒ **A, C,** and **D** are incorrect. **A** is incorrect because the organizational system doesn't define the roles and responsibilities of the project team members. **C** is incorrect—standards and regulations are not defined by the organizational system. **D** is incorrect because the organizational structure doesn't provide accountability to the project manager, project team, or stakeholders.

11. You are the project manager of the JHK Project and working with the IT department and the accounting department on some project requirements. There is a relationship and dynamic between IT and accounting that is likely to affect the project requirements. What is this relationship between these two components called?
   A. Business links
   B. Matrix
   C. System dynamics
   D. Functional structuring

   ☑ **C.** System dynamics is a way of describing the relationship between the components, such as the relationship between the IT and accounting departments.
   ☒ **A, B,** and **D** are incorrect. These are not valid descriptions of the relationship between the components of the system.

12. An organization has created a program for a new endeavor. The program manager is establishing all of the rules, policies, and approved approaches for project management within the program. What term best describes the rules, policies, and approved project management approaches that the program manager is creating?
   A. Framework
   B. Program governance
   C. Constraints
   D. Program threshold management

   ☑ **B.** The program manager is creating the program governance for all projects that operate within the program.
   ☒ **A, C,** and **D** are incorrect. **A** is incorrect because, although frameworks can establish the boundaries of the projects, the better choice is program governance. **C** is incorrect because constraints describe things that limit the project manager's options, such as a deadline or predetermined budget. **D** is incorrect because program threshold management isn't a valid project management term.

13. You are the project manager for the ERP Project. Your organization uses a PMO. The primary purpose of a project office is to do which of the following?
    A. Support the project manager
    B. Support the project sponsor
    C. Support the project team
    D. Identify the stakeholder objectives

    ☑ **A.** The PMO supports the project manager.
    ☒ **B, C,** and **D** are incorrect. **B** and **C** are incorrect because the project office does not support the project sponsor and project team. **D** is incorrect because stakeholder objectives can vary from stakeholder to stakeholder on a project.

14. An organization has multiple departments, and within each department is an IT structure that supports only that department. IT projects are launched within one department and not all departments in the organization as the whole. What type of organizational structure is this?
    A. Multidivisional structure
    B. Functional structure
    C. Hybrid structure
    D. Strong matrix structure

    ☑ **A.** In this multidivisional organization, there will likely be replication of functions for each division.
    ☒ **B, C,** and **D** are incorrect. **B** is incorrect because functional structures are project-centric to each function, but there likely is not a replication of functions across the organization. In a true functional structure, there is not a replication of function, such as an IT group within each department, but rather just an IT department within the organization. **C** is incorrect because a hybrid structure is blend of organizational structure types. **D** is incorrect because strong matrix structures utilize resources from across the organization, rather than isolate them within each department.

15. You are the project manager of a project. The project is nearing its completion and the project team is experiencing some anxiety as to what their next project will be. What type of organizational structure are you operating in?
    A. Matrix
    B. Project-oriented
    C. Functional
    D. Multidivisional

☑ **B.** In a project-oriented structure, the project team works on one project full time. Near the end of the project the team members may experience some anxiety as to what their next project will be.
☒ **A, C,** and **D** are incorrect. These organizational structures allow the project team members to return to their day-to-day operations after the project is completed.

16. What type of project management office manages and controls all projects within the organization?
    A. Controlling project management office
    B. Supportive project management office
    C. Directive project management office
    D. Functional project management office

☑ **C.** A directive project management office manages and controls all projects within the organization. The PMO control is considered high.
☒ **A, B,** and **D** are incorrect. Controlling project management offices define project governance through project management frameworks, templates, forms, project management activities, and communications. Supportive project management offices act as a consultative role by offering advice, best practices, lessons learned, forms and software, and project information from similar projects. **D** is incorrect because there is no such thing as a functional project management office type.

17. Beth is a project manager in small startup company. The project team is loosely organized and people chip in to help however they can, based on their skills and the work that needs to be completed. The organization owner, Sarah, has control over the project resources. What structure is Beth likely operating in?
    A. Organic
    B. Functional
    C. Weak matrix
    D. Strong matrix

☑ **A.** An organic or simple organizational structure means that the work groups within the organization are flexible. People work alongside one another regardless of their roles in the organization, and the project manager may have little to no authority over the project resources.
☒ **B, C,** and **D** are incorrect. **B** is incorrect because functional structures are based on functions and don't use resources from across the organization. **C** and **D** are incorrect because matrix structures do use resources from across the organization, but the structure is more clearly defined than in an organic structure. Also, in a strong matrix, the project manager, rather than the functional manager, will have authority over the project resources.

18. An organization that typically operates as a weak matrix has decided that for a high-priority project, the team will work on the project full time. In addition, the project manager will manage just this one project full time. What type of organization structure is this?

A.   Simple

B.   Project-oriented

C.   Strong matrix

D.   Hybrid

☑   **D.** This organization is a hybrid because it's shifting from its usual weak matrix structure to a project-oriented structure for just this one project.

☒   **A, B,** and **C** are incorrect. **A** is incorrect because organic or simple organizational structures allow individuals within the organization to be flexible and work alongside one another regardless of their roles in the organization. **B** is a tempting choice, but the organization isn't project-oriented all the time, just for this one project. **C,** strong matrix, isn't the best answer because this structure utilizes resources from all over the organization and people don't always work on just one project.

19. Henry, the project manager of the MHB Project, is operating within a multidivisional organizational structure. Who will make decisions about the project budget?

A.   Henry

B.   Functional manager

C.   Program manager

D.   Portfolio manager

☑   **B.** In a multidivisional structure, the functional manager makes decisions about the project budget.

☒   **A, C,** and **D** are incorrect. The project manager, program manager, and portfolio manager aren't making decisions about the budget.

20. A company has hired you as a project manager to lead a new software development project. You have an assigned budget and several milestones in the project. The project sponsor has asked you to wait on launching the project execution a month or two because of some unsettling news in the marketplace. The marketplace conditions are best described as which one of the following?

A.   High costs and high demand for resources

B.   External organizational process assets

C.   Internal enterprise environmental factors

D.   External enterprise environmental factors

☑   **D.** Marketplace conditions are external enterprise environmental factors that can affect project decisions in the organization.

☒   **A, B,** and **C** are incorrect. High costs and high demand for resources isn't a good answer for this question. There is no category of external organizational process assets. Marketplace conditions are outside of the organization, so they are considered external enterprise environmental factors, rather than internal enterprise environmental factors.

21. All the following are organizational process assets that can be used within a project except for which one?
   A. Templates for project documents
   B. Historical information
   C. Regulations
   D. Performance measurements

> ☑ **C.** Regulations are an example of external enterprise environmental factors, not organizational process assets.
> ☒ **A, B,** and **D** are incorrect. Templates, historical information, and performance measurements are all examples of organizational process assets.

22. Tracey is the project manager of the KHG Project. Her organization is a classic functional environment. Her level of authority as a project manager can be best described as which of the following?
   A. Low
   B. Moderate
   C. Balanced
   D. High

> ☑ **A.** Tracey will most likely have a low amount of authority in a functional organizational structure.
> ☒ **B, C,** and **D** are incorrect. **B** and **C** are incorrect because they describe matrix structures. **D** is incorrect because it is relevant to a project-oriented structure.

23. Project team members are most likely to work full time on a project in which of the following organizational structures?
   A. Functional
   B. Weak matrix
   C. Organizational
   D. Project-oriented

> ☑ **D.** Project-oriented structures often have project team members assigned to the project on a full-time basis.
> ☒ **A, B,** and **C** are incorrect. **A** and **B** are incorrect because these structures are part-time project teams. **C** is not a valid organization structure.

24. A project manager is operating in a weak matrix. She has asked management for information from a past project that is similar to her project. Where is the best place for the project manager to find this information?

    A. Organizational knowledge repository
    B. Organizational process assets
    C. Internal enterprise environmental factors
    D. From the project manager of the past project

    ☑ **A.** A knowledge repository will have the information needed from the past project and is the best place to locate the information.
    ☒ **B, C,** and **D** are incorrect. These choices don't reflect the best places to find the knowledge. Though the knowledge repository could be an example of an organizational process asset, organizational process assets isn't the best choice for this question. Historical information isn't part of enterprise environmental factors. And although it's logical to consult with the previous project manager, this isn't the best place to find the information needed.

25. Stacey is the project manager of the GBN Project for her company. She'll be using several templates for a project, but she's not certain where these templates should originate. Where can a project manager usually expect to receive templates?

    A. Commercial databases
    B. The project management office
    C. The project sponsor
    D. PMIS

    ☑ **B.** The project management office is the best choice, since its role is to support the project manager.
    ☒ **A, C,** and **D** are incorrect. **A,** commercial databases, may be feasible, but it is not the best choice presented. Project sponsors, **C,** are not typically going to provide the project manager with templates. **D,** project management information systems, may have project templates available, but the project management office is the best choice presented.

Chapter 3

Serving as a Project Manager

CERTIFICATION OBJECTIVES

3.01	Defining the Project Management Role	3.04		Leading and Managing the Project
3.02	Exploring the Project Manager Influence	3.05		Performing Project Integration
3.03	Building the Project Management Competencies	✓		Two-Minute Drill
		Q&A		Self Test

I f you're aiming to pass the PMP exam, you're obviously already working as a project manager. So often, PMP candidates will try to answer the PMP exam questions based on how they manage projects in their environment, rather than how the *PMBOK Guide* suggests as best practices. I'm not saying that you aren't effectively managing projects where you work, but I am saying that you need to answer exam questions according to the *PMBOK Guide* rather than basing your answers solely on your project management experience.

Where you work as a project manager is likely different from where any other reader of this book works as a project manager. Just as every project is unique, so is the environment in which a project exists. Consider software development projects, construction projects, IT infrastructure projects, learning and development projects, and various other types of projects. Each of these different projects operates in a distinct environment. The environment is a factor of influence in these projects and in your projects.

The project's environment can influence how you manage the project, the expectations of the project manager, how stakeholders contribute to the project, and a myriad of other concerns. It's important to understand the environment and what's expected of the project manager—including the formalities, processes, rules and regulations, and even simpler things like templates and forms.

The *PMBOK Guide* includes a clear profile of the ideal project manager and an ideal environment. Part of the profile is the ability to be flexible, to adapt, and to follow best practices. That's what you'll be tested on—determining the next best thing to do in any given scenario. It all begins, really, with a clear understanding of what the project manager does and the *PMBOK Guide*'s expectations of what a project manager is. The goal of this chapter is to give you a solid foundation of the project manager role that you'll be tested on so you can clear the exam and continue on with your life and career.

CERTIFICATION OBJECTIVE 3.01

Defining the Project Management Role

The project manager's role is to get things done by leading the project team through the challenges of the project to achieve the project goals and objectives. Most often, project managers get involved with a project after the vision of the project has been created. Consider a project to build a house, design some software, or move employees from one building to another. Each of these projects and its objectives can be defined well before the project manager is involved.

It's not unusual, however, for project managers to be involved in the project formulation before the project is initiated. A project manager could consult with the portfolio review board, customers, and management to offer input before a project is selected, funded, and initiated. Project managers may work with business analysts (or take on the role of a business analyst) to gather requirements, create high-level estimates, and develop business cases and feasibility studies—all work that precedes project initiation.

It's tempting to put roles into boxes and keep people isolated with titles and boundaries, but that's just not the way it works. Project team members, like the project manager, may play multiple roles on any given project. While the project manager is responsible for leading and managing the project team, the project team is responsible for executing the project plan to get things done. The project manager and the project team work together to plan and execute the project work. As the project manager leads and manages the project team, she will rely on the project team's expertise, experience, skills, and technical abilities to complete the project work. It's unrealistic for the project manager to be able to have the skills of each project team member, but it's realistic for the project manager to understand the type of work each project team member can perform in the project.

Leading the Project Team

Project managers manage things, but lead people. What's the difference? Management is the process of getting the results that are expected by project stakeholders. Leadership is the ability to motivate and inspire individuals to work toward those expected results.

Ever work for a project manager who wasn't motivating or inspiring? A good project manager can motivate and inspire the project team to see the vision and value of the project. The project manager as a leader can inspire the project team to find a solution to overcome the perceived obstacles to get the work done. Motivation is a constant process, and the project manager must be able to motivate the team to move toward completion—with passion and a profound reason to complete the work. Finally, motivation and inspiration must be real; the project manager must have a personal relationship with members of the project team to help them achieve their goals.

Communicating Project Information

Project communication can be summed up as "who needs what information, when do they need it, and what's the best modality to deliver the message." Project managers spend the bulk of their time communicating information—not doing other activities. Therefore, they must be good communicators, promoting a clear, unambiguous exchange of information. Communication is a two-way street; it requires a sender and a receiver.

A key part of communication is *active listening*. This is the process by which the receiver restates what the sender has said to clarify and confirm the message. For example, a project team member tells the project manager that a work package will be done in seven days. The project manager clarifies and confirms by stating the work package will be done a week from today. This gives the project team member the opportunity to clarify that the work package will actually be done nine days from today because of the upcoming weekend.

There are several communication avenues:

- Listening and speaking
- Written and oral
- Internal to the project, such as project team member to team member
- External to the project, such as the project manager to an external customer
- Formal communications, such as reports and presentations
- Informal communications, such as e-mails and "hallway" meetings
- Vertical communications, which follow the organizational flowchart
- Horizontal communications, such as director-to-director within the organizational flowchart

Included with management communication skills are variables and elements unique to the flow of communication. Although we'll discuss communications in full in Chapter 10, here are some key facts to know for now:

- **Sender–receiver models** Communication requires a sender and a receiver. Within this model may be multiple avenues to complete the flow of communication, but barriers to effective communication may be present as well. Other variables within this model include recipient feedback, surveys, checklists, and confirmation of the sent message.
- **Media selection** There are multiple choices when it comes to sending a message. Which one is appropriate? Based on the audience and the message being sent, the media should be in alignment. In other words, an ad hoc hallway meeting is probably not the best communication avenue to explain a large variance in the project schedule.
- **Style** The tone, structure, and formality of the message being sent should be in alignment with the audience and the content of the message.
- **Presentation** When it comes to formal presentations, the presenter's oral and body language, visual aids, and handouts all influence the message being delivered.
- **Facilitation** Project managers sometimes serve as facilitators of group events, such as meetings and workshops. Facilitators keep people involved in the conversation, guide the conversation to be certain that all participants' opinions and ideas are considered, and help the participants come to an agreed-upon decision.
- **Meeting management** Meetings are forms of communication. How the meeting is led, managed, and controlled all influence the message being delivered. Agendas, minutes, and order are mandatory for effective communications within a meeting.

See the video "Role of the Project Manager."

Negotiating Project Terms and Conditions

Project managers must negotiate for the good of the project. In any project, the project manager, the project sponsor, and the project team will have to negotiate with stakeholders, vendors, and customers to reach a level of agreement acceptable to all parties involved in the negotiation process. In some instances, typically in less-than-pleasant circumstances, negotiations may have to proceed with assistance. Specifically, mediation and arbitration are examples of assisted negotiations. Negotiation proceedings typically center on the following:

watch **The purpose of negotiations is to reach a fair agreement among all parties.**

- Priorities
- Technical approach
- Project scope
- Schedule
- Cost
- Changes to the project scope, schedule, or budget
- Vendor terms and conditions
- Project team member assignments and schedules
- Resource constraints, such as facilities, travel issues, and team members with highly specialized skills

Active Problem Solving

Like riddles, puzzles, and cryptology? If so, you'll love this area of project management. Problem solving is the ability to understand the heart of a problem, look for a viable solution, and then make a decision to implement that solution. In any project, countless problems require viable solutions. And like any good puzzle, the solution to one portion of the problem may create more problems elsewhere.

The premise for problem solving is problem definition. Problem definition is the ability to discern between the cause and effect of the problem. This centers on root-cause analysis. If a project manager treats only the symptoms of a problem rather than its cause, the symptoms will perpetuate and continue throughout the project's life. Root-cause analysis looks beyond the immediate symptoms to the cause of the symptoms, which then affords opportunities for solutions.

watch **Completing the PMP exam is an example of having problem-solving skills. Even though you may argue that things described in this book don't work this way in your environment, remember that the exam is not based on your environment. Learn the Project Management Institute (PMI) method for passing the exam and allow that to influence your "real-world" implementations.**

Once the root of a problem has been identified, the project manager must make a decision to address the problem effectively. Solutions can be presented from vendors, the project team, the project manager, or various stakeholders. A viable solution focuses on more than just the problem. It looks at the cause and effect of the problem itself. In addition, a timely decision is needed, or the window of opportunity may pass and then a new decision will be needed to address the problem. As in most cases, the worst thing you can do is nothing.

CERTIFICATION OBJECTIVE 3.02

Exploring the Project Manager Influence

As a project manager, you have tremendous influence on the project's success, the people on the project team, the management of your organization, and stakeholders that can span your organization, region, or even the entire globe. The project's sphere of influence describes the parties affected by the role of the project manager. Your project can send ripples into all areas of your organization: resources, monetary constraints, politics, and many other factors can all be influenced by you, the project manager, and the project you lead.

Influence isn't something we often think of as project managers, but it's a factor that should be considered when we plan, execute the project, and certainly when we communicate with stakeholders. Not that the project manager must play politics, but the project manager must consider the implications of the project's success, the communication between the project manager and project team, and the perceptions of the stakeholders regarding the project and its leadership. Over time and with experience in your organization, you'll find it easier to understand the undercurrent of politics and the hidden messages in questions and comments, and you'll have a broader, wiser view into what's happening in the organization and how your project (and you) affects the environment. Everyone involved in the project, from stakeholders to the project manager, can influence others involved, as shown in Figure 3-1.

For your PMP exam, consider the different levels of influence the project manager has on the following stakeholders:

- **Project team**   The project manager leads and directs the team to reach the project's objectives.
- **Organizational managers**   The project manager will likely need to work with managers to have access to people, process, and resources.
- **Project management office**   The project manager will work with the project management office, if one exists, to manage the project and provide assets, directions, and support.

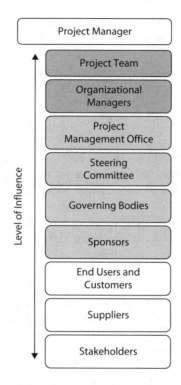

FIGURE 3-1

Stakeholder and
project manager
influence are
connected.

- **Steering committee** The project manager may have to report on the project status and progress.

- **Governing bodies** The project manager may have to report on project governance internally or to government agencies regarding how the project is adhering to laws and regulations.

- **Sponsors** The project sponsor will want information on the project status and decisions the project manager has made to keep the project moving forward toward its objectives.

- **End users and customers** The project manager is responsible to these people with regard to what the project is creating and how the project may interfere with their lives as the project is in progress.

- **Suppliers** When resources and services are needed, suppliers are influenced by the project manager's planning and the procurement policies of the organization.

- **Stakeholders** All of the people and groups that are affected by the project and that can affect the project are stakeholders that the project manager can influence for the betterment of the project.

All of these different categories are linked to the project manager and influenced by the project manager. The better the project manager coordinates, plans, and communicates within each of these spheres, the better she can influence these groups for continued project support, improved synergy, and sustainability of the project within the organization.

Influencing the Project

The success, or failure, of a project is often a reflection of how well the project manager led the project team, balanced constraints, executed the project plan, and monitored the project progress. The person with the greatest influence over a project is the project manager, and the project's outcome is largely based on the project manager's ability to influence the project to reach its objectives. And, sure, some projects may be doomed from the start due to lack of finances or qualified resources, an unrealistic schedule, or other problems, but these are the exceptions, not the rule. Besides, a good project manager will address these issues and risks with management and stakeholders and find a solution that works, not an excuse that sticks.

The influence of the project manager on the project is demonstrated in two key aspects: communications skills and a positive attitude. Communication is paramount in successful project management. Project managers will effectively communicate with stakeholders through a variety of methods: verbal, written, and nonverbal. Messages are direct and appropriate for the audience, and the communication style is tailored based on what's being communicated to whom.

Project managers must communicate good and bad news, status of the project, and other project information throughout the project. Communication isn't one-way, however. The project manager will need to work with the team, clients, vendors, and other stakeholders to get these individuals to contribute to the conversation. This means asking questions, listening to stakeholder concerns, following up on ideas and promises, and keeping the project stakeholders involved, excited, and motivated to continue the project.

A positive attitude does wonders for the success of the project manager. People like to be around other people who have a positive outlook and a "can-do" attitude. Having a positive attitude is really part of project leadership: The project team will mimic your attitude and behavior, and will look to you, the project manager, for guidance and an outlook of what's happening in the project. When the project manager has a sour disposition, that communicates that things aren't going well and likely aren't going to be getting better.

I'm not saying that as project managers we ignore problems and issues. What I am saying is that having a positive attitude, being cheerful, and showing the project team how to be optimistic communicates confidence and inspires others to do the work with gusto and determination. A positive attitude costs you nothing, but it can make a big difference in project team leadership and management.

Influencing the Organization

Project management is about getting things done. Every organization is different in its policies, modes of operations, and underlying culture. There are political alliances, differing motivations, conflicting interests, and power struggles within every organization. So where does project management fit into this rowdy scheme? Smack dab in the middle.

A project manager must understand all of the unspoken influences at work within an organization as well as the formal channels that exist. A balance between the implied and the explicit will enable the project manager to take the project from launch to completion. We all reference organizational politics with disdain; however, politics aren't always a bad thing. Politics can be used as leverage to align and direct people to accomplish activities— with motivation and purpose.

e x a m

ⓌatcH **The exam questions are shallow. Don't read too much into the questions as far as political aspirations and** **influences go. Take each question at face value and assume all of the information provided in the question is correct.**

Project managers also interact with other project managers within the organization. They'll discuss projects, competition for resources, priorities on project funding, and alignment of project goals with organizational goals. This network among project managers isn't just gossip, because it helps them see how other projects are faring, how decisions and events in the organization can affect projects and decisions, and even each project's viability and quality.

Managing Social, Economic, and Environmental Project Influences

Social, economic, and environmental influences can cause a project to falter, stall, or fail completely. Your awareness of potential influences outside of traditional management practices will help complete the project. The acknowledgement of such influences, from internal or external sources, enables the project manager and the project team to plan how to react to these influences in order for the project to succeed.

For example, consider a construction project that may reduce traffic flow to one lane over a bridge. Obviously, stakeholders in this instance are the commuters who travel over the bridge. Social influences are the people who are frustrated by the construction project, the people who live in the vicinity of the project, and even individuals or groups that believe the need for road repairs is more pressing than the need to repair the bridge. These issues must all be addressed, on some level, for the project team to complete the project work quickly and efficiently.

The economic conditions in any organization are always present. The cost of a project must be weighed against the project's benefits and perceived worth. Projects may succumb to budget cuts, project reprioritization, or their own failure based on the performance to date. Economic factors inside the organization may also hinder a project from moving forward. In other words, if the company sponsoring the project is not making money, projects may get axed in an effort to curb costs.

Finally, environmental influence on, and created by, the project must be considered. Let's revisit the bridge construction project. The project must consider the river below the bridge and how construction may affect the water and wildlife. Consideration must be given not only to short-term effects that arise during the bridge's construction but also to long-term effects that the construction may have on the environment.

In most projects, the social, economic, and environmental concerns must be evaluated, documented, and addressed within the project plan. Project managers can't have a come-what-may approach to these issues and expect to be successful.

Considering International Influences

If a project spans the globe, how will the project manager effectively manage and lead the project team? How will teams in Paris communicate with teams in Sydney? What about the language barriers, time zone differences, currency differences, regulations, laws, and social influences? All of these concerns must be considered early in the project. Tools can include teleconferences, travel, face-to-face meetings, team leaders, and subprojects.

As companies and projects span the globe to offer goods and services, the completion of those projects will rely more and more on individuals from varying educational backgrounds, social influences, and values. The project manager must create a plan that takes these issues into account.

Reviewing Cultural and Industry Influences

Good project managers stay abreast of what's happening in the project management community. They subscribe to newsgroups, read magazine articles, and take training to become more proficient in their role as a project manager. By staying current on what's happening in project management trends, you can identify opportunities, new standards, and best practices. In addition, you'll also monitor what's happening in your application field, be it healthcare, construction, or information technology, for example. This will help you as a project manager to identify trends, market conditions, and potential projects your organization may take on.

Once you earn your PMP, you'll likely take continuing education to earn professional development units (PDUs) to maintain your PMP certification. Don't view this education as a chore, but rather an opportunity to continue to advance your career and the project management profession.

CERTIFICATION OBJECTIVE 3.03

Building the Project Management Competencies

By earning the PMP, you're showing that you have both project management experience and project management knowledge. Once you're a PMP, you'll need to maintain your certification with continuing education by earning PDUs. Your PMP certification is actually a three-year cycle, in which time you'll earn 60 PDUs to maintain your PMP. If you fail to earn the 60 PDUs, you'll lose your PMP status and will have to start the entire journey over—not a wise decision.

It's not terribly difficult to earn PDUs. You can earn some PDUs by serving as a project manager, by volunteering for PMI events, by writing books and articles, and via many other activities. On PMI's web site, look for the *Continuing Certification Requirements* handbook for complete rules and opportunities to earn PDUs. Not all of your development can be through volunteering and events, however. As of this writing, PMPs will have to earn a minimum of 35 education PDUs and are allowed a maximum of 25 "giving back" PDUs. Giving back PDUs means that you're volunteering or contributing to the project management community.

Considering Your Skills and Competencies

Once you earn the PMP, you'll be attending training online or in person to maintain your certification. It's a good idea to take stock of what you do, or don't, know and to choose your training accordingly. Consider your career goals, areas of your project management expertise that may be lacking, or what's interesting to you. All of the training you take should benefit you—don't just trudge through training because you have to. Be smart! Choose training and education that will make you a better person and a better project manager, and that will also help you to keep your PMP.

The *PMBOK Guide* walks through the five steps of competence, as shown in Figure 3-2, that we all move through as we learn new things:

1. **Unconsciously incompetent**   You're unaware of a skill that you don't have.
2. **Consciously incompetent**   You become aware that you don't have the skill.
3. **Consciously competent**   You learn and practice the skill to gain competence.
4. **Unconsciously competent**   You can do the skill without even thinking about it.
5. **Chosen conscious competence**   You practice and maintain the skill.

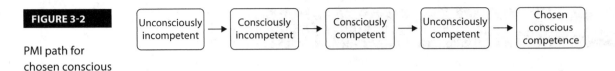

FIGURE 3-2

PMI path for
chosen conscious
competence

That's pretty much how we all started in our careers. We begin by not even knowing
that we don't have a skill. Then we learn about the skill, practice the skill, and so on. To
become an expert, we have to learn, practice, and maintain that skill. There are several steps
involved in becoming skilled and remaining skilled as an individual. We gather data, such
as observations and facts about the skill and process that raw data into useable information.
The useable information helps us to gain knowledge and find a deeper understanding and
practice of the skill. Over time, and through practice and knowledge, we gain wisdom and
mastery of the skill.

Exploring the PMI Talent Triangle

PMI has established a Talent Triangle to illustrate the three domains of education required
for PMPs, as shown in Figure 3-3. As a PMP, you'll need a total of 35 minimum education
hours. These 35 hours are distributed across the three domains of technical, leadership,
and strategic PDUs. You must have at least 8 PDUs from each category of education, which
is 24 of your 35 PDUs. The remaining 11 PDUs can be distributed across any of the three
domains—you pick.

FIGURE 3-3

The PMI Talent
Triangle requires
education in all
three domains.

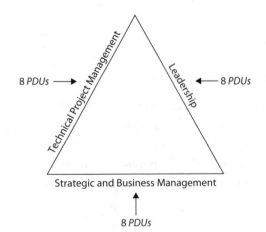

I know this can seem a little confusing at first glance, but here's a way of looking at all these PDUs and categorization of learning: As a PMP, you have three years to earn 60 PDUs to maintain your PMP. You can earn all 60 PDUs through education—attend a few seminars or online courses and you're all set. Or you can volunteer at some events to earn up 25 PDUs for your service. That leaves 35 PDUs to keep your PMP. Of those 35 PDUs, you'll need 8 PDUs from technical training, 8 PDUs from leadership training, and 8 PDUs from strategic training. The remaining 11 PDUs can come from any category in the PMI Talent Triangle.

Technical project management skills are the core skills you apply in your role as a project manager. You'll focus on what it'll take to get the project done: planning the project work, executing the plan, monitoring and controlling the project, and closing out phases and eventually the entire project. Within these process groups is where you'll choose and apply the needed processes to keep the project moving toward the goals and objectives. You'll also communicate the project status, keep stakeholders involved and informed, track finances, control changes, and manage issues. We'll spend the bulk of our time in the balance of this book in the technical project management arena.

The PMI Talent Triangle also includes strategic and business management skills. As a project manager, you're not only working on the project, but you also must look at the organization's bigger picture of why the project is important and has been initiated and funded in the first place. The goal is to understand and communicate the business strategy, effectively plan and deliver the project for the organization, and maximize the business value of the project. You'll need to understand how your project fits into the organization's strategy, mission, tactics, and overall prioritization of projects. You'll do this in the project by managing the following:

- Risks and issues
- Finances
- Costs and benefits
- Business value
- Benefits realized by delivering the project
- Balance of competing objectives, such as time, cost, and quality

Project managers must also provide leadership. Leadership, the third angle of the PMI Talent Triangle, focuses on dealing with people. You'll manage the project team, work with vendors, and keep stakeholders informed, involved, and excited about the project. Leadership means that you'll be optimistic, collaborative, and able to manage conflicts that will creep up within the project. Project managers must build trust, address concerns with stakeholders, and be able to persuade, gain consensus, compromise, network, and provide a long-term view of how the project fits into the overall business strategy. A term you'll see in Agile project management is "servant leadership," which means that while you're the leader, you're also supporting the project team and ensuring that they have what they need to do their work on the project.

Leadership in a project manager means you'll have the following:

- Respect for others
- Integrity and cultural sensitivity
- Problem-solving abilities
- Ability to give others credit
- Desire to learn and improve

Leadership in project management is about helping the team and business succeed. It's about doing what's right for the project, for the project team, and for the stakeholders. You'll focus on what's most important by prioritizing work, needs, and wants. Leaders take action, make decisions, are flexible and courageous, and can go directly to problems to rectify issues and keep the project moving forward.

Recognizing Politics in Project Management

Without a doubt, politics in an organization can affect project management. Unfortunately, project managers often get mired in between stakeholders' competing objectives and succumb to office politics that can affect the project for the worse. Politics are really a way of describing how organizations operate—the undocumented, but present, undercurrent of how decisions are made within the organization. Project managers have to understand how organizations work and who wields authority, and navigate through the politics, good or bad, to keep the project moving toward a successful conclusion.

Though the project manager may want to avoid politics, it's nearly impossible to do, because politics can begin with the perception of the project manager and the power he has. Perception of power is how other people—from the project team, to management, to stakeholders—view not just the project but also the project manager. The project manager does have power, to an extent, over the project and the perceptions others have the of the project manager. Every scenario is different, but you should be familiar with several types of power for your role as a project manager and for your PMP exam:

- **Positional power**   The project manager's power is a result of the position she has as the project manager. This is also known as formal, authoritative, and legitimate power.
- **Informational power**   The project manager has control of data gathering and distribution of information.
- **Referent power**   The project manager is respected or admired because of others' past experiences with the project manager. This is about the project manager's credibility in the organization.

- **Situational power**   The project manager has power because of certain situations in the organization.
- **Personal or charismatic power**   The project manager has a warm personality that others like.
- **Relational power**   The project manager networks, make connections, and creates alliances with others.
- **Expert power**   The project manager has deep skills and experience in a discipline. (For example, years of working in IT helps an IT project manager better manage IT projects.)
- **Reward power**   The project manager can reward the project team.
- **Punitive or coercive power**   The project manager can punish the project team.
- **Ingratiating power**   The project manager aims to gain favor with the project team and stakeholders through flattery.
- **Pressure-based power**   The project manager can restrict choices to get the project team to perform and do the project work.
- **Guilt-based power**   The project manager can make the team and stakeholders feel guilty in order to gain compliance in the project.
- **Persuasive power**   The project manager can persuade people toward a specific outcome or decision.
- **Avoiding power**   The project manager refuses to act, get involved, or make decisions.

You'll notice that I've framed all of these types of power from the project manager's point of view, but the reality is that any stakeholder, such as a customer or even the project sponsor, can apply these powers. This is all part of politics, and being able to recognize the power being wielded can help the project manager better manage the project and its outcomes.

exam

watch   Recognize these types of power and how they can be implemented in a project. You may be presented with a scenario and have to determine what type of power is being demonstrated.

CERTIFICATION OBJECTIVE 3.04

Leading and Managing the Project

Leadership and management are not the same things. Leadership is about aligning and motivating to achieve goals. Leadership is more about emotional intelligence and inspiring people to work together to achieve great things. Management is about getting things done. Management is concerned with the results and the work of directing people to achieve those results. Certainly project management has attributes of both leadership and management, and you'll need to recognize both as a PMP candidate.

As a project manager, you'll serve as both leader and manager. You'll lead the team by giving them the opportunity to accomplish the project, to create something new, and to complete the project work with an eye toward how the project contributes to business value for the organization. As a manager, you'll keep the team organized, keep the work authorization moving, and address the knowledge areas of project management. You'll be accountable, and hold the team accountable, for the scope, costs, quality, risk management, and other facets of project management. Successful project management requires both leadership and management.

People work hard when they feel valued, are inspired, and see others working hard, too. When the project manager leads the project team, she does so by being personally invested in the project. Project management isn't barking out orders, but serving the project team and working with the team to get the needed results and achieve the project objectives.

Exploring Leadership Styles

Chances are you've worked for people you've admired. Think of how they led the organization or project. Their characteristics, such as their temperaments and their values, made you admire them. And project team members often reflect their moods, values, and ethics. What the team sees in management, including project managers, is how they'll tend to act as team members. Leadership styles are the methods you, and others, can take to offer leadership within the project. That's an important concept: it's not just the project manager that can offer leadership, because the team, stakeholders, and even vendors can offer leadership at different times throughout the project.

Six leadership styles are utilized within organizations, and you should recognize these for your exam:

- **Servant leadership**   The leader puts others first and focuses on the needs of the people he serves. Servant leaders provide opportunity for growth, education, autonomy within the project, and the well-being of others. The primary focus of servant leadership is service to others.

- **Transactional leadership**   The leader emphasizes the goals of the project and rewards and provides disincentives for the project team. This is sometimes called management by exception, because it's the exception that is rewarded or punished.

- **Laissez-faire leadership**   The leader takes a "hands-off" approach to the project. This means the project team makes decisions, takes initiative in the actions, and creates goals. Though this approach can provide autonomy, it can make the leader appear absent when it comes to project decisions.

- **Transformational leadership**   The leader inspires and motivates the project team to achieve the project goals. Transformational leaders aim to empower the project team to take action, be innovative in the project work, and accomplish through ambition.

- **Charismatic leadership**   The leader is motivating, has high energy, and inspires the team through strong convictions about what's possible and what the team can achieve. Positive thinking and a can-do mentality are characteristics of a charismatic leader.

- **Interactional leadership**   The leader is a hybrid of transactional, transformational, and charismatic leaders. The interactional leader wants the team to take action, is excited and inspired about the project work, yet still holds the team accountable for their results.

Applying a Leadership Personality

When you think of a leader, you'll likely think of a person who's excited, inspiring, and leads by doing. Or maybe you think of a football coach giving a great half-time speech about overcoming the odds and winning the game. Or some combination of personality characteristics that are motivating, inspiring, and admirable. All of those traits are at the center of the personality of a good leader. For your PMP exam, you'll need to recognize some personality traits that directly affect your ability to serve as a leader for your project team.

These personality traits stem from experience, maturity, patterns of thinking, feelings, and repeated behavior. Recognize these personality traits:

- **Authentic**   Shows concern for others and accepts who they are
- **Courteous**   Is polite and shows respectful behavior toward others
- **Creative**   Creates, thinks through problems, seeks solutions through creativity
- **Cultural**   Is sensitive to cultural norms and beliefs
- **Emotional**   Shows empathy and understanding, and manages personal emotions

- **Intellectual**   Demonstrates intelligence and respects the intelligence of others
- **Managerial**   Shows management aptitude in all aspects of the project
- **Political**   Understands the politics at play within an organization
- **Service-oriented**   Provides others what they need to be successful
- **Social**   Is friendly and approachable, and understands the needs and wants of the project team and stakeholders
- **Systemic**   Understands existing frameworks and systems and builds project systems to get things done in an orderly fashion

INSIDE THE EXAM

This chapter focuses on the foundations of what it means to be a project manager. I'd not be surprised if you already recognize most of the information in this chapter, as you're currently serving as a project manager and working toward your PMP certification. However, don't shrug off these elements, because you'll likely see this information on your exam. This chapter is based on Chapter 3 of the *PMBOK Guide*, and it's fair to assume it's part of what you'll be tested on when it comes to your exam day.

One of the most important points in this chapter is the difference between project management and leadership. Management is about directing people to get things done. Leadership is about aligning, motivating, and inspiring people. Be familiar with both aspects of project management, not just the mechanics of getting things done.

Management utilizes positional power to

- Maintain the project
- Administrate duties
- Focus on project systems
- Control the project work
- Focus on the next project achievements

- Question how and when things will happen
- Control and administer finances
- Maintain the status quo
- Do the right things at the right time
- Address issues and problem solving

Leadership influences and inspires people to

- Develop personality and skills
- Perform their work with innovation
- Build relationships
- Trust one another
- Examine the long-range vision of the project
- Question why and what will happen
- Challenge the status quo
- Do the right things at the right time
- Align with the organization vision with motivation and inspiration

There's some overlap between management and leadership, but the difference is in the attitude, the desire to do things well, and a positive mindset focused on serving others and serving the good of the stakeholders, team, and organization.

All of these characteristics are commendable traits for a successful project manager. Project managers need these traits, which they'll develop over time with experience, maturity, and a conscious effort to incorporate them into thoughts, actions, and leadership of others.

Performing Project Integration

Integration, in this context, differs from project integration management. Instead of addressing the interrelationship among the project processes, project integration in this context addresses how the project is integrated with the goals, tactics, and vision of the organization, not just the project scope and knowledge areas. Integration at this level means that you're working with the project sponsor to ensure that the goals and objectives of the project mesh with the goals and objectives of the organization. Projects must support the broader vision and purpose of the organization or the project likely isn't contributing to business value and may have challenges garnering support within the organization.

Within the project, the project manager continues integration by leading and managing the project team. The people that have the greatest effect on project success are the project team members. The project manager can't do everything, of course, and the project team will execute the project plan. When the project team executes the project plan, their work needs to support the goals of the project, which in turn must support the goals of the organization. If those two things are not in synch, the project will no doubt face challenges, issues, and unrest.

Examining Process-Level Integration

In Chapter 4 of this book and the *PMBOK Guide*, you'll see that project integration management addresses the interrelationship among the project processes. Processes are the predefined actions, such as quality control, that bring about a specific result. Process-level integration means that the processes are largely integrated and affect one another throughout the project. Some processes might occur just one time, such as creating the project charter, while other processes can happen over and over as needed in the project. Still, some processes may not happen at all—consider the procurement processes in a project that won't be purchasing anything from vendors.

Many project managers miss this important point: You complete only the processes that are needed within a project, and you complete the most appropriate process only when it's needed. There is no "paint-by-number" approach to project management, and processes can generally happen in any order that's needed once the project is initiated and the charter is created. Yes, you'll generally move into planning once the charter is created, but as the project is in motion, especially on larger projects, you'll move on to the process that's next required, not necessarily the next process described in the *PMBOK Guide*. Of course, what you do with one process has a direct effect on other processes in your project.

Projects can be complex, and the larger and more complex the project, the more processes you are likely to use. The more processes are introduced and needed in a project, the more you'll need project integration management. Project managers need not address only the processes of a project, but must also consider three other factors that contribute to the project's complexity:

- **Ambiguous nature of projects** Some projects aren't clear in requirements and what will happen throughout the project life cycle. Consider software development, extremely long projects, and unknowns that are lurking in the nature of the work.
- **Human behavior** Perhaps the most complex aspect of project management is human behavior. People don't always get along, and this can cause problems within the project that stem from behavior outside of the project.
- **System behavior** How your organization works is entirely different from how other organizations work You'll need to understand the business framework of what it takes to interact with employees, departments, and systems in order to manage the project.

Examining Cognitive-Level Integration

When you first started in project management, did you manage the construction of a skyscraper? Or did you manage a project with clear expectations, not too many moving parts, and what you might today consider an easy project? When we first begin as project managers, we're often assigned projects that are low priority and that have easily achievable objectives. As we become more mature in the role of a project manager, and have gained experience and insight into project management, we're allowed to take on more complex projects. It's the experience that gives us the wisdom to manage the more complex projects.

The idea of integration at the cognitive level means that we not only rely on our experience—an excellent teacher—but we also learn from others. We take classes, read books, and attend PMI chapter meetings. We make a deliberate effort to learn more so that we can manage projects more effectively. Cognitive-level integration is the act of learning on purpose, not just by doing, to ensure that we're well-rounded in all knowledge areas of project management, even those areas we don't touch frequently. That's why your PMP exam will cover the whole breadth of project management even if you have little experience in procurement, or risk management, or any of the knowledge areas.

Examining Context-Level Integration

Context-level integration is the management of a project with consideration for how the project environment has changed, and is changing, in our organizations today. Consider a project 20 or 30 years ago. Social networking, texting, and virtual teams weren't a reality back then, but they certainly are in play in most organizations today. As project managers, we need insight into how our projects will take advantage of these and other evolving project landscapes and how these elements can create benefits, and perhaps some disruptions, to the project.

Your organization may allow texting and virtual teams in a project, while another organization doesn't use those elements. This doesn't mean that one is better than the other—they are just different. Each facet of the context level brings benefits but also costs that can affect how the project moves forward. The project manager needs to understand what's allowed to use, what's being ignored, what's not allowed, and why.

CERTIFICATION SUMMARY

The role of the project manager is to manage the project work, lead the project team, and get things done. The project manager works with the project team to achieve the project objectives, contribute to business value, and coordinate the activities, communications, and events that happen within a project. Project managers facilitate processes to reach predefined expectations and usher the project through initiating, planning, execution, monitoring, and controlling—and, ultimately, to project closing.

Through experience and training, the project manager's competency increases. The project manager should ascertain his level of skill in management and leadership areas; identify strengths, weaknesses, opportunities, and threats; and then decide to improve upon his management prowess. The PMI Talent Triangle aims to address the three common areas of education for project managers: technical project management, leadership, and strategic and business management.

The role of the project manager isn't just about managing project work and resources; it also includes leadership. Leadership provides the alignment, motivation, and inspiration for people to complete the project work, succeed in their lives, and focus on the long-range vision of the project. Leadership styles are the methods a project manager can utilize to help the project team members be inspired and motivated to complete their tasks and complete the project.

KEY TERMS

To pass the PMP exam, you will need to memorize these terms and their definitions. For maximum value, create your own flashcards based on these definitions and review them daily.

active listening   The message receiver restates what's been said to confirm the message, providing an opportunity for the sender to clarify the message if needed.

active problem-solving   Begins with problem definition, the ability to discern between the cause and effect of the problem. Root-cause analysis looks beyond the immediate symptoms to the cause of the symptoms—which then affords opportunities for solutions.

avoiding power   Power gained by refusing to act, getting involved, or making decisions.

charismatic leadership   The leader is motivating, has high energy, and inspires the team through strong convictions about what's possible and what the team can achieve. Positive thinking and a can-do mentality are characteristics of a charismatic leader.

expert power   Power gained by deep skills and experience in a discipline. (For example, years of working in IT helps an IT project manager better manage IT projects.)

guilt-based power   Power gained by making the team and stakeholders feel guilty in order to gain compliance in the project.

informational power   Power gained by controlling the gathering and distribution of information.

ingratiating power   Power gained by flattering, or ingratiating oneself, with the project team members and stakeholders.

interactional leadership   A hybrid of transactional, transformational, and charismatic leaders. The interactional leader wants the team to take action, is excited and inspired about the project work, and holds the team accountable for results.

laissez-faire leadership   The leader takes a hands-off approach to the project. The project team makes decisions, takes initiative in the actions, and creates goals. Although this approach can provide autonomy, it can make the leader appear absent when it comes to making project decisions.

leadership   Aligning, motivating, and inspiring the project team members to do the right thing, build trust, think creatively, and to challenge the status quo.

management   Management uses positional power to direct, maintain, administrate, control, and focus on getting things done without challenging the status quo of the project and organization.

media selection   Based on the audience and the message being sent, the media should be in alignment with the message.

meeting management   Meetings are forms of communication. How the meeting is led, managed, and controlled all influence the message being delivered. Agendas, minutes, and order are mandatory for effective communications within a meeting.

personal or charismatic power   Power gained by a warm personality that others like.

persuasive power   Power gained by persuading people to move toward a specific outcome or decision.

PMI Talent Triangle   Defines three areas of PDUs for PMI-certified professionals to maintain their certification: technical project management, leadership, and strategic and business management.

positional power   Power gained by the position one holds in the organization or project. This is also known as formal, authoritative, or legitimate power.

presentation   In formal presentations, the presenter's oral and body language, visual aids, and handouts all influence the message being delivered.

pressure-based power   Power gained by restricting choices to get the project team to perform the desired project work.

professional development units (PDUs)   Hours of education or experiences that the PMP must earn after obtaining the PMP to maintain the PMP certification. PMPs are required to earn 60 PDUs per three-year certification cycle. Of the 60 PDUs, a minimum of 35 hours must come from educational opportunities.

project manager   The role of leading the project team and managing the project resources to achieve the objectives of the project effectively and efficiently.

punitive or coercive power   Power gained by punishing the people.

referent power   Power gained by credibility, respect, and admiration resulting from others' past experiences with the person.

relational power   Power gained by networking, making connections, and creating alliances with others.

reward power   Power gained by rewarding people.

sender–receiver models   Communication requires a sender and a receiver. Within this model may be multiple avenues to complete the flow of communication, but barriers to effective communication may be present as well.

servant leadership   The leader puts others first and focuses on the needs of the people she serves. Servant leaders provide opportunity for growth, education, autonomy within the project, and the well-being of others. The primary focus of servant leadership is service to others.

situational power   Power gained by specific situations within the organization.

style   The tone, structure, and formality of the message being sent should be in alignment with the audience and the content of the message.

transactional leadership   The leader emphasizes the goals of the project and offers rewards and disincentives for the project team. This is sometimes called management by exception, because it's the exception that is rewarded or punished.

transformational leadership   The leader inspires and motivates the project team to achieve the project goals. Transformational leaders aim to empower the project team to take action, be innovative in the project work, and accomplish through ambition.

TWO-MINUTE DRILL

Defining the Project Management Role

❑ The project manager's role involves getting things done. The project manager is responsible for managing the project work, project resources, and characteristics of the project, but you must also provide leadership for the project team members. Project managers aim to coordinate the efforts of the project in a logical approach to achieve the project objectives.

❑ Communicating project information is a key aspect of successful project management. You'll need to communicate the right information, to the right people, and at the right time. The message you're communicating will affect how you communicate. It's been said that 90 percent of project manager's time is spent communicating.

❑ Problem solving is a skill that all project managers need. Problem solving means you're examining a problem at face value, but then digging deeper into the problem and looking for causal factors and the root cause of the problem. Problem solving doesn't mean just dealing with issues, but solving the logistics of a project, planning for project work, and working with project constraints and boundaries.

Exploring the Project Manager Influence

❑ The project manager is influenced by, and can influence, all of the project stakeholders. Certainly the project team is influenced by the project manager, but so, too, are managers, steering committee members, and other stakeholders. Understanding the roles, power, and interests of these stakeholders can help the project manager better manage the project and operate more efficiently within an organization.

❑ Politics are a natural part of any organization. Effective project managers understand how things really get done in an organization, who has what power, and how politics can influence decisions, progress, and the project team. Politics are often reflected in the behavior of the project manager and how she may manage the project based on the politics she has to deal with in the organization.

❑ International projects can have a variety of influences on the project manager. The project manager must be educated regarding how people and businesses in other cultures operate and how these conditions can affect the project, the project team, and stakeholders. Completing projects in an international environment will challenge the project manager to work with people with varying beliefs, values, educational backgrounds, and social influences.

Building the Project Management Competencies

❑ Once you earn the PMP, you'll enter your three-year certification cycle. Within these three years, you'll need to accrue 60 professional development units (PDUs). Of the 60 PDUs, a maximum of 25 can be earned by giving back to the profession by volunteering. The other 35 PDUs must come from continuing education. Within these 35 education PDUs, you must earn 8 in technical project management, leadership, and strategic and business management skills.

❑ Politics are a part of every organization, and projects are not immune from politics. Project managers must understand the political landscape and how politics can affect project decisions, stakeholder involvement, and how things get done in an organization. Politics often stem from the perception of the project and the project manager.

❑ The project manager can utilize several types of power to keep the project moving forward. Understanding and recognizing these powers are important for the PMP exam. You'll need to be able to identify which power may be used, depending on the given scenario.

Leading and Managing the Project

❑ You will lead people and manage the project. Leadership and management are connected, but they are different things in project management. Leadership is about aligning, motivating, and inspiring people. Management is about getting key results—getting things done. Effective project managers, through experience, will learn how to be both leaders and managers for the project.

❑ Leadership styles are the methods you'll use to lead the project team. There are six leadership styles you should recognize for the exam: servant leadership, transactional, laissez-faire, transformational, charismatic, and interactional. Know these leadership types and their characteristics so you can identify which leadership type is being used in a given scenario.

❑ Personality affects leadership. Effective leaders are authentic, courteous, and creative. They are aware of the culture the project is operating within and respectful of the project team, have emotional intelligence, and are sociable. Know the characteristics of a good leadership personality.

Performing Project Integration

❑ Process-level integration is project integration management. It's the coordination of the project management processes within the five knowledge areas. Project integration management is the understanding that what you do with one process can affect other processes. The processes are not isolated in a project, but relative to one another, and many processes can be repeated many times.

❑ Cognitive-level integration is about obtaining experience, knowledge, and ultimately wisdom. Over time, project managers learn by doing, by managing more and more projects within an organization. It's also about acting and recognizing opportunities for additional learning through training and education.

❑ Context-level integration is the management of a project in consideration for how the project environment has changed, and is changing, in organizations today. By understanding where the project is taking place, the trends and advances in technologies, and the different methods people have for working and communicating, the project manager can adapt and better lead the project within the boundaries and framework of the organization.

SELF TEST

1. Leadership and project management are connected. As a leader and a manager, you will rely on communications within a project to help motivate, manage, and ensure that the project is moving forward toward its objectives. In one component of communication, the receiver restates what the sender has said to clarify the message and to give the sender an opportunity to offer clarity if needed. What is this communication component called?
   A. Active listening
   B. Sender–receiver model
   C. Communications planning
   D. Leader listening

2. Beth is a project manager for the HGF Electricians Company, and she's working with a client to start a new project. Beth and the client are negotiating the price, schedule, and other concerns for a contract for the new project that HGF Electricians Company may take on. In the negotiating, Beth and the client should be negotiating for what result?
   A. Best price for the contracted work
   B. Fair agreement for both the client and the vendor
   C. Most profit for the contracted work
   D. Risk distribution between the two parties

3. You are the project manager of the NHQ Project. In your project management role, you want to influence the organization and the project team for the better. What two key aspects are most helpful in influencing the organization as a project manager?

    A. Management and leadership

    B. Communication skills and a positive attitude

    C. Experience and knowledge

    D. Experience and willingness to learn

4. Beth is a new project manager for her company, and she's working with her project team to develop the project management plan. Beth knows that she must rely on several different skills to make her first project successful. Of the following management skills, which will she use most?

    A. Leading

    B. Communicating

    C. Influencing the organization

    D. Negotiating

5. Sammy is the project manager for her organization. Sammy is examining her skills and her career and she's determined that more training in a project management information system would make her a better project manager in her organization. In the five steps of competence, where is Sammy with this realization?

    A. Unconsciously competent

    B. Consciously competent

    C. Consciously incompetent

    D. Unconsciously incompetent

6. As a PMP candidate, you should be familiar with the PMI Talent Triangle. You'll be earning professional development units to maintain your PMP certification status once you've cleared the exam. Of the following choices, which answer is *not* part of the PMI Talent Triangle?

    A. Leadership

    B. Technical project management

    C. Continuing education

    D. Strategic and business management

7. Leadership is a desirable trait for a project manager and is heavily referenced throughout the *PMBOK Guide*. Which one of the following characteristics is *not* an attribute of leadership?

    A. Fiscal responsibility

    B. Respect for others

    C. Problem-solving ability

    D. Desire to learn and improve

8. You are the project manager for your organization. Influencing your organization requires which of the following?

A. An understanding of the organizational budget

B. Research and documentation of proven business cases

C. An understanding of formal and informal organizational systems

D. Positional power

9. Mark is new project manager in the Donaldson Consulting Company. Before joining this company, Mark worked as a project manager for more than 20 years in The Briane Firm, a technical company. Mark has a deep understanding of electronics, software development, and data warehouse technology and is considered an expert in his field. His current project team, however, is pushing back on recommendations from Mark and challenging his knowledge on the project. Since Mark is so new, the project team reasons, he likely doesn't understand how Donaldson Consulting Company works. What type of power does Mark have in this scenario?

A. Expert

B. Positional

C. Situational

D. Informational

10. What type of power does a project manager have when the team admires the project manager because they've worked with her before the current project or they know of her reputation as a project manager?

A. Situational

B. Referent

C. Personal

D. Expert

11. Martha is the project manager for her company and her team likes working for her. Martha has a good attitude, is easy to work with, and is a good planner. The project team views Martha as a member of management who can give them a good review and possibly affect a bonus payment for each project team member if the project is completed on time. What type of power does Martha have?

A. Punitive

B. Situational

C. Reward

D. Guilt-based

12. You can adopt several different tactics and leadership styles in a project. Which one of the following is the best description of being a servant leader?

    A. The leader emphasizes the goals of the project and offers rewards and disincentives for the project team.

    B. The leader puts others first and focuses on the needs of the people he serves.

    C. The leader takes a "hands-off" approach to the project.

    D. The leader inspires and motivates the project team to achieve the project goals.

13. You are the project manager for the ERP Project. As such, you will have to use some positional power to keep the project moving forward. You'll also need to develop leadership skills to align, motivate, and inspire people. Of the following choices, which one is most likely associated with management skills?

    A. Focus on the next project achievements

    B. Build relationships

    C. Support the project team

    D. Challenge status quo

14. You are the project manager of the Finance Project for your organization. In this project you're coaching Maria on the project management knowledge areas. Maria is having questions about project integration management at the process level. Which one of the following is the best example of project integration management at the process level?

    A. Poor quality management planning will likely affect the quality of the project deliverable.

    B. A robust communications management plan is dependent on the number of stakeholders involved in the project.

    C. Larger projects require more detail than smaller projects.

    D. Planning is an iterative activity that will happen throughout the project.

15. You are the project manager of a project. The project team is experiencing some trouble with a new material that the project will utilize. You gather the team to lead an active problem-solving session. Which one of the following is the best definition of problem solving?

    A. Define the problem and the desired solution.

    B. Discern the cause and the effect of the problem.

    C. Document the problem and its characteristics to see the whole effect.

    D. Test the materials to identify the solution.

16. Dwight was the project lead for the IT Upgrade Project, while Jim was serving as the project manager. Because of a family emergency, Jim has stepped down from the project and has taken a leave of absence. Management has asked that Dwight to serve as the project manager for the remainder of the project. What type of power does Dwight now have?
    A. Personal
    B. Expert
    C. Situational
    D. Reward

17. A project manager is meeting with his project team. In this meeting, the top 10 percent of project team members are openly praised for their hard work. The bottom 10 percent of the project team members are disciplined and scolded in the meeting. The balance of the project team is not addresses. What type of leadership is happening in this scenario?
    A. Transactional leadership
    B. Laissez-faire leadership
    C. Interactional leadership
    D. Pressure-based power

18. Who is responsible for executing the project plan and creating the project deliverables?
    A. Project lead
    B. Project manager and the project team
    C. Project manager
    D. Project team

19. As a project manager, you need both leadership and management skills. Which one of the following statements best describes the difference between leadership and management in a project?
    A. Management is the process of getting the results that are expected by project. Leadership is the ability to motivate and inspire individuals.
    B. Management is the process of getting the results that are expected by project stakeholders. Leadership is the ability to motivate and inspire individuals to work toward those expected results.
    C. Leadership is about creating excitement to be managed.
    D. Leadership is the process of getting the project team excited to create results that are expected by project stakeholders. Management is the ability to keep track of the project results.

20. Communication is paramount in project management and best summed up by defining who needs what information, when do they need it, and what other factor? (Choose the best answer.)
    A. Person
    B. Resource
    C. Format
    D. Modality

21. Tracy is the project manager for her organization. She's working with Tim, a project team member, to garner information about an activity. Tim reports that he's nearly done with the task and will likely be done next week. Tracy responds by confirming that Tim is nearly done with the activity and that he could be done by next Monday. This is an example of what?

    A. Leadership
    B. Management
    C. Active listening
    D. Scrum

22. You are the project manager in a large organization, and you instruct the project team that you and the project team should follow vertical communications throughout the project whenever risks are discussed. What is vertical communications?

    A. Communications that follow the organizational flow chart.
    B. Communications that follow the project phases.
    C. Communication that always flow through the project manager.
    D. Communication that is open and any project team member can discuss the risks with anyone associated with the project.

23. Terri is the project manager of the IT Development Project for her company. She and a stakeholder are having a heated disagreement about what was to be included in the project. Terri decides it's best to bring the project sponsor into the conversation to help everyone find an agreeable conclusion to the disagreement. What is happening in this scenario?

    A. Poor requirements gathering
    B. Sender–receiver model
    C. Strong negotiation
    D. Mediation

24. The project manager can influence people and people can also influence the project manager. One such group of influence comprises the organizational managers. Why will the project manager need to influence the organizational managers?

    A. To have access to people, processes, and resources
    B. To have control over project team members' time
    C. To determine when the organizational managers expect the project to be completed
    D. To negotiate for project funding

25. Once you earn the PMP, the certification is valid for how long?

    A. One year
    B. Three years
    C. Five years
    D. Forever

SELF TEST ANSWERS

1. Leadership and project management are connected. As a leader and a manager, you will rely on communications within a project to help motivate, manage, and ensure that the project is moving forward toward its objectives. In one component of communication, the receiver restates what the sender has said to clarify the message and to give the sender an opportunity to offer clarity if needed. What is this communication component called?

   A. Active listening
   B. Sender–receiver model
   C. Communications planning
   D. Leader listening

   ☑ **A.** Active listening is the participatory component of a conversation that confirms what was said and enables the sender to offer clarity, if needed.
   ☒ **B, C,** and **D** are incorrect. **B** is incorrect because the sender–receiver model is a model regarding how communication moves between two people. **C** is incorrect because communications planning is a project management process plan for who needs what information, when the information is needed, and in what modality. **D,** leader listening, is not a valid project management term, so this choice is incorrect.

2. Beth is a project manager for the HGF Electricians Company, and she's working with a client to start a new project. Beth and the client are negotiating the price, schedule, and other concerns for a contract for the new project that HGF Electricians Company may take on. In the negotiating, Beth and the client should be negotiating for what result?

   A. Best price for the contracted work
   B. Fair agreement for both the client and the vendor
   C. Most profit for the contracted work
   D. Risk distribution between the two parties

   ☑ **B.** The purpose of negotiations is to reach a fair agreement for all parties involved.
   ☒ **A, C,** and **D** are incorrect. **A** and **C** are incorrect because these two choices are mutually exclusive and not concerned with the other party in the contract. **D,** risk distribution, is not a valid choice as the fair agreement among the parties would address the risk distribution. If the HGF Electricians Company takes on more risk, the client may pay more for the service.

3. You are the project manager of the NHQ Project. In your project management role, you want to influence the organization and the project team for the better. What two key aspects are most helpful in influencing the organization as a project manager?
   A. Management and leadership
   B. Communication skills and a positive attitude
   C. Experience and knowledge
   D. Experience and willingness to learn

   ☑ **B.** Communication skills and a positive attitude are most helpful in influencing an organization.
   ☒ **A, C,** and **D** are incorrect. **A** is incorrect because management and leadership are values for a project manager, but they aren't the most helpful aspects of influence. **C** is incorrect because experience and knowledge are self-contained skills and don't do much to influence, inspire, and motivate others. **D** is incorrect because experience and a willingness to learn are good attributes, but they are intrinsic for a good project manager and are not an external influence on the organization.

4. Beth is a new project manager for her company, and she's working with her project team to develop the project management plan. Beth knows that she must rely on several different skills to make her first project successful. Of the following management skills, which will she use most?
   A. Leading
   B. Communicating
   C. Influencing the organization
   D. Negotiating

   ☑ **B.** Communication is the key general management skill a project manager will use the most.
   ☒ **A, C,** and **D** are incorrect. These choices are important to project management, but communication accounts for the majority of a project manager's time.

5. Sammy is the project manager for her organization. Sammy is examining her skills and her career and she's determined that more training in a project management information system would make her a better project manager in her organization. In the five steps of competence, where is Sammy with this realization?
   A. Unconsciously competent
   B. Consciously competent
   C. Consciously incompetent
   D. Unconsciously incompetent

   ☑ **C.** Sammy is consciously incompetent because she is aware that she needs more training to be competent in a new skill.
   ☒ **A, B,** and **D** are incorrect. **A** is incorrect because unconsciously competent project managers have a skill without even thinking about it. **B** is incorrect because consciously competent managers learn and practice a skill to gain competence. **D,** unconsciously incompetent, would indicate that Sammy doesn't know that she is incompetent in the skill.

6. As a PMP candidate, you should be familiar with the PMI Talent Triangle. You'll be earning professional development units to maintain your PMP certification status once you've cleared the exam. Of the following choices, which answer is *not* part of the PMI Talent Triangle?

A. Leadership

B. Technical project management

C. Continuing education

D. Strategic and business management

☑ **C.** Continuing education is not part of the PMI Talent Triangle.

☒ **A, B,** and **D** are incorrect. Leadership, technical project management, and strategic and business management are the three components of the PMI Talent Triangle.

7. Leadership is a desirable trait for a project manager and is heavily referenced throughout the *PMBOK Guide*. Which one of the following characteristics is *not* an attribute of leadership?

A. Fiscal responsibility

B. Respect for others

C. Problem-solving ability

D. Desire to learn and improve

☑ **A.** This is an example of a management skill. Fiscal responsibility is also a desirable trait for project managers, but it's a management skill rather than a leadership skill.

☒ **B, C,** and **D** are incorrect. Leadership attributes include respect for others, problem-solving abilities, and a desire to learn and improve.

8. You are the project manager for your organization. Influencing your organization requires which of the following?

A. An understanding of the organizational budget

B. Research and documentation of proven business cases

C. An understanding of formal and informal organizational systems

D. Positional power

☑ **C.** To influence an organization (to get things done), a project manager must understand the explicit and implied organizational system within the organization.

☒ **A, B,** and **D** are incorrect. **A** is incorrect because the project manager may not have access to an organizational budget. **B** is incorrect because a proven business case may not map to every scenario when influencing an organization. **D** is incorrect because positional power may relate only to a small portion of an organization, not to multiple facets of influence.

9. Mark is new project manager in the Donaldson Consulting Company. Before joining this company, Mark worked as a project manager for more than 20 years in The Briane Firm, a technical company. Mark has a deep understanding of electronics, software development, and data warehouse technology and is considered an expert in his field. His current project team, however, is pushing back on recommendations from Mark and challenging his knowledge on the project. Since Mark is so new, the project team reasons, he likely doesn't understand how Donaldson Consulting Company works. What type of power does Mark have in this scenario?

   A. Expert
   B. Positional
   C. Situational
   D. Informational

   ☑ **B.** Mark has positional power in this scenario, because he's new to the organization and the team doesn't recognize his expertise in the technology. Positional power is also known as formal, authoritative, or legitimate power.

   ☒ **A, C,** and **D** are incorrect. **A** is incorrect because expert power means the team would recognize his expertise in the technology and respect his decisions. **C** is incorrect because situational power relies on situations within the organization. **D** is incorrect because informational power means the individual has control of the data gathering and distribution of information.

10. What type of power does a project manager have when the team admires the project manager because they've worked with her before the current project or they know of her reputation as a project manager?

    A. Situational
    B. Referent
    C. Personal
    D. Expert

    ☑ **B.** Referent power of the project manager indicates that she is respected or admired because of her team's past experiences with her. This is about the project manager's credibility in the organization.

    ☒ **A, C,** and **D** are incorrect. **A** is incorrect because situational power means the project manager has power because of certain situations in the organization. **C** is incorrect because the project manager is liked because of her personality rather than her experiences with the project team in the past. **D** is incorrect because expert power means the project manager has deep skills and experience in a particular discipline.

11. Martha is the project manager for her company and her team likes working for her. Martha has a good attitude, is easy to work with, and is a good planner. The project team views Martha as a member of management who can give them a good review and possibly affect a bonus payment

for each project team member if the project is completed on time. What type of power does Martha have?

A. Punitive
B. Situational
C. Reward
D. Guilt-based

☑ **C.** When the project team sees the project manager as someone who can reward them, the project manager has reward power.

☒ **A, B,** and **D** are incorrect. **A,** punitive power, means the team thinks the project manager can punish them. **B,** situational power, is when the project manager has power based on unique situations within the organization. **D,** guilt-based power, is when the team feels guilty if they don't complete their project work according to plan.

12. You can adopt several different tactics and leadership styles in a project. Which one of the following is the best description of being a servant leader?

A. The leader emphasizes the goals of the project and offers rewards and disincentives for the project team.
B. The leader puts others first and focuses on the needs of the people he serves.
C. The leader takes a "hands-off" approach to the project.
D. The leader inspires and motivates the project team to achieve the project goals.

☑ **B.** The leader puts others first and focuses on the needs of the people he serves. Servant leaders provide opportunity for growth, education, autonomy within the project, and the well-being of others. The primary focus of servant leadership is service to others.

☒ **A, C,** and **D** are incorrect. **A** is incorrect because this answer describes transactional leadership. **C** is incorrect because this answer describes a laissez-faire leadership approach. **D** is incorrect because this answer describes the transformational leadership style.

13. You are the project manager for the ERP Project. As such, you will have to use some positional power to keep the project moving forward. You'll also need to develop leadership skills to align, motivate, and inspire people. Of the following choices, which one is most likely associated with management skills?

A. Focus on the next project achievements
B. Build relationships
C. Support the project team
D. Challenge status quo

☑ **A.** Management focuses on the next project achievements.

☒ **B, C,** and **D** are incorrect. These choices are attributes of leadership. Leaders build relationships, support the project team, and challenge the status quo. This isn't to say that managers don't do these things, but **A** is the best answer in this case.

14. You are the project manager of the Finance Project for your organization. In this project you're coaching Maria on the project management knowledge areas. Maria is having questions about project integration management at the process level. Which one of the following is the best example of project integration management at the process level?
    A. Poor quality management planning will likely affect the quality of the project deliverable.
    B. A robust communications management plan is dependent on the number of stakeholders involved in the project.
    C. Larger projects require more detail than smaller projects.
    D. Planning is an iterative activity that will happen throughout the project.

    ☑ **A.** Of all the choices presented, this answer is the best example of project integration management. Project integration management at the process level means that what you do in one process can have a direct effect on other processes. Poor quality management planning will likely affect the quality of the deliverables is a true statement linked to project integration management.
    ☒ **B, C,** and **D** are incorrect. These are examples of project integration management at the process level. We'll discuss more about project integration management in the next chapter of this book.

15. You are the project manager of a project. The project team is experiencing some trouble with a new material that the project will utilize. You gather the team to lead an active problem-solving session. Which one of the following is the best definition of problem solving?
    A. Define the problem and the desired solution.
    B. Discern the cause and the effect of the problem.
    C. Document the problem and its characteristics to see the whole effect.
    D. Test the materials to identify the solution.

    ☑ **B.** Problem solving begins with problem definition. Problem definition is the ability to discern between the cause and effect of the problem. Root-cause analysis looks beyond the immediate symptoms to the cause of the symptoms, which then affords opportunities for solutions.
    ☒ **A, C,** and **D** are incorrect. These approaches don't first define the effect and the causes, which is crucial to problem solving.

16. Dwight was the project lead for the IT Upgrade Project, while Jim was serving as the project manager. Because of a family emergency, Jim has stepped down from the project and has taken a leave of absence. Management has asked that Dwight to serve as the project manager for the remainder of the project. What type of power does Dwight now have?
    A. Personal
    B. Expert
    C. Situational
    D. Reward

☑ **C.** Dwight now has situational power. The project manager has power because of certain situations in the organization.

☒ **A, B,** and **D** are incorrect. Personal power means the project manager has a warm personality that others like. Expert means that the project manager has deep skills and experience in a discipline. Expert isn't the best choice because Dwight is made project manager only because of the situation with Jim having to leave the project. Reward power means the project manager can reward the project team.

17. A project manager is meeting with his project team. In this meeting, the top 10 percent of project team members are openly praised for their hard work. The bottom 10 percent of the project team members are disciplined and scolded in the meeting. The balance of the project team is not addresses. What type of leadership is happening in this scenario?

    A. Transactional leadership

    B. Laissez-faire leadership

    C. Interactional leadership

    D. Pressure-based power

☑ **A.** Transactional leadership means the leader emphasizes the goals of the project and offers rewards and disincentives for the project team. This is sometimes called management by exception because it's the exception that is rewarded or punished.

☒ **B, C,** and **D** are incorrect. **B** is incorrect because laissez-faire leadership means the leader takes a hands-off approach to the project. **C** and **D** are incorrect because the leader is a hybrid of transactional, transformational, and charismatic leaders. The interactional leader wants the team to act, is excited and inspired about the project work, yet still holds the team accountable for their results. **D**, pressure-based power, is not a leadership type, but rather a type of power where the project manager can restrict choices to get the project team to perform the project work.

18. Who is responsible for executing the project plan and creating the project deliverables?

    A. Project lead

    B. Project manager and the project team

    C. Project manager

    D. Project team

☑ **D.** The project team members are responsible for executing the project plan and creating the project deliverables.

☒ **A, B,** and **C** are incorrect. **A** is incorrect because the project lead isn't the only role responsible for executing the plan. Answer **B** is tempting, but the project team is responsible for executing the plan—that is, doing the work to create the project deliverables. **C**, the project manager, isn't the best answer, because the project manager may be accountable for the project, but it's the project team that builds the project deliverables.

19. As a project manager, you need both leadership and management skills. Which one of the following statements best describes the difference between leadership and management in a project?

   A. Management is the process of getting the results that are expected by project. Leadership is the ability to motivate and inspire individuals.

   B. Management is the process of getting the results that are expected by project stakeholders. Leadership is the ability to motivate and inspire individuals to work toward those expected results.

   C. Leadership is about creating excitement to be managed.

   D. Leadership is the process of getting the project team excited to create results that are expected by project stakeholders. Management is the ability to keep track of the project results.

   ☑ **B.** Of all the choices, this is the best answer. Management is the process of getting the results that are expected by project stakeholders. Leadership is the ability to motivate and inspire individuals to work toward those expected results.

   ☒ **A, C,** and **D** are incorrect. These statements do not reflect the difference between management and leadership in a project.

20. Communication is paramount in project management and best summed up by defining who needs what information, when do they need it, and what other factor? (Choose the best answer.)

   A. Person

   B. Resource

   C. Format

   D. Modality

   ☑ **D.** Project communication can be summed up as "who needs what information, when do they need it, and what's the best modality to deliver the message."

   ☒ **A, B,** and **C** are incorrect. Although these answers are tempting choices, these aren't the best answers. Communication is best summed up by defining who needs what information, when do they need it, and the modality.

21. Tracy is the project manager for her organization. She's working with Tim, a project team member, to garner information about an activity. Tim reports that he's nearly done with the task and will likely be done next week. Tracy responds by confirming that Tim is nearly done with the activity and that he could be done by next Monday. This is an example of what?

   A. Leadership

   B. Management

   C. Active listening

   D. Scrum

☑ **C.** This is an example of active listening because Tracy is repeating the information and giving Tim an opportunity to clarify which day next week he could have the task completed.
☒ **A, B,** and **D** are incorrect. This is not an example of leadership, management, or scrum.

22. You are the project manager in a large organization, and you instruct the project team that you and the project team should follow vertical communications throughout the project whenever risks are discussed. What is vertical communications?
    A. Communications that follow the organizational flow chart.
    B. Communications that follow the project phases.
    C. Communication that always flow through the project manager.
    D. Communication that is open and any project team member can discuss the risks with anyone associated with the project.

    ☑ **A.** Vertical communication follows the organizational flow chart.
    ☒ **B, C,** and **D** are incorrect. **B** is incorrect because vertical communication doesn't follow the project phase. **C** is incorrect because not all communication must flow through the project manager. **D** is incorrect because the project team shouldn't discuss risks with anyone in the project in a vertical communications models.

23. Terri is the project manager of the IT Development Project for her company. She and a stakeholder are having a heated disagreement about what was to be included in the project. Terri decides it's best to bring the project sponsor into the conversation to help everyone find an agreeable conclusion to the disagreement. What is happening in this scenario?
    A. Poor requirements gathering
    B. Sender-receiver model
    C. Strong negotiation
    D. Mediation

    ☑ **D.** By bringing in the project sponsor to help resolve the disagreement, Terri is starting a mediation session for the requirements wanted by the stakeholder.
    ☒ **A, B,** and **C** are incorrect. Though there may have been poor requirements gathering prior to this meeting, we don't know enough from the question to determine that this is the case. Though communication should follow the sender–receiver model, this isn't the best choice for the question. Strong negotiation isn't a valid project management term.

24. The project manager can influence people and people can also influence the project manager. One such group of influence comprises the organizational managers. Why will the project manager need to influence the organizational managers?
    A. To have access to people, processes, and resources
    B. To have control over project team members' time
    C. To determine when the organizational managers expect the project to be completed
    D. To negotiate for project funding

    ☑ **A.** The project manager will likely need to work with and influence managers to have access to people, process, and resources.
    ☒ **B, C,** and **D** are incorrect. These choices aren't the best answers for why the project manager will need to influence the organizational managers. The project manager may need to influence the organizational managers for project team members' time, but this isn't the best choice. Understanding when the project work needs to be completed is part of project requirements gathering and isn't the best answer. Project funding will likely be established prior to the project initiation and is backed by the project sponsor.

25. Once you earn the PMP, the certification is valid for how long?
    A. One year
    B. Three years
    C. Five years
    D. Forever

    ☑ **B.** The PMP is valid for three years. You maintain the certification by earning 60 PDUs within the three-year certification cycle.
    ☒ **A, C,** and **D** are incorrect. The PMP is valid for three years.

Part II

PMP Exam Essentials: Knowledge Areas

CHAPTERS

4   Implementing Project Integration Management

5   Managing the Project Scope

6   Introducing Project Schedule Management

7   Introducing Project Cost Management

8   Introducing Project Quality Management

9   Introducing Project Resources Management

10 Introducing Project Communications Management

11 Introducing Project Risk Management

12 Introducing Project Procurement Management

13 Introducing Project Stakeholder Management

14 The PMI Code of Ethics and Professional Conduct

Chapter 4

Implementing Project Integration Management

CERTIFICATION OBJECTIVES

4.01	Developing the Project Charter		4.05	Monitoring and Controlling the Project Work
4.02	Developing the Project Management Plan		4.06	Performing Integrated Change Control
4.03	Directing and Managing the Project Work		4.07	Closing the Project or Phase
4.04	Managing Project Knowledge		✓	Two-Minute Drill
			Q&A	Self Test

hat the heck is *project integration management*? Project integration management is the heart of project management and comprises the day-to-day processes the project manager relies on to ensure that all of the parts of the project work together.

Put simply, project integration management is the way the gears of the project work together.

Within any project are many moving parts: schedule management, cost management, schedule conflicts, human resource issues, iterative planning, alternative methods of doing the project work, and much, much more. Project integration management is the art and science of ensuring that your project moves forward and that your plan is fully developed and properly implemented. Project integration management requires that your project—regardless of its size and impact—meshes with the existing operations of your organization. This knowledge area encompasses integrated change control, too; you'll need to manage changes that are bound to happen within your project.

Project integration management requires finesse. As the project manager, you will have to negotiate with stakeholders to resolve competing project objectives. This requires organization, since you'll have to develop, coordinate, and record your project plan. It requires the ability to accomplish your project plan. It requires leadership, record-keeping, and political savvy, given you'll have to deal with potential changes throughout your project implementation. And, perhaps most importantly, it requires flexibility and adaptability throughout the project plan execution.

In this chapter, we'll cover the big topics you have to master to pass your PMP exam, as well as the skills necessary to implement projects successfully out in the real world. These topics include the following:

- Developing the project charter
- Developing the project plan
- Directing and managing the project work
- Managing project knowledge
- Monitoring and controlling the project work
- Managing integrated change control
- Closing the project or the project phase

As you've learned already, all projects need a project plan—it's up to the project manager and the project team to create one. Then the project manager must work with the project team to ensure that the work is being completed as planned. You'll also manage the information that comes into the project and seek out information that's needed for the project to be successful. Finally, the project manager must work throughout the project to control changes across all facets of the project. Figure 4-1 shows the complete picture of project integration management.

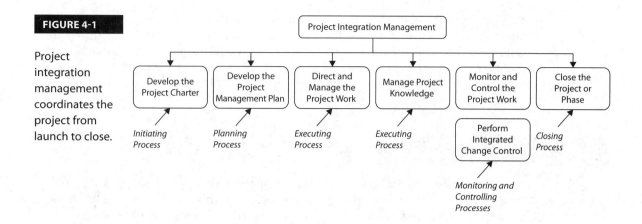

FIGURE 4-1

Project integration management coordinates the project from launch to close.

Exploring Project Integration Management

Of all the project management knowledge areas, project integration management is the one that's totally managed by the project manager. Cost management, schedule management, risk management, and other knowledge areas can be managed within the project by specialists from your organization. But project integration management is totally led by the project manager—in fact, it's the day-to-day work of the project manager. And like most things in project management, the larger and more complex the project, the more detail, organization, and sophistication is needed within project integration management.

Project integration management is the only knowledge area that has processes in each of the five process groups. We'll explore seven processes in this chapter:

- Develop the project charter (Initiating)
- Develop the project management plan (Planning)
- Direct and manage the project work (Executing)
- Manage project knowledge (Executing)
- Monitor and control the project work (Monitoring and Controlling)
- Perform integrated change control (Monitoring and Controlling)
- Close project or phase (Closing)

With the exception of creating the project charter, the processes in this knowledge area are broad, iterative in nature, and really coordinate the activities of the project. You'll plan, execute, control, and close phases many times. To be clear, these processes are iterative, so you'll always move to the most appropriate process depending on what needs to be done next in the project. Although there is a logical progression of moving through the five process groups, the process groups are not phases of the project.

e x a m

ⓦatch Throughout the *PMBOK Guide*, you'll see special sections on emerging practices in each knowledge area. You'll also find a little scoop on agile project management and how the knowledge area fits within the Agile methodology. Will you see this stuff on your exam? Very likely! I'll be addressing these components at the start of each chapter.

Considering Trends for Project Integration Management

One of the nice things about project management is that it's not concrete; it's fluid, evolving, developing from year to year and between organizations. Project management can be adapted, twisted, pared down, or sized up. There's no law or regulations from stopping you from managing a project however you best see fit. Several trends have found success and favor in the project management community when it comes to project integration management.

Because project integration management is all about coordinating the other knowledge areas, there is lots information to gather, store, process, and share. You should explore the following emerging trends in project integration management:

- ▪ **Automation** Software tools, such as Microsoft Project and Basecamp, help with the scheduling, cost tracking and estimating, workflow management, and communications. These tools are commonly called the *project management information system (PMIS)*, and that's how you'll see it referenced throughout the balance of this book. You won't be tested on any specific PMIS for your exam.

- ▪ **Visual management tools** In the olden days, I used giant sheets of paper to map out project schedules, task lists, and deliverables. Not anymore. Now it's dashboards of these items. Visual management tools provide a quick way of seeing project status, activities in motion, issues, and other project information. Visual management tools can be customized for your project and help you share information quickly with the entire project team.

- **Project knowledge management** All projects create data that needs to be managed to be useable information. The information needs to be available: reports, electronic viewing, and even mobile access. And you'll have to control who has access to what data. This is a new process in the *PMBOK Guide*, sixth edition.

- **Project management responsibilities** Traditionally project initiation, business case development, and benefits management were outside of the project manager's responsibility. Today, that's changing. Project managers often help management, the project management office (PMO), and the steering committee to define objectives, build requirements, work with stakeholders, and create benefits for the organization.

- **Hybrid approaches to project management** New practices in project management, such as agile and Extreme Programming (XP), are being utilized by more than just software development project managers. Organizations are cherry-picking the best of these approaches and melding them with other practices to streamline projects, have more control, and create a project management system that works in their environment.

Tailoring Project Integration Management

No two projects are identical—there are always one or more different factors that distinguish one project from projects that have happened in the past. Because of this unique nature of projects, it's not uncommon to tailor the project integration management processes to fit the project and the organization. The goal of project management isn't to fall in love with the project management processes or the bureaucracy of a framework, but to get things done.

Tailoring the project integration management processes help organizations better manage the project with an eye toward balancing the need for process and the need to work expediently in the execution of the project work. Consider these points for tailoring project integration management:

- **Project life cycle** The project life cycle is made up of the phases of the project. In your industry, the phases may be predefined and readily identified. In other projects, you may need to identify logical phases that aren't too large or small, that create a deliverable, and that serve as ideal segments to the project.

- **Development life cycle** You may need to identify how the project output will be built. You may use a traditional predictive life cycle, where you plan most everything up front in the project. Or you may embrace the adaptive life cycle, where you'll move through increments or iterations to define what's most important and what should be created next.

- **Management approach** Larger projects require more detail than smaller projects. Depending on the size of your project, your organization, and the project management framework your organization utilizes, you may need to tailor the management approach to keep the project moving quickly without heavy, unneeded processes.

- **Knowledge management** Project managers need a systematic way of collecting, distributing, and storing information. They also need to control who has access to the information, when the information is needed, and what directions are needed for stakeholders to get information they need quickly. This is knowledge management.

- **Change management** The *PMBOK Guide* (and this chapter) will define a generally accepted practice of change management. The model I'll discuss is fine, but chances are that in your organization you'll need to tweak this model to work best for you and your projects. Change isn't unusual in a project—in fact, it's expected—but how you manage the changes is entirely up to the project manager and the organization.

- **Governance** Every organization needs some governance for the project. Governance needs to be defined and communicated, and its expectations must be met. Governance includes steering committees, change control boards, user groups, or whatever entity is required in your organization that sets the rules that you need to follow. Governance will control how you manage the project and what the project team does, and it will greatly influence communication of project status.

- **Lessons learned** Lessons learned is knowledge that the project manager and the project team create throughout the project, not just at the end. Your tailoring will define the lessons learned creation, where the information is stored, and how you and others may access the information.

- **Benefits management** Projects create benefits, and you'll need to define when the benefits will become available. On some projects, there may be intermittent benefits that the stakeholders can begin using as the benefits become available. Other projects, such as a technology cutover project, won't have benefits available for the stakeholders until late in the project.

Considering Project Integration Management in Agile Environments

Although project integration management is the focal point of work for project managers in a predictive approach, it's a bit different in an agile or adaptive environment. In an agile environment, the project team members have much more control over the integration of project management plans and project components. Agile is more fluid than the predictive environment, so documentation isn't a value-added component to the project.

Though the project manager still oversees the coordination of the project management knowledge areas, the agile and adaptive approaches rely more on the project team defining what needs to be done at the current point of the project, and the team plans and does the work accordingly. The project manager doesn't necessarily control and direct the project work, but ensures that the project team has what it needs to get the work done.

CERTIFICATION OBJECTIVE 4.01

Developing the Project Charter

Let's not linger. You know what the project charter is and what it does: It authorizes the project and enables the project manager to assign resources to the project work. It's all about power. The project manager is officially identified in the project charter, though the project manager should be selected as early as possible during the project—hopefully while the charter is being developed—but she must be identified before project planning commences. The project charter also demonstrates the organization's commitment to the project and the investment in the endeavor.

The project manager, however, doesn't issue the project charter. Nope. The project charter comes from outside of the project. The project manager may help develop the project charter, but it's not signed or issued by the project manager; the charter needs the authority of someone in the organization who has oversight of the needed resources and finances the project will require. The project manager is, though, accountable for the project charter getting issued. Specifically, the project charter should be issued outside the confines of the project by any of the following:

- Sponsor
- Project management office
- Portfolio governing body, such as a steering committee
- Program organization
- Portfolio organization
- Authorized organizational representative

And the reason why a project is chartered? It can be because of opportunities, problems that need to be solved, business requirements, and lots of other reasons. The project manager or business analyst may create a business case that defines why a project needs to be chartered. A business case determines whether the investment in the project is worth making. The business case will define the project purpose and characteristics, such as the following:

- Market demand
- Business need
- Customer request
- Technological advance
- Legal requirements
- Ecological impacts
- Social need

Creating the Project Charter

The point of the charter, other than authorizing the project and the project manager, is to launch the project officially and to enable the project manager to go about the business of getting the project work planned and then finished. The charter gives the project a definite start and maps out the high-level objectives for the project. The project charter needs to communicate all of the following directly or through references to other documents:

- **Project purpose** The charter needs to answer why the project is being launched and why it's important to the organization.

- **Project requirements for satisfaction** The charter must identify what it'll take to complete the project—in other words, it should identify the metrics for success.

- **High-level project description** The charter provides a description of what the project will create and what the project boundaries may be, and it provides an overview of the key project deliverables.

- **High-level requirements** The charter should identify the high-level purpose of the project, the business need the project aims to accomplish, and/or the product requirements the project will create.

- **High-level risks** Any of the known risks should be referenced in the project charter.

- **Milestone schedule** Milestones are timeless events that show the progress within a project.

- **Summary budget** The charter should have preapproved financial resources.

- **Stakeholder list** The charter needs to identify the key stakeholders who will influence the project.

- **Project approval requirements** The project charter needs to state clearly what it takes for the project to be successful and who signs off on project deliverables, project decisions, and project completion.

- **Exit criteria** The project charter defines what constitutes completion of the project and, in some cases, what scenarios would cause the project or phase to be cancelled.

- **Project manager**   The project charter defines who the project manager is and what level of power the project manager has in the project.
- **Project sponsor**   The project charter defines who the project sponsor is; if the project sponsor is not the person signing the project charter, it should define who is authorizing the project (it's almost always the project sponsor who signs the charter). The sponsor has the authority to authorize the project and to help resolve project issues during execution.

watch   Assumptions should be documented in an assumptions log. This includes assumptions estimates, planning, scheduling, and so on. Assumptions can be considered risks, because false assumptions can alter the entire project.

To develop the project charter, the project manager will most likely rely on expert judgment. Expert judgment, a tool and technique you'll see often in project processes, simply means the project manager is relying on someone with more knowledge and wisdom to help make the best decisions for the project. For the project charter, expert judgment can be from people with insight into the organization's strategy, benefits management techniques, technical knowledge, estimating skills for schedule and costs, and risk management.

The project charter will also need data in order to communicate the goals of the project. Data-gathering techniques for creating the project charter include the following:

- **Brainstorming**   A group of people generates as many ideas as possible about the project. The first step of brainstorming is the most common: generate ideas. The second step, unfortunately, is often overlooked: analyze the ideas.
- **Focus groups**   A focus group of stakeholders has a conversation about the project, its goals, any concerns, and other project charter attributes. You'll see focus groups again when I discuss the project scope creation.
- **Interviews**   Unlike a focus group with its conversational approach, an interview is a one-on-one discussion with stakeholders to gather data through specific questions.

During this early process, the project manager will need to implement meeting management skills to keep people on track and keep the charter creation process moving forward. The project manager may also need some conflict management skills to manage disagreement among stakeholders; I'll discuss this in more detail in Chapter 9 on project resources. Finally, the project manager may be serving as a facilitator when meeting with large groups of project stakeholders.

In most cases, creating the project charter is a process that's done only once. However, in the *PMBOK Guide*, sixth edition, creating the project charter can happen once or be revisited at predefined times throughout the project, such as at project phases or during interactions with other groups in the project.

Relying on the Business Documents

Before the project charter is created, the organization may have created a business case and a benefits management plan. The business case justifies the investment in the project and often is the document upon which the project charter is based. The business case also defines the cost-benefit analysis of doing the project, project boundaries, and why the project should be initiated. The benefits management plan defines when the project benefits will be delivered to the organization. This document contributes to the project charter.

Documenting Project Agreements and Contracts

If your company is completing projects for other entities, your contract will probably define what your company will provide for the client and what the client will pay for the work and contribute to the work, and other terms. Your project charter may reference the details of the contract directly, define the agreements of the contract, and include service-level agreements, letters of intent, a memorandum of understanding, or even just a verbal agreement for the work. Your company might also use this approach if you're operating in a functional environment and completing work for other lines of service within your business. In any case, if there's an agreement, written or verbal, between the project initiators and the project customer, it should be documented and referenced as part of the project charter.

Considering Enterprise Environmental Factors

Project managers know that many things influence a project's success; it's not all planning, execution, and good luck. Projects take place within organizations, and many components of any organization can, and will, affect a project's success. These enterprise environmental factors have to be considered throughout the project and should be identified in the project charter. Enterprise environmental factors include the following:

- Government and industry standards
- Regulations or legal requirements

- Marketplace conditions
- Organizational governance, culture, political climate, and framework
- Stakeholder risk tolerances

Identifying Organizational Process Assets

Has anyone in the organization ever done something like this project before? Historical information is an organizational process asset that resource project managers can use to make decisions about their current projects. Historical information provides proven documentation of the success or failure of performance and can be referenced for project selection criteria. For instance, has management squelched similar projects for specific reasons? Historical information can be referenced for comparable projects to see how they performed through to execution, as well as how the deliverables of the project performed according to prediction.

In addition, historical information is one of the key elements in determining whether an existing project should move forward into the next project phase. If the completed project phase has proven successful and provided some merit or value, it's likely to move forward. Projects that don't prove valuable—based on the performance of the phase or less-than-desirable phase results—will likely be axed.

Organizational process assets can also include the standard policies of your organization, reporting methods, and templates your organization may rely upon.

Examining the Project Selection Criteria

Project selection methods are about resolving the unknown, predicting the likelihood of project success, and determining the expected value of that project's success—or the cost of its failure. The process of selecting those projects to keep and those to discard is based on the following two methods:

- Benefit measurement methods
- Constrained optimization methods

Benefit measurement methods are the most common approaches to project selection and are usually defined before the project charter and documented in the business case and the benefits management plan. Benefit measurement methods are tools that enable management and key stakeholders to examine the benefits of a project and how the project completion will contribute to the organization. *Constrained optimization methods* are also tools for selecting projects, but their approach is much more scientific and math-driven. Don't worry—you won't need to know much, if anything, about constrained optimization on the PMP exam. We'll examine both selection types later in this chapter.

Project selection is also known as "Go/No Go decision-making." Projects with many variables are excellent candidates for phase gates. The project is allowed a Go decision to the end of the first phase. Another Go/No Go decision happens at the end of each phase based on the performance and deliverables.

Meet Tracy. Tracy has a great project she'd like to see authorized. She has to "sell" the project to management in order to have it authorized. She needs to determine what's so great about her project and why management should buy into it. She is looking for project selection criteria—reasons why her project should be authorized. Following are some possible considerations Tracy can include:

- Return on investment
- Realized opportunities
- Market share
- Customer perspective
- Demand for the product
- Social needs
- Increased revenues
- Reduced costs
- Regulatory compliance

exam

Watch **Historical information is always a key source for project information—even more important than project team members' opinions. Why? Because historical** **information is proven and documented, and it comes from reliable sources. If you must choose, choose historical information as a key input.**

Examining Benefit Measurement Methods

The various benefit measurement methods are all about comparing values of one project against the values of another. As you might expect, the projects with higher, positive values typically get selected over projects with low values. The following sections describe some common benefit measurement methods you may encounter.

Scoring Models

Scoring models (sometimes called weighted scoring models) use a common set of values for all of the projects up for selection. For example, values can be profitability, complexity, customer demand, and so on. Each of these values has a weight assigned to it—values of high importance have higher weights, while values of lesser importance have lower weights. The projects are measured against these values and assigned scores by how well they match the predefined values. The projects with high scores take priority over projects with lower scores. Figure 4-2 demonstrates the scoring model.

Estimating Benefit/Cost Ratios

Just like they sound, *benefit/cost ratio (BCR)* models examine the cost-to-benefit ratio. For example, a typical measurement is the cost to complete the project plus the cost of ongoing operations of the project product compared against the expected benefits of the project. For example, consider a project that will require $575,000 to create a new product, market the product, and provide ongoing support for the product for one year. The expected gross

	Cost	ROI	Marketplace	Demand	Prototype	Score
Project A	45	65	80	45	25	260
Project B	65	76	50	58	46	295
Project C	34	80	80	90	66	350
Project D	65	25	66	40	75	271
Project E	85	90	45	25	80	325
Project F	50	65	25	90	40	270

FIGURE 4-2

The weighted model bases project selection on predefined values.

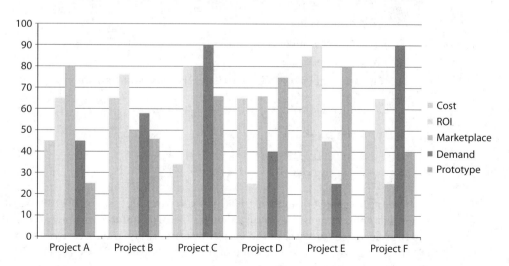

return on the product, however, is $980,000 in year 1. The benefit of completing the project is greater than the cost to create the product.

Estimating the Payback Period

How long does it take the project to "pay back" its costs? For example, the AXZ Project will cost the organization $500,000 to create over five years. The expected cash inflow (income) on the project deliverable, however, is $40,000 per quarter. From here, it's simple math: $500,000 divided by $40,000 is 12.5 quarters, or a little over three years to recoup the expenses.

This selection method, while one of the simplest, is also the weakest. Why? The cash inflows are not discounted against the time it takes to begin creating the cash. This is the time value of money. The $40,000 per quarter five years from now is worth less than $40,000 in your pocket today. Remember when sodas were a quarter? It's the same idea. The soda hasn't gotten better; a quarter is just worth less today than it was way back then.

See the video "Time Value of Money."

Considering the Discounted Cash Flow

Discounted cash flow accounts for the time value of money. If you were to borrow $100,000 from your uncle for five years, you'd be paying interest on the money, yes? (If not, you've got a terrific uncle.) If the $100,000 were invested for five years and managed to earn a whopping 6 percent interest per year, compounded annually, it'd be worth $133,822.60 at the end of five years. This is the future value of the money in today's terms.

The magic formula for future value is $FV = PV (1 + i)^n$, where

- FV is future value
- PV is present value
- i is the interest rate
- n is the number of time periods (years, quarters, and so on)

Here's the formula with the $100,000 in action:

1. $FV = 100,000(1 + 0.06)^5$
2. $FV = 100,000(1.338226)$
3. $FV = 133,822.60$

The future value of the $100,000 five years from now is worth $133,822.60 today. So how does that help? Now we've got to calculate the discounted cash flow across all of the projects up for selection. The discounted cash flow is really just the inverse of the preceding formula. We're looking for the present value of future cash flows: $PV = FV \div (1 + i)^n$.

In other words, if a project says it'll be earning the organization $160,000 per year in five years, that's great. But what's $160,000 five years from now really worth today? This puts the amount of the cash flow in perspective with what the projections are in today's money. Let's plug it into the formula and find out (assuming the interest rate is still 6 percent):

1. $PV = FV \div (1 + i)^n$
2. $PV = 160,000 \div (1.338226)$
3. $PV = \$119,561$

So, $160,000 in five years is worth only $119,561 today. If we had four different projects with various times to completion and various costs, and we expected project cash inflows at completion, we'd calculate the present value and choose the project with the best PV, since it'll likely be the best investment for the organization.

Calculating the Net Present Value

The *net present value (NPV)* is a somewhat complicated formula, but it allows a more precise prediction of project value than the lump-sum approach of the PV formula. NPV evaluates the monies returned on a project for each time period the project lasts. In other words, a project may last five years, but there may be a return on investment in each of the five years the project is in existence, not just at the end of the project.

For example, a retail company may be upgrading the facilities at each of its stores to make shopping and purchasing easier for customers. The company has 1000 stores. As each store makes the conversion to the new facility design, the project deliverables will begin, hopefully generating cash flow as a result of the project deliverables. (Uh, we specifically want cash inflow from the new stores, not cash outflow. That's some nerdy accounting humor.) The project can begin earning money when the first store is completed with the conversion to the new facilities. The faster the project can be completed, the sooner the organization will see a complete return on its investment. In this example, an interest rate of 6 percent per year is assumed.

The following outlines how the NPV formula works:

1. Calculate the project's cash flow per time unit (typically quarters or years).
2. Sum the cash flows for all time units; this yields the total cash flow.
3. Calculate the present value of each cash flow.
4. Sum the present value of each time unit; this yields the total present value.
5. Subtract the investment for the project from the total present value, this yields the NPV.
6. Take two aspirins.
7. Examine the NPV. An NPV greater than zero is good and the project should be approved. An NPV less than zero is bad and the project should be rejected.

When comparing two projects, the project with the greater NPV is typically better, although projects with high returns (PV) early in the project are better than those with low returns early in the project. The following is an example of an NPV calculation:

Time Period	Cash Flow	Present Value
1	$15,000.00	$14,150.94
2	$25,000.00	$22,249.91
3	$17,000.00	$14,273.53
4	$25,000.00	$19,802.34
5	$18,000.00	$13,450.65
Totals	$100,000.00	$83,927.37
Investment		$78,000.00
NPV		$5,927.37

I bet you're wishing you could try some of these out for yourself, right? You're in luck. I've created for you a Microsoft Excel file called "Time Value of Money" that has a few exercises and all of the formulas to test your work. Enjoy!

Considering the Internal Rate of Return

The last benefit measurement method is the *internal rate of return (IRR)*. The IRR is a complex formula used to calculate when the present value of the cash inflow equals the original investment. Don't get too lost in this formula—it's a tricky business, and you won't need to know how to calculate the IRR for the exam. You will need to know, however, that when comparing multiple projects' IRRs, projects with high IRRs are better choices than projects with low IRRs. This makes sense. Would you like an investment with a high rate of return or a low rate of return?

Examining Constrained Optimization Methods

Constrained optimization methods are complex mathematical formulas and algorithms that are used to predict the success of projects, the variables within projects, and the tendencies to move forward with selected project investments. For the exam, thankfully, all you need to know about these selection methods is that they are not typically used for most projects, being instead utilized for multiphase, complex projects. The following are the major constrained optimization methods:

- Linear programming
- Nonlinear programming

- Integer algorithms
- Dynamic programming
- Multiobjective programming

CERTIFICATION OBJECTIVE 4.02

Developing the Project Management Plan

The project plan is not a museum piece. You'll use, wrinkle, update, and depend on your project plan like a Super Bowl coach depends on the playbook. The project plan is developed with the project team, stakeholders, and management. It is the guide to how the project should flow and how the project will be managed, and it reflects the values, priorities, and conditions influencing the project. The project plan should be baselined to show the expectations for schedule, costs, and scope.

Project plan development requires an iterative process of progressive elaboration. The project manager will revise and update the plan as research and planning reveal more information and as the project develops. For example, an initial project plan may describe a broad overview of what the project entails, what the desired future state should be, and the general methods used to achieve the goals of the plan. Then, after research, careful planning, and discovery, the project plan will develop into a concise document that details the work involved in, and the expectations of, the project; how the project will be controlled, measured, and managed; and how the project should move. In addition, the project plan will contain all of the supporting details, specify the project organization, and allow for growth in the plan through a disciplined change control process.

exam
watch

The project plan guides the project manager throughout the project execution, monitoring and controlling, and project or phase closing. The project plan is designed to control the project. As a whole, the point of the project plan is to communicate to the project team, stakeholders, and management how the project will be managed and controlled. The project management plan is the foundation and guideline for all project work.

Understanding the Project Plan's Purpose

The project plan is more than a playbook to determine what work needs to be accomplished. The project plan is a fluid document that will control several elements:

- **Provide structure**   The project plan is developed to provide a structure that advances the project toward completion. It is a thorough but concise collection of documents that will serve as a point of reference throughout the project execution, monitoring and controlling, and project or phase closing.

- **Provide documentation**   A documented project plan is needed for truly successful projects. They provide a historical reference and the reasons why decisions were made. A project plan must provide documentation of the assumptions and constraints influencing the project plan development. The size of the project, the application the project exists within, and enterprise environmental factors can all affect the depth of detail the project management plan provides.

- **Provide communication**   Project plans are documents that provide the information, explanations, and reasoning underlying the decisions made for the project. The project plan serves as a source of communication among stakeholders, the project team, and management regarding how the project plan will be controlled.

- **Provide baselines**   A project plan contains several baselines. As the project moves toward completion, management, stakeholders, and the project manager can use the project plan to see what was predicted as far as costs, scheduling, quality, and scope—and then see how these predictions compare with what is being experienced.

Preparing to Develop the Project Plan

To develop the project plan effectively, the project manager and the stakeholders must be in agreement about the project objectives. For this agreement to exist, the project manager works with the stakeholders to negotiate a balance of expectations and required objectives. Competing objectives is a recurring theme in project management (and on the PMP exam). Project managers must be able to negotiate among stakeholders for the best solution to the problem or opportunity. The project plan is created based on the organization's project management methodology, the nature of the work to be implemented, and the overall scope of the project.

To develop the project management plan, you'll need the project charter, enterprise environmental factors, organizational process assets, and outputs from other processes. Because project management planning is an iterative process, you won't know everything as you begin the creation of the plan. Outputs from other processes, such as risk identification, will then require you to go back to your project management plan and update it accordingly. All of the ten knowledge areas (project integration management, scope, time, cost, quality, resources, communications, risk, procurement, and stakeholder management) will have processes that contribute to the comprehensive project management plan.

Applying Tools and Techniques for Project Plan Development

All the planning is done, right? Of course not. The planning processes are iterative and allow the project manager and the project team to revisit them as needed. But at what point do we push back from the planning buffet and move on with a working, feasible plan? Every project is different when it comes to planning, but a project team will continue in the planning stage until it is knowledgeable about the project work and has a clear vision of what needs to be done.

Figure 4-3 depicts the evolution of the planning to action process for a typical technology project. Once the business and the functional requirements have been established through iterations and revisions, the planning processes move into the specifics. Recall that the business requirements establish the project vision and the functional requirements establish the goals for the project. The technical requirements and the design plan shift the focus onto the specifics the project will accomplish.

All of the inputs to the project plan should be readily available for the project manager, because she may need to rely on this information for additional planning. With all of the "stuff" the project manager has to work with, it should be a snap to create the actual project plan, right? Well, not exactly. The tools and techniques for developing the project management plan are simply expert judgment and facilitation techniques. Expert judgment isn't just the project manager's job alone; it involves several stakeholders: the project

FIGURE 4-3

The planning processes require documentation and a logical, systematic approach.

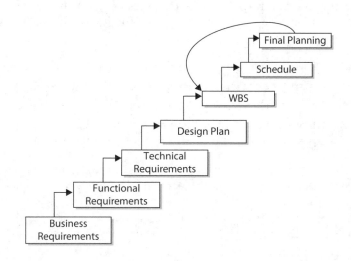

manager, the project team, stakeholders, and management work together to finalize the project plan. The contributions from each include the following:

- **Project manager** Leadership, facilitation, organization, direction, and expert judgment
- **Project team members** Knowledge of the project work and time estimates; also influence the schedule, provide advice and opinions on risk, as well as expert judgment
- **Customer** Objectives, quality requirements, expert judgment, and some influence over budget and schedule
- **Management** Budget, resources, project management methodology, quality requirements, and project plan approval

Facilitation techniques require the project manager to direct and control the planning meetings and to use different techniques to encourage participation among the stakeholders participating in the planning. Common interpersonal and data-gathering techniques are interviews, focus groups, checklists, brainstorming, facilitation, conflict resolution, and good meeting management to help the stakeholders reach a consensus on what should be included in the project management plan.

Using a Project Management Information System

The *PMBOK Guide* will repeatedly recommend using a PMIS. Here's the scoop: The PMIS is an automated system to create, manage, and streamline the project management processes quickly. In the development portion of the project, the PMIS can be used to help the project management team create the schedule, estimates, and risk assessments, and to gather feedback from stakeholders.

The PMIS also includes a configuration management system. Configuration management is an approach for tracking all approved changes, versions of project plans, blueprints, software numbering, and sequencing. A configuration management system aims to do the following:

- Manage functional and physical characteristics of the project deliverables
- Control, track, and manage any changes to the project deliverables
- Track any changes within the project
- Allow the project management team to audit the project deliverables to confirm conformance to defined criteria for acceptance

Let's say that, for the moment, the project manager and the project team have finished their project plan. Before the project team can set about implementing it, the plan must be approved, even though the project manager is accountable for the plan itself. Let's hear that again: The project plan is a formal, documented plan that must be approved by management. Once management has signed off on the project plan, the work is truly authorized to begin.

Examining the Typical Project Plan

The project plan is actually a collection of subsidiary plans and documents. Which ones, you ask? Well, let's take a peek.

Scope Management Plan

The scope management plan details how the project scope should be maintained and protected from change, as well as how a change in scope may be allowed. The plan also provides information on how likely it is that the project scope will change, and if changes do occur, how drastic those changes may be. We'll discuss scope management and change control in Chapter 5.

Requirements Management Plan

The requirements management plan works in tandem with the scope management plan. It defines how requirements will be identified, prioritized, documented, and then managed throughout the project. This plan also addresses the process for when changes are approved for a requirement and how the project team will manage new changes within the project. We'll discuss scope management and change control in Chapters 5, 6, 7, and 12.

Change Management Plan

Changes are likely to happen within a project, so you'll need a clearly defined plan that describes how to manage the changes. Ideally, all changes follow the change control process before they're implemented in the project, but some changes do bypass the process, and this can mean corrective actions for the unapproved change. The change management plan also addresses the change control board (CCB), if your company uses one, and how stakeholders can submit and query changes to the project. Changes can affect the entire project, but they stem from four specific areas: scope, costs, schedule, and contract.

Configuration Management Plan

Configuration management ensures consistency and makes certain that the customer receives exactly what was expected and defined. Configuration management is concerned with controlling and documenting the features and functions of the product the project is creating. This plan defines the elements of the product that are configurable and that will require change control should the elements change or be desired to be changed. This plan is tightly linked to the change management plan and the project's scope management plan.

Schedule Management Plan

The project plan details the scheduled work, milestones, and target completion dates for the project phases and the project itself. The schedule management plan, on the other hand, identifies circumstances that may change the project schedule, such as the completion of project phases or reliance on other projects and outside resources. The schedule management plan identifies the likelihood that the schedule will change and the impact of such changes, should they occur. Finally, the schedule management plan details the approval and accountability process for changes within the project. Along with the schedule management plan, the project manager creates the schedule baseline. We'll discuss the schedule management and schedule baseline in Chapter 6.

Cost Management Plan

The project plan includes the project budget, the cash-flow forecast, and procedures for procurement and contract administration. The subsidiary cost management plan explains how variances to the costs of the project will be managed. This plan may be based on a range of acceptable variances and the expected response to variances over a given threshold. The cost management plan also includes a cost performance baseline to measure accuracy of estimates and budgeting. Variances are revealed by comparing the actual project costs to the original cost performance baseline. We'll cover cost management in Chapter 7.

Quality Management Plan

The quality management plan describes how the project will operate and meet its quality expectations. It details the quality improvement and quality controls, and how the project will map to the quality assurance program of the performing organization. The quality management plan provides information on the required resources and time to meet the quality expectations. We'll discuss quality management in Chapter 8.

Resource Management Plan

The project plan includes information on the resources needed to complete the project work. The resource management plan, however, provides details on how the project team members and other physical resources will be brought onto the project and released from the project. For example, a project may have a need for an electrical engineer and a set of electrical tools for three months during a ten-month project. The resources plan will determine how the engineer's time and the tools are accounted for on the project and how the engineer can later be released and tools refurbished/repaired and returned to general stock; it also considers an accounting of the depletion of consumables when they're no longer needed on the project. We'll discuss resource management in Chapter 9.

Communications Management Plan

It's been said that project managers spend 90 percent of their time communicating. When you consider all of the different communication requirements for a project, it's easy to believe that statistic. The communications management plan describes the required communications and how they will be fulfilled. It also explains the methods used for gathering, storing, and dispersing information to appropriate parties.

In addition, the communications management plan maps out the schedule of when the expected communication needs will be met. For example, milestone reports, timely status reports, project meetings, and other expected communication events are included in the communications management plan. The communication schedule also includes accepted procedures to update, access, and revise communications between scheduled communication events. We'll discuss communications in Chapter 10.

Risk Management Plan

The risk management plan details the identified risks within the project, the risks associated with the constraints and project assumptions, and how the project team will monitor, react, or avoid the risks. The risk management plan, and the processes to create it, will be detailed in Chapter 11.

Procurement Management Plan

If the project includes vendors, the project plan needs a procurement management plan. This plan describes the procurement process, from solicitation to source selection. The plan may also include the requirements for selection as set by the organization. The selected offers, proposals, and bids from vendor(s) should be incorporated into the procurement management plan. We'll discuss procurement processes in Chapter 12.

Stakeholder Engagement Plan

Stakeholders need to be engaged and included in communication throughout the project. This plan defines the approach the project manager and the project team will take with the project stakeholders. The stakeholder engagement plan defines the level of engagement, the interrelationships among stakeholders, communications requirements, and the timing of stakeholder engagement. This plan may contain sensitive information about the project stakeholders, so it's often guarded rather than openly distributed to all of the project stakeholders.

PMP
Coach   **Loads of project plans and documents are covered in this chapter. I highly recommend that you remember all of the project plans and documents. Knowing these documents will help you in all of the other knowledge areas, too, as you'll see these plans there. Keep at it—if it were easy, everyone would do it.**

Project Baseline Documents

The project management plan also includes four baselines. The most prevalent baseline is the project's scope baseline. This baseline is made up of the project's scope document, the project work breakdown structure (WBS), and the WBS dictionary. These three documents are used to compare what was promised to the project customer and what the project delivered. A difference between the two can mean quality errors or scope validation rejections.

The cost baseline and the schedule baseline help show project performance. The cost baseline reflects the project's accumulative costs in relation to the project's predicted cost. Like the cost baseline, the schedule baseline is also used to compare the project's planned schedule against the actual progress. A difference between what was planned and what was experienced is called a *variance*. Variances mean that the project is losing money, is off schedule, or both.

The performance measurement baseline is a combination of the scope, schedule, and cost plans. Project measurement and performance are compared to the performance measurement baseline for an overall view of how well the project is doing. The integrated nature of time, cost, and scope are the reason for this baseline view; events in one of these three knowledge areas will likely directly affect the other two knowledge areas.

Project Documents and Files

In addition to the compilation of project management subsidiary plans, you'll rely on many project documents that help you plan and execute the project. These are not officially part of the project plan, but you should be familiar with them for your PMP exam.

- **Activity list**   This is a shopping list of all the activities the project team must complete to satisfy the project. This list is an input to the project network diagram.
- **Activity attributes**   Activities are documented in the activity list to include a coding structure, successor and predecessor activity identification, resource requirements, imposed dates, constraints, assumptions, and other pertinent information.
- **Assumption log**   This document clearly identifies and tracks all constraints and assumptions that are made in the project. All assumptions need to be tested for their validity, and the outcomes of the tests should be recorded.
- **Basis of estimates**   This document contains an explanation of how you and the project team arrived at the predicted cost and duration of the project.
- **Change log**   As changes to the project time, cost, or scope enter the project, they should be recorded with their status in the change log for future reference.
- **Cost estimates**   The cost of resources, including materials, services, and, when warranted, labor should be estimated.

- **Cost forecasts**   This document predicts what the project and its activities will cost based on current project performance. Forecasting may also include when the costs will happen.
- **Duration estimates**   This document includes a prediction of how long the project activities will take to complete.
- **Issue log**   Issues are conditions or situations that need decisions. They are recorded in the issue log, along with an issue owner designation, an issue date for resolution, and the eventual outcome of the issue.
- **Lessons learned register**   Lessons learned are recorded in the lessons learned register throughout the project.
- **Milestone list**   This is a listing of the project milestones and anticipated completion dates.
- **Physical resource assignments**   This document indicates when people and facilities are available or scheduled to work on the project. Materials, equipment, and facilities may need to be procured and scheduled in the project.
- **Project calendar**   You'll need to define when the project work will take place. This includes any special accommodations, such as working weekends or after hours, holidays, or pauses in the project so as not to interfere with operations.
- **Project communications**   The project manager, team, and stakeholders will generate much information and communication throughout the project. This information should be organized and kept as part of the project.
- **Project schedule**   Predictions of when project events will happen, such as milestones accomplished, phases completed, and project closed.
- **Project schedule network diagram**   This diagram illustrates the flow of the project activities and reveals the project's critical path and opportunities for float.
- **Project scope statement**   This document defines the project scope—major deliverables the project is required to create in order to satisfy the project objectives, along with the assumptions and constraints.
- **Quality control measurements**   Quality control is an inspection-driven process; quality control measurements are predefined values that signal problems with quality within the project deliverables. These can vary, based on the discipline the project centers on—for example, manufacturing or information technology.
- **Quality metrics**   These are predefined values that the results of project work should match in order to be acceptable for the project deliverables and project performance.
- **Quality report**   This report communicates how well the project is adhering to the quality requirements. These documents are ideal for repetitive activities to ensure that each activity is done identically to the other activities in the project. They are also ideal for safety procedures.

- **Requirements documentation**   These documents include a refined list of requirements of the product scope. They include everything the project is expected to create by the project closing.

- **Requirements traceability matrix**   This table identifies all of the project requirements, when the requirements are due, when the requirements are created, and any other pertinent information about the requirements.

- **Resource assignments**   These define who will do what in the project activities and may include a roles and responsibility matrix chart.

- **Resource breakdown structure**   This chart identifies the resources utilized in the project in each section of the WBS.

- **Resource calendars**   This document indicates when people and facilities are available or scheduled to work on the project.

- **Resource requirements**   The identification of what resources are needed to complete the project work is required as a supporting document for planning. This includes people, materials, equipment, facilities, and services.

- **Risk register**   A risk is an uncertain event or condition that can have a positive or negative effect on the project. All risks, regardless of their probability or impact, are recorded in the risk register, and their status is kept current.

- **Risk report**   This document communicates the status of risk events that are pending, passed, or are in motion within the project.

- **Schedule data**   This document stores raw data about the activities, project progress, and schedule information.

- **Schedule forecast**   This forecast predicts when events are going to happen in the project, such as milestone achievement, project phase completion, and project completion.

- **Stakeholder register**   All stakeholders, their positions within the project, contact information, and other characteristics are recorded in this document.

- **Team charter**   This document defines the team values, meeting guidelines, communication rules, and agreements among the project team.

- **Team resource assignments**   The team resource assignments list who will do what activities during project execution.

- **Test and evaluation documents**   These documents define what will be tested and evaluated during the project and the results of the testing.

CERTIFICATION OBJECTIVE 4.03

Directing and Managing the Project Work

So you've got a project plan—great! Now the work of executing the project plan begins. The project manager and the project team will go about completing the promises made in the project plan to deliver, document, measure, and complete the project work. The project plan will communicate to the project team, the stakeholders, management, and even vendors what work happens next, how it begins, and how it will be measured for quality and performance.

The product of the project is created during these execution processes. The largest percentage of the project budget will be spent during the project execution processes. The project manager and the project team must work together to orchestrate the timing and integration of all the project's moving parts. A flaw in one area of the execution can have ramifications in cost and additional risk and can cause additional flaws in other areas of the project.

As the project work is implemented, the project manager refers to the project plan to ensure that the work is meeting the documented expectations, requirements, quality demands, target dates, and more. The completion of the work is measured and then compared against the cost, schedule, and scope baselines as documented in the project plan. Should there be—GASP!—discrepancies between the project work and the scope, time, and cost baselines, prompt and accurate reactions are needed to adjust the slipping components of the project.

Executing the project plan includes the following:

- Doing the work to satisfy the project objectives
- Managing the project knowledge
- Spending funds to satisfy the project objectives
- Managing, developing, and leading the project team
- Completing procurement requirements and managing the vendors and buyers
- Acquiring, managing, and using resources such as materials, tools, facilities, and equipment to get the project work completed
- Implementing risk responses
- Incorporating approved changes into the project

■ Managing communications

■ Collecting project data on schedules, costs, quality, and overall project progress—and then reporting on these components

■ Managing the project stakeholders to keep them engaged and supportive of the project work

■ Completing lessons learned documentation

Applying Corrective Action

Things go awry. Corrective actions are methods the project manager and the project team can undertake to bring the project back into alignment with the project plan. For example, if a delay in the project work has shifted the project schedule by a month, the project manager, the project team, and even the stakeholders can examine the project schedule to see what possible changes can be made in the schedule to complete the project on time. Solutions may include adding resources, fast tracking, changing the order of work packages, and so on. Corrective actions bring the project performance back in line with the project plan. In addition to communicating, project managers spend a great deal of their time applying corrective actions.

Considering Preventive Actions

Do you wear your seatbelt? Take an umbrella when there's a chance of rain? These are preventive actions. In project management, preventive actions are steps the project manager and the project team can take to help ensure that potential problems don't affect the project. The project manager is taking action to make sure that future work is done properly and in accordance with the project management plan.

Managing Defect Repair

Sometimes the project team will screw up. Defect repair is the action required to fix the problem and to fix it correctly. The project manager will need to ensure that the actions taken to fix the problem have indeed corrected the defect and allowed the project to move forward as planned. Sometimes when a project team member faces a defect, he or she will rush through the defect repair, causing more errors and waste. The project manager must work with the project team to ensure that the defect is fixed efficiently and properly.

Managing Change Requests

As the project team completes the work, the project manager will be faced, challenged, or even bombarded with change requests. Part of project execution is to evaluate the worthiness of the proposed change, feed the change through the change control system, and then act on the approval or denial of the change request. All change requests are documented for future reference, while approved changes are incorporated into the project plan. Change requests can include the following:

■ Any change that affects the project's schedule, cost, or scope baseline
■ Contract changes from the vendor or client
■ Updates to project assets, such as the project plans or documents
■ Corrective action to bring the project work back into alignment with the project plan
■ Preventive action to take new steps to prevent problems from entering the project
■ Defect repair to fix a mistake in the project deliverables
■ Changes to project policies and procedures

Implementing Tools and Techniques for Project Execution

You have completed a workable, approved project plan. Now it's time to implement the thing. This is the heart of project management: taking your project plan and putting it into action. You'll act, do, adjust, and repeat. The project manager will use several tools and techniques to execute the project plan.

Using Expert Judgment

It should come as no surprise that one of the leading tools and techniques required to direct and manage the project work is expert judgment. You'll use your experience, savvy, and management abilities to communicate what actions need to take place in the project based on current project conditions. But it's not all up to you—you'll also rely on guidance and know-how from your project team, as they're closest to the work being performed. You may also seek expert judgment for this process from lines of service within your company, consultants, professional organizations to which you subscribe, and project stakeholders.

Employing a PMIS

A PMIS is typically a computer-driven system (though it can be paper-based) to aid a project manager in the development of the project. It is a tool for, not a replacement of, the project manager. A PMIS can calculate schedules, costs, expectations, and likely results. It cannot, however, replace the expert judgment of the project manager and the project team.

The goal of the system is to automate, organize, and provide control of the project management processes. A typical PMIS software system offers the following:

■ Work breakdown structure creation tools
■ Calendaring features

- Scheduling abilities
- Work authorization tools
- Earned value management controls
- Quality control charts, program evaluation and review technique (PERT) charts, Gantt charts, and other charting features
- Calculations for the critical path, earned value management (EVM), target dates based on the project schedule, and more
- Resource tracking and leveling
- Reporting functionality

watch   **Don't worry too much about**   **with any PMIS systems—they're just tools for**   **PMIS brand names such as Microsoft Project**   **the project manager to work with.**   **and Primavera. The exam doesn't fall in love**

on the **Collaborative PMIS packages can also serve as a work authorization system—if** **job**   **they are configured and used properly. Any PMIS, electronic or paper-based, is**   **only as good as the person (or persons) keeping the information up to date.**

Meeting to Execute Project Work

Project managers need to meet with the project team, vendors, managers from other business units in the organization, and other stakeholders as the work is being executed. Meetings help the project manager, the project team, and other key stakeholders come together and form a consensus on how the work in the project management plan is about to commence. As a project manager, you'll go to lots of meetings to discuss the project work, ensure communication, and maintain stakeholder buy-in for the project. It's best for all meetings to have an agenda and for someone to keep minutes to ensure that documentation exists regarding what's to be discussed and what was accomplished in the meeting.

Examining the Outputs of Project Plan Execution

The project is being completed, and you have visible evidence that it is moving toward the desired future state. Inspections by the project manager and scope verification by the customer also prove the project team is completing work as planned. Status meetings provide opportunities for the project team members to report their work and evaluate it against the WBS and the network diagram. Things are moving along smoothly.

And then it happens. The project team begins to slip on the quality of the project work. Team members begin to take longer than what was scheduled to complete their project work. The scope verification with the clients takes longer—and their satisfaction with the project work begins to wane. What's a project manager to do?

This scenario is typical of project plan execution. The team completes the work, and then the project manager reviews the work and makes adjustments to bring the project back into alignment with the baselines created in the project plan. Several major components of project plan execution happen throughout project execution, not just at the end:

- Project deliverables
- Change requests
- Project management plan updates for approved change requests
- Work performance information
- Project document updates
- Project management plan updates

Examining the Project Work Results

The team completes their work based on the project plan. The end result of the work should be measured against the quality metrics, scope requirements, and expected outcomes of the work as defined in the project plan. In addition, the project manager must examine the time and cost required to reach the work results and compare them against the baselines recorded in the project plan. Any difference between what was experienced and what was planned is a variance.

Work results are not always physical, tangible things—the creation of a service, the completion of a training class, the completion of a certification process can also be measured as work results.

Executing the project plan will also create work performance data. Work performance data are observations, measurements, and facts that aren't necessarily useful without some context. You'll see coming up that work performance data is analyzed and processed into work performance information. Work performance information will then help you create work performance reports to communicate information about your project. A little tip—these happen in alphabetical order: data, information, and then reports.

Updating the Issue Log

Issues will happen throughout the project and these issues need to be documented and added to the project's issue log. Whenever there are inconsistencies between what was planned and what was experienced, you've likely got an issue. You can sometimes refer to issues as risk events: problems, conflicts, gaps. When you document the issue in the issue log, you'll also assign an issue owner and a target resolution date for the issue. Each issue in the log should include the following:

- Classification of the issue
- Person who identified the issue
- Description of the issue
- Priority level
- Issue owner
- Resolution date
- Status
- Final solution or outcome

Examining Change Requests

How many times have stakeholders begged, pleaded, or demanded a change in the project scope? Probably more times than you can count, right? Change requests are any requested deviation from, or addition to, the project scope, schedule, budget, quality, or resources. Change requests will predominantly trickle (or flood) in to the project manager during project plan execution. Change requests almost always affect one of four facets of a project:

- **Schedule** This is a desire to shorten or lengthen the project duration—for example, a key stakeholder would like the project to be completed before a particular business cycle begins. If the project can't be completed by that time, the project will be delayed until the business cycle has completed, so the project won't interfere with the business operations.

- **Cost** This involves a reduction or increase in the project's budget. For example, the project's priority has been reduced in the organization, so the budget may, unfortunately, be reduced as well. Budgets can also be increased: A functional manager may want to spend the entire remaining departmental budget at the end of the fiscal year so that next year's budget may meet or exceed the current year's budget. In this questionable instance, additional funds, new features, and more resources, needed or not, are added to a project's budget to "help" the functional manager spend the budget.

- **Scope** This is the most common instance of change. Stakeholders may request additional features, different features, or small changes to the project product. Each change must be evaluated against the project plan, the project scope, and supporting details to determine the cost, time, and risks implied.

Change requests do include changes for corrective actions, preventive actions, defect repair, and updates to the project plans and documentation.

■ **Combination**   This is a change made to the schedule, cost, or scope that may affect more than one facet of the project. This goes back to the idea of the "Triple Constraints of Project Management" and the project's performance measurement baseline. For example, a change to finish the schedule more quickly may be reasonable if more resources are applied to the project. More resources, in turn, mean more money.

Updating the Project Documents

Change is expected in projects, though it's not always welcome. When changes are approved, the project management plan should be updated to reflect the approved changes. This means that the project management scope baseline, schedule baseline, cost baseline, and the performance measurement baseline should all be updated to reflect the new project deliverables. You'll also need to update the project activities lists to reflect the new activities the project changes will require, and, in turn, you'll update the project network diagram. You may also need to update the assumptions log, activity list, lessons learned register, risk register, and the stakeholder register. Finally, changes can cause a ripple effect into the project management subsidiary plans and the project documents, which all need to be updated to reflect the changes in the project.

CERTIFICATION OBJECTIVE 4.04

Managing Project Knowledge

When you manage a project, you'll rely on your existing knowledge, based on your education and experience, but you might also learn new things to manage the project better. That's what this new to *PMBOK Guide*, sixth edition, process is all about—managing both existing knowledge and new knowledge while managing the project. It's not just about documenting information, but documenting knowledge to share with others openly in the current project, future projects, and in operations to support the solution the project creates.

There are two types of knowledge you'll need to know for you exam:

- **Explicit knowledge**   Knowledge that can be quickly and easily expressed through conversations, documentation, figures, or numbers
- **Tacit knowledge**   Knowledge that's more difficult to express, because it's about personal beliefs, values, knowledge gained from experience, and know-how when performing a task

Though it's tempting to lump this process into lessons learned, it's actually more than documenting what was learned in the project. Lessons learned includes more explicit knowledge because it's easily codified, but often lacks the deeper understanding that tacit knowledge provides. Tacit knowledge is more difficult to communicate through lessons learned, but it might be expressed by working alongside an experienced project team member or through in-depth training.

Preparing to Manage Knowledge

It's difficult to set start and end points for managing knowledge within a project because a project is an ongoing, iterative activity. There are, however, several inputs that can help you manage knowledge within a project:

- **Project management plan**   All parts of the project management plan are inputs to managing knowledge.
- **Lessons learned register**   The lessons learned register defines what's worked well in the project (and other projects in the organization).
- **Project team assignments**   Team assignments are made according to identified skills needed in the project and any skills that might be missing in the project.
- **Resource breakdown structure**   This visualizes the utilization of resources, but also what knowledge may be collectively used based on the composition of project team resources.
- **Source selection criteria**   When choosing a vendor, this component can help you identify what knowledge you're obtaining from an outside resource.
- **Stakeholder register**   This help you understand what knowledge stakeholders bring to the project.

Understanding the project deliverables can help you ascertain knowledge. Project deliverables are the products, results, or services that are created as a result of the project work. Deliverables take knowledge to create; therefore, understanding the nature of the deliverables, how the deliverables were created, and what it will take to support and maintain the deliverables will help you better manage the knowledge surrounding project deliverables. While deliverables are usually things the customer of the project receives, they can also be documents and items from the project management plan.

As with most process inputs, knowledge management can also rely on enterprise environmental factors and organizational process assets. For enterprise environmental factors, the culture of the customers, organization, and stakeholders can contribute to knowledge management. You'll also consider the geography of facilities and resources, rely on organization experts, and align with any legal and regulatory requirements. For organizational process assets, you'll consider policies, processes, and procedures. Organizational process assets also include personnel administration, communication requirements, and formal knowledge-sharing procedures (such as learning reviews throughout the project).

Reviewing Knowledge Management Tools and Techniques

One of the primary knowledge management tools you'll use is your expert judgment. You'll also work with people who are skilled in knowledge and information management. This may include trainer and instructors, technical writers, or people who are skilled in knowledge management software. Whatever approach you take to knowledge management, the goal is the same: to capture, document, and share knowledge in the project.

Knowledge management can also depend on the size of the project and the number of stakeholders involved. Projects with a large number of stakeholders will likely need a more formal knowledge management strategy than what's required for a smaller project. Although expert judgement is an accessible tool for knowledge management, many other tools and techniques are available to consider, especially in a larger project:

- **Networking (live and web-based)**   Informal conversations and questions can occur live or via intranet or the Internet.
- **Communities of practice**   Sometimes called special interest groups, these communities can be live or web-based.
- **Meetings**   Both live and web-based meetings help inform and educate.
- **Work shadowing and reverse shadowing**   Following, or shadowing, an expert can help you learn new skills. In reverse shadowing, the expert follows you as you perform tasks to learn new skills; in this case, the expert can offer coaching or feedback at the end of the session.
- **Discussion forums and focus groups**   Like communities of practices, these can be live or online to help participants learn from others in an informal setting.
- **Training events**   Seminars, conferences, workshops, and training require participants to interact with one another.
- **Storytelling**   By using storytelling, team members and experts can help other learners better relate to tacit knowledge.
- **Creativity and ideas management techniques**   Blogs, journals, meeting scribes, and even software tools can help the project manager, team, and stakeholders capture their ideas from brainstorming and planning sessions.

■ **Knowledge fairs and cafes**   Like a traditional fair, participants can move between "tents," or stations, to learn quick lessons about a topic from a trainer. Knowledge fairs and cafes are a fun and quick way to learn lots of information, at a high-level, from a variety of speakers and on a variety of topics.

Another tool and technique in knowledge management is information management. Information management helps link people to the information they need. These tools are useful for providing fast and direct access to document explicit knowledge, such as adding or accessing information in the lessons learned register. Depending on the size of your organization, you may also have library services for information. Of course, a robust PMIS can include document and information management as well.

Information management is often driven by a tool such as software, but knowledge management shouldn't be just data-driven. People have knowledge, not machines. Interaction with others and working process owners in the organization can often provide a richer, more meaningful way to learn and share information than a search engine. Face-to-face communication, active listening, facilitation, and leadership are all people skills. With such skills, people on both ends of the knowledge management equation will need political awareness of what's being asked and what information is being provided.

Reviewing the Results of Knowledge Management

Knowledge management creates three outputs, but these three items will be appended and updated throughout the project; they are not the final outputs of a simple process. As more knowledge becomes available, you'll need to revisit knowledge management and then update these three items accordingly:

■ **Lessons learned register**   This is an register of knowledge management that you'll create early in the project, not at closing. Your lessons learned register can be a simple recording of what's been learned in the project—or, more likely, you can create categories of learning, the effects of what was learned, and any recommendations you and the team have for different scenarios.

■ **Project management plan updates**   You'll see project management plan updates as an output of many processes, and knowledge management is no different. Note that when you need to change the project management plan, you'll follow the project's change management system.

■ **Organizational process assets updates**   When a project creates new knowledge, that knowledge can be used not only in the current project, but in future projects and operations. New knowledge can be documented, shared, and implemented as a benefit of doing the current project.

CERTIFICATION OBJECTIVE 4.05

Monitoring and Controlling the Project Work

Sure, sure, it'd be nice to have a project plan and a team that follows orders and to have all the work requests completed on budget and on time every time—but this book isn't fiction. One of the key activities for the project manager is to monitor the project team and control the work that they complete as part of the project. This is the hands-on portion of project management. By monitoring and controlling the project, you help stakeholders see where the project is and better understand what's needed to keep the project in alignment with the project plan.

Monitoring and controlling the project work is a process that happens with project execution. There is overlap between the two process groups: the project is executed according to the plan, and the project is monitored and controlled according to the plan.

Preparing for Monitoring and Controlling Processes

Throughout the project, you will monitor and control the process. You and the project team will consistently measure, examine, and inspect the project work to make certain it is correct and in accordance with the project plan. These iterative processes help ensure that the project is done properly and that you're meeting objectives for the project stakeholders. To monitor and control the project, you'll use several inputs throughout the life of the project:

■ Assumptions log

■ Basis of estimates

■ Cost forecasts

■ Issue log

- Lessons learned register
- Milestone lists
- Quality reports
- Risk register
- Risk report
- Schedule forecast

The project manager, with this list and the project management plan in hand, will examine what was promised in the plan and what's been executed by the project team. This means the project manager needs work results to compare to the plan to ensure that the project is being completed as planned. The project manager will examine the forecasted schedule milestones, cost estimates, changes that have been approved for the project scope, and actual project deliverables as part of this process.

Creating Work Performance Information

Recall that work performance data is just data—raw, unprocessed data, facts, and figures. Work performance data comes from executing processes. This data is shuffled over into the monitoring and controlling processes, where it is analyzed by comparing the raw data against what was planned and expected to ensure that what's being created is actually what's needed in the project.

Consider the metrics established in the project performance measurement baseline: time, cost, and scope. The data gathered will include facts about the percentage of activities complete, the running cost of project work, and the amount of time utilized to complete the project work. That data will then be compared against the goals for the project to determine whether the project is off schedule, off budget, or out of scope. Through analysis during monitoring and controlling, the gathered data becomes information. You'll see more about work performance data and work performance information throughout this book and in the *PMBOK Guide*.

Reviewing the Final Inputs for Monitoring and Controlling

Three other inputs to monitoring and controlling the project are somewhat more flexible. First, if your project involves vendors, you'll have contracts and agreements with them. When you create an agreement with the vendor, it will include terms and conditions that both parties must adhere to. Agreements could apply to a portion of the project, which means the subcontractor must abide by the terms of the contract, which should also support the goals of the project. In some instances, your company may be completing a project for a client, which will also require a contract that includes terms and conditions with which your company must comply in order for the project to be successful.

Other inputs for monitoring and controlling the project work are your enterprise's environmental factors. You'll use the tools required by your organization to track costs, schedule the project work, manage resources, and track the project's performance. Enterprise environmental factors can also include the stakeholder's expectations regarding what the project will create and how the project will perform. In addition, your organization may have rules regarding risk tolerance (which we'll dive into in Chapter 11). Your industry may also be required to work with certain regulations in order to meet compliance requirements.

The final inputs, which you'll see over and over, are organizational process assets. The organizational process assets you'll consider for monitoring and controlling the project work are the policies, processes, and procedures unique to your organization. They can include how your organization manages finances, contracts, accounting codes, and human resources. Organizational process assets can also include tools and approaches used by your organization for reporting project status and conditions, issue management, defect management, and how you'll track these items throughout the project.

Using Monitoring and Controlling Tools and Techniques

Recall that the product scope is the vision of what the customer expects, while the project scope is the work completed by the project team to create the product scope. If the project team is completing activities outside of the project scope, they are not contributing to the project scope, which in turn means they're creating a product scope that's different from what the customer is expecting. Not a good thing. This leads to waste, frustration, delays, and unhappy customers—and unhappy project managers. We don't want this. We want control and accuracy.

Relying on Expert Judgment

You may need help to monitor and control the project work, and this means working with experts. Specifically, you may call upon experts to help with earned value management (EVM), data analysis, cost and duration estimating, and trend analysis. Experts can also be from your discipline, including those who have insight into best practices, risk management, and even contract management. You'll see that expert judgment is a common tool and technique used by many processes in a project.

Relying on Data Analysis

Based on current conditions in the project, you may be able to forecast future performance and outcomes in the project. Analytical techniques can help the project manager and experts predict the likelihood of success, or failure, based on what's happened in the project to date. For the PMP, you should be topically familiar with these analytical techniques:

- **Alternatives analysis**   When something goes awry in your project, you'll need to consider the different corrective and prevent actions that you can take to fix the current problem, but also to prevent the problem from happening again in the project.

- **Cost-benefit analysis**   In monitoring and controlling, this involves the examination of the cost of the proposed corrective actions you may take and the consideration of the benefit these actions will bring to the project.

- **Earned value analysis**   This suite of formulas helps to show project performance on time and costs. We'll discuss this in detail in Chapter 7, but know that the analysis of this data helps you gain insight to scope, schedule, and cost performance in the project.

- **Root cause and causal analysis**   This approach aims to determine what activities, people, organizational processes, or other factors are contributing to an effect in the project. Through analysis, which is really detective work, you'll determine contributing causes and causal factors. This approach helps you identify actual causes, not just symptoms of the cause, so that you can take recommended corrective and preventive actions. One approach is to ask "why?" five times to help lead you to the root cause.

- **Trend analysis**   This analysis technique examines recurring problems, threats, and even opportunities, so that you can react to the situation based on the trends you've identified.

- **Variance analysis**   The difference between what was planned and what was experienced in the project will reveal a variance. Variance analysis can be performed on duration estimates, costs, resource utilization, overall project costs, technical performance, and other project aspects. You'll use variance analysis throughout the project and in each knowledge area.

exam
watch

Voting is a tool and technique you can use in monitoring and controlling the project work. Discussed in more detail in Chapter 5, voting can help you and the team or key stakeholders make decisions through unanimity, majority, plurality, or even an autocratic method.

Hosting Meetings

You'll host meetings to discuss and review the status and conditions within the project. In these meetings, you'll be reviewing the project, issues, and any problems that must be addressed. Most likely, you'll be using expert judgment and meeting with team members and stakeholders. Recall that expert judgment is simply relying on a resource who is especially knowledgeable in one or more areas to help the project manager make the best decision. Expert judgment can come from many different sources:

- Third-party consultants
- Subject matter experts
- Project team members
- Stakeholders
- Individuals within the organization who may not be directly affected by the project

Examining the Results of Project Work

As a project moves toward completion and the project manager monitors and controls the project, there will be evidence of the project's success, failures, or, at a minimum, some results of the work as performed by the project team. Here's the business you can expect to be tested on when it comes to the PMP exam:

- **Work performance reports**   The work performance data is analyzed and becomes useable work performance information. Then the work performance information is formatted, combined, and made readable in work performance reports. These are the project reports you'll distribute to help management, customers, and stakeholders make decisions about project work and stay informed. We'll talk more about reports and the communications management plan in Chapter 10.

- **Requested changes**   Yep, change requests can come out of monitoring and controlling. Change requests usually mean that the project scope will widen— although in some instances, the project scope may be trimmed due to lack of funds, time constraints, or other reasons. Change requests can also affect the schedule and costs. All requested changes should be documented and passed through integrated change control. Change requests can also include the following:

  - **Recommended corrective actions**   Corrective actions must be followed to bring future project results into alignment with expected project performance. To implement these corrective actions, documented change requests are required.

  - **Recommended preventive actions**   These actions ensure that mistakes don't get repeated within a project. For example, if a piece of electrical equipment fails because it overheats, the project manager and the project team will take action to ensure that the equipment doesn't overheat and delay the project work. To implement these actions, documented change requests are required.

■ **Recommended defect repair** Quality control is an inspection-driven process of finding mistakes or errors with the project work results before the customer does. When a defect is found, the project manager should document the defect and then, usually, ask the project team to fix the problem. To implement defect repairs, documented change requests are required.

■ **Project management plan and project document updates** When project work changes, the project manager must update the corresponding project documents and project plans. Updates can include updates to cost and schedule forecasts, the issue log, the risk register, and the lessons learned register. This is a recurring theme throughout project management, so you can bet dollars to donuts you'll see this concept on your PMP exam.

e x a m

w a t c h You may need to create a burnup or burndown chart as part of your work performance reports. A burndown chart predicts when the project will be completed—it burns down to completion. Your burnup chart can also show scope changes throughout the project and how these changes contributed to the project as a whole. A burnup chart graphs the work accumulating in an upward curve to predict project completion.

CERTIFICATION OBJECTIVE 4.06

Performing Integrated Change Control

Integrated change control examines a change request to determine the total effect the change may have on all parts of the project: deliverables, project documents, and the project management plan. It determines the value of the change on the project to help determine whether the change should be approved, declined, or postponed. Integrated change control examines changes that stem from scope, cost, schedule, and contract, though scope changes are the most common (and we'll discuss these in detail in Chapter 5).

When changes are proposed to the project, the project manager must route the proposed changes through a change control system (CCS). The CCS may also include the review of proposed changes through a change control board (CCB). Changes may be discarded or approved on the basis of different criteria, such as benefit/cost ratios (BCRs), value-added changes, risk, and political capital.

When changes are approved, the project manager must then update the project baselines, as changes will likely affect a combination of scope, cost, and time. The updated baselines enable the project to continue with the new changes incorporated into the project and provide for accurate measurement of the performance of the project as changed.

This is an important concept: *Update the project baselines*. Consider a project scope to which requirements have been added but for which the schedule baseline has not been updated: The project's end date will thus be sooner than what is possible, because the project baseline does not reflect the additional work that would extend that date. In addition, a failure to revise the project baseline could skew reporting, variances, future project decisions, and even future projects.

Consider a project manager who does not update the performance measurement baseline after a change. The completion of the project goes into the archives and can serve as historical information for future projects. In such cases, the historical information would be skewed, since it doesn't accurately account for the added work and the projected end date or budget.

Changes, small or large, must be accounted for throughout the project plan. While change requests can start out with a verbal change request, the change request must be documented and entered into the change management system. Notice how the integrated change control processes influence the communications of the change, including the change approval or denial. That's the whole point: to integrate proposed changes into the project processes. Figure 4-4 details integrated change control.

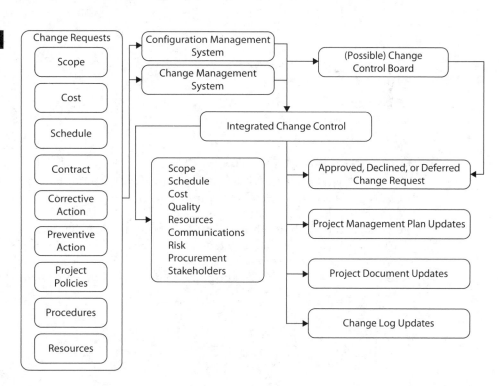

FIGURE 4-4

All change requests must pass through integrated change control.

Implementing Tools and Techniques for Integrated Change Control

Given that changes, or requests for change, are likely to happen during the project, what tools are available to evaluate and squelch or approve the proposed changes? And how can the project manager organize change requests in an orderly system so he is not constantly evaluating change requests instead of focusing on project completion? And how do change requests get approved, worked into the project plan, and accounted for in costs, schedule, and risk?

Many tools can be applied to requests for change: consistency, scope comparison, BCRs, risk analysis, and an estimate of the time and cost to incorporate the change, among others. The tools will guide the project manager, the project team, and the stakeholders through the process of approving and declining changes. The best approach for integrated change control is a constant, purposeful process of reviewing, considering, and evaluating, followed by a decision as to whether the change is needed.

A seemingly tiny change in costs, schedule, scope, or a contract can mushroom into large problems throughout the project. Integrated change control examines a change to determine what effect it will have on all parts of the project:

- Project scope
- Project schedule
- Project costs
- Project quality
- Project resources
- Project communications
- Project risks
- Project procurement
- Project stakeholder management

Relying on a Change Control System

A *change control system (CCS)* is a formal process of documenting and reviewing proposed changes. It establishes the flow of change from proposal to decision. The CCS process describes how project performance will be monitored, how changes may occur, and then how the project plan may be revised and sent through versioning when the changes are approved.

A CCS is a collection of documented activities, factors for decisions, and performance measurements—it is not a computer program. Although many electronic project management information systems offer a CCS, know that a CCS is a documented approach to change, not an automated approval structure.

INSIDE THE EXAM

What must you know from this chapter to pass the exam? Know the purpose of the project plan: to guide the project manager through the execution and control groups. The project plan is also in place to provide communication to the project team, stakeholders, and management. Additionally, it will guide all future project decisions.

You should know all of the components of the project plan. Know what each of the subsidiary project plans are used for, how they can be updated, and what their objectives are. Remember that the point of planning is to create the project plan. The project plan, then, provides leadership and direction for the project execution and control processes. It is a formal, management-approved document—and once it's approved, work can begin.

Historical information from organizational process assets is another big factor on the exam. Why? Historical information is proof from other project managers. It enables the current project manager to rely on what has been proven, what has been accomplished, and what has been archived for reference. And remember that the current project plan will become a future historical reference. Knowledge management is key here.

Assumptions and constraints are present on every project. Assumptions are beliefs held to be true but not *proven* to be true. They should be documented in the project plan. Constraints are restrictions within which the project must operate. The Triple Constraints of Project Management—time, cost, and scope—will visit you on exam day, as will other internal and external constraints.

To begin the project, you need a project charter. Project charters come from a manager external to the project. Once the charter is present, the project manager is named. The project manager then assembles the project team and begins the planning processes. The primary output of any planning is a project plan, and its execution cannot begin until management approves the plan. All work described in the project plan must pass through a work authorization system, either a formal system on a larger project or an informal system on smaller projects.

Integrated change control requires the evaluation of change requests to determine their worthiness for approval—or lack thereof for denial. Change requests must be documented and may originate from stakeholders or external sources such as government agencies, laws, or industry mandates.

Some organizations may have a CCS that is used across all projects and maps to common guidelines within the organization. If the performing organization does not have a CCS, it is the responsibility of the project manager and the project team to create one. A CCS is mandatory for effective project management.

Within a CCS may be a collection of management, key stakeholders, and project team members who review the changes for approval or denial. This group is defined in the project plan, and its roles and responsibilities are defined prior to project plan execution. Common names for the board include the following:

- Change control board (CCB)
- Schedule change control board
- Technical review board (TRB)
- Technical assessment board (TAB)
- Engineering review board (ERB)

Implementing Configuration Management

While the change control system addresses project changes, the configuration management system addresses changes to the product. The product—the thing the project is creating as the end result of the project—directly correlates to the project scope. Imagine a house construction project. If the homeowners want wood floors now instead of tile, or they decide to add a swimming pool, or they choose a different cabinet type, these are all changes to the product and need to be documented in the configuration management system. Changes to the product pass through the configuration management system to document and control the changes. Approved changes to the product scope will require a corresponding change to the project scope.

Configuration management focuses on controlling the characteristics of a product or service. It is a documented process of controlling the features, attributes, and technical configuration of any product or service. When it comes to project management, configuration management focuses on the project deliverables. In some organizations, configuration management is a part of the CCS, but in other industries, such as manufacturing, configuration management refers to the control of existing operations. In a general sense, configuration management consists of the following:

- **Configuration item identification**   The documentation and labeling of the features, characteristics, and functions of a product or service.
- **Configuration item status accounting**   The management and coordination of efforts to change the product or service. This includes status of proposed changes, both pending and implemented.
- **Configuration item verification and audit**   The process of documenting any changes to the product or service. It is the ongoing auditing of products and services to ensure their conformance to documented requirements, including tracking approved changes to the product's features and functions.

The configuration management system and the change control system work together to control and identify changes within the project and product. All changes should be identified, documented, and then moved through the appropriate system. A decision-maker, or group of decision-makers, will determine whether the change is approved, declined, or deferred. You'll also have to track changes and communicate the outcome to the appropriate project stakeholders. Change management happens throughout the project.

Deciding on Project Changes

When it comes to making a decision about the change, I purposefully used the term "decision-maker." This may or may not be the project manager; it could be the project sponsor, a change control board, or some other entity unique to your project and organization. Some organizations allot change power based on the price or impact of the change. For example, a change less than $10,000 and/or two weeks of duration could be within the power of the project manager to approve, decline, or defer. Changes above that threshold would be escalated to the CCB, PMO, or steering committee.

When making a decision about change, the group can use a voting approach, as discussed earlier, or a multicriteria decision analysis. A multicriteria decision analysis relies on a matrix of possibilities and outcomes for the change, and this provides a more systematic, analytical approach to the change decision. The matrix could have qualifiers or dequalifiers included, such as time, cost, amount of labor, risks, and any other factor the organization elects to use. Changes that exceed a qualifier or combination of qualifiers could be declined.

All changes can also move through alternative analysis as part of the research to determine whether or not the change can be implemented. Alternative analysis could determine whether the change is approved, declined, or needs to modified and negotiated before it can be approved. You'll also implement a cost-benefits analysis of changes to analyze what the change will cost the project; this determines financial concerns, but also other costs such as labor, morale, and schedule.

Revisiting Planning Processes

Planning is iterative. Because a project rarely, if ever, happens exactly the way the project team and project manager planned it, the project freely moves between the controlling, executing, and planning processes. This is most evident when changes enter the project scene. The project manager and the project team must evaluate the proposed changes for additional cost, time, and risk concerns.

If the project work slips from the expected performance, quality, or schedule, adjustments are needed. Planning also considers the effect of a risk that a new change can introduce. These adjustments will require the consideration of project activities, the critical path, resources, cost, sequence of activities, and other refinements to the project plan.

Evaluating the Outputs of Integrated Change Control

As the project follows the project plan and changes are presented, the project manager will implement integrated change control. Some changes will be denied or deferred, and archived for reference if needed. Other changes will be approved and factored into the project scope and have their schedules, costs, and risks documented and accounted for. All changes—approved, declined, and deferred—should be documented in a project's change log for reference and supporting detail. The process of integrated change control is ongoing until project closure. Integrated change control can spur the following:

- Approved change requests
- Rejected change requests
- Change log updates
- Project management plan updates
- Project scope statement updates
- Approved corrective actions
- Approved preventive actions
- Approved defect repair
- Project deliverables

CERTIFICATION OBJECTIVE 4.07

Closing the Project or Phase

The project management plan defines what the project or phase is, how the project or phase will be completed, and finally—the good part—how the project or phase will be closed. The close project processes are activities that the project manager, the project management team, vendors, and the organization's management will undertake to close out the project work. If a project has multiple phases, as most projects do, the closing processes will be implemented at the end of each phase.

Preparing to Close the Project or Phase

The project manager must rely on several documents to prepare the close project processes. Specifically, the project manager relies on the project management plan to guide the required actions needed to close out the project. The project manager will review the results of the project with the project management plan to ensure that all of the requirements of the project have been met.

While project managers often think of closing as the end of the project, it also includes closing a phase. When closing a phase, the project manager should define the required phase exit criteria to move onto the next phase of the project. Administrative closure of a phase, and also at the conclusion of the project, require the following:

- All documents updated
- All issues resolved
- Customer approved and accepted the deliverables
- Vendors work formally accepted
- Open claims are closed
- Contractual information archived
- Project records gathered for archive
- Project or phase audit completed
- Knowledge shared and transferred
- Lessons learned identified
- Project information archived to be part of the organizational process assets

Of course, other components contribute to the start of the closing processes:

- **Project charter**   The project charter defines what the project will accomplish, what constitutes project success, and who will sign off on the project completion.
- **Project management plan**   The project management plan includes the project scope, the project requirements, and expectations for the project objectives. When a project is being completed for another organization, the contract serves as a guide for how the project may be closed. The project plan may also reference the enterprise environmental factors to consider as part of project closing.
- **Project documents**   You may rely on some (or all) of the project documents to close the project. This can include the assumptions log, basis of estimates, change log, issue log, lessons learned register, milestone list, communications, quality control measurement, quality reports, requirements documentation, risk register, and any risk reports.
- **Deliverables**   The project has to create something, so it's no surprise that the deliverables serve as input to the project closing processes.
- **Business documents**   The business case that justified the need for the project and the benefits management plan are referenced in closing.
- **Agreements**   Any contracts that need to be closed are included as part of the closing project phase or project process. The terms of contract closure are part of the contract.

■ **Procurement documentation** Along with the contract, all procurement documents are gathered and filed. This includes all vendor performance, contract change information, payments, and inspection results. Your project may also have "as-built" or "as-developed" plans, drawings, and documentation that also need to be archived.

■ **Organizational process assets** An organization may have procedures and processes that every project manager must follow to close a phase or project. These can include financial, reporting, and human resource obligations.

Closing the Project or Phase

Formally closing the project or phase involves documenting and archiving all of the work necessary to formalize the closing process. The formal closing process updates the organizational process assets as the current information about the project's performance, lessons learned, and other documents becomes future historical information. This requires more than just the project manager and involves the project team, project sponsor, key stakeholders, and vendors. The project manager may rely on expert knowledge for management control, audits of the project and vendors, legal and procurement issues, and any legislation or regulations that are required as part of project closing.

Administrative closure includes all of the following activities:

■ Collecting and assembling all project records

■ Analyzing the project's success or failure

■ Gathering lessons learned documentation

■ Archiving project information for future reference

PMP
Coach At the end of the project, project teams and the project manager are often rewarded. How will you reward yourself for finishing the project to pass your PMP exam? Set a reward for earning your PMP—you'll deserve it!

Data analysis is also a result of closing your project. In data analysis, four techniques can be utilized:

■ **Document analysis** Review the available project documentation to help with lessons learned and knowledge sharing activities for future projects within the organization.

■ **Regression analysis** Study the interrelationships of the project variables to determine how the different components of the project affected one another. This understanding will help with future projects.

- **Trend analysis**   Identify trends in the project performance at closure so that the project manager and stakeholders can see what went awry and when. This also helps with future projects.
- **Variance analysis**   Analyze project variances in schedule, costs, scope, and performance to help the organization better understand root causes and plan more accurately in future projects.

Reviewing the Results of Project Closure

The final closure of the project creates four official items for the project and the organization:

- **Project document updates**   All of the project documents are updated as needed to reflect the final results of the project. These should be stamped as "Final" so that future projects referencing the outcome of this project have a clear sense as to what the final results were.
- **Final product, service, or result transition**   This is the primary objective of the project that is then transitioned from being owned by the project to now being owned, managed, and maintained by the organization, the customer, or some other entity according to the project management plan.
- **Final project report**   This report summarizes the project or phase; defines the completed scope objectives and exit criteria, quality objectives that were met, and schedule results (including planned and actual dates); and summarizes the final product benefits, how the final product will or will not achieve the business benefits the project aimed to achieve, and the project risks, their outcomes, and how the risks were managed.
- **Organizational process assets updates**   Current project information becomes future historical information. Historical information is part of the organizational process assets. You'll update, distribute, and archive a copy of the project documents, operational and support documentation, project and phase closure documentation, customer acceptance documentation, and the lessons learned register.

The two favorite days in a project are the day the project is launched and the day the project is closed. The business in between is project management. Should a project be cancelled before successfully reaching its objectives, the project manager should still move through the closing activities. This will include a report on why the project was terminated and what benefits were transitioned to the organization or customer. Projects can be cancelled for a number of reasons, and it's important to document why the project ended, even if it the end wasn't a happy one.

CERTIFICATION SUMMARY

Project integration management is an ongoing process the project manager completes to ensure that the project moves from start to completion. It is the gears, guts, and grind of project management—the day-in, day-out business of completing the project work. Project integration management takes your project plans; coordinates the activities, project resources, constraints, and assumptions; and massages them into a working model.

Of course, project integration management isn't an automatic process; it requires you, the project manager, to negotiate, finesse, and adapt to the project's circumstances. Project integration management relies on general business skills such as leadership, organizational skills, and communication to get all the parts of the project working together.

The process of project management can be broken down into three chunks:

- **Developing the project charter and plan**   The project charter authorizes the project and names the project manager. You'll usually create only one charter in a project, but an organization could also create a charter for each phase within a project. Project plan development is an iterative process that requires input from the project manager, the project team, the project customers, and other stakeholders. It communicates the details of how the project work will accomplish the project goals.

- **Directing and managing the project work**   After the plan has been created, the project execution processes authorize the work to begin, enabling the project manager to manage procurement and quality assurance, host project team meetings, and manage conflict between stakeholders. On top of managing all these moving parts, the project manager must actively work to develop the individuals on the project to work as a team for the good of the project.

- **Managing changes to the project**   Changes can kill a project. Change requests must be documented and sent through a formal change control system to determine their worthiness for implementation. Integrated change control manages changes across the entire project. Change requests are evaluated and considered for impacts on risk, costs, schedule, and scope. Not all change requests are approved—but all change requests should be documented for future reference.

As the project moves from start to completion, the project manager and the project team must update the lessons learned register as part of managing project knowledge. The lessons learned serve as future historical information to the current project and to future projects within the organization. The project manager and project team should update the lessons learned at the end of project phases, when major deliverables are created, and at the project's completion.

Project Integration Management

Project integration management relies on project plan development, project plan execution, and integrated change control. Integrated change control manages all the moving parts of a project.

- Project integration management is a fancy way of saying that the project components need to work together—and the project manager sees to it that they do. Project integration management requires negotiation between competing objectives.

- Project integration management calls for general management skills, effective communications, organization, familiarity with the product, and more. It is the day-to-day operations of the project execution.

Project Planning

On your exam, you'll need to know that planning is an iterative process and that the results of planning are inputs to the project plan. The project plan is a fluid document, authorized by management, and it guides all future decisions on the project.

The project plan is a fluid work in progress. Updates to the plan reflect changes to the project, discoveries made during the project plan execution, and changes to the conditions of the project. The project plan serves as a point of reference for all future project decisions, and it becomes future historical information to guide other project managers. When changes occur, the cost, schedule, and scope baselines in the project plan must be updated.

w a t c h   **You should be familiar with the work breakdown structure (WBS)—a tool for listing, organizing, and decomposing the project work. You should know that the WBS is an input to many of the planning,** **execution, and control processes. If you're stumped on a question and one of the answers is WBS, hedge your bets and choose WBS. The WBS is part of the scope baseline.**

Project Constraints

All projects have one or more constraints in time, cost, and scope. Constraints are factors that can hinder project performance:

- **Time constraints** include project deadlines, availability of key personnel, and target milestone dates. Remember that all projects are temporary: they have a beginning and an end.

■ **Cost constraints** are typically predetermined budgets for project completion. It's usually easier to get more time than more money.

■ **Scope constraints** are requirements for the project deliverables, regardless of the cost or time to implement the requirements (safety regulations or industry mandates are examples).

Integrated Change Control Management

Integrated change control is the process of documenting and controlling the features of a product, measuring and reacting to project conditions, and revisiting planning when needed.

■ Projects need change control systems to determine how changes will be considered, reviewed, and approved or declined. A change control system is a documented approach to how a stakeholder may request a change and then what factors are considered when approving or declining the requested change. There are four project change control systems: scope, schedule, cost, and contract.

■ Configuration management is part of change control. It is the process of controlling how the characteristics of the product or the services the project is creating are allowed to be changed.

KEY TERMS

If you're serious about passing the PMP exam, memorize these terms and their definitions. For maximum value, create your own flashcards based on these definitions and review them daily.

activity attributes   Activities that have special conditions, requirements, risks, successor activities, predecessor activities, coding structure, and other conditions should be documented.

activity list   A shopping list of all the activities the project team must complete in order to satisfy the project. This list is an input to the project network diagram.

alternative analysis   Data analysis technique used to consider the corrective and preventive actions to take in the project. You are analyzing the different options available.

assumption log   A document that clearly identifies and tracks all constraints and assumptions that are made in the project. All assumptions need to be tested for their validity, and the outcome of the tests should be recorded.

basis of estimates   Explanation of how the activity duration and cost estimates were created.

benefit/cost ratio   Shows the proportion of benefits to costs; for example 4:1 would equate to four benefits and just one cost.

benefit measurement methods   Project selection methods that compare the benefits of projects to determine into which project the organization should invest its funds.

benefits management   The management and control of when the benefits of the project will become available. Some projects have benefits only once the project is complete; other projects will have intermittent benefits for the organization.

brainstorming   People generating as many ideas a possible and then analyzing the ideas.

burndown chart   A graph that tracks the project's completeness, including scope changes, in a downward curve against the project timeline.

burnup chart   A graph that tracks the project's completeness in an upward curve against the project timeline.

causal analysis   The analysis of why a problem exists to understand why the problem is happening. Root cause analysis defines the problem, or the effect you're trying to resolve, and then identifies all of the causal factors that may be independently or collaboratively contributing to the defect.

change control board   A group of decision-makers that reviews proposed project changes.

change control system   A predefined set of activities, forms, and procedures that establishes how project change requests may proceed.

change log   As changes to the project time, cost, or scope emerge during the project, they should be recorded with their status in the change log for future reference.

communications management plan   Defines the required communications and how they will be fulfilled, and explains the methods used for gathering, storing, and dispersing information to appropriate parties. In addition, it maps out the schedule of when the expected communication needs will be met.

configuration management   The control and documentation of the project's product features and functions.

constraints   Anything that limits the project manager's options; time, cost, and scope are always project constraints.

contract   A legally binding agreement between the buyer(s) and seller(s) that defines the roles and responsibilities of all parties in the agreement.

corrective actions   Actions taken to correct problems and to ensure that the project work is in alignment with the project management plan.

cost-benefit analysis   A data analysis technique used to examine of the cost of the proposed corrective actions you might take and the consideration of the benefits these actions will bring to the project.

cost management plan   A subsidiary plan of the overall project management plan that defines how cost management will be planned, how costs will be structured, and how they will be controlled. This plan addresses how variances to the costs of the project will be managed. The plan may be based on a range of acceptable variances and the expected response to variances over a given threshold.

defect repair   Actions taken to fix defects within the project or product. Defect repair will also require validation that the defects were corrected properly.

development life cycle   One or more phases of the project life cycle that define how the product, service, or result will be built The life cycle is typically a predictive or adaptive life cycle depending on the project and the enterprise environmental factors of the organization.

duration estimates   The prediction of how long the project work will take to complete based on the resources available, nonworking hours, and other factors.

earned value management   A suite of formulas used to measure the project's overall performance for time, costs, and progress.

exit criteria   Defines the criteria that must be present for the project to move from one phase to the next.

explicit knowledge   Knowledge that can be quickly expressed through documentation, conversations, facts, and figures.

focus groups   A meeting for stakeholders to have a conversation about the project goals, concerns, requirements, and other project information.

forecast   Throughout the project, the project manager will create forecasts about the expected project's completion date and projected project costs.

future value   A formula used to predict the future value of a current amount of funds. The formula is Future Value = Present Value $(1 + i)^n$, where i is the interest rate and n is the number of time periods.

historical information   Any information created in the past that can help the current project succeed.

integrated change control   The analysis of a change's effect on all components of the project. It examines the proposed change and how it may impact scope, schedule, costs, quality, resources, communications, risk, procurement, and stakeholder management.

internal rate of return   A benefit measurement formula to calculate when the present value of the cash inflow equals the project's original investment.

interview   Formal, direct discussion used in project integration management as part of the data gathering technique to create the project charter.

issue log   Issues are conditions or situations that need decisions. They are recorded in the issue log, along with an issue owner designation, an issue date for resolution, and the eventual outcome of the issue.

knowledge management   A systematic way of collecting, distributing, and storing useable knowledge in the project.

lessons learned register   A log of the ongoing collection of documentation regarding what has and has not worked in the project; the project manager and the project team participate in lessons learned creation.

net present value A benefit measurement formula that provides a precise measurement of the present value of each year the project generates a return on investment.

payback period The duration of time it takes a project to earn back the original investment.

performance reports Formal reports that define how the project is performing with regard to time, cost, scope, quality, and other relevant information.

present value A benefit measurement formula to determine what a future amount of funds is worth today. The formula is Present Value = Future Value / $(1 + i)^n$, where i is the interest rate and n is the number of time periods.

preventive actions Actions taken to ensure that potential problems don't enter the project and that future project work is in alignment with the project management plan.

procurement documents All of the documents for purchasing, such as request for quotes, invitation to bid, request for proposal, and the responses, are stored as part of the project documentation.

procurement management plan Describes the procurement process, from solicitation to source selection. The plan may also include the requirements for selection as set by the organization.

project baselines Four baselines in a project are used to measure project performance: cost, schedule, scope, and the performance measurement baseline.

project charter A document that authorizes the project, defines the high-level requirements, identifies the project manager and the project sponsor, and provides initial information about the project.

project funding requirements In larger projects, this document identifies the timeline of when capital is required for the project to move forward. This document defines the amount of funds a project needs and when the project funds are needed in order to reach its objectives.

project integration management The art and science of ensuring that your project moves forward and that your plan is fully developed and properly implemented. Ten knowledge areas (project integration management, scope, time, cost, quality, resources, communications, risk, procurement, and stakeholder management) have processes that contribute to the comprehensive project management plan.

project knowledge management   The project management process of managing all knowledge within the project. This includes refining the knowledge, documenting what was learned, making the information available to others, and archiving the documentation to be part of organizational process assets.

project management information system   A PMIS is typically a software system, such as Microsoft Project, used to assist the project manager in managing the project.

project plan   A comprehensive document comprising several subsidiary plans that communicates the intent and direction of the project.

proposal   An exposé on ideas, suggestions, recommendations, and solutions to an opportunity provided by a vendor for a seller. A proposal includes a price for the work and documents how the vendor would provide the service to the buyer.

quality management plan   Details the quality improvement, quality controls, and how the project will map to the quality assurance program of the performing organization.

regression analysis   A forecasting tool used to measure and predict the link between two variables within a project. This analysis tool and technique examines a series of variables and their results to determine how closely related the relationship among the variables may be.

requirements management plan   Defines how project requirements will be identified, prioritized, documented, and managed throughout the project.

requirements traceability matrix   A table that identifies all of the project requirements, when the requirements are due, when the requirements are created, and any other pertinent information about the requirements.

resource breakdown structure   A chart that identifies the resources utilized in the project in each section of the work breakdown structure.

resource calendar   Indicates when people and facilities are available or scheduled to work on the project.

resource requirements   A planning document that identifies what resources are needed to complete the project work. This includes people, materials, equipment, facilities, and services.

resources plan   Details on how the project team members and other physical resources will be brought onto and released from the project.

reverse shadowing   An expert follows someone learning to perform a skill to offer coaching or feedback at the end of the session.

risk   An uncertain event or condition that can have a positive or negative effect on the project.

risk management plan   Details the identified risks within the project, the risks associated with the constraints and project assumptions, and how the project team will monitor, react to, or avoid risks.

risk register   All risks, regardless of their probability or impact, are recorded in the risk register, and their status is kept current in the risk register. Should a risk be identified, the issue log is also updated to reflect the risk event that is now a likely issue in the project.

roles and responsibilities   Maps project roles to responsibilities within the project; roles are positions on the project team, and responsibilities are project activities.

schedule management plan   Identifies circumstances that may change the project schedule, such as the completion of project phases or the reliance on other projects and outside resources. The plan details the approval and accountability process for changes within the project.

scope management plan   Details how the project scope should be developed, maintained, monitored, controlled, and validated.

scoring models   A project selection method that assigns categories and corresponding values to measure a project's worthiness of investment.

source selection criteria   A predefined listing of the criteria to determine how a vendor will be selected—for example, cost, experience, certifications, and the like.

stakeholder management plan   Defines the level of engagement, the interrelationships among stakeholders, communications requirements, and the timing of stakeholder engagement.

supporting detail for estimates   The project manager should document how time and cost estimates were created.

storytelling   By telling stories, team members can better understand tacit knowledge and interact with one another.

tacit knowledge   Knowledge that's more difficult to express because it's about personal beliefs, values, knowledge gained from experience, and know-how when performing a task.

trend analysis   Examines recurring problems, threats, and even opportunities so you can react to the situation based on the trends you've identified.

work performance data   Raw data about the project work. This can include data on activities completed, costs, schedule, and other items measured for analysis.

work performance information   Useable information based on the work performance data, which is analyzed and becomes work performance information.

work performance reports   The communication devices used to share the work performance information with the appropriate stakeholders as defined in the project's communications management plan.

work shadowing   Following, or shadowing, an expert as they work to learn how to perform certain tasks.

TWO-MINUTE DRILL

Developing the Project Charter
- ❑   The project charter authorizes the project and names the project manager.
- ❑   The project charter is not authorized by the project manager, but by a person or party who has the power to grant the project manager the authority over the project resources.
- ❑   The project charter defines the high-level requirements for the project and the conditions for success.

Developing the Project Management Plan

❑ The project plan is a collection of subsidiary project plans.

❑ The project plan communicates the intent of the project.

❑ Project planning is an iterative process that may require updates to the project plan and other project documents.

Directing and Managing the Project Work

❑ The project manager directs and manages the work, while the project team executes the project plan.

❑ The project team executes the project plan in order to create the requirements of the project.

❑ The majority of the project's time and budget are spent during project execution.

❑ Team development and team management are executing processes.

❑ The procurement requirements are completed during project execution.

Managing Project Knowledge

❑ New and existing knowledge from the project is documented, catalogued, shared, and archived.

❑ Explicit knowledge is easy to convey through facts and figures.

❑ Tacit knowledge is more difficult to convey because it's based on personal beliefs, values, and experiences.

Monitoring and Controlling the Project Work

❑ Monitoring and controlling processes happen in tandem with the project execution processes.

❑ Earned value management (EVM) is a suite of formulas that can help the project management team monitor the project performance.

❑ Expert judgment comes from someone with more experience, who helps the project manager make the best decisions.

❑ Change requests include scope changes, recommended corrective actions, recommended preventive actions, and defect repairs.

Performing Integrated Change Control

❑ Integrated change control examines the effect of a change on the entire project.

❑ All changes from scope, schedule, costs, and contract must pass through integrated change control to determine whether the changes can be permitted in the project.

❑ Changes approved, declined, or deferred are documented in the project's change control log.

Closing the Project or Phase

❑ Closing the project or phase requires that the project manager follow the guidelines of the organization and the project plan.

❑ The project's contract documentation can help guide the procedures for closing a project or phase when the project is being completed by a vendor for a buyer.

❑ Project documentation should be archived as part of project closure.

SELF TEST

1. You are a project manager for your organization. Management has asked you to help determine which projects should be selected for implementation. In a project selection model, which of the following is the most important factor?
   A. Business needs
   B. Type of constraints
   C. Budget
   D. Schedule

2. Beth is the project manager of a software development project. She and her project team are done with a phase and Beth needs to make certain the lessons learned register is complete before moving the project onto the next phase. On any project, the lessons learned document is created by which of the following?
    A. Customers
    B. Project sponsor
    C. Project team
    D. Stakeholders

3. Your project is moving ahead of schedule. Management elects to incorporate additional quality testing into the project to improve the quality and acceptability of the project deliverable. This is an example of which one of the following?
    A. Scope creep
    B. Change control
    C. Quality assurance
    D. Integrated change control

4. You are the project manager of a new web site design project. There are 45 stakeholders with this project, and you are anticipating many change requests in the project. Which of the following is *not* true about change requests?
    A. They happen while the project work is being done.
    B. They always require additional funding.
    C. They must be documented.
    D. They can be requested by a stakeholder.

5. You are the project manager for a pharmaceutical company. You are currently working on a project for a new drug your company is creating. A recent change in a law governing drug testing will change your project scope. Since the project must be completed within two years, what's the first thing you should do as project manager?
    A. Create a documented change request.
    B. Proceed as planned, since the project will be grandfathered in and unaffected by the new change in the law.
    C. Consult with the project sponsor and the stakeholders.
    D. Stop all project work until the issue is resolved.

6. During project execution activities, a project sponsor's role in a functional organization can best be described as doing which one of the following?
    A. Acting as a sounding board for the project stakeholders
    B. Helping the project manager and stakeholders resolve any issues ASAP
    C. Deflecting change requests for the project manager
    D. Showing management the project progress and status reports

7. You are the project manager for the HALO Project. You and your project team are preparing the project plan. Of the following, which one is a project plan development constraint you and your team must consider?

A. The budget as assigned by management

B. Project plans from similar projects

C. Project plans from similar projects that have failed

D. Interviews with subject matter experts (SMEs) who have experience with the project work in your project plan

8. You are the project manager of HYH Project for your company, and you're working with the project team and several key stakeholders to develop the project management plan. Which of the following is the primary purpose of the project management plan?

A. To define the work to be completed to reach the project end date

B. To define the work needed in each phase of the project life cycle

C. To prevent any changes to the scope

D. To define how the project is executed, monitored, controlled, and then closed

9. John is a new employee and he's learning how to perform a task in your organization. Mary, a senior network engineer, is working with John to perform the new task. Rather than just show John the procedure, Mary is watching John and coaching him through the task. What is happening in this knowledge management activity?

A. Reverse shadowing

B. Project planning methodology

C. On-the-job training

D. Storytelling

10. You are examining the project management plan and its components with the project team. The team doesn't understand why so much information is needed for the project. What is the difference between a project baseline and a project plan?

A. Project plans change as needed, while baselines change only at milestones.

B. Project plans and baselines do not change—they are amended.

C. Project plans change as needed, while baselines are snapshots of the project plan.

D. Baselines are control tools, while project plans are execution tools.

11. Which one of the following is *not* beneficial to the project manager during the project plan development process?

A. Gantt charts

B. PMIS

C. Project management methodology

D. Stakeholder knowledge

12. Yoli is the project manager for her company and she's reviewing the project budget with management. Management is concerned about the capital expenses in the project, and they'd like more information about when Yoli will actually spend the project budget. Which one of the following represents the vast majority of a project's budget?

A. Project planning

B. Project plan execution

C. Labor

D. Cost of goods and services

13. The project plan provides a baseline for several things. Which one of the following does the project plan *not* provide a baseline for?

A. Scope

B. Cost

C. Schedule

D. Control

14. Natasha is the project manager for her organization. She is meeting with her project stakeholders to review the project plan and the different elements she'll use as part of project execution. Which of the following can best help Natasha during project execution?

A. Stakeholder analysis

B. Change control boards

C. PMIS

D. Scope verification

15. You are the project manager for your organization. When it comes to integrated change control, you must ensure that which one of the following is present?

A. Supporting detail for the change

B. Approval of the change from the project team

C. Approval of the change from an SME

D. Risk assessment for each proposed change

16. Jeff is the project manager of the Bridge Construction Project for his company. This project requires strict change control because of government regulations, the cost of the project deliverables, and the approved scope. The project plan provides what with regard to project changes?

A. A methodology to approve or decline CCB changes

B. A guide to all future project decisions

C. A vision of the project deliverables

D. A fluid document that may be updated as needed based on the CCB

17. You are the project manager for the DGF Project. This project is to design and implement a new application that will connect to a database server. Management of your company has requested that you create a method to document technical direction on the project and to document any changes or enhancements to the technical attributes of the project deliverable. Which one of the following would satisfy management's request?

    A. Configuration management
    B. Integrated change control
    C. Scope control
    D. Change management plan

18. Baseline variances, a documented plan to management variances, and a proven methodology to offer corrective actions to the project plan are all part of which process?

    A. Change management
    B. Change control system
    C. Scope change control
    D. Integrated change control

19. One of the requirements of project management in your organization is to describe your project management approach and methodology in the project plan. You can best accomplish this requirement through which one of the following actions?

    A. Establishing a project office
    B. Establishing a program office
    C. Compiling the management plans from each of the knowledge areas
    D. Creating a PMIS and documenting its inputs, tools and techniques, and outputs

20. You have just informed your project team that each team member will be contributing to the lessons learned register. Your team does not understand this approach and wants to know what the documentation will be used for. Which one of the following best describes the purpose of the lessons learned documentation?

    A. Offers proof of concept for management
    B. Offers historical information for current and future projects
    C. Offers evidence of project progression as reported by the project team
    D. Offers input to team member evaluations at the project conclusion

21. Which one of the following is a formal document to manage and control project execution?

    A. WBS
    B. Project management plan
    C. Organizational management plan
    D. Work authorization system

22. Configuration management is a process for applying technical and administrative direction and surveillance of the project implementation. Which activity is *not* included in configuration management?
    A. Controlling changes to the project deliverables
    B. Scope verification
    C. Automatic change request approvals
    D. Identification of the functional and physical attributes of the project deliverables

23. You are preparing to enter into the project execution with your project team. As part of your preparation, you'll rely on your project management plan and several tools and techniques. Which of the following contains parts of the project plan execution?
    A. PMIS, WBS, and EVM
    B. General management skills, status review meetings, and EVM
    C. Project management methodology and the PMIS
    D. General management skills, EVM, status review meetings, and interpersonal skills

24. You are the project manager of the GHQ Project for your company. Management has required that you utilize earned value management as part of your project and their enterprise environmental factors. EVM is used during the _____.
    A. Controlling processes
    B. Executing processes
    C. Closing processes
    D. Entire project

25. You are the project manager for your organization. Management would like you to use a tool that can help you plan, schedule, monitor, and report findings on your project. Which of the following is the correct tool to use?
    A. PMIS
    B. EVM
    C. Status review meetings
    D. Project team knowledge and skill set

SELF TEST ANSWERS

1. You are a project manager for your organization. Management has asked you to help determine which projects should be selected for implementation. In a project selection model, which of the following is the most important factor?
    A. Business needs
    B. Type of constraints
    C. Budget
    D. Schedule

    ☑ **A.** Projects are selected based on business needs first.
    ☒ **B, C,** and **D** are incorrect. **B** is incorrect because project constraints are typically not an issue when a project is selected, but the feasibility of a project to operate within the project constraints may be. **C,** project budget, is incorrect, because the project budget is a project constraint. **D** is incorrect because the project schedule is also a constraint.

2. Beth is the project manager of a software development project. She and her project team are done with a phase and Beth needs to make certain the lessons learned register is complete before moving the project onto the next phase. On any project, the lessons learned document is created by which of the following?
    A. Customers
    B. Project sponsor
    C. Project team
    D. Stakeholders

    ☑ **C.** The project team contributes to the lessons learned document. The project manager also contributes, or leads, the creation, but this is not a choice in the question.
    ☒ **A, B,** and **D** are incorrect. **A** is incorrect because the customers do not always contribute to the lessons learned document. **B** is incorrect because the project sponsor does not always contribute to the lessons learned document. **D** is incorrect because stakeholders, other than the project manager and the project team, do not always contribute.

3. Your project is moving ahead of schedule. Management elects to incorporate additional quality testing into the project to improve the quality and acceptability of the project deliverable. This is an example of which one of the following?

A. Scope creep
B. Change control
C. Quality assurance
D. Integrated change control

☑ **D.** Additional quality testing will require additional time and resources for the project. This is an example of integrated change control.

☒ **A, B,** and **C** are incorrect. **A** is incorrect because scope creep includes small, undocumented changes to the project execution. **B,** change control, is incorrect because change control falls within integrated change control. **C** is incorrect because QA is an organization-wide program.

4. You are the project manager of a new web site design project. There are 45 stakeholders with this project, and you are anticipating many change requests in the project. Which of the following is *not* true about change requests?

A. They happen while the project work is being done.
B. They always require additional funding.
C. They must be documented
D. They can be requested by a stakeholder.

☑ **B.** Change requests do not always require more money. Approved changes may require more funds, but not always. The change request may be denied, so no additional funds are needed for the project.

☒ **A, C,** and **D** are incorrect. These are characteristics of change requests that occur during a project. For more information, see Section 4.6 in the *PMBOK Guide*.

5. You are the project manager for a pharmaceutical company. You are currently working on a project for a new drug your company is creating. A recent change in a law governing drug testing will change your project scope. Since the project must be completed within two years, what's the first thing you should do as project manager?

A. Create a documented change request.
B. Proceed as planned, since the project will be grandfathered in and unaffected by the new change in the law.
C. Consult with the project sponsor and the stakeholders.
D. Stop all project work until the issue is resolved.

☑ **A.** A formal, documented change request is the best course of action for a change request stemming from a law or regulation.

☒ **B, C,** and **D** are incorrect. **B** is incorrect because the law or regulation will likely override any existing project implementation. **C** is incorrect because the project manager should first document the change through a change request. **D** is incorrect because all project work shouldn't stop just because of a change request.

6. During project execution activities, a project sponsor's role in a functional organization can best be described as doing which one of the following?
   A. Acting as a sounding board for the project stakeholders
   B. Helping the project manager and stakeholders resolve any issues ASAP
   C. Deflecting change requests for the project manager
   D. Showing management the project progress and status reports

☑ **B.** The project sponsor can help the project manager and the stakeholders resolve issues during project execution.

☒ **A, C,** and **D** are incorrect. **A** is incorrect because the project sponsor is going to have an active rather than passive role in the process of integration management. **C** is incorrect because the project sponsor will guide changes through the change control system. **D** is not a valid choice, because the project sponsor is part of management and will do more than report the status to other management roles.

7. You are the project manager for the HALO Project. You and your project team are preparing the project plan. Of the following, which one is a project plan development constraint you and your team must consider?
   A. The budget as assigned by management
   B. Project plans from similar projects
   C. Project plans from similar projects that have failed
   D. Interviews with subject matter experts (SMEs) who have experience with the project work in your project plan

☑ **A.** If management has assigned the project the constraint of a fixed budget, the project manager and the project team must determine how the project can operate within that constraint.

☒ **B, C,** and **D** are incorrect. **B** describes historical information, not a project constraint. **C** is also historical information and not a project constraint, so it is incorrect. **D** is a valuable tool to use as input into the project plan development, but it is not a constraint.

8. You are the project manager of HYH Project for your company, and you're working with the project team and several key stakeholders to develop the project management plan. Which of the following is the primary purpose of the project management plan?
   A. To define the work to be completed to reach the project end date
   B. To define the work needed in each phase of the project life cycle
   C. To prevent any changes to the scope
   D. To define how the project is executed, monitored, controlled, and then closed

   ☑ **D.** Of all the choices presented, **D** is the best choice. Project management plans communicate to the project team, the project sponsor, and stakeholders how the entire project will operate.
   ☒ **A, B,** and **C** are incorrect. **A** and **B** are incorrect because they do not define the primary purpose of the project plan. **C** is also incorrect because the project plan is intended not to prevent changes, but to communicate the project management life cycle.

9. John is a new employee and he's learning how to perform a task in your organization. Mary, a senior network engineer, is working with John to perform the new task. Rather than just show John the procedure, Mary is watching John and coaching him through the task. What is happening in this knowledge management activity?
   A. Reverse shadowing
   B. Project planning methodology
   C. On-the-job training
   D. Storytelling

   ☑ **A.** Of the choices, reverse shadowing is the best choice. Mary is letting John learn by doing, and she's coaching and watching him perform the task.
   ☒ **B, C,** and **D** are incorrect. **B** is incorrect because it describes a tool and technique used to develop the project plan. **C** is incorrect; although this is a tempting choice, reverse shadowing is the best choice. **D** is incorrect because storytelling is a knowledge management technique used to convey tacit information.

10. You are examining the project management plan and its components with the project team. The team doesn't understand why so much information is needed for the project. What is the difference between a project baseline and a project plan?
    A. Project plans change as needed, while baselines change only at milestones.
    B. Project plans and baselines do not change—they are amended.
    C. Project plans change as needed, while baselines are snapshots of the project plan.
    D. Baselines are control tools, while project plans are execution tools.

☑   **D.** A project baseline serves as a control tool. Project plan execution and work results are measured against the project baselines.

☒   **A, B,** and **C** are incorrect. **A** is incorrect, given that baselines can change with the project plan. **B** is incorrect because project plans and baselines do change. **C** is incorrect because baselines are more than snapshots of the project plans—they are expectations of how the work should be performed.

11.   Which one of the following is *not* beneficial to the project manager during the project plan development process?
   A.   Gantt charts
   B.   PMIS
   C.   Project management methodology
   D.   Stakeholder knowledge

☑   **A.** Gantt charts are excellent tools to measure and predict the project progress, but they are not needed during the project plan development process.

☒   **B, C,** and **D** are incorrect. These choices are needed and expected during the development of the project plan.

12.   Yoli is the project manager for her company and she's reviewing the project budget with management. Management is concerned about the capital expenses in the project, and they'd like more information about when Yoli will actually spend the project budget. Which one of the following represents the vast majority of a project's budget?
   A.   Project planning
   B.   Project plan execution
   C.   Labor
   D.   Cost of goods and services

☑   **B.** The project plan execution represents the majority of the project budget.

☒   **A, C,** and **D** are incorrect. **A,** project planning, does not reflect the majority of the project budget, although it may contain the most project processes. **C,** labor, does not reflect the biggest project expense in all projects. **D,** cost of goods and services, is incorrect because the procurement of the goods and services will fall within the project plan execution. In addition, not every project will procure goods and services.

13. The project plan provides a baseline for several things. Which one of the following does the project plan *not* provide a baseline for?
    A. Scope
    B. Cost
    C. Schedule
    D. Control

    > ☑ **D.** Control is not a baseline.
    > ☒ **A, B,** and **C** are incorrect. These choices describe the project baselines included within the project plan. Incidentally, scope, cost, and schedule are also the attributes of the Triple Constraints of Project Management.

14. Natasha is the project manager for her organization. She is meeting with her project stakeholders to review the project plan and the different elements she'll use as part of project execution. Which of the following can best help Natasha during project execution?
    A. Stakeholder analysis
    B. Change control boards
    C. PMIS
    D. Scope verification

    > ☑ **C.** A PMIS can assist the project manager the most during project execution. It does not replace the role of the project manager, however.
    > ☒ **A, B,** and **D** are incorrect. **A** is incorrect because stakeholder analysis should have been completed during the project planning processes. **B** also is incorrect, because CCBs can assist the project manager, but not as much as the control and assistance offered through a PMIS. **D** is incorrect because scope verification is proof of the project work and does not assist the project manager.

15. You are the project manager for your organization. When it comes to integrated change control, you must ensure that which one of the following is present?
    A. Supporting detail for the change
    B. Approval of the change from the project team
    C. Approval of the change from an SME
    D. Risk assessment for each proposed change

    > ☑ **A.** Integrated change control requires detail for implementing the change. Without evidence of the need for the change, there is no reason to implement it.
    > ☒ **B, C,** and **D** are incorrect. **B** is incorrect because the project team's approval is not necessary for changes. **C** is incorrect because a subject matter expert isn't always needed to determine the need for change. **D** is also incorrect because, although risk assessment is needed for changes, some changes may be discarded based on reasons other than risk.

16. Jeff is the project manager of the Bridge Construction Project for his company. This project requires strict change control because of government regulations, the cost of the project deliverables, and the approved scope. The project plan provides what with regard to project changes?

   A. A methodology to approve or decline CCB changes

   B. A guide to all future project decisions

   C. A vision of the project deliverables

   D. A fluid document that may be updated as needed based on the CCB

> ☑ **B.** The project plan serves as a guide to all future project decisions.
> ☒ **A, C,** and **D** are incorrect. **A** is incorrect because the project plan details more than how changes may be approved or denied. Recall that the change control board (CCB) approves and declines changes. **C** is also incorrect, because the project plan describes how to obtain the project vision, not just what the project vision may be. **D** does describe the project plan, but not as fully as choice **B.** In addition, the project plan can be updated without changing the project scope.

17. You are the project manager for the DGF Project. This project is to design and implement a new application that will connect to a database server. Management of your company has requested that you create a method to document technical direction on the project and to document any changes or enhancements to the technical attributes of the project deliverable. Which one of the following would satisfy management's request?

   A. Configuration management

   B. Integrated change control

   C. Scope control

   D. Change management plan

> ☑ **A.** Configuration management is the documentation of the project product, its attributes, and its changes to the product.
> ☒ **B, C,** and **D** are incorrect. **B** is incorrect because integrated change control describes how to incorporate all of the project changes across the knowledge areas. **C** is incorrect because scope control describes how to manage changes, or potential changes, to the project scope. **D** is also incorrect, because the change management plan does not describe the project product, its features, or changes to the product.

18. Baseline variances, a documented plan to manage variances, and a proven methodology to offer corrective actions to the project plan are all part of which process?
    A. Change management
    B. Change control system
    C. Scope change control
    D. Integrated change control

    ☑ **D.** Integrated change control is a process to document changes, variances within the project, impact of changes and variances, the response to those changes, and offer corrective actions to the project plan.
    ☒ **A, B,** and **C** are incorrect. **A** is incorrect because change management does not respond to variances as integrated change control does. **B** is incorrect because the change control system is a documented procedure, which is part of integrated change control, to manage change requests. **C** is incorrect because scope change control is the process of managing changes that affect the work only in the project scope.

19. One of the requirements of project management in your organization is to describe your project management approach and methodology in the project plan. You can best accomplish this requirement through which one of the following actions?
    A. Establishing a project office
    B. Establishing a program office
    C. Compiling the management plans from each of the knowledge areas
    D. Creating a PMIS and documenting its inputs, tools and techniques, and outputs

    ☑ **C.** The management approach is best described as a compilation of the individual management plans from each knowledge area.
    ☒ **A, B,** and **D** are incorrect. **A** is incorrect because a project office is not needed to describe the management approach. **B** is incorrect for the same reason. **D** may be a good practice for project control, but it does not describe management approach and methodologies.

20. You have just informed your project team that each team member will be contributing to the lessons learned register. Your team does not understand this approach and wants to know what the documentation will be used for. Which one of the following best describes the purpose of the lessons learned documentation?
    A. Offers proof of concept for management
    B. Offers historical information for current and future projects
    C. Offers evidence of project progression as reported by the project team
    D. Offers input to team member evaluations at the project conclusion

☑   **B.** The lessons learned register offers historical information for current and future projects.
☒   **A, C,** and **D** are incorrect. **A** is incorrect because proof of concept likely comes early in the project's planning processes. **C** is also incorrect, because lessons learned may offer evidence of project progression, but this is not the purpose of the lessons learned document. **D** is also incorrect, given that lessons learned offers historical information for future projects, not the current one.

21.   Which one of the following is a formal document to manage and control project execution?
   A.   WBS
   B.   Project management plan
   C.   Organizational management plan
   D.   Work authorization system

☑   **B.** The project management plan is the formal document used to manage and control project execution.
☒   **A, C,** and **D** are incorrect. **A** is incorrect because the WBS is an input to the project plan. **C** is incorrect because the organizational management plan is part of the project plan. **D** is incorrect because the work authorization system enables work to be approved and new work to begin.

22.   Configuration management is a process for applying technical and administrative direction and surveillance of the project implementation. Which activity is *not* included in configuration management?
   A.   Controlling changes to the project deliverables
   B.   Scope verification
   C.   Automatic change request approvals
   D.   Identification of the functional and physical attributes of the project deliverables

☑   **C.** Hopefully, automatic change request approvals are not included in any project. They are not a part of configuration management.
☒   **A, B,** and **D** are incorrect. These choices all describe attributes of configuration management.

23.   You are preparing to enter into the project execution with your project team. As part of your preparation, you'll rely on your project management plan and several tools and techniques. Which of the following contains parts of the project plan execution?
   A.   PMIS, WBS, and EVM
   B.   General management skills, status review meetings, and EVM
   C.   Project management methodology and the PMIS
   D.   General management skills, EVM, status review meetings, and interpersonal skills

☑   **C.** The project management methodology and the PMIS are tools and techniques used for project execution.
☒   **A, B,** and **D** are incorrect. **A** is incorrect because EVM and the WBS are not tools used in the project plan execution. **B** is incorrect because it includes EVM, which is not a tool used in the project plan execution. **D** is incorrect because it also includes EVM.

24. You are the project manager of the GHQ Project for your company. Management has required that you utilize earned value management as part of your project and their enterprise environmental factors. EVM is used during the _____.
    A. Controlling processes
    B. Executing processes
    C. Closing processes
    D. Entire project

    ☑   **D.** EVM, earned value management, is used throughout the project processes. It is a planning and control tool used to measure performance.
    ☒   **A, B,** and **C** are incorrect. These choices are correct in that EVM is used during these processes, but none of these answers is as good a choice as **D.**

25. You are the project manager for your organization. Management would like you to use a tool that can help you plan, schedule, monitor, and report findings on your project. Which of the following is the correct tool to use?
    A. PMIS
    B. EVM
    C. Status review meetings
    D. Project team knowledge and skill set

    ☑   **A.** PMIS is the best answer because it helps the project manager plan, schedule, monitor, and report findings.
    ☒   **B, C,** and **D** are incorrect. **B** is incorrect because EVM does not help the project manager schedule. **C** is incorrect because status review meetings do not help the project manager schedule. **D** is incorrect because the project team's knowledge and skills do not necessarily help the project manager plan, schedule, monitor, and report findings.

Chapter 5

Managing
the Project Scope

CERTIFICATION OBJECTIVES

5.01	Planning Project Scope Management	5.05	Validating the Project Scope
5.02	Collecting and Eliciting Project Requirements	5.06	Controlling the Project Scope
		✓	Two-Minute Drill
5.03	Defining the Project Scope	Q&A	Self Test
5.04	Creating the Work Breakdown Structure		

Have you ever set out to clean your garage and ended up cleaning your attic? It usually starts by needing to move the car out of the garage so you can really dig in and clean. As you move your car, you realize the car could really use a cleaning, too.

So you clean out the car. You dust it down, clean the windows inside and out, and vacuum out pennies, old pens, and some green French fries. The vacuum, you discover, has something caught in the hose, so you have to fight to clear the blockage to finish cleaning out the car. Once the inside's spick-and-span, you think, "Might as well wash and wax the car, too."

This calls for the garden hose. The garden hose, you notice, is leaking water at the spigot by the house. Now you've got to replace the connector. This calls for a pair of channel-lock pliers. You run to the hardware store, get the pliers—and some new car wax. After fixing the garden hose, you finally wash and wax the car.

As you're putting on the second coat of wax, you see a few scratches on the car that could use some buffing. You have a great electric buffer but can't recall where it is. Maybe it's in the attic? You check the attic only to realize how messy things are there, too. So, you begin moving out old boxes of clothes, baby toys, and more interesting stuff.

Before you know it, the garage is full of boxes you've brought down from the attic. The attic is somewhat cleaner, but the garage is messier than when you started this morning. As you admire the mess, you realize it's starting to rain on your freshly waxed car, the garden hose is tangled across the lawn, and there are so many boxes in the garage you can't pull the car in out of the rain.

So what does this have to do with project management? Plenty! Project management requires concentration, organization, and a laser-like focus. In this chapter, we'll be covering project scope management, the ability to get the required work done—and only the required work—to complete the project. We'll look at how a project manager should create and follow a plan to complete the required work to satisfy the scope without wandering off or embellishing on the project deliverables.

Exploring Project Scope Management

Two types of scopes are involved in project management: the project scope and the product scope. The *product scope* includes all the details and specifications of the result of the project for the recipients of the project: the user, the customer, and the organization. The *project scope* describes all the work required to create the product scope. In some instances, the product scope and the project scope are melded together into one project scope, while in other projects, these are two distinct scopes. Your exam may include a question or two about the concept of product scope, but the overwhelming concern of this book, and project management, is the project scope.

The approach that you take with your project has a direct effect on how you'll manage the project scope. In a predictive life cycle, the deliverables are all defined up front before the project execution begins. In an adaptive or agile life cycle, the project scope and deliverables are defined through iterations of planning and executing. The elements of the project scope in an agile environment are agreed upon at the launch of each iteration.

Predictive life cycles have a reputation for wanting all requirements and deliverables defined early in the project, and then the project tends to be somewhat rigid and against changes to the project scope. An agile environment is practically the opposite: change is expected, welcome, and part of the overall project management approach. Predictive life cycles protect the project scope and requirements from change, whereas agile and adaptive life cycles define and prioritize requirements in a backlog and determine how many requirements the team can create in the current iteration.

Tailoring Project Scope Management

The project scope is based largely on the requirements, which are typically gathered before the project is initiated. Requirements gathering has long been the responsibility of a business analyst, though project managers may take on this role. Requirements gathering can also be part of the organization's portfolio planning or program planning, or even set up as a separate project. Requirements elicitation, technically and from the *PMBOK Guide* point of view, takes place within the project scope management knowledge area.

Your organization may utilize the business analyst approach, and that's fine; but for your exam, you should know that stakeholder requirements elicitation and documentation will fall under project scope management. As the project manager, you may work with a business analyst or take on the role of business analyst to do the following:

- Define business needs and/or problems the project will address.
- Recommend solutions for the business needs and/or problems identified.
- Perform requirement elicitation and document the stakeholder requirements.
- Lead the project to implement the solutions.
- Close out the requirements by transitioning the solution to the project stakeholders.

Of course, when appropriate, the project manager and the business analyst work together to identify problems and solutions, elicit requirements, and document the requirements the project must satisfy. There should not be an antagonistic relationship between the project manager and the business analyst. By clearly identifying roles and responsibilities, having open communications, and working in a spirit of collaboration, the project manager and business analyst should have no problems working together on the requirements gathering activities.

Each project and organization is unique, and this uniqueness allows for the tailoring of the scope management processes. Consider the following key project management processes and how they could be tailored for a project and an organization:

- **Knowledge and requirements management** Knowledge and requirements management systems may be in play to help organize, document, and communicate the requirements. The knowledge and management systems may also help the project manager and the business analyst access requirements from previous projects and apply them to the current endeavor.

- **Scope validation and scope control**   Each organization can have unique scope validation and scope control processes that supersede the information I'll share in this chapter about these processes.
- **Development approaches**   An organization may use an agile, adaptive, or predictive approach to manage its projects. In addition, the life cycle could be incremental or iterative, depending on what the project is creating and the preferences of the organization. Some organizations could even create a hybrid approach for their projects.
- **Requirements stability**   Loosely defined requirements can hinder a predictive approach, but they may work well in an agile or adaptive approach to project management. Unstable requirements mean the requirements could evolve and change as the project moves forward.
- **Governance**   Each organization can have its own governance to implement its rules, policies, and procedures. The project must operate within the governance boundaries to be successful in the organization.

A big consideration in this project management knowledge is the difference between the predictive and the agile and adaptive environments. While the predictive environment is keen on defining and documenting all requirements upfront in a project, agile and adaptive environments are not. Adaptive and agile projects release prototypes of the solution to allow requirements to move through requirements refinement. Requirements in an agile environment are added and prioritized in a backlog. At the start of each iteration, the requirements are prioritized, and the team decides how many of the prioritized requirements can be delivered in the iteration.

CERTIFICATION OBJECTIVE 5.01

Planning Project Scope Management

This first process in project scope management is to create the *scope management plan*, which defines how the project scope will be defined, the techniques you and the project team will use to validate the scope, and what approach is in place or will be created to control changes to the scope. Project scope management has several purposes:

- It defines what work is needed to complete the project objectives.
- It determines what is included in the project.
- It serves as a guide to determine what work is not needed to complete the project objectives.

- It serves as a point of reference for what is not included in the project.
- It defines how the scope will be controlled.
- It communicates how scope validation will occur in the project.

So what is a project scope statement? A *project scope statement* is a description of the work required to deliver the product of a project along with the assumptions and constraints that may affect the work of building the project scope. The project scope statement defines what work will, and will not, be included in the project work. A project scope guides the project manager on decisions to add, change, or remove work in the project.

Project Scope vs. Product Scope

Project scope and product scope are different entities.

A project scope deals with the work required to create the project deliverables. For instance, a project to create a new barn would focus only on the work required to complete the barn with the specific attributes, features, and characteristics called for by the project plan. The project scope is specific to the work required to complete the project objectives.

Product scope, on the other hand, is the attributes and characteristics of the deliverables the project is creating. For the barn project, the product scope would specifically define the features and attributes of the barn: the materials to be used, the dimensions of the different rooms and stalls, the expected weight the hayloft should carry, electrical requirements, and more. The project scope would not include features of a flower garden, a wading pool, or a fence.

The project scope and the product scope are bound to each other. Throughout the project execution, the work is measured against the project plan to verify that the project is on track to fulfill the project scope. The product scope is measured against requirements, while the project scope is measured against the project plan.

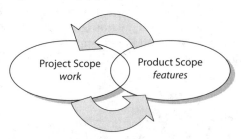

Creating the Scope Management Plan

Planning the project scope involves progressive elaboration. The project scope begins broad and through refinement becomes focused on the required work to create the product of the project. The project manager and the project team must examine the product scope—what the customer expects the project to create—to plan on how to achieve that goal. Based on the project requirements documentation, the project scope can be created.

In order to build the scope management plan fully, you'll rely on four inputs:

- **Project charter**   The project purpose and high-level objectives
- **Project management plan**   The quality management plan, the project life cycle description, and a definition of the project development approach
- **Enterprise environmental factors**   The organization's culture, infrastructure, personnel administration, and marketplace conditions
- **Organizational process assets**   The organization's policies, procedures, historical information, and lessons learned from past projects

Using Scope Planning Tools and Techniques

The goal of scope planning is to create the scope management plan and the requirements management plan. The project manager and the project team must have a full understanding of the project requirements, the business need of the project, and stakeholder expectations to be successful in creating the scope statement and the scope management plan. Recall that there are two types of scope:

- **Product scope**   Features and functions of the product of the project
- **Project scope**   The work needed to create the product of the project

The project manager and the project team can rely on three tools and techniques to plan the project scope:

- **Expert judgment** Use someone more knowledgeable than the project team, the project manager, and even the key stakeholders to guide the scope planning process. Expert judgment can come from experts within the organization or outside, such as consultants.
- **Data analysis** The project manager can rely on data analysis, such as alternatives analysis. Data analysis also reviews the options for collecting and refining requirements, creating the product scope, scope validation options, and scope control.
- **Meetings** The planning meetings' approach is really part of the organization's culture and will likely include the project sponsor, project team members, key stakeholders, and other experts. Consider, for example, what work is like for a project manager in a bank versus a project manager in a small, entrepreneurial company. The culture of both entities differs regarding how a project is initiated, planned, and then managed. Of course, the project charter, the requirements documentation, and organizational process assets will guide the scope planning process as well.

Creating the Scope Management Plan

The scope management plan explains how the project scope will be managed and how scope changes will be factored into the project plan. Based on the conditions of the project, the project work, and the confidence of the exactness of the project scope, the scope management plan should also define the likelihood of changes to the scope, how often the scope may change, and how much the scope can change. The scope management plan also details the process of how changes to the project scope will be documented and classified throughout the project life cycle. Every scope management plan should define four processes:

- The process to create the project scope statement
- The process to create the work breakdown structure (WBS) based on the project scope statement—and the methods for maintaining the WBS integrity and the process for WBS approval
- The process for formal acceptance of the project deliverables by the project customer
- The process for evaluating and approving or declining scope change requests

The process of creating the scope management plan also includes creating the requirements management plan, which defines how you and the project team will collect, document, and protect the project requirements. The requirements management plan defines configuration management for the product and the tracking approach you'll utilize in this project. This plan also defines how requirements may be prioritized, any metrics for requirements measurements, and the requirements traceability matrix. The requirements management plan maps out how requirements will be tracked, reported, and prioritized. The requirements management plan can also define the configuration management activities, such as product changes, reporting requirements, and authorization levels for changes to the product.

The requirements management plan defines how requirements will be managed throughout the phases of the project. This plan also defines how any changes to the requirements will be allowed, documented, and tracked through project execution. You'll also need to prioritize the project requirements and define what metrics will be used to measure requirement completion and acceptability.

CERTIFICATION OBJECTIVE 5.02

Collecting and Eliciting Requirements

Projects don't exist without stakeholders. Sure, sure, sometimes they are a pain in the neck, but if it weren't for them, there would be no reason to have projects—or project managers. Stakeholders and project managers need to work together as a team; the stakeholders know what they want as the result of your work, and the project manager and the project team can make that result a reality. The project manager's role, often along with a business analyst, is to elicit requirements from the stakeholders to create the best possible solution to satisfy the needs of the stakeholders and the organization, and to ensure the longevity of the solution.

The goal, whether the project manager or a business analyst is leading the work, is the same: Find detailed specifications about exactly what the stakeholders want and expect from the project. Once the requirements have been identified—clearly identified—the project manager and team can work toward specific results. Though loose, open-ended, foggy requirements waste time, money, and effort in a predictive project life cycle, such requirements are more likely in an agile environment.

You'll be gathering broad categories of requirements:

■ **Business requirements** These define why the project has been initiated and what are the high-level expectations for the project.

■ **Stakeholder requirements** These are the individual stakeholder and stakeholder group requirements for the project.

- **Solution requirements** These describe the features, function, and characteristics of the project deliverable. Solution requirements are more fully described by two sub-requirement categories:
  - **Functional requirements** These describe how the solution will work, what the solution will manage, and all the capabilities the solution will provide for the stakeholder. It's how your project deliverable will operate.
  - **Nonfunctional requirements** These describe the conditions within which the functional requirements must operate. You might hear this also described as the quality requirements or environmental requirements, where the solution will operate at its ideal level or performance. You can recognize nonfunctional requirements when stakeholders talk about speed, capacity, security, user interfaces, or production.
- **Transition and readiness requirements** These requirements describe the needed elements to move from the current state to the desired future state—for example, training requirements or dual-supporting systems.
- **Project requirements** The project may have requirements in the way it is managed, specific processes that are to be followed, and other objectives that the project manager is obligated to meet.
- **Quality requirements** Any condition, metric, performance objective, or condition the project must meet to be considered of quality. These should be measurable and not ambiguous goals.

The project charter may rely on a current state assessment and compare it to the desired future state assessment. This is basically a project before-and-after—your project deliverables create the future state. Other charters simply define the high-level goals of the project, and then it's up to you, your project team, and any other experts to figure out how to make it happen.

You'll also rely on project documents, such as the assumptions log and the lessons learned register. A key project document is the stakeholder registry to confirm that you're communicating, interviewing, and eliciting requirements from all the stakeholders. Recall that some stakeholders won't want your project to succeed at all—those nasty, negative stakeholders. Just because they despise the project doesn't mean you get to ignore them. You'll need to work with both positive and negative stakeholders during requirements gathering and throughout the project. Expert judgement is a tool and technique you'll use to begin eliciting requirements, and this will include stakeholders and experts in your discipline.

Interview the Stakeholders

One of the most reliable data-gathering techniques is *interviewing*, which is a conversation between you and the project stakeholders about their needs, wants, and demands for the project. It's a learning process for you to absorb information from the project customer by asking them questions. You need and want the interviewees to talk to you, so you've got to ask questions. Let me rephrase that: You need to ask good questions.

The interviewer should go into the interview armed with some questions that allow the stakeholder to ramble a bit and other questions that allow the stakeholder to be precise about the project deliverables. You probably aren't going to ask the stakeholder how to create the deliverable, but you'll likely ask how they'll be using the product that you'll be creating. You want to see how they'll be using the deliverable as part of their day-to-day lives. This is where you'll categorize the requirements as functional or nonfunctional.

Interviews are usually done one-on-one, but there's no reason why a project manager can't have several interviewers participating in the session. As a rule, however, the more people who participate in the interview, the more complex the elicitation process becomes. Smaller groups allow for a more conversational tone to the meeting. Sometimes, however, the project manager will need a subject matter expert to help the conversation along.

Leading a Focus Group

Focus groups provide an opportunity for a group of stakeholders to interact with a moderator about the requirements of the project, the current state of an organization, or how they'll see the project deliverables affecting the organization once the project is completed. Like an interviewer, the moderator is armed with questions, but he should be well versed on the topic to branch into new contributing discussions on the project requirements.

An ideal focus group has six to twelve people in one room, and the moderator should encourage open, conversational discussion. The moderator, often not the project manager, should be neutral to the project, have the ability to draw people into the conversation, and keep the session on track to the goals of the project. A scribe or recorder should document the discussion in the session so the project manager and team can review the results of the meeting and act accordingly.

Relying on Surveys

Surveys are a fine approach to eliciting requirements from a large group of stakeholders in a relatively short amount of time. The challenge with surveys, however, is that they must be responded to and tabulated, and the survey questions must be well written to generate accurate responses. When the general requirements are known, closed-ended questions are ideal, but you should restrict the type of information the respondent may provide. Open-ended questions allow the respondent to write essays about a topic, but it takes more time to tabulate the responses.

Survey writers need to determine the best type of questions, and they must consider the audience of the survey. You'll also want to consider how quickly you'd like respondents to complete the survey and how you'll collect and tabulate the results. Obviously, electronic surveys are ideal, as you can quickly sort the data, create charts, and track who has responded.

Leveraging Data Analysis

One of the best data analysis tools to use in requirements gathering is document analysis. You, the team, and any experts will review all the project documentation and information. You'll identify requirements through the documentation and identify information and specifics about the requirements. While your project may have tons of documentation, here are some good examples of documents for data analysis:

- Agreements and contracts
- Business plans
- Business process documentation
- Business rules repositories
- Process flow information for the organization
- Marketing information
- Problems and issues logs from the current and past projects
- Regulatory documentation
- Request for proposal (if one exists)
- Use cases

Making Group Decisions on Requirements

Rarely are all the requirements for a project clearly defined when the project launches. There are probably some cases, such as in manufacturing or construction, in which certain types of projects are repeated over and over, and theses projects may be based on the same initial set of requirements, but usually the requirements for each project vary wildly, because each project is unique. When you're managing a large project, you need to work with groups of stakeholders to elicit their requirements for the project deliverables.

Sometimes stakeholders have a general idea of what they'd like you to create, but they aren't certain. Consider market opportunities, problems that need to be solved, and implementations of new materials, software, or organization-wide changes. The requirements in these instances can go in multiple directions and demand a good plan and uniformity to create a successful project and useable deliverable.

When multiple solutions exist for a project, or the stakeholders aren't entirely certain what the exact project requirements should be, group creativity techniques can be useful. These techniques help the key stakeholders generate ideas, solutions, and requirements for the project. Here are some examples you should know for your PMP exam:

- **Brainstorming** The group of participants brainstorms about a topic and throws out as many ideas as possible to generate solutions and requirements.
- **Nominal group technique** Like brainstorming, this approach generates ideas, but the ideas are voted on by the stakeholders and ranked based on usefulness. There are four steps to implementing the nominal group technique:
    1. Each participant brainstorms the problem or opportunity with her ideas.
    2. The facilitator writes all ideas from each person on a white board.
    3. Each idea is discussed for clarity and understanding.
    4. The participants privately vote on each idea from a low score of 1 to a high score of 5. Rounds of voting and discussion can take place to reach a consensus on the highest scoring ideas.
- **Mind mapping** Mind maps link ideas, thoughts, requirements, and objectives to one another. You might use mind maps after a brainstorming or nominal group technique to organize possible solutions and requirements, and to show where differences exist between the stakeholders (see Figure 5-1).
- **Affinity diagram** This group creativity technique is often used for solutions. It groups ideas into clusters, each of which can be broken down again to analyze each subset. It's basically a decomposition and organization of project ideas and requirements.
- **Multicriteria decision analysis** This approach relies on a systematic approach of determining, ranking, and eliminating project criteria such as performance metrics, risks, requirements, and other project elements. These approaches use a table called a "decision matrix" to measure and score these project elements.
- **Delphi Technique** This approach uses rounds of anonymous surveys to foster consensus. Each round of surveys is based on answers from the past round so each participant can freely and anonymously comment on others' thoughts and inputs about the project requirements. The idea is that the comments will lead the group toward the most appropriate answer without the political attachment that may occur if the process were not anonymous.

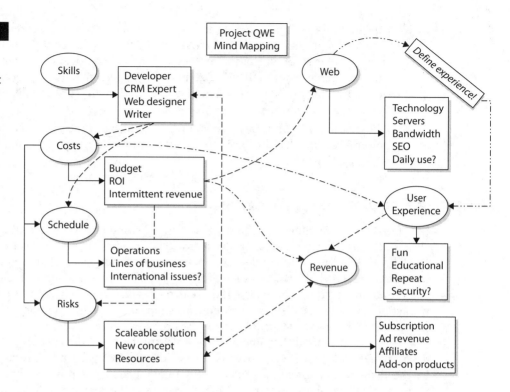

FIGURE 5-1

Mind maps visualize project requirements while they're being created.

on the **job**   **If you're wondering why it's called the Delphi Technique, it's named after the Oracle at Delphi—the most important oracle from Greek mythology. The technique was first used in 1944 at the start of the Cold War to predict how technology may affect warfare.**

Using Group Decisions

When many project stakeholders have loads of different competing objectives about the project deliverables, it's sometimes best for the project manager to hand the decision back to the project stakeholders. This approach generally allows the majority to vote on the project direction, but it doesn't always garner goodwill, cohesion, or buy-in from all the project stakeholders. You should be familiar with four different models of group decisions:

- **Unanimity** All the stakeholders agree on the project requirements (and then rainbows appear, the sun shines, and bluebirds sing).
- **Majority** This is probably the most common group decision, in which a vote is offered and the majority wins.

- **Plurality** Like a majority rule, this approach allows the biggest section of a group to win, even if a majority doesn't exist. You might experience this when there are three possible solutions for the project and the stakeholders vote their opinion for each solution in uneven thirds of 25 percent, 35 percent, and 40 percent. The group that represents the 40 percent would win, even though more people (60 percent) are opposed to the solution.

- **Autocratic** The project manager, project sponsor, or the person with the most power forces the decision, even though the rest of the group may oppose the decision. No warm, fuzzy feelings here.

Hosting a Requirements Workshop

Let's face facts: Sometimes stakeholders have agendas. And by sometimes, I mean they always do. When you're managing a project with stakeholders from across the organization, you'll be dealing with different departments, different functions, and different lines of business. The stakeholders from each of these groups may have different expectations and requirements for the project, and these expectations will often clash. A requirements workshop, sometimes called a facilitated workshop, aims to find commonality, consensus, and cohesion among the stakeholders for the project requirements.

If you're in software development work, you've probably participated in a joint application design (JAD) workshop. These strive to gather all the requirements and to create a well-rounded, balanced application for all the stakeholders. In manufacturing, project managers use a requirements workshop, sometimes called the voice of the customer (VOC), where the voice of the customer dictates what the project will create. You might also know VOC as quality function deployment (QFD). The idea is that quality is achieved by giving the customer exactly what they expect.

Your workshop might create user stories; these are short narratives about what the solution should provide and how the deliverables will work for the end users or customers. User stories follow a role-goal-motivation sequence. For example, it describes the stakeholder role, what they are trying to accomplish as their goal, and how the requirement equates to a benefit to the stakeholder.

Utilizing a Context Diagram

Imagine that your project is to install, configure, and roll out an organization-wide e-mail and calendaring server. A context diagram would illustrate all the components that would interact with your server. It would show the other computers on the network; the network itself; other servers, routers, and switches; and other hardware. Then the context diagram would show the people who interact with the server and their different roles, such as administrators, users, and support personal. These things and people that interact with the server are called *actors* in the context diagram.

Creating Prototypes

Have you ever seen a model of a skyscraper, or what about a mockup for a new web site, application, or even a brochure? These are *prototypes* that allow the stakeholder to see how the result is going to function. Prototypes help the project manager confirm that she understands the requirements the stakeholder expects from the deliverable. Some prototypes are considered throw-away, and they don't really work beyond communicating the idea of the deliverable. Others are considered functional or working prototypes and evolve into the final deliverable of the project.

A common prototype is a storyboard to show the flow of the interaction, activities, or information in a business system. Though you might be familiar with the idea of the Hollywood movie storyboard, the storyboard in project management helps to uncover the requirements the project needs for all the steps to be taken in the workflow. For example, a storyboard could show the flow of activities a customer could take to search a web-based catalogue, add an item to the shopping cart, set the shipping preferences, and then pay for the product. The storyboard could continue with the payment being processed, a confirmation page and e-mail, and order fulfillment from the warehouse all the way to the customer's address.

Observing Stakeholders

When it comes to learning a new skill, one of the best pieces of advice out there is this: It's easier to watch someone peel a banana than it is to describe how to peel a banana. This is true in requirements gathering, too—by observing someone do his work, you can see the processes, approaches, and challenges of his work more clearly than by just hearing about his work. Observing stakeholders is an excellent way to gather requirements, especially when your project is likely to affect their day-to-day work life, processes, and methods of operation in your organization.

As an observer, you can shadow a person and watch how he does his work. You might complete the shadowing as a passive or invisible observer. In this role, you work quietly, stay out of the way, and take notes on the processes you see. As an active or visible observer, you're stopping the person doing the work, asking loads of questions, and seeking to understand how the person is completing his work.

Benchmarking the Requirements

Benchmarking is an approach you can use throughout the project. Benchmarking compares two similar things to see which is performing better. For example, you might compare software packages, organizations, or different pieces of equipment. Benchmarking, in requirements collections, enables you to compare the requirements for your project against organizations that have completed similar work to see how their projects and products performed to help you better define what's needed in your project.

Managing the Requirements

The goal of eliciting the project requirements is to identify clearly and manage the requirements so the project scope can be created and the in-depth project planning can begin. It's ever so important for the project manager, the project team, and the key project stakeholders to be in agreement with the intent, direction, and requirements of the project before the project scope is created.

You should be familiar with two outputs of the process to collect project requirements:

- **Requirements documentation**   The clearly defined requirements must be measurable, complete, accurate, and approved by the project stakeholders. The requirements documentation may start broadly and, through progressive elaboration, become more distinct, but the identification and agreement of what is required and demanded of the project is paramount. This includes definitions of the functional and nonfunctional requirements, acceptance criteria, documentation of the impact of the deliverable on the organization, and any assumptions or constraints that have been identified.

- **Requirements traceability matrix (RTM)**   A requirements traceability matrix will track each requirement from its first entry, through executing, all the way into the operational transfer. When you're managing loads of requirements, an RTM can help you track several characteristics for each requirement:
  - Requirement name
  - Requirement's link to the business and project objectives
  - Project scope and WBS entry
  - Any relevant data, coding, cost, or schedule about a requirement
  - Requirement's current status as active, cancelled, deferred, added, approved, assigned, or completed
  - Testing activities for each requirement
  - Comments or notes about the requirement

An RTM can help you ensure that every requirement in the project has been created to specification. This will help in quality control processes and in scope validation later in the project. Figure 5-2 shows an example of an RTM.

An RTM can track elements and delivery of requirements.

Data and function

	Op1	Op2	Op3	Op4	Op5	Data	Status	Owner	Comments
REQ1	X		X	X	X	487	Fun	PM1	Currently functional
REQ2	X	X	X		X	7,321	Open	PM1	Open for review
REQ3	X	X		X		.99	Test	Pr2	Currently testing
REQ4		X	X			12.32	Prog	Pr2	Development
REQ5	X			X			Prog	BA3	Development
REQ6			X	X			Init	FM1	Initiating
REQ7	X			X		7.55	Test	IT1	Testing
REQ8			X		X		Fun	ITCIN	Currently functional
REQ9						475	Open	PS	Open for review

Requirements

CERTIFICATION OBJECTIVE 5.03

Defining the Project Scope

The process of scope definition is all about defining the project and product scope. It creates the project scope statement that fully communicates what the project will, and will not, create as a result of the project work. The project scope statement is a clear vision of what the result of the project will create. If you wanted to create a new house, you probably wouldn't stop by the lumberyard; pick up a truck of lumber, some cement, and nails; and set about building your dream house. You'd follow a logical approach: you'd first define the house and would then go about planning and creating the house.

The same is true with project management. Your organization and stakeholders may have a general idea of where the project should end up, but a detailed, fully developed plan is needed to get you there. Scope definition is the process of breaking down the broad vision for the project into logical components to reach its completion.

Examining the Inputs to Scope Definition

You should be very familiar with the inputs to scope definition; you've seen these several times already in the book. The following is a quick refresher of each input and its role in this process:

- **The project charter**   The project charter authorizes the project and the project manager and provides a high-level view of the project, the product, and the requirements for approval.
- **Project management plan**   The project management plan includes the scope management plan, which defines the approach for creating the project scope statement.
- **Project documents**   The project documents can be useful in creating the project scope statement. The assumption log, requirements documentation, and risk register are needed for this process.
- **Requirements documentation**   The project scope is founded on the requirements documentation, as this is what's expected of the project.
- **Enterprise environmental factors**   Consideration of the enterprise environmental factors, such as the organization's culture, infrastructure, personnel administration, and the marketplace conditions, can contribute to the creation of the project scope statement.
- **Organizational process assets**   The formal and informal guidelines, policies, and procedures that influence how a project scope is managed, and lessons learned from past projects, can help define the scope statement.

on the job   **You'll rely on the project's scope management plan, because it defines how the scope will be defined, managed, and controlled. Once your project is in motion, you can also expect change requests to influence the definition of your project scope.**

Consulting with Experts

Throughout the *PMBOK Guide* you'll see references to "expert judgment." It should come as no surprise that developing the project scope also includes this tool and technique. The experts for the project scope are the stakeholders, customers, users, and consultants to the project work. For a project to be successful, the project manager and the project team must know what the stakeholders of the project expect. This means communication must occur between the project manager and the stakeholders. Business analysts may be involved or may even facilitate the process of scope definition, but the result is the same: the expectations of the project stakeholders must be identified, documented, and then prioritized.

This is also the time to define what constitutes project success. Unquantifiable metrics, such as customer satisfaction, "good," and "fast," don't cut it. The project manager and the stakeholders must agree on metrics that indicate a project's success or failure. These are the key performance indicators (KPIs) that projects are often measured against.

Finding Alternatives

Project managers, project team members, and stakeholders must resist the temptation to fall in love with a solution too quickly. Alternative identification is any method of creating alternative solutions to the project's needs. This is typically accomplished through brainstorming and lateral thinking. Lateral thinking challenges assumptions, shifts perception, and uses creativity to find better solutions.

Facilitating Meetings and Workshops

A tool and technique that the project manager may utilize to create the project scope statement is facilitation. Good meeting management techniques, workshop leadership, and facilitating conversations are all needed during the creation of the project scope statement. Because you'll likely be working with stakeholders with differing backgrounds, differing understanding of the project work, and differing goals for the project, facilitation is a valuable interpersonal skill for the project manager.

Using Product Analysis

Product analysis is, as the name implies, the process of analyzing the product the project will create. Specifically, it involves understanding all facets of the product, its purpose, how it works, and its characteristics. Product analysis can be accomplished through one or more of the following:

- **Product breakdown**   Breaks down the product into components, examining each component individually and to determine how it may work with other parts of the product. This approach can be used in chemical engineering, for example, to see how a pharmaceutical product is created and how effective it is.
- **Systems engineering**   Focuses on satisfying the customers' needs, cost requirements, and quality demands through the design and creation of the product. An entire science is devoted to systems engineering in various industries.
- **Value engineering**   Deals with reducing costs and increasing profits, all while improving quality. Its focus is on solving problems, realizing opportunities, and maintaining quality improvement. Value engineering is also concerned with the customers' perception of the value of the different aspects of the product versus the project's cost to create the product's features and functions.
- **Value analysis**   Similar to value engineering, focuses on the cost/quality ratio of the product. For example, your expected level of quality of a $100,000 automobile versus a $6700 used car is likely relevant to the cost of each. Value analysis focuses on the expected quality against the acceptable cost.

Examining the Project Scope Statement

The *project scope statement*, an output of scope planning, clearly defines the project and product scope of the project, major deliverables, assumptions, and constraints. It is the guide for all future project decisions when it comes to change management. It is the key document to provide understanding of the project purpose. The scope statement provides justification for the project's existence, lists the high-level deliverables, and quantifies the project objectives. The scope statement is a powerful document that the project manager and the project team will use as a point of reference for potential changes, added work, and any project decisions.

The scope statement includes or references the following:

- **Product scope description**   Recall that the product scope description defines the characteristics and features of the thing or service the project is aiming to create. In most projects, the product scope will be vague early in the scope planning process, and then more details will become available as the product scope is progressively elaborated.

- **Project deliverables**   The high-level deliverables of the project should be identified. These deliverables, when predefined metrics are met, signal that the project scope has been completed. When appropriate, the scope statement should also list what deliverables are excluded from the project deliverables. For example, a project to create a new food product may state that the packaging of the food product is not included as part of the project. Items and features not listed as part of the project deliverables should be assumed to be excluded.

- **Product acceptance criteria**   The scope statement defines the requirements for acceptance. Product acceptance criteria establish what exactly qualifies a project's product as a success or failure.

- **Project exclusions**   Every project has boundaries. The scope statement defines the boundaries of the project by defining what's included and what's excluded in the project scope. For example, a project to create a piece of software may include the created compilation of a master software image but exclude the packaging and delivery of the software to each workstation within an organization. The project scope must clearly state what will be excluded from the project so there's no ambiguity as to what the stakeholders will receive as part of the product.

Obviously, the project scope statement is a hefty document that aims to create the confines of the project and the expectations of the project manager, the project team, and the project customers. It defines what's in and what's out of the project scope. Overall, the project scope statement sets the tone of the project expectations and paints a picture of what the project will create and how long and how much it'll take to get there.

During the scope statement creation, the project manager may also face, believe it or not, change requests from the project stakeholders. Change requests are managed through the integrated change control process, which basically means that any proposed change is reviewed and its impact on all areas of the project are considered. If a change is approved, the scope statement should be updated to reflect the approved change.

Reviewing the Project Document Updates

When you create the project scope statement, several project documents may need to be updated:

- **Assumption log**   Any new assumptions are added to the log.
- **Requirement documentation**   The scope statement creation can result in new requirements to be identified and documented.
- **Requirements traceability matrix**   The matrix is populated with the requirements, and the project manager and team begin tracking the requirements in the project.
- **Stakeholder register**   Ideally, stakeholders are identified early in the project, but the project scope creation could uncover new stakeholders for the project.

INSIDE THE EXAM

You'll encounter three big themes from this chapter on the project exam: project scope management, the WBS, and scope validation.

There are two types of scope: project scope and product scope. Unless the exam is talking about features and characteristics of the project deliverables, it will be referring to the project scope. If you think this through, it makes sense: Think of all the billions of different product scopes that can exist—the exam will offer big hints if it's talking about product scope. Project scope focuses on the work that must be done to create the product. Recall that the project scope is concerned with the work required—and only the work required—to complete the project.

Here's a nifty hint: WBS templates come from previous projects and/or the project management office, if the organization has one. WBS work packages are defined in the WBS dictionary.

Scope validation is all about the project customer accepting the project deliverables. Scope validation uses inspection as the tool to complete the process, which makes perfect sense. After all, how else will the customer know if the deliverable meets the project requirements unless they examine it?

CERTIFICATION OBJECTIVE 5.04

Creating the Work Breakdown Structure

As you hopefully know by now, the WBS is a deliverables-oriented collection of project components. It is a breakdown of the project work into smaller components. Work that doesn't fit into the WBS does not fit within the project. The point of the WBS is to organize and define the project scope. As you can see in Figure 5-3, each level of the WBS becomes more detailed.

The WBS is not a list of activities or a chart of the activities required to complete the work—it is a visual representation of the high-level deliverables divided up into manageable components. The smallest element in the WBS is called the *work package.* The components in the WBS are typically mapped against a code of accounts, which is a tool to number and identify the elements within the WBS. For example, a project manager and a stakeholder could reference work package 7.3.2.1, and both would be able to find the exact element in the WBS.

The components in the WBS should be included in a WBS dictionary, a reference tool to explain the WBS components, the nature of the work package, the assigned resources, and the time and billing estimates for each element. The WBS dictionary includes the following:

- Code of account identifier
- Description of each work package
- Related assumptions and constraints

FIGURE 5-3

A sample structure for a technology project

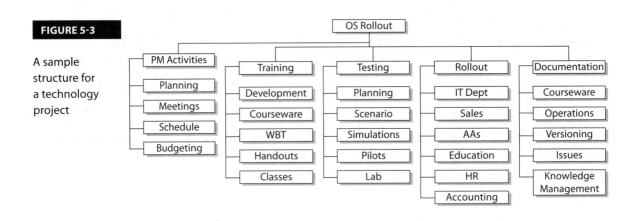

- Related milestones
- Activities linked to each WBS dictionary entry
- Responsible party for each entry
- Needed resources, time, and costs
- Quality metrics
- References for technical specifications
- Acceptance criteria for each element
- Cost estimates
- Agreement information

The WBS also identifies the relationship between work packages. Finally, the WBS should be updated to reflect changes to the project scope. The following are some essential elements you must know about the WBS:

- It serves as a major component of the project scope baseline.
- It's one of the most important project management tools.
- It serves as the foundation for planning, estimating, and project control.
- It visualizes the entire project.
- Work not included in the WBS is not part of the project.
- It builds team consensus and project buy-in.
- It serves as a control mechanism to keep the project on track.
- It allows for accurate cost and schedule estimates.
- It serves as a deterrent to scope change.

Using a Work Breakdown Structure Template

One of the tools you can use in scope definition is a WBS template. A WBS breaks down work into a deliverables-orientated collection of manageable pieces (see Figure 5-4). It is not a list of activities necessary to complete the project. A WBS template uses a similar project's WBS as a guide for the current work. This approach is recommended, since most projects in an organization are similar in their project life cycles—and the approach can be adapted to fit a given project.

Depending on the organization and its structure, an entity may have a common WBS template that all projects follow. The WBS template may have common activities included in the form, a common lexicon for the project in the organization, and a standard approach to the level of detail required for the project type.

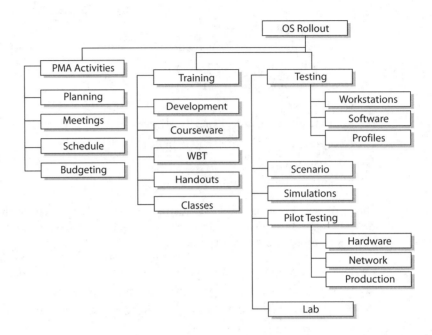

FIGURE 5-4

This section of the WBS has been expanded to provide more detail.

Decomposing the Project Deliverables

Decomposition is the process of breaking down the major project deliverables into smaller, more manageable components. So what's a manageable component? It's a unit of the project deliverable that can be assigned resources, measured, executed, and controlled. So how do you decompose the project deliverables? It's done this way:

1. Identify the major deliverables of the project, including the project management activities. A logical approach includes identifying the phases of the project life cycle or the major deliverables of the project.

2. Determine whether adequate cost and time estimates can be applied to the lowest level of the decomposed work. What is adequate is subjective to the demands of the project work. Deliverables that won't be realized until later portions of the project may be difficult to decompose, since many variables exist between now and when the deliverable is created. The smallest component of the WBS is the work package. A simple heuristic of decomposition is the 8/80 rule: no work package smaller than 8 hours and none larger than 80 hours.

3. Identify the deliverable's constituent components. This is a fancy way of asking whether the project deliverable can be measured at this point of decomposition. For example, the decomposition of a user manual may have the constituent components of assembling the book, confirming that the book is complete, shrink-wrapping the book, and shipping it to the customer. Each component of the work can be measured and may take varying amounts of time to complete, but it all must be done to complete the requirement.

4. Verify the decomposition. The lower-level items must be evaluated to ensure they are complete and accurate. Each item within the decomposition must be clearly defined and deliverable-orientated. Finally, each item should be decomposed to the point that it can be scheduled, budgeted, and assigned to a resource.

5. Other approaches include breaking it out by geography or functional area, or even breaking the work down by in-house and contracted work.

There are many approaches to creating the WBS. You can arrange the WBS by the project life cycle, by elements of the product scope, or even by simply identifying the major deliverables of the project. Whatever approach you select, you should identify all deliverables in the WBS. Some deliverables, however, may not be clear at the start of the project, and a marker can be added to the WBS signifying more information will be coming later—that marker is called a *planning package*.

Planning packages are often part of a control account. A *control account* is a control point within the WBS to track scope, costs, and schedule for a portion of the project deliverables. For example, you're constructing a home and you have allotted $125,000 of your budget for the kitchen deliverable. That's $125,000 for everything in the kitchen deliverable: lights, cabinets, plumbing, appliances, and so on. The control account is like a budget and schedule for the scope portion of the kitchen. The items to be determined within the kitchen, such as what appliances will be installed, are planning packages. You don't have to know on the first day of the project what cabinets will be installed, but there is a deadline for the cabinets to be selected to finish the project on time. Control accounts track schedule, costs, and scope for a portion of the project.

Defining the Scope Baseline

Traditionally, the scope baseline is made up of three documents: the project scope statement, the WBS, and the WBS dictionary. Technically, however, there are a few more elements that go into the scope baseline. Here's everything that's considered to be part of the scope baseline:

- Project scope statement
- WBS

- Work packages
- Planning packages
- WBS dictionary

When a change enters the project scope, you'll likely have to update these items, with the assumption that the change will affect the planning packages. The scope baseline must be in balance with the schedule and costs for the project.

CERTIFICATION OBJECTIVE 5.05

Validating the Scope

Imagine a project to create a full-color, slick catalog for an electronics manufacturer. The project manager has completed the initiation processes and moved through planning, and now the team is executing the project work. The only trouble is that the project manager and the experts on the project team aren't sharing their work progress with the customer. Plus, the work they're completing isn't in alignment with the product description or the customer's requirements.

The project team has created a trendy 1950s-style catalog with funky green and orange colors, lots of beehive hairdo models, horn-rimmed glasses, and tongue-in-cheek jokes about "the future" of electronics. The manufacturer wants to demonstrate a professional, accessible, current look for its publications. What do you think will happen if the project manager presents the catalog with his spin rather than following the request of the customer?

Scope validation is the process of the project customer accepting the project deliverables. Scope validation occurs at the end of each project phase or as major deliverables are created. Scope validation ensures that the deliverables the project creates are in alignment with the project scope. It is concerned with the acceptance of the work. A related activity, quality control, is concerned with the correctness of the work. Scope validation and quality control work together, as the quality of the work contributes to scope validation. Poor quality processes will typically result in scope validation failure. In the catalog example, working closely with the customer throughout the project, not just at the end, will save time, prevent frustration, and help the project team better understand what the customer wants—and that'll make the project more successful, save time, and money.

PMP Coach You'll be doing some scope validation when you pass the PMP examination. Your project is to pass the exam, and once you do, you'll have verified that you've completed your project scope. Study smart, work hard, and keep after it. If you've made it this far, you can go just a bit farther. You can do it!

Should a project get cancelled before it has completed the scope, scope validation is measured against the deliverables up to the point of the project's cancellation. In other words, scope validation measures the completeness of the work up to cancellation, not the work that was to be completed after project termination.

Examining the Inputs to Scope Validation

To validate the project scope, which is accomplished through inspection, there must be something to inspect—namely, work results. The work results are compared against the project plan to check for their completeness and against the quality control measure to check the correctness of the work.

One of the biggest inputs of scope validation is the requirements documentation you created as part of the collect requirements process. This information describes the requirements and expectations of the product, its features, and its attributes. The product documentation may go by many different names, depending on the industry:

- Plans
- Specifications
- Technical documentation
- Drawings
- Blueprints

The project manager will also rely on the project management plan, the scope baseline, and the traceability matrix to help compare what was promised to the customer and what was created. Work performance data such as nonconformance, degree of accuracy, and other performance metrics are also needed to see how well the deliverable conforms to the criteria for acceptance by the project customer.

Inspecting the Project Work

To complete scope validation, the work must be inspected. This may require measuring, examining, and testing the product to prove it meets customer requirements. Inspection usually involves the project manager and the customer inspecting the project work for validation, which in turn results in acceptance. Depending on the industry, inspections may also be known as the following:

- Reviews
- Product reviews
- Audits
- Walkthroughs

Formally Accepting the Project Deliverables

Assuming the scope has been validated, the customer accepts the deliverable. This is a formal process that requires signed documentation of the acceptance by the sponsor or customer. Scope validation can also happen at the end of each project phase or at major deliverables within the project. In these instances, scope validation may be conditional, based on the work results. When the scope is not validated, the project may undergo one of several actions: it may be cancelled and deemed a failure, sent through corrective actions, or put on hold while a decision is made based on the project or phase results.

<table>
<tr><td>

e x a m

ⓦatch   **If a project scope has been completed, the project is complete. Resist the urge to do additional work once the project scope has been fulfilled. Also, be cautious of instances in which the scope**

</td><td>

is fulfilled and the product description is exact, but the customer is not happy with the product. Technically, for the exam, the project is complete even if the customer is not happy.

</td></tr>
</table>

Scope validation creates work performance information about the project, scope validation, customer feedback, and status of deliverables that have, or have not, been accepted. When the deliverables are not accepted, you may need to issue a change request for defect repair. This change request will follow the project integration management approach. When the defect has been corrected and passed through quality control, it may then move back to scope validation for acceptance by the customer.

CERTIFICATION OBJECTIVE 5.06

Controlling the Scope

When it comes to project management, the one constant thing is change. Changes happen, or try to happen, all the time in projects. The project manager must have a reliable system to track, monitor, manage, and review changes to the project scope. Scope control focuses on three things:

- It facilitates scope changes to determine that changes are agreed upon.
- It determines whether a scope change has happened.
- It manages the scope changes when, and if, they happen.

Examining the Inputs to Scope Control

Throughout a project's life, the need and desire for change will come from project team members, the sponsor, management, customers, and other stakeholders. These change requests must be coupled with supporting evidence to determine the need of the change, the change's impact on the project scope (and usually on other processes as well), and the required planning, schedule, and budget to account for the changes.

 See the video "Change Control."

Using the Project Management Plan

The project management plan does offer some specific direction on how changes are allowed into the project. Although most project managers are resistant to changes in the project once the scope has been created and agreed upon, changes are sometimes valid. You'll rely on the change management plan as a general direction of the flow of decisions to determine whether a change is valid for your project. This assumes, of course, that you, the project manager, have control over change management decisions.

You'll also rely on the configuration management plan to determine how change is allowed specifically to the product scope. Configuration management is the control and documentation of the features and functions of the project's product. It's important for you to communicate the impact of change on the product to all the stakeholders as part of the change control review.

A project document that you'll reference in scope control is the performance measurement baseline. The results of earned value management, which I'll discuss in Chapter 7, are compared against what was planned to show how well the project is performing overall. This information can help determine whether corrective or preventive actions or a scope change is required to rectify problems within the project.

Finally, you'll rely on your favorite project management tool, the scope baseline. The scope baseline represents the sum of the components and ultimately the project work that makes up the project scope. The change requests may be for additional components in the project deliverables, changes to product attributes, or changes to different procedures to create the product. The WBS and WBS dictionary are referenced to determine which work packages would be affected by the change and which may be added or removed because of the change.

Relying on the Scope Management Plan

Remember this plan mentioned earlier in the chapter? It's an output of scope planning and controls how the project scope can be changed. The scope management plan also defines the likelihood of the scope to change, how often the scope may change, and how much it may change. You don't have to be a mind reader to determine how often the project scope may change and by how much; you just must rely on your level of confidence in the scope, the variables within the project, and the conditions under which the project must operate. The scope management plan also details the process of how changes to the project scope will be documented and classified throughout the project life cycle.

Referencing the Requirements Management Plan and Documentation

The requirements management plan, the requirements traceability matrix, and the actual requirements documentation are inputs to the control scope process. The requirements management plan defines how changes to the requirements are allowed and how they're to be managed. The actual requirements documentation is also needed, because it contains the specific elements that the scope change may be affecting. You'll use the requirements traceability matrix to see how a change in the requirements may directly affect other requirements in the project.

Considering the Change Management Plan

Some project managers despise change requests. Change requests can mean additional work, adjustments to the project, or a reduction in scope. They mean additional planning for the project manager and time for consideration, and they can be seen as a distraction from the project execution and control. Change requests can address preventive actions, corrective actions, defect repair, or scope enhancements. Change requests are an expected part of project management.

Why do change requests happen? Which ones are most likely to be approved? Most change requests are a result of the following:

- **Value-added events**   The change will reduce costs (often due to technological advances since the time the project scope was created).
- **External events**   These could be things such as new laws or industry requirements.
- **Errors or omissions**   Ever hear this one: "Oops! We forgot to include this feature in the product description and WBS!" Errors and omissions can happen both to the project scope (the work to complete the project) and the product scope and typically constitute an overlooked feature or requirement.
- **Risk response**   A risk has been identified and changes to the scope are needed to mitigate the risk.

w a t c h   Change requests are more than just changes to the project scope. They include preventive action, corrective action, and defect repairs.

e x a m

The *PMBOK Guide* lists only one tool and technique for controlling the project scope: data analysis. Data analysis includes variance analysis and trend analysis. This is really a broad approach to controlling the scope, because variance analysis addresses the difference between the planned scope baseline and what was experienced. Trend analysis identifies trends that maybe causing correct actions and defect repairs to enter the project. Corrective or preventive actions may be needed to correct project variances.

Considering the Results of Controlling Scope

Work performance information is an output of the control scope process. Work performance data is an input to scope change control; the contents of work performance data—the actual measurements of the project—are evaluated to determine what the needed changes may be, which will be an output of control scope as work performance information. The information is not meant to expose variances as much as it's meant to drive root-cause analyses of the variances. Project variances happen for a reason: the correct actions required to eliminate the variances may require changes to the project scope.

There is a distinct difference between work performance information and performance measurement, as shown in Table 5-1.

Creating More Change Requests

It sounds funny, but it's not: controlling scope can create more change requests. More change requests will mean more planning, and you know that planning is iterative. As change requests are presented, evidence of change exists, or corrective actions are needed within the project, the project manager and the project team will need to revisit the integrated change control process. Change within the project may require alternative

TABLE 5-1	Performance Information	Performance Measurement
Performance Reports vs. Performance Measurement	Signals an inconsistency	Evaluates the degree of inconsistency
	Makes analyzed data useable	Defines expected and experienced performance levels
	Serves as an output of the control scope process	Measures current performance against what was planned

identification, study of the change impact, analysis of risks introduced by the change, and solutions to problems within the project execution. Changes made as part of this planning could cause the project plan, WBS, and baselines to be revised.

Often, the reasons for change include faulty deliverables, quality problems, or poor performance of the project deliverables. Corrective actions are activities that will make an effort to bring the project back in line with the project plan. Errors and omissions in the product specifications are scope changes, not corrective action changes.

Updating the Project Management Plan

Changes to the project management plan will also go through the project's integrated change control process. This includes changes to the scope management, scope baseline, schedule baseline, cost baseline, and the performance measurement baseline. The change management plan within the project management plan and governance will determine how significant of a change to the project management plan will require a change request and the formal change control.

When changes to the project scope have been approved, the documented project scope must be updated to reflect these new changes. The stakeholders affected by the scope changes must be notified. The WBS must also be updated to reflect the components added or removed from the project. Scope changes can include cost updates, schedule updates, quality updates, or changes to the project deliverables.

When the project scope is to be changed, the new requirements must pass through the planning processes. The changes must be evaluated for cost and schedule estimates, risk, work considerations, product specification, and technical specification.

Updating Project Documents

The lessons-learned documentation should be updated as an output of scope change control. The project manager should document reasons why changes were approved, corrective actions were taken, and components were added or removed from the scope, and she should also document the reasoning behind these decisions. Lessons learned will serve as future historical information to help guide other project managers.

When changes are made, the project baselines will need to be adjusted to reflect these changes. Such changes can affect cost, schedule, and scope. The changes that affect the appropriate baseline should be updated to reflect the new project scope. The new baselines serve as a point of reference for the remainder of the project (assuming there are no additional changes). Should other changes occur, the baseline should be updated, enabling the project to continue. Scope changes will cause the requirements documentation and the requirements traceability matrix to be updated to reflect the new set of project requirements.

CERTIFICATION SUMMARY

Projects exist to satisfy the project requirements. Project requirements are discovered through interviews, focus groups, workshops, and other elicitation techniques to help the stakeholders and the project team clearly understand what the project should create. The requirements documentation, the requirements management plan, and a requirements traceability matrix all help the project stay focused on expected deliverables and serve as input to the project scope. A business analyst may lead the requirements collection process along with a project manager, or even before the project manager is selected and the project initiated.

Project scope management is the ability to complete all the project's required work—and only the required work. This means no extras, no favors, and no cutting corners. The project scope is the focus of the project—or rather, the work necessary to complete the project. Project scope management is a tool the project manager uses to determine what work is necessary in the project and what work is extraneous.

Projects big or small fit within the confines of the performing operation's strategic plans. Projects don't meander, at least not often, outside of the business focus of the organization. You won't find too many car manufacturers creating projects to make chocolate pies. Projects fit within the vision and function of the organization within which they operate.

Determining the project scope takes plenty of scope planning. The project manager and the project team must have a clear vision of the project, the business need for the project, the requirements, and the stakeholder expectations for the project. The result of the scope planning processes is the scope statement. The scope statement says, in no uncertain terms, what is included in the project and what is excluded.

For your PMP exam, focus on protecting the project scope. This includes finding the real purpose of the project so the scope is in alignment with identified needs. Once the scope has been created, the project team, the stakeholders, the project sponsor, and even the project manager should not change the scope—unless there is overwhelming evidence of why the scope needs to be changed.

KEY TERMS

To pass the PMP exam, you'll need to memorize these terms and their definitions. For maximum value, create your own flashcards based on these definitions and review them daily. The definitions can be found within this chapter and in the glossary.

affinity diagram   Clusters similar ideas together and allows for decomposition of ideas to compare and contrast project requirements.

brainstorming   People generating as many ideas a possible and then analyzing the ideas.

business analyst   Organizational role that is responsible for eliciting requirements from stakeholders and analyzing the requirements to predict feasibility, likelihood of project success, and estimated time and costs to create the requirements.

business requirements   Why the project has been initiated and what the high-level expectations are for the project deliverables and performance.

context diagram   A diagram that illustrates all of the components, called "actors," that interact with a project's solutions, such as systems, software, hardware, and people.

decomposition   The process of breaking down the major project deliverables into smaller, manageable components. The smallest item of the project's decomposition into the WBS is called the "work package."

Delphi Technique   A consensus-building group creativity technique that uses rounds of anonymous surveys during requirements elicitation. The Delphi Technique may also be used during risk assessment.

facilitated workshop   A collection of stakeholders from throughout the organization who come together to analyze, discuss, and determine the project requirements.

focus group   A conversation of stakeholders led by a moderator to elicit project requirements.

interview   Formal, direct discussion used in project integration management as part of the data gathering technique to create the project charter.

majority decision   A group decision process by which a vote is offered and the majority wins.

mind mapping   A visual representation of like and opposing ideas, thoughts, and project requirements.

multicriteria decision analysis   An approach that relies on a systematic method of determining, ranking, and eliminating project criteria such as performance metrics, risks, requirements, and other project elements.

nominal group technique   A group creativity technique that follows the brainstorming model but scores each brainstorm idea.

observation   A requirements elicitation process whereby an observer shadows a person to understand how the person completes a process. An observer may be a participant observer or an invisible observer.

plurality decision   A group decision process approach that allows the biggest section of a group to win even if a majority doesn't exist.

product scope   The attributes and characteristics of the deliverables the project is creating.

project scope statement   The definition of what the project will create for the project stakeholders. It includes the product scope description, product acceptance criteria, project deliverables, project exclusions, project assumptions, and project constraints.

prototype   A mockup of the project deliverable to confirm, adapt, or develop the project requirements.

quality requirements   Any condition, metric, performance objective, or condition the project must meet in order to be considered of quality.

requirements documentation   A clearly defined explanation of the project requirements. The requirements must be measurable, complete, accurate, and approved by the project stakeholders.

requirements management plan   Defines how requirements will be managed throughout the phases of the project. This plan also defines how any changes to the requirements will be allowed, documented, and tracked through project execution.

requirements traceability matrix   A table that helps the project team identify the characteristics and delivery of each requirement in the project scope.

scope baseline   Comprises the project scope statement, the work breakdown structure, and the WBS dictionary.

scope management plan   Explains how the project scope will be managed and how scope changes will be factored into the project plan. Based on the conditions of the project, the project work, and the confidence of the project scope, the scope management plan should also define the likelihood of changes to the scope, how often the scope may change, and how much the scope can change.

scope validation   An inspection-driven process led by the project customer to determine the exactness of the project deliverables. Scope validation is a process that leads to customer acceptance of the project deliverables.

stakeholder requirements   The individual stakeholder and stakeholder group requirements for the project.

systems engineering   Focuses on satisfying the customers' needs, cost requirements, and quality demands through the design and creation of the product. An entire science is devoted to systems engineering in various industries.

unanimity decision   A group decision process whereby all participants are in agreement.

value analysis   Like value engineering, this focuses on the cost/quality ratio of the product. Value analysis focuses on the expected quality against the acceptable cost.

value engineering   Deals with reducing costs and increasing profits, all while improving quality. Its focus is on solving problems, realizing opportunities, and maintaining quality improvement.

voice of the customer   The initial collection of customer requirements that serves as part of quality function deployment in a facilitated workshop.

work breakdown structure   A decomposition of the project scope statement into work packages. The WBS is an input to seven project management processes: developing the project management plan, defining the project activities, estimating the project costs, determining the project budget, planning the project quality, identifying the project risks, and planning the project procurement needs.

work breakdown structure dictionary   A companion to the WBS, this document defines all of the characteristics of each element of the WBS.

work breakdown structure templates   Based on historical information, this is a WBS from a past project that has been adapted to the current project.

TWO-MINUTE DRILL

Planning Project Scope Management

❑ The scope management plan communicates how the project scope will be managed and how scope changes will be allowed. It defines how the scope statement is created, how the WBS is created, the scope validation process, and the project's change control system.

❑ All change requests should be written and entered into the project's change control system. Changes to the project scope may affect all the project's knowledge areas: schedule, cost, quality, resources, communication, risk, procurement, and stakeholder management. The knowledge area of project integration management evaluates the project change and its impact on the entire project.

❑ Scope management is the process that follows the scope management plan. It ensures that the scope includes all the required work—and only the required work—to complete the project. It documents how changes may enter the scope and how frequently the scope is expected to change.

Collecting and Eliciting Project Requirements

❑ Collecting the project requirements is the process of eliciting the requirements from the project stakeholders so that the project manager and the project team may create the project deliverables. The project manager, the project team, and/or a business analyst elicit requirements from the stakeholders.

❑ Eight tools and techniques can be used to collect requirements: expert judgment, data gathering, data analysis, decision-making, data representation, interpersonal and team skills, context diagrams, and prototypes.

❑ A requirements traceability matrix is a table that maps all the project requirements; their characteristics, related data, and expected delivery dates; and any comments or notes about each requirement. The RTM helps the project manager, the project team, and the stakeholders confirm that all the requirements have been included in the project and have been created as expected.

Defining the Project Scope

❑ Progressive elaboration is the process of allowing the project scope to start broad, and then, through iterations of analysis, development, and refinement, making the project scope more specific.

❑ The project scope builds the product scope. If the project scope contains work that's not needed, the product scope has changed from what the project customer is expecting. The product scope and the project scope support each other.

❑ Projects move through product-oriented processes to create the project's product. These processes are typically marked by phases unique to the project work—for example, foundation, framing, roofing, finishing, and so on. Project management processes are the activities universal to all projects.

❑ There are two scopes: the project scope and the product scope. The project scope is the work to be completed to create the product. The product scope describes the features of the product and its characteristics.

❑ Project scope definition is concerned with what the project will include for the project stakeholders, but it's also concerned with what won't be included in the project. By establishing and communicating boundaries for the project, the project manager and the project team can focus on creating the agreed-upon project requirements.

Creating the Work Breakdown Structure

❑ The WBS is a deliverables-oriented decomposition of the project scope. It is not the activity list, but the predecessor to creating the activity list. The WBS reflects, in detail, the elements and components that contribute to the project scope.

❑ The smallest item in the WBS is called the "work package." The work package should follow the 8/80 rule, which means it should not take fewer than 8 hours and no more than 80 hours of labor to create the work package item. (Don't worry; this is just a heuristic. There may be small items that you want to account for in your WBS that don't follow this guideline.)

❑ A WBS dictionary is a reference tool that explains the WBS components, the nature of the work package, the assigned resources, and the schedule and billing estimates for each element. The WBS also identifies the relationship between work packages.

Validating the Project Scope

❑ At the end of the project or project phase—or even at major deliverables within the project—scope validation happens. Scope validation is the process of formally accepting the project work as defined in the product documentation, in the project scope, or in the contractual agreement, if relevant. Formal acceptance requires sign-off for acceptance of the product.

❑ Scope validation involves two techniques: decision and inspection. It's completed by the project stakeholders to determine whether the project has delivered on its promises. The goal of scope validation is for the project customer to sign off on the project deliverables.

Controlling the Project Scope

❑ By accurately defining the project scope, communicating how the scope will be managed, and then working with project stakeholders to control changes to the scope, the schedule and cost objectives are easier to maintain.

❑ Should a change occur to the project scope, configuration management must be enacted. Configuration management documents and controls changes to the features and function of the project's product. Configuration management strives for consistency between the project scope and the product scope.

❑ "Scope creep" is a loose term used to describe the small, seemingly innocent but unapproved changes the project team may allow into the project execution that can rob the project of time and costs. Scope creep can also be known as project poison.

SELF TEST

1. You are the project manager of the OQH Project and are working with the project stakeholders to determine the project requirements. You and the stakeholders are brainstorming privately to come up with as many solutions to the project as possible. After the brainstorming session, a recorder documents all the solutions on a white board so everyone can see the ideas and how they may be related. After the solutions have been documented, you lead the group through a voting process to discuss and rank each idea and requirement that has been proposed. What is this requirements gathering technique called?

   A. Brainstorming
   B. Nominal group technique
   C. Affinity diagram creations
   D. Mind mapping

2. You are the project manager for the HGD Project and will need as many inputs to the scope planning as possible. Mary, your project assistant, recommends that you use some of the organizational process assets to help with your project scope planning. Of the following, which one is *not* an organizational process asset?
   A. Organizational procedures
   B. Organizational policies
   C. WBS
   D. Historical information

3. You are a project manager for your organization. In your role as the lead project manager, you are required to cross-train and coach your project team members. Sarah, a project manager in training, wants to know which project documents can stem from templates? What should be your answer?
   A. Risk policies
   B. Organizational policies
   C. Scope management plans
   D. Historical information

4. You are the project manager for a technical project. The project product is the complete installation of a new operating system on 4500 workstations. You have, in your project cost and schedule estimates, told the customer that the estimates provided will be accurate if the workstations meet the hardware requirements of the new operating system. This is an example of which of the following?
   A. Risk
   B. Assumption
   C. Constraint
   D. Order of magnitude

5. You are the project manager for the NBG Project. The project is to develop new software that is supported on mobile devices. The project customer has defined a maximum budget, performance metrics, and other quality metrics for the project deliverable to be acceptable. One requirement of the project is that it must be completed within six months; this is an example of which of the following?
   A. Schedule
   B. Assumption
   C. Constraint
   D. Planning process

6. As a PMP candidate, you must be familiar with the project management terms. Sometimes the terms seem confusing, such as project scope statement, scope baseline, or even the scope control process. Which of the following best describes the project scope statement?

   A. The description of the project deliverables

   B. The authorizing document that allows the project manager to move forward with the project and to assign resources to the tasks

   C. A document that defines all the required work—and only the required work—to create the project's deliverables

   D. The process of planning and executing all the required work to deliver the project to the customer

7. During the planning phase of your project, your project team has discovered another method to complete a portion of the project scope. This method is safer for the project team, but it may cost more for the customer. This is an example of which of the following?

   A. Risk assessment

   B. Alternative identification

   C. Alternative selection

   D. Product analysis

8. You are the project manager of a large software development project. Hundreds of requirements need to be documented, annotated, and communicated to the project stakeholders. Management would also like you to report when the requirements should be created and when they're actually created by the project team. What document can help you monitor all the characteristics of each requirement?

   A. Project management plan

   B. Configuration management plan

   C. Requirements traceability matrix

   D. Communications management plan

9. You are the project manager for the JHN Project. Mike, a project manager you are mentoring, does not know which plan he should reference for guarding the project scope. Which plan does Mike need?

   A. The scope management plan

   B. The scope change control system

   C. The scope validation

   D. The scope charter

10. You are the project manager for the JKL Project. This project has more than 45 key stakeholders and will span the globe when implemented. Management has deemed that the project's completion should not cost more than $34 million. This is an example of which of the following?

    A. Internationalization

    B. Budget constraint

    C. Management constraint

    D. Hard logic

11. You are the project manager for your organization. Your project is to construct a new house for a client. You and the client have agreed to meet at the end of each phase of the project to walk through the house as it's being built to confirm the quality and accuracy of the build. You need to ensure that the customer formally accepts the deliverables of each project phase. This process is known as _____.
    A. Earned value management
    B. Scope validation
    C. Quality control
    D. Quality assurance

12. It's important to know what each project management process creates. For example, which of the following is an output of scope validation?
    A. WBS template
    B. Rework
    C. Formal acceptance
    D. SOW acceptance

13. Where can the project manager find work package information such as the code of an account identifier, a statement of work, information on the responsible organization, quality requirements, and information on the required resources? Choose the best answer.
    A. Execution plan
    B. WBS
    C. WBS dictionary
    D. Project management plan

14. You are a project manager for a large manufacturer. Your current project is to create a new manufacturing assembly line that will enable your organization to create its products with less downtime and faster turnaround time for its clients. A stakeholder has presented a change request for your project, which will likely increase the cost and time needed to complete the project. All the following components are *not* part of the change control system except for which one?
    A. Adding more team members to the project to get the project work done faster
    B. Outsourcing portions of the project execution to transfer risk
    C. Creating tracking systems for the proposed change
    D. Documenting the project and how the manufacturing assembly should work

15. A project team member has, on his own initiative, added extra vents to an attic to increase air circulation. The project plan did not call for these extra vents, but the team member decided they were needed based on the geographic location of the house. The project team's experts concur with this decision. This is an example of which of the following?
    A. Cost control
    B. Ineffective change control
    C. Self-led teams
    D. Value-added change

16. Which of the following is an output of scope control?
   A. Workarounds
   B. Recommended corrective action
   C. Transference
   D. Risk assessment

17. You are the project manager for the JHG Project. Your project is to create a new product for your industry. You have recently learned that your competitor is also working on a similar project, but their offering will include a computer-aided program and web-based tools, which your project does not offer. You have implemented a change request to update your project. This is an example of which of the following?
   A. A change due to an error or omission in the initiation phase
   B. A change due to an external event
   C. A change due to an error or omission in the planning phase
   D. A change due to a legal issue

18. You are the project manager for a pharmaceutical company. A new government regulation will change your project scope. For the project to move forward and be in accordance with the new regulation, what should be your next action?
   A. Prepare a new baseline to reflect the government changes.
   B. Notify management.
   C. Present the change to the CCB.
   D. Create a feasibility study.

19. Your project is to document all the computer systems in your company. Your project team was required to document the operating systems, the hardware, the network configuration, and the software on each computer. You have finished the project scope according to plan. For the customer to accept the project, what must happen next?
   A. Nothing. The plan is complete, so the project is complete.
   B. Scope validation should be conducted.
   C. Lessons learned should be finalized.
   D. Proof-of-concept should be implemented.

20. You are the project manager for an airplane manufacturer. Your project concerns the development of lighter, stronger material for commercial jets. As the project moves toward completion, different material composition is considered for the deliverable. This is an example of which of the following?
   A. Program management
   B. Alternatives identification
   C. Quality assurance
   D. Regulatory guidelines

21. You are the project manager of a large project. Your project sponsor and management have approved your outsourcing portions of the project plan. The _____ must document project scope management decisions.

   A. Project sponsor

   B. Organization's management

   C. Vendor(s)

   D. Project management team

22. A project team member has asked you what project scope management is. Which of the following is a characteristic of project scope management?

   A. It defines the baseline for project acceptance.

   B. It defines the requirements for each project within the organization.

   C. It defines the processes to ensure that the project includes all the work required—and only the work required—to complete the project successfully.

   D. It defines the functional managers assigned to the project.

23. One of the stakeholders of the project you are working with asks why you consider the scope statement so important in your project management methodology. You answer her question with which of the following?

   A. It is mandatory to consult the plan before authorizing any change.

   B. Project managers must document any changes before approving or declining them.

   C. The project scope statement serves as a reference for all change requests to determine if the change is in or out of scope.

   D. The project plan and EVM work together to assess the risk involved with proposed changes.

24. The project scope statement is decomposed into the work breakdown structure. The WBS then becomes an important part of the project for planning, execution, and control. A WBS serves as an input to many of the project processes. Of the following, which is *not* true?

   A. WBS serves as an input to activity sequencing.

   B. WBS serves as an input to activity definition.

   C. WBS serves as an input to risk identification.

   D. WBS serves as an input to cost budgeting.

25. You are the project manager of the WIFI Project. You would like to meet with a stakeholder for scope validation. Which of the following is typical of scope validation?

   A. Reviewing changes to the project scope with the stakeholders

   B. Reviewing the performance of the project deliverables

   C. Reviewing the performance of the project team to date

   D. Reviewing the EVM results of the project to date

SELF TEST ANSWERS

1. You are the project manager of the OQH Project and are working with the project stakeholders to determine the project requirements. You and the stakeholders are brainstorming privately to come up with as many solutions to the project as possible. After the brainstorming session, a recorder documents all the solutions on a white board so everyone can see the ideas and how they may be related. After the solutions have been documented, you lead the group through a voting process to discuss and rank each idea and requirement that has been proposed. What is this requirement gathering technique called?
   A. Brainstorming
   B. Nominal group technique
   C. Affinity diagram creations
   D. Mind mapping

   ☑ **B.** This is an example of the nominal group technique, in which you ask for as many ideas and solutions as possible, and then the group ranks the concepts to help guide the requirements development.
   ☒ **A, C,** and **D** are incorrect. **A** is incorrect because brainstorming is similar to this concept, but it does not include the ranking of the concepts identified. **C** is incorrect because affinity diagrams cluster ideas into similar groups for further analysis. **D** is incorrect because mind mapping shows the relationship between ideas but it does not rank them.

2. You are the project manager for the HGD Project and will need as many inputs to the scope planning as possible. Mary, your project assistant, recommends that you use some of the organizational process assets to help with your project scope planning. Of the following, which one is *not* an organizational process asset?
   A. Organizational procedures
   B. Organizational policies
   C. WBS
   D. Historical information

   ☑ **C.** The WBS is not an organizational process asset.
   ☒ **A, B,** and **D** are incorrect. These responses are examples of organizational process assets.

3. You are a project manager for your organization. In your role as the project manager, you are required to cross-train and coach your project team members. Sarah, a project manager in training, wants to know which project documents can stem from templates? What should be your answer?
   A. Risk policies
   B. Organizational policies
   C. Scope management plans
   D. Historical information

   ☑ **C.** Scope management plans can be based on templates. For the record, so can the WBS and project scope change control forms.
   ☒ **A, B,** and **D** are incorrect. These documents do not stem from templates.

4. You are the project manager for a technical project. The project product is the complete installation of a new operating system on 4500 workstations. You have, in your project cost and schedule estimates, told the customer that the estimates provided will be accurate if the workstations meet the hardware requirements of the new operating system. This is an example of which of the following?
   A. Risk
   B. Assumption
   C. Constraint
   D. Order of magnitude

   ☑ **B.** This is an example of an assumption, since the workstations must meet the hardware requirements.
   ☒ **A, C,** and **D** are incorrect. **A** and **C** are incorrect because the scenario did not describe a risk or constraint. **D** is incorrect because the order of magnitude refers to the level of confidence in an estimate.

5. You are the project manager for the NBG Project. The project is to develop new software that is supported on mobile devices. The project customer has defined a maximum budget, performance metrics, and other quality metrics for the project deliverable to be acceptable. One requirement of the project is that it must be completed within six months; this is an example of which of the following?
   A. Schedule
   B. Assumption
   C. Constraint
   D. Planning process

☑ **C.** A project that must be completed by a deadline is dealing with schedule constraints.

☒ **A, B,** and **D** are incorrect. **A** is incorrect because the condition does not offer a schedule, but includes a "must finish no later than" constraint. **B** is incorrect because the condition is not an assumption. **D** is incorrect because this is not a planning process.

6. As a PMP candidate you must be familiar with the project management terms. Sometimes the terms seem confusing, such as project scope statement, scope baseline, or even the scope control process. Which of the following best describes the project scope statement?
    A. The description of the project deliverables
    B. The authorizing document that allows the project manager to move forward with the project and to assign resources to the tasks
    C. A document that defines all the required work—and only the required work—to create the project's deliverables
    D. The process of planning and executing all the required work to deliver the project to the customer

☑ **C.** A project scope statement focuses on defining all the required work, and only the required work, to create the project's deliverables.

☒ **A, B,** and **D** are incorrect. **A** is a product description, not a scope. **B** is incorrect because this choice describes the charter. **D** is incorrect because it does not define the project scope as completely as choice C.

7. During the planning phase of your project, your project team has discovered another method to complete a portion of the project scope. This method is safer for the project team, but it may cost more for the customer. This is an example of which of the following?
    A. Risk assessment
    B. Alternative identification
    C. Alternative selection
    D. Product analysis

☑ **B.** Alternative identification is a planning process to find alternatives to completing the project scope.

☒ **A, C,** and **D** are incorrect. **A** is incorrect because this is not a risk assessment activity. **C** is incorrect because the team has identified the alternative but has not selected it. **D** is incorrect because this is not product analysis.

8. You are the project manager of a large software development project. Hundreds of requirements need to be documented, annotated, and communicated to the project stakeholders. Management would also like you to report when the requirements should be created and when they're actually created by the project team. What document can help you monitor all the characteristics of each requirement?

   A. Project management plan
   B. Configuration management plan
   C. Requirements traceability matrix
   D. Project communications management plan

   ☑ **C.** The requirements traceability matrix can help the project manager track and monitor all the characteristics of each project requirement. It helps to communicate the requirement's status and completion, and it records any notes or comments about each requirement.
   ☒ **A, B,** and **D** are incorrect. **A,** the project management plan, does define how all the components of the project will be planned, executed, and monitored, but it does not answer the question as completely as choice C. **B,** the configuration management plan, defines how changes to the product scope will be allowed, controlled, and documented. **D,** the communications management plan, defines who needs what information, when the information is needed, and the expected modality.

9. You are the project manager for the JHN Project. Mike, a project manager you are mentoring, does not know which plan he should reference for guarding the project scope. Which plan does Mike need?

   A. The scope management plan
   B. The scope change control system
   C. The scope validation
   D. The scope charter

   ☑ **A.** The scope management plan provides details about how the project scope may be changed.
   ☒ **B, C,** and **D** are incorrect. **B** is not a valid choice, because the scope change control system is part of the project's integrated change control. **C** is incorrect because scope validation is the process of formally accepting the product. **D** is incorrect because the charter does not define how changes to the project may happen.

10. You are the project manager for the JKL Project. This project has more than 45 key stakeholders and will span the globe when implemented. Management has deemed that the project's completion should not cost more than $34 million. This is an example of which of the following?

    A. Internationalization
    B. Budget constraint
    C. Management constraint
    D. Hard logic

☑ **B.** This is an example of a budget constraint. The budget must not exceed $34 million. In addition, the metric for the values to be in U.S. dollars can affect the budget if most of the product is to be purchased in a foreign country.

☒ **A, C,** and **D** are incorrect. **A** is incorrect because this does not define a constraint. Internationalization focuses on time zones, languages, cultural differences, and so on. **C** is incorrect because a management constraint describes a management decision such as resources, risk policies, or control over the project budget. **D** is also incorrect, because hard logic describes the most logical or required method for events or conditions to happen.

11. You are the project manager for your organization. Your project is to construct a new house for a client. You and the client have agreed to meet at the end of each phase of the project to walk through the house as it's being built to confirm the quality and accuracy of the build. You need to ensure that the customer formally accepts the deliverables of each project phase. This process is known as _____.

  A. Earned value management
  B. Scope validation
  C. Quality control
  D. Quality assurance

☑ **B.** Scope validation is the process of formally accepting the deliverable of a project or phase.

☒ **A, C,** and **D** are incorrect. **A** is incorrect because earned value management measures project performance. **C** is incorrect because quality control is concerned with the correctness of the work, not the acceptance of the work. **D,** quality assurance, is incorrect because this describes the quality program for the organization as a whole.

12. It's important to know what each project management process creates. For example, which of the following is an output of scope validation?

  A. WBS template
  B. Rework
  C. Formal acceptance
  D. SOW acceptance

☑ **C.** Scope validation results in one thing: formal acceptance.

☒ **A, B,** and **D** are incorrect. **A** is incorrect because WBS templates come from past projects or the PMO. **B** is incorrect because rework does not come from validation. **D** is incorrect because SOW (statement of work) acceptance is not the best choice.

13. Where can the project manager find work package information such as the code of an account identifier, a statement of work, information on the responsible organization, quality requirements, and information on the required resources? Choose the best answer.
    A. Execution plan
    B. WBS
    C. WBS dictionary
    D. Project management plan

    ☑ **C.** The WBS dictionary provides all this information—along with information on milestones and contract information—and then cross-references each work package with related work package information.
    ☒ **A, B,** and **D** are incorrect. **A,** the execution plan, is technically not an accurate term for the project management plan. This also does not define the question as accurately as the WBS dictionary. **B,** the WBS, is incorrect because the WBS does not define the work to the extent the WBS dictionary does. **D** is incorrect because the project management plan communicates the project intent. The subsidiary plans, which are part of the project management plan, communicate information on specific knowledge areas.

14. You are a project manager for a large manufacturer. Your current project is to create a new manufacturing assembly line that will enable your organization to create its products with less downtime and faster turnaround time for its clients. A stakeholder has presented a change request for your project, which will likely increase the cost and time needed to complete the project. All the following components are not *part* of the change control system except for which one?
    A. Adding more team members to the project to get the project work done faster
    B. Outsourcing portions of the project execution to transfer risk
    C. Creating tracking systems for the proposed change
    D. Documenting the project and how the manufacturing assembly should work

    ☑ **C.** The only answer that describes a component of the change control system is the tracking system for the proposed change.
    ☒ **A, B,** and **D** are incorrect. **A** is incorrect because this describes crashing and is not part of the change control system. **B** is incorrect because transference is not a value-added change and is not part of the change control system. **D** is incorrect because this process should be part of the product description already included in the project management plan and is not part of the change control system.

15. A project team member has, on his own initiative, added extra vents to an attic to increase air circulation. The project plan did not call for these extra vents, but the team member decided they were needed based on the geographic location of the house. The project team's experts concur with this decision. This is an example of which of the following?

A. Cost control
B. Ineffective change control
C. Self-led teams
D. Value-added change

☑ **B.** The project team member did not follow the change management plan's method of incorporating changes into the scope.

☒ **A, C,** and **D** are incorrect. **A** is incorrect because this scenario describes change control, although the decision may lead to additional expenses. **C** is incorrect because self-led teams are not described in this scenario. **D** is also incorrect, because the added vents do not apparently reduce cost in this example.

16. Which of the following is an output of scope control?
A. Workarounds
B. Recommended corrective action
C. Transference
D. Risk assessment

☑ **B.** Recommended corrective actions, which are change requests, are outputs of change control. Poor performance leads to corrective actions to bring the project back in alignment with the project management plan. Recall that a corrective action is a change request.

☒ **A, C,** and **D** are incorrect. **A** is incorrect because a workaround is a reaction to an identified risk or issue. **C** and **D** are incorrect because transference is the process of transferring the risk, and risk assessment is the process of identifying and analyzing risk within the project or phase.

17. You are the project manager for the JHG Project. Your project is to create a new product for your industry. You have recently learned that your competitor is also working on a similar project, but their offering will include a computer-aided program and web-based tools, which your project does not offer. You have implemented a change request to update your project. This is an example of which of the following?
A. A change due to an error or omission in the initiation phase
B. A change due to an external event
C. A change due to an error or omission in the planning phase
D. A change due to a legal issue

☑ **B.** The change is requested to remain competitive with the competition—an external event. Change is inevitable and requires a change control process to manage.

☒ **A, C,** and **D** are incorrect. These choices are based on the conditions of the change request.

18. You are the project manager for a pharmaceutical company. A new government regulation will change your project scope. For the project to move forward and be in accordance with the new regulation, what should be your next action?
    A. Prepare a new baseline to reflect the government changes.
    B. Notify management.
    C. Present the change to the CCB.
    D. Create a feasibility study.

    ☑ **C.** Presenting the change to the change control board is the best choice.
    ☒ **A, B,** and **D** are incorrect. **A** is incorrect because the change has not been approved—the project could be stopped based on the required change. **B** is tempting, but it is incorrect for two primary reasons: The project manager should never contact management with a problem, and no solution is offered for the problem. It is also incorrect because **C** more fully answers the question, since management is likely part of the group of appropriate stakeholders. **D** is incorrect because a feasibility study is not appropriate for the conditions surrounding the change.

19. Your project is to document all the computer systems in your company. Your project team was required to document the operating systems, the hardware, the network configuration, and the software on each computer. You have finished the project scope according to plan. For the customer to accept the project, what must happen next?
    A. Nothing. The plan is complete, so the project is complete.
    B. Scope validation should be conducted.
    C. Lessons learned should be finalized.
    D. Proof-of-concept should be implemented.

    ☑ **B.** Scope validation concerns itself with the formal acceptance of the product.
    ☒ **A, C,** and **D** are incorrect. **A** is incorrect because acceptance must happen for closure. **C** is incorrect—lessons learned do not close out the project. **D** is incorrect because it is not relevant to the issue.

20. You are the project manager for an airplane manufacturer. Your project concerns the development of lighter, stronger material for commercial jets. As the project moves toward completion, different material composition is considered for the deliverable. This is an example of which of the following?
    A. Program management
    B. Alternatives identification
    C. Quality assurance
    D. Regulatory guidelines

    ☑ **B.** Alternatives identification is the technique to consider different approaches, materials, and solutions for the project work.
    ☒ **A, C,** and **D** are incorrect. **A** is incorrect because program management is not relevant. **C** is incorrect because QA describes the quality assessment system of an organization. **D** is incorrect because regulatory guidelines do not refine the project scope.

21. You are the project manager of a large project. Your project sponsor and management have approved your outsourcing portions of the project plan. The _____ must document project scope management decisions.
   A. Project sponsor
   B. Organization's management
   C. Vendor(s)
   D. Project management team

   ☑ **D.** The responsibility to document project scope management decisions rests with the project management team.
   ☒ **A, B,** and **C** are incorrect. These stakeholders do not have the responsibility of the project manager in this scenario.

22. A project team member has asked you what project scope management is. Which of the following is a characteristic of project scope management?
   A. It defines the baseline for project acceptance.
   B. It defines the requirements for each project within the organization.
   C. It defines the processes to ensure that the project includes all the work required—and only the work required—to complete the project successfully.
   D. It defines the functional managers assigned to the project.

   ☑ **C.** Project scope management defines the processes to ensure that the project includes all the work required—and only the work required—to complete the project successfully.
   ☒ **A, B,** and **D** are incorrect. **A** is incorrect because the scope statement document will provide information on the project product acceptance. **B** is incorrect because project scope management does not address all projects within an organization. **D** is incorrect because functional managers are not addressed in project scope management.

23. One of the stakeholders of the project you are working with asks why you consider the scope statement so important in your project management methodology. You answer her question with which of the following?
   A. It is mandatory to consult the plan before authorizing any change.
   B. Project managers must document any changes before approving or declining them.
   C. The project scope statement serves as a reference for all change requests to determine if the change is in or out of scope.
   D. The project plan and EVM work together to assess the risk involved with proposed changes.

   ☑ **C.** The scope statement serves as a point of reference when considering whether change requests are in or out of scope.
   ☒ **A, B,** and **D** are incorrect. **A** is incorrect because it is too vague. **B** is incorrect because some changes may come orally and be declined immediately based on historical information or other factors. **D** is incorrect because EVM is not an issue in this scenario.

24. The project scope statement is decomposed into the work breakdown structure. The WBS then becomes an important part of the project for planning, execution, and control. A WBS serves as an input to many of the project processes. Of the following, which is *not* true?

    A. WBS serves as an input to activity sequencing.
    B. WBS serves as an input to activity definition.
    C. WBS serves as an input to risk identification.
    D. WBS serves as an input to cost budgeting.

    ☑ **A.** The WBS does not directly serve as an input to activity sequencing.
    ☒ **B, C,** and **D** are incorrect. The WBS does serve as an input to these processes. Incidentally, the WBS is needed for developing the project management plan, defining the project activities, estimating the project costs, determining the project budget, identifying the project risks, performing qualitative risk analysis, and validating the project scope.

25. You are the project manager of the WIFI Project. You would like to meet with a stakeholder for scope validation. Which of the following is typical of scope validation?

    A. Reviewing changes to the project scope with the stakeholders
    B. Reviewing the performance of the project deliverables
    C. Reviewing the performance of the project team to date
    D. Reviewing the EVM results of the project to date

    ☑ **B.** When it comes to scope validation, the customer is concerned with the performance of the product.
    ☒ **A, C,** and **D** are incorrect. **A** may seem correct, but the stakeholder should already know about the changes prior to scope validation. **C** and **D** are incorrect because these reviews are not relevant to scope validation.

Chapter 6

Introducing Project Schedule Management

CERTIFICATION OBJECTIVES

6.01   Creating the Schedule Management Plan

6.02   Defining the Activities

6.03   Sequencing Activities

6.04   Estimating Activity Durations

6.05   Developing the Schedule

6.06   Controlling the Schedule

✓   Two-Minute Drill

Q&A   Self Test

H ere's an old joke about project management schedules: "The first 90 percent of a project schedule takes 90 percent of the time. The last 10 percent takes the other 90 percent of the time."

And isn't that the way it goes? You always hope it won't be like this, but far too often that's precisely what happens. Projects, especially projects that are running behind schedule, fail at the beginning, not at the end. The importance of planning a project is never more evident than when you rush to reach completion. The final actions to complete a project are dependent on the plans and motivations set early on during the project planning processes.

Schedule management is an essential element on the PMP exam. You'll need a solid understanding of the activities and methods required to predict and account for project time. Schedule management is crucial not only to passing the PMP exam, but also to managing projects successfully.

Exploring Project Schedule Management

Project schedule management used to be called "time management" in the *PMBOK Guide*. Time management, however, implies more of a personal management of how you spend your time, and you can't you really manage and manipulate time like you can manage a schedule. Schedule management in project management is about completing the work of the project scope within a predicted amount of time. Lots of things affect the schedule and the project's duration, and it's the project manager's role, or the role of an expert scheduler, to predict how long the project should take based on what the scope requires. This is tricky business, but fortunately, on your PMP exam the questions won't have time or space to consider every nuanced situation, but it will test your understanding of the generally accepted principles of schedule management within a project.

To pass this portion of your exam, you'll need to be familiar with the six processes of schedule management:

- Create the schedule management plan.
- Define the activities.
- Sequence the activities.
- Estimate the activities duration.
- Develop the schedule.
- Control the schedule.

These six processes are very logical: plan how you'll manage the schedule, define the work to be scheduled, sequence the activities, predict durations, massage the schedule, and control the schedule. I'll follow this same approach to the six processes throughout this chapter. There's a lot of information to cover in this chapter, but I'm confident that you can get it done.

Tailoring Project Schedule Management

Like all knowledge areas, project schedule management can be tailored to fit any organization's needs. The uniqueness of each organization and each project means that there's no one-size-fits-all approach to schedule management. For starters, the project manager will consider the size of the project and the chosen life cycle approach. Larger projects generally require a more detailed schedule because there's more work to coordinate with the project team, vendors, and stakeholders. This means more planning and communication.

You'll also have to consider the organizational structure. Matrix structures require more coordination with the resources you'll utilize on the project. Project managers also need to consider physical resources in the schedule: materials, equipment, and facilities that will require thought and logistics to make certain these resources are available when the project team needs them. It's a disappointment when human resources are available to do the work, but someone has forgotten to schedule the equipment, order materials, or ensure that other resources are available.

All projects will require some level of control. Complex projects need certainty in the schedule so everyone knows what's in motion, what's pending, and when activities should occur within the project. You'll track the progress of the project through approaches such as earned value management, burnup or burndown charts based on percent complete, and perhaps red/yellow/green markers to show how activities are moving in the project. Whatever approach you take, you'll document it in the schedule management plan and communicate the approach with the project team. Finally, it's unlikely that you'll do all this scheduling work with a pencil. Your favorite project management information system will likely help you plan and control the project schedule—but no software can take the place of a human project manager.

Considerations for Agile and Adaptive Environments

Projects embrace either the critical path method or the agile method when it comes to project scheduling. I'll discuss the critical path in this chapter. On the agile side, you should be familiar with two emerging approaches to schedule management for your PMP exam: *iterative scheduling with a backlog* and *on-demand scheduling*.

Iterative scheduling uses a rolling wave planning method and a backlog of requirements in an agile environment. The backlog of requirements, called *user stories*, are prioritized at the start of each iteration. The team determines how many user stories they can develop, and then the iteration begins.

On-demand scheduling also uses a backlog of requirements, but as resources become available in the project, the next requirement is launched. This pull-based approach to scheduling stems from lean manufacturing and is used with a Kanban system. *Kanban* is

Japanese for visual sign or card—as a "sign board" is used to show what's being worked on (called the work in progress, or WIP), how many requirements are completed, and how many requirements remain to be worked on. The Kanban board is a table that shows all the requirements and phases until "done" is reached in a work process. For example, you'd start with requirements on the left, and then design, develop, test, deploy, and done (or other phases, as appropriate to your project). You'd pull the requirements from left to right as the project moves through the phases of production. Figure 6-1 shows a simple Kanban board for a video project.

Agile approaches use shorter increments of project work versus longer phases you might enjoy in a predictive environment.

Although the flexible nature of agile is great, there are caveats to scheduling work and prioritizing requirements with the project team. The first few iterations in an agile environment can help the team establish a user-story baseline of what's feasible to accomplish in each iteration. Though the PMP exam is likely to have a few questions on agile and adaptive environments, these are unique approaches to project management that require the project manager and the project team to understand fully the flow of the work and expectations of the methodology.

FIGURE 6-1

Kanban boards show work in progress and completed requirements.

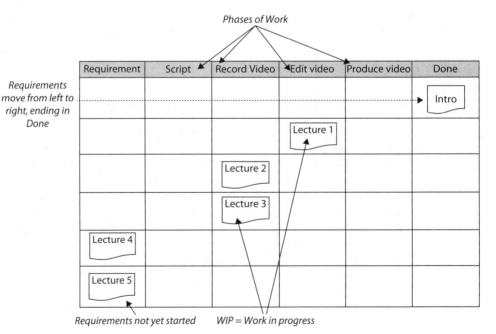

CERTIFICATION OBJECTIVE 6.01

Creating the Schedule Management Plan

As soon as you initiate the project, stakeholders will want to know when the project will be completed. On some projects, you, the project team, and experts will have to dig into the project scope, the work breakdown structure (WBS), and the technical details of the project to determine how long the project will take to complete. On other projects, you won't have that luxury, as customers, management, and other stakeholders will have already created a deadline—a constraint—for the project. The process of creating the schedule management plan defines how the schedule will be created and includes the type of work to be completed, the resources, and other attributes to predict when the project will be completed. Creating the schedule management plan can happen once in a project, but it will likely be an iterative process based on the conditions within the project.

Two of the biggest factors in this process are the organizational process assets and enterprise environmental factors. If your organization is completing the same types of projects over and over, chances are that you and the key stakeholders will already have a rough estimate of how long the project will take. If the project work is unique and new, then more uncertainties and assumptions are made about the duration of the project, which means the estimates could be unreliable because you don't know what you don't know. Enterprise environmental factors can also affect the schedule management plan, as the organizational culture, limits on working hours, resource heuristics, work authorization systems, and other policies can directly influence how the schedule is planned and maintained.

Other inputs include the project charter, because it includes the summary milestone schedule to help you better plan the work and when the project will take place. You'll also rely on the project management plan as an input to this process. Specifically, the scope management plan defines how the work will be determined and decomposed for scheduling. Also in the project management plan is the development approach for the project, which addresses how you'll schedule the work in your organization, how the work will be estimated for duration, and what scheduling tools and techniques you'll be required to use in the project.

Building the Schedule Management Plan

Imagine you're a new project manager in your company and you've just been assigned a new project. One of your first tasks, assuming the project scope is defined, is to create a project schedule. It's time to gather experts for a meeting to explore the project scope and understand the work it'll take to make the scope a reality. You'll also have to know the constraints of the work environment, who will be on your project team, the skill sets of the project team members, whether the project team is full-time or part-time, what time constraints exist (such as procurement details and working hours), bottlenecks within the work authorization system, and lots of other bits of information to help you predict how long the project will take to complete.

The schedule management plan is the foundation for all the activities that you, as a project manager, would undertake to create a schedule. The *PMBOK Guide*, in predictive environments, advises that you first create a schedule management plan for most projects, and then you can get into the gory details of creating duration estimates and a schedule for the project. To build the schedule management plan, you might rely on organizational process assets and just adapt a plan from a previous, similar project—nothing wrong with that. Or, if you must create a schedule management plan from scratch, you'll use just three tools and techniques:

- **Expert judgment** Involve people who are closest to the project work and who know the organization and how the work may proceed. Experts can help with schedule development, methodologies, software, and scheduling concerns specific to your industry.
- **Data analysis techniques** Decisions are made about the project approach, how the work will be scheduled, duration compression techniques, modeling approaches, analytical techniques, and software that can help create and control the project schedule.
- **Meetings** You'll attend lots of meetings regarding project management. Schedule management meetings bring the key stakeholders together to discuss the development and the contents of the schedule management plan.

Exploring the Schedule Management Plan

One of the goals of the schedule management plan is to define how the other processes in this knowledge area are performed. The schedule management plan considers the scope baseline, the project, organizational process assets, and the enterprise environmental factors, which enable the experts to create the content of the plan. The schedule management plan is part of the comprehensive project management plan, and it defines the following:

- **Model for schedule development** This includes the methodology for creating the schedule and any tools that will be used to facilitate the schedule development.
- **Release and iteration length** If you're using an adaptive life cycle, you'll have segments of work iterations. These time-boxed durations are defined as part of the project approach, and they help control scope creep as the project team focuses on only the selected user stories for the current iteration of the project.
- **Level of accuracy** More information translates into a more accurate schedule. This component of the plan allows for a range of variance based on the project information, the size of the project, contingency for delays, and the demand for an accurate schedule.

- **Units of measure** This defines how the schedule will measure time (hours, days, weeks, or other units).
- **Organizational procedures links** These connect the schedule management to the components of the work breakdown structure for consistency.
- **Project schedule model maintenance** This defines how the schedule model will be updated based on work performed, work in progress, and work remaining in the project.
- **Control thresholds** These are predefined ranges of variances for tasks, milestones, and project completion, such as +/– 10 percent.
- **Rules of performance measurement** These metrics will be used to measure the project performance regarding schedule. The most common approach is earned value management (EVM).
- **Reporting formats** These techniques, forms, templates, and metrics are used for reporting the completion of tasks.
- **Process descriptions** The schedule management plan defines the processes addressed in this knowledge area (activity definition, activity sequencing, activity resource estimating, activity duration estimating, schedule development, and schedule control).

Planning, as you know, is an iterative activity in the project. As more information becomes available, you and the project team can revise the schedule management plan and the other processes in this knowledge area. For example, the project scope may be defined in high-level objectives, so the schedule estimate is also provided at a high level. As the project scope is more clearly defined, the WBS is created, and the activity list is generated, the duration estimate can become more accurate as well. This is an example of progressive elaboration and a good example of the iterative nature of project planning.

CERTIFICATION OBJECTIVE 6.02

Defining the Activities

Projects are temporary undertakings that create a unique product or service. The idea of time is inherent to the very definition of a project, in that all projects are temporary. Even though they might seem to last forever, sooner or later they must end. Adequate planning of the temporary project can predict when a project will end. Within this short and limited time, the project manager must create something: a product, a result, or a service. The creation is about change—and change, as you may know, takes time.

Creation of the product, result, or service comes about when the work the project team completes. The sum of the durations of the work equates to when the project is completed.

In addition to the duration of activities, other factors of time must be considered, such as the following:

- Project management activities
- Planning processes
- The sequence of activities
- Procurement of resources
- Reliance on internal and external events
- Known and unknown events affecting the project

Project schedule management is based predominantly on planning, but it is also about control and execution. Planning for project schedules may stem from deadlines, customer demands, hard and soft logic, and a bit of prediction. You'll use the schedule management plan, the scope baseline, enterprise environmental factors, and organizational process assets as inputs to this process.

Getting to Work: Defining the Activities

The activity list is an output of activity definition that includes all the activities to be performed within the project. The list must be in line with the project scope. Remember the project scope? It's a description of all the required work, and only the required work, to complete the project. In a sense, the activity list is a further definition of the project scope, because it includes only those actions needed to complete the project scope.

Creating the activity list relies on knowledge, actions, and several completed documents. The creation of the activity list uses the following as inputs to the process:

- **Schedule management plan**   This defines and directs the process of defining the project activities. This plan is part of the comprehensive project management plan.
- **Scope baseline**   This comprises the WBS, the WBS dictionary, the project scope statement, constraints, and assumptions. You'll need these elements to define the project activities.
- **Enterprise environmental factors**   This is all the stuff an organization and external entities can offer the project manager to assist with or constrain the activity definition. In particular, it's the project management information system and scheduling software. Also included are any commercial databases to help predict duration for project work in your industry. (Think manufacturing and construction, for instance.)
- **Organizational process assets**   Organizations have a way of getting things done. The process assets are the methods and procedures an organization must follow to create the activity list. This also includes historical information from past projects that can help the project team define activities on the current project.

Relying on Templates

Why reinvent the wheel? If similar projects have been completed in the past, you can rely on the WBS and activity lists from this historical information to serve as a template for the current project. Even if a portion of a project is similar, a project manager can use the activity list and focus on the similarities of the current project.

A template can include several elements that make a project manager's life easier and the new project more successful:

- Required actions to complete the project scope
- Required resources and skills
- Required hours of efforts for activities
- Known risks
- Outputs of the work
- Descriptions of the work packages
- Supporting details

Decomposing the Project Work Packages

The WBS, the collection of deliverable-orientated components, must now be broken down into activities. Specifically, the work packages within the WBS must be decomposed into manageable work elements. What's the difference between decomposing the project deliverables and the project work? The elements in the WBS are deliverables; this process is concerned with the actions needed to create the deliverables.

The creation of the WBS and the activity list is not a solo activity. You'll create the WBS and the activity list along with the project team.

It's quite possible to create the WBS and the activity list in tandem. Don't get too caught up in the timing of the activity list definition and the WBS. Simply put, the WBS describes the components of the deliverables, and the activity list defines the actions needed to create the deliverables. Typically, the project manager and the project team work together to decompose the work packages. In some instances, you'll find it ideal to use expert judgment to help with the decomposition.

Using Rolling Wave Planning

Have you ever stood in the ocean? Wave after wave knocks up against you. And way out in the distance, you can see a crest of water that glides along the surface until it crashes at your knees. In project management, the concept of a rolling wave plan is similar to your ocean visit.

Work that is imminent is planned in detail, while work that is way off in the future is planned at a high level. As the work in the future approaches, more detail is allotted to planning for it. Rolling wave planning enables the project team to focus planning on pressing matters as the project moves toward completion. This is a form of progressive elaboration.

Project teams that subscribe to the agile project management methodology use a form of the rolling wave plan. In the agile approach, you'll create deliverables through shorter cycles of work, with lots of evidence of quick planning, quick bursts of execution, and a deliverable to show for the work, before the team starts the cycle again.

Using Planning Components

Sometimes the project scope doesn't include enough detail to help you decompose everything to the smallest level: the work package level in the WBS. This isn't a problem, but it should be acknowledged during planning. For example, a project to build a home may have defined the room dimensions, lighting needs, and windows, but the specifics on paint color, flooring choices, and exact light fixtures haven't been defined. You can still plan for these elements with a to-be-determined-later characteristic.

When there isn't enough information in the project scope to decompose the work to the work packages, the project team can use two planning components:

- **Management control account**   This account is a marker that indicates that additional decisions and planning for the work exist below the control account in the WBS. All work and effort for the associated deliverables is documented through a control account plan.
- **Planning packages**   These allow the project team to position planning activities below the control account but still above the work packages. A planning package is the planning time and activities to determine what should exist within the control account. You could say that the planning package is a visual marker of planning that's yet to come. This acknowledges the need for future planning while not delaying immediate work on the project.

Compiling the Activity List

Ta-da! The primary output of decomposing the work is the activity list, which is a collection of all the work elements required to complete the project. The activity list is not the same as the WBS, but it does correlate to the work packages of the WBS and will serve as a fundamental tool in creating the project schedule. The activity list is needed to ensure that all the deliverables of the WBS are accounted for and that the necessary work is mapped to each deliverable, as shown in Figure 6-2.

The activity list also ensures that no extra work is included in the project. Extra work costs time and money—and it defeats the project scope. The WBS comprises all the components

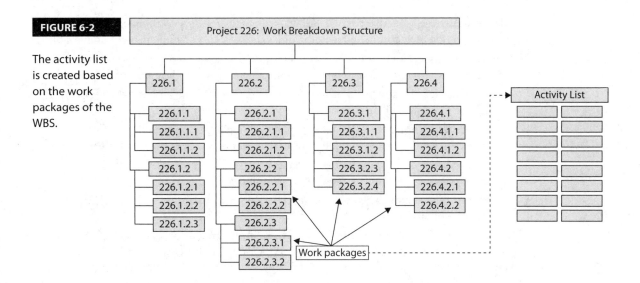

FIGURE 6-2

The activity list is created based on the work packages of the WBS.

the project will create, while the activity list is made up of all the work required to create the components within the WBS.

In addition, the work on the activity list includes attributes of each identified activity. This accomplishes four things:

■ It ensures that each activity has an identifier.
■ It ensures that the team members agree on what the work package accomplishes.
■ It ensures that the work supports and creates the WBS deliverables.
■ It ensures that the work is within the project scope.

Documenting the Activity Attributes

You'll need to do more than create a shopping list of activities for the project to plan, execute, and control the project work effectively. By documenting the activity attributes, you're communicating the intent of the project work, the supporting detail of the project decisions, and more. As information becomes available, the activity attributes should be updated to include the following:

■ **Activity name and description**   Each activity should have its name and description recorded.
■ **Activity ID**   This is a unique number for each activity in the activity list. It's especially useful when there are repetitions in the project work, similar activities, or similar activities throughout the project life cycle.

- **WBS identifier** Each activity is linked to a corresponding WBS package through the WBS code of accounts. This helps link the work to a specific project deliverable.

- **Relationships** The predecessor and successor tasks of each activity may be identified to help with planning and monitoring and controlling processes.

- **Leads and lags** If any leads or lags have been added to the activity, this information should be documented as part of the activity attributes.

- **Resource requirements** The people, materials, facilities, tools, equipment, and any other resources required to complete the activity should be documented for each activity.

- **Imposed dates** Any constraints, such as must-start-on dates or other deadlines attached to the project activities should be documented.

- **Constraints and assumptions** All activity-based constraints and assumptions should be documented.

- **Activity attributes** Activities may have attributes that affect the schedule. Consider geographical locations for the work, specific project team members to complete the activity, required materials and equipment, and other factors.

- **Additional information** Additional information may be unique to the discipline and application area of the project for the project activities.

Finalizing Activity Definition

Activity definition will happen throughout the project, and you'll revisit the activity list frequently to track activities, predict work that needs to be done, and to track the activities and their completion information. When you create the activities list, there are three additional outputs of this process:

- **Milestone list** A milestone is a timeless event that shows progress. The milestone list documents all the milestones in the project. Milestones can be optional, based on historical information from other projects, or mandatory due to contractual obligations.

■ **Change requests**   As you might expect, defining activities for the project can result in change requests for the project. By defining the activities, you and the team may uncover scope items that need to be added, changes to the predetermined deadline for the project, or any number of changes that must flow through integrated change control.

■ **Project management plan updates**   Updates to the project management plan will also flow through integrated change control. In this process, you may be updating the schedule and cost baselines as you're identifying the activities and associated resources needed to complete the activities.

CERTIFICATION OBJECTIVE 6.03

Sequencing Activities

After you've created the activity list, you need to arrange the activities in a logical sequence. This process calls on the project manager and the project team to identify the logical and preferred relationships among activities. This can be accomplished in a few different ways:

■ **Computer-driven**   Many different scheduling and project management software packages are available. These programs can help the project manager and the project team determine which actions need to happen and in what order.

■ **Manual process**   On smaller projects, and on larger projects in the early phases, manual sequencing may be preferred. An advantage of manual sequencing is that it can be easier to move around dependencies and activities than it is in some programs.

■ **Blended approach**   A combination of manual and computer-driven scheduling methods is fine. It's important to determine the finality of the activity sequence, however. Sometimes a blended approach can be more complex than relying on just one or another.

on the **job**

Using "sticky notes" can help you sequence events. Put your activities on sticky notes and then plot them out on a white board. Draw arrows to show the relationships between activities. Want to make a change? It's easy to rearrange the notes and the relationships.

Considering the Inputs to Activity Sequencing

There are many approaches to completing the activity sequencing. Perhaps the best approach, however, is to sequence activities with the project team, rather than as a solo activity. The project manager must rely on the project team and the inputs to activity sequencing:

- **The schedule management plan**   The schedule management plan defines and directs the process of sequencing the project's activities.
- **Scope baseline**   The scope baseline is required because it may influence the sequence of events. For example, in construction, technology, or community planning (among other project types), the scope statement may include requirements, constraints, and assumptions that will logically affect the planning of activity sequencing.
- **The activity list**   This list shows the actions needed to complete the project deliverables.
- **Activity attributes**   Each scheduled activity includes attributes that need to be documented. For example, the successor and predecessor of each activity, the lead and lag information, and the person responsible for completing the activity should all be documented. This information is important when it comes to schedule development and project control.
- **Milestone list**   Milestones must be considered and evaluated when sequencing events to ensure that all the work needed to complete the milestones is included.
- **Enterprise environmental factors**   Enterprise environmental factors can include government and industry standards you must adhere to, your organization's PMIS and scheduling tool, and a work authorization system.
- **Organizational process assets**   When you consider how most organizations repeat the same type of projects, it's easy to see why project managers rely on historical information as much as they do. After all, historical information and lessons learned are proven information that can be adapted to the current project. It is part of your organizational process assets. Organizational process assets can also vary if you're part of a program or have portfolio interdependencies.

Creating Network Diagrams

Network diagrams visualize the project work and show the relationship of the work activities and how they will progress from start to completion. They can be extremely complex or easy to create and configure. Most network diagrams in today's project management environment use the *activity-on-node (AON)* approach to illustrate the activities and the relationship between those activities.

Using the Precedence Diagramming Method

The *precedence diagramming method (PDM)* is the most commonly used method for arranging the project work visually. The PDM puts the activities in boxes or circles, called nodes, and connects the nodes with arrows. The arrows represent the relationship and the dependencies of the work packages. The following illustration shows a simple network diagram using PDM.

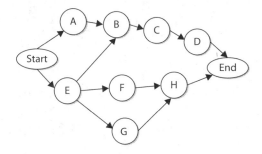

Relationships between activities in a PDM constitute one of four different types (as shown in Figure 6-3):

- **Finish-to-start (FS)**   In this relationship, Task A must be completed before Task B can begin. This is the most common type of relationship. In construction, for example, the foundation must be set before the framing can begin. This is most common type of relationship in the PDM.

- **Start-to-start (SS)**   In this relationship, Task A must start before Task B can start. Then both activities can happen in tandem. For example, a crew of painters is painting a house. Task A is to scrape the flaking paint off the house, and Task B is to prime the house. The workers scraping the house must start before the other workers can begin priming the house. All the scraping doesn't have to be completed before the priming can start—just some of it.

- **Finish-to-finish (FF)**   In this relationship, Task A must finish before Task B does. Ideally, the two tasks should finish at exactly the same time, but this is not always the case. For example, two teams of electricians may be working together to install new telephone cables throughout a building by Monday morning. Team A is pulling the cable to each office. Team B, meanwhile, is connecting the cables to wall jacks and connecting the telephones. Team A must pull the cable to the office so Team B can complete their activity. The activities need to complete at nearly the same time, by Monday morning, so that the new phones are functional when office workers return to work.

FIGURE 6-3

Task relationships can vary, but finish-to-start is the most common.

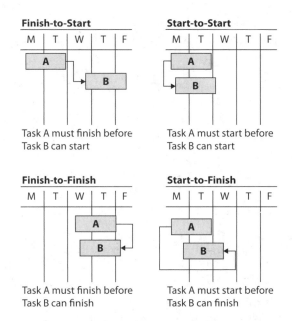

Finish-to-Start

Task A must finish before Task B can start

Start-to-Start

Task A must start before Task B can start

Finish-to-Finish

Task A must finish before Task B can finish

Start-to-Finish

Task A must start before Task B can finish

- **Start-to-finish (SF)**   This relationship is unusual and is rarely used. It requires Task A to start so that Task B may finish. Such relationships may be encountered in construction and manufacturing. It is also known as just-in-time (JIT) scheduling. An example is a construction of a shoe store. The end of the construction is soon, but an exact date is not known. The owner of the shoe store doesn't want to order the shoe inventory until the construction is nearly complete. The start of the construction tasks dictates when the shoe inventory is ordered.

Determining the Activity Dependencies

The progression of the project is built on the sequence of activities. Activities are dependent on their predecessor activities completing before successor activities may begin. The following are the dependencies you should know for your PMP exam:

- **Mandatory dependencies**   These dependencies are the natural order of activities. For example, you can't begin building your house until its foundation is in place. These relationships are called *hard logic*.

- **Discretionary dependencies**   These dependencies are the preferred order of activities. Project managers should use these relationships at their discretion and document the logic behind the decision. Discretionary dependencies allow activities to happen in a preferred order because of best practices, conditions unique to the project work, or external events. For example, a painting project typically allows the paint to be applied within hours of applying the primer. Due to expected high humidity during the project, however, all the building will be completely primed before the paint can be applied. These relationships are also known as *soft logic*, *preferred logic*, or *preferential logic*.

- **External dependencies** As its name implies, these dependencies are outside of the project's control. Examples include the delivery of equipment from a vendor, the deliverable of another project, or the decision of a committee, lawsuit, or expected new law.

- **Internal dependencies** These dependencies are internal to the organization or even to the project. For example, the project members who are responsible for testing the software can't test it until the developers complete the software. The project manager can schedule testers, but the start of their activity depends on the completion of the software development by other project team members.

Considering Leads and Lags

Leads and lags are values added to work packages to slightly alter the relationship between two or more work packages. For example, a finish-to-start relationship may exist between applying primer to a warehouse and applying the paint. The project manager in this scenario has decided to add one day of lead time to the work package for painting the warehouse. Now the painting can begin one day before the priming is scheduled to end. Lead time is considered a negative value, because time is subtracted from the downstream activity to bring successor activities closer to the start of the project.

Lag time is waiting time. Imagine a project to install wood floors in an office building. Currently, there is a finish-to-start relationship between staining the floors and adding a layer of shellac to seal the wood floors. The project manager has elected, because of the humidity in the building, to add two days of lag time to the downstream activity of sealing the floors. Now the shellac cannot be applied immediately after the stain but must wait two additional days. Lag is considered a positive value, since time is added to the project schedule.

PMP Coach **How is your lead time? You should be thinking about scheduling your PMP exam soon (if you've not done so already). You'll need lead time to complete the application, get PMI's approval, and find an open slot at the testing center. You don't want to complete all your studying and then schedule to pass your exam. Be a good project manager and look for opportunities to save time by completing activities in tandem.**

The following illustration shows the difference between lead and lag:

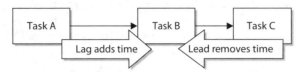

Leads and lags must be considered in the project schedule, since an abundance of lag time can increase the project duration. An abundance of lead time, while decreasing duration, may increase risks. When a project is using an abundance of lead time, it's often in a rush to meet a deadline. Rushing the project can lead to a rush in the execution, quality control, and inspections, and ultimately to rejection from the stakeholders. Too much lead can also cause some wonky scheduling issues, as a resource may be needed on two overlapping tasks due to the added lead time. It's okay to use lead time, but always consider the risks that too much lead can have on the project.

In a project network diagram, lag time is shown as positive time and lead is shown as negative time. For example, Activities C and D could be a start-to-start, but D could lag three days after activity C. That'd be represented as C SS +3.

Utilizing Network Templates

Just as a project manager can rely on WBS templates, network templates may be available to help streamline the planning process or to conform to a predetermined standard. Network templates can represent an entire project if appropriate, though portions of a network template, such as the required project management activities, are common.

The portions of a network template are also known as subnets, or fragnets. Subnets are often associated with repetitive actions within a network diagram. For example, each floor in a high-rise apartment building may undergo the same or similar actions during construction. Rather than complete the network diagram for each floor, a subnet can be implemented.

Examining the Sequencing Outputs

There are many approaches to using activity sequencing: a project manager and the project team can use software programs, the approach can be done manually, or the team can manually do the scheduling and then transfer the schedule into a project management information system (PMIS). Whichever method is selected, the project manager must remember four things:

- Only the required work should be scheduled.
- Finish-to-start relationships are the most common and preferred.
- Activity sequencing is not the same thing as a schedule.
- Scheduling comes after activity sequencing.

Using a Project Network Diagram

Once the activity list has been put into sequential order, the flow of the project work can be visualized. A project network diagram (PND) illustrates the flow of the project work and the relationship between the work packages. PNDs are typically AON, and most PMIS packages use the PDM method. The following illustration is a typical example of a network diagram.

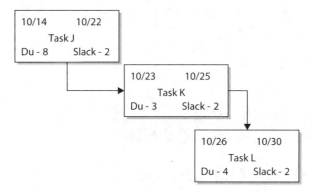

Network diagrams may include summary activities, also known as hammock activities. Accompanying the network diagram should be an explanation of the workflow, why decisions were made, and details on any preferred logic the project manager may have used. A network diagram is just a flow chart: it shows how the project work should flow from its launch to its conclusion. Should changes enter the project scope, the WBS will need to be updated, which will likely cause the activity list to be updated, which will, in turn, cause the network diagram to be updated to reflect the new project requirements.

ⓦatch   **Risks in the project can affect the project schedule, too. Rushed work, unrealistic deadlines, and a lack of resources are all common risks that affect the project completion.**

Updating the Project Documents

When sequencing the project work, the project team and the project manager may discover discrepancies or inadequacies in the existing WBS. Updates to the WBS enable the project manager to ensure that all the needed project deliverables are included in the WBS, and then she can map the discovered deliverables to the identified work in the activity list. Updates to the WBS are called refinements. As the project moves toward completion, refinements ensure that all the deliverables are accounted for within the WBS. They may also indirectly call for updates to the activity list.

Four project documents may be updated as a result of this process:

- **Activity attributes** Any information regarding a required sequence, leads, or lags should be included as part of the attributes.
- **Activity list** Relationships among activities that have changed during the sequencing activities should be updated.
- **Assumption log** Any assumptions and constraints in the assumptions log that affect the activity sequencing should be updated.
- **Milestone list** Any target or imposed dates for milestones may need to be updated based on the activities sequenced.

CERTIFICATION OBJECTIVE 6.04

Estimating Activity Durations

Ready for a loaded question? "Now how long will all of this take?" Project managers hear this one all the time, right? And maybe right after that, "How much will all of this cost?" We'll talk about cost estimates in Chapter 7. For now, let's talk about time.

The answer to the question "How long will it take?" depends on the accuracy of the estimates, the consistency of the work, and other variables within the project. The best a project manager can do is create honest estimates based on the information he's been provided. Until the schedule is finalized, and the project is complete, no one will know the duration of the project.

Usually, the tasks are first identified, the sequencing of the activities takes place, resources are defined, and then durations are estimated. However, it's perfectly normal for the sequencing of activities to be created apart from resource definition and even the duration estimating. These activities are required to complete the project schedule and the estimated project duration. These four activities are iterated as more information becomes available. If the proposed schedule is acceptable, the project can move forward. If the proposed schedule takes too long, the scheduler can use a few strategies to compress the project. We'll discuss the art of scheduling shortly.

Activity duration estimates, like the activity list and the WBS, don't come from the project manager—they come from the people completing the work. They may also undergo progressive elaboration. In this section, we'll examine the approach to completing activity duration estimates, the basis of estimates, and the allowance for activity list updates.

Considering the Activity Duration Estimates Inputs

The importance of accurate estimates is paramount. The activity estimates will be used to create the project schedule and predict when the project should end. Inaccurate estimates could cost the performing organization thousands of dollars in fines, lost opportunities, lost customers, or worse. To create accurate estimates, the project manager and the project team will rely on several inputs:

- **Schedule management plan**   The schedule management plan defines the approved approach for estimating the duration of project activities.
- **Scope baseline**   Identification of the project constraints and assumptions is needed, since they may influence the estimates. The project scope statement provides this information.
- **Activity attributes**   Effort is the amount of labor applied to a task. Duration, on the other hand, is how long the task is expected to take with the given amount of labor. For example, a task to unload a freight truck may take eight hours with two people assigned to the task. If the effort is increased by adding more labor to the task (in this instance, more people), then the duration of the task is decreased. Some activities, however, have a fixed duration and are not affected by the amount of labor assigned to the task. For example, installing a piece of software on a computer will take the same amount of time if one computer administrator is completing the work or if two computer administrators are doing it.
- **Activity list**   You know this, right? The activity list is the work elements necessary to create the deliverables.
- **Assumption log**   This log lists all assumptions and constraints that can affect the activities to be schedule and estimated in the project.
- **Lessons learned register**   Lessons learned can help the project manager and team better create estimates for the current project.
- **Milestone list**   The milestones give an ordering of activities, to a degree, and they'll help you plan the work in order to hit the high-level milestone dates.
- **Project team assignments**   Work assignments will help the project manager plan for when work can happen, make certain there aren't resource shortages, and plan for who'll be doing what work when.
- **Resource breakdown structure**   The breakdown of the project scope and the needed resources for the activities helps the project manager and the project team visualize when resources will be needed and for what duration.
- **Resource calendars**   Resource calendars are needed to predict when people, equipment, and facilities are available for scheduling. The total labor may not change on a task, but the duration could be affected by other commitments of project team members, facilities, and equipment.
- **Activity resource requirements**   Activity resource requirements define the resources that are needed to complete an activity. For example, a project to build a home will require lots of different resources: plumbers, electricians, architects, framers, and landscapers. The project manager would not, however, assign all the different resources to every task, but only to the tasks that the resource was qualified to complete. Remember that resources also include equipment and materials, so those are identified as part of the activity resource requirements as well.

- **Risk register**   The risk register is considered because the risk's probability and impact may affect the predicted duration of an activity. A risk response may require additional work in the project that could cause activity durations to increase.

- **Enterprise environmental factors**   Organizational policies can affect the duration estimating techniques the project manager uses. For example, the organization may limit the number of hours employees can contribute to a project, or agreements with unions could affect the duration of the activities in the project.

- **Commercial duration estimating database**   Commercial duration estimating databases can offer information on how long industry-specific activities should take. These databases should take into consideration the materials and the experience of the resources and define the assumptions the predicted work duration is based upon.

- **Organizational process assets**   Okay, the big one here is historical information. Historical information is always an excellent source for information on activity duration estimates. It can come from several sources, such as the following:

  - Historical information can come from project files of other projects within the organization.

  - Project team members may recollect information regarding the expected duration of activities. While these inputs are valuable, they are generally less valuable than documented sources such as project files from other projects or the commercial databases.

on the job   **The project manager and the project team should evaluate the project risks when it comes to project duration. We'll discuss risk in detail in Chapter 11. Risks, good or bad, can influence the estimated duration of activities. The risks on each activity should be identified, analyzed, and then predicted as to their probability and impact. If risk mitigation tasks are added to the schedule, the mitigation activities will need their durations estimated and then sequenced into the schedule in the proper order. The project activity cost estimates, if they exist yet, should also be referenced during activity duration estimates to determine the most cost-effective amount of labor or resources to apply to any given activity.**

Estimating the Project Work Considerations

The identified resource requirements will affect the project schedule. Remember the difference between duration and effort? Duration is how long the activity will take, and effort is the labor applied to the task. For example, painting a building may take 80 hours to complete with two workers assigned to the job. Add two more workers, and now the work will take only 40 hours. The duration to complete the painting is 40 hours, but there will still be 160 hours of effort expended on the activity. At some point in the work, the "duration to effort ratio" becomes saturated, and adding laborers will become counterproductive. This is the law of diminishing returns. The following illustration demonstrates the example.

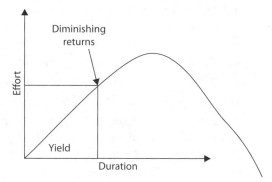

In agile projects, you'll host planning meetings at the beginning of iterations, called sprints, to determine how many user stories the team will be able to create in each time-boxed sprint session. Recall that user stories are prioritized requirements from the product backlog. A sprint planning session is held on the first day of the iteration, and the product owner, the person that helps prioritize the backlog, the project manager, and the project team will work together to determine how many user stories the team can realistically accomplish in the current iteration. The meeting's goal is also to create an iteration backlog for the current sprint; to identify any assumptions, risks, and activity dependencies for ordering; and to assign actions to the project team.

Considering Resource Availability

In a perfect world, all the needed resources for a project would be available whenever the project manager says so. In the real world, however (and on your PMP exam), the availability of project resources fluctuates due to the demands of other projects, the demands of ongoing operations, personal lives, vacations, sick days, and more. Organizational process assets and enterprise environmental factors can also guide the project manager and project team as to when certain resources may be needed, or allowed, in a project.

The availability of the project pool must be evaluated. If certain activities require a worker with a highly specialized skill, these activities are resource-dependent. Should the worker not be available for the time frame of the required activity, one of several things must happen:

- The project manager must negotiate to make the resource available for the activity in the project schedule.
- The activity must be moved in the schedule to when the resource is available.
- The activity, and possibly the project, must wait for the resource to become available.
- The project may incur additional costs in finding other resources to complete the scheduled work.

Resources mean more than just people. The project manager must also consider physical resources such as equipment, facilities, software, and other materials. With each nonhuman resource, the project manager must consider the cost and procurement procedures needed to acquire it. We'll discuss procurement in more detail in Chapter 12.

e x a m

ⓦatch When a resource is needed but is not available, the project manager must negotiate to secure the resource. This may involve tradeoffs between projects or additional expenses as the activity is outsourced to a vendor to complete the work. The project manager does not want to delay the project because of having to wait on a resource.

Considering the Calendars

Two calendar types will affect the project:

- **The project calendar** This calendar shows when work is allowed on the project. For example, a project may require the project team to work nights and weekends so as not to disturb the ongoing operations of the organization during working hours. In addition, the project calendar accounts for holidays, working hours, and work shifts that the project will cover.
- **The resource calendar** The resource calendar controls when resources such as project team members, consultants, and SMEs are available to work on the project. It considers vacations, other commitments within the organization, or restrictions on contracted work, overtime issues, and so on.

The consideration of the project calendar and the resource calendar is mandatory to predict when a project may realistically begin and end. Figure 6-4 shows the project calendar setting from Microsoft Project. Keep in mind that the PMP exam is not concerned with which PMIS system is used, only that you understand the role of the PMIS.

Creating a Resource Breakdown Structure

A resource breakdown structure, like the work breakdown structure, is a decomposition of the utilization of the project resources by category, phases, or types of resources. It's a visual mapping of the types of resources the project requires, organized by logical groupings. In a construction project, the project manager may create a resource breakdown structure using the construction phases, whereas in an IT project, the project manager may use hardware, software, network, and data as the categories. In either instance, the project manager would include all resources needed—both people and things.

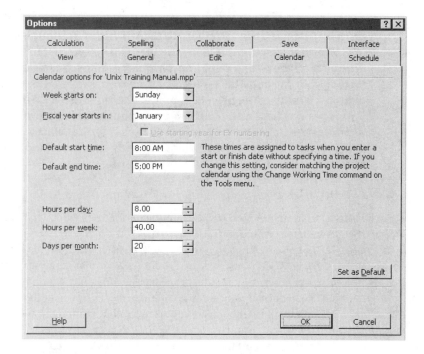

FIGURE 6-4

Project calendars determine when the project work may take place.

Updating the Activity List

During the creation of the network diagram, assumptions about the activity sequence may reveal missing activities in the activity list. Just as the creation of the activity list may prompt the project team and the project manager to update the WBS, the creation of the network diagram may prompt the project team to update the activity list.

While this may seem redundant—updating the activity list illustrated in the project network diagram—it is essential documentation. A reflection of the WBS, the activity list and the network diagram should both support the project scope. A key stakeholder should thus be able to follow the logic of the WBS to the activity list, and from the activity list, find all the activities mapped in order.

Applying Expert Judgment

The project manager and the project team should utilize expert judgment, if possible, to predict the duration of project activities. Expert judgment can come from SMEs, project team members, and other resources, internal or external to the performing organization, who are familiar with the activities the project demands.

Estimating durations is not easy, as many variables can influence an activity's duration. Consider the amount of resources that can be applied to the activities, the experience of the resources completing this type of work, and their competence with the work packages.

on the job A big dose of reality is also needed with activity duration estimates. Imagine an activity that has been estimated to take 40 hours. Although on paper that looks like a typical workweek, it's unlikely the task will be completed within one week. Why? Consider all the phone calls, impromptu meetings, e-mail, and other interruptions throughout the day. These slivers of time chip away at the actual productive hours within a workday. The project manager should find a base of actual productive hours per day based on typical interruptions, meetings, and so on—for example, 6 productive hours out of 8 working hours is typical. Based on this assumption, a task slated to last 40 hours will take nearly seven working days to complete.

Creating an Analogy

Analogous estimating relies on historical information to predict what current activity durations should be. Analogous estimating, also known as top-down estimating, is a form of expert judgment. In analogous estimating, the durations of activities from a historical project that are similar in nature are used to predict the durations of similar activities in the current project.

A project manager must consider whether the work has ever been done before and, if so, what help the historical information will provide. The project manager must consider the resources, project team members, and equipment that completed the activities in the previous project compared to the resources available for the current project. Ideally, the activities should be more than similar; they should be identical. And the resources that completed the work in the past should be the same resources used in completing the current work.

When the only source of activity duration estimates is the project team members instead of expert judgment and historical information, your estimates will be uncertain and inherently risky.

exam watch   Analogous estimating uses historical information and is more reliable than recollections from project team members. It's a fast method to duration estimating, but it's also less accurate than other estimating approaches.

Applying Parametric Estimates

Quantitatively based durations use mathematical formulas to predict how long an activity will take based on the "quantities" of work to be completed. For example, a commercial printer needs to print 100,000 brochures. The workers include two pressmen and two bindery experts to fold and package the brochures. The duration is how long the activity will take to complete, and the effort is the total number of hours (labor) invested because of the resources involved. The decomposed work, with quantitative factors, is shown in Table 6-1.

TABLE 6-1	Workers	Units per Hour	Duration for 100,000 Brochures	Effort
Decomposed Work with Quantitative Factors	Pressman (two)	5000	20 hours	40 hours
	Bindery (two)	4000	25 hours	50 hours
	Totals		45 hours	90 hours

e x a m

ⓦatch **Duration is how long an activity takes, while effort is the billable time for the labor to complete the activity. Consider an activity that is scheduled to last 40 hours. The project manager must consider the cost of the person's time assigned to complete the project work—for example, a senior full-time engineer versus a part-time person at a lower cost. The senior engineer may be able to complete the activity in 40 consecutive work hours, but the cost of this employee's time may be more than the value of the activity. The part-time employee may be able to complete the task in two segments of 25 hours, but his time is billed at a substantially lower rate.**

Creating a Three-Point Estimate

How confident can a project manager be when it comes to estimating? If the project work has been done in past projects, the level of confidence in the duration estimate is probably high. But if the work has never been done before, there are lots of unknowns—and with that comes risk. To mitigate the risk, the project manager can use a three-point estimate, which requires that for each activity, optimistic, most likely, and pessimistic time estimates are created. Based on these three time estimates, the project manager can create an average to predict how long the activity should take (see Figure 6-5).

e x a m

ⓦatch **If you're thinking this sounds a lot like the program evaluation and review technique (PERT), you're correct. The formula for PERT is similar to a three-point estimate but differs slightly: (Optimistic time + (4 × Most likely time) + Pessimistic time)/6. It's six factors instead of three, because you're using six factors in the numerator. PERT, as you can tell from the formula, uses a weighted average, because the "most likely" estimate is overrepresented in the calculation. The three-point estimate is an average of all the equal factors.**

Three-point
estimates rely
on averages to
predict duration.

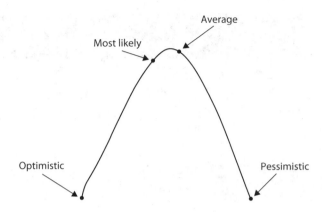

A three-point estimate using the average of optimistic, most likely, and pessimistic is also known as triangular distribution. The PERT approach, using (Optimistic time + (4 × Most likely time) + Pessimistic time)/6 is also known as beta distribution.

Creating a Bottom-Up Estimate

Bottom-up estimating is usually a term associated with cost estimates, but you can use this for resource estimating, too. The approach requires you to have a fully decomposed WBS for each work package, and then you estimate how many and what type of resources you'll need to create that work package. Each work package can have multiple activities associated with it, so the duration of each work package is estimated for its duration based on the number of resources you'll assign to do the work. This approach takes longer than other approaches, but it's also the most accurate. It's called bottom-up because you're starting at the bottom and working your way up to predict the total duration for the project.

Using the Delphi Technique

The Delphi Technique uses rounds of anonymous surveys to build consensus on project decisions. In activity duration estimating, this approach could be utilized to predict how long an activity should take the project team to complete. For example, consider an activity to create a web site as part of the project deliverable. On the project team, there may be six people who are qualified to predict how long the web site creation would take, and each web designer may give a different estimate of the duration for that task. Or the designers may create some conformance based on what others say for the duration.

Using the Delphi Technique, the six designers would submit an anonymous prediction of how long the task would take to complete. Then the project manager would create a second survey so each designer could comment, consider, and even repredict their estimate based on what others have said. The project manager would continue to create rounds of surveys for this task to build a consensus among the designers regarding how long the task is likely to take to complete.

Using the Fist-to-Five Approach

This decision-making technique calls for the project team members and experts participating in the estimating planning sessions to vote on the decision. Participants will show their level of support for a decision by showing their fist, which means zero support, or any number of fingers from one to five, where one is low and five is high. Though you'll usually see this approach in agile projects, you can use it in predictive approaches, too, for a quick understanding of the participants' confidence in a duration estimate decision.

When an individual holds up less than three fingers, that person can explain their reasoning for the low score. A conversation follows to support, or debunk, the opinion and the participants can revote. The process continues until there is a consensus on what the duration of the activity should be.

Factoring in Reserve Time

Parkinson's Law states, "Work expands to fill the time available for its completion." This little nugget of wisdom is oh-so-true. Consider a project team member who knows an activity should last 24 hours. The team member decides, in his own wisdom, to say the activity will last 32 hours. This extra 8 hours, he figures, will allow plenty of time for the work to be completed should any unforeseen incidents pop up. The trouble is, however, that the task will magically expand to require the complete 32 hours. Why does this happen? Consider the following:

- **Hidden time**   Hidden time, the time factored in by the project team member, is secret. No one, especially the project manager, knows why the extra time has been factored into the activity. The team member can then "enjoy" the extra time to complete the task at her leisure.

- **Procrastination**   Most people put off starting a task until the last possible minute. The trouble with bloated, hidden time is that people may wait through the additional time they've secretly factored into the activity. Unfortunately, if something does go awry in completing the activity, the work result is later than predicted.

- **Demands**   Project team members may be assigned to multiple projects with multiple demands. The requirement to move from project to project can shift focus, result in a loss of concentration, and require additional ramp-up time as workers shift from activity to activity. The demand for multitasking enables project team members to take advantage of hidden time.

- **On schedule** Activities are typically completed on schedule or late, but rarely early. A user who has bloated the activity duration estimates may finish his task ahead of what he promised, but he may tend to hold onto those results until the activity's due date. This is because workers aren't usually rewarded for completing work early. In addition, workers don't want to reveal the inaccuracies in their time estimates. Workers may believe future estimates may be based on actual work durations, rather than estimates, so they'll "sandbag" the results to protect themselves—and finish "on schedule."

Contingency reserve is time, usually in the form of money to pay for the labor usage, built into the project schedule for known-unknowns, which are risk events. Contingency reserve can be quickly created with an overall percentage of the project schedule or assigned to activities. Contingency reserve is calculated through quantitative risk analysis, something I'll discuss in more detail in Chapter 11 on project risk management.

Another reserve type is management reserve. Management reserve time is a percentage of the project duration or a preset number of work periods and is usually added to the end of the project schedule. Management reserve time may also be added to individual activity durations based on risks or uncertainties in the activity durations. When an activity is completed late, the additional time for the activity is subtracted from the reserve time. As the project moves forward, the reserve time can be reduced or eliminated as the project manager sees fit. Management reserve is for unknown-unknowns, also risk events, but are specific to activities. Management reserve is not part of the schedule baseline, because you don't know for certain where, or if, the reserve will be utilized in the project. Management reserves are included as part of the overall project duration, however.

Evaluating the Estimates

The result of estimating activities provides the following three things:

- **Activity duration estimates** Activity duration estimates reflect how long each work package will take to complete. A duration estimate should include an acknowledgment of the range of variance. For example, an activity whose duration is expected to be one week may have a range of variance of one week ± three days. This means the work can take up to eight days or as little as two days. This is assuming a week is five days. You might also add a degree of confidence to the activity estimates, such as being 90 percent certain the task duration estimates are accurate.

- **Basis of estimates** Documentation of how you and the team arrived at the duration estimates is also important. You'll define how an estimate was created, assumptions made about the estimate, and known constraints, and you'll identify any risks associated with the activity that could affect the project schedule.

■ **Project document updates**   Estimating the duration of the project activities may prompt the project manager to update the project documents. Any assumptions made during the activity estimating process should be identified. In addition, any historical information, SMEs, or commercial estimating databases that were used should also be documented for future reference. The project manager may also need to update the activity attributes to describe the nature of the work, specific directions for the work, timing concerns, and other relevant information. You'll update the activity attributes, assumption log, and lessons learned register as needed.

INSIDE THE EXAM

There's a ton of information in this chapter—all of it important—but you must know some key facts to pass the PMP exam. For starters, you should understand how activity estimates are created.

Analogous estimates use historical information to predict how long current project activities will last. These estimates are considered top-down estimates and are part of expert judgment. Quantifiable estimates, on the other hand, use a quantity to predict how long activities will take. Consider any unit, such as square feet painted per hour or the number of units created per day.

Lag is positive time added to a task to indicate waiting. Lead is negative time added to a task to "hurry up." Fast tracking arranges activities to happen in tandem rather than in succession, which increases risk. Crashing adds more resources to activities to decrease their duration, which typically adds cost.

Monte Carlo analysis (named after the world-famous gambling city) is a computer program that is typically used to estimate the

many possible variables within a project schedule. Monte Carlo simulations predict probable end dates, not an exact end date. Another tool the project manager can use is resource leveling, which smooths out the project schedule so resources are not overallocated. As a result, projects are often scheduled to last longer than initial estimates.

The critical path in a project has zero float (the amount of time a task can be delayed without delaying the project's completion); it is the path with the longest duration to completion. There can be more than one critical path in a network diagram, as two paths could have the same duration that's the longest duration of all paths. Should delays happen on noncritical paths and consume all float, the critical path may change.

The project schedule is a calendar-based system used to predict when the project, and work, will start and end. Gantt charts map activities against a calendar and may show the relationship between activities. Milestone charts show when key deliverables are expected; they do not show the relationship between activities

CERTIFICATION OBJECTIVE 6.05

Developing the Schedule

Now that the estimates for the activities are completed, it's time to work some magic and see how long the entire project will take by putting the activities in the order they should, and can, happen. The project manager specifically pursues the start date and, more importantly, the completion date. Projects that don't provide realistic schedules aren't likely to get approved. Or worse, the projects will get approved, but they will most likely fail, as the project team will not be able to meet the unrealistic schedule.

The creation of the project schedule model is iterative. It's rare for a schedule to get created, approved, and implemented without some iterative examination, arrangement, and management input—though on smaller projects it may be possible. When activity list updates, constraints, assumptions, and other inputs are considered, it's easy to see why scheduling can become complex.

There are five inputs to the schedule development process:

- **Project management plan**   This plan specifies schedule management plan and the scope baseline.
- **Project documents**   You'll reference the activity list and attributes, assumption log, basis of estimates, duration estimates, lessons learned register, milestone list, project schedule network diagram, team assignments, resource calendars, resource requirements, and risk register.
- **Agreements**   The contracts with vendors and agreements with other departments or organizations can affect your schedule development.
- **Enterprise environmental factors**   This is where rules and policies are referenced.
- **Organizational process assets**   Historical information, templates, and other historical information can be an input.

Revisiting the Project Network Diagram

The PND illustrates the project. Recall that the PND shows the sequence of activities and the relationship between activities. It is important during schedule creation, because it allows the project manager and the project team to evaluate the decisions, constraints, and assumptions that were made earlier in the process to determine why certain activities must occur in a particular order.

Hard logic and soft logic must be evaluated to confirm that the decisions and logic are feasible and accurate, and that they fit within the expected completion of the project. The following illustration shows a simple PND for a small project.

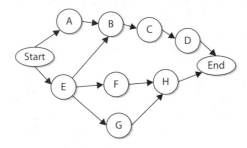

Relying on Activity Duration Estimates

Another key input to schedule creation is the activity duration estimates and the basis of estimates. Makes sense, right? The project manager needs to know how long the whole project will take, so the activity duration estimates will help calculate that. Recall, however, the range of variances for each activity—these possible variances need to be accounted for in the actual project schedule creation. We'll discuss the schedule creation shortly.

Evaluating the Project Constraints

Constraints will restrict when and how the project may be implemented. They are added to a project for a purpose, not just to rush the work to completion. It's important to understand why a constraint has been imposed. The following offers a few common examples as to why constraints exist:

- To take advantage of an opportunity to profit from a market window for a product or service
- To work within the parameters of expected weather conditions (for seasonal or outdoor projects)
- To adhere to government requirements
- To adhere to industry regulations, best practices, or guidelines
- To work within time frames that incorporate the expected delivery of materials from vendors or other projects

Perhaps one of the biggest constraints is the predetermined project deadline. Imagine a company creating a product to take to a trade show. If the creation of the product is running late, the trade show isn't going to move its date back so the product has enough time to be completed for the show.

There are four time constraints to consider:

- **Start no earlier than (SNET)** This constraint requires that the project or activity not start earlier than the predetermined date. Consider an activity to add software to an existing network server in a IT project. The project manager adds a "start no earlier than" constraint to the activity to ensure the activity begins on a Saturday when the server is not in use by the organization. The activity can begin any time after the preset date, but not before it.

- **Start no later than (SNLT)** This constraint requires the activity to begin by a predetermined date. For example, the creation of a community flower garden must "start no later than" May 15. The creation of the garden may, weather permitting, begin earlier than the preset date, but it must start by that date.

- **Finish no later than (FNLT)** This constraint requires that the project or activity finish by a predetermined date. For example, the installation of flooring tile in a restaurant must be finished by October 25 so the kitchen equipment can be installed. The constraint "finish no later than" is tied to the date of October 25. The activity can end sooner than October 25, but not after that date.

- **Finish no earlier than (FNET)** This somewhat unusual constraint requires the activity to be in motion up until the predetermined date. Consider a project to create a special blend of wine. The wine must be aged a specific amount of time before the winemaking process can continue. Thus, the process requires a set amount of time so it may "finish no earlier than" the determined time. The activity can end any time after the preset date, but not before it.

Project constraints can also include milestones. The project sponsor may request, for example, a milestone for a deliverable within the project on April 28. Based on this milestone, all the work needed to create a deliverable must be scheduled against the expected due date. In addition, once these milestones are set, it's darn tough to change them.

Milestone constraints can also be tied to activities outside of the project. Consider a scheduled walkthrough with a customer on a construction project. Or consider the demands of a project to create a product or service by a scheduled milestone that another project within the performing organization is expecting.

exam

ⓦatch The "start no earlier than" and "finish no later than" constraints are your best bets for exam answers, since these are the most common constraints. Remember that constraints can be tied to individual activities within the project or to the entire project.

Reevaluating the Assumptions

Assumptions are beliefs that are held to be true but that may not necessarily be so. Assumptions—such as being able to have access to a building 24 hours a day, seven days a week—can wreak havoc on the project schedule if they are proved false. Consider a schedule that plans on working three shifts during the remodeling of an office building only to discover late in the project planning that the customer will not allow the work to happen during daytime hours. Assumptions factored into the project should be documented and accounted for.

Evaluating the Risk Management Register

Risk and risk management are discussed completely in Chapter 11. For now, know that risks can alter the project schedule—for better or for worse. This isn't difficult to see. A risk in the project may be identified as delays from the vendor for the equipment needed to complete the project. The response to this risk, should it happen, may be to secure an alternative vendor that charges slightly more for the same equipment but has it in stock. The delay of the equipment with the original vendor may throw the project off schedule, and the additional time to find, purchase, and ship the needed equipment could also add extra time to the project. This is why the risk register is an input to developing the project schedule.

Examining the Activity Attributes

The activity attributes can have a direct impact on the project schedule. Some activities are effort-driven, which means more effort can reduce the duration. Other activities are of fixed duration—that is, additional effort does nothing to reduce their expected duration. Activity attributes are the characteristics of the work to be completed, including the following:

- The person(s) responsible for completing each work package
- Where the work will take place (building, city, outdoors)
- The type of activity (electrical, technical, supervised, and so on)
- When the activity must take place (business hours, off-hours, more unusual times)

Defining the Project Timeline

The project manager, the project team, and possibly even the key stakeholders will examine the inputs previously discussed and apply the techniques discussed in this section to create a feasible schedule for the project. The point of the project schedule is to complete the project scope in the shortest amount of time possible without incurring exceptional costs or risks, or a loss of quality.

Creating the project schedule is part of the planning process group. It is calendar based and relies on both the project network diagram and the accuracy of time estimates.

See the video "Calculating Float."

Performing Schedule Network Analysis

Schedule network analysis is the process of factoring theoretical early and late start dates and theoretical early and late finish dates for each activity within the PND. The early and late dates are not the expected schedule, but rather a potential schedule based on the project constraints, the likelihood of success, the availability of resources, and other constraints.

The most common approach to calculating when a project may finish is by using the critical path method (CPM). It uses "forward" and "backward" passes to reveal which activities are considered critical. Activities on the critical path may not be delayed; otherwise, the project end date will be delayed. The critical path is the path with the longest duration to completion. To find the critical path, just add up the duration of path from the project start to finish. The longest path is the critical path. Activities not on the critical path have some float (also called slack) that allows some amount of delay without delaying the project end date. In the following illustration, the path EGH is the longest path, with 14 days of duration, so it's the critical path.

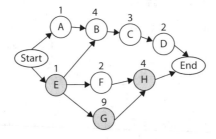

Calculating Float in a PND

Float, or slack, is the amount of time a task can be delayed without delaying the project's completion time. Technically, there are four different types of float:

- **Free float** This is the total time a single activity can be delayed without delaying the early start of any successor activities.
- **Total float** This is the total time an activity can be delayed without delaying project completion. It's possible to have positive total float when the project will take less time to complete than the imposed deadline for the project.
- **Negative total float** A constraint on an activity, such as "the activity must start on a specific date," or a deadline for the project completion, can cause negative float. This means the activities on the critical path don't have enough time to meet the defined finish date for the project or the constrained activity.
- **Project float** This is the total time the project can be delayed without passing the customer-expected completion date.

Most project management software will automatically calculate float. Project management software can also help you identify near-critical paths, try what-if scenarios by adding labor, or quickly rearranging the order of tasks to see the effect on the project. On the PMP exam, however, candidates will be expected to calculate float manually. Don't worry; it's not too tough. Give it a try:

Follow along with the PND illustrations to find the critical path. The critical path is typically the path with the longest duration and will usually have zero float. The critical path is technically found once you complete the forward and backward passes. Start with the forward pass. After the backward pass, you can identify the critical and near-critical paths, as well as float. In all the illustrations that follow, the activity duration is centered above each node.

1. The early start (ES) and early finish (EF) dates are calculated first by completing the forward pass. The ES of the first task is 1. The EF for the first task is its ES, plus the task duration, minus 1. Don't let the "minus 1 value" throw you. If Task A is scheduled to last one day, it would only take one day to complete, right? The ES would be 1, the duration is 1, and the EF would also be 1, because the activity would finish within one day, not two days. The following illustration shows the start of the forward pass.

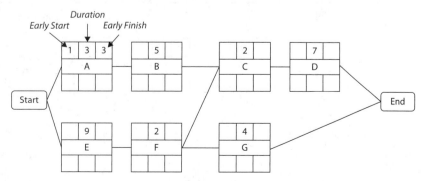

2. The ES of the next task(s) will be the EF for the previous activity, plus 1. In other words, if Task A finishes on day eight, Task B will begin on day nine.

3. The EF for the next task(s) equals its ES, plus the task duration, minus 1. Sound familiar?

4. Now each task moves forward with the forward pass. Use caution when there are predecessor activities; the EF with the largest value is carried forward. The following illustration shows the completed forward pass.

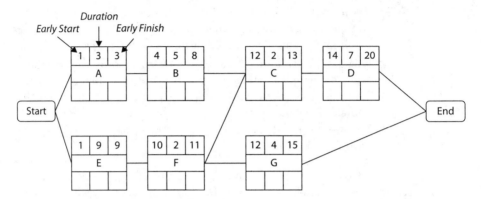

5. After the forward pass is completed, the backward pass starts at the end of the PND. The backward pass is concerned with the late finish (LF) and the late start (LS) of each activity. The LF for the last activity in the PND equals its EF value. The LS is calculated by subtracting the duration of the activity from its LF, plus 1. The 1 is added to accommodate the full day's work; it's just the opposite of subtracting the one day in the forward pass. Here's a tip: The last activity is on the critical path, so its LS will equal its ES.

6. The next predecessor activity's LF equals the LS of the successor activity, minus 1. In other words, if Task Z has an LS of 107, Task Y will have an LF of 106. The following illustration shows the process of the backward pass.

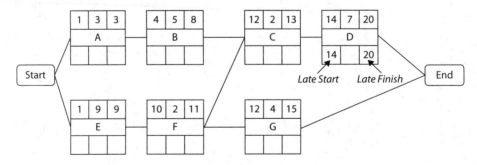

7. The LS is again calculated by subtracting the task's duration from the task's LF, plus 1. The following shows the completed backward pass.

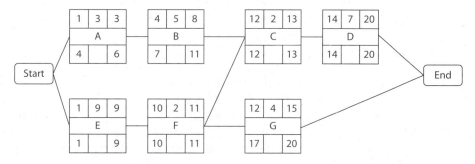

8. To calculate float officially, the LS is subtracted from the ES and the LF is subtracted from the EF. Recall the total float is the amount of time a task can be delayed without delaying the project completion date. The next illustration shows the completed PND with the float exposed.

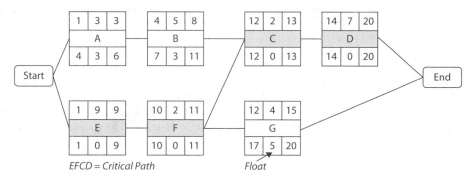

EFCD = Critical Path   Float

I bet you're wishing you could try this one out for yourself, right? You're in luck! Included with this book is an Adobe PDF document titled "Chapter Six Float Exercise." This document has a project network diagram that you can print and use to test your float-ability. You can also just create your own diagrams and practice finding float.

See the video "Float Exercise Explained" once you've completed the exercise.

Encountering Scheduling on the PMP Exam

You'll encounter float, scheduling, and critical path activities on the PMP exam. You should count these questions as "gimmies" if you remember a few important rules:

- Always draw out the network diagram presented on your scratch paper. It may be used in several questions.
- Know how to calculate float. (The complete process was shown earlier in the "Calculating Float in a PND" section.)
- You may encounter questions that ask on what day of the week a project will end if no weekends or holidays are worked. No problem. Add up the critical path, divide by 5 (Monday through Friday), and then figure out on which day of the week the activity will end.
- You may see something like Figure 6-6 when it comes to scheduling. When three numbers are presented, think three-point estimate. Optimistic is the smallest number, pessimistic is the largest, so most likely it's somewhere between the two. When a number is positioned directly over the tasks, it is the task duration. When a number is positioned to the upper-right corner of a task, this represents the early finish date.

Optimizing Resource Utilization

Resource leveling is a method to flatten the schedule when resources are overallocated. Resource leveling can be applied using different methods to accomplish different goals. One of the most common methods is to ensure that workers are not overextended on activities. Figure 6-7 shows a Microsoft Project screen, which shows where resource leveling has been applied.

FIGURE 6-6

Scheduling follows many rules to arrive at project completion.

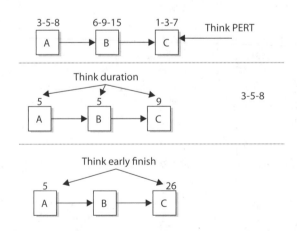

FIGURE 6-7

Resource leveling flattens the project schedule and will likely extend the project duration.

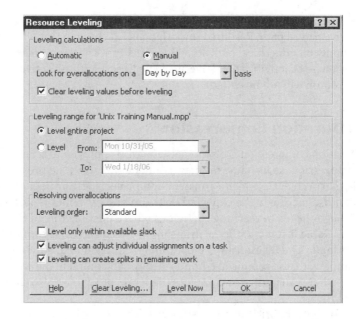

For example, Sarah is assigned to Task C and Task H, which are planned to happen concurrently. Sarah cannot be in two places at once, so resource leveling changes the timing of the activities so Sarah can complete Task C and then move on to Task H. As expected, however, resource leveling often extends the project end date.

Another method for resource leveling is to take resources from noncritical path activities and apply them to critical path activities to ensure that the project end date is met. This method takes advantage of available slack and balances the expected duration of the noncritical path with the expected duration of the critical path.

Resource leveling also provides for changing the project schedule to allow for long work hours to complete the project work—such as weekends and evenings, or even a second or third shift to bring the project back in alignment. Another approach, also part of resource leveling, is to change the resources, tools, or equipment used to complete the project work faster. For example, a project manager could request that the printer use a different, faster printing press to complete the printing activity than what was originally planned for. Of course, these approaches often increase cost.

Some resources may be scarce to the project. Consider a highly skilled technician or consultant who is available only on a particular date to contribute to the project. These resources are scheduled from the project end date, rather than the start date. This is known as reverse resource allocation scheduling.

Often in project management, you don't want to change anything dealing with the activities on the critical path. Resource smoothing is a technique that allows you to do resource leveling, but only on noncritical path activities. This approach levels resource utilization by taking advantage of activities that have available float. For those activities with no float, the resource utilization will not be edited.

Applying Duration Compression

Duration compression is also a mathematical approach to scheduling. The trick with duration compression, as its name implies, is calculating ways the project can be completed sooner than expected. Consider a construction project. The project may be slated to last eight months, but due to the expected cold and nasty weather typical of month seven, the project manager needs to rearrange activities where possible to end the project as soon as possible.

In some instances, the relationship between activities cannot be changed due to hard or soft logic. The relationships must remain as scheduled. Now consider the same construction company that is promised a bonus if they can complete the work by the end of month seven. Now there's incentive to complete the work, but there's also the fixed relationship between activities.

To apply duration compression, the performing organization can rely on two different methods, which can be used independently or together and are applied to activities or the entire project based on need, risk, and cost:

- **Crashing** This approach adds more resources to activities on the critical path to complete the project earlier. When crashing a project, costs are added as the labor expenses increase. Crashing doesn't always work. Consider activities that have a fixed duration and won't be finished faster with additional resources. The project manager must also consider the expenses in relation to the gains of completing on time. For example, a construction company may have been promised a bonus to complete the work by a preset date, but the cost incurred to hit the targeted date is more than what the bonus offers.

- **Fast tracking** This method changes the relationship of activities. With fast tracking, activities that would normally be done in sequence can be done in parallel or with some overlap. Fast tracking can be accomplished by changing the relationship of activities from FS to SS or by adding lead time to downstream activities. For example, a construction company could change the relationship between painting the rooms and installing the carpet by adding lead time to the carpet installation task. Before the change, all the rooms had to be painted before the carpet installers could begin. With the added lead time, the carpet can be installed hours after a room is painted. Fast tracking increases risk and may cause rework in the project. Can't you just imagine those workers getting fresh paint on the new carpet? However, it's often ideal to fast track the project. When it's done properly and with qualified resources, it's a huge timesaver.

Using a Project Simulation

Project simulation is a data analysis technique that enables a project manager to examine the feasibility of the project schedule under different conditions, variables, and events. For example, the project manager can see what would happen to a project if activities were delayed, a vendor missed a shipment date, or external events affected the project.

Simulations are often completed with the Monte Carlo analysis, which predicts how scenarios may work out given any number of variables. The process doesn't churn out a specific answer, but a range of possible answers. When Monte Carlo is applied to a schedule, it can examine, for example, the optimistic completion date, the pessimistic completion date, and the most likely completion date for each activity in the project.

As you can imagine, in a typical network diagram, there are likely thousands, if not millions, of combinations of tasks that complete early, late, or as expected. The Monte Carlo analysis shuffles these combinations, usually through computer software, and offers a range of possible end dates coupled with an expected probability for achieving each end date.

In other words, the Monte Carlo analysis is an odds-maker. The project manager chooses, or is at least influenced by, the end date with the highest odds of completion relative to the demands for completion by an expected time. The project manager can then predict with some certainty that the project has, for example, an 85 percent chance of completion by a specific date. The Monte Carlo analysis can help predict the probability of reaching a project completion date, milestones, or a specific activity based on current project status or what-if scenarios.

Simulations also provide time to factor in what-if questions, worst-case scenarios, and potential disasters. The result of simulations is to create responses to the feasible situations. Then, should the situations come into play, the project team is ready with a planned response.

Using Project Management Software

When it comes to project management software, take your pick: the market is full of options. Project management applications are tools, not replacements, for the project management process. Many of the software titles today automate the processes of scheduling, activity sequencing, work authorization, and other activities. The performing organization must weigh the cost of the PMIS against the benefits the project manager will gain.

Relying on a Project Coding Structure

The coding structure identifies the work packages within the WBS and is then applied to the PND. This enables the project manager, the project team, experts, and even key stakeholders to extract areas of the project to examine, evaluate, and inspect. For example, a project to create a catalog for a parts distributor may follow multiple paths to completion. Each path to completion has its own "family" of numbers that relate to each activity on the path (see Table 6-2).

TABLE 6-2	Path	Coding for Path	Typical Activities
Possible Paths in Creating a Catalog	Artwork	4.2	Concept (4.2.1) Logos (4.2.2) Font design (4.2.3)
	Photography	4.3	Product models (4.3.1) Airbrushing (4.3.2) Selection (4.3.3)
	Content	4.4	Message (4.4.1) Copywriting (4.4.2) Editing (4.4.3) Rewrites (4.4.4)
	Print	4.5	Signatures (4.5.1) Plates (4.5.2) Four-color printing (4.5.3)
	Bind	4.6	Assembly (4.6.1) Bindery (4.6.2) Trimming (4.6.3) Shrink-wrap (4.6.4)
	Distribution	4.7	Packaging (4.7.1) Labeling (4.7.2) Shipping (4.7.3)

Examining the Project Schedule

The project schedule includes, at a minimum, a date when the project begins and a date when the project is expected to end. The project schedule is considered proposed until the resources needed to complete the project work are ascertained. In addition to including the schedule, the project manager should include all the supporting details. Project schedules can be presented in many different formats, such as the following:

- **Project network diagram** Illustrates the flow of work, the relationship between activities, the critical path, and the expected project end date. PNDs, when used as the project schedule, should have dates associated with each project activity to show when the activity is expected to start and end.

- **Bar charts** Show the start and end dates for the project and the activity duration against a calendar. They are easy to read. Scheduling bar charts are also called Gantt charts.

- **Milestone charts** Plot out the high-level deliverables and external interfaces, such as a customer walkthrough, against a calendar. Milestone charts are like Gantt charts, but with less detail regarding individual activities. The following is an example of a milestone chart.

Milestone	July	Aug	Sep	Oct	Nov	Dec
Customer	△▼					
Architect signature		△	▼			
Foundation			△			
Framing					△ ▼	
Roofing					△	

Legend

△ Planned
▼ Actual

- **Schedule baseline** The agreed-upon project schedule based on your project network diagram. It's part of the project management plan, and your project progress is compared against the schedule baseline.

- **Schedule data** The supporting detail and relevant information for the project schedule. It includes details about the project milestones, project activities and their attributes, and relevant assumptions and constraints.

Utilizing the Schedule Management Plan

The schedule management plan is a subsidiary plan of the overall project plan. It is used to control changes to the schedule. A formal schedule management plan has procedures that control how changes to the project plan can be proposed, accounted for, and then implemented. An informal schedule management plan may consider changes on an instance-by-instance basis.

Updating the Resource Requirements

Due to resource leveling, resources may need to be added to the project. For example, a proposed leveling may extend the project beyond an acceptable completion date. To reach the project end date, the project manager elects to add resources to the critical path activities. The resources the project manager adds should be documented, and the associated costs should be accounted for and approved.

Planning the Schedule in Agile Environments

Agile relies on a product roadmap, sometimes called the product vision, to help the project manager, product owner, and project team see the expectations for the project. Agile planning takes a high-level approach to project schedule planning, usually a three- to six-month view, to predict how the project will move forward. The time-boxed iterations, or sprints, are predetermined durations of project work. Based on how long the project is expected to take and the duration of the sprints, it's easy to work backward and see how many sprints the project is likely to have. For example, a high-level schedule of six months with four-week sprints will offer a total of six sprints to map to the six-month anticipated schedule for the project work.

A clear understanding of the number of sprints helps the product owner and the team quickly and accurately prioritize the product backlog based on value to be delivered at the start of each iteration. At each iteration, a group of user stories, based on their values, is selected to tackle first. User stories are assigned story points based on their degree of difficulty to create; the more story points a user story has, the more hours of labor it will take to create the requirement.

Reviewing the Results of Developing the Schedule

There are seven outputs of developing the project schedule. Two of the most important outputs are the schedule baseline and the project schedule. The schedule baseline is an approved version of the schedule model. Once the baseline is created and approved, it can be changed only through the project's integrated change control. The baseline represents what you believe will happen in the project; what actually happens in the project is compared to the baseline. When there is a difference between what was expected and what the baseline predicts, it is called a schedule variance.

The project schedule is the actual schedule of when the work will happen, the relationship between activities, the flow of the activities, the duration of activities, the milestones, and the resources you'll utilize to complete the project. In almost all cases, the project schedule is presented in a chart or diagram to be most effective. Typical charts include the following:

- **Gantt charts**   Bar charts that show the duration of tasks against a calendar. This is the default view you've probably seen in Microsoft Project when creating and linking tasks.
- **Milestone charts**   Bar charts that show the target and actual dates for milestone completion.
- **Project schedule network diagram**   Shows the flow of the project work and relationship between activities. Project schedule network diagrams can also show a time scale for the nodes, activity dates, and other information. These schedule network diagrams are called time-scaled logic diagrams.

The schedule development process will also create schedule data, such as resource requirements, alternative schedules for best- and worst-case scenarios, consumption of schedule reserves, and possibly resource histograms, cash-flow forecasting, and other scheduling information unique to your organization and project.

Recall the two calendars—the project calendar and the resource calendar. These two calendars will be updated as needed to reflect the scheduling of project work, considerations for project hours, and other data that affects when the project work can take place and when resources are available. You'll also update the project management plan and documents as needed: schedule management plan, cost baseline, activity attributes, assumption log, duration estimates, lessons learned register, resource requirements, and risk register.

CERTIFICATION OBJECTIVE 6.06

Controlling the Schedule

Throughout a typical project, events will happen that may require updates to the project schedule. Schedule control is concerned with four factors:

- It documents the status of the project schedule and manages the schedule baseline.
- The project manager works with the factors that can cause schedule changes to confirm that the changes are needed, may have already happened, and cannot be avoided, and that the changes are agreed upon. Factors can include project team members, stakeholders, management, customers, and project conditions.

- The project manager examines the work results and conditions to determine whether the schedule has changed.
- The project manager manages the actual change in the schedule.

Managing the Inputs to Schedule Control

Schedule slippage can be caused by several things: scope creep, underestimating the project work, risks, decisions, and much more. The project manager needs to communicate with the resources and factors that can affect the project schedule throughout the project. This is one area where the project manager can't assume that everything's going to work out just fine. Schedule control, the process of managing changes to the project schedule, is based on several inputs:

- Project management plan
- Schedule management plan
- Schedule baseline
- Performance measurement baseline
- Project documents (lessons learned register, project and resource calendars, schedule, schedule data)
- Work performance data
- Organizational process assets

All changes to the schedule baseline must follow the integrated change control process. Schedule control is a formal approach to managing changes to the project schedule. It considers the conditions, reasons, requests, costs, and risks of making changes. It includes methods of tracking changes, approval levels based on thresholds, and the documentation of approved or declined changes. Schedule control is part of integrated change management.

Measuring Project Performance

Data analysis is needed to gain insight into project schedule performance. Poor performance may result in schedule changes. Consider a project team that is completing its work on time, but all the work results are unacceptable. The project team members may be rushing through their assignments to meet their deadlines. To compensate for this, the project may be changed to allow for additional quality inspections and more time for activity completion.

Though a burndown chart is typically used in agile projects, you can implement one to illustrate the amount of work left to do in the project or iteration. A burndown chart, such as the one shown in Figure 6-8, starts in the upper-right corner and predicts the amount of remaining work distributed over the timeline. As work is completed a second line representing the actual work is added to the chart to show any variances between what is happening and what was predicted. Based on current completion of tasks, you can add a third line to represent a trend and offer a new prediction of when the project will be done.

Examining the Schedule Variance

The project manager must actively monitor the variances between when activities are scheduled to end and when they actually end. An accumulation of differences between schedule baseline and actual dates may result in a schedule variance.

The project manager must also pay attention to the completion of activities on paths with float, not just on the critical path. Consider a project that has eight different paths to completion. The project manager should first identify the critical path, but he should also identify the float on each path. The paths should be arranged and monitored in a hierarchy from the path with the smallest float to the path with the largest float. As activities are completed, the float of each path should be monitored to identify any paths that may be slipping from the scheduled end dates.

Burndown charts show the balance of activities, the predicted completion of activities, and the forecast for when activities are likely to be finished.

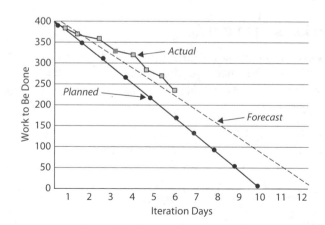

Updating the Project Schedule

So what happens when a schedule change occurs? The project manager must ensure that the project schedule is updated to reflect the change, document the change, and follow the guidelines within the schedule management plan. Any formal processes, such as notifying stakeholders or management, should be followed.

Revisions are a special type of project schedule change that cause the project start date and, more likely, the project end date to be changed. They typically stem from project scope changes. Because of the additional work the new scope requires, additional time is needed to complete the project.

Schedule delays, for whatever reason, may be so drastic that the entire project must be rebaselined. Rebaselining is a worst-case scenario and should occur only when adjusting for drastic, long delays. When rebaselining happens, all the historical information up to the point of the rebaseline is eliminated. Schedule revision is the preferred, and most common, approach to changing the project end date.

Applying Corrective Action

Corrective action is any method applied to bring the project schedule back into alignment with the original dates and goals for the project end date. Corrective actions are efforts to ensure that future performance meets the expected performance levels. It includes the following:

- Extraordinary measures to ensure that work packages complete as scheduled
- Extraordinary measures to ensure that work packages complete with as little delay as possible
- Root-cause analysis of schedule variances
- Measures to recover from schedule delays

Writing the Lessons Learned

Lessons learned on creating the schedule, changes to the project schedule, and responses to variances are needed as part of the project's historical information. Recall that lessons learned documentation happens throughout the project plan, not just at the conclusion of the project.

CERTIFICATION SUMMARY

Projects cannot last forever—thankfully. To finish and manage a project effectively, a project manager must be able to manage time effectively. Within a project, many factors can affect the project length: activity duration, project calendars, resource calendars, vendors, activity sequencing, and more. Schedule management begins with the constraints of the product schedule, the project calendar, and the resource calendars, as well as the activities and their expected duration.

Many projects can rely on project templates that were created for prior successful and similar projects. Other projects, including new and never-attempted technologies, require that a project schedule be created from scratch. The WBS contributes to the activity list, which, in turn, enables the project manager and the project team to begin activity sequencing.

Activities to be sequenced must be estimated. The project manager and the project team must evaluate the required time to complete the work packages. The project manager can rely on several estimating methods to arrive at a predicted duration for activities. For example, a project manager may use analogous estimation of historical data to provide the needed estimate. Or the project manager may use parametric estimating to predict the amount of time required for the activities. The important aspects of estimating are that each work package is considered and its duration calculated.

Within the process of activity sequencing will be hard logic and soft logic. Hard logic is the mandatory relationships between activities: the foundation must be in place before the house framing can begin. Soft logic allows the relationship and order of activities to be determined based on conditions, preferences, or other factors: the landscaping will happen before the house is painted so that dirt and dust won't ruin the fresh paint.

The relationships of activities are illustrated within a network diagram. Network diagrams show the path from start to completion and identify which activities are on the critical path. Of course, the critical path is the path with the longest duration and typically has zero slack or float. Activities on the noncritical paths may be delayed to the extent that they do not delay activities on the critical path.

Finally, project team members may tend to bloat their duration estimates. Bloating the work to allow for "wiggle room" on assignments can cause durations to swell way beyond the practical completion date of the project. In lieu of bloated estimates, project team members and the project manager should use a percentage of the project time as management reserve. Management reserve is a percentage of the overall project duration estimate, and it is set aside just for schedule slippage. When activities are late, the tardiness of the work is borrowed from management reserve rather than tacked on to the conclusion of the project.

KEY TERMS

To pass the PMP exam, you will need to memorize these terms and their definitions. For maximum value, create your own flashcards based on these definitions and review them daily. The definitions can be found within this chapter and in the glossary.

activity list   A listing of all the project activities required to complete each project phase or the entire project.

activity-on-node   A network diagramming approach that places the activities on a node in the project network diagram.

activity sequencing   The process of mapping the project activities in the order in which the work should be completed.

analogous estimating   A duration-estimating technique that bases the current project duration estimate on historical information from similar projects.

crashing   A duration-compression technique that adds project resources to the project in an effort to reduce the amount of time allotted for effort-driven activities.

critical path method   A network diagramming approach that identifies the minimum project duration. This includes project activities that cannot be delayed or the project completion date will be late.

discretionary dependencies   These project activities do not have to be completed in a particular order; instead, these tasks can be completed in the order determined by the project manager or at the project team's discretion.

fast tracking   A duration-compression technique that allows entire phases of a project to overlap other phases.

finish no earlier than (FNET)   A project constraint that requires an activity to finish no earlier than a specific date.

finish-to-finish   A relationship between project activities whereby the predecessor activities must finish before successor activities may finish.

finish-to-start   A relationship between project activities whereby the predecessor activities must finish before the successor activities may start; this is the most common network diagramming relationship type.

fist-to-five voting   Team members vote on the accuracy of an activity duration estimate by showing their fists, which represent low confidence, or up to five fingers, which show highest confidence. Votes of three fingers or lower are discussed to gain consensus.

float   A generic term that describes the amount of time an activity may be delayed without delaying any subsequent activities' start dates.

Gantt chart   A bar chart against a calendar to show the duration of activities and the sequence of activities in a project.

hard logic   The project activities must be completed in a particular order; this is also known as mandatory dependencies.

internal dependencies   Dependencies that are internal to the project that are often related to the nature of the work that's being completed.

Kanban   A sign board to show work in progress as requirements move through the predefined stages of a project. Most often used in lean and agile environments.

lag   Time added to a project activity to delay its start time; lag time is considered positive time and is sometimes called waiting time.

lead   Time added to an activity to allow its start time to begin earlier than scheduled; lead time is negative time, as it moves the activities closer to the project's start date.

mandatory dependencies   Project activities must happen in a particular order due to the nature of the work; also known as hard logic.

milestone chart   Shows when milestones are expected to be reached in the project schedule and when the milestones were achieved.

Monte Carlo analysis   A "what-if" scenario tool to determine how scenarios may work out, given any number of variables. The process doesn't create a specific answer, but a range of possible answers. When Monte Carlo is applied to a schedule, it can present, for example, the optimistic completion date, the pessimistic completion date, and the most likely completion date for each activity in the project.

negative total float   When a project or task is running late on its implementation, or if there's a predefined deadline for the project, you may experience negative float. This means the activities on the critical path are allotted enough time to meet the defined late finish date for the project.

network template   A network diagram based on previous similar projects that is adapted for the current project work.

parametric estimating   Ideal for projects with repetitive work, in which a parameter, such as five hours per unit, is used to estimate the project duration.

Parkinson's Law   Work expands to fill the amount of time allotted to it.

precedence diagramming method   The most common method of arranging the project work visually. The PDM puts the activities in boxes, called nodes, and connects the boxes with arrows. The arrows represent the relationship and the dependencies of the work packages.

project calendar   A calendar that defines the working times for the project. For example, a project may require the project team to work nights and weekends so as not to disturb the ongoing operations of the organization during working hours. In addition, the project calendar accounts for holidays, working hours, and work shifts the project will cover.

resource calendar   Shows when resources, such as project team members, consultants, and SMEs, are available to work on the project. It considers vacations, other commitments within the organization, restrictions on contracted work, overtime issues, and so on.

resource leveling   A method to reduce resources overallocated or allocated unevenly, also known as flattening. Resource leveling can be applied in different methods to accomplish different goals. One of the most common methods is to ensure that workers are not overextended on activities.

resource smoothing   A technique that enables you to do resource leveling, but only on noncritical path activities. This approach levels resource utilization by taking advantage of activities that have available float. For those activities with no float, the resource utilization will not be edited.

schedule control   Schedule control is concerned with three processes: the project manager confirms that any schedule changes are agreed upon, the project manager examines the work results and conditions to know if the schedule has changed, and the project manager manages the actual change in the schedule. The schedule baseline cannot be changed without using the integrated change control process.

schedule management plan   A subsidiary plan of the overall project plan, used to develop, manage, and control the schedule. A formal schedule management plan has procedures that control how changes to the project plan can be proposed, accounted for, and then implemented.

schedule variance   The difference between the schedule baseline and the performance to schedule.

soft logic   The preferred order of activities. Project managers should use these relationships at their discretion and document the logic behind making soft logic decisions. Also known as discretionary dependencies, soft logic allows activities to happen in a preferred order because of best practices, conditions unique to the project work, or external events.

sprint   Time-boxed duration, typically two-to-four weeks, of project execution in an agile environment. Sprints are iterations of executing the prioritized list of product backlog requirements.

Start no earlier than (SNET)   A project constraint that demands that a project activity start no earlier than a specific date.

start-to-finish   A relationship that requires an activity to start so that a successor activity may finish; it is unusual and is rarely used.

start-to-start   A relationship structure that requires a task to start before a successor task activity may start. This relationship allows both activities to happen in tandem.

three-point estimate   An estimate that uses optimistic, most likely, and pessimistic values to determine the cost or duration of a project component. Also called triangular distribution.

user stories   A backlog of prioritized requirements. User stories are prioritized by value with the product owner and project team in an agile environment. User stories are assigned story points to predict the difficulty of creating the requirement. Only so many story points are allowed per iteration.

TWO-MINUTE DRILL

Creating the Schedule Management Plan

❑ The schedule management plan is part of the overall project management plan. It defines how the project schedule will be created, how you'll monitor the project's schedule, and how you'll protect and control the project schedule.

❑ The schedule management plan includes the rules for performance measurement. This component of the plan defines how exactly you'll measure the project on its schedule performance, how you'll know progress is happening in the project, and how you might use earned value management as part of your project measurement.

❑ The process of creating the schedule management plan uses four inputs: the project management plan, the project charter, enterprise environmental factors, and organizational process assets. Through analysis and meetings, the project manager, the project team, and expert judgment, will create the schedule management plan.

Defining the Activities

❑ Based on the project management plan, enterprise environmental factors, and organizational process assets, the project manager and the project team will define the activities that are required to be completed to create the project scope.

❑ Just as the project team decomposes the project scope into work packages, the work packages can be broken down into project activities. Decomposition is a project management tool that breaks down deliverables into activities to execute the project more successfully.

❑ Rolling wave planning is a project management approach to progressive elaboration. Imminent work is planned in detail, while future work is planned only at a high level. Rolling wave planning is ideal for projects in which the current work may shape future project requirements.

Sequencing Activities

❑ Projects are made up of sequential activities to create a product. The WBS and the activity list serve as key inputs to the sequencing of project activities. The science of arranging, calculating, and predicting how long the activities will take to complete allows the project manager to create a schedule and then predict when the project will end.

❑ Hard logic is the approach that requires activities to happen in a specific order due to the nature of the work—for example, configuring a computer workstation's operating systems before adding the software.

❑ Soft logic is a "preferred" method of arranging activities based on conditions, guidelines, or best practices—for example, the project manager prefers to have the artwork for the user manual created before the contents of the user manual are written.

❑ The sequence of activities is displayed in a project schedule network diagram. The network diagram illustrates the flow of activities and the relationship between activities. The precedent diagramming method is the most common approach to arranging activities visually.

❑ Free float is the total time a single activity can be delayed without delaying the early start of any subsequent activities.

❑ A schedule constraint on an activity or the project completion date may cause negative float in the project or a task. This means there's not enough time to complete the activities, based on their duration, to meet the time constraint on the task or project.

❑ Total float is the total time an activity can be delayed without delaying project completion.

❑ Project float is the total time the project can be delayed without passing the customer-expected completion date.

Estimating Activity Durations

❑ Activity duration estimates are needed to calculate how long the project will take to complete. Estimates can come from project team members, commercial databases, expert judgment, and historical information.

❑ Analogous estimating relies on historical information to predict how long current project activities should last.

❑ Parametric estimates use a mathematical model to calculate how long activities should take based on units, duration, and effort.

Developing the Schedule

❑ The critical path is the longest path to completion in the network diagram. Activities on the critical path typically have no float or slack. Free float is the amount of time an activity can be delayed without affecting the next activity's scheduled start date. Total float is the amount of time an activity can be delayed without affecting the project end date.

❑ Duration compression is applied to reduce the length of the project or to account for project delays. Crashing adds resources to project activities and usually increases cost. Fast tracking allows activities to happen in tandem and usually increases risk.

❑ The schedule management plan must be consulted when project schedule changes occur, are proposed, or are needed. The schedule control system implements the schedule management plan and is part of integration change management.

❑ The project timeline defines the sequence of project activities, the consideration of available resources, constraints that may affect when the work can be completed, and sets expectations for when the project may be completed.

❑ A project network diagram visualizes the sequencing of project activities. The most common method is the critical path method and shows the early start, early finish, late start, and late finish possibilities for each project activity. This critical path method illustrates the ordering of events and the relationship between activities among several possible paths to project completion.

❑ In the critical path method of creating the project network diagram, the critical path is the longest duration of connected activities to reach the project completion. There can be more than one critical path if two or more paths have the same duration. The critical path can also change because of delays, changes to the project scope or schedule, availability of resources, and other constraints.

❑ Float is the amount of time a task can be delayed without delaying the project's completion. There are four types of float. Free float is the total time a single activity can be delayed without delaying the early start of any successor activities. Total float is the total time an activity can be delayed without delaying project completion. Project float is the total time the project can be delayed without passing the customer-expected completion date. Negative float, which is based on constraints and deadlines for certain activities, means the activities on the critical path don't have enough time to meet the defined finish date for the project or the constrained activity.

Controlling the Schedule

❑ The project management plan, the project schedule, work performance information, and organizational process assets are all inputs to controlling the project schedule.

❑ Schedule compression is an approach to bring the project back into alignment with the project baseline. Crashing adds resources to the project work, which usually increases project costs. Fast tracking allows entire phases of the project to overlap, which may increase risks.

❑ Updates to the project schedule may cause the schedule baseline, schedule management plan, and the cost baseline to be updated. All changes must flow through the schedule change control system and integrated change control.

SELF TEST

1. You are the project manager of the JHG Project. This project has 32 stakeholders and will require implementation activities in North and South America. You have been requested to provide a duration estimate for the project. Of the following, which will offer the best level of detail in your estimate?
   A. The resource calendar
   B. An order of magnitude
   C. A requirements document
   D. A stakeholder analysis

2. Michael is the project manager of the 78GH Project. This project requires several members of the project team to complete a certification class for another project the week of November 2. This class causes some of the project activities on Michael's activities to be delayed from his target schedule. This is an example of which of the following?
   A. Hard logic
   B. External dependencies
   C. Soft logic
   D. Conflict of interest

3. You are managing an interior decorating project. The walls are scheduled to be painted immediately after the primer is applied. You have allowed 36 hours between the primer activity and the painting activity to ensure that the primer has cured. This is an example of which one of the following?
   A. Lead
   B. Lag
   C. Soft logic
   D. Finish-to-start relationship

4. You are the project manager of the DFK Project and you're reviewing your project network diagram. You are considering changing the relationship of some of the project activities to reduce the duration of the project work. Consider your project's network diagram (as shown in the following illustration).

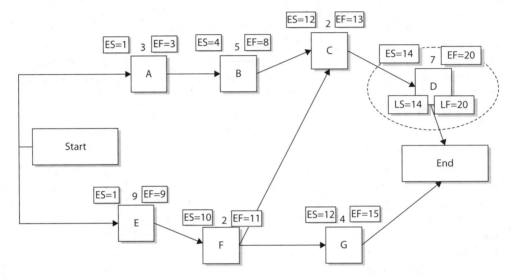

Given the diagram, what is the relationship between tasks F and G?

A. FS

B. SS

C. FF

D. SF

5. You are the project manager for the LLL Project. Steven, a project team member, is confused about network diagrams. Specifically, he wants to know what the critical path is in a network diagram. Your answer is which one of the following?

A. The critical path is the network that hosts the activities most critical to the project's success.

B. The critical path is a path with the longest duration.

C. The critical path is always one path that cannot be delayed, or the entire project will be delayed.

D. The critical path is the path from start to completion with no deviation from the project plan.

6. You are the project manager of the HQQ Project and you're working with your customer stakeholder. The stakeholder has asked that you find a method to reduce the overall project duration for her organization. She has promised a bonus to your company of $10,000 per day that you finish ahead of schedule. Which duration compression technique could you utilize on activities that are effort-driven?
   A. Crashing
   B. Fast tracking
   C. Effort-driven activities cannot be compressed
   D. Resource smoothing

7. You are creating a schedule duration estimate for the activities in the PDR Project. You're working with your project team and comparing the results of a past similar project to predict the schedule for the current project. What estimating approach are you using?
   A. Organizational process assets
   B. Parametric
   C. Analogous
   D. PERT

8. You are the project manager for your organization, which utilizes an agile approach to project management. The development team is rating the difficulty of completing the requirements in the current sprint. What term describes rating of the requirements to determine how many requirements can be completed in a sprint?
   A. Fist-to-five voting
   B. Value analysis
   C. Sprint backlog
   D. Story points

9. You are the project manager for the POL Project. This project will use a three-point estimate to calculate the estimates for activity duration. For Activity D, you have the following information: P = 9 weeks, O = 4 weeks, M = 5 weeks. What is the result of this estimate?
   A. 18 weeks
   B. 6 weeks
   C. 33.33 days
   D. 3 weeks

10. You are the project manager for the YKL Project. This project will affect several lines of business at completion. You have elected to schedule each milestone in the project to end so the work does not affect current business cycles. This is an example of which one of the following?
    A. Constraint
    B. Expert judgment
    C. WBS scheduling
    D. Soft logic

11. You are the project manager for the MNB Project. You and your project team are about to enter the activity duration estimating process. Which of the following will *not* be helpful in your meeting?
    A. Constraints
    B. Assumptions
    C. The project charter
    D. Identified risks

12. You are the project manager for a new training program at your customer's site. This program will require each of the customer's employees to attend a half-day class and complete an assessment exam. You will be completing the training at the customer's facility and will need a trainer for the duration of the training, which is six months. This is an example of which of the following?
    A. Resource requirements
    B. Assumption
    C. Cost constraint
    D. A human resource issue

13. You are the project manager for a construction company. Your firm has been contracted to complete the drilling of a well for a new cabin in Arkansas. The specification of the well is documented, but your company has little experience in well drilling in Arkansas. The stakeholder is concerned that your time estimates are not accurate, since the soil and rock in Arkansas are quite different from the soil in your home state. Which one of the following can you use to ensure your project estimates are accurate?
    A. An order of magnitude
    B. A commercial duration estimating database
    C. Local contractors
    D. Soil samplings from the Arkansas government

14. You are the project manager for your organization. You and your project team are in conflict on the amount of time allotted to complete certain activities. Several of the team members want to bloat the time associated with activities to ensure they will have enough time to complete their tasks should something go awry. The law of economics that these tasks may suffer from is which one of the following?
    A. Parkinson's Law
    B. The law of diminishing returns
    C. Hertzberg's theory of motivation
    D. Oligopoly

15. You are the project manager for your organization. You and your project team are in conflict regarding the amount of time allotted to complete certain activities. Several of the team members want to bloat the time associated with activities to ensure they will have enough time to complete

their tasks should some risk events cause the schedule to change. Instead of overestimating their project activities, the project team should use which of the following?

A. Capital reserve

B. Contingency plans

C. Contingency reserve

D. Assumptions of plus or minus a percentage

16. You are the project manager for your organization and part of your role requires that you coach the project team on the project management processes. At this point in your project, you're estimating the activity durations with the project team and need to review the tools and techniques that are appropriate for use with this process. Which one of the following is *not* a tool and technique for the estimate activity duration process?

A. Risk identification

B. Analogous estimating

C. Reserve analysis

D. Three-point estimating

17. You are the project manager for the 987 Project. Should this project run over schedule, it will cost your organization $35,000 per day in lost sales. With four months to completion, you realize the project is running late. You decide, with management's approval, to add more project team members to the plan to complete the work on time. This is an example of which of the following?

A. Crashing

B. Fast tracking

C. Expert judgment

D. Cost-benefit analysis

18. You are the project manager for the 987 Project. Should this project run over schedule, it will cost your organization $35,000 per day in lost sales. With four months to completion, you realize the project is running late. You decide, with management's approval, to change the relationship between several of the work packages so they begin in tandem rather than sequentially. This is an example of which one of the following?

A. Crashing

B. Fast tracking

C. Expert judgment

D. Cost-benefit analysis

19. Chris, a project manager for his company, is explaining the difference between a Gantt chart and a milestone chart. Which of the following best describes a Gantt chart?

A. A Gantt chart depicts what was planned against what occurred.

B. A Gantt chart compares the work in the project against the work that has been completed.

C. A Gantt chart depicts the work in the project against a calendar.

D. A Gantt chart depicts the work in the project against each resource's calendar.

20. Beth is a project manager for her organization. Management has asked Beth to use the CPM approach in her network diagram. She is not familiar with this approach and she's asked you to help her complete this portion of her project work. Which of the following is a correct attribute of the critical path?

A. It determines the earliest completion date.

B. It has the largest amount of float.

C. It has the most activities in the PND.

D. It is the path with the most expensive project activities.

21. You are the project manager for a construction project. Your foreman informs you that, because of the humidity, the concrete will need to cure for an additional 24 hours before the framing can begin. To accommodate the requirement, you add _____ time to the framing activity.

A. Lead

B. Lag

C. Delay

D. Slack

22. Management has informed you that you must flatten your project through resource leveling. What is likely to happen to your project schedule if your project team members are allowed to contribute only 30 hours per week?

A. The project schedule will increase.

B. The project schedule will decrease.

C. The project critical path will change.

D. The project manager will need to use the critical path method.

23. You are the project manager for a project with the following network diagram. Study the following diagram: Which path is the critical path?

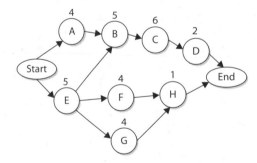

A. ABCD

B. EBCD

C. EFH

D. EGH

24. Bertha is the project manager for the HAR Project. The project is behind schedule, and Bertha has elected, with management's approval, to crash the critical path. This process adds more what? (Choose the best answer.)

A. Cost

B. Time

C. Risk

D. Documentation

25. Bertha is the project manager for the HAR Project. It's currently behind schedule, and Bertha has elected, with management's approval, to fast track the critical path. This process adds more what? (Choose the best answer.)

A. Cost

B. Time

C. Risk

D. Documentation

SELF TEST ANSWERS

1. You are the project manager of the JHG Project. This project has 32 stakeholders and will require implementation activities in North and South America. You have been requested to provide a duration estimate for the project. Of the following, which will offer the best level of detail in your estimate?

A. The resource calendar

B. An order of magnitude

C. A requirements document

D. A stakeholder analysis

☑ **A.** The resource calendar is the best choice for this scenario because it is the only activity duration estimating input listed.

☒ **B, C,** and **D** are incorrect. **B** is incorrect because the order of magnitude provides little information for accurate estimating. **C,** while tempting, is incorrect because the requirements document lists the high-level deliverables, while the WBS provides more detail. **D** is incorrect because stakeholder analysis does not provide enough information to predict accurately when the project will end.

2. Michael is the project manager of the 78GH Project. This project requires several members of the project team to complete a certification class for another project the week of November 2. This class causes some of the project activities on Michael's activities to be delayed from his target schedule. This is an example of which of the following?

A. Hard logic
B. External dependencies
C. Soft logic
D. Conflict of interest

☑   **B.** Before the work can begin, the certification class external to the work must be completed.
☒   **A, C,** and **D** are incorrect. **A** is incorrect; hard logic is the mandatory sequencing of events. **C** is incorrect because there is no preferential (soft) logic. **D** is incorrect because it does not apply to this scenario.

3. You are managing an interior decorating project. The walls are scheduled to be painted immediately after the primer is applied. You have allowed 36 hours between the primer activity and the painting activity to ensure that the primer has cured. This is an example of which one of the following?

A. Lead
B. Lag
C. Soft logic
D. Finish-to-start relationship

☑   **B.** The time between the activities is lag time. The painting activity must wait 36 hours before it can begin.
☒   **A, C,** and **D** are incorrect. **A**, lead time, is when the activities are brought closer together or even overlap. **C**, soft logic, describes when activities are scheduled based on preferences, guidelines, or external conditions. **D** is incorrect, because, although this does describe a finish-to-start relationship, lag is a better choice because of the added waiting time.

4. You are the project manager of the DFK Project and you're reviewing your project network diagram. You are considering changing the relationship of some of the project activities to reduce the duration of the project work. Consider your project's network diagram (as shown in the following illustration).

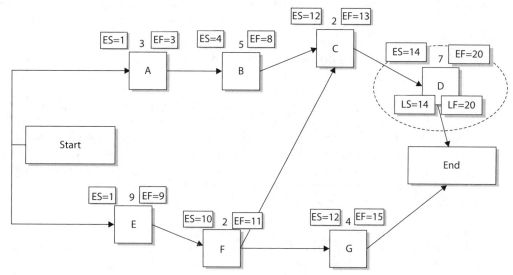

A. FS
B. SS
C. FF
D. SF

  ☑ **A.** G is slated to start immediately after F, so this is a finish-to-start (FS) relationship. In other words, F must finish so G may start.
  ☒ **B, C,** and **D** are incorrect. These relationships do not fit the scenario.

5. You are the project manager for the LLL Project. Steven, a project team member, is confused about network diagrams. Specifically, he wants to know what the critical path is in a network diagram. Your answer is which one of the following?
A. The critical path is the network that hosts the activities most critical to the project's success.
B. The critical path is a path with the longest duration.
C. The critical path is always one path that cannot be delayed, or the entire project will be delayed.
D. The critical path is the path from start to completion with no deviation from the project plan.

  ☑ **B.** The critical path is always the path with the longest duration; it's also the minimum amount of time needed to complete the project.
  ☒ **A, C,** and **D** are incorrect. **A** is incorrect because the critical path hosts the activities, not a network. **C** is a distraction answer and is incorrect because there can be more than one critical path in a network diagram. **D** is incorrect because it does not adequately describe the critical path.

6. You are the project manager of the HQQ Project and you're working with your customer stakeholder. The stakeholder has asked that you find a method to reduce the overall project duration for her organization. She has promised a bonus to your company of $10,000 per day that you finish ahead of schedule. Which duration compression technique could you utilize on activities that are effort-driven?

    A. Crashing
    B. Fast tracking
    C. Effort-driven activities cannot be compressed
    D. Resource smoothing

> ☑ **A.** Crashing enables you to add more labor to effort-driven activities. By adding more labor, or effort, you are reducing the duration of the activity.
> ☒ **B, C,** and **D** are incorrect. **B** is incorrect because fast tracking enables you to overlap phases in your project and isn't the best choice for the question. **C** is incorrect because effort-driven activities are ideal activities to be reduced through additional labor. **D** is incorrect because resource smoothing refers to the leveling of resources on noncritical path activities. This approach doesn't reduce the duration of activities.

7. You are creating a schedule duration estimate for the activities in the PDR Project. You're working with your project team and comparing the results of a past similar project to predict the schedule for the current project. What estimating approach are you using?

    A. Organizational process assets
    B. Parametric
    C. Analogous
    D. PERT

> ☑ **C.** This is an example of an analogous estimate. You can remember this estimate approach by identifying the "analogy" between the two similar projects.
> ☒ **A, B,** and **D** are incorrect. **A** is incorrect because, although the previous project data is part of organizational process assets, the assets are not an estimating approach. **B** is incorrect because parametric estimates use a parameter, such as five hours per unit. **D** is also incorrect because PERT uses an average of the optimistic, most likely, and pessimistic time estimates for each activity.

8. You are the project manager for your organization, which utilizes an agile approach to project management. The development team is rating the difficulty of completing the requirements in the current sprint. What term describes rating of the requirements to determine how many requirements can be completed in a sprint?

    A. Fist-to-five voting
    B. Value analysis
    C. Sprint backlog
    D. Story points

    ☑ **D.** Requirements are written as user stories. Story points score the difficulty of the tasks needed to complete a user story in a sprint.

    ☒ **A, B,** and **C** are incorrect. These terms are not processes that rate requirements to determine how many requirements can be completed in a sprint.

9. You are the project manager for the POL Project. This project will use a three-point estimate to calculate the estimates for activity duration. For Activity D, you have the following information: P = 9, O = 4, M = 5. What is the result of this estimate?

  A. 18 weeks

  B. 6 weeks

  C. 33.33 days

  D. 3 weeks

    ☑ **B.** The formula is (P + M + O)/3. In this instance, the outcome is 6 weeks.

    ☒ **A, C,** and **D** are incorrect. These calculations are incorrect.

10. You are the project manager for the YKL Project. This project will affect several lines of business at completion. You have elected to schedule each milestone in the project to end so the work does not affect current business cycles. This is an example of which one of the following?

  A. Constraint

  B. Expert judgment

  C. WBS scheduling

  D. Soft logic

    ☑ **D.** Soft logic enables the project manager to make decisions based on conditions outside of the project, best practices, or guidelines.

    ☒ **A, B,** and **C** are incorrect. **A** is incorrect because this is not an example of constraints, since the project manager is not required to use soft logic. **B** and **C** are incorrect; they do not describe the scenario fully.

11. You are the project manager for the MNB Project. You and your project team are about to enter the activity duration estimating process. Which of the following will *not* be helpful in your meeting?

  A. Constraints

  B. Assumptions

  C. The project charter

  D. Identified risks

    ☑ **C.** The project charter is not an input to the activity duration estimating process.

    ☒ **A, B,** and **D** are incorrect. These are inputs to activity duration estimating.

12. You are the project manager for a new training program at your customer's site. This program will require each of the customer's employees to attend a half-day class and complete an assessment exam. You will be completing the training at the customer's facility and will need a trainer for the duration of the training, which is six months. This is an example of which of the following?
    A. Resource requirements
    B. Assumption
    C. Cost constraint
    D. A human resource issue

    ☑ **A.** The trainer resource is required for the project for six months.
    ☒ **B, C,** and **D** are incorrect. They do not describe the resource requirement of the trainer on the project.

13. You are the project manager for a construction company. Your firm has been contracted to complete the drilling of a well for a new cabin in Arkansas. The specification of the well is documented, but your company has little experience in well drilling in Arkansas. The stakeholder is concerned that your time estimates are not accurate, since the soil and rock in Arkansas are quite different from the soil in your home state. Which one of the following can you use to ensure your project estimates are accurate?
    A. An order of magnitude
    B. A commercial duration estimating database
    C. Local contractors
    D. Soil samplings from the Arkansas government

    ☑ **B.** Commercial duration-estimating databases are valid resources to confirm or base time estimates on.
    ☒ **A, C,** and **D** are incorrect. **A** is incorrect because an order of magnitude offers very little detail on time estimates. **C** is incorrect because local contractors are not the best source for confirming time estimates; the question does not define whether the contractors are local to Arkansas or to your home state. **D** is incorrect because commercial duration estimating databases are much more reliable in this scenario.

14. You are the project manager for your organization. You and your project team are in conflict on the amount of time allotted to complete certain activities. Several of the team members want to bloat the time associated with activities to ensure they will have enough time to complete their tasks should something go awry. The law of economics that these tasks may suffer from is which one of the following?
    A. Parkinson's Law
    B. The law of diminishing returns
    C. Hertzberg's theory of motivation
    D. Oligopoly

☑   **A.** Parkinson's Law states that work will expand to fulfill the time allotted to it. Bloated tasks will take all the time allotted. Management reserve should be used instead.

☒   **B, C,** and **D** are incorrect. **B** is incorrect because this describes the relationship between effort, duration, and the maximum yield. **C** is incorrect because Hertzberg's theory of motivation describes personalities and worker motivation. **D** is incorrect because an oligopoly is a procurement issue in which there are few vendors available to choose from. Plus, the vendors may seemingly have checks and balances with each other.

15. You are the project manager for your organization. You and your project team are in conflict regarding the amount of time allotted to complete certain activities. Several of the team members want to bloat the time associated with activities to ensure they will have enough time to complete their tasks should some risk events cause the schedule to change. Instead of overestimating their project activities, the project team should use which of the following?

A. Capital reserve

B. Contingency plans

C. Contingency reserve

D. Assumptions of plus or minus a percentage

☑   **C.** Rather than bloat activities, projects should use a contingency reserve. A contingency reserve is a portion of the project schedule allotted for time overruns on activities.

☒   **A, B,** and **D** are incorrect. **A** is incorrect because it does not describe the scenario. **B** is incorrect because contingency plans are a response to risk situations. **D** is incorrect because it describes a range of variance.

16. You are the project manager for your organization and part of your role requires that you coach the project team on the project management processes. At this point in your project, you're estimating the activity durations with the project team and need to review the tools and techniques that are appropriate for use with this process. Which one of the following is *not* a tool and technique for the estimate activity duration process??

A. Risk identification

B. Analogous estimating

C. Reserve analysis

D. Three-point estimating

☑   **A.** Risk identification is not a tool and technique of the estimate activity durations process.

☒   **B, C,** and **D** are incorrect. These are tools and techniques of activity duration estimating. This process has six tools to consider: expert judgment, analogous estimating, parametric estimating, three-point estimating, Delphi technique, and reserve analysis.

17. You are the project manager for the 987 Project. Should this project run over schedule, it will cost your organization $35,000 per day in lost sales. With four months to completion, you realize the project is running late. You decide, with management's approval, to add more project team members to the plan to complete the work on time. This is an example of which of the following?

A. Crashing

B. Fast tracking

C. Expert judgment

D. Cost-benefit analysis

☑ **A.** When more resources are added to a project to complete the work on time, it is called crashing.

☒ **B, C,** and **D** are incorrect. **B** is incorrect because fast tracking is the process of changing the relationship between activities to allow tasks to overlap. **C** is incorrect because expert judgment is not used in this scenario. **D** is incorrect; cost-benefit analysis may be part of the process to decide the value of adding more workers to the schedule, but it is not the process described.

18. You are the project manager for the 987 Project. Should this project run over schedule, it will cost your organization $35,000 per day in lost sales. With four months to completion, you realize the project is running late. You decide, with management's approval, to change the relationship between several of the work packages so they begin in tandem rather than sequentially. This is an example of which one of the following?

A. Crashing

B. Fast tracking

C. Expert judgment

D. Cost-benefit analysis

☑ **B.** Fast tracking allows activities to operate in tandem with each other rather than sequentially.

☒ **A, C,** and **D** are incorrect. **A** is incorrect; when more resources are added to a project to complete the work on time, it is called crashing. **C** is incorrect because expert judgment is not used in this scenario. **D** is incorrect; cost-benefit analysis may be part of the process to decide the value of fast tracking the schedule, but it is not the process described.

19. Chris, a project manager for his company, is explaining the difference between a Gantt chart and a milestone chart. Which of the following best describes a Gantt chart?

A. A Gantt chart depicts what was planned against what occurred.

B. A Gantt chart compares the work in the project against the work that has been completed.

C. A Gantt chart depicts the work in the project against a calendar.

D. A Gantt chart depicts the work in the project against each resource's calendar.

☑ **C.** A Gantt chart is a bar chart that represents the duration of activities against a calendar. The length of the bars represents the length of activities, while the order of the bars represents the order of activities in the project.

☒ **A, B,** and **D** are incorrect. **A** and **B** are incorrect because they describe a tracking Gantt. **D** is incorrect because this does not describe a Gantt chart.

20. Beth is a project manager for her organization. Management has asked Beth to use the CPM approach in her network diagram. She is not familiar with this approach and she's asked you to help her complete this portion of her project work. Which of the following is a correct attribute of the critical path?
    A. It determines the earliest completion date.
    B. It has the largest amount of float.
    C. It has the most activities in the PND.
    D. It is the path with the most expensive project activities.

☑ **A.** Of all the choices presented, **A** is the best description of the critical path. The critical path is the path with the longest duration and it tells the earliest and the latest day the project can be completed. There can be instances, however, when the project's expected end date is well beyond the duration of the scheduled work. In such cases, the critical path is considered the path with the least amount of float.

☒ **B, C,** and **D** are incorrect. These are false descriptions of the critical path. The critical path has the smallest amount of float, is the longest duration, and does not necessarily have the most expensive activities.

21. You are the project manager for a construction project. Your foreman informs you that, because of the humidity, the concrete will need to cure for an additional 24 hours before the framing can begin. To accommodate the requirement, you add _____ time to the framing activity.
    A. Lead
    B. Lag
    C. Delay
    D. Slack

☑ **B.** You will add lag time to the framing activity. Lag is waiting time.

☒ **A, C,** and **D** are incorrect. **A** is incorrect; lead time allows activities to overlap. **C** is not the correct choice, because a delay isn't the correct nomenclature for the scenario. Lag time is what's added to the schedule, not a delay. **D** is also incorrect because slack is the amount of time a task can be delayed without delaying the scheduled start date of dependent activities.

22. Management has informed you that you must flatten your project through resource leveling. What is likely to happen to your project schedule if your project team members are allowed to contribute only 30 hours per week?
  A. The project schedule will increase.
  B. The project schedule will decrease.
  C. The project critical path will change.
  D. The project manager will need to use the critical chain method.

☑ **A.** When the project schedule is flattened through resource leveling, the project duration (schedule) will likely increase.
☒ **B, C,** and **D** are incorrect. The project schedule will not decrease, and there's no evidence that the critical path will change. The project manager can use the critical chain method or not, and it will likely not affect the project duration.

23. You are the project manager for a project with the following network diagram. Study the diagram: Which path is the critical path?

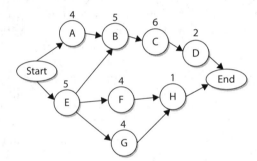

  A. ABCD
  B. EBCD
  C. EFH
  D. EGH

☑ **B** is the critical path because EBCD is the longest path to completion at 18 days.
☒ **A, C,** and **D** are incorrect. These paths have float.

24. Bertha is the project manager for the HAR Project. The project is behind schedule, and Bertha has elected, with management's approval, to crash the critical path. This process adds more what? (Choose the best answer.)

    A. Cost
    B. Time
    C. Risk
    D. Documentation

    > ☑ **A.** Crashing involves adding resources, which typically increases cost.
    >
    > ☒ **B, C,** and **D** are incorrect. **B** is incorrect because crashing is an effort to reduce time, not add it. **C** may be correct, but it is not the best answer. **D** is incorrect because crashing doesn't necessarily add more documentation. Crashing adds resources, which will add costs to the project.

25. Bertha is the project manager for the HAR Project. It's currently behind schedule, and Bertha has elected, with management's approval, to fast track the critical path. This process adds more what? (Choose the best answer.)

    A. Cost
    B. Time
    C. Risk
    D. Documentation

    > ☑ **C.** Fast tracking adds risk because tasks can overlap.
    >
    > ☒ **A, B,** and **D** are incorrect. **A** may be correct in some instances, but it is not the best choice here. **B** is incorrect because Bertha wants to remove time, not add it. **D** is also incorrect, because fast tracking doesn't necessarily add documentation to the project. Fast tracking allows phases and activities to overlap and this increases risk for the project.

Chapter 7

Introducing Project Cost Management

CERTIFICATION OBJECTIVES

7.01	Planning the Project Costs		7.05	Measuring Project Performance
7.02	Estimating the Project Costs		✓	Two-Minute Drill
7.03	Creating a Project Budget		Q&A	Self Test
7.04	Implementing Cost Control			

Projects cost money. Ever worked with a client who had a huge vision for a project but little capital to invest in that vision? Or worked with a client who gasped when you revealed how much it would cost to complete her desired scope of work? Or have you been fortunate with customers who accepted the costs for the project at face value, made certain that funds were available, and sent you on your way to complete the work? As a rule, management and customers are always concerned with how much a project is going to cost in relation to how much a project is going to earn as a return on the investment (ROI). And stakeholders will measure costs and return on investment with different approaches. Some organizations define costs when the invoice is received, others when the order is placed, and even others only when the payment is actually made.

Most likely, there is more need for negotiating, questioning, and evaluating for larger projects than for smaller ones. The relationship between the project cost and the project scope should be direct: You get what you pay for. Think it's possible to buy a mansion at ranch home prices? Not likely. Think it's possible to run a worldwide marketing campaign at the cost of a postcard mailer? Not likely. A realistic expectation of what a project will cost will give great weight to the project's scope.

As the business need undergoes analysis, progressive elaboration and estimates are completed based on varying levels of detail, and eventually the cost of the project emerges. Often, however, predicted costs and actual costs vary. Poor planning, skewed assumptions, and overly optimistic estimates all contribute to this. A successful project manager must be able to plan, predict, budget, and control the costs of a project.

Exploring Project Cost Management

Costs associated with projects are not just the costs of goods procured to complete the project. The cost of the labor may be one of the biggest expenses of a project. The project manager must rely on time estimates to predict the cost of the labor to complete the project work. In addition, the cost of the equipment and materials needed to complete the project work must be factored into the project expenses. This chapter examines the management of project costs, how to predict them, account for them, and then, with plan in hand, to control them. We'll examine exactly how costs are planned for and taken into consideration by the performing organization and how the size of the project affects the cost estimating process.

One of the most popular topics I'm asked about in my project management exam prep classes is earned value management (EVM). EVM is a suite of formulas to show project performance. While most of EVM deals with the cost of the project in relation to what was created, there's another facet we'll look at called *earned schedule*. Earned schedule looks at the actual time it took to complete a portion (or all) of the project. I'll talk about that in detail a bit later in this chapter.

Tailoring the Project Cost Management Approach

How your organization manages project costs is likely different from how my organization manages project costs. Every organization, like every project, is different, and cost management can be managed any number of different ways. Organizations might use a database of past projects' financial information to guide the current project's finances. Organizations can also use special estimating and budget approaches they've developed over years of experience. Earned value management can be implemented fully, partially, or not all—there's no requirement to use it. Project and program governance can also affect cost management techniques, financial audits for projects, and special procedures unique to the organization.

Agile projects usually don't have the in-depth planning and estimating approaches that predictive life cycle projects use. This is because when things are consistently changing, as you'd expect in an agile project, estimates aren't very reliable. More likely, agile projects are going to have a high-level cost estimate for the project, based on past projects, the expertise of the project manager or other experts, or the predicted hours of labor for the size of the known project work.

For your PMP exam, you'll want to know about the cost management processes covered in this chapter:

- Planning cost management
- Estimating costs
- Determining the budget
- Controlling costs

CERTIFICATION OBJECTIVE 7.01

Planning the Project Costs

You need to create a plan for how you'll manage the costs of the project. This direct-forward cost management process is part of the project's planning process group and defines how you, the project manager, will manage the costs of the project. Like most of the subsidiary project management plans, this plan directs the other processes in the process group. It serves as a guidebook for how the process groups should operate within your organization.

If you're thinking that a cost management plan could be standardized for your organization, you're on the right track. Most organizations could create a standard project cost management plan that serves as a template for all projects. You'd then adapt that template to all future projects. That's something important to remember for your PMP exam: You don't have to start from scratch when creating a subsidiary plan, cost management plan, or others; just take what's been created in the past and adapt it to the present. That's part of utilizing your organizational process assets to make your life easier, but it also keeps the projects consistent by using what has worked in the past.

 on the job **You might be wondering whether you need to create a cost management plan for every project that you're managing. Let me answer that for you: No, you don't. Remember that these processes are not required, but available. You might have a small project, a project that's based on previous work, or a project for which all the funds are controlled and managed by functional management. There's probably no need to create an in-depth cost management plan in these instances.**

Considering the Cost Planning Inputs

If you're tasked with creating the cost management plan, you'll need several components to help you do the planning. Bear in mind that this is a planning process, so you may be returning to this process many times throughout the project. Chances are you want to have in-depth information for the entire project when you start planning costs, so you'll have to revisit the process to complete the planning. Yes, that can be a pain, but the cyclic nature of project management planning helps you create more accurate project plans and provide better insight and control to the project's cost performance.

Here are the four inputs you'll use for cost management planning:

- **Project charter** The project charter provides a high-level summary budget that can help guide the cost planning process.
- **Project management plan** In particular, you'll need the schedule management plan and the risk management plan.
- **Enterprise environmental factors** These factors include things like the market conditions, exchange rates for international projects, and resource cost rates.
- **Organizational process assets** Your organization may have rules and a structure that affect how you manage costs. Historical information, templates, financial controls, and formal and informal cost management policies can also serve as an input to cost management planning.

Creating the Cost Management Plan

After considering expert judgment, undergoing analysis, and attending lots of meetings, you and the project team will create the cost management plan. This project management process is part of the project planning process group. The cost management plan defines how the project costs will be estimated, how the budget will be created, and how you'll control the costs within the project. The plan also defines any analytical tools you'll use for performance of the project costs, such as EVM.

The cost management plan accomplishes many things for the project manager, but chief among them is that it defines how costs will be planned, managed, and controlled. Here are the contents of the cost management plan you'll create:

- **Units of measure** Currency, staffing time, quantity metrics, and resource utilization costs
- **Level of precision** How precise your measurements need to be: for example, you may be required to list costs down to two decimal places, or you may round cents to the nearest dollar.
- **Level of accuracy** The acceptable range of variance for project costs, such as +/−10 percent or a dollar amount.

- **Control thresholds**   The amount of variance that is allowed before an action must be taken, such as a variance report or predefined cuts in the project scope to maintain overall costs.

- **Rules of performance measurement**   The method you'll use to measure project performance; if your WBS is using control account plans, you'll reference those. For your PMP examination, you'll want to know EVM.

- **Organizational procedure links**   How the project's costs will be linked to the deliverables in the WBS. The midlevel components of the WBS that have a dollar amount associated with the deliverables are called the *control account*.

- **Additional planning details**   Funding information for the project, cash flow expectations, fluctuations in currency exchanges, inflation, and overall cost recording.

CERTIFICATION OBJECTIVE 7.02

Estimating the Project Costs

Cost estimating is the process of calculating the costs of the identified resources required to complete the project work. The person or group doing the estimating must consider the possible fluctuations, conditions, and other causes of variances that could affect the total cost of the estimate.

There is a distinct difference between cost estimating and pricing. A cost estimate is the cost of the resources required to complete the project work. Pricing, however, includes a profit margin. In other words, a company performing projects for other organizations may do a cost estimate to see how much the project is going to cost to complete. Then, with this cost information, they'll factor a profit into the project work, as shown next.

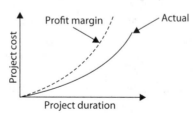

More and more companies are requiring that the project manager calculate the project costs and then factor the ROI and other benefit models into the project product. The goal is to see the value of the project once its deliverables are in operation. While the ROI on a project rarely happens while the project is in motion, the concept is that the project will create an ROI.

Considering the Cost Estimating Inputs

Cost estimating relies on several project components from the initiation and planning process groups. This process also relies on enterprise environmental factors, the processes and procedures unique to your organization, and the organizational process assets such as historical information and forms and templates.

Referencing the Project Management Plan

The primary input to creating the cost estimates is the cost management plan. Recall that this plan defines the acceptable approach for cost estimating in your organization and for the project. The cost management plan is based on your company's enterprise environmental factors—specifically the rules and procedures for how you may estimate costs. If you're doing a project that's internal to your company, you may have a looser approach to cost estimating than you would if you were doing a project for a client of your company. The project for your client has a profit margin and cash inflows, while the internal project, though still important, is funded by existing funds rather than incoming funds. The quality management plan is also needed, because it defines quality objectives required and that'll help estimate the costs to ascertain the quality expectations.

You'll need the scope baseline, because the goal of the project team and the stakeholders is to create all of the elements in the project scope to satisfy the requirements of the project. The project scope statement is with the project manager throughout the entire project, and it's useful to ensure that all of the requirements are being met.

At a deeper level, however, you'll want to rely on the work breakdown structure (WBS). Of course, the WBS is included—it's an input to several major planning processes, all of which deal with costs:

- **Developing the project management plan** This is the overarching project management plan that includes not only the cost management plan but also the information about how the project may be financed and contracted, and what the expectations in the organization are for cost management.
- **Defining the project activities** In some, but not all, projects, the project includes the cost of labor as part of its project expenses. Any resources, such as equipment and material, will need to be paid for as part of the project budget.
- **Estimating the project costs** You'll use the WBS to help you identify how much each work package will cost, and this can help you create a definitive estimate (details coming up).
- **Determining the project budget** You can estimate all you want, but you never know how much a project costs until it's done. The project budget is the cost aggregation and cost reconciliation for each thing, service, and expense the project needs.
- **Planning the project quality** A cost is associated with achieving the expected quality in a project. We'll discuss that more in Chapter 8.

- **Identifying the project risks**   Risks often have a cost element associated with them, and the project manager and organization may create a contingency reserve to offset the risk exposure.
- **Planning the project procurement**   When the project needs to procure materials, labor, or services, the project manager must follow a cost element and purchasing process.

Along with the WBS, you'll rely on the WBS dictionary as the third element of the scope baseline. The WBS dictionary provides information on each deliverable and the associated work needed to create the WBS component. In addition, the WBS may be referenced to an organization's code of accounts. The code of accounts is a coding system used by the performing organization's accounting system to account for the project work. Estimates within the project must be mapped to the correct code so that the organization's ledger reflects the actual work performed, the cost of the work performed, and any billing (internal or external) that was charged to the customer for the completed work.

Referencing the Resource Plan

The estimator must know how much each resource costs, and the resource plan may include this information, depending on the organizational policies, application area, and the type of project being completed. The cost should be in some unit of time or measure—such as cost per hour, cost per metric ton, or cost per use. If the rates of the resources are not known, the rates themselves may also have to be estimated. Of course, skewed rates on the estimates will result in a skewed estimate for the project. There are four categories of cost:

- **Direct costs**   These costs are attributed directly to the project work and cannot be shared among projects (airfare, hotels, long-distance phone charges, and so on).
- **Indirect costs**   These costs are representative of more than one project (utilities for the performing organization, access to a training room, project management software license, and so on).
- **Variable costs**   These costs vary, depending on the conditions applied in the project (the number of meeting participants, the supply and demand of materials, and so on).
- **Fixed costs**   These costs remain constant throughout the project (the cost of a piece of rented equipment for the project, the cost of a fixed-price consultant brought onto the project, and so on).

Referencing the Project Schedule

Resources are more than just people—though people are a primary expense on most projects. The estimate activity resource process (as part of resource management) identifies what resources are needed; the project schedule identifies when they're needed and the frequency at which they're needed. Essentially, the project schedule enables the project manager and the project team to estimate how much the resources will cost the project, when the funds will be used to employ or consume the resources, and the cost impact should the identified resources miss deadlines within the project.

Estimates of the duration of the activities, which predict the length of the project, are required for decisions on financing the project. The length of the activities will help the performing organization calculate what the total cost of the project will be, including the finance charges. Recall the formula for present value? It's Present Value = FV / $(1 + i)^n$; FV is the future value, i is the interest rate, and n is the number of time periods. The future value of the monies the project will earn may need to be measured against the present value to determine whether the project is worth financing, as shown next:

Present value = $317,000	Future value = $550,000
Interest rate = 6%	Interest rate = 6%
Years = 5 years	Years = 5 years
Formula: 317,000 (1.33)	Formula: 550,000/(1.33)
Future value = $424,218	Present value = $410,992

Calculations of the duration of activities are needed to extrapolate the total cost of the work packages. For example, if an activity is estimated to last 14 hours and Suzanne's cost per hour is $80, then the cost of the work package is $1120 (14 × $80). The duration shows management how long the project is expected to last and which activities will cost the most. It also provides the opportunity to re-sequence activities to shorten the project duration—which consequently shortens the finance period for the project.

on the job

Straight-line depreciation allows the organization to write off the same amount each year. The formula for straight-line depreciation is

(purchase value – salvage value) / number of years in use

For example, if the purchase price of a photocopier is $7000 and the salvage value of the photocopier in five years is $2000, the formula would read ($7000 – $2000) / 5 = $1000. This means that the value of the copier decreases $1000 each year; so do the values of your project's assets, and many organizations want to know this for doing their corporate taxes.

Resources can also cost the project if they miss deadlines with penalties, such as a schedule change in a union's contract, the cost of materials based on seasonal demand, and fines and penalties for failing to adhere to scheduled regulations.

Using the Risk Register

We've not said much about the risk register in the project, and it's discussed in detail in Chapter 11 on project risk management. However, due to the integrated nature of projects, this is one of those examples where we'll need to jump ahead just a bit. Risks, as you probably know from your project management experience, can have a positive or a negative effect on the outcome of a project. All identified risks, their characteristics, statuses, and relevant notes are recorded in the risk register.

Most risks, especially the probable, high-impact, negative ones, need to pass through quantitative analysis to determine how much the risk may cost the project in time and money. Based on risk analysis, the project manager creates a special budget just for the impact of project risks: this is called the risk contingency reserve. You use the risk register here in cost estimating to determine how much cash you'll need to offset the risk events as part of your cost estimates.

Management reserves can also be created to deal with those pesky "unknown unknowns" that practically every project has to deal with. The unknown unknowns are essentially risks that are lurking within the project but that haven't been specifically identified by name, source, or probability. Management reserves (both schedule and cost) are not included in baseline but are part of the project budget.

Contingency reserves can be managed in a number of different ways. The most common is to set aside an allotment of funds for the identified risks within the project. Another approach is to create a slush fund for the entire project for identified risks and known unknowns. The final approach is an allotment of funds for categories of components based on the WBS and the project schedule. You'll see this again in much more detail later in this book. (I hope you'll be able to sleep between now and Chapter 11.)

Referencing Enterprise Environmental Factors

Enterprise environmental factors are an input to the cost estimating process because these are the processes and rules regarding how the project manager will estimate the costs within the organization. Enterprise environmental factors also include the market conditions that can affect the procurement process and the costs vendors provide. You'll also want to consider any commercially available databases for pricing information. Commercial cost-estimating databases for pricing include industry-standard rates for different types of labor, cost per unit of materials, average costs based on geographical conditions, and other factors depending on the industry. They provide estimates of what the project should cost based on the variables of the project, resources, and other conditions.

Using Organizational Process Assets

One of the preferred organizational process assets is historical information. After all, if the same project's been done before, why reinvent the wheel? Historical information is proven information and can come from several places:

- **Project files** Past projects within the performing organization can be used as a reference to predict current costs and time. Ensure that the records referenced are accurate, somewhat current, and reflective of what was actually experienced in the historical project.

- **Team members** Team members may have specific experience with the project costs or estimates. Recollections may be useful but are highly unreliable when compared to documented results.

- **Lessons learned** Lessons learned documentation can help the project team estimate the current project if the lessons are from a project with a similar scope.

Estimating Project Costs

Management, customers, and certain stakeholders are all going to be interested in what the project will cost to complete. Several approaches to cost estimating exist, as you'll learn in a moment. First, however, you need to understand that cost estimates have a way of following the project manager around—especially the lowest initial cost estimate.

The estimates you'll want to know for the PMP exam, and for your career, are reflective of the accuracy of the information the estimate is based upon. The more accurate the information, the better the cost estimate will be. If you're steeped in experience in a particular industry, you'll probably have a good idea of what a project should cost based on your experience. Sometimes you may hire a consultant or rely on experts within your organization to help you predict the cost of a project. That's great! That's an example of expert judgment.

Using Analogous Estimating

Analogous estimating relies on historical information to predict the cost of the current project. It is also known as top-down estimating. The analogous estimating process considers the actual cost of a historical project as a basis for the current project. The cost of the historical project is applied to the cost of the current project, taking into account the scope and size of the current project as well as other known variables.

Analogous estimating is a form of expert judgment. This estimating approach takes less time to complete than other estimating models, but it is also less accurate. This top-down approach is good for fast estimates to get a general idea of what the project may cost.

The following is an example of analogous estimating: The Carlton Park Project was to grade and pave a sidewalk around a pond in the community park. The sidewalk of Carlton Park was 1048 feet-by-6 feet, had a textured surface, had some curves around trees, and cost $25,287 to complete. The current project, King Park, will have a similar surface and will cover 4500 feet-by-6 feet. The analogous estimate for this project, based on the work in Carlton Park, is $108,500. This is based on the price per foot of material at $4.02.

on the **J** ob
As part of the planning process, the project manager must determine what resources are needed to complete the project. Resources include the people, equipment, and materials that will be utilized to complete the work. In addition, the project manager must identify the quantity of the needed resources and when the resources are needed for the project. The identification of the resources, the needed quantity, and the schedule of the resources are directly linked to the expected cost of the project work.

Using Parametric Estimating

Parametric estimating uses a mathematical model based on known parameters to predict the cost of a project. The parameters in the model can vary based on the type of work being completed and can be measured by cost per cubic yard, cost per unit, and so on. A complex parameter can be cost per unit, with adjustment factors based on the conditions of the project. The adjustment factors may have additional modifying factors, depending on additional conditions. For example, parametric estimating could say that the cost per square foot of construction is $28 using standard materials, and could then charge additional fees if the client varies the materials.

To use parametric modeling, the factors upon which the model is based must be accurate. The factors within the model are quantifiable and don't vary much based on the effort applied to the activity. And, finally, the model must be scalable between project sizes. The parametric model using a scalable cost-per-unit approach is depicted next.

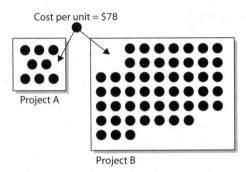

There are two types of parametric estimating:

■ **Regression analysis** This statistical approach predicts what future values may be, based on historical values. Regression analysis creates quantitative predictions based on variables within one value to predict variables in another. This form of estimating relies solely on pure statistical math to reveal relationships between variables and predict future values.

■ **Learning curve** This approach is simple: The cost per unit decreases the more units workers complete, because workers learn as they complete the required work and perform the tasks more quickly and efficiently. The estimate is considered parametric, since the formula is based on repetitive activities, such as wiring telephone jacks, painting hotel rooms, or performing other activities that are completed over and over within a project. The cost per unit decreases as the experience increases, because the time to complete the work becomes shorter. Of course, there will always be some cost associated with the work, but there is a reduction in costs as the workers become more experienced in completing the activities.

Using Bottom-Up Estimating

Bottom-up estimating starts from zero, accounts for each component of the WBS, and arrives at a sum for the project. It is completed with the project team and can be one of the most time-consuming methods used to predict project costs. Although this method is more expensive because of the time invested to create the estimate, it is also one of the most accurate methods. A fringe benefit of completing a bottom-up estimate is that the project team may buy into the project work since they see the cost and value of each activity in the project.

Creating a Three-Point Cost Estimate

It's sometimes risky to use just one cost estimate for a project's activity, especially when the work hasn't been completed before. And like any project work, you don't know how much it's really going to cost until you pay for it. Issues, errors, delays, and unknown risks can affect the project cost. Three-point estimates are also known as simple averaging estimates. A three-point cost estimate attempts to find the average of the cost of an activity using three factors:

- Optimistic cost estimate
- Most likely cost estimate
- Pessimistic cost estimate

You can then simply sum up the three cost estimate values and divide by 3. Or you can use the program evaluation and review technique (PERT) approach, which is slightly different. PERT is a weighted average to the most likely cost estimate value. The PERT formula is

(optimistic cost estimate + (4 × most likely cost estimate) + pessimistic cost estimate) / 6

Figure 7-1 shows the slight difference between a true average of the costs and the PERT approach.

In either approach, simple averaging or PERT, you have to create three cost estimates for each activity. This can get tiresome and overwhelming, especially on a larger project. And if you elect to use an average estimate, be certain to document the approach you took and record the actual costs of the project activities for future historical information.

FIGURE 7-1

Costs can be averaged with PERT or three-point estimates.

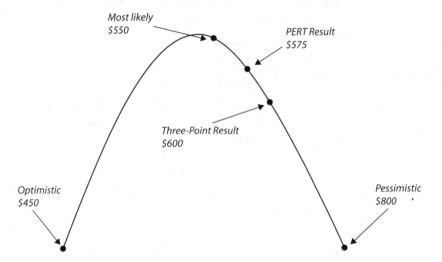

Three-Point Estimate
Optimistic – $450
Most likely – $550
Pessimistic – $800
(450 + 550 + 800)/3 = $600

PERT Estimate
Optimistic – $450
Most likely – $550
Pessimistic – $800
(450 + (4 × 550) + 800)/6 = $575

Most likely
$550

PERT Result
$575

Three-Point Result
$600

Optimistic
$450

Pessimistic
$800

Analyzing Data for Cost Estimating

Data analysis with cost estimating helps the project manager examine the possibilities for cost in a project and provides a broad view of costs. There are three data analysis factors in cost estimating:

- **Alternatives analysis** Examines the different approaches to the project work, materials, equipment, and supplies. This will expose not only possible cost differences, but also tradeoffs between the alternatives identified.

- **Reserve analysis** Management and contingency reserves are amounts of monies set aside for risk events related to unknown and known risks in the project, respectively. When risks enter your project and it takes time to deal with the risk events, the project is consuming these reserves. The quicker the project spends the reserves, the more likely the project is going to be over budget.

- **Costs of quality** I'll discuss this in more detail in Chapter 8, but for now, the cost of quality describes the monies you'll have to spend to achieve the quality expectations within the project. Cost of quality can be training, purchasing the right tools and equipment, and other factors that drive costs to achieve quality.

Using Computer Software

Although the PMP examination is vendor-neutral, having a general knowledge of how computer software can assist the project manager is necessary. Several computer programs are available that can streamline project work estimates and increase their accuracy. These tools can include project management software, spreadsheet programs, and simulations.

Making Decisions in Cost Estimating

Decisions have to be made in cost estimating, like in all areas of project management. Decision-making isn't always a solo activity for the project manager. Experts, the project team, and stakeholders can make cost estimating decisions if it's appropriate for them to do so. You might also rely on voting for cost estimates, just as you can with duration estimates, to create accurate, reliable estimates for the project.

Analyzing Cost Estimating Results

The output of cost estimating is the actual cost estimates of the resources required to complete the project work. The estimate is typically quantitative and can be presented in detail against the WBS components or summarized in terms of a grand total according to various phases of the project or its major deliverables. Each resource in the project must be accounted for and assigned to a cost category. Categories include the following:

- Labor costs
- Material costs
- Travel costs
- Supplies costs
- Hardware costs
- Software costs
- Special categories (inflation, cost reserve, and so on)

The cost of the project is expressed in monetary terms, such as dollars, euros, or yen, so management can compare projects based on costs. It may be acceptable, depending on the demands of the performing organization, to provide estimates in staffing hours or days of work to complete the project along with the estimated costs.

Because projects have risks, the cost of the risks should be identified along with the cost of the risk responses. The project manager should list the risks, their expected risk event values, and the response to each risk should it come into play. We'll cover risk management in detail in Chapter 11.

Change requests often affect the project cost. Chances are, if the project scope increases in size, the project budget will reflect these changes. When a change request is approved, the project manager must make the appropriate change to the cost baseline. A failure to offset approved changes with an appropriate monetary amount will skew the project's cost baselines and show a false variance. With all costs estimates, you'll also include a basis of estimates; you have to document how the estimate was created and a range of variance or degree of confidence for the estimate created.

Refining the Cost Estimates

Cost estimates can also pass through progressive elaboration. As more details are acquired as the project progresses, the estimates are refined. Industry guidelines and organizational policies may define how the estimates are refined, but there are three generally accepted categories of estimating accuracy:

- **Rough order of magnitude (ROM)** This estimate is "rough" and is used during the initiating processes and in top-down estimates. The range of variance for the estimate can be from –25 percent to +75 percent.
- **Budget estimate** This estimate is also somewhat broad and is used early in the planning processes and also in top-down estimates. The range of variance for the estimate can be from –10 percent to +25 percent.
- **Definitive estimates** This estimate type is one of the most accurate. It's used late in the planning processes and is associated with bottom-up estimating. The range of variance for the estimate can be from –5 percent to +10 percent.

Considering the Supporting Detail

Once the estimates have been completed, the basis of the estimates must be organized and documented to show how they were created. This material, even the notes that contributed to the estimates, may provide valuable information later in the project. Specifically, the supporting detail includes the following:

- **Information on the project scope work** This may be provided by referencing the WBS.
- **Information on the approach used in developing the cost estimates** This can include how the estimate was accomplished and the parties involved with creating the estimate.
- **Information on the assumptions and constraints made while developing the cost estimates** Assumptions and constraints can be wrong and can change the entire cost estimate. The project manager must list what assumptions and constraints were made during the cost estimate in order to communicate with stakeholders how she arrived at the estimate.

- **Information on the range of variance in the estimate**   For example, based on the estimating method used, the project cost may be $220,000 ± $15,000. This project cost may be as low as $205,000 or as high as $235,000.
- **Risk considerations**   Risks must be considered for their financial impact on the project.
- **Confidence level in the estimate**   The degree of confidence in the estimate is also included. If you've never done a project like this one before, the confidence level may be low, as opposed to a project for which you've done this type of work many times before.

CERTIFICATION OBJECTIVE 7.03

Creating a Project Budget

Cost budgeting is the process of assigning a cost to an individual work package. The sum of the costs of the individual work packages contribute to the predicted cost for the entire project. This is cost aggregation. The goal of this process is to assign costs to the work in the project so it can be measured for performance. This is the creation of the cost baseline, as shown here:

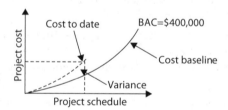

Cost budgeting and cost estimates may go hand in hand, but estimating should be completed before a budget is requested—or assigned. Cost budgeting applies the cost estimates over time. This results in a time-phased estimate for cost, which enables an organization to predict cash flow needs. Cost estimates show costs by category, whereas a cost budget shows costs across time. There are six process inputs for developing the project budget:

- **Project management plan**   Specifically, the cost management plan, resource management plan, and the scope baseline
- **Project documents**   You'll reference the basis of estimates, cost estimates, project schedule, and the risk register

- **Agreements**   Contracts with suppliers, or if you're completing the work for another entity, the contractual agreement between your organization and your customer
- **Business documents**   Business case and the benefits management plan
- **Enterprise environmental factors**   Exchange rates for international projects
- **Organizational process assets**   Cost-budgeting policies, historical information, cost-budgeting tools, and reporting methods

Developing the Project Budget

Many of the tools and techniques used to create the project cost estimates are also used to create the project budget. The following is a quick listing of the tools you can expect to see on the PMP exam:

- **Cost aggregation**   Costs are parallel to each WBS work package. The costs of each work package are aggregated to their corresponding control accounts. Each control account is then aggregated to the sum of the project costs.

- **Reserve analysis**   You should be familiar with two reserves for your PMP exam. The first you've already learned about: the risk contingency reserve. The second cost reserve is the management reserve, and this chunk of cash is for unplanned changes to the project scope and cost. It's a buffer of cash for fluctuations for cost, errors, or other increases in project cost. These reserves are not part of the cost baseline but are part of the project budget. In other words, you don't use these funds unless there's a problem in the project.

- **Expert judgment**   Subject matter experts can be consultants, vendors, internal stakeholders, project team members, and other stakeholders who can help budget the project work. You might also rely on trade groups and other entities within your organization.

- **Historical information review**   This approach uses a parametric model to extrapolate what costs will be for a project (for example, cost per hour and cost per unit). It can include variables and points based on conditions. This approach might also use a top-down estimate type based on historical information. A top-down estimate is also known as an analogous estimate type.

- **Funding limit reconciliation**   Organizations have only so much cash to allot to projects—and no, you can't have all the monies right now. Funding limit reconciliation is an organization's approach to managing cash flow against the project deliverables based on a schedule, milestone accomplishments, or data constraints. This helps an organization plan when monies will be devoted to a project rather than using all of the funds available at the start of a project. In other words, the monies for a project budget will become available based on dates and/or deliverables. If the project doesn't hit predetermined dates and products that were set as milestones, the additional funding becomes questionable.

- **Financing** On larger projects you may experience financing concerns and the cost of the financing. Interest rates, depreciation, and time value of money are all considerations when financing a project.

Creating the Cost Baseline

A project's cost baseline measures performance and predicts the expenses over the life of the project, including the management reserve. It's usually shown as an S-curve, as in Figure 7-2. The cost baseline allows the project manager and management to predict when the project will be spending monies and over what time period. Any discrepancies early on between the predicted baseline and the actual costs serve as a signal that the project is slipping.

Large projects that have multiple deliverables may use multiple cost baselines to illustrate the costs within each phase. In addition, larger projects may use cost baselines to predict spending plans, cash flows of the project, and overall project performance.

Establishing Project Funding Requirements

The project's cost baseline can help the project manager and the organization determine when the project will need cash infusions. Based on phases, milestones, and capital expenses, the project funding requirements can be mapped to the project schedule and the organization can plan accordingly. This is where the concept of project step funding originates. The curve of the project's timeline is funded in steps, where "step" is an amount of funds allotted to the project to reach the next milestone in the project.

FIGURE 7-2

Cost baselines show predicted project and phase performance.

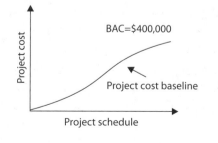
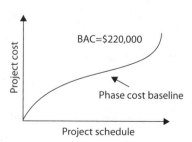

CERTIFICATION OBJECTIVE 7.04

Implementing Cost Control

Cost control focuses on the ability of costs to change and on the ways of allowing or preventing cost changes from happening. When a change does occur, the project manager must document the change through the integrated change control process, update the cost baseline, define the reason why the change occurred, and, if necessary, create a variance report. Cost control is concerned with understanding why the cost variances, both good and bad, have occurred. The "why" behind the variances enables the project manager to make appropriate decisions on future project actions.

Ignoring the project cost variances may cause the project to suffer from budget shortages, additional risks, or scheduling problems. When cost variances happen, they must be examined, recorded, and investigated. Cost control allows the project manager to confront the problem, find a solution, and then act accordingly. Specifically, cost control focuses on the following activities:

- Controlling causes of change to ensure that the changes are needed
- Controlling and documenting changes to the cost baseline as they happen
- Controlling changes in the project and their influence on cost
- Performing cost monitoring to recognize and understand cost variances
- Recording appropriate cost changes in the cost baseline
- Preventing unauthorized changes to the cost baseline
- Communicating the cost changes to the proper stakeholders
- Working to bring and maintain costs within an acceptable range

Considering Cost Control Inputs

To implement cost control, the project manager must rely on several documents and processes:

- **Cost management plan**   The cost management plan dictates how cost variances will be managed.
- **Cost baseline**   The cost baseline is the expected cost the project will incur. This time-phased budget reflects the amount that will be spent throughout the project. Recall that the cost performance baseline is a tool used to measure project performance. And, yes, it's the same thing as the cost baseline.
- **Performance measurement baseline**   Used with earned value management to determine if corrective actions, preventive actions, or a change is required in the project.
- **Project funding requirements**   The funds for a project are not allotted all at once, but stair-stepped in alignment with project deliverables. Thus, as the project moves toward completion, additional funding is allotted. This allows for cash-flow forecasting. In other words, an organization doesn't need to allot all of the project's budget at the start of the project, but it can predict, based on expected income, that all of the project's budget will be available in incremental steps.
- **Work performance data**   This includes raw data on project progress, status of project activities, status of project deliverables, and information about the project costs and the cost of the balance of the project work.
- **Organizational process assets**   One category of inputs for cost control are the existing methods, forms, templates, and guidelines in the organization's organizational process assets.
- **Lessons learned register**   Lessons learned are also updated as a result of this process. You'll update the lessons learned register throughout the project.

Managing Changes to Costs

Sometimes a project manager must add or remove costs from a project. The cost change control system is part of the integrated change control system and documents the procedures to request, approve, and incorporate changes to project costs.

When a cost change enters the system, the project manager must create the appropriate paperwork and follow a tracking system and procedures to obtain approval on the proposed change. If a change gets approved, the cost baseline is updated to reflect the approved changes. If a request gets denied, the denial must be documented for future reference.

CERTIFICATION OBJECTIVE 7.05

Measuring Project Performance

Earned value management (EVM) is the process of measuring the performance of project work against a plan to identify variances. It can also be useful in predicting future variances and the final costs at completion. EVM is a system of mathematical formulas that compares work performed against work planned and measures the actual cost of the work performed. It's an important part of cost control because it allows a project manager to predict future variances from the expenses to date within the project.

See the video "Earned Value Management."

In regard to cost management, EVM is concerned with the relationships among three formulas that reflect project performance. Figure 7-3 demonstrates the connection between the following EVM values:

- **Planned value (PV)** Planned value is the work scheduled and the budget authorized to accomplish that work. For example, if a project has a budget of $100,000 and month six represents 50 percent of the project work, the PV for month six is $50,000. The entire project's planned value—that is, what the project should be worth at completion—is known as the budget at completion (BAC). You might also see the sum of the planned value called the performance measurement baseline.

- **Earned value (EV)** Earned value is the physical work completed to date and the authorized budget for that work. For example, if a project has a budget of $100,000 and the work completed to date represents 25 percent of the entire project work, its EV is $25,000.

FIGURE 7-3

Earned value management measures project performance.

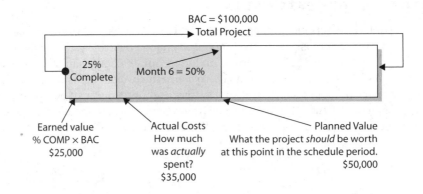

■ **Actual cost (AC)**   Actual cost is the actual amount of monies the project has required to date. For example, if a project has a budget of $100,000 and $35,000 has been spent on the project to date, the AC of the project would be $35,000.

These three values offer key information about the worth of the project to date (EV), the cost of the project work to date (AC), and the planned value of the work to date (PV).

Finding the Variances

At the end of the project, will there be a budget variance (VAR)? Any variance at the end of the project is calculated by subtracting the actual costs (ACs) of the project work from the budget at completion (BAC). The term "budget at completion" refers to the estimated budget at completion—what you and the project customer agree the project will likely cost. Of course, you don't actually know how much the project will cost until it's completely finished. So throughout the project, a variance is any result that is different from what is planned or expected.

Cost Variances

The cost variance (CV) is the difference between the earned value (EV) and the actual costs (AC). For example, for a project that has a budget of $200,000 and has earned, or completed, 10 percent of the project value, the EV is $20,000. However, due to some unforeseen incidents, the project manager had to spend $25,000 to complete that $20,000 worth of work. The AC of the project, at this point, is $25,000 and the cost variance is –$5000. Thus, the equation for cost variance is CV = EV – AC.

Schedule Variances

A schedule variance (SV) is the value that represents the difference between where the project was planned to be at a certain point in time and where the project actually is. For example, consider a project with a budget of $200,000 that's expected to last two years. At the end of year one, the project team has planned that the project be 60 percent complete. Thus, the planned value (PV) for 60 percent completion equates to $120,000—the expected worth of the project work at the end of year one. But let's say that at the end of year one the project is only 40 percent complete. The EV at the end of year one is, therefore, $80,000. The difference between the PV and the EV is the SV: –$40,000. The equation for schedule variance is SV = EV – PV.

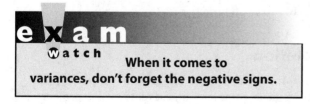

Calculating the Cost Performance Index

The cost performance index (CPI) shows the amount of work the project is completing per dollar spent on the project. In other words, a CPI of 0.93 means it is costing $1.00 for every 93 cents' worth of work. Or you could say the project is losing 7 cents on every dollar spent on the project. Let's say a project has an EV of $25,000 and an AC of $27,000. The CPI for this project is thus 0.93. The closer the number is to 1, the better the project is doing. The equation for cost performance index is CPI = EV / AC.

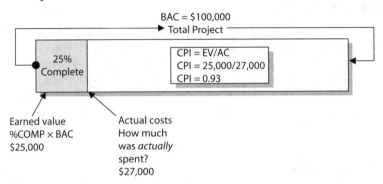

CPI is a value that shows how the project costs are performing to plan. It relates the work you've accomplished to the amount you've spent to accomplish it. A CPI of less than 1.00 means the project is performing poorly against the plan. However, a CPI of more than 1.00 does not necessarily mean that the project is performing well. It could mean that estimates were inflated or that an expenditure for equipment is late or sitting in accounts payable and has not yet been entered into the project accounting cycle.

Finding the Schedule Performance Index

The schedule performance index (SPI) is similar to the CPI. The SPI, however, reveals how closely the project is on schedule. Again, as with the CPI, the closer the quotient is to 1, the better. The formula for schedule performance index is SPI = EV / PV. In our example, the EV is $20,000, and let's say the PV, where the project is supposed to be, is calculated as $30,000. The SPI for this project is then 0.67—way off target!

Preparing for the Estimate at Completion

The estimate at completion (EAC) is a hypothesis of what the total cost of the project will be. Before the project begins, the project manager completes an estimate for the project deliverables based on the scope baseline. As the project progresses, in most projects there will be some variances between the cost estimate and the actual cost. The difference between these is the variance for the deliverable.

FIGURE 7-4

There are many approaches to calculating the EAC.

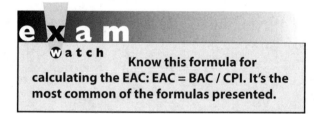

$$EAC = \frac{BAC}{CPI} \qquad EAC = \frac{\$575,000}{.91} \qquad EAC = \$631,868$$

$$EAC = AC+ETC \qquad EAC = \$20,000+\$175,000 \qquad EAC = \$195,000$$

$$EAC = AC+BAC-EV \qquad EAC = \$7,000+24,500-\$2,450 \qquad EAC = \$29,050$$

$$EAC = AC + \frac{(BAC-EV)}{(CPI \times SPI)} \qquad EAC = \$45,000 + \frac{(250,000-37,500)}{(0.83 \times 0.89)} \qquad EAC = \$332,667$$

e x a m

ⓦ a t c h **Know this formula for calculating the EAC: EAC = BAC / CPI. It's the most common of the formulas presented.**

The EAC is based on experiences in the project so far. There are several different formulas for calculating the EAC, as Figure 7-4 demonstrates. For now, and for the exam, here's the EAC formula you'll need to know: EAC = BAC / CPI. In our project, the BAC is $200,000. The CPI was calculated to be 0.80. The EAC for this project, then, is $250,000.

Considering Project Performance

Another variation of the EAC is to consider the project performance beyond just the CPI. This approach looks at the project performance, good or bad, and considers the actual costs of the project to date, the budget at completion, and the project's earned value. This EAC formula is EAC = AC + BAC − EV.

For example, consider a project with a BAC of $350,000 that's 45 percent complete, though it's supposed to be 60 percent complete at this point. The EV for this project is 45 percent of the $350,000, which is $157,500. In this scenario, the project has actually spent $185,000—considerably more than what the project should have spent. Let's plug in this EAC formula. EAC = $185,000 + $350,000 − $157,500. The EAC for this project using this formula would be $377,500.

Consider Project Variances

Sometimes a project may have some wild swings on the project cost variances and the project schedule variances, and you want to take these variances into consideration when predicting the project's estimate at completion. Usually, it's the project schedule that's affecting the project's ability to meet its cost obligations because the planned value continues to slip, which wrecks the SPI. Add to that the concept that the longer a project takes to complete, the more likely the project costs will increase.

Here's this windy formula (get out your slide rule): EAC = AC + [(BAC − EV) / (CPI × SPI)]. Let's try this one using the same values used in the last example. Consider a project with a BAC of $350,000 that's 45 percent complete, though it's supposed to be 60 percent complete. The earned value for this project is 45 percent of $350,000, which is $157,500. In this scenario, the project has actually spent $185,000—considerably more than what the project should have. Here are the parts of our formula:

Actual cost = $185,000
Planned value = $210,000
Budget at completion = $350,000
Earned value = $157,500
Cost performance index = 0.85
Schedule performance index = 0.75

Let's plug these values into the formula EAC = AC + [(BAC − EV) / (CPI × SPI)]:

EAC = $185,000 + [($350,000 − $157,500) / (0.85 × 0.75)]
EAC = $185,000 + (192,500 / 0.64)
EAC = $185,000 + 300,781.25
EAC = $485,781.25

Calculating the To-Complete Performance Index

Imagine a formula that would tell you if the project can match the budget at completion based on current conditions. Or imagine a formula that can predict whether the project can even achieve your new estimate at completion. Well, forget your imagination and just use the to-complete performance index (TCPI). This formula can forecast the likelihood of a project to achieve its goals based on what's happening in the project currently. There are two different flavors for the TCPI, depending on what you want to accomplish:

- If you want to see whether your project can meet the budget at completion, you'll use this formula: TCPI = (BAC − EV) / (BAC − AC).
- If you want to see whether your project can meet the newly created estimate at completion, you'll use this version of the formula: TCPI = (BAC − EV) / (EAC − AC).

Any result greater than 1 in either formula means that you'll have to be more efficient than you planned to achieve the BAC or the EAC, depending on whichever formula you've used. Basically, the larger the resulting number (greater than 1), the less likely you'll be able to meet your BAC or EAC. For results less than 1, the lower the number, the more likely you'll be able to reach your BAC or EAC (again, depending on which formula you've used).

Finding the Estimate to Complete

The estimate to complete (ETC) shows how much more money will be needed to complete the project. To calculate the ETC, you need to know another formula: the estimate at completion (EAC). Remember that the EAC is what you predict the project will cost based on current conditions. The ETC is a pretty straightforward formula: EAC − AC. Let's say our EAC was calculated to be $250,000 and our AC is currently $25,000; our ETC would then be $225,000.

Accounting for Flawed Estimates

Imagine a project to install a new operating system on 1000 workstations. One of the assumptions the project team made was that each workstation had the correct hardware to install the operating system automatically. As it turns out, this assumption was wrong, and now the project team must change their approach to installing the system.

Because the assumption to install the operating system was flawed, a new estimate to complete the project is needed, which also means a change request. This is the most accurate approach in estimating how much more the project will cost, but it's the hardest to do. This new estimate to complete the work is the ETC, which represents how much more money is needed to complete the project work, and its formula is simply a revised estimate of how much more the remaining work will cost to complete. Nothing tricky here.

Accounting for Anomalies

During a project, sometimes weird stuff happens. These anomalies, or weird stuff, can cause project costs to be skewed. For example, consider a project with a $10,000 budget to construct a wooden fence around a property line. One of the project team members makes a mistake while installing the wooden fence and reverses the face of the fencing material. In other words, the material for the outside of the fence faces the wrong direction.

The project now has to invest additional time to remove the fence material, correct the problem, and replace any wood that may have been damaged in the incorrect installation. The project, mistakes and all, is thus considered 20 percent done, so the earned value is $2000. This anomaly likely won't happen again, but it will add costs to the project.

For these instances, when events happen but the project manager doesn't expect similar events to happen again, the following ETC formula should be used: ETC = (BAC − EV). Let's try this out with our fencing project. The project's EV is only $2000 since the project has barely started. The formula would read ETC = $10,000 − $2000.

Accounting for Typical Variances

This last ETC formula is used when existing variances in the project are expected to be typical of the remaining variances in the project. For example, a project manager has overestimated the competence of the workers to complete the project work. Because the project team is not performing at the level the project manager expected, work is completed late and in a faulty manner. Rework has been a common theme for this project.

The formula for these instances is ETC = (BAC − EV) / CPI. In our example, let's say the AC is $45,000, the BAC is $250,000, the EV is $37,500, and our CPI is calculated to be 0.83. The ETC formula for this project is ETC = ($250,000 − $37,500) / 0.83. The result of the formula (following the order of operations) is thus $256,024.

Finding the Variance at Completion

A variance is the difference between what was expected and what was experienced. The formula for the variance at completion (VAC) is VAC = BAC − EAC. In our example, the BAC was $200,000 and the EAC was $250,000, so the VAC is predicted to be $50,000.

The Five EVM Formula Rules

For EVM formulas, remember the following five rules:

- ■ Always start with EV.
- ■ Variance means subtraction.
- ■ Index means division.
- ■ Less than 1 is bad in an index (unless it's the TCPI).
- ■ Negative is bad in a variance.

The formulas for earned value analysis can be completed manually or through project management software. For the exam, you'll want to memorize these formulas. Table 7-1 shows a summary of all the formulas.

PMP Coach These aren't much to memorize, I know, but you should. Although you won't have an overwhelming amount of EVM questions on your exam, they are free points if you know the formulas and can do the math.

Media I have a present for you. It's a Microsoft Excel spreadsheet called "EV Worksheet." It has all of these formulas in action. I recommend you make up some numbers to test your ability to complete these formulas and then plug your values into Excel to confirm your math. Enjoy!

| TABLE 7-1 | A Summary of EVM Formulas |

Name	Formula
Planned value	PV= percent complete of where the project should be
Earned value	EV = percent complete × budget at completion
Cost variance	CV = EV – AC
Schedule variance	SV = EV – PV
Cost performance index	CPI = EV / AC
Schedule performance index	SPI = EV / PV
Estimate at completion, if the CPI is going to remain constant for the remainder of the project	EAC = BAC / CPI
Estimate at completion, if flawed work and cost overruns are not likely to happen again	EAC = AC + BAC – EV
Estimate at completion, if the cost estimate is no longer valid due to cost overruns (use a re-estimate for the bottom-up ETC)	EAC = AC + Bottom-up ETC
Estimate at completion, if the CPI and SPI are likely to fluctuate for the remainder of the project	EAC = AC + [(BAC – EV) / (CPI × SPI)]
Estimate to complete	ETC = EAC – AC
To-complete performance index (using the BAC)	(BAC – EV) / (BAC – AC)
To-complete performance index (using the EAC)	(BAC – EV) / (EAC – AC)
Variance at completion	VAC = BAC – EAC

Additional Planning

Planning is an iterative process. Throughout the project, there will be demands for additional planning—and an output of cost control is one of those demands. Consider a project that must complete by a given date and that also has a set budget. The balance between the schedule and the cost must be maintained. The project manager can't assign a large crew to complete the project work if the budget won't allow it. The project manager must, through planning, get as creative as possible to figure out an approach to accomplish the project without exceeding the budget.

The balance between cost and schedule is an ongoing battle. Although it's usually easier to get more time than money, this isn't always the case. Consider, for example, deadlines that can't be moved—perhaps fines and penalties will be imposed if a deadline is missed, or a deadline centers on the date of a tradeshow, an expo, or the start of the school year.

Using Computers

It's hard to imagine a project, especially a large project, moving forward without the use of computers. Project managers can rely on project management software and spreadsheet programs to assist them in calculating actual costs, earned value, and planned value.

 It's not difficult to create a spreadsheet with the appropriate earned value formulas. After you've created the spreadsheet, you can save it as a template and use it on multiple projects. If you want, and if your software allows it, you can tie in multiple earned value spreadsheets to a master file to track all of your projects at a glance.

Considering the Cost Control Results

Cost control is an ongoing process throughout the project. The project manager must actively monitor the project for variances to costs. Specifically, the project manager should always do the following:

- Monitor cost variances and then understand why variances have occurred.
- Update the cost baseline as needed based on approved changes.
- Work with the conditions and stakeholders to prevent unnecessary changes to the cost baseline.
- Communicate to the appropriate stakeholders cost changes as they occur.
- Maintain costs within an acceptable and agreed-upon range.
- Collect work performance information to compare the work against the cost baseline.

Creating Change Requests

As the project progresses and more detail becomes available, there may be a need to update the cost estimates. A revision to the cost estimates requires communication with the key stakeholders to share why the costs were revised. A revision to the cost estimates may have a ripple effect: Other parts of the project may need to be adjusted to account for the changes in cost, the sequence of events may need to be reordered, and resources may have to be changed. In some instances, the revision of the estimates may be expected, as with phased-gate estimating in a lengthy project.

Throughout a project, the project manager will apply corrective actions. Corrective actions are applied to project performance to bring the project back into alignment with the project plan. Corrective actions can be scheduling changes, a shift in resources, or a different approach to completing the project work—essentially any action, even nudges or shoves, designed to bring the project back to its expected level of performance.

Updating the budget is slightly different from revising a cost estimate. Budget updates allow the cost baseline to be changed. The cost baseline is the "before project snapshot" of what the total project scope and the individual WBS components should cost. Should the project scope grow, as shown next, the cost will also likely change to be able to fulfill the new scope.

If a project undergoes drastic changes—due to large changes to the project scope, false assumptions, or new demands from the customer—it may be necessary to rebaseline the project cost. Rebaselining is done only in drastic changes, because it essentially resets the project.

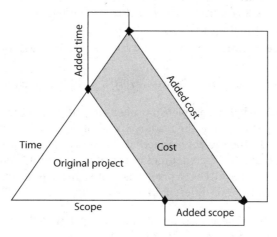

Updating Lessons Learned

As part of cost control, the project manager should update the lessons learned document to reflect the decisions behind the actions taken. For example, the project manager should identify the following:

- Any changes to the cost baseline and why they were approved
- Corrective actions and why they were implemented
- Cost control challenges and issues, and how they were resolved
- Other cost control information that may be beneficial for other projects

CERTIFICATION SUMMARY

Several factors contribute to the costs on any project: the expense of the labor to complete the project, the expense of materials needed to complete the project, and the expense of the equipment needed to complete a project. These expenses must be estimated, planned for, and monitored for a project to finish on budget.

Management and customers will want to know how much a project is going to cost so that they can determine whether the project is worth doing, whether the project deliverable will be worth the cost, and if the project will be profitable. The estimates for project costs can come in several forms:

- **Analogous estimating** Uses similar historical information to predict the cost of the current project.
- **Top-down estimating** Uses a similar project as a cost baseline and factors in current project conditions to predict costs. Note that analogous estimating is also top-down estimating.
- **Parametric estimating** Uses a parameter, such as cost per metric ton, to predict project costs.
- **Bottom-up estimating** Starts at zero and adds expenses from the bottom up.

The resources needed to complete a project may be one of the biggest expenses in the project's budget. The activities the resources complete must be worthy of the resources' time. In other words, the project manager does not want to assign a $125-per-hour engineer to perform filing that a $15-per-hour administrative assistant is qualified to do. Accurate assignment of project resources to project activities helps prevent waste.

Projects also involve four different kinds of costs:

- **Direct costs** These costs are attributed directly to the project and cannot be shared with operations or other projects.
- **Indirect costs** These costs can be shared across multiple projects that use the same resources—such as for a training room or piece of equipment.
- **Variable costs** These costs vary depending on the conditions within the project.
- **Fixed costs** These costs remain the same throughout the project.

There is one last cost, called opportunity cost, that's usually calculated by the business, not the project manager, but is still important to understand. This is a special cost, because it really doesn't cost the organization anything out of pocket but represents the cost of a lost opportunity. Opportunity costs are an expense that companies that complete projects for other organizations should realize. When an organization that completes projects for others must forgo one project in order to complete the other, the value of the forgone project is the opportunity cost. For example, let's say a company has two projects it can complete, but it must choose only one of them. Project A is worth $75,000, while Project B is worth $50,000. If the company chooses Project A, the opportunity cost is thus $50,000 because the company misses out on the opportunity.

KEY TERMS

If you're serious about passing the PMP exam, memorize these terms and their definitions. For maximum value, create your own flashcards based on these definitions and review them daily.

actual costs   The amount of funds the project has spent to date. The difference between earned value and actual costs will reveal the cost variance.

analogous estimating   A technique that relies on historical information to predict estimates for current projects. Analogous estimating is also known as top-down estimating and is a form of expert judgment.

bottom-up estimating   A technique by which an estimate for each component in the WBS is developed and then totaled for an overall project budget. This is the most time-consuming method to complete, but it provides the most accurate estimate.

budget at completion   The predicted budget for the project; what the project should cost when it is completed. Budget at completion represents 100 percent of the planned value for the project's completion.

cost baseline   Usually shown in an S-curve, the cost baseline indicates the expected project cost. It enables the project manager and management to predict when the project will be spending monies and over what duration. The purpose of the cost baseline is to measure and predict project performance.

cost budgeting   A process of assigning a cost to an individual work package. This process shows costs over time. The cost budget results in an S-curve that becomes the cost baseline for the project.

cost change control   This is part of the integrated change control system and documents the procedures to request, approve, and incorporate changes to project costs.

cost control   An active process to control causes of cost changes, to document cost changes, and to monitor cost fluctuations within the project. When changes occur that affect cost, the cost baseline must be updated.

cost estimating   The process of calculating the costs, by category, of the identified resources to complete the project work.

cost management plan   A subsidiary plan of the overall project management plan that defines how costs will be estimated, budgeted, and controlled.

cost performance index   The process of calculating the costs, by category, of the identified resources to complete the project work.

cost variance   The difference between the earned value and the actual costs.

direct costs   Costs that are attributed directly to the project and cannot be shared with operations or other projects.

earned value   The value of the work that has been completed and the budget for that work: $EV = \% \text{ Complete} \times BAC$.

earned value management   EVM integrates scope, schedule, and cost to provide an objective, scalable, point-in-time assessment of the project. EVM calculates the performance of the project and compares current performance against plan. It can also be a harbinger of things to come. Results early in the project can predict the likelihood of the project's success or failure.

estimate at completion   A hypothesis of what the total cost of the project will be. Before the project begins, the project manager completes an estimate for the project deliverables based on the WBS. As the project progresses, there will likely be some variances between the cost estimate and the actual cost. The EAC is calculated to predict the new estimate at completion.

estimate to complete   Represents how much more money is needed to complete the project work.

estimating publications   Typically, a commercial reference to help the project estimator confirm and predict the accuracy of estimates. If a project manager elects to use one of these commercial databases, the estimate should include a pointer to this document for future reference and verification.

fixed costs   Costs that remain the same throughout the project.

indirect costs   Costs that can be shared across multiple projects and that use the same resources—such as costs for a training room or piece of equipment.

parametric modeling   A mathematical model based on known parameters to predict the cost of a project. The parameters in the model can vary based on the type of work being done. A parameter can be cost per cubic yard, cost per unit, and so on.

planned value   The value of the work that should be completed by a specific time in the project schedule.

risk   An uncertain event that can have a positive or negative influence on a project's success. Risk can affect the project costs, project schedule, and often both. All risks and their statuses should be recorded in the risk register.

schedule performance index   Reveals the efficiency of work. The closer the quotient is to 1, the better: SPI = EV / PV.

schedule variance   The difference between the planned work and the earned work.

to-complete performance index   An EVM formula that can forecast the likelihood of a project to achieve its goals based on what's currently happening in the project.

top-down estimating   A technique that bases the current project's cost estimate on the total cost of a similar project. A percentage of the similar project's total cost may be added to or subtracted from the total, depending on the size of the current project.

variable costs   Costs that vary, depending on the conditions within the project.

variance   The time or cost difference between what was planned and what was actually experienced.

INSIDE THE EXAM

The PMP examination requires that the exam candidate know how to estimate, budget, and manage costs. The WBS is an input to estimating costs because it reflects the whole of the project. When creating the estimates, you should rely on documented historical information over team members' recollections. There are three estimating approaches:

- **Analogous**   A top-down approach that is less costly and less accurate than others and that offers an idea of what the project will cost.

- **Bottom-up**   Starts with zero and adds up all the expenses. This is more costly and takes longer but gains team buy-in to the project.

- **Parametric modeling**   Uses a parameter for labor and goods to calculate the cost of the project.

The accuracy of the estimates is based on available information. As the project manager and the project team progressively elaborate on the project plan, more details become available. The more details a project has, the more accurate the estimate. Know the following facts on estimating:

- **Rough order of magnitude**   The accuracy of the estimate ranges from −25 percent to +75 percent and is used both in the initiation process and in top-down estimating.

- **Budget estimate**   The accuracy of the estimate ranges from −10 percent to +25 percent. This is used early in the planning process and in top-down estimating.

- **Definitive estimate**   The accuracy of the estimate ranges from −5 percent to +10 percent. This is used late in the planning process and in bottom-up estimating.

The resources on a project can include people, materials, and equipment. If the people working on a project do not have the necessary skill sets to complete the work, hire an SME to guide the project implementation, outsource the project work, or train the current people in the needed skills.

EVM is a tool to measure project performance. It is the budget at completion multiplied by the percentage of the project work that has been completed. The cost performance index shows how well the project is performing financially, and is calculated by dividing EV by the actual costs spent on the project. Use the most common formula for finding the estimate at completion: EAC = BAC / CPI.

TWO-MINUTE DRILL

Planning the Project Costs

❑ Planning the project costs is the first process you'll encounter in the project cost management knowledge area. This process creates the cost management plan, which defines how the project costs will be estimated, spent, managed, and controlled throughout all of the project activities.

❑ To plan the project costs, you'll need the project management plan, the project charter, the rules of the enterprise environmental factors, and any organizational process assets. Organizational process assets can help with planning if you've done similar projects in the past and can use the historical information as a template for the current project.

❑ The cost management plan also defines the earned value management formulas your project will utilize if appropriate. Recall that the purpose of earned value management is to show performance in the project and allow for forecasting of the project's overall performance based on current information.

Estimating the Project Costs

❑ The project manager must know what resources are needed to complete the project work. How will the project be completed without the resources? The project manager must know the people, the equipment, materials, and other resources needed to make the vision of the project a reality. Once the resources are identified, the costs of the resources can be calculated.

❑ The resources also must be known so the project manager can predict, monitor, and control what the project costs are expected to be. The relationship between the project vision and the needed resources can help the project manager work within the predicted costs.

❑ Resources to complete a project also include services, leases, real estate, and other components that contribute to the project work being completed.

❑ The rough order of magnitude estimate is used during the initiating processes and in top-down estimates. The range of variance for the estimate can be from −25 percent to +75 percent.

❑ The budget estimate is also somewhat broad and is used early in the planning processes and in top-down estimates. The range of variance for the estimate can be from −10 percent to +25 percent.

❑ The definitive estimate is one of the most accurate. It's used late in the planning processes and is associated with bottom-up estimating. The range of variance for the estimate can be from –5 percent to +10 percent.

❑ In analogous estimating, the project manager uses a similar project to predict what the costs of the current project should be. It is less accurate but easier and faster to complete than other methods.

❑ In parametric estimating, the project manager uses a parameter for units of goods and time to calculate what the project will cost—for example, cost per hour, cost per metric ton, or cost per cubic yard.

Creating a Project Budget

❑ Cost aggregation maps the overall costs to each WBS work package. The costs of each work package are aggregated to their corresponding control accounts. Each control account then is aggregated to the sum of the project costs.

❑ Funding limit reconciliation is an organization's approach to managing cash flow against the project deliverables based on a schedule, milestone accomplishment, or data constraints. This helps an organization plan when monies will be devoted to a project rather than using all of the funds available at the start of a project. In other words, the monies for a project budget will become available based on dates and/or deliverables.

Implementing Cost Control

❑ The cost management plan documents how the project manager will react to cost variances within the project. The performing organization will likely have policies and procedures on unacceptable variances.

❑ Variances that cross a given threshold may require the project manager to create a variance report to explain the variance, why it has happened, and what corrective action has been applied to prevent the variance from reoccurring.

❑ Cost control is the process of monitoring and documenting cost changes, whether they are allowed to occur or are prevented from occurring. The project manager studies the cost changes to understand why the change has happened and then makes corrective actions to the project if needed.

Measuring Project Performance

❏ Planned value (PV) includes the work scheduled and the budget authorized to accomplish that work. The entire project's planned value—that is, what the project should be worth at completion—is known as the budget at completion. You might also see the sum of the planned value called the performance measurement baseline.

❏ Earned value (EV) is the physical work completed to date and the authorized budget for that work.

❏ Actual cost is the actual amount of monies the project has required to date.

❏ The cost variance is the difference between the earned value and the actual cost.

❏ A schedule variance (SV) is the value that represents the difference between where the project actually is (EV) and where the project was planned to be at a certain point in time (PV).

❏ The cost performance index (CPI) shows the amount of work the project is completing per dollar spent on the project.

❏ The schedule performance index (SPI) reveals the efficiency of work by comparing where the project is currently against where it was scheduled to be.

❏ The estimate at completion (EAC) is a hypothesis of what the total cost of the project will be.

❏ The estimate to complete (ETC) shows how much more money will be needed to complete the project.

❏ The to-complete performance index (TCPI) can forecast the likelihood of a project to achieve its goals based on what's happening in the project currently.

❏ Cost control can cause changes and updates within the project for the project scope, schedule, or overall costs. If the cost of material increases, there may be tradeoffs in the project scope to afford the existing materials. For example, the stakeholders or project manager could elect to use a lower grade of material or remove the deliverable from scope, if that's feasible, to keep the costs in check. Either way, if the cost of materials increases, there will be ripples throughout the project.

❏ Updating the budget is slightly different from revising a cost estimate. Budget updates enable the cost baseline to be changed. The cost baseline is the "before project snapshot" of what the total project scope and the individual WBS components should cost.

❏ Errors in the project can cause costs to increase. Corrective actions are an effort, technically a change request, to bring the project back into alignment with the cost baseline and what was planned.

SELF TEST

1. You are the project manager for your organization and you need to create a cost estimate for your current project. This project is similar to the ABG Project you completed a few months ago, so you report to your program manager that you'll be using analogous estimating. Which of the following best describes analogous estimating?
    A. Regression analysis
    B. Bottom-up estimating
    C. Less accurate
    D. More accurate

2. You are the project manager for the GHG Project. You are about to create the cost estimates for the project. Which input to this process will help you the most?
    A. Parametric modeling
    B. WBS
    C. Project scope
    D. Requirements document

3. You are the project manager for the JKH Project. You have elected to use parametric estimating in your cost estimating for the project. Which of the following is an example of parametric estimating?
    A. $750 per ton
    B. Historical information from a similar project
    C. Estimates built bottom-up based on the WBS
    D. Estimates based on top-down budgeting

4. You are the project manager for a new technology implementation project. Management has requested that your estimates be as exact as possible. Which one of the following methods of estimating will provide the most accurate estimate?
    A. Top-down estimating
    B. Top-down budgeting
    C. Bottom-up estimating
    D. Parametric estimating

5. Your company has been hired to install tile in 1000 hotel rooms. All rooms will be identical in nature and will require the same amount of materials. Your project team has completed the first three hotel rooms, which took an average of six hours each to complete. You calculate the time to install the tile in each hotel room at six hours. The cost for the labor for your new project team is calculated at $700 per room. Your project sponsor disagrees with your labor estimate. Why?

   A. You haven't completed one hotel room yet, so you don't know how long the work will actually take.

   B. You have not factored in all of the effort applied to the work.

   C. You have not considered the law of diminishing returns.

   D. You have not considered the learning curve.

6. You are the project manager for a construction project to build 17 cabins. All of the cabins will be identical in nature. The contract for the project is set at a fixed cost, the incentive being that the faster the project work is completed, the more profitable the job. Management has requested that you study the work method to determine a faster, less costly, and better method of completing the project. This is an example of which of the following?

   A. Time constraint

   B. Schedule constraint

   C. Value engineering

   D. Learning curve

7. You are the project manager for a technical implementation project. The customer has requested that you factor in the after-the-project costs, such as maintenance and service. This is an example of which one of the following?

   A. Life-cycle costs

   B. Scope creep

   C. Project spin-off

   D. Operations

8. You are the project manager for your organization and you need to create a cost estimate for your current project. Your manager informs you that this project requires a precise cost estimate so you need to choose the most accurate estimating approach possible. Which one of the following provides the least accuracy in estimating?

   A. Rough order of magnitude

   B. Budget estimate

   C. Definitive estimate

   D. WBS estimate

9. As a PMP candidate, you need to be able to compare and contrast project plans, their components, and how the plans are used within a live project. Based on this information, which one of the following is true?
   A. The cost management plan controls how change management affects the BAC.
   B. The cost management plan controls how cost variances will be managed.
   C. The cost management plan controls how the project manager may update the cost estimates.
   D. The cost management plan controls how the BAC may be adjusted.

10. You are the project manager for project with a manufacturer. Project team members report they are 30 percent complete with the project. You have spent $25,000 out of the project's $250,000 budget. What is the earned value for this project?
    A. 10 percent
    B. $75,000
    C. $25,000
    D. Not enough information to know

11. You and your project team are about to enter a meeting to determine project costs. You have elected to use bottom-up estimating and will base your estimates on the WBS. Which one of the following is *not* an attribute of bottom-up estimating?
    A. People doing the work create the estimates.
    B. It creates a more accurate estimate.
    C. It's more expensive to do than other methods.
    D. It's less expensive to do than other methods.

12. What is the present value if an organization expects to make $100,000 four years from now and the annual interest rate is 6 percent?
    A. $100,000
    B. $79,000
    C. $25,000
    D. Zero

13. You are the project manager for the construction of a new hotel. Before you begin the cost budgeting process, what is needed?
    A. Cost estimates and project schedule
    B. Cost estimates and supporting detail
    C. EAC and BAC
    D. A parametric model to arrive at the costs submitted

14. You are the project manager of the MNJ Project. Your project is falling behind schedule, and you have already spent $130,000 of your $150,000 budget. What do you call the $130,000?

A. Planned value

B. Present value

C. Sunk costs

D. Capital expenditure

15. You are the project manager of the JHD Project. Your project will cost your organization $250,000 to complete over the next eight months. Once the project is completed, the deliverables will begin earning the company $3500 per month. Which of the following represents the time to recover the costs of the project?

A. Not enough information to know

B. 8 months

C. 72 months

D. 5 years

16. You are the project manager for a consulting company. Your company has two possible projects to manage, but they can choose only one. Project KJH is worth $17,000, while Project ADS is worth $22,000. Management elects to choose Project ADS. The opportunity cost of this choice is which one of the following?

A. $5000

B. $17,000

C. $22,000

D. Zero, because project ADS is worth more than Project KJH

17. You are the project manager for the CSR Training Project, and 21,000 customer service reps are invited to attend the training session. Attendance is optional. You have calculated the costs of the training facility, but the workbook expense depends on how many students register for the class. For every 5000 workbooks created, the cost is reduced by a percentage of the original printing cost. The workbook expense is an example of which one of the following?

A. Fixed costs

B. Parametric costs

C. Variable costs

D. Indirect costs

18. You are the project manager of a construction project scheduled to last 24 months. You have elected to rent a piece of equipment for the duration of the project, even though you will need the equipment only periodically throughout the project. The cost of the equipment rental per month is $890. This is an example of which of the following?

A. Fixed costs

B. Parametric costs

C. Variable costs

D. Indirect costs

19. You are the project manager for the Hardware Inventory Project. You have a piece of equipment that was purchased recently for $10,000 and is expected to last five years in production. At the end of the five years, the expected worth of the equipment will be $1000. Using straight-line depreciation, what is the amount that can be written off each year?

A. Zero

B. $1000

C. $1800

D. $2000

20. You are the project manager of the LKG Project. The project has a budget of $290,000 and is expected to last three years. The project is now 10 percent complete and is on schedule. What is the BAC?

A. $29,000

B. $290,000

C. $96,666

D. $9,666

21. Your project has a budget of $130,000 and is expected to last ten months, with the work and budget spread evenly across all months. The project is now in month three, the work is on schedule, but you have spent $65,000 of the project budget. What is your variance?

A. $65,000

B. $39,000

C. $26,000

D. $64,999

22.   You are the project manager of the Carpet Installation Project for a new building. Your BAC is $600,000. You are now 40 percent complete with the project, though your plan called for you to be 45 percent complete with the work by this time. What is your earned value?

    A. $240,000

    B. $270,000

    C. $30,000

    D. −$30,000

23.   You are the project manager of the Carpet Installation Project for a new building. Your BAC is $600,000. You have spent $270,000 of your budget. You are now 40 percent done with the project, though your plan called for you to be 45 percent done with the work by this time. What is your CPI?

    A. 100

    B. 89

    C. 0.89

    D. 0.79

24.   You are the project manager for the Facility Installation Project. The project calls for 1500 units to be installed in a new baseball stadium. Your team wants to know why you have not assigned the same amount of time for the last 800 units that you assigned for the first 500 units. You tell them it is because of the learning curve. Which one of the following best describes this theory?

    A. Production increases as workers become more efficient with the installation procedure.

    B. Efficiency increases as workers become more familiar with the installation procedure.

    C. Costs decrease as workers complete more of the installation procedure.

    D. Time decreases as workers complete more of the installation procedure in the final phases of a project.

25.   Beth is a project manager for her company and she has been assigned a new project. During project planning, Beth needs to create a cost estimate for her project. Of the following, which one is the most reliable source of information for estimating project costs that Beth may use?

    A. Historical information from a recently completed project

    B. An SME's opinion

    C. Recollections of team members that have worked on similar projects

    D. Vendors' whitepapers

SELF TEST ANSWERS

1. You are the project manager for your organization and you need to create a cost estimate for your current project. This project is similar to the ABG Project you completed a few months ago, so you report to your program manager that you'll be using analogous estimating. Which of the following best describes analogous estimating?
   A. Regression analysis
   B. Bottom-up estimating
   C. Less accurate
   D. More accurate

   ☑ **C.** Analogous estimating is less accurate than other estimating methods.
   ☒ **A, B,** and **D** are incorrect. **A** is incorrect because regression analysis is a type of parametric modeling. **B** is incorrect because bottom-up estimating starts with zero and adds up the project costs. **D** is incorrect because analogous estimating is not more accurate.

2. You are the project manager for the GHG Project. You are about to create the cost estimates for the project. Which input to this process will help you the most?
   A. Parametric modeling
   B. WBS
   C. Project scope
   D. Requirements document

   ☑ **B.** The WBS is the input that can help you the most with the cost estimates.
   ☒ **A, C,** and **D** are incorrect. **A** is incorrect because parametric modeling is a form of estimating, not an input. **C** is incorrect because the project scope is not an input to the estimating process. **D** is incorrect because the requirements document is also not an input to the estimating process.

3. You are the project manager for the JKH Project. You have elected to use parametric estimating in your cost estimating for the project. Which of the following is an example of parametric estimating?
   A. $750 per ton
   B. Historical information from a similar project
   C. Estimates built bottom-up based on the WBS
   D. Estimates based on top-down budgeting

   ☑ **A.** The answer, $750 per ton, is an example of parametric estimating.
   ☒ **B, C,** and **D** are incorrect. **B** is incorrect because historical information is analogous, not parametric. **C** and **D** are incorrect because these do not describe parametric modeling.

4. You are the project manager for a new technology implementation project. Management has requested that your estimates be as exact as possible. Which one of the following methods of estimating will provide the most accurate estimate?

A. Top-down estimating

B. Top-down budgeting

C. Bottom-up estimating

D. Parametric estimating

☑ **C.** Bottom-up estimating provides the most accurate estimates. The project manager starts at zero, the bottom, and accounts for each cost within the project.

☒ **A, B,** and **D** are incorrect. They do not reflect the most accurate methods to create an estimate.

5. Your company has been hired to install tile in 1000 hotel rooms. All rooms will be identical in nature and will require the same amount of materials. Your project team has completed the first three hotel rooms, which took an average of six hours each to complete. You calculate the time to install the tile in each hotel room at six hours. The cost for the labor for your new project team is calculated at $700 per room. Your project sponsor disagrees with your labor estimate. Why?

A. You haven't completed one hotel room yet, so you don't know how long the work will actually take.

B. You have not factored in all of the effort applied to the work.

C. You have not considered the law of diminishing returns.

D. You have not considered the learning curve.

☑ **D.** As the project team completes more and more units, the time to complete a hotel room should take less and less time. **D** is the best choice.

☒ **A, B,** and **C** are incorrect because these choices do not reflect that learning curve – as more work is done, the more efficient the project team doing the work will become.

6. You are the project manager for a construction project to build 17 cabins. All of the cabins will be identical in nature. The contract for the project is set at a fixed cost, the incentive being that the faster the project work is completed, the more profitable the job. Management has requested that you study the work method to determine a faster, less costly, and better method of completing the project. This is an example of which of the following?

A. Time constraint

B. Schedule constraint

C. Value engineering

D. Learning curve

☑ **C.** Value engineering is a systematic approach to finding less costly ways to complete the same work.

☒ **A, B,** and **D** are incorrect. **A** and **B** are incorrect because this situation does not describe a specific time or schedule constraint. **D** is incorrect because the learning curve happens as the project team completes the work.

7. You are the project manager for a technical implementation project. The customer has requested that you factor in the after-the-project costs, such as maintenance and service. This is an example of which one of the following?
   A. Life-cycle costs
   B. Scope creep
   C. Project spin-off
   D. Operations

   ☑ **A.** The after-project costs are known as the life-cycle costs.
   ☒ **B, C,** and **D** are incorrect. **B** and **C,** though tempting, are incorrect because they do not describe the process of calculating the ongoing expenses of the product the project is creating. **D** is incorrect because operations do not fully describe the expenses unique to the product.

8. You are the project manager for your organization and you need to create a cost estimate for your current project. Your manager informs you that this project requires a precise cost estimate so you need to choose the most accurate estimating approach possible. Which one of the following provides the least accuracy in estimating?
   A. Rough order of magnitude
   B. Budget estimate
   C. Definitive estimate
   D. WBS estimate

   ☑ **A.** The rough order of magnitude is the least accurate approach, since it may vary from −25 percent to +75 percent.
   ☒ **B, C,** and **D** are incorrect. **B** and **C** are incorrect because they are more accurate estimates than the rough order of magnitude. **D** is not a valid answer for this question, as a WBS estimate isn't an estimating type.

9. As a PMP candidate, you need to be able to compare and contrast project plans, their components, and how the plans are used within a live project. Based on this information, which one of the following is true?
   A. The cost management plan controls how change management affects the BAC.
   B. The cost management plan controls how cost variances will be managed.
   C. The cost management plan controls how the project manager may update the cost estimates.
   D. The cost management plan controls how the BAC may be adjusted.

   ☑ **B.** The cost management plan controls how cost variances will be managed.
   ☒ **A, C,** and **D** are incorrect. These are not true descriptions of the cost management plan.

10. You are the project manager for project with a manufacturer. Project team members report they are 30 percent complete with the project. You have spent $25,000 out of the project's $250,000 budget. What is the earned value for this project?

   A. 10 percent

   B. $75,000

   C. $25,000

   D. Not enough information to know

   ☑ **B.** The earned value is 30 percent of the project's budget.

   ☒ **A, C,** and **D** are incorrect. They are not valid answers for the question.

11. You and your project team are about to enter a meeting to determine project costs. You have elected to use bottom-up estimating and will base your estimates on the WBS. Which one of the following is *not* an attribute of bottom-up estimating?

   A. People doing the work create the estimates.

   B. It creates a more accurate estimate.

   C. It's more expensive to do than other methods.

   D. It's less expensive to do than other methods.

   ☑ **D.** Using bottom-up estimating is not less expensive to do.

   ☒ **A, B,** and **C** are incorrect. These are attributes of a bottom-up estimating process.

12. What is the present value if an organization expects to make $100,000 four years from now and the annual interest rate is 6 percent?

   A. $100,000

   B. $79,000

   C. $25,000

   D. Zero

   ☑ **B.** The present value of $100,000 four years from now is $79,000. This can be calculated by using this formula: present value = $FV / (1 + i)^n$. FV is the future value, i is the interest rate, and n is the number of time periods.

   ☒ **A, C,** and **D** are incorrect. They don't reflect the present value.

13. You are the project manager for the construction of a new hotel. Before you begin the cost budgeting process, what is needed?
   A. Cost estimates and project schedule
   B. Cost estimates and supporting detail
   C. EAC and BAC
   D. A parametric model used to arrive at the costs submitted

   ☑ **A.** Cost estimates and the project schedule are inputs to the cost budgeting process.
   ☒ **B, C,** and **D** are incorrect. They are not inputs to cost budgeting.

14. You are the project manager of the MNJ Project. Your project is falling behind schedule, and you have already spent $130,000 of your $150,000 budget. What do you call the $130,000?
   A. Planned value
   B. Present value
   C. Sunk costs
   D. Capital expenditure

   ☑ **C.** Sunk costs are monies that have been spent.
   ☒ **A, B,** and **D** are incorrect. **A** is incorrect because planned value is the amount the project should be worth at this point in the schedule. **B** is also incorrect; present value is the current value of future monies. **D** is incorrect because a capital expenditure is money spent to purchase a long-term asset, such as a building.

15. You are the project manager of the JHD Project. Your project will cost your organization $250,000 to complete over the next eight months. Once the project is completed, the deliverables will begin earning the company $3500 per month. Which of the following represents the time to recover the costs of the project?
   A. Not enough information to know
   B. 8 months
   C. 72 months
   D. 5 years

   ☑ **C.** The time to recoup the monies from the project is 72 months. This is calculated by dividing the ROI of $3500 per month into the project cost.
   ☒ **A, B,** and **D** are incorrect. **A** is incorrect because there is enough information to make this calculation. **B** is incorrect because 8 months is the amount of time left in the project schedule. **D,** 5 years, is also incorrect.

16. You are the project manager for a consulting company. Your company has two possible projects to manage, but they can choose only one. Project KJH is worth $17,000, while Project ADS is worth $22,000. Management elects to choose Project ADS. The opportunity cost of this choice is which one of the following?

   A. $5000

   B. $17,000

   C. $22,000

   D. Zero, because project ADS is worth more than Project KJH

   ☑ **B.** The opportunity cost is the amount of the project that was not chosen.
   ☒ **A, C,** and **D** are incorrect. **A** is incorrect because $5000 is the difference between the two projects. It is not the opportunity cost. **C** is incorrect because $22,000 is the amount of the project that was selected. **D** is also an incorrect answer.

17. You are the project manager for the CSR Training Project, and 21,000 customer service reps are invited to attend the training session. Attendance is optional. You have calculated the costs of the training facility, but the workbook expense depends on how many students register for the class. For every 5000 workbooks created, the cost is reduced by a percentage of the original printing cost. The workbook expense is an example of which one of the following?

   A. Fixed costs

   B. Parametric costs

   C. Variable costs

   D. Indirect costs

   ☑ **C.** This is an example of variable costs, which are costs that can be affected by conditions within the project.
   ☒ **A, B,** and **D** are incorrect. **A** is incorrect because the cost of the books varies, depending on the number of students who register for the class. **B** is incorrect because fixed costs do not vary. **B,** parametric costs, would remain the same, regardless of how many books were created. **D** is incorrect because this example is not an indirect cost, which is a cost that can be shared across multiple projects.

18. You are the project manager of a construction project scheduled to last 24 months. You have elected to rent a piece of equipment for the duration of the project, even though you will need the equipment only periodically throughout the project. The cost of the equipment rental per month is $890. This is an example of which of the following?

   A. Fixed costs
   B. Parametric costs
   C. Variable costs
   D. Indirect costs

   ☑ **A.** This is a fixed-cost expense of $890 per month—regardless of how often the piece of equipment is used.
   ☒ **B, C,** and **D** are incorrect. **B** is incorrect because a parametric cost is a value used to calculate cost per use, cost per metric ton, or cost per unit. While it may at first appear that **B** is the correct choice, there is no historical information mentioned upon which to base the parametric model. **C** is incorrect because the cost does not vary within the project. **D** is also incorrect; this is a cost attributed directly to the project work.

19. You are the project manager for the Hardware Inventory Project. You have a piece of equipment that was purchased recently for $10,000 and is expected to last five years in production. At the end of the five years, the expected worth of the equipment will be $1000. Using straight-line depreciation, what is the amount that can be written off each year?

   A. Zero
   B. $1000
   C. $1800
   D. $2000

   ☑ **C.** The straight-line depreciation takes the purchase value of the item, minus the salvage price of the item, divided by the number of time periods. In this instance, it would be $10,000 minus $1000, or $9000. The $9000 is divided by five years and equates to $1800 per year.
   ☒ **A, B,** and **D** are incorrect. They do not reflect the correct calculation.

20. You are the project manager of the LKG Project. The project has a budget of $290,000 and is expected to last three years. The project is now 10 percent complete and is on schedule. What is the BAC?

   A. $29,000
   B. $290,000
   C. $96,666
   D. $9,666

   ☑ **B.** The BAC is the budget at completion, which is $290,000.
   ☒ **A, C,** and **D** are incorrect. **A** is incorrect because it describes the earned value for the project. **C** and **D** are both incorrect values.

21. Your project has a budget of $130,000 and is expected to last 10 months, with the work and budget spread evenly across all months. The project is now in month three, the work is on schedule, but you have spent $65,000 of the project budget. What is your variance?
   A. $65,000
   B. $39,000
   C. $26,000
   D. $64,999

   ☑ **C.** $26,000 is the variance. This is calculated by subtracting the actual costs of $65,000 from the earned value of $39,000. EV is calculated by taking the 30 percent completion of the project against the BAC. The project is considered to be 30 percent complete because it's slated for 10 months, is currently in month three, and is on schedule.
   ☒ **A, B,** and **D** are incorrect. These are not the correct calculations for the problem.

22. You are the project manager of the Carpet Installation Project for a new building. Your BAC is $600,000. You are now 40 percent complete with the project, though your plan called for you to be 45 percent complete with the work by this time. What is your earned value?
   A. $240,000
   B. $270,000
   C. $30,000
   D. −$30,000

   ☑ **A.** The earned value is calculated by multiplying the percentage of completion, 40 percent, by the BAC, which is $600,000, for a value of $240,000.
   ☒ **B, C,** and **D** are incorrect. There are not calculations of the earned value formula.

23. You are the project manager of the Carpet Installation Project for a new building. Your BAC is $600,000. You have spent $270,000 of your budget. You are now 40 percent done with the project, though your plan called for you to be 45 percent done with the work by this time. What is your CPI?
   A. 100
   B. 89
   C. 0.89
   D. 0.79

   ☑ **C** is the correct answer. The EV of $240,000 is divided by the AC of $270,000 for a CPI value of 0.89.
   ☒ **A, B,** and **D** are incorrect. **B** is incorrect because the value needs a decimal. **A** and **D** are incorrect calculations.

24. You are the project manager for the Facility Installation Project. The project calls for 1500 units to be installed in a new baseball stadium. Your team wants to know why you have not assigned the same amount of time for the last 800 units that you assigned for the first 500 units. You tell them it is because of the learning curve. Which one of the following best describes this theory?

 A.   Production increases as workers become more efficient with the installation procedure.
 B.   Efficiency increases as workers become more familiar with the installation procedure.
 C.   Costs decrease as workers complete more of the installation procedure.
 D.   Time decreases as workers complete more of the installation procedure in the final phases of a project.

☑   **B.** The learning curve allows the cost to decrease as a result of decreased installation time, because workers will complete more of the installation procedure as they become more familiar with it.
☒   **A, C,** and **D** are incorrect. These choices do not correctly describe the learning curve in relation to time and cost.

25. Beth is a project manager for her company and she has been assigned a new project. During project planning, Beth needs to create a cost estimate for her project. Of the following, which one is the most reliable source of information for estimating project costs that Beth may use?

 A.   Historical information from a recently completed project
 B.   An SME's opinion
 C.   Recollections of team members that have worked on similar projects
 D.   Vendors' whitepapers

☑   **A.** Of the choices presented, historical information from a recently completed project is the most reliable source of information.
☒   **B, C,** and **D** are incorrect. **B,** an SME's opinion, is valuable, but historical information is a more reliable way to estimate costs. **C** is incorrect because recollections are the least reliable source of information. **D** is also incorrect, although it may prove valuable in the planning process.

Chapter 8

Introducing Project Quality Management

CERTIFICATION OBJECTIVES

8.01	Preparing for Quality	8.04	Implementing Control Quality
8.02	Planning for Quality Management	✓	Two-Minute Drill
8.03	Managing Quality	Q&A	Self Test

What is *quality*? Quality, in project management, is about fulfilling requirements. Quality is about satisfying stated and implied needs. Quality is a conformance to project requirements. Every project has an anticipated level of quality for the project deliverables. Project quality management is the process of ensuring that the project fulfills its obligations to satisfy the project needs. As projects vary, so, too, will the anticipated level of quality.

Picture this: It's late on a hot summer night and you're hungry. You pull onto a gravel road and see a diner with a neon "Open" sign. The sign, you notice, really says "Ope" since the "n" is burned out. Inside the diner, stale smoke drifts around like fog. Grease, onions, and garlic seep into your clothes. You opt for a booth, only to find the table smeared with catsup, a little gravy, and, guessing by the stickiness, a glob of maple syrup.

Now picture this: You step off the elevator on the 43rd floor. A maître d' welcomes you and guides you to a table next to a window offering a sweeping view of the city. A piano player massages a song into the evening. The waiter snaps open a napkin and drapes it across your lap. Another waiter pours you a glass of cold, crisp water and presents the menu. By the soft candlelight, everything looks, and feels, grand.

With these two contrasting scenarios, which one do you think will have the better quality? Or can they both have an *acceptable* level of quality? For the first scenario—the diner—you expect a certain level of quality when it comes to service, food, and atmosphere. With the second scenario—the fancy restaurant—you also have an expected level of quality regarding service, food, and atmosphere. Both experiences are measured by that expected level of quality.

In the diner, you might get one of the best bacon cheeseburger and milkshake combos you can find late at night in the middle of nowhere. Just what you'd expect from this kind of place. And the fancy downtown restaurant? A fancy meal cooked to perfection—also what you'd expect. The difference between the two restaurants is in their grade. *Quality* and *grade* are not the same thing. The expected level of service, food, and atmosphere is the quality of the experience.

Looking at the Big Quality Picture

Before we hop into the three different facets of project quality management, let's establish a few "PMI-isms" on quality. Because quality means so many different things to so many different people, it's important to confirm that we're working with a common understanding of what quality is and what quality management hopes to accomplish from the PMI's point of view.

Accepting the Quality Management Approach

The details and specifications set out by the customer determine the expected level of quality. Project quality management, as far as your exam goes, is compatible with ISO 9000 and ISO 10000 quality standards and guidelines.

Project quality management also is concerned with both the management of the project and the product of the project. It's easy to focus on the product (the thing or service the project creates), but project managers must also provide quality for the project management activities. Aspects of the downside of focusing too much on the product include the following:

- **Overworking the project team to complete the project** This may result in unacceptable work, a decline in team morale, and the slow, steady destruction of the project team's willingness to work.

- **Hurrying to complete the project work by speeding through quality inspections** This can result in unacceptable deliverables.

a t c h ISO 9000 is an international standard that helps organizations follow their own quality procedures. It is not a quality system, but a method of following procedures created internally in an organization. And for the curious, *ISO* means "uniform" in Greek and it's from the International Organization for Standardization.

See the video "Quality Facts."

Quality vs. Grade

Quality and grade are not the same.

Quality is the sum of the characteristics of a product that allow it to meet the demands or expectations of the project. Quality is all about fulfilling requirements. Grade, according to the *PMBOK Guide*, "is a category or rank given to entities having the same functional use but different technical characteristics." For example, there are different grades of paint, different grades of metal, and even different grades of travel.

a t c h Know that low quality is always a problem, but low grade may not be. Depending on the requirements of the customer, low grade may be completely acceptable, but low quality never is.

Implementing Quality Project Management

Quality management and project management have similar characteristics:

- **Customer satisfaction**   The project must satisfy the customer requirements by delivering what it promised to satisfy the needs of the customer. The *PMBOK Guide* states it as "conformance to requirements" and "fitness for use."

- **Prevention**   Quality is planned into a project, not inspected in. It is always more cost-effective to prevent mistakes than to correct them.

- **Attribute sampling**   When you measure the results of a work, the results either will conform to quality or will not. In addition, variable sampling will measure the degree of conformity for the result of project work.

- **Tolerances**   There's usually a window of tolerance when it comes to measurements of work results (for example, five defects per 100 units). Control limits define the boundaries of tolerance and acceptability for work results.

- **Management responsibility**   The project team must work toward the quality goal, but management must provide the needed resources to deliver on the quality promises.

- **Plan-do-check-act**   Dr. W. Edwards Deming, arguably the world's leader in quality management theory thanks to his management methods implemented in Japan after World War II, set the bar with his "plan-do-check-act" approach to quality management. This approach is similar to the project management processes that every project passes through.

- **Kaizen technology**   Kaizen is a quality management philosophy of applying continuous small improvements to reduce costs and to ensure consistency of project performance.

- **Quality improvement programs**   One of the goals of any organization is to improve quality, reduce errors, and effectively become more efficient and more productive. Two quality improvements the *PMBOK Guide* mentions directly are Total Quality Management and Lean Six Sigma. Both programs aim to reduce waste, eliminate non-value-added efforts, and help the organization become more efficient and achieve quality goals.

There are five levels of quality management:

- **Let the customer find the defects**   This is the most expensive, and often the most embarrassing, approach to quality management. Warranty claims, rework, loss of income, and damage to reputation are all attributes of letting the customer find the defects.

- **Quality control inspections**   Inspect the work and correct the defects before the customer finds the defects. This approach can still be expensive and time-consuming, as rework must be done to correct the defects before the customer sees the work results.
- **Quality assurance programs**   Aim to perfect the processes, not just the errors that are a result of a poor work process.
- **Build quality into work**   Do the work correctly the first time by implementing quality planning and designing quality into the project.
- **Quality culture**   Build a culture of quality in the organization, where everyone aims to achieve quality in all processes and work results

Tailoring Quality in Project Management

The first step in achieving quality is to define what constitutes quality in your project. To define quality, there must be agreement on what the scope requirements are, what the tolerances for quality are, and what expectations the project stakeholders have for quality. In other words, there must be quantifiable goals for quality to achieve quality in the project. To tailor quality in project management means that you'll build a quality approach, or adapt a quality approach, for your organization that supports the vision of quality.

Considerations for tailoring quality in any organization include the following:

- **Policy compliance and auditing**   Your industry may have regulation and compliance concerns to which you must adhere. Your organization may have a quality assurance department or group that sets internal policies for quality, and they may audit the project and project results to confirm adherence.
- **Continuous improvements**   You'll need to define up front what the quality aspirations are and how you'll achieve those aspirations. You'll also define quality improvement for the project work, the processes, and the project management approach to be implemented throughout the project.
- **Stakeholder engagement**   You want stakeholders to be engaged with the project work and to feel a sense of ownership in the project. The stakeholder management plan, which I'll discuss in Chapter 13, is key for improving stakeholder engagement.

Considering Quality in Agile Environments

Quality in agile projects is still about meeting the project requirements. Of course, the project requirements are defined in the iteration planning sessions and directly before the project team takes on the work for the current iteration. As the product owner and the development team review the number of user stories that can be completed within the current iteration, the team, product owner, and project manager seek clarification on what exactly is required to deliver on the selected user stories.

In agile and adaptive environments, quality reviews are built into the process, rather than waiting until the end of the project or iteration to check for quality. At the end of each iteration, the project manager and the project team attend a special meeting, called a retrospective, to look back on what's worked (or didn't work) in the last iteration. This enables the project manager and team to make changes to processes and make adjustments to improve upon the project processes and the execution of the work to create the user stories.

CERTIFICATION OBJECTIVE 8.01

Preparing for Quality

Before a project manager can plan for quality, he must know what the quality expectations are. Specifically, what are the quality standards of the performing organization, and which quality standards are applicable to the project? As part of the planning processes, the project manager and the project team must identify the requirements of planning, determine how the requirements may be met, and identify the costs and schedule demands to meet the identified requirements.

One of the key principles of project quality management is that quality is planned in, not inspected in. Planning for quality is more cost-effective than inspecting work results and doing the work over or correcting problems to adhere to quality demands.

The project manager must consider the costs of achieving the expected level of quality in contrast to the costs of nonconformance. The costs of quality include training, safety measures, and action to prevent poor quality. The costs of nonconformance can far outweigh the costs of quality with possible loss of customers, rework needed, lost time, lost materials, and danger to workers.

e x a m

ⓦ a t c h As part of planning, the project manager must be wary of *gold plating*. Gold plating happens when the project manager sees that money remains in the budget, so she adds features and extras to the project scope to consume the entire budget. The customer does not need or want more than what was requested. Gold plating can be considered unethical.

Determining the Quality Policy

Top management should define the quality policy; this is part of the organizational process assets. The quality policy of the organization may follow a formal approach, such as ISO 9000, Six Sigma, or Total Quality Management, or it may have its own direction and approach to satisfying the demand for quality. There are loads of proprietary quality management methodologies, and you won't need to know much about any of them for your PMP exam. Out in the real world, however, you'll need to be familiar with the rules, policies, and procedures of whatever quality management methodology your organization subscribes to. Lucky you.

The project team should adapt the quality policy of the organization to guide the project implementation. This ensures that the management of the project and the deliverables of the project are in alignment with the performing organization's quality policy. In addition, the project manager should document how the project will fulfill the quality policy both in management and in the project deliverable.

What if the performing organization doesn't have a quality policy? Or what if two different entities are working together on a project and they use differing quality policies? In these circumstances, the project management team should create the quality policy for the project. The quality policy, in these instances, will accomplish the same goals as a company's quality policy: define quality requirements and determine how to adhere to them.

Regardless of where the quality policy comes from—management or the project team—the project stakeholders must be aware of the policy. This is important because the quality policy and associated quality methodology may require actions that could lengthen the project schedule—for example, quality audits, peer reviews, and other quality-centric activities. In addition to the required time to fulfill the quality requirements, other costs may be incurred.

Reviewing the Scope Baseline

Just as project quality management is focused on fulfilling the needs of the project, the project scope baseline is a key input to the quality planning process. I know you know that the scope baseline comprises the project scope statement, the WBS, and the WBS dictionary. Recall that the scope statement defines what will and will not be delivered as part of the project, as well as objectives regarding cost, schedule, and scope. The deliverables, and the expectations of the customers, will help guide the quality planning session to ensure that the customer requirements are met with regard to quality.

While the project scope will define the initial product description, the product description may have supporting detail that the project manager and project team will need to review. Consider a project to create an apartment building. The requirements, specifications, and details of the building will need to be evaluated and reviewed since this information will, no doubt, affect the quality planning.

The WBS and WBS dictionary are needed during quality planning because they define the specific things that will satisfy the project requirements for deliverables. The WBS is like a catalog of customer expectations. When you and your project team fulfill the elements of the WBS, you're meeting customer satisfaction, which maps to quality. The WBS dictionary tags along because it has the specific details of what each element of the WBS requires.

PMP
Coach

So, what is quality in project management? Quality is the accurate completion of the project scope and the satisfaction of the stated and implied project needs. In your quest for your PMP certification, do you have quality? What is the scope of your certification goal and how will you reach it? Focus on quality as you're studying, in your preparation, and in your mental mindset, and you'll find quality in the execution of your PMP test-taking.

Consider Schedule and Costs

From the project management plan you will also need to consider the schedule and costs baselines. Recall that quality is affected by the balance of the schedule, costs, and scope, so it stands to reason that you'll need the baselines of these components of the project management plan as part of quality planning. The balance of time, cost, and scope are the Iron Triangle of project management. If your organization has high demands for quality, but the project is rushed or insufficient funds are available to achieve the quality demanded in the project scope, then there is a risk that the project will not be successful because quality could not be achieved.

The schedule of the project does affect quality. Consider a schedule that is perfect only for the project activities and doesn't consider time for the quality inspections. If the quality inspections are rushed—or, worse, skipped entirely—there will probably be errors in the project work. The project schedule should include time for the project management work, including the quality control activities discussed in this chapter, for the quality expectations to be met.

Costs can also influence the ability of the project to meet quality expectations. If the costs are not adequate to meet the demands of the project scope—such as purchasing the correct materials, tools, and equipment—then quality is likely to suffer as well. Costs affect the elements of the project quality, because to achieve the expected quality, you'll have to pay for the correct tools, equipment, material, and resources. If there are errors and mistakes in the project execution, quality again can be adversely affected by costs. Consider a project that wastes materials due to an error. If the organization can't afford to replace the materials, the quality of the project suffers because of the error and ultimately because of the cost of the wasted materials.

Reviewing the Standards and Regulations

The standards and regulations of each industry should be reviewed to determine that both the project plan and the plan for quality are acceptable. For example, a project to wire a building for electricity will have certain regulations to which it must adhere. The relevance of the regulations must be understood and planned into the project to ensure conformance with regulatory requirements. Standards and regulations are considered part of the enterprise environmental factors that affect the project planning and execution.

CERTIFICATION OBJECTIVE 8.02

Planning for Quality Management

Once the project manager has assembled the needed inputs and evaluated the product description and project scope, she can get to work creating a plan on how to satisfy the quality demands. She'll need to rely on the documentation created to date, her project team, and the project's key stakeholders for much of the input. In addition, the project manager will use several different techniques to plan on meeting quality. But first, she must consider five inputs to planning quality management in a project:

- **Project charter**   A high-level project description of what the project will create. The charter also defines what constitutes success and the measurable project objectives.
- **Project management plan**   The project management plan is needed because of the integration of quality management. Specifically, the requirements management plan, risk management plan, stakeholder engagement plan, and the scope baseline are referenced in quality management planning.
- **Project documents**   The project documents that are needed in quality management planning are the assumption log, requirements documentation, requirements traceability matrix, the risk register, and the stakeholder register.
- **Enterprise environmental factors**   The project manager will need to review any regulations, rules, and standards for the organization; the geographic makeup of the project; the organizational structure; marketplace conditions; working conditions of the project; and any cultural perceptions that could affect achieving quality.
- **Organizational process assets**   The project manager will also need to abide by the organization's quality management system, policies, procedures, and guidelines. Organizational process assets leveraged here may also include templates, check sheets, and historical information.

As planning is an iterative process, so, too, is quality planning. As events happen within the project, the project manager should evaluate the events and then apply corrective actions. This is a common PMI theme: plan, implement, measure, react—and document! Throughout the project implementation, things will go awry, team members may complete less-than-acceptable work, stakeholders will demand changes, and so on; these variables must be evaluated for their impacts on project quality. What good is a project if it's "completed" on time, but the quality of the deliverable is unacceptable? Technically, if the product is unacceptable, the project is not finished, because it failed to meet the project scope. Let's look at some tools and techniques the project manager will use to plan for quality.

Applying Benchmarking Practices

Benchmarking, when it comes to quality project management, is all about comparing one project to another. This technique considers what the project manager has planned or experienced regarding quality and compares it to another project to see how things measure up. The current project can be measured against any other project—not just projects within the performing organization or within the same industry.

The goal of benchmarking is to evaluate the differences between the two projects and then to take corrective actions for the current project if necessary. For example, Project A may have better quality performance than Project B. When the project manager compares the two projects, she'll want to determine the differences between them. She'll look for what's missing in Project B or what activities the folks in Project A are doing that she's not.

Benchmarking allows the project manager and the project team to see what's possible and then strive toward that goal. Benchmarking can also be used as a measurement against industry standards, competitors' pricing, or competitors' level of performance.

Brainstorming and Interviews

Brainstorming and interviews are two data-gathering techniques that a project team can use in planning for quality. Brainstorming, as discussed earlier in this book, enables the team to generate as many ideas as possible, so that the ideas can be discussed to be adapted into the project. Interviews can query stakeholders, subject matter experts, and management on quality needs and expectations for the project.

Using a Benefit/Cost Analysis

Benefits should outweigh costs.

A benefit/cost analysis is a process of determining the pros and cons of any process, product, or activity. The straightforward approach when it comes to project management is concerned with the benefits versus the costs of the quality management activities. There are two major considerations with the benefit/cost analysis in quality management:

- ■ **Benefit**   Completing quality work increases productivity because shoddy work does not have to be redone. When work is completed correctly the first time as expected, the project does not have to spend additional funds to redo the work.

- ■ **Costs**   Completing quality work may cost more than the work is worth. To deliver a level of quality beyond what is demanded costs the project additional funds. The types of quality management activities that guarantee quality may not be needed for every project.

Although quality is required on every project, not every project has the same quality expenses based on the demands. For example, consider a project to create a temporary drainage ditch for a field. Specifications are set for the ditch, but the project may not require the expense of a landscape architect to evaluate the slant and descent of the temporary ditch.

Another project, to create and secure an information technology department, may require the expense of a security consulting firm to evaluate, test, and certify the security of the software code, the network servers, and the physical security of the department. The cost of the quality requirements is in alignment with the demands of the project.

Considering the Cost of Quality

The cost of quality considers the expense of all the activities within a project that are undertaken to ensure its quality. The cost of quality is divided into three major categories:

- **Prevention costs** Defines the costs of preventing poor quality in the project. This approach is the cost of completing the project work to satisfy the project scope and the expected level of quality. Examples of this cost include training, safety measures, and acquiring the right tools and equipment to do the project work.

- **Appraisal costs** The cost of measuring, testing, auditing, and evaluating the project's product to confirm that quality has been achieved in the work results.

- **Failure costs** This approach is the cost of completing the project work without quality. The biggest issue here is the money lost by having to redo the project work; it's always more cost-effective to do the work right the first time. Internal failure costs are the rework and scrap caused by poor quality. External failure costs include loss of sales, loss of customers, downtime, and damage to the organization's reputation.

The optimal cost quality is about balancing the prevention and appraisal costs against the failure costs. For example, a manufacturer could slow down a piece of equipment to ensure that every widget created is perfect, but the cost of doing so is greater than running the equipment at a faster pace and losing a few widgets due to poor quality.

exam

ⓦatch You might use some additional quality management planning tools, such as the affinity diagram, brainstorming, nominal group techniques, or—here's a new one—force-field analysis. It sounds like something out of *Star Wars*, but it's a diagram that captures the forces that are for or against a change. The forces could be people, policies, or other constraints in the organization. When you think about "may the force be with you," it could mean you want the people, policies, and other factors on your side as you move toward project execution.

Utilizing Multicriteria Decision Analysis Tools

Multicriteria decision analysis tools, also called multiple-criteria decision-making tools, help the project manager evaluate multiple facets of decisions when it comes to quality. The tool can help determine tradeoffs for achieving quality expectations, but it can also help keep the project's costs, schedule, and workflow all in balance. The project manager can examine the competing objectives of a predetermined budget against the requirements for quality, risks in the project, schedule, and the business value the project will bring. There are software packages to help you make the best choice, if not the best solution, for the decision.

Representing Data in Quality Management Planning

You can use several tools for data representation in quality management planning (and in other processes):

- **Flowcharts**   Also called process maps, they show the flow of process, possibilities for branching, loops, and possible outcomes for a process. (I'll cover flowcharting in more detail later in this chapter.)
- **Logical data model**   Visualizes the data and helps to uncover where quality issues may be lurking.
- **Matrix diagrams**   Compares and contrasts objectives, metrics, and other factors that may affect quality in the project.
- **Mind mapping**   Helps to visualize thoughts and information.

Planning for Testing and Inspection

Quality control is inspection-driven, but you'll need a plan for how you'll inspect the work. As part of quality management planning, the project manager and the project team will define how the work will be tested and inspected to ensure that quality has been met. This is an example of an appraisal cost, because the inspection activities will take time, may require materials or tools to test, and may have other cost factors depending on the industry in which the project is being undertaken. For example, consider the testing costs in manufacturing versus construction or IT projects.

Creating the Quality Management Plan

The result of quality planning is to identify a method for implementing the quality policy. Because planning is iterative, the quality planning sessions often require several revisits to the quality planning processes. Longer projects may include scheduled quality planning sessions to compare the performance of the project in relation to the quality that was planned.

One of the major outputs of quality planning is the quality management plan. This document describes how the project manager and the project team will fulfill the quality policy. In an ISO 9000 environment, the quality management plan is referred to as the "project quality system." The quality management plan addresses the following three things about the project and the project work:

- **Quality control**   Work results are monitored to see if they meet relevant quality standards. If the results do not meet the quality standards, the project manager applies root-cause analysis to determine the cause of the poor performance and then eliminates the cause. Quality control is inspection-oriented.

■ **Quality assurance** The overall performance is evaluated to ensure that the project meets the relevant quality standards. Quality assurance maps to an organization's quality policy and is typically a managerial process. Quality assurance is generally considered the work of applying the quality plan.

■ **Quality improvement** The project performance is measured and evaluated, and corrective actions are applied to improve the product and the project. The improvements can be large or small, depending on the condition and the quality philosophy of the performing organization.

Identifying the Quality Metrics

Quality metrics are the quantifiable terms and values used to measure a process, activity, or work result. An example of an operational definition could be an expected value for the required torque to tighten a bolt on a piece of equipment. Testing and measuring the torque could determine the operational definition to prove or disprove the quality of the product. Other examples can include hours of labor to complete a work package, required safety measures, cost per unit, and so on.

Quality metrics are clear, concise measurements. Designating that 95 percent of all customer service calls should be answered by a live person within 30 seconds is a metric; a statement that all calls should be answered in a timely manner is not. The project can also have a quality metric, such as the cost performance index or the number of user stories completed per iteration.

CERTIFICATION OBJECTIVE 8.0

Managing Quality

Managing quality is an executing process. It is the sum of the planning and the implementations of the plans the project manager, the project team, and management apply to ensure that the project meets the demands of quality. Managing quality is sometimes referred to as quality assurance (QA). QA is not done only at the end of the project, but it should occur before and during the project as well. Because QA is an executing process, you should link it to continuous process improvement, because its aim is to make the project better. In project management, managing quality includes not only managing the quality of the processes, but also managing the quality of the product design. Managing quality is everyone's responsibility: the project manager, project team, project sponsor, management, and even the project customer.

In some organizations, the QA department or another entity will complete the QA activities. QA is interested in finding the defects and then fixing the problems. There are many different approaches to QA, depending on the quality system the organization or project team has adopted.

Preparing to Manage Quality

The project manager and the project team will need to prepare several inputs for managing quality:

- **Lessons learned register**   Lessons from the current project can help improve quality for the remainder of the current project.
- **Results of quality control**   The measurements taken by the project manager and the project team to inspect the project deliverables' quality are fed back into the quality management process.
- **Quality metrics**   Quality control tests will provide these measurements. The values must be quantifiable so results may be measured, compared, and analyzed. In other words, "pretty close to on track" is not adequate; "95 percent pass rate" is more acceptable.
- **Risk report**   Risks can affect the quality of the project, so a review of the risk report is needed to ensure that quality is not adversely affected.
- **The quality management plan**   This plan defines how the project team will implement and fulfill the quality policy of the performing organization.
- **Organizational process assets**   Considerations include the organization quality management system, quality templates, previous quality audit results, and lessons learned from similar projects.

Managing Quality for a Project

You can use several tools and techniques to manage quality within a project. You don't have to use all of these tools—just the ones that are most appropriate for your organization. One of the most common tools is a data-gathering tool: the checklist. The checklist ensures that all the required steps were correctly taken to create a quality result. For example, you could use a checklist in a project to install light fixtures. The checklist would ensure that all installations, regardless of the team member, were done in the same way to get the same results.

Here are other tools and techniques to consider:

- **Alternatives analysis**   Determines quality options and chooses the best option for the project
- **Document analysis**   Reviews project documentation, such as performance and risk reports, to see if quality may be threatened by what's occurring in the project
- **Process analysis**   Reviews processes in the project and organization to identify improvement opportunities
- **Root cause analysis**   Finds the root cause of project variances, defects, or risk (if root causes of poor quality are corrected or eliminated the poor quality won't happen again)

- **Multicriteria decision analysis**   Reviews, compares, and contracts project and product characteristics that may affect quality
- **Affinity diagrams**   Group similar ideas, deliverables, or concepts together; the WBS could be considered an example of an affinity diagram
- **Cause-and-effect diagrams**   Also known as fishbone diagrams, Ishikawa diagrams, and why-why diagrams, they help to identify causal factors and root cause of quality problems
- **Flowcharts**   Demonstrate the flow of information or activities in a process, project, or organization
- **Histograms**   Bar charts that can help show distribution of errors, issues, metrics accomplished, and other data
- **Matrix diagrams**   Compare and contrast objectives, metrics, and other factors that may affect quality in the project
- **Scatter diagrams**   Track the relationship between two variables, which are considered related the closer they track against a diagonal line

Completing a Quality Audit

Quality audits are about learning. A quality audit identifies compliance with organizational policies, processes, and procedures to make things better for this project and other projects within the organization. The idea, for example, is that project manager Susan can learn from the implementations of project manager Bob, and vice versa.

Quality audits are formal reviews of what's been completed within a project, what worked, and what didn't work. The result of the audit is to improve performance for the current project, other projects, or the entire organization. Quality audits aim to do the following:

- Document the best practices the project is using.
- Document any variances in the project quality approach.
- Recommend best practices that should be implemented in the current project.
- Assist the project manager and project team in implementing recommendations for quality improvement.
- Document the outcomes of the quality audit in the project's lessons learned documentation.

Quality audits can be scheduled at key intervals within a project, or—surprise!—they can occur without warning. The audit process can vary, depending on who is completing the audit: internal auditors or hired, third-party experts. The goal of a quality audit is to ensure that the project is adhering to the requirements of managing quality, and the goal of managing quality is to reduce the overall cost of quality. As you probably know from your experience, it's usually more cost-effective to do something right the first time than to do it right the second time. That's managing quality—do the work according to plan, and you'll save time and money.

Utilizing the Design for X Approach

Design for X is a philosophy in product design, where the X can mean excellence, or, more often, a specific characteristic of a solution. Design for X is also known as DfX. X is usually a variable that the project is trying to address, such as cost, uptime, return on investment, or some other facet the organization is pursuing. Design for X considers all components of the design and how the component affects the X variable for better or for worse. Common project goals for Design for X include lowered costs and improved service, reliability, safety, and overall quality.

Implementing Problem-Solving Techniques

When there's a problem in the project, it's the responsibility of the project manager and the project team to attempt to resolve the problem and to ensure that the project can continue and overcome the setback or challenge. In the quality management process, problem solving will address quality issues and concerns by following a six-step problem-solving approach:

1. Define the problem.
2. Define the problem's root cause.
3. Generate solutions to the problem.
4. Select the best solution for the problem.
5. Implement the selected solution.
6. Test and verify the effectiveness of the selected solution.

Reviewing the Results of Managing Quality

The primary output of managing quality? Quality improvement. But it's not just about the quality of the project's deliverables; it's also about the process to complete the project work. This is process analysis, and it follows the guidelines of the process improvement plan. There are five outputs of the process:

- Quality reports
- Test and evaluation documentation

- Project management plan updates (which can include quality management plan, scope baseline, schedule baseline, and cost baseline)
- Project document updates (which include issue log, lessons learned register, and risk register)

Quality improvement requires action to improve the project's effectiveness. The actions to improve the effectiveness may have to be routed through the change control system, which means change requests, analysis of the costs and risks, and involvement of the change control board.

Implementing Control Quality

Quality control (QC) requires the project manager, or another qualified party, to monitor and measure project results to determine whether the results are up to the demands of the quality standards. If the results are unsatisfactory, root-cause analysis follows the quality control processes. Root-cause analysis enables the project manager to determine the cause and apply corrective actions. QC occurs throughout the life of a project, not just at its end.

QC is also not concerned only with the product the project is creating, but with the project management processes. QC measures performance, scheduling, and cost variances. The management of the project should be of quality—not just the product the project creates. Consider a project manager who demands the project team work extreme hours to meet an unrealistic deadline; team morale suffers and likely so does the project work the team is completing.

The project team should do the following to ensure competency in quality control:

- Conduct statistical quality control, such as sampling and probability.
- Inspect the product to keep errors away from the customer.
- Perform attribute sampling to measure conformance to quality on a per-unit basis.
- Conduct variable sampling to measure the degree of conformance.
- Study special causes to determine anomalies to quality.
- Research random causes to determine expected variances of quality.
- Check the tolerance range to determine whether the results are within or without an acceptable level of quality.
- Observe control limits to determine whether the results are in or out of quality control.

Preparing for Quality Control

Quality control relies on several inputs, such as the following:

- **The quality management plan**   The quality management plan defines how QA will be applied to the project, the expectations of QC, and the organization's approach for continuous process improvement.
- **Lessons learned register**   Lessons learned from the current project can help the remainder of the project improve upon its quality outcome.
- **Quality metrics**   The operational definitions that define the metrics for the project are needed so QC can measure and react to the results of project performance.
- **Test and evaluation documents**   Documentation on the outcomes of the testing and review of project deliverables are used to determine how well they achieved the project objectives.
- **Approved change requests**   Approved change requests have an effect on how the project work is scheduled and performed, which may affect the project's overall quality.
- **Deliverables**   Execution brings about deliverables. The results of both the project processes and the product results are needed to measure the results of the project team's work and compare it to the quality standards. The expected results of the product and the project can be measured from the project plan.
- **Work performance data**   The key performance metrics about the work the project team has performed are needed. The project manager will need to inspect the variances between what was planned and what was implemented for schedule, costs, and scope.
- **Enterprise environmental factors**   The project management information system, plus any quality management software, regulations, rules, and standards that the project must adhere to are considered inputs for quality control.
- **Organizational process assets**   The organization's quality policy, standards for quality control techniques, and communication requirements based on the outcomes of quality control inspections are all needed for the quality control process.

Inspecting Results

Although quality is planned into a project, not inspected in, inspections are needed to prove conformance to requirements. An inspection can be done on the project as a whole, on a portion of the project work, on the project deliverable, or even on an individual activity. Inspections are also known as the following:

- Reviews
- Product reviews

- Audits
- Walkthroughs

Data gathering is also utilized in the QC process. You should be familiar with two data-gathering tools:

- **Checklists**   Ensure that the work is done the same way each time to reach the same quality result.
- **Checksheets**   Help organize data about a quality issue. Checksheets, also known as tally sheets, are not the same thing as checklists. Checksheets can be used to "tally" up the type of defects in a project to organize a plan of defect repair or corrective actions.

Another type of inspection is testing, which tests the product against the quality standards to see if the deliverable meets the quality objectives. Testing is unique to the discipline in which the project takes place. For example, testing in software development aims to find bugs and errors, while testing in construction may occur to confirm electrical, plumbing, and HVAC systems. Testing is typically done throughout the project, not just at the end, to ensure that work isn't built on faulty results.

Statistical sampling is an inspection tool and technique in which you randomly select a few items from the pool of deliverables to measure quality on these items as a representative of the whole population. For example, if you were installing 1000 doors in a project, you might select 200 doors to inspect randomly to see how quality is being implemented across the task of installing doors.

Finally, you can use questionnaires and surveys to collect information on customer satisfaction after the project, or after a portion of the project, is completed. The surveys can be a fast way to see how happy the customers are with the project results and give you some insight to how well the project team ascertained the needed quality in the project.

Data Representation Tools

Data representation tools are charts that can illustrate the results of your quality control efforts. You'll need to be concerned with several types of charts for the exam—these first two are pretty easy:

- **Cause-and-effect diagrams**   These diagrams show the relationships between the variables within a process and how those relationships may contribute to inadequate quality. They can help organize both the process and team opinions, as well as generate discussion on finding a solution to ensure quality. Figure 8-1 shows an example of a cause-and-effect diagram. To create a diagram, start with the effect—the problem you want to solve—and then fill out the diagram with possible causes that contribute to the effect. These diagrams are also known as Ishikawa diagrams and fishbone diagrams.

FIGURE 8-1

Cause-and-effect diagrams show the relationship of variables to a problem.

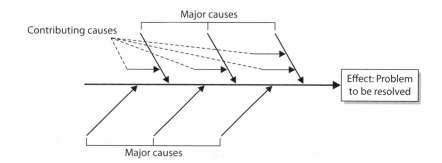

System or process flowcharts These flowcharts illustrate the flow of a process through a system, such as a project change request through the change control system or work authorization through a quality control process. A process flowchart does not have to be limited to the project management activities. It could instead demonstrate how a manufacturer creates, packages, and ships the product to the customer, as shown in Figure 8-2.

e x a m
ⓦ a t c h   **A cause-and-effect diagram is also called an Ishikawa diagram, why-why chart, and a fishbone diagram—these terms refer to the same thing.**

FIGURE 8-2

Flowcharts demonstrate how processes within a system are related.

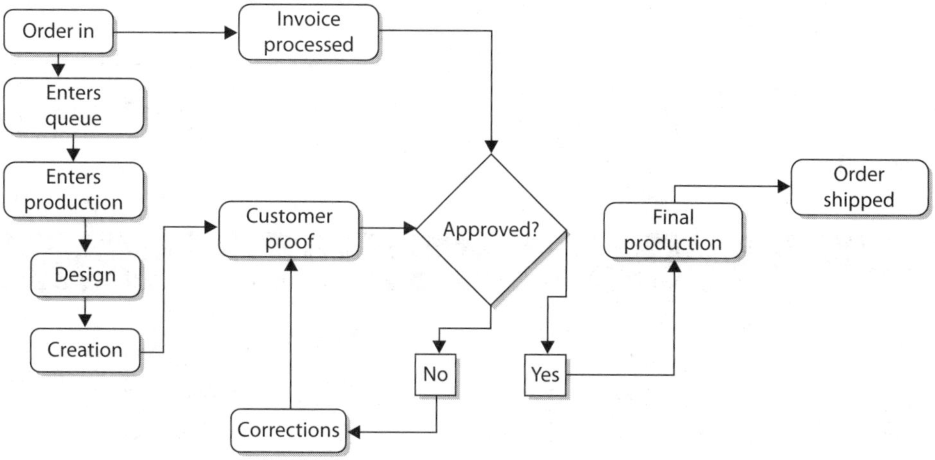

Creating a Control Chart

Ever feel like your project is out of control? A control chart can prove it. Control charts illustrate the performance of an aspect of a project over time. They map the results of inspections against a chart, as shown in Figure 8-3. Control charts are typically used in projects or operations that involve repetitive activities—such as projects for manufacturing, a testing series, or help desks.

The outer limits of a control chart are established by customer requirements. Within the customer requirements are the upper control limits (UCLs) and the lower control limits (LCLs). The UCL is typically set at +3 or +6 sigma, while the LCL is set at −3 or −6 sigma. Sigma results show the degree of correctness. Table 8-1 outlines the four sigma values representing normal distribution. You'll need to know these for the PMP exam.

So, what happened to sigma 4 and sigma 5? Nothing. They're still there; it's just that the difference between 3 sigma at 99.73 and 6 sigma at 99.99 is so small that statisticians just jump to 6 sigma. The mean in a control chart represents the expected result, while the sigma values represent the expected spread of results based on the inspection. A true

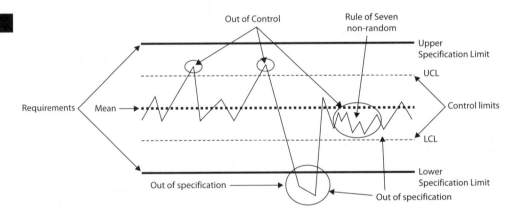

FIGURE 8-3

Control charts demonstrate the results of inspections.

TABLE 8-1	Value	Percent Correct
The Four Sigma Values Representing Normal Distribution	+/− 1 sigma	68.26 percent
	+/− 2 sigma	95.46 percent
	+/− 3 sigma	99.73 percent
	+/− 6 sigma	99.99 percent

6 sigma allows only two defects per million opportunities, and the percentage to represent that value is 99.99985 percent. For the exam, you can go with 99.99 percent.

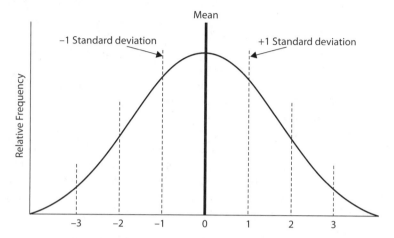

For example, if a manufacturer creates 1000 units per hour and expects an average of 50 units each hour to be defective, the mean would be 950 units. Of course, a better approach would be to create a mean based on a history of what's been produced, but for now let's assume that the expectation is 50 units defective per hour out of 1000 units created. If the control limits were set at +/−3 sigma, the results of testing would actually expect up to 953 correct units and down to 947 correct units. The upper and lower specifications, identified as the solid lines in Figure 8-3, are the boundaries for acceptable performance.

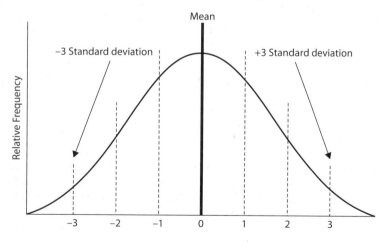

Over time, the results of testing are plotted in the control chart. Whenever a result of testing is plotted beyond the UCL or LCL values, it is considered to be "out of control." When a value is out of control, there is a reason why—it's called an assignable cause. Something caused the results to change for better or for worse, and the result must be investigated to understand the why behind the occurrence.

Another reason to look for an assignable cause is The Rule of Seven, which states that whenever seven consecutive results are all on one side of the mean or there are seven consecutive measures trending up or down, this is an assignable cause. Thus, some change has caused the results to shift to one side of the expected mean. Again, the cause must be investigated to determine why the change happened.

Although control charts are easily associated with recurring activities, such as manufacturing, they can also be applied to project management. Consider the number of expected change requests, delays within a project, and other recurring activities. A control chart can plot out these activities to measure performance, evaluate positive and negative results, and track corrective actions based on previous similar projects or from historical information within the current project.

 on the job   **Some project managers may believe that there should be no variance at all in the results of testing—they expect it to be 100 percent correct all the time. In some instances, this is valid; consider hospitals, military scenarios, and other situations dealing with life and death. When a project manager demands 100 percent perfection, the cost of quality issues needs to be revisited. What is the cost of obtaining perfection versus the cost of obtaining 98 percent correctness?**

Creating Pareto Diagrams

A Pareto diagram is somewhat related to Pareto's Law: 80 percent of the problems come from 20 percent of the issues. This is also known as the *80/20 rule*. A Pareto diagram illustrates the problems by assigned cause from smallest to largest, as Figure 8-4 shows. The project team should first work on the largest problems and then move on to the smaller problems.

Creating a Histogram

A histogram is a bar chart showing the frequency of variables within a project. For example, a histogram could show which states have the most customers for a retailer. Within project management, a common histogram is a resource histogram, which shows the frequency of resources used on project work. It's nothing more than a bar chart.

FIGURE 8-4

A Pareto diagram is a histogram that ranks issues from largest to smallest.

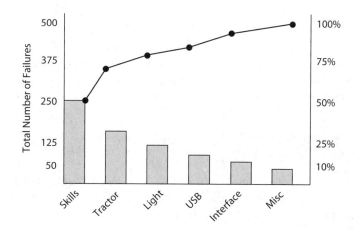

Creating a Run Chart

A run chart, as Figure 8-5 shows, is a line graph that shows the results of inspections in the order in which they've occurred. The goals of a run chart are first to demonstrate the results of a process over time and then to use trend analysis to predict when certain trends may reemerge. It is similar to a control chart, but it tracks the outcomes of measurements against when the outcome happened and the time between the measurements. This gives insight into the measurements that differs from what the control chart offers. Based on this information, an organization can work to prevent the negative trend or work to capitalize on an identified opportunity.

FIGURE 8-5

A run charts track the results of inspections over time.

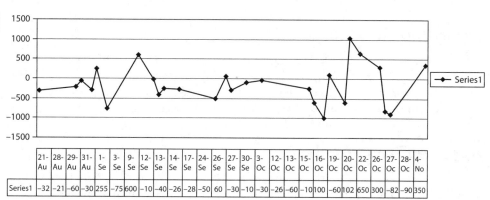

	21-Au	28-Au	29-Au	31-Au	1-Se	3-Se	9-Se	12-Se	13-Se	14-Se	17-Se	24-Se	26-Se	27-Se	30-Se	3-Oc	12-Oc	13-Oc	15-Oc	16-Oc	19-Oc	20-Oc	22-Oc	26-Oc	27-Oc	28-Oc	4-No
Series1	−32	−21	−60	−30	255	−75	600	−10	−40	−26	−28	−50	60	−30	−10	−30	−26	−60	−10	100	−60	102	650	300	−82	−90	350

Creating a Scatter Diagram

A scatter diagram is like a run chart, but it instead tracks the relationship between two variables. The two variables are considered related the closer they track against a diagonal line. For example, a project manager could track the performance of two team members, the time and cost, or even changes between functional managers and the project's schedule.

The seven basic quality management tools are scatter diagrams, control charts, histograms, Pareto diagrams, checksheets, flowcharts, and cause-and-effect diagrams.

Completing a Statistical Sampling

Statistical sampling is the process of choosing a percentage of results at random. For example, a project creating a medical device may have 20 percent of all units randomly selected to check quality. This process must be completed on a consistent basis throughout the project, rather than on a sporadic schedule.

Statistical sampling can reduce the costs of quality control, but results can be mixed if an adequate testing plan and schedule are not followed. The science of statistical sampling (and its requirements to be effective) is an involved process. Many books, seminars, and professionals are devoted to the process. For the PMP exam, know that statistical sampling uses a percentage of the results to test for quality. This process can reduce quality control cost.

Revisiting Flowcharting

Flowcharts are used to illustrate how the different parts of a system operate. Flowcharting is valuable in quality control because the process can be evaluated and tested to determine where in the process quality begins to break down. Corrective actions can then be applied to the system to ensure that quality continues as planned—and as expected.

Applying Trend Analysis

Trend analysis is the science of analyzing past results to predict future performance. Sports announcers use trend analysis all the time: "The Cubs have never won in St. Louis, on a Tuesday night, in the month of July, when the temperature at the top of the third inning was above 80 degrees."

The results of trend analysis enable the project manager to apply corrective actions to intervene and prevent unacceptable outcomes. Trend analysis on a project requires adequate records to predict results and set current expectations. Trend analysis can monitor the following:

- **Technical performance**   Trend analysis can ask, "How many errors have been experienced up to this point in the project schedule, and how many additional errors were encountered since the last testing of the technical performance?"
- **Cost and schedule performance**   Trend analysis can ask, "How many activities were completed incorrectly, came in late, or had significant cost variances?"

The Results of Quality Control

Quality control should, first and foremost, result in quality improvement. Based on the results of the tools and techniques used to implement quality control, the project manager and project team apply corrective actions to prevent unacceptable quality and improve the overall quality of the project management processes.

INSIDE THE EXAM

Quality, in project management, has many different meanings. For the PMP exam, you should know the following four key facts:

- Customer satisfaction is the conformance of the requirements and fitness for use.
- Quality is distinct from grade.
- Quality is obtained by the project team doing what was promised at the start of the project.
- Quality is concerned with prevention over inspection.

The quality management plan spans all areas of project quality—not just the product the project is creating—and considers quality after the project is complete. The experience of the project as led by the project manager should be of quality as well. There is a direct relationship between the project deliverables and the quality of project management.

Another area of quality is scheduling. A project manager must examine resources and how they are allocated, and pay attention to the cost of quality for the assigned resources. One scheduling technique, just-in-time (JIT) scheduling, demands higher quality. JIT scheduling means, for example, that you do not order inventory, such as supplies and materials, until it is needed. This improves cash flow and reduces the cost of inventory not in use. However, a lack of quality in the project may cause defects. Because of the defects, the material in use is thus wasted and downtime occurs. This downtime results because no additional materials are on hand and the project is waiting for new materials to arrive.

Finally, spend some time learning the values for the four sigmas shown in Table 8-1. You'll need to know them.

The corrective actions and the defect repairs that the project manager and the project team want to incorporate into the project may require change requests and management approval. The value and importance of the change should be evident so the improvement to quality is approved and folded into the project. In addition to quality improvement, there are other results of quality control:

■ **Verified deliverables and changes**   The work results are either accepted or rejected. Rejected items typically mean rework. When changes are approved and executed, these changes also need to be validated, as they're now part of the project scope baseline. Verified deliverables mean that the work is of quality and may now be an input to validate scope process.

■ **Rework**   Nonconformance to quality results in change requests for corrective action. Rework costs time and money, and it contributes to projects being late, over budget, or both. It is always more cost-effective to do the work right the first time than to do it correctly the second time.

■ **Project management plan updates**   When results of inspections indicate quality is out of control, process adjustments may be needed to make immediate corrective actions or planned preventative actions to ensure that quality improves. Process adjustments that affect the project management plan will qualify for a change request and will be funneled through the change control system as part of integration management.

■ **Project document updates**   Quality control can result in updates to the issue log, lessons learned register, risk register, and test and evaluation documents.

CERTIFICATION SUMMARY

What good is a project deliverable if it doesn't work, is unacceptable, or is faulty? Project quality management ensures that the deliverables that project teams create meet the expectations of the stakeholders. For your PMP examination, quality means delivering the project at the exact level of the design specifications and the project scope. No more, no less.

Quality and grade are two different things. Grade is the ranking assigned to different components that have the same functional purpose. For example, sheet metal may come in different grades based on how it will be used. The grade of paper is based on its thickness, ability to retain ink, and so on. Low quality is always a problem; low grade may not be.

Quality planning happens before project work begins, but also as work is completed. Quality planning can confirm the preexistence of quality or the need for quality improvements. Quality is planned into a project, not inspected in. However, quality control uses inspections to prove the existence of quality within a project deliverable. Quality management is based upon the quality management plan and addresses the quality of the project, but also the design of the product and the processes.

There is a distinct difference between quality management and quality control. Quality management is a prevention-driven process. The organization's management wants the project manager and the project team to do the work right the first time. Quality control, however, is an inspection-driven process—the project team, the project manager, and sometimes third-party inspectors examine the work to confirm that it is correct and of quality. Quality assurance is usually a program for the entire organization, or at least a line of business or department. In project management, quality management is specific to the actual project work.

The prevention costs are concerned with the monies invested in the project to ascertain the expected level of quality. Examples of this cost include training, safety measures, and the acquisition of appropriate tools and equipment to do the project work. The failure costs centers on the monies lost by not completing the project work correctly the first time. In addition, this cost includes external failure costs the loss of sales, loss of customers, and damage to the organization's reputation.

KEY TERMS

If you're serious about passing the PMP exam, memorize these terms and their definitions. For maximum value, create your own flashcards based on these definitions and review daily.

affinity diagram   A tool that groups similar ideas, deliverables, or concepts together. The WBS could be considered an example of an affinity diagram.

appraisal costs   The cost of measuring, testing, auditing, and evaluating the project's product to confirm that quality has been achieved in the work results.

benchmarking   The process of using prior projects internal or external to the performing organization to compare and set quality standards for processes and results.

benefit/cost analysis   The process of determining the pros and cons of any project, process, product, or activity.

checklist   A listing of activities that workers check to ensure the work has been completed consistently; used in quality control.

checksheet   Also called a tally sheet. Used to count errors and defects in different categories of failure in the project.

control chart Illustrates the performance of a project over time. It maps the results of inspections against a chart. Control charts are typically used in projects or operations that have repetitive activities, such as manufacturing, testing series, or help desk functions. Upper and lower control limits indicate whether values are in control or out of control.

Design for X A philosophy in product design in which the X can mean excellence or, more often, a specific characteristic of a solution. In Design for X, or DfX, the X is usually a variable that the project is trying to address, such as cost, uptime, return on investment, or another facet the organization is pursuing.

failure costs The cost of not completing the project with quality, including wasted time for corrective actions and rework, and wasted materials. Failure costs include internal failure costs, which include the cost of corrective actions and defect repair incurred by doing the work twice. External failure costs describe the loss of sales, loss of opportunities, and damage to the organization's reputation due to poor quality.

flowchart A chart that illustrates how the parts of a system occur in sequence.

histogram A bar chart, such as a Pareto diagram.

ISO 9000 An international standard that helps organizations follow their own quality procedures. ISO 9000 is not a quality system, but a method of following procedures created by an organization.

Multicriteria Decision Analysis Tools Also called multiple-criteria decision-making tools, these help the project manager evaluate multiple facets of decisions with regard to quality. They can also help determine tradeoffs for achieving quality expectations, but they also keep the project's costs, schedule, and flow of work in balance.

Pareto diagram A diagram related to Pareto's Law, which states that 80 percent of the problems come from 20 percent of the issues (also known as the 80/20 rule). A Pareto diagram illustrates problems by assigned cause, from smallest to largest.

prevention costs The cost of completing the project work to satisfy the project scope and the expected level of quality. Examples include training, safety measures, and acquiring the appropriate tools to do the project work.

process adjustments   When quality is lacking, process adjustments are needed for immediate corrective actions or for future preventive actions to ensure that quality improves. Process adjustments may qualify for a change request and may be funneled through the change control system as part of integration management.

quality assurance (QA)   An executing process to ensure that the project is adhering to the quality expectations of the project customer and organization. QA is a prevention-driven process that seeks to perform the project work with quality to avoid errors, waste, and delays.

quality audit   A process to confirm that the quality processes are being performing correctly on the current project. The quality audit determines how to make things better for the project and other projects within the organization and measures the project's ability to maintain the expected level of quality.

quality control (QC)   A process in which the work results are monitored to see if they meet relevant quality standards.

quality management plan   A document that describes how the project manager and the project team will fulfill the quality policy. In an ISO 9000 environment, the quality management plan is referred to as the project quality system.

quality policy   The formal policy an organization follows to achieve a preset standard of quality. The project team should either adapt the quality policy of the organization to guide the project implementation or create its own policy if one does not exist within the performing organization.

run chart   Similar to a control chart, a run chart tracks trends over time and displays those trends in a graph with the plotted data mapped to a specific date.

scatter diagram   Tracks the relationship between two or more variables to determine whether one variable affects the other. It enables the project team, quality control team, or project manager to make adjustments to improve the overall results of the project.

statistical sampling   A process of choosing a percentage of results at random for inspection. Statistical sampling can reduce the costs of quality control.

trend analysis   Analyzes past results to predict future performance.

TWO-MINUTE DRILL

Looking at the Big Quality Picture

❑ The project manager is responsible for the overall quality management of the project and must set quality expectations based on the requirements of the customers and stakeholders.

❑ The project manager must integrate the quality control of the project with the quality assurance program of the performing organization.

❑ Quality is planned into a project, not inspected in.

Preparing for Quality

❑ Quality doesn't happen by accident. Quality is satisfying the expectations of the project scope baseline.

❑ The project team members (the people completing the project work) are responsible for the quality of the deliverables.

❑ The project team, as guided by the project manager and the quality management plan, should be empowered to stop the project work when preset quality thresholds are exceeded.

Planning for Quality Management

❑ Quality planning is an iterative process. As quality concerns enter into the project, the planning processes are revisited to ensure that actions—both preventive and corrective—are taken to ensure quality.

❑ The quality management plan is a subsidiary plan of the overall project management plan. It defines how the project will accomplish the quality expectations of the organization and how the project will adhere to the quality policy of the organization.

❑ The quality management plan is a subsidiary plan of the overall project management plan. It defines how project processes will be analyzed and improved upon. The goal of this plan is to improve the value of the project by removing non-value-added activities.

❑ The cost of quality is the amount of monies the performing organization must spend to satisfy the quality standards. This can include prevention costs, appraisal costs, and failure costs.

❑ The cost of nonconformance to quality is the monies or events attributed to not satisfying the quality demands. These can include loss of business, downtime, wasted materials, rework, and cost and schedule variances.

Managing Quality

❑ Managing quality aims to do the work properly and correctly the first time, according to plan.

❑ Managing quality may use a QA program to set quality standards.

❑ Managing quality represents the implementation of the quality plan.

❑ Managing quality is the process to ensure the project is completed with no deviations from the requirements.

❑ The Kaizen philosophy is used in an organization to apply small changes to products and processes to improve consistency, reduce costs, and provide overall quality improvements.

Implementing Quality Control

❑ Quality control monitors specific results within a project.

❑ A fishbone diagram is a cause-and-effect diagram that illustrates the factors that may be contributing to quality issues or problems. It is also known as an Ishikawa diagram or a why-why chart.

❑ Pareto diagrams are histograms that are related to Pareto's 80/20 rule: 80 percent of the problems come from 20 percent of the issues. The diagram charts the problems, categories, and frequency. The project team should first solve the larger problems and then move on to smaller issues.

❑ A run chart is a line graph that shows the results of inspection in the order in which each inspection occurred. The goal of a run chart is first to demonstrate the results of a process over time and then use trend analysis to predict when certain trends may reemerge.

❑ Control charts plot out the results of inspections against a mean and specification limits to examine performance against expected results. Upper and lower control limits are typically set to ±3 or 6 sigma. Results that are beyond the control limit value are considered out of control.

SELF TEST

1. Gary is the project manager of the HBB Project for his organization. He's working with project customers to define the specifics of the project requirements, the project scope, and the defined product scope to help define the quality of the project. The customer asks Gary who is responsible for the quality of the project deliverables. Which of the following is responsible for managing quality?
   A. The project champion
   B. The project team
   C. Stakeholders
   D. Everyone

2. As a PMP candidate, you'll need to recognize all the quality control charts and their usage. What type of chart is the following?

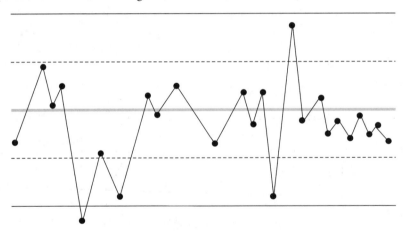

   A. Control
   B. Pareto
   C. Scatter
   D. Flow

3. You are the project manager for the BBB Project. Stacy, a project team member, is confused about what QA is. You need all the project team members and the project stakeholders to be clear on the quality management processes. To help Stacy, which of the following best describes QA?
   A. QA is quality assurance for the overall project performance.
   B. QA is quality acceptance according to scope verification.
   C. QA is quality assurance for the project deliverable.
   D. QA is quality assurance for the project stakeholders.

4. You are the project manager for the Photo Scanning Project. This project is similar to another project you have completed. Your project is to store thousands of historical photos electronically for your city's historical society. Quality is paramount on this project. Management approaches you and asks why you have devoted so much of the project time for planning. Your response is which of the following?
   A. This is a first-time, first-use project, so more time is needed for planning.
   B. Planning for a project of this size, with this amount of quality, is mandatory.
   C. Quality is planned into a project, not inspected in.
   D. Quality audits are part of the planning time.

5. You are the project manager for the Floor Installation Project. Today you will meet with your project team to ensure that the project is completed with no deviations from the project requirements. This process is which of the following?
   A. Quality planning
   B. Quality management
   C. Quality control
   D. Quality assurance

6. You are the project manager for the ASE Project, which must map to industry standards in order to be accepted by the customer. You and your team have studied the requirements and have created a plan to implement the deliverables with the appropriate level of quality. What is this process called?
   A. Quality planning
   B. Quality management
   C. Quality control
   D. Quality assurance

7. You are the project manager of the NHQ Project, which is part of the HQQ Program to construct a condominium building. Samuel, the program manager, has required that you document any variances to costs, schedule, scope, and quality expectations as part of the program governance. You believe that your project team now has an internal failure cost that needs to be documented for Samuel. Which of the following is an example of internal failure cost?
   A. Rework
   B. Quality audits
   C. Random quality audits
   D. Project team training

8. Quality assurance is an organization-wide initiative and is part of your enterprise environmental factors. All projects must adhere to the quality assurance initiatives in your company. Within your project, however, you also have quality assurance efforts and you have quality control efforts. Quality control is typically a(n) _____ process.
   A. Management
   B. Project manager
   C. Audit
   D. Inspection

9. Quality assurance is an organization-wide initiative and is part of your enterprise environmental factors. All projects must adhere to the quality assurance initiatives in your company. Within your project, however, you also have quality assurance efforts and you have quality control efforts. Managing quality is typically a(n) _____ process.
   A. Executing
   B. Project manager
   C. Audit
   D. Inspection

10. You are the project manager for a large manufacturer of wood furniture. Your new project is the Shop Table Project, which will involve the creation and manufacture of a new table for woodworkers to use in their wood shops. For this project, you have elected to use JIT for scheduling. Which of the following is an advantage to using JIT?
    A. It requires materials to be readily available.
    B. It enables the project team to have control over the materials.
    C. It decreases the inventory investment.
    D. It allows for a broad range of deviation compared to other inventory solutions.

11. You are the project manager of the HHQ Project for your company. Your company is a manufacturer of paper products. Your company has elected to use ISO 9000 standards. What is an attribute of ISO 9000?
    A. It ensures that your company follows its own quality procedures.
    B. It ensures that your company follows the set phases in each project from initiation to closure.
    C. It ensures that your company maps its processes to a proven process within the program.
    D. It ensures that QA and QC are integrated into the product or service your organization offers.

12. You are the project manager of the Halogen Installation Project. As this project gets underway, you receive notice from the program manager that the organization will be moving to a Kaizen methodology as part of its quality management program. What is a Kaizen methodology?
    A. Small improvements for small results
    B. Small improvements for all projects
    C. Small process and product improvements that are carried out on a continuous basis
    D. Small process improvements that are made to shorten the project duration

13. Holly Ann is a project manager for her organization. She is working with Jeff, the manufacturing rep, to analyze the errors in the deliverables as part of their quality control approach. Jeff recommends that they create a fishbone diagram to help analyze the problem. A fishbone diagram is the same as a(n) _____ diagram.
    A. Ishikawa
    B. Pareto
    C. Flow
    D. Control

14. Management has asked you to define the correlation between quality and the project scope. Which of the following is the best answer?
    A. The project scope will include metrics for quality.
    B. Quality metrics will be applied to the project scope.
    C. Quality is the process of completing the scope to meet stated or implied needs.
    D. Quality is the process of evaluating the project scope to ensure quality exists.

15. Quality is about conforming to requirement and the deliverables' fitness for use. Quality also has some attributes that must be considered as part of the project planning, project costs, and the project schedule. Considering these factors, which of the following is most true about quality?
    A. It will cost more money to build quality into the project.
    B. It will cost less money to build quality into the project process.
    C. Quality is inspection-driven.
    D. Quality is prevention-driven.

16. Which of the following can be described as a business philosophy to find methods that will continuously improve products, services, and business practices?
    A. TQM
    B. ASQ
    C. QA
    D. QC

17. Yolanda is the project manager for her company and she's working with the project team to identify errors in the project deliverables. As part of the process, Yolanda and the team must calculate the cost of the error, the materials, the time, and the cost to redo the work. In this instance, in regard to quality management, which of the following is *not* an attribute of failure costs that Yolanda will need to consider?
    A. Loss of customers
    B. Downtime
    C. Safety measures
    D. Rework

18. You are the project manager for the KOY Project, which requires quality that maps to federal guidelines. To ensure that you can meet these standards, you have elected to put the project team through training specific to the federal guidelines to which your project must adhere. The costs of these classes can be assigned to which of the following?
    A. Cost of doing business
    B. Cost of quality
    C. Cost of adherence
    D. Cost of nonconformance

19. You are the project manager for the KOY Project, which requires quality that maps to federal guidelines. During a quality audit, you discover that a portion of the project work is faulty and must be redone. The requirement to correct the work is an example of which of the following?
    A. Prevention cost
    B. Appraisal cost
    C. Failure cost
    D. Cost of doing business

20. You are the project manager of the GHQ Project. Your organization has a requirement that you use only the seven basic quality tools. Which one of the following is *not* one of the seven basic quality tools?
    A. Cause-and-effect diagram
    B. Histogram
    C. Control chart
    D. Network diagrams

21. You are the project manager of the JKL Project, which currently has some production flaws. Which analysis tool will enable you to determine the cause and effect of the production faults?
    A. A flowchart
    B. A Pareto diagram
    C. An Ishikawa diagram
    D. A control chart

22. Linda is the project manager of a manufacturing project. She and her project team are using root-cause analysis. How will Linda know they have found the root cause?
    A. She will never know because root-cause analysis creates a hypothesis of causes.
    B. When she has asked why seven times she will find the root cause.
    C. When the root causes are removed and the problem doesn't recur.
    D. When she has found three root causes that are linked by process design.

23. You are the project manager of the Global Upgrade Project. Your project team consists of 75 project team members around the world. Each project team will be upgrading a piece of equipment in many different facilities. Which of the following could you implement to ensure that the project team members are completing all the steps in the install procedure with quality?
   A. Checklists
   B. WBS
   C. PND
   D. The WBS dictionary

24. Mark is the project manager of the PMH Project. Quality audits of the deliverables show several problems. Management has asked Mark to create a chart showing the distribution of problems and their frequencies. Given this, management wants which of the following?
   A. A control chart
   B. An Ishikawa diagram
   C. A Pareto diagram
   D. A flowchart

25. You are the project manager of the NHH Project for your company and you're reviewing the results of quality control. In your analysis, you've created a quality control chart. In the following graphic, what does the highlighted area represent?

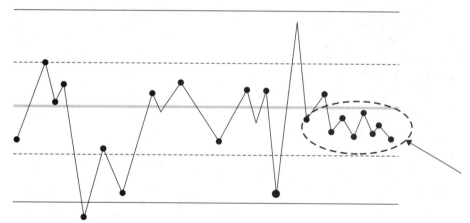

   A. Out-of-control data points
   B. In-control data points
   C. The Rule of Seven
   D. Standard deviation

SELF TEST ANSWERS

1. Gary is the project manager of the HBB Project for his organization. He's working with project customers to define the specifics of the project requirements, the project scope, and the defined product scope to help define the quality of the project. The customer asks Gary who is responsible for the quality of the project deliverables. Which of the following is responsible for managing quality?
   A. The project champion
   B. The project team
   C. Stakeholders
   D. Everyone

   ☑ **B.** The project team (the individuals completing the project work) is responsible for the quality of the project deliverables.
   ☒ **A, C,** and **D** are incorrect. **A** is incorrect because the project champion may review the work, but the responsibility of quality does not lie only with this individual. **C** and **D** are also incorrect choices; the stakeholders are not solely responsible for the quality of the project, and everyone can't be solely responsible.

2. As a PMP candidate, you'll need to recognize all the quality control charts and their usage. What type of chart is the following?

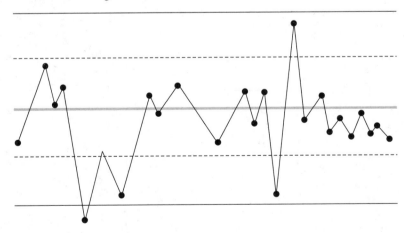

A. Control
B. Pareto
C. Scatter
D. Flow

> ☑ **A.** The chart shown is a control chart.
> ☒ **B, C,** and **D** are incorrect. **B** is incorrect because a Pareto diagram maps categories of issues and their frequency. **C** is incorrect because a scatter chart compares common values across multiple categories. **D,** a flowchart, is also incorrect. Flowcharts illustrate how a process moves through a system and how the components are interrelated.

3. You are the project manager for the BBB Project. Stacy, a project team member, is confused about what QA is. You need all the project team members and the project stakeholders to be clear on the quality management processes. To help Stacy, which of the following best describes QA?
   A. QA is quality assurance for the overall project performance.
   B. QA is quality acceptance according to scope verification.
   C. QA is quality assurance for the project deliverable.
   D. QA is quality assurance for the project stakeholders.

> ☑ **A.** QA is concerned with overall project quality performance.
> ☒ **B, C,** and **D** are incorrect. They do not correctly explain quality assurance.

4. You are the project manager for the Photo Scanning Project. This project is similar to another project you have completed. Your project is to store thousands of historical photos electronically for your city's historical society. Quality is paramount on this project. Management approaches you and asks why you have devoted so much of the project time for planning. Your response is which of the following?
   A. This is a first-time, first-use project, so more time is needed for planning.
   B. Planning for a project of this size, with this amount of quality, is mandatory.
   C. Quality is planned into a project, not inspected in.
   D. Quality audits are part of the planning time.

> ☑ **C.** Of all the choices presented, this is the best answer. Quality is planned into the project, and the planning requires time.
> ☒ **A, B,** and **D** are incorrect. **A** is incorrect because a project of this nature has been completed before. **B** is incorrect because there isn't enough information provided to determine the quality demands of the project. **D** is incorrect because quality audits are not part of the planning processes.

5. You are the project manager for the Floor Installation Project. Today you will meet with your project team to ensure that the project is completed with no deviations from the project requirements. This process is which of the following?
   A. Quality planning
   B. Quality management
   C. Quality control
   D. Quality assurance

   ☑ **A.** Quality planning should be completed prior to the work beginning—and should thereafter be revisited as needed.
   ☒ **B, C,** and **D** are incorrect. **B** is incorrect because quality management is not an applicable answer to the scenario. **C** and **D** are incorrect because QC and QA are part of quality management.

6. You are the project manager for the ASE Project, which must map to industry standards in order to be accepted by the customer. You and your team have studied the requirements and have created a plan to implement the deliverables with the appropriate level of quality. What is this process called?
   A. Quality planning
   B. Quality management
   C. Quality control
   D. Quality assurance

   ☑ **A.** Quality planning is the process of creating a plan to meet the requirements of quality.
   ☒ **B, C,** and **D** are incorrect. They do not explain the process in the question's scenario.

7. You are the project manager of the NHQ Project, which is part of the HQQ Program to construct a condominium building. Samuel, the program manager, has required that you document any variances to costs, schedule, scope, and quality expectations as part of the program governance. You believe that your project team now has an internal failure cost that needs to be documented for Samuel. Which of the following is an example of internal failure cost?
   A. Rework
   B. Quality audits
   C. Random quality audits
   D. Project team training

☑ **A.** Internal failure cost is attributed to failure that results in rework. It is an example of the cost of nonconformance to quality.

☒ **B, C,** and **D** are incorrect. B and C are incorrect because quality audits are not a cost associated with nonconformance. D is incorrect because project team training is an example of the cost of conformance to quality.

8. Quality assurance is an organization-wide initiative and is part of your enterprise environmental factors. All projects must adhere to the quality assurance initiatives in your company. Within your project, however, you also have quality assurance efforts and you have quality control efforts. Quality control is typically a(n) _____ process.
    A. Management
    B. Project manager
    C. Audit
    D. Inspection

☑ **D.** QC requires an inspection of the work results. Although quality is planned into a project, inspections ensure it exists.

☒ **A, B,** and **C** are incorrect. A is incorrect because QA is a managerial function, not QC. B is incorrect because another department, team member, or SME can complete QC. C is incorrect; an audit is too broad an answer for this question. Audits can be financially driven, schedule-driven, or quality-driven.

9. Quality assurance is an organization-wide initiative and is part of your enterprise environmental factors. All projects must adhere to the quality assurance initiatives in your company. Within your project, however, you also have quality assurance efforts and you have quality control efforts. Managing quality is typically a(n) _____ process.
    A. Executing
    B. Project manager
    C. Audit
    D. Inspection

☑ **A.** Managing quality is typically an executing process.

☒ **B, C,** and **D** are incorrect. B is incorrect because another department, team member, or SME can complete QC. C is incorrect because an audit is too broad of an answer for this question. Audits can be financially driven, schedule-driven, or quality-driven. D is incorrect because QA is typically not an inspection process.

10. You are the project manager for a large manufacturer of wood furniture. Your new project is the Shop Table Project, which will involve the creation and manufacture of a new table for woodworkers to use in their wood shops. For this project, you have elected to use JIT for scheduling. Which of the following is an advantage to using JIT?
    A. It requires materials to be readily available.
    B. It enables the project team to have control over the materials.
    C. It decreases the inventory investment.
    D. It allows for a broad range of deviation compared to other inventory solutions.

> ☑ **C.** JIT (just-in-time) scheduling decreases the investment in inventory. However, mistakes with the materials can cause downtime if no additional materials are on hand.
>
> ☒ **A, B,** and **D** are incorrect. **A** is incorrect because materials are available only when they're needed. **B** is incorrect; the project team must use caution not to waste the materials. **D** is incorrect because JIT does not allow for a broad range of deviation.

11. You are the project manager of the HHQ Project for your company. Your company is a manufacturer of paper products. Your company has elected to use ISO 9000 standards. What is an attribute of ISO 9000?
    A. It ensures that your company follows its own quality procedures.
    B. It ensures that your company follows the set phases in each project from initiation to closure.
    C. It ensures that your company maps its processes to a proven process within the program.
    D. It ensures that QA and QC are integrated into the product or service your organization offers.

> ☑ **A.** ISO 9000 is not a quality management system, but a system to ensure that an organization follows its own quality procedures.
>
> ☒ **B, C,** and **D** are incorrect. These choices do not correctly describe ISO 9000.

12. You are the project manager of the Halogen Installation Project. As this project gets underway, you receive notice from the program manager that the organization will be moving to a Kaizen methodology as part of its quality management program. What is a Kaizen methodology?
    A. Small improvements for small results
    B. Small improvements for all projects
    C. Small process and product improvements that are carried out on a continuous basis
    D. Small process improvements that are made to shorten the project duration

☑   **C.** Kaizen technologies are small changes to processes and products on a steady, continuous basis to save costs and improve quality.

☒   **A, B,** and **D** are incorrect. **A** is incorrect. Although Kaizen does implement small process changes, it does not aim for small results. **B** and **D** are also incorrect. Kaizen does not have to be implemented in all projects, although it often is. Kaizen is also not interested in necessarily reducing the project duration.

13. Holly Ann is a project manager for her organization. She is working with Jeff, the manufacturing rep, to analyze the errors in the deliverables as part of their quality control approach. Jeff recommends that they create a fishbone diagram to help analyze the problem. A fishbone diagram is the same as a(n) _____ diagram.

A. Ishikawa
B. Pareto
C. Flow
D. Control

☑   **A.** A fishbone diagram is the same as an Ishikawa diagram, also called a why-why chart.

☒   **B, C,** and **D** are incorrect. These charts and diagrams accomplish goals other than the cause-and-effect of the Ishikawa.

14. Management has asked you to define the correlation between quality and the project scope. Which of the following is the best answer?

A. The project scope will include metrics for quality.
B. Quality metrics will be applied to the project scope.
C. Quality is the process of completing the scope to meet stated or implied needs.
D. Quality is the process of evaluating the project scope to ensure quality exists.

☑   **C.** Quality, with regard to the project scope, is about completing the work as promised and defined in the project scope. It is what the customer is expecting as part of the project deliverables.

☒   **A, B,** and **D** are incorrect. **A** and **B** are incorrect because although the project scope will have requirements for acceptance, it may not have metrics for quality defined. **D** is also incorrect, because this statement defines quality control, as you and the project team will inspect the results of the work that creates the project scope to determine if quality exists within the project.

15. Quality is about conforming to requirement and the deliverables' fitness for use. Quality also has some attributes that must be considered as part of the project planning, project costs, and the project schedule. Considering these factors, which of the following is most true about quality?
    A. It will cost more money to build quality into the project.
    B. It will cost less money to build quality into the project process.
    C. Quality is inspection-driven.
    D. Quality is prevention-driven.

    ☑ **D.** Quality is prevention-driven. Quality wants to complete the work correctly the first time to prevent poor results, a loss of time, and a loss of funds.
    ☒ **A, B,** and **C** are incorrect. **A** and **B** are incorrect because there is no guarantee that a project will cost more or less, depending on the amount of expected quality. Incidentally, lack of quality will likely cost more than quality planning because of the cost of nonconformance. **C** is incorrect because quality is planned into a project, not inspected in.

16. Which of the following can be described as a business philosophy to find methods that will continuously improve products, services, and business practices?
    A. TQM
    B. ASQ
    C. QA
    D. QC

    ☑ **A.** TQM, total quality management, is a business philosophy to find methods that will continuously improve products, services, and business practices.
    ☒ **B, C,** and **D** are incorrect. **B,** ASQ (American Society of Quality), is not a business philosophy. **C** and **D** are attributes of TQM but are incorrect answers for this question.

17. Yolanda is the project manager for her company and she's working with the project team to identify errors in the project deliverables. As part of the process, Yolanda and the team must calculate the cost of the error, the materials, the time, and the cost to redo the work. In this instance, in regard to quality management, which of the following is *not* an attribute of failure costs that Yolanda will need to consider?
    A. Loss of customers
    B. Downtime
    C. Safety measures
    D. Rework

    ☑ **C.** A safety measure is not an attribute of the cost of nonconformance, but rather a prevention cost.
    ☒ **A, B,** and **D** are incorrect. These are all attributes of the cost of nonconformance.

18. You are the project manager for the KOY Project, which requires quality that maps to federal guidelines. To ensure that you can meet these standards, you have elected to put the project team through training specific to the federal guidelines to which your project must adhere. The costs of these classes can be assigned to which of the following?
A. Cost of doing business
B. Cost of quality
C. Cost of adherence
D. Cost of nonconformance

☑ **B.** Training to meet the quality expectations is attributed to the cost of quality.
☒ **A, C,** and **D** are incorrect. These choices do not describe training as a cost of quality.

19. You are the project manager for the KOY Project, which requires quality that maps to federal guidelines. During a quality audit, you discover that a portion of the project work is faulty and must be redone. The requirement to correct the work is an example of which of the following?
A. Prevention cost
B. Appraisal cost
C. Failure cost
D. Cost of doing business

☑ **C.** When project work results are faulty and must be redone, it is attributed to the cost of nonconformance to quality, which is a failure cost.
☒ **A, B,** and **D** are incorrect. These values do not describe faulty work or the cost of nonconformance.

20. You are the project manager of the GHQ Project. Your organization has a requirement that you use only the seven basic quality tools. Which one of the following is *not* one of the seven basic quality tools?
A. Cause-and-effect diagram
B. Histogram
C. Control chart
D. Network diagrams

☑ **D.** Network diagrams are not part of the seven basic quality tools. The tools are cause-and-effect diagrams, flowcharts, checksheets, Pareto diagrams, histograms, control charts, and scatter diagrams.
☒ **A, B,** and **C** are incorrect. These answers are three of the seven basic quality tools.

21. You are the project manager of the JKL Project, which currently has some production flaws. Which analysis tool will enable you to determine the cause and effect of the production faults?
    A. A flowchart
    B. A Pareto diagram
    C. An Ishikawa diagram
    D. A control chart

    ☑ **C.** The key words "cause and effect" equate to the Ishikawa diagram.
    ☒ **A, B,** and **D** are incorrect. **A,** a flowchart, will show how a process moves through the system, but it won't show the cause and effect of the problems involved. **B** is incorrect because a Pareto chart maps out the causes and frequency of problems. **D,** a control chart, plots out the results of sampling but doesn't show the cause and effect of problems.

22. Linda is the project manager of a manufacturing project. She and her project team are using root-cause analysis. How will Linda know they have found the root cause?
    A. She will never know because root-cause analysis creates a hypothesis of causes.
    B. When she has asked why seven times she will find the root cause.
    C. When the root causes are removed and the problem doesn't recur.
    D. When she has found three root causes that are linked by process design.

    ☑ **C.** Of all the choices presented, **C** is the best choice. When Linda removes the root causes, the problem will not recur and she will know that she has found the root causes to the problem.
    ☒ **A, B,** and **D** are incorrect. **A** is incorrect because she will know when the root causes are found by the problem not recurring. **B** and **D** are also incorrect because these are not valid statements about root cause analysis.

23. You are the project manager of the Global Upgrade Project. Your project team consists of 75 project team members around the world. Each project team will be upgrading a piece of equipment in many different facilities. Which of the following could you implement to ensure that the project team members are completing all the steps in the install procedure with quality?
    A. Checklists
    B. WBS
    C. PND
    D. The WBS dictionary

    ☑ **A.** Checklists are simple but effective quality management tools that the project manager can use to ensure that the project team is completing the required work.
    ☒ **B, C,** and **D** are incorrect. The WBS, PND, and WBS dictionary are not tools the project team can necessarily use to prove they've completed required work. Checklists are the best approach for this scenario.

24. Mark is the project manager of the PMH Project. Quality audits of the deliverables show several problems. Management has asked Mark to create a chart showing the distribution of problems and their frequencies. Given this, management wants which of the following?

   A. A control chart

   B. An Ishikawa diagram

   C. A Pareto diagram

   D. A flowchart

   ☑ **C.** Management wants Mark to create a Pareto diagram. Recall that a Pareto diagram maps out the causes of defects and illustrates their frequency.

   ☒ **A, B,** and **D** are incorrect. **A** is incorrect because a control chart does not identify the problems, only the relationship of the results to the expected mean. **B** is incorrect because an Ishikawa diagram does not map out the frequency of problems. **D** is also incorrect. Flowcharts show how a process moves through a system and how the components are related.

25. You are the project manager of the NHH Project for your company and you're reviewing the results of quality control. In your analysis you've created a quality control chart. In the following graphic, what does the highlighted area represent?

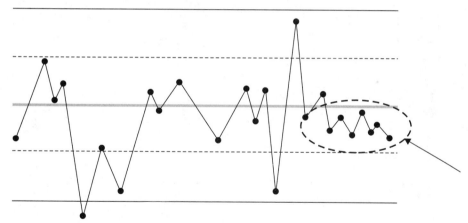

   A. Out-of-control data points

   B. In-control data points

   C. The Rule of Seven

   D. Standard deviation

   ☑ **C.** The highlighted area shows seven consecutive sampling results all on one side of the mean. This is known as the Rule of Seven and is an assignable cause.

   ☒ **A, B,** and **D** are incorrect. **A** is incorrect because these values are in control. **B** is correct, but it does not fully answer the question as well as choice C. **D** is incorrect because standard deviation is a predicted measure of the variance from the expected mean of a sampling.

Chapter 9

Introducing Project Resource Management

CERTIFICATION OBJECTIVES

9.01	Preparing for Resource Planning	9.05	Managing the Project Team
9.02	Estimating Project Activity Resources	9.06	Controlling Resources
9.03	Acquiring the Project Resources	✓	Two-Minute Drill
9.04	Developing the Project Team	Q&A	Self Test

P roject resource management is a multifaceted task that addresses how to determine what resources are needed for the project, how to get the needed resources, and then how to control the resources throughout the project. Project resource management addresses both physical resources, such as equipment and facilities, and people on the project team. Managing project resources requires that you lead, direct, and orchestrate the project team, customers, project partners, contributors, and any other stakeholders to achieve the desired results for the project's purpose.

Project managers cannot, and must not, do everything. They must rely on the project team to complete the project work. Have you ever worked on a project in which the project manager wanted to do all the work? Or the project manager assigned the mundane tasks to the project team and did the most important activities himself? Or the project manager completed the activities with the highest exposure? Not good. Project managers must delegate activities.

Project managers must find ways to motivate the project team to complete the work. There is a tendency in many projects for the project team to be excited about the project at the start, and then the excitement wanes as the project moves toward completion. The project manager must coach and mentor to develop the project team and ensure that the excitement, willingness, and dedication to the project work continue.

Throughout the project, the project manager will have to address project team retention, labor relations, performance appraisals, and, depending on the nature of the project work, health and safety issues. As projects are temporary, so, too, are most of the relationships between the project team members and the project manager.

Project resources management may not be completely in the hands of the project manager. The performing organization's HR department may have control over the majority of the assignments and recruitment of the project team. It's important for the project manager to know his responsibilities and levels of power and autonomy to comply with the organization's policies.

Just as the project manager works to secure the needed human resources for the project, he will also have to work to secure the physical resources needed for the project. Physical resources are the things the project needs to be successful: equipment, materials, hardware, software, facilities, infrastructure, vendor-provided solutions, and anything else that's not a person that the project needs.

Exploring Project Resource Management

In the *PMBOK Guide*, 6th edition, the knowledge area of human resource management was changed to project resource management. Resource management includes people and things. You need people to do the work of the project, to provide expert judgment, and to contribute to the project's success. You also need physical resources to do the project work or complete the project on time.

There are six processes in this knowledge area:

- Plan resource management
- Estimate activity resources
- Acquire resources

- Develop team
- Manage team
- Control resources

Wherever you see "resources," think of people and the skills you'll need to complete the tasks required for the project. And then swap out "resources" for "things," and think of the skills and actions you'll need to perform the tasks with the things a project might need. A project manager will use two different types of skills to deal with people and deal with things—something to be on the lookout for in this chapter and on your PMP exam.

Reviewing Project Resource Management Foundations

There's an old adage in project management: "When a project fails it's the project manager's fault. And when a project is successful, it's everyone's fault." There may be a little truth to that statement, and that's the basis of project resource management. Project team members have roles and responsibilities, but it takes all the team members working together to help with planning, identify risk, and offer their expert judgment to succeed with the project. The project manager's role is to keep folks involved, keep the excitement going, and keep things organized to get things done.

The project manager is both the leader and the manager of the project—not just one or the other. The project manager leads people and manages things. The project team and stakeholders will look to the project manager to lead the project, to keep the synergy, and to offer guidance and direction. People will also look to the project manager to be a good communicator about the project, to make effective decisions, to balance objectives, and to act when action is needed. The project manager influences the project team and looks for influences on the team, such as these:

- Team environment and politics
- Communication demands
- Organizational change management
- Culture and organization issues
- Challenges of virtual teams and geographic concerns

The project manager makes certain the project team member have the skills they need to do the work. The project manager leads team development. The project manager works on behalf of the project team to make certain the team is protected, engaged, and feels valued in the project.

Exploring Trends in Managing Resources

Project management is becoming more and more about empowering the project team members to make decisions rather than the project manager making all the project decisions. This collaborative approach fosters trust, shared ownership, and a reliance on experts on the project team. For your PMP exam, you should be familiar with this approach and these other trends in managing resources:

- **Just-in-time (JIT) manufacturing** Resources are in place only as they are needed. This approach reduces waste, keeps inventory at a minimum, and helps the project manager forecast resource utilization more accurately.

- **Kaizen** Small changes to the organization and project team over time result in large changes overall. Kaizen posits that small changes in processes are easier to accept and incorporate than large, sweeping changes for the organization or project.

- **Total productive maintenance** Continuous maintenance on equipment and quality systems keeps equipment working well and efficiently. This approach aims to reduce downtime by avoiding equipment failure.

- **Theory of constraints** A management system is limited by its weakest components—the constraints—and works to remove those constraints. It's an adaption of the phrase "a chain is only as strong as its weakest link."

- **Emotional intelligence** A person is aware of his inbound and outbound emotions; by becoming emotionally competent, the person can better control his emotions and understand the emotions of others.

- **Self-organizing teams** In agile environments, the project manager may be called a scrum master or servant leader. The project team takes charge on who'll do what tasks to accomplish the project objectives.

- **Virtual teams/distributed teams** These teams are non-collocated, dispersed around the globe, and rely on technology to interact, communicate, and contribute to the project. Communication becomes a central focal point in virtual teams.

Resource management is a process that can be tailored to fit your project and organization. The project manager will consider the diversity of the project team and the strengths, weaknesses, opportunities, and threats (SWOT) that the diverse group may bring to the project. When work is completed by virtual teams, the physical location of each team member is also evaluated for how best to manage the resources.

Your industry may have special resources considerations, such as unions or inspectors, that must be considered. All project managers, regardless of the industry, will also have to follow the organization's policies for acquiring and managing the project team. Finally, the project life cycle can affect how you manage project team members. Specifically, you'll consider the peaks and valleys of team utilization depending on the type of work that's taking place in the project at any given time.

Preparing for Resource Planning

Resource planning is the process of mapping the roles, responsibilities, and reporting relationships to the appropriate people or groups of people on the project team. Resource planning identifies the people involved with the project and determines their roles in the project, their overall influence on the project work, to whom they may report, and from whom they may receive a report. Resource planning also includes the planning for the physical resources the project will need.

Consider a project to create a community park. The project manager works for a commercial entity that will complete the project work. She identifies the roles responsible for activities within her organization—the designers, engineers, installers, management, and so on. She will also have functional managers who coordinate employees' availability, financing to arrange procurement of resources needed for project completion, and senior management to which she must report the status of the project work. The project will also require equipment, materials, tools, and other physical resources such as plans and permits.

The project manager will also work and communicate with government officials for approval of the design, change requests, and overall schedule of the project. There'll be safety issues, landscaping questions, and other concerns that will come up as the project progresses.

Finally, the project manager will likely communicate with stakeholders who are not internal to her organization—for example, the people who live in the community and various government officials. These stakeholders will need to be involved in the planning and design of the park to ensure that it satisfies the community's needs.

As you can see, resource planning can involve both internal and external stakeholders. In most projects, organizational planning happens early in the project planning phase—but it should be reviewed and adjusted as the environment changes. Organizational planning is all about ensuring that the project performs properly in the working environment and ensuring that the team has the physical resources they'll need to do the project work.

exam

watch

The resource plan defines four terms for the project management team: The *role* is the generic project team name, such as application developer or instructor. The *authority* is the level of decision-making ability a project team member has. The *responsibility* includes the actions and expectations of project team members to complete project work. *Competency* refers to the project role's depth of skills, knowledge, and experience in the project.

There are five inputs to plan resource management:

- Project charter for the high-level description and requirements
- Project management plan—specifically, the quality management and the scope baseline
- Project documents, specifically the schedule, requirements, risk register, and stakeholder register
- Enterprise environmental factors to consider the culture, geographical concerns, resources and competencies, and marketplace conditions
- Organizational process assets, such as human resource policies, physical resource management, safety and security consideration, templates, and historical information

Identifying the Resource Requirements

Every project needs people to complete the work, and expert judgment is a key technique to identify the resources the project will need. Resource requirements are the identified human and physical resources needed on a project to complete the assigned work. For example, a project to install a new telephone system throughout a campus would require a menagerie of workers with varying skill sets: hardware and software gurus, telephony experts, electricians, installers, and others. The identified staff would be pulled from the resource pool. Any skill gaps would need to be addressed through staff acquisition, additional training, or procurement. The resource requirements will also include the physical resources needed on the project.

Expert judgment can help identify the best resources for the project, estimate the lead time needed for the resource acquisition, and help the project manager comply with regulations that affect the project. Consideration is also given to talent management, personnel development, risk identification with acquisition and release planning, and working with sellers to ensure that procured physical resources are correct and delivered as needed in the project.

The contractual agreements between employee groups, unions, equipment providers, or other labor organizations may serve as a constraint on the project. In these instances, there may be additional reporting relationships regarding the project status, work, and performance of project team members.

Completing Organizational Planning

Organizational planning calls upon the project manager to consider the requirements of the project and the stakeholders involved—and how the nature of the project will require the project manager and the project team to interact with the stakeholders. In addition, the project manager must consider the project team itself and how the team will be managed, led, and motivated to complete the project work according to plan.

The goal of organizational planning is to identify and plan for the constraints and opportunities brought about by the nature of the project work, the team's competence, and the demands of the performing organization and stakeholders. Scores of books have been written on organizational planning, theory, and project team motivation. The goal of this conversation is to help you know the essentials to pass the PMP exam.

Charting the Project Resources

The project manager can utilize several different charts to map the hierarchy of the project and the roles and responsibilities of the project team. These are the most common charts:

- **Work breakdown structure (WBS)**   The decomposition of the project scope into work packages can help reveal the need for resources and areas of responsibility for different project team members.
- **Organizational charts**   These show how an organization, such as a company or large project team, is ordered, the reporting structures, and the flow of information.
- **Organizational breakdown structure**   Although these charts are similar to the WBS, the breakdown is by department, by units, or by team.
- **Resource breakdown structure**   This type of chart breaks down the project by types of resources utilized, no matter where the resource is being used in the project.
- **Responsibility assignment matrix chart**   This chart type designates the roles and responsibilities of the project team.
- **RACI chart**   This chart designates each team member against each project activity as Responsible, Accountable, Consulted, or Informed (RACI). A RACI chart is technically a type of responsibility assignment matrix chart. At least one person is responsible, and only one person is accountable. One person can be both responsible and accountable for an activity. Table 9-1 is an example of a RACI chart in which each activity is mapped to each team member with the RACI legend. Only one person is accountable per activity.

TABLE 9-1		Steve	Shannon	Sammi	Laura	Morgan
RACI Chart	Install doors	R	A	I	C	I
	Install windows	A	C	R	I	I
	Sand trim	A	R	R	I	I
	Priming	R	A	C	C	I
	Painting	R	R	R	A	I
	Site cleanup	I	I	I	R	A

R = Responsible   A = Accountable   C = Consulted   I = Informed

Creating the Role and Responsibility Assignments

Here are some slick definitions for roles and responsibilities:

- **Role**   Defines the accountable person by label or function
- **Authority**   Has the authority to assign project resources, make decisions, and sign off on project documents
- **Responsibility**   Defines the work assigned to a project team member
- **Competency**   Determines what skill set is needed to complete an activity

The assignment of the roles and responsibilities determines what actions the project manager, project team member, or individual contributor will have in the project. Roles and responsibilities generally support the project scope, since this is the required work for the project.

An excellent tool that the project manager should create is the responsibility assignment matrix (RAM). A RAM can be high-level—for example, mapping project groups to the high-level components of a WBS, such as architecture, network, or software creation. A RAM can also be specific to the activities within the project work. Figure 9-1 is an example of a RAM.

Relying on Templates

All projects are different, but some may resemble historical projects. This resemblance to historical projects means the project manager can use proven plans as templates for current projects. Specifically, considering organizational planning, the project manager can use the roles and responsibility matrixes and the reporting structure of historical projects as models for the current project. As a rule, current projects should emulate successful historical projects.

FIGURE 9-1	WBS Component	Resource I	Resource 2	Resource 3	Resource 4	Resource 5	Resource 6
A responsibility assignment matrix (RAM) can map work to project team members.	Architectural	RS		R		A	
	Foundation	A	R	I			
	Framing	S		A		I	
	Electrical	S			R		A
	Interior	S	A			I	R

A = Accountable   R = Resource   I = Informed   S = Sign off

Applying Resource Practices

The performing organization will likely have policies and procedures for the project manager to follow. Enterprise environmental factors, usually through management or a resources department, should specify the following:

- Job responsibilities
- Reporting structures
- The project manager's role and autonomy
- Policies regarding project team member discipline
- The definition for customized organizational terms, such as coach, mentor, or champion

Relating to Organizational Theories

A project manager can rely on many different organizational theories to identify weaknesses and strengths, guide the project team, and move the project forward. The entire context of these theories is beyond the scope of this book; however, you should be familiar with several of these theories to pass the PMP exam.

See the video "Resource Theories."

FIGURE 9-2

Maslow's
hierarchy: people
work for self-
actualization.

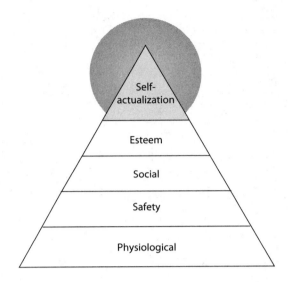

Maslow's Hierarchy of Needs

Maslow's hierarchy asserts that people work to take care of a "hierarchy of needs." The pinnacle of their needs is self-actualization. People want to contribute, prove their work, and use their skills and abilities. Figure 9-2 shows the pyramid of needs that all people try to ascend by fulfilling each layer, one at a time.

Following are Maslow's five layers of needs, from the bottom up:

- **Physiological**   Several necessities are required for human life: air, water, food, clothing, and shelter.
- **Safety**   People need safety and security; this can include stability in life, work, and culture.
- **Social**   People are social creatures and need love, approval, and friends.
- **Esteem**   People strive for the respect, appreciation, and approval of others.
- **Self-actualization**   At the pinnacle of needs, people seek personal growth, knowledge, and fulfillment.

Herzberg's Theory of Motivation

According to Frederick Herzberg, a psychologist and authority on the motivation of work, there are two catalysts for creating job satisfaction and success:

- **Hygiene agents**   These elements are the expectations all workers have: job security, a paycheck, clean and safe working conditions, a sense of belonging, civil working relationships, and other basic attributes associated with employment.

FIGURE 9-3

The absence of
hygiene factors
causes a worker's
performance to
suffer.

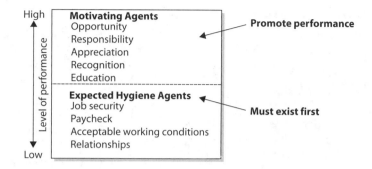

Motivating agents   These elements motivate people to excel. They include responsibility, appreciation of work, recognition, the chance to excel, education, and other opportunities associated with work other than just financial rewards.

Herzberg's theory says the presence of hygiene factors will not motivate people to perform because these are expected attributes. However, the absence of these elements will demotivate performance. For people to excel, the presence of motivating factors must exist. Figure 9-3 illustrates Herzberg's Theory of Motivation.

McGregor's Theory of X and Y

McGregor's theory states that management believes there are two types of workers, good and bad, as shown in Figure 9-4:

■ *X is bad.* These people need to be watched all the time, micromanaged, and distrusted. X people avoid work, shirk responsibility, and have no ability to achieve.

■ *Y is good.* These people are self-led, motivated, and can accomplish new tasks proactively.

FIGURE 9-4

Management
believes X people
are bad and Y
people are good.

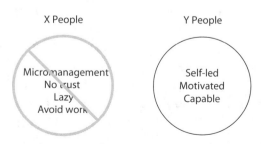

Ouchi's Theory Z

William Ouchi's Theory Z is based on the Japanese participative management style. This theory states that workers are motivated by a sense of commitment, opportunity, and advancement. Workers in an organization subscribing to Theory Z learn the business by moving up through the ranks of the company.

Ouchi's Theory Z also credits the idea of "lifetime employment." Workers will stay with one company until they retire because they are dedicated to the company, which is, in turn, dedicated to them.

exam

Watch **If you need a way to keep McGregor's Theory of X and Y and Ouchi's Z separate in your mind, think of this: X is bad, Y is good, and Z is better.**

McClelland's Theory of Needs

David McClelland developed his acquired-needs theory based on his belief that a person's needs are acquired and develop over time. These needs are shaped by circumstance, conditions, and life experiences for each individual. McClelland's Theory of Needs is also known as the three needs theory because it asserts that each individual has three basic needs. Depending on the person's experiences, the order and magnitude of each need shifts:

- **Need for achievement** These people need to achieve so they avoid both low-risk and high-risk situations. Achievers like to work alone or with other high achievers, and they need regular feedback to gauge their achievement and progress.

- **Need for affiliation** People who have a driving need for affiliation look for harmonious relationships, want to feel accepted by people, and conform to the norms of the project team.

- **Need for power** People who have a need for power are usually seeking either personal or institutional power. Personal power-seekers generally want to control and direct other people. Institutional power-seekers want to direct the efforts of others for the betterment of the organization.

McClelland developed the Thematic Apperception Test to determine what needs are driving individuals. The test is a series of pictures, and the test taker has to create a story about what's happening in the picture. Through the storytelling, the test taker will reveal which need is driving his life at that time.

Vroom's Expectancy Theory

Vroom's Expectancy Theory states that people will behave based on what they expect as a result of their behavior. In other words, people will work in relation to the expected reward of the work. If the attractiveness of the reward is desirable to the worker, she will work to receive the reward. People expect to be rewarded for their effort.

Creating a Resource Management Plan

The resource management plan, the output of planning resources, details how project team members will be brought onto the project and excused from the project. The resource management plan addresses how physical resources, such as equipment and facilities, will be acquired for the project. This plan also defines how long the project resources will be needed—something that's important in all organizational structures, but especially so in the matrix environment. This subsidiary plan documents the process the project manager is expected to complete to bring new project team members aboard and acquire the needed physical resources based on the conditions of the project.

For example, the third phase of a project may require an application developer. The project manager may have to complete a job description that includes the application developer's responsibilities, how her time will be used, and how long the role is needed on the project. HR or other functional managers may have to approve the request.

Management may also want to see a resource histogram, as Figure 9-5 illustrates, so they may plan employees' time and activities accordingly. Management may elect to hold off on the launch of a project based on the requirement for resources and the conflict with business cycles or other projects with higher priorities within the organization.

Each performing organization will likely have policies and procedures that should be documented and followed to bring resources onto the project team. In addition, the organization may have similar ways to excuse project team members from a project once their contribution has been completed. This plan can also communicate when physical resources will be released from the project so other projects can utilize the resources. If a project has "reserved" a piece of equipment for six months, but needs the equipment for only three months, the reserved time is wasted and causes other projects to suffer as they wait for the equipment to be released. You may also need to address consumable resources that will be used throughout the project; consumable resources are materials that need to be replenished as they're used (paint, wood, network cables, and the like).

FIGURE 9-5

Resource histograms are bar charts that illustrate the utilization of labor.

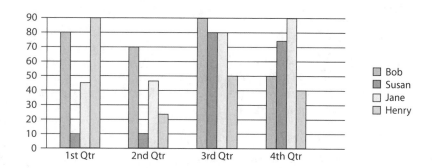

The resource management plan should do the following:

- Identify human resources and physical resources for the project
- Define how physical resources will be acquired for the project
- Detail how project team members are brought onto and released from the project
- Account for employees' time on the project
- Use employees as needed and when needed
- Define timetables outlining when project team members are needed
- Provide resource calendars
- Define the training needs and plans for the project team
- Remove or reduce worries about employment by communicating the expected need for resources
- Define the project's reward and recognition system
- Define the project's compliance with government regulations, union contracts, and policies and procedures
- Provide a resource control mechanism to plan for when physical resources are needed, the processes for acquiring the physical resources, consideration of lead time for procurement activities, vendor fulfillment, and the work to ensure that the team has the needed physical resources at the right time to prevent project delays

e x a m

ⓦ a t c h   Scheduling unneeded resources is a waste of time and money. Schedule resources on a project only when they are needed. Functional managers may want you, the project manager, to schedule resources on a project even though you don't need them. Not only is this outside of the resource management plan, it is a violation of the project management Code of Ethics and Professional Conduct.

Creating a Team Charter

A team charter is a document typically created by the project team to define their values, agreements, and ground rules for the project. In some organizations, the team charter may be developed for the project team, though the charter works best when the project team creates the document—or at least has a part in creating it. The team charter includes the following:

- Team values
- Communication guidelines

- Decision-making process
- Conflict resolution process
- Meeting guidelines
- Team agreements

When ground rules are created and agreed upon, it's up to all project team members to enforce them. The team charter helps to establish the values and agreement as to how the project team will operate and abide by the ground rules.

CERTIFICATION OBJECTIVE 9.02

Estimating Project Activity Resources

Way back in Chapters 6 and 7, I discussed project schedules and costs. Now consider what you are actually scheduling and paying for: resources. You'll need human resources to do the project work and you need physical resources such as materials, equipment, software, and hardware for the project. This process of estimating activity resources is directly related to your project's schedule and cost activities. In fact, you'll see that many of the activities are very similar to what's already been discussed in the sections on schedule management and cost management.

Estimating the activity resources is a prediction of what you believe you'll need to complete the project. You'll rely on your project team, experts, and historical information to help you make the best decisions.

Let's be practical for a moment: When you're managing a project, you don't just think about the activities and the costs of the project; you think about the activities and the role or individual who'll perform those activities in the project. A project is not segmented into knowledge areas—it comprises people, materials, schedules, costs, and the actual work of the project. However, when you're studying to pass the PMP, you need to segment things into knowledge areas that sometimes seem disconnected from the actual application of the knowledge area.

For your exam, you should know that schedule, cost, and resource management are different knowledge areas that are closely related. You need resources, of course, and the activities take time to complete, and you'll need to pay for the resources. And this is a great example of project integration management.

Preparing to Estimate Activity Resources

Estimating the activity resources is something that you'll do throughout the project. There are four inputs for this process:

- **Project management plan** Resource management plan and scope baseline
- **Project documents** Activity attributes, activity list, assumptions, cost estimates, resource calendars, and risk register
- **Enterprise environmental factors** Location of resources, skills, published estimating data, and marketplace conditions
- **Organizational process assets** Policies for acquiring and scheduling resources and historical information from similar projects

Estimating the Resources for Activities

Once you have defined the activities, you'll need to think through what resources you'll need to do the activities. You'll have to think about roles and responsibilities, materials, equipment, and other physical resources. Don't forget to include facilities, too, such as rental space, and consider shipping costs, airfare, and other related expenses and needs.

You'll can use seven tools and techniques for estimating activity resources (all of which you have seen in the schedule and cost knowledge areas):

- **Expert judgment** Experts, such as the project team and consultants, can help identify what resources you'll need.
- **Bottom-up estimating** This approach starts at the work package and works its way up through the WBS to create a definitive estimate.
- **Analogous estimating** Estimates are based on a similar project to predict the cost and/or duration of the current project activities.
- **Parametric estimating** Costs and time are based on parameters, such as historical data, $200 per square foot of construction, or four hours per fixture to install.
- **Data analysis** Alternatives identification enables you to determine whether there are alternative resources for the activities. This can help with scheduling conflicts, costs, and physical resource availability from different vendors.
- **Project management information system** Your PMIS can help identify where resources haven't been assigned to find skills gaps or needed resources, costs of resources, tradeoffs, reporting, and other project management tasks.
- **Meetings** Of course, you'll need to meet with the project team, vendors, functional managers, and other stakeholders.

Reviewing the Results of Estimating Activity Resources

The primary output of estimating activity resources are the resource requirements. Based on the work packages identified in the WBS and the associated activities, this process will help the project manager define what resources are needed. This process also includes documentation on how the estimates were created, assumptions used, constraints, any range of variances included with the estimates, documentation of any associated risks, and what your confidence level is with the estimates provided.

On some projects, especially larger projects, you may create a resource breakdown structure. The resource breakdown structure visualizes the resources needed throughout the project. It can follow the same structure as the WBS, or you can arrange the RBS by types of resources, such as roles, equipment, facilities, and materials. The RBS can help you define what resources you need to acquire, procure, and what roles are needed in the project work.

The estimating activity resources process will also mean you'll need to update three project documents as needed:

- **Activity attributes**   The activities will be updated to reflect the resource requirements you've identified with this process.
- **Assumption log**   Any assumptions about the resource type, quantity, constraints, and other related information is recorded.
- **Lessons learned register**   If any lessons were learned during the process, such as the effectiveness of how the estimates were created, they should be documented.

CERTIFICATION OBJECTIVE 9.03

Acquiring the Project Resources

Have you ever managed a project in which the resources you want on the project are not available? Or have you managed a project in which the resources you've been assigned aren't the best resources to complete the project work? Staff acquisition is the process of getting the needed human resources on the project team to complete the project work. Staff acquisition focuses on working within the policies and procedures of the performing organization to obtain the needed human resources to complete the project work. Negotiation, communication, and political savvy are the keys to getting the desired resources on the project team. Resource acquisition also includes getting the needed physical resources for your project.

First, a project needs a project team. A project needs a good, qualified, and competent project team. Their competency, experience, and availability will directly influence the success of the project. Armed with this notion, the project manager may rely on a few different tools and techniques to obtain the needed project team resources.

Second, almost all projects need some physical resources: equipment, materials, tools, and access to meeting rooms and other facilities. After identifying the resources you'll need, you'll work through the environmental factors of your organization to acquire the physical resources for your project. Internal resources, such as facilities and team members, are often assigned to the project. External resources, such as special equipment or consultants, follow the procurement process for your organization.

Preparing to Acquire Project Resources

The project manager will rely on the project management plan as an input to acquiring project team members. The resource management plan details how project team members will be brought on to the project and excused from the project as conditions within the project demand. The project management plan also includes the needed procurement management plan for how the project manager may go about procuring resources. I'll talk about creating and using this plan in Chapter 12. You'll also rely on the cost baseline as an input to acquiring the needed resources, as resources cost money.

You'll use four inputs to begin this process:

- **Project management plan**   Resource management plan, procurement management plan, and the cost baseline
- **Project documents**   Project schedule, resource calendars, resource requirements, and the stakeholder register
- **Enterprise environmental factors**   Your organization's information on resource availability, skill sets, experience, and resource costing, along with marketplace conditions, your organization structure (such as weak matrix or functional), and the location of the resources
- **Organizational process assets**   Policies, procedures, historical information from similar projects, and lessons learned repository

Acquiring the Resources

In some organizations, the project manager has little or no say regarding project team assignments. Not fun. In other organizations, project managers have the ability to recruit, or at least influence, the project team assignments and should ask questions about the following:

- **Availability**   Will the project team members desired for the project be available? Project managers should confer with functional managers on the availability of the potential team members.

- **Costs**   How much will each individual team member cost the project?
- **Ability**   What is the competency and proficiency of the available project team members?
- **Experience**   What is the experience of the project team members? Have they done similar work in the past—and have they done it well?
- **Knowledge and skills**   Does a prospective project team member have the right knowledge and skills to do the work?
- **Attitude**   Are the project team members interested in working on this project? Can they work well the project team?
- **International factors**   Does the project span countries, and if so, how will the local culture, time zones, and languages affect the project?

Negotiating for Resources

Project managers need negotiating skills to acquire the best resources for the project's success. Most projects require that the project manager negotiate for resources. The project manager will likely have to negotiate with functional managers to obtain the needed resources to complete the project work. The functional managers and the project manager may struggle over an employee's time due to demands in ongoing operations, other projects, and the effective utilization of resources. In other instances, functional managers may want to assign underutilized resources on projects to account for their employees' time.

Project managers may also have to negotiate with other project managers to share needed resources among projects. Scheduling the needed resources between the project teams will need to be coordinated so that both projects may complete successfully. Project managers may also have to negotiate with vendors when acquiring physical resources or subcontractors to be part of the project team.

Organizational politics certainly come into play with staff acquisitions. Functional managers may want project managers to carry extra resources on the project in exchange for key personnel, added deliverables to the project, or other "favors" for the manager. In all instances, the project manager should follow the PMI Code of Ethics and Professional Conduct. We'll discuss this infamous code of conduct in Chapter 13.

ⓦatch   **When recruitment policies or guidelines are in place within the performing organization, they act as a project constraint.**

Recruiting Project Team Members

The project manager has to follow the rules of the organizations involved in the project. For example, an organization may forbid a project manager from approaching a worker directly to discuss her availability and desire to work on a project. The project manager may instead have to speak with the employee's functional manager to obtain the resource.

Working with Preassigned Staff

Team members and physical resources are often preassigned to a project for several reasons, such as the following:

- The resource was preassigned as part of the project charter or planning processes.
- The individual is available.
- He was promised as part of a competitive contract.
- She was required as part of the project charter of an internal project.
- The staff member has an opportunity to complete on-the-job training.

Whatever the reasoning behind the assignment of the resource to the project, the project manager should evaluate the project team for skills gaps, the availability to complete the project work, and the expectations of the project team members. The project manager must address any discrepancies between the requirements of the project work and the project team members' ability to complete the work.

Acquiring Human Resources

In some instances, the project manager may have no alternative but to procure the project team or individuals to complete the project work. Procurement will be discussed in detail in Chapter 12. In regard to project team procurement, reasons why the project manager can use this alternative include, but are not limited to, the following:

- The performing organization lacks the internal resources with the needed skills to complete the project work.
- The work is more cost-effective to procure.
- The project team members are present within the organization, but they are not available for the current project because of their workload in their current job.
- The project team members are present within the organization, but they cannot complete the needed work due to other project assignments.

Working with Virtual Teams

Virtual teams are project teams that share a common goal—to complete the project work—but they are not collocated and may rarely, if ever, meet face-to-face with other project team members. The virtual team relies on e-mail, video conferences, and teleconferences to communicate about the project. Virtual teams involve the following:

- Teams composed of geographically dispersed individuals
- The ability to add experts to the project team who may not be in the same geographical area

- The inclusion of workers from home offices
- The ability to create project teams of individuals with varying working hours
- The inclusion of people with mobility issues
- The deletion or reduction of travel expenses

Reviewing the Outputs of Acquiring Resources

Congratulations! The project team has been recruited or assigned to the project. With the project team assembled, the project manager can continue planning, assigning activities, and managing the project's progression. Project team members can be assigned to the project on a full- or part-time basis, depending on the project conditions.

Once the project team is built, a project team directory should be assembled that includes the following:

- Team members' names
- Phone numbers
- E-mail addresses
- Assignments
- Mailing addresses if not collocated
- Contact information for key stakeholders
- Any other relevant contact information for each team member, such as photos, web addresses, and so on

The acquire project resources process creates or updates eight things:

- Assignments for the physical resources
- Assignments for the project team members
- Change requests
- Updates to the resource calendars
- Project management plan updates
- Project document updates
- Enterprise environmental factors updates
- Organizational process assets updates

CERTIFICATION OBJECTIVE 9.04

Developing the Project Team

Throughout the project, the project manager will need to develop the project team. The project manager may have to develop the abilities of the individual team members so that each member can complete his assignment. The project manager will also be required to develop the project team so that the team can work together to complete the project.

In matrix organizations, the project team members are accountable to the project manager and their functional managers. The development of the project team can prove challenging, because the project team members may feel pulled between multiple bosses. The project manager must strive to involve and develop the project team members as individuals completing project work—and as team members completing the project objectives together.

Preparing to Develop the Project Team

The project manager will rely on several pieces of information to prepare for team development, such as the following:

- **Project management plan**   The resource management plan, part of the project management plan, defines the training needs, the reward and recognition systems, and the process for disciplinary actions. The assignments of the project team members define their skills, their need for development, and their ability to complete the project work as individuals and as part of the collective team.

- **Lessons learned register**   Lessons learned from earlier in the current project can help the project manager better manage the team.

- **Project schedule**   The schedule will help the project manager identify opportunities and requirements for training and team development.

- **Project team assignment**   Assignments identify who will do what in the project.

- **Resource calendars**   Project managers will use the resource calendar to determine when resources are needed and when they're available to participate in team development activities.

- **Team charter**   The charter defines the values and ground rules to serve as guidelines for the project team.

- **Enterprise environmental factors**   The project manager will need to follow the organizational rules for hiring and terminating project team members, performance reviews, training, and rewards and recognition policies.

■ **Organizational process assets**   Historical information can help the project manager better manage the current project team based on what did, or did not, work well in the past.

Dealing with Team Locales

Collocated teams work in the same physical location to improve team dynamics and team relations. On large projects, it may be particularly valuable to bring all the project team members together to a central location to work collectively on the project. A project headquarters or war room may be ideal.

When collocation is not feasible, the project manager must make attempts to bring the project team together for team interaction, face-to-face meetings, and other avenues of communication to bolster relations. Communication is paramount in all of project management; when dealing with virtual teams, consider communication technologies for effective communication:

■ **Shared portal**   Use a web site or repository for sharing information for easy access for the project team.
■ **Videoconferencing**   Help virtual teams communicate via web-based technology for video calls and chats.
■ **Audioconferencing**   Like video conferencing, conference calls can bring everyone together to communicate in a forum-like environment.
■ **E-mail and chat**   E-mail and chat sessions are common communication tools that project teams can utilize to communicate and share information quickly.

Creating Team-Building Activities

Team-building activities are approaches to develop the team through facilitated events. Events can include the following:

■ Training the project team
■ Team involvement during the planning processes
■ Defining rules for handling team disagreements
■ Offsite activities
■ Quick team-involvement activities
■ Activities to improve interpersonal skills and form relationships

Naturally Developing Project Teams

There's a general belief that project teams go through their own natural development processes. These processes can shift, linger, stall, and even regress based on the dynamics of the project team. This theory of team development was created by educational psychologist Bruce Tuckman in 1965. Here are the five phases of team development that project managers may face:

- **Forming**   The project team meets and learns about their roles and responsibilities on the project. Little interaction among the project team members happens in this stage, because they are learning about the project and the project manager.

- **Storming**   The project team struggles for project positions, leadership, and project direction. The project team can become hostile toward the project leader, challenge ideas, and try to establish and claim positions about the project work. The amount of debate and fury varies depending on whether the project team is willing to work together, the nature of the project, and the control of the project manager.

- **Norming**   Project team members go about getting the project work done, begin to rely on one another, and generally complete their project assignments.

- **Performing**   If a project team can reach the performing stage of team development, they trust one another and work well together, and issues and problems are resolved quickly and effectively.

- **Adjourning**   Once the project is done, the team moves on to other assignments as a unit, or the project team is disbanded and individual team members go on to other work.

 on the Job   **Face-to-face communication is vital to effective communications. Collocation, the concept of project team members being physically close together, is also known as a tight matrix. You might know this concept as a war room, the project meeting room, or the project headquarters. Remember that collocation helps project team members communicate quickly and through ad hoc conversations.**

Relying on General Management Skills

A chunk of project management relies on general management skills. Specifically, the project manager relies on the following:

- **Leading**   Leading is the art of establishing direction, aligning people, and motivating the project team to complete the project work.

- **Communicating**   Good project managers are good communicators. Remember that half of communicating is listening.

■ **Negotiating**   Project managers will likely negotiate for scope, cost, terms, assignment, and resources.

■ **Problem-solving**   Project managers must have the ability to confront and solve problems.

■ **Influencing**   Project managers use their influence to get things done.

Rewarding the Project Team

A reward and recognition system encourages, emphasizes, and promotes good performance and behavior by the project team. The reward and recognition system should be a formal, achievable approach for the project team to perform and be rewarded for their outstanding performance.

The relationship between the requirements for the reward and the power to achieve should not be limited. In other words, if the project manager is rewarded for completing a project by a given date, she needs the autonomy to schedule resources and make decisions so the goal is achievable.

The project team should be rewarded for good work only. For example, a project team should not be rewarded for completing a crucial assignment on schedule if the work is unacceptable because of quality issues.

Finally, the culture in which the project is taking place should also be considered. It may be inappropriate to reward individual team members over an entire group, or vice versa. The project manager should be aware of the cultural environment and operate within the customs and practices of the environment to reward the project team without causing offense.

Training the Project Team

The project team may require training to complete the project work, function as a project team, or participate in management skills such as finance or formal communications. Training can include the following:

■ Formal education
■ Classroom training
■ On-the-job training
■ Cross-training (shadowing)

Completing Project Performance Appraisals

Project team members need feedback. They need to know when they're doing a good job and when they're doing a not-so-good job. But before the project manager can begin offering appraisals, organizational policies and procedures must determine the type of appraisals the project manager provides. The project manager should understand the organizational policies, labor contracting requirements, and whether the project even qualifies for formal appraisals. Smaller, lower priority projects may not need appraisals at all.

One popular approach for completing project team member appraisals is the *360-degree feedbac*k approach. This method offers appraisals from more than just the project manager. They can also come from peers, supervisors, managers, and even project team members' subordinates.

Examining the Results of Team Development

Team development is an ongoing process. Optimum team performance doesn't happen on the first day of the project, but hopefully it does kick in well before the final day of the project. The primary goal of team development is to improve project team performance. Improvements can include the following:

- **Individuals**   Improvements to individual skill sets may enable the individual to complete his assigned work better, faster, or with more confidence.
- **Team**   Improvements to the project team may enable the team to perform with a focus on technical requirements, project work, and working together (in harmony) to complete the project work.
- **Individuals and team**   Improvements either to team members or to the project team may lead to the better good of the project by finding better ways of completing the project work.

Another result of team development is the input to performance reviews of the project team members. Hopefully, all goes well and the project manager can report successful, willing, and cooperative team members. Honesty is paramount in reporting the performance of project team members. Team development can also result in change requests, updates to the project management plan, project documents, enterprise environmental factors, and organizational process assets.

CERTIFICATION OBJECTIVE 9.05

Managing the Project Team

Wouldn't it be great if the project team just did what was assigned to them and did it well? And the project manager could then just organize, document, and plan for future phases of the project? Sure, it would—but then project management would be way, way too easy.

One of the trickiest parts of project management is managing the project team, which involves the following (and then some):

- Tracking each project team member's performance
- Providing feedback to the project team members about their performance and project work
- Finding solutions and facilitating conversations to find solutions for project issues
- Managing changes to the project and project processes to improve overall project performance
- Providing communications among the project team, project stakeholders, and in a matrix structure, communicating with functional managers

There are six inputs to the manage team process:

- **Project management plan** The resource management plan, part of the project management plan, will help guide the activities of this process.
- **Project documents** The issue log, lessons learned register, project team assignments, and the team charter will be used throughout this process.
- **Work performance reports** Work performance data is analyzed and then made into work performance information. Work performance information is then communicated through work performance reports to offer insight into how the team is performing.
- **Team performance assessments** Feedback on how the different team members are performing in the project is needed for effect management of the team.
- **Enterprise environmental factors** Your organization's human resources policies are needed for this process.
- **Organizational process assets** Certificates of appreciation, coffee mugs and corporate apparel, and other rewards for the project team are well received and part of managing the team.

Dealing with Team Disagreements

In most projects, there will be instances when the project team, management, and other stakeholders disagree on the progress, decisions, and proposed solutions within the project. It's essential for the project manager to keep calm, lead, and direct the parties to a sensible solution that's best for the project. Following are seven reasons for conflict:

- Schedules
- Priorities
- Resources

■ Technical beliefs

■ Administrative policies and procedures

■ Project costs

■ Personalities

So, what's a project manager to do with all the potential for strife in a project? A project manager can take five different approaches to conflict resolution:

■ **Collaborate/problem-solving**   This approach confronts the problem head-on and is the preferred method of conflict resolution. You may see this approach as "confronting" rather than problem-solving, however. Problem-solving calls for additional research to find the best solution for the problem and should be a win-win solution. It should be used if there is time to work through and resolve the issue. It also serves to build relationships and trust.

■ **Forcing/directing**   The person with the power makes the decision; the person with the power "forces" their way onto the other parties. The decision made may not be the best decision for the project, but it's fast. As expected, this autocratic approach does little for team development and is a win-lose solution. It's used when the stakes are high and time is of the essence, or if relationships are not important.

■ **Compromising/reconcile**   This approach requires that both parties give up something. The decision made is a blend of both sides of the argument. Because neither party really wins, it can result in a lose-lose solution. The project manager can thus use this approach when the relationships are equal and no one can truly "win." This approach can also be used to avoid a fight.

■ **Smoothing/accommodating**   This approach smooths out the conflict by minimizing the perceived size of the problem to keep harmony in the team relationship. It is a temporary solution but can calm team relations and boisterous discussions. Smoothing may be acceptable when time is of the essence or when none of the proposed solutions will settle the problem. This can be considered a lose-lose situation because no one really wins in the long term. The project manager can use smoothing to emphasize areas of agreement between disagreeing stakeholders, thus minimizing areas of conflict. It's typically used to maintain relationships and when the issue is not critical.

■ **Withdrawing/avoiding**   This is the worst conflict resolution approach, because one side of the argument essentially walks away from the problem, usually in disgust. The conflict is not resolved and it is considered a yield-lose solution, because the "loser" in the argument yields to the other person's point of view. The approach can be used, however, as a cooling-off period or when the issue is not critical. Withdrawing can also be a tactic to delay the issue to be better prepared for the discussion or to allow the issue to be resolved by others.

INSIDE THE EXAM

Most project managers taking the PMP exam can rely on their practical experience to ace these questions. But as reinforcement, let's examine some key issues you should know going into the examination. Project resources management questions on the exam center around four big points:

- **Role** Defines the accountable person by label or function
- **Authority** Provides the authority to assign project resources, make decisions, and sign off on project documents
- **Responsibility** Describes the work assigned to a project team member
- **Competency** Determines what skill set is needed to complete an activity

Because project managers are responsible for the success of the project, they have power that they can exert over the project team. Table 9-2 is a quick list of project manager powers.

You may encounter six organizational theories on the exam:

- **Maslow's Hierarchy of Needs** People don't work for money, but for self-actualization.

- **Herzberg's Theory of Motivation** The presence of hygiene factors doesn't motivate people; the absence of hygiene factors, however, hinders people's performance.
- **McGregor's Theory of X and Y** X people are lazy and do not want to work. Y people are self-led, motivated, and want to accomplish tasks.
- **Ouchi's Theory Z** Workers and management cooperate for the good of the organization. Everyone wins!
- **McClelland's Theory of Needs** People have three needs: achievement, affiliation, and power. One of these needs drives the person's actions.
- **Vroom's Expectancy Theory** People expect to be rewarded for their behavior.

Many methods can be used to resolve conflicts in a project. Table 9-3 lists various resolution methods you should know.

TABLE 9-2	Power	Definition
Powers of the Project Manager	Expert	The project manager is an expert with the technology the project focuses on.
	Reward	The project manager can reward the project team members.
	Coercive	The project manager can punish the project team members.
	Positional	The project manager is formally assigned to the role of project manager.
	Referent	The project team knows the project manager, and the project manager refers to the power of the person who assigned him the role of project manager.

TABLE 9-3	Conflict Resolution	Quick Example
Conflict Resolution Methods	Problem-solving/collaborate	"Let's put our heads together, research the problem, and find the best solution."
	Forcing/directing	"Bob's got seniority here, so we'll go with his opinion on the solution."
	Compromising/reconciling	"Let's take a little of both sides of the argument and create a blended solution."
	Smoothing/accommodating	"Let's smooth this issue out. It's not that big of a problem and it'll keep the project moving forward."
	Withdrawing/avoiding	"I'm leaving. Do whatever solution works for you, or let senior management decide what's best to do."

CERTIFICATION OBJECTIVE 9.06

Controlling Resources

Controlling resources sounds like a process to prevent your project team from running wild. It's really a process to control the physical resources your project team will need to do the work. You want to ensure that the project team has the right physical resources at the right time to do the project activities. Delayed physical resources can introduce all sorts of problems for the project: delays in the work, issues and risks, ripple effects into new resource conflicts, frustration among the stakeholders, and a decrease in confidence in the project manager.

Controlling resources is about monitoring and controlling resource allocation for the project, tracking the cost and utilization of resources, communicating any problems with resources, and managing changes when they may occur in the project. Changes to resources can result from vendor issues; conflicts with other people utilizing the resource, such as equipment or facilities; and issues that happen because of defects in the project work. When defects happen, you'll likely need to do a change request to order more materials, and this means the cost of the project increases.

Preparing to Control Resources

To control resources you'll rely on five inputs to this straightforward process:

- **Project management plan**   The subsidiary resource management plan
- **Project documents**   The issue log, lessons learned register, physical resource assignments, schedule, resource breakdown structure, resource requirements, and the risk register.
- **Work performance data**   Raw data gathered on project status and resource utilization
- **Agreements**   Contracts and agreements with vendors and groups regarding the project resources
- **Organizational process assets**   Policies for resource control, resource assignment, escalation processes, and lessons learned from similar projects

Reviewing the Tools and Techniques to Control Resources

Data analysis is used with controlling resources to examine alternatives analysis. When a resource is not available—perhaps a vendor can't deliver the physical resource as promised—alternative analysis is used to determine whether another resource could work or a different vendor could deliver the solution. Analysis can also involve an examination of what the late delivery would mean to the project schedule and whether the project team can work on other tasks while waiting for the delivery for the resource from the vendor.

Performance reviews are also part of controlling resources. The project manager can compare the actual performance of physical resources to the planned performance of the resources. If the performance of a planned resource is not meeting expectations, the project manager can use cost-benefits analysis to determine whether changing vendors, materials, or both is cost efficient.

The final data analysis technique you can use to control resources is trend analysis. Trend analysis will enable you to examine how well physical resources have performed and identify trend lines in the analysis to plan for future work. For some materials or equipment, the trend line may reflect the learning curve of using the resource. If the project team members have never used a material before, for example, it will likely take some time for the team to learn the best application of the material, develop an approach to doing the work, and master the use of the material. A trend line can track this progress over time.

Resolving issues concerning materials is a common activity of the project manager or experts on the project team. When materials aren't working as expected, you'll need to create a solution to keep the project moving forward. Problems can come from inside the organization, such as equipment damaged by a team member, or from outside the organization, such as vendor that can't deliver, weather, or other external issues. When problem-solving, use methodical, logical steps to find a solution:

- Identify the problem, not the evidence of the problem.
- Break the problem down into manageable chunks.
- Investigate the problem, collect data, experience the problem.
- Analyze the problem to discover the root causes.
- Find a solution that's time and cost efficient.
- Confirm the solution is working.

Reviewing the Results of Controlling Resources

Controlling resources is an ongoing activity throughout the project. The first output of the process is work performance information. Work performance information is useable data about the performance of the physical resources in the project. This information can help the project manager determine whether a change request is needed for the materials. Change requests are the second output of this process; all change requests must be submitted to the project's integrated change control process.

The project management plan could need to be updated as a result of controlling resources. When the project management plan is updated, a change request should be submitted as well. Project management plan changes as a result of controlling resources can include the following:

- **Resource management plan**   Results of resources should be compared to what was planned for the resources.
- **Schedule baseline**   Any changes to the project schedule resulting from controlling resources should be reflected in the schedule baseline.
- **Cost baseline**   Defects, change in the price of materials, and other changes to the costs of the resources must be updated and reflected in the cost baseline.

The process of controlling resources can also cause several project documents to be updated:

- **Assumption log**   Any assumptions about the physical resources that could affect the project should be logged.
- **Issue log**   Issues are risks that have happened; issues with physical resources must be documented, tracked, and monitored.
- **Lessons learned register**   What was learned about the physical resources is documented.

- ■ **Physical resource assignments**   Should the assignments for the physical resources change, the change needs to be documented and updated.
- ■ **Resource breakdown structure**   Where the resources are utilized in the project can be reflected in the resource breakdown structure.
- ■ **Risk register**   Any risks that are introduced or changed as a result of physical resources must be updated in the risk register.

CERTIFICATION SUMMARY

Project resource management requires that the project manager lead and direct the project team, customers, and other stakeholders in unison to complete the project scope. Resource management isn't just about managing people, but also the physical resources of the project. It requires working within the confines of the organizational policies, as well as the ability to relate to the concerns and expectations of the stakeholders. Perhaps most importantly, it is tightly integrated with project communications management.

The PMP candidate should be familiar with several resource theories to pass the PMP examination successfully. Here's a quick listing of these theories and their core beliefs:

- ■ **Maslow's Hierarchy of Needs**   People work for self-actualization.
- ■ **Herzberg's Theory of Motivation**   Hygiene agents are expected by workers and can demotivate only if they aren't present. Motivating agents include the opportunity both to exceed and advance, and to acquire rewards other than mere financial gain.
- ■ **McGregor's Theory of X and Y**   This management theory posits that X people must be micromanaged and should be distrusted and Y people are self-led and motivated.
- ■ **Ouchi's Theory Z**   Workers are motivated by a sense of commitment, opportunity, and advancement. This theory centers on lifetime employment.
- ■ **McClelland's Theory of Needs**   People have three needs: achievement, affiliation, and power. One of the needs drives the person's actions.
- ■ **Vroom's Expectancy Theory**   People expect to be rewarded for their behavior.

Within a project are roles and responsibilities. A role can be defined as "who does what," and a responsibility can be defined as "who decides what." A responsibility assignment matrix (RAM) can map project work to specific project team members. This matrix clarifies which project team member is responsible for what actions within the project.

The RAM can help the project manager determine which resources are needed for which activities, but it can also ensure that the adequate amount of resources is assigned to the project work. The project manager must work to ensure that extra resources are not assigned to project activities. It is wasteful to add unneeded resources to project work.

The resource management plan dictates how resources are brought on to the project—and taken off the project. Should a functional manager want to add unneeded team members, the resource management plan can restrict the functional manager. The plan should work with the operational policies of the performing organization.

KEY TERMS

If you're serious about passing the PMP exams, memorize these terms and their definitions. For maximum value, create your own flashcards based on these definitions and review them daily. You can find additional information on these terms in the book's glossary.

360-degree appraisal   A performance review completed by a person's peers, managers, and subordinates. It's called a 360-degree appraisal because it's a circle of reviews by people at different levels of an organization.

adjourning   The final stage of team development; once the project is done, the team moves on to other assignments, or the project team is disbanded and individual team members go on to other work.

autocratic   The project manager or some other authority makes all of the decisions.

coercive power   The project manager or some other authority uses fear and threats to manage the project team.

collective bargaining agreements   Contractual agreements initiated by employee groups, unions, or other labor organizations; they may act as a constraint on the project.

compromising   A conflict resolution approach that requires both parties to give up something. The decision ultimately made is a blend of both sides of the argument. Because neither party completely wins, it often results in a lose-lose solution.

emotional intelligence   A person is aware of his inbound and outbound emotions; by becoming emotionally intelligent, the person can better control his emotions and understand the emotions of others.

expert power   A type of power in which the authority of the project manager comes from experience with the area that the project focuses on.

forcing   A conflict resolution method whereby one person dominates or forces his point of view or solution to a conflict.

formal power   The type of power with which the project manager or other person has been assigned by her position.

forming   The initial stage of team development; the project team meets and learns about their roles and responsibilities on the project.

halo effect   When one attribute of a person influences a decision.

Herzberg's Theory of Motivation   Posits that there are two catalysts for workers: hygiene agents and motivating agents. Hygiene agents do nothing to motivate, but their absence demotivates workers. Hygiene agents are the expectations all workers have: job security, paychecks, clean and safe working conditions, a sense of belonging, civil working relationships, and other basic attributes associated with employment. Motivating agents are components such as reward, recognition, promotion, and other values that encourage individuals to succeed.

Just-in-time (JIT) manufacturing   Resources are in place only as they are needed. This approach reduces waste, keeps inventory at a minimum, and helps the project manager forecast resource utilization more accurately.

Kaizen   Posits that small changes in processes are easier to accept and incorporate than large, sweeping changes for the organization or project; implementing small changes to the organization and project team over time will result in large changes overall.

Maslow's Hierarchy of Needs   A theory that states that all humans have five layers of needs: physiological, safety, social, esteem, and the crowning jewel, self-actualization.

McClelland's Theory of Needs   A theory that states that all humans have three needs: achievement, affiliation, and power. One of the needs drives the person's actions.

McGregor's Theory of X and Y   A theory that states that X people are lazy, don't want to work, and need to be micromanaged. Y people are self-led, motivated, and strive to accomplish.

norming   Project team members go about getting the project work done, begin to rely on one another, and generally complete their project assignments.

organizational breakdown structure Though these charts are similar to the WBS, the breakdown is by department, unit, or team.

organizational charts Show how an organization, such as a company or large project team, is ordered, its reporting structures, and the flow of information.

Ouchi's Theory Z Theory that posits that workers are motivated by a sense of commitment, opportunity, and advancement. Workers will work if they are challenged and motivated.

performing If a project team can reach the performing stage of team development, they trust one another, they work well together, and issues and problems are resolved quickly and effectively.

problem-solving The ability to determine the best solution for a problem in a quick and efficient manner.

RACI chart A chart that designates each team member against each project activity as responsible, accountable, consulted, or informed (RACI). It is technically a type of responsibility assignment matrix chart.

referent power Power that is present when the project team is attracted to or wants to work on the project or with the project manager. Referent power also exists when the project manager references another, more powerful person, such as the CEO.

resource breakdown structure A chart that breaks down the project by types of resources utilized on the project no matter where a resource is being used in the project.

resource histogram A bar chart reflecting when physical resources, individual employees, groups, or communities are involved in a project. It's often used by management to see when employees or items are most or least active in a project.

resource management plan A subsidiary project management plan that documents how project team members and physical resources will be included in the project and excused from the project. This plan is included in the resources plan.

responsibility The person who performs the duties of the assignment.

responsibility assignment matrix chart   A chart type designating the roles and responsibilities of the project team.

reward power   The project manager's or other party's authority to reward the project team.

role   Designates the type of activities a person performs in a project.

smoothing   A conflict resolution method that smooths out the conflict by minimizing the perceived size of the problem. It is a temporary solution, but it can calm team relations and reduce boisterousness of discussions. Smoothing may be acceptable when time is of the essence or when any of the proposed solutions would work.

storming   The second stage of team development; the project team struggles for project positions, leadership, and project direction.

Theory of constraints   A management system is limited by its weakest components or bottlenecks, the constraint. Adapts the phrase "a chain is only as strong as its weakest link."

virtual teams   Project teams that are not collocated and that may rarely, if ever, meet face-to-face with other project team members. The virtual team relies on e-mail, video conferences, and teleconferences to communicate on the project.

Vroom's Expectancy Theory   A theory that claims people will behave based on what they expect as a result of their behavior. In other words, people will work in relation to the expected reward of the work.

war room   A centralized office or locale for the project manager and the project team to work on the project. It can house information on the project, including documentation and support materials. It enables the project team to work in close proximity.

withdrawal   A conflict resolution method that is used when the issue is not important or the project manager is outranked. The project manager pushes the issue aside for later resolution or resolution by someone else. It can also be used as a method for cooling down. The conflict is not resolved, and it is considered a yield-lose solution.

TWO-MINUTE DRILL

Preparing for Resource Planning

❑ Project resources management focuses on utilizing the people and physical resources involved in the project in the most effective way. These people include more than just the project team members, although they're the most obvious resources.

❑ The project manager must involve other stakeholders: customers, management, individual contributors, the project sponsor, and any other stakeholder unique to the project.

❑ Organizational planning calls on the project manager to identify the roles and responsibilities of the project and the reporting relationship within the organization.

Completing Organizational Planning

❑ Because projects are often similar, the project manager can rely on templates to re-create the success of historical projects. Reporting structures, role and responsibility matrixes, and other resource models can be replicated and adjusted between projects.

❑ Maslow's Hierarchy of Needs says that people work for five needs: physiological, safety, social, esteem, and self-actualization.

❑ Herzberg's Theory of Motivation says that hygiene agents do not promote performance, but their absence can lower performance. Motivating agents, such as rewards and recognition, can improve performance.

❑ McClelland's Theory of Needs states that people are driven primarily by one of three needs: achievement, affiliation, or power.

❑ McGregor's Theory of X and Y states that management believes there are two types of workers. X workers are lazy, unproductive, and need to be micromanaged. Y workers are self-led, productive, and want the organization to succeed.

❑ Vroom's Expectancy theory states that people will behave based on what they expect as a result of their behavior.

❑ William Ouchi's Theory Z is based on the Japanese participative management style. This theory states that workers are motivated by a sense of commitment, opportunity, and advancement.

Preparing for Project Team Management

❑   The resource management plan describes the process that the project manager must follow to bring resources on to a project or to dismiss them from a project when the resources are no longer needed.

❑   The policies and procedures of the performing organization should be documented within the resource management plan to ensure that the guidelines are followed as management intends.

❑   The resource management plan also details the policies regarding how the project manager can recruit project team members. In addition, the plan may detail the procedure to procure resources for the project from vendors or consultants.

Acquiring the Project Resources

❑   The resource management plan, part of the project management plan, defines how members and physical resources will be brought on to the project team and how the team members and physical resources will be released from the project once their work has been completed. It's not cost-effective to keep project team members on the project once their work has been completed. This plan is based on the project's resource requirements.

❑   Virtual teams are project teams that are not collocated and may rarely, if ever, meet face-to-face with other project team members. The virtual team relies on e-mail, video conferences, and teleconferences to communicate on the project. Communication demands increase when working with virtual teams.

Developing the Project Team

❑   Ideally, the project is collocated and has access to a war room in which to refer to project information, research, and schedules, and to meet with other project team members.

❑   The goal of team development is outstanding performance for the good of the project. Through training, the project team may increase their ability to work together and individually, with a higher level of confidence, performance, and teamwork.

❑   A reward and recognition system can help the project manager motivate the project team to perform as required.

❑   The project manager must be certain to involve the entire project team when team members are scattered geographically. The project manager can rely on face-to-face meetings, videoconferences, or teleconferences to promote non-collocated teams.

❑   The result of team development is project performance improvements. The improvements should be noted in an honest appraisal of the project team members' efforts and contributions to the project.

Managing the Project Team

- ❑ Communication is an important factor in managing the project team. The project manager must communicate the expectations, responsibilities, and performance of the project team members so they can work accordingly.

- ❑ Problem-solving is a conflict resolution method by which both parties work together to find a solution. This approach is also known as confronting.

- ❑ Forcing is a conflict resolution approach whereby the person with the power forces her decision.

- ❑ Compromising requires that both parties give up something they want to reach a resolution.

- ❑ Smoothing solves the issue by minimizing the perceived size of the problem. It is a temporary solution but can calm team relations and boisterous discussions. Smoothing may be acceptable when time is of the essence or when none of the proposed solutions will settle the problem.

- ❑ Withdrawal happens when one party retreats from the conflict and avoids a resolution.

SELF TEST

1. You are the project manager for the JHG Project. This project requires coordination with the directors of manufacturing, resources, the IT department, and the CIO. You will be acquiring resources for the project only as the resources are needed. The goal is to reduce waste, minimize inventory, and forecast resource utilization. What type of approach is this?

   A. Just-in-time manufacturing

   B. Schedule ALAP

   C. Schedule ASAP

   D. Resource recurring factoring

2. You are the project manager of the GHY Project. This project will remove old lights throughout your building and replace the fixtures with new, cost-saving lights. In this project, you'll work with internal and external vendors. Your project requires an electrician at month eight. This is an example of which of the following?

    A. Organizational interfaces

    B. Resource requirements

    C. Contractor requirements

    D. Resource constraints

3. You are the project manager of the PUY Project. This project requires a chemical engineer for seven months of the project, but there are no available chemical engineers within your department. This is an example of which of the following?

    A. Organizational interfaces

    B. Resource requirements

    C. Contractor requirements

    D. Resource constraints

4. As a PMP, you need to recognize the different organizational structures and the expected amount of authority a project manager will have in these environments. For example, suppose you are the project manager in an organization with a weak matrix. Who will have the authority on your project?

    A. The project manager

    B. The customer

    C. Functional management

    D. The team leader

5. You are the project manager for the LMG Project. Your project will have several resource issues that must be coordinated and approved by the union. Which of the following statements is correct about this scenario?

    A. The union is considered a resource constraint.

    B. The union is considered a management constraint.

    C. The union is considered a project stakeholder.

    D. The union is considered a project team member.

6. You are the project manager of the PLY Project. This project is like the ACT Project you completed earlier. What method can you use to expedite the process of organization planning?

    A. Use the project plan of the ACT Project on the PLY Project.

    B. Use the roles and responsibilities definitions of the ACT Project on the PLY Project.

    C. Use the project team reward structure of the ACT Project on the PLY Project.

    D. Use the project team of the ACT Project on the PLY Project.

7. In your organization, management is referred to as coaches. As a project manager, you are referred to as a project coach. A resource document should be created to handle this scenario. What should it cover?

    A. How coaches are separate from managers

    B. How coaches are the same as managers

    C. How a coach is to complete his job

    D. How the project team is to work for a coach

8. You are the project manager of the JQA Project. This project will last for eight months, and you have 12 project team members. Management has requested that you create a chart depicting all the project resource needs and the associated activities. Management is looking for which type of chart?

    A. A roles chart

    B. A roles matrix

    C. A roles and responsibilities matrix

    D. A Gantt chart

9. Many theories and philosophies can affect the approach a manager uses to lead and manage the project team. Based on your knowledge of the different management theories, which of the following is an example of the X in Theory of X and Y?

    A. Self-led project teams

    B. Micromanagement

    C. Team members able to work on their own accord

    D. EVM

10. You are the project manager of the PLN Project. Management has asked you to identify the weakest link in the project chain. What approach is management likely using in your organization?

    A. Formal power

    B. Theory of constraints

    C. Critical path networking

    D. Referent power

11. Beth is a great application developer and has been in that role for 12 years. Because of her experience, she would make a great project manager of an application development project. What does this scenario best describe?

    A. Halo effect

    B. Coercive power

    C. Expert power

    D. Halo power

12. Management has approached Tyler, one of your project team members. Tyler is a database administrator and developer whose work is always on time, accurate, and of quality. He also has a reputation of being a "good guy" and is well liked. Because of this, management has decided to move Tyler into the role of a project manager for a new database administration project. This is an example of which of the following?

A. Management by exception

B. The halo effect

C. Management by objectives

D. McGregor's Theory of X and Y

13. Susan is the project manager for the PMG Project. She makes all the decisions on the project team, regardless of the project team's objections. This is an example of which of the following management styles?

A. Forcing

B. Democratic

C. Laissez faire

D. Exceptional

14. You are a new project manager in your company. Many of the project team members do not know you, haven't worked with you before, and don't seem interested in working on the project goal now. Some problems have come up in the project and need to be addressed immediately for the project to be successful. Which problem-solving technique is the best for most project management situations?

A. Confronting

B. Compromising

C. Forcing

D. Avoidance

15. Harold is an outspoken project team member. All the project team members respect Harold for his experience with the technology, but things usually have to be done as Harold sees fit; otherwise, things don't go well. During a discussion on a solution, a project team member throws up her arms and says, "Fine, Harold, do it your way." This is an example of which of the following?

A. A win-win solution

B. A leave-lose solution

C. A lose-lose solution

D. A yield-lose solution

16. You are the project manager for the GBK Project. This project affects a line of business, and the customer is anxious about the success of the project. Which of the following is likely not a top concern for the customer?
    A. Project priorities
    B. Schedule
    C. Cost
    D. Personality conflicts

17. As a project manager in your organization, you believe that projects operate better when the project team is involved in the management processes. You like to include the project team in decisions, listen to their input, and create a familial environment. Which theory believes that workers need to be involved with the management process?
    A. McGregor's Theory of X and Y
    B. Ouchi's Theory Z
    C. Herzberg's Theory of Motivation
    D. Vroom's Expectancy Theory

18. Employees and employers enter the employment contract with certain obligations. The employee is obligated to work and perform according to requirements. The employer is obligated to abide by the employment offer and pay the worker accordingly. Which of the following states that if workers are rewarded they will remain productive?
    A. McGregor's Theory of X and Y
    B. Ouchi's Theory Z
    C. Herzberg's Theory of Motivation
    D. Vroom's Expectancy Theory

19. Mary has created a RACI chart for her project team. What does the C in RACI mean?
    A. Continue
    B. Coercive
    C. Consulted
    D. Character

20. You are the project manager for the GHB Project. You have served as a project manager for your organization for the past ten years. Practically all your projects are completed on time and on budget. The project team has worked with you in the past, and they consider you to be an expert project manager. They also like working with you. Given all of this, you likely have what type of power on this project?
    A. Formal power
    B. Coercive power
    C. Expert power
    D. Referent power

21. Several types of power can be used in project management. Some of the powers are based on the project manager's experience, knowledge, perception, or even relationship. Which of the following scenarios is an example of coercive power?
    A. A project manager who has lunch with the project team every Thursday
    B. A project manager who will openly punish any team member who is late with an activity
    C. A project manager who has worked with the technology on the project for several years
    D. A project manager who is friends with all the project team members

22. Charles is the project manager for the WAC Project. The customer and a project team member are in conflict over the level of quality needed on a sampling. Charles decides to split the difference between what the two stakeholders want. This is an example of which of the following?
    A. A win-win solution
    B. A win-lose solution
    C. A lose-lose solution
    D. A leave-lose solution

23. Mike is the project manager for a project with a very tight schedule. The project is running late, and Mike thinks that he does not have time to consider all the possible solutions that two team members are in disagreement over. Mike quickly decides to go with the team member with the largest amount of seniority. This is an example of which of the following?
    A. Problem-solving
    B. Compromising
    C. Forcing
    D. Withdrawal

24. You are a project manager in a project-oriented organization. Your job as a project manager can be described best by which of the following?
    A. Full-time
    B. Part-time
    C. Expeditor
    D. Coordinator

25. You are the project manager of the NHH Project for your organization. This project will span three countries and utilize four languages: English, Flemish, French, and Spanish. In this project, you'll rely heavily on a virtual project. Of the following, which one is a benefit of using a collocated team?
    A. The project team is dispersed, so the team is self-led.
    B. The project team is dispersed, so communication increases.
    C. The project team is in the same physical location, so their ability to work as a team is enhanced.
    D. The project team is in the same physical location, so project costs are greatly reduced.

SELF TEST ANSWERS

1. You are the project manager for the JHG Project. This project requires coordination with the directors of manufacturing, resources, the IT department, and the CIO. You will be acquiring resources for the project only as the resources are needed. The goal is to reduce waste, minimize inventory, and forecast resource utilization. What type of approach is this?
   A. Just-in-time manufacturing
   B. Schedule ALAP
   C. Schedule ASAP
   D. Resource recurring factoring

   ☑ **A.** With just-in-time manufacturing, the physical resources are put in place only as they are needed. This approach reduces waste, keeps inventory at a minimum, and helps the project manager forecast resource utilization more accurately.
   ☒ **B, C,** and **D** are incorrect. **B,** schedule ALAP, means to schedule as late as possible to schedule the work against a deadline for the project. **C,** schedule ASAP, means to schedule the work as soon as possible. **D,** resource recurring factoring, is not a valid project management term.

2. You are the project manager of the GHY Project. This project will remove old lights throughout your building and replace the fixtures with new, cost-saving lights. In this project, you'll work with internal and external vendors. Your project requires an electrician at month eight. This is an example of which of the following?
   A. Organizational interfaces
   B. Resource requirements
   C. Contractor requirements
   D. Resource constraints

   ☑ **B.** Because the project requires the electrician, a project role, this is a resource requirement.
   ☒ **A, C,** and **D** are incorrect. **A** is incorrect because it does not accurately describe the situation. **C** is incorrect because contractor requirements would specify the procurement issues, the minimum qualifications for the electrician, and so on. **D** is incorrect because a resource constraint, while a tempting choice, deals more with the availability of the resource or the requirement to use the resource.

3. You are the project manager of the PUY Project. This project requires a chemical engineer for seven months of the project, but there are no available chemical engineers within your department. This is an example of which of the following?

A. Organizational interfaces

B. Resource requirements

C. Contractor requirements

D. Resource constraints

☑ **B.** The project needs the resource of the chemical engineer to be successful. When the project needs a resource, it is a resource requirement.

☒ **A, C,** and **D** are incorrect. This situation does not describe an organizational interface or contractor requirement. Resource constraints might include a requirement to use a particular resource or a requirement that a resource must be available when certain project activities are happening.

4. As a PMP, you need to recognize the different organizational structures and the expected amount of authority a project manager will have in these environments. For example, suppose you are the project manager in an organization with a weak matrix. Who will have the authority on your project?

A. The project manager

B. The customer

C. Functional management

D. The team leader

☑ **C.** In a weak matrix structure, functional management will have more authority than the project manager.

☒ **A, B,** and **D** are incorrect. They do not have as much authority on a project in a weak matrix environment as functional management will have.

5. You are the project manager for the LMG Project. Your project will have several resource issues that must be coordinated and approved by the union. Which of the following statements is correct about this scenario?
   A. The union is considered a resource constraint.
   B. The union is considered a management constraint.
   C. The union is considered a project stakeholder.
   D. The union is considered a project team member.

   ☑ **C.** In this instance, the union is considered a project stakeholder because it has a vested interest in the project's outcome.
   ☒ **A, B,** and **D** are incorrect. **A** is incorrect because the union is not a resource constraint—it is interested in the project management methodology and the project resources management. **B** is incorrect because the union is the counterweight to the management of the organization—not to the project itself. **D** is also incorrect, because the union is not a project team member.

6. You are the project manager of the PLY Project. This project is like the ACT Project you completed earlier. What method can you use to expedite the process of organization planning?
   A. Use the project plan of the ACT Project on the PLY Project.
   B. Use the roles and responsibilities definitions of the ACT Project on the PLY Project.
   C. Use the project team reward structure of the ACT Project on the PLY Project.
   D. Use the project team of the ACT Project on the PLY Project.

   ☑ **B.** When projects are similar in nature, the project manager can use the roles and responsibilities definitions of the historical project to guide the current project.
   ☒ **A, C,** and **D** are incorrect. **A** is incorrect because the entire project plan of the ACT Project isn't needed. Even the roles and responsibilities matrix of the historical project may not be an exact fit for the current project. **C** is incorrect because copying the project team reward structure is not the best choice of all the answers presented. **D** is incorrect because using the same project team may not be feasible at all.

7. In your organization, management is referred to as coaches. As a project manager, you are referred to as a project coach. A resource document should be created to handle this scenario. What should it cover?
   A. How coaches are separate from managers
   B. How coaches are the same as managers
   C. How a coach is to complete his job
   D. How the project team is to work for a coach

☑ **C.** When project managers, or managers in general, are referred to by different terms, a job description is needed so that the project manager can successfully complete the required obligations.

☒ **A, B,** and **D** are incorrect. **A** and **B** are incorrect because the project manager must know what the specific responsibilities are, not the similarities and differences between the current role and management. **D** is also incorrect, because by the project manager knowing how to complete his job, the role of the project team should be evident.

8. You are the project manager of the JQA Project. This project will last for eight months, and you have 12 project team members. Management has requested that you create a chart depicting all the project resource needs and the associated activities. Management is looking for which type of chart?

   A. A roles chart

   B. A roles matrix

   C. A roles and responsibilities matrix

   D. A Gantt chart

☑ **C.** Management is looking for a roles and responsibility matrix. This chart lists the roles and responsibilities, and depicts the intersection of the two.

☒ **A, B,** and **D** are incorrect. **A** and **B** are incorrect because management is looking for more than a listing of the roles and the associated responsibilities. **D** is not an acceptable answer for the scenario presented, because Gantt charts are visual representation of the flow and duration of the project work against a calendar.

9. Many theories and philosophies can affect the approach a manager uses to lead and manage the project team. Based on your knowledge of the different management theories, which of the following is an example of the X in Theory of X and Y?

   A. Self-led project teams

   B. Micromanagement

   C. Team members able to work on their own accord

   D. EVM

☑ **B.** The X in the Theory of X and Y states that workers have an inherent dislike of work and will avoid it if possible. Micromanagement is a method with regard to X that helps to make certain workers complete their work.

☒ **A, C,** and **D** are incorrect. **A** and **C** are not examples of McGregor's Theory of X and Y. **D** is incorrect because EVM is not directly related to McGregor's Theory of X and Y.

10. You are the project manager of the PLN Project. Management has asked you to identify the weakest link in the project chain. What approach is management likely using in your organization?
    A. Formal power
    B. Theory of constraints
    C. Critical path networking
    D. Referent power

    ☑ **B.** When looking for the weakest link in the project management chain, management is likely using the theory of constraints. The theory of constraints says a management system is limited by its weakest components, the constraints. Adapts the phrase "a chain is only as strong as its weakest link."
    ☒ **A, C,** and **D** are incorrect. These describe power over the project and the project network diagramming technique.

11. Beth is a great application developer and has been in that role for 12 years. Because of her experience, she would make a great project manager of an application development project. What does this scenario best describe?
    A. Halo effect
    B. Coercive power
    C. Expert power
    D. Halo power

    ☑ **A.** The perception that Beth would make a great project manager of an application development project solely because she has been an application developer is an example of the halo effect.
    ☒ **B, C,** and **D** are incorrect. **B** is incorrect because coercive power is the associated fear of the project manager. **C** is incorrect because expert power is derived from the project manager's experience with the technology being implemented. **D** is incorrect because halo power is not a viable answer to the question.

12. Management has approached Tyler, one of your project team members. Tyler is a database administrator and developer whose work is always on time, accurate, and of quality. He also has a reputation of being a "good guy" and is well liked. Because of this, management has decided to move Tyler into the role of a project manager for a new database administration project. This is an example of which of the following?
    A. Management by exception
    B. The halo effect
    C. Management by objectives
    D. McGregor's Theory of X and Y

    ☑   **B.** The halo effect is the assumption that because a person is good at a certain technology, he will also be good at managing a project dealing with said technology.
    ☒   **A, C,** and **D** are incorrect. These do not describe the scenario.

13. Susan is the project manager for the PMG Project. She makes all the decisions on the project team, regardless of the project team's objections. This is an example of which of the following management styles?
  A. Forcing
  B. Democratic
  C. Laissez faire
  D. Exceptional

    ☑   **A.** Susan is an autocratic decision maker, also known as forcing.
    ☒   **B, C,** and **D** are incorrect. **B** is incorrect because a democracy counts each project team member's opinion. **C** is incorrect because laissez faire enables the project team to make all the decisions. **D** is incorrect because this is not exceptional project management.

14. You are a new project manager in your company. Many of the project team members do not know you, haven't worked with you before, and don't seem interested in working on the project goal now. Some problems have come up in the project and need to be addressed immediately for the project to be successful. Which problem-solving technique is the best for most project management situations?
  A. Confronting
  B. Compromising
  C. Forcing
  D. Avoidance

    ☑   **A.** Confronting is the best problem-solving technique, since it meets the problem directly.
    ☒   **B, C,** and **D** are incorrect. **B** is incorrect because compromising requires both sides of an issue to give up something. **C** is incorrect because forcing requires the project manager to force a decision based on external inputs, such as seniority, experience, and so on. **D** is incorrect because avoidance ignores the problem and does not solve it.

15. Harold is an outspoken project team member. All the project team members respect Harold for his experience with the technology, but things usually have to be done as Harold sees fit; otherwise, things don't go well. During a discussion on a solution, a project team member throws up her arms and says, "Fine, Harold, do it your way." This is an example of which of the following?

   A. A win-win solution

   B. A leave-lose solution

   C. A lose-lose solution

   D. A yield-lose solution

> ☑ **D.** When Harold always must win an argument and team members begin to give in to Harold's demands simply to avoid arguments rather than find an accurate solution, this is a yield-lose situation.
>
> ☒ **A, B,** and **C** are incorrect. **A** is incorrect because both parties do not win. **B** is incorrect because the project team member did not leave the conversation, but rather ended it. **C** is incorrect because a lose-lose solution is a compromise in which both parties give up something.

16. You are the project manager for the GBK Project. This project affects a line of business, and the customer is anxious about the success of the project. Which of the following is likely not a top concern for the customer?

   A. Project priorities

   B. Schedule

   C. Cost

   D. Personality conflicts

> ☑ **D.** Personality conflicts are likely a concern for the customer but are not as important as project priorities, schedule, and cost. The customer hired your company to solve the technical issues.
>
> ☒ **A, B,** and **C** are incorrect. These are most likely the top issues for a company in a project of this magnitude.

17. As a project manager in your organization, you believe that projects operate better when the project team is involved in the management processes. You like to include the project team in decisions, listen to their input, and create a familial environment. Which theory believes that workers need to be involved with the management process?

   A. McGregor's Theory of X and Y

   B. Ouchi's Theory Z

   C. Herzberg's Theory of Motivation

   D. Vroom's Expectancy Theory

☑ **B.** Ouchi's Theory Z states that workers need to be involved with the management process.

☒ **A, C,** and **D** are incorrect. A is incorrect because McGregor's Theory of X and Y posits that X workers don't want to work and need constant supervision. Y workers will work if the work is challenging, satisfying, and rewarding. C is incorrect because Herzberg's Theory of Motivation describes the type of people and what excites them to work. **D,** Vroom's Expectancy Theory, describes how people will work based on what they expect as a result of the work they do.

18. Employees and employers enter the employment contract with certain obligations. The employee is obligated to work and perform according to requirements. The employer is obligated to abide by the employment offer and pay the worker accordingly. Which of the following states that if workers are rewarded they will remain productive?
    A. McGregor's Theory of X and Y
    B. Ouchi's Theory Z
    C. Herzberg's Theory of Motivation
    D. Vroom's Expectancy Theory

☑ **D.** Vroom's Expectancy Theory describes how people will work based on what they expect as a result of the work they do. If people are rewarded because of the work they complete and they like the reward (payment), they will continue to work.

☒ **A, B,** and **C** are incorrect. These theories do not accurately describe the scenario presented.

19. Mary has created a RACI chart for her project team. What does the C in RACI mean?
    A. Continue
    B. Coercive
    C. Consulted
    D. Character

☑ **C.** The C in RACI means consulted.

☒ **A, B,** and **D** are incorrect. These do not describe the C in RACI. RACI stands for responsible, accountable, consulted, and informed and describes the role the associated project team member will take with an assignment.

20. You are the project manager for the GHB Project. You have served as a project manager for your organization for the past ten years. Practically all your projects are completed on time and on budget. The project team has worked with you in the past, and they consider you to be an expert project manager. They also like working with you. Given all of this, you likely have what type of power on this project?
    A. Formal power
    B. Coercive power
    C. Expert power
    D. Referent power

    ☑ **D.** This is referent power because the project team knows you, the project manager, personally.
    ☒ **A, B,** and **C** are incorrect. **A** and **B** are incorrect because they do not describe the scenario. **C** is incorrect because expert power does not deal with the ability to lead and complete a project, but instead focuses on being an expert with the technology that the project deals with.

21. Several types of power can be used in project management. Some of the powers are based on the project manager's experience, knowledge, perception, or even relationship. Which of the following scenarios is an example of coercive power?
    A. A project manager who has lunch with the project team every Thursday
    B. A project manager who will openly punish any team member who is late with an activity
    C. A project manager who has worked with the technology on the project for several years
    D. A project manager who is friends with all the project team members

    ☑ **B.** Coercive power is the power a project manager yields over the project team, which is essentially formal authority.
    ☒ **A, C,** and **D** are incorrect. **A** is incorrect because only referent power may result from lunch meetings. **C** is incorrect because experience is expert power. **D** is incorrect because interpersonal relationships are examples of referent power.

22. Charles is the project manager for the WAC Project. The customer and a project team member are in conflict over the level of quality needed on a sampling. Charles decides to split the difference between what the two stakeholders want. This is an example of which of the following?
    A. A win-win solution
    B. A win-lose solution
    C. A lose-lose solution
    D. A leave-lose solution

☑ **C.** When both parties give up something, it is a compromise. A compromise is an example of a lose-lose solution.

☒ **A, B,** and **D** are incorrect. **A** is incorrect because win-win is accomplished through confrontation. **B** is incorrect because win-lose allows only one party to get what she wants from the scenario. **D** is incorrect because a leave-lose solution occurs when one party walks away from the problem.

23. Mike is the project manager for a project with a very tight schedule. The project is running late, and Mike thinks that he does not have time to consider all the possible solutions that two team members are in disagreement over. Mike quickly decides to go with the team member with the largest amount of seniority. This is an example of which of the following?

A. Problem-solving

B. Compromising

C. Forcing

D. Withdrawal

☑ **C.** Forcing happens when the project manager makes a decision based on factors not relevant to the problem. Just because a team member has more seniority does not mean this individual is correct.

☒ **A, B,** and **D** are incorrect. **A** is incorrect because problem-solving is not described in the scenario. **B** is incorrect because compromising occurs when both parties agree to give up something. **D** is incorrect because withdrawal occurs when a party leaves the argument.

24. You are a project manager in a project-oriented organization. Your job as a project manager can be described best by which of the following?

A. Full-time

B. Part-time

C. Expeditor

D. Coordinator

☑ **A.** Project managers are typically assigned to a project on a full-time basis in a project-oriented organization.

☒ **B, C,** and **D** are incorrect. They do not accurately describe the work schedule of a project manager in a project-oriented environment.

25. You are the project manager of the NHH Project for your organization. This project will span three countries and utilize four languages: English, Flemish, French, and Spanish. In this project, you'll rely heavily on a virtual project. Of the following, which one is a benefit of using a collocated team?
    A. The project team is dispersed, so the team is self-led.
    B. The project team is dispersed, so communication increases.
    C. The project team is in the same physical location, so their ability to work as a team is enhanced.
    D. The project team is in the same physical location, so project costs are greatly reduced.

> ☑ **C.** When a project team is collocated, all the project team members are in the same physical location, which increases their ability to work as a team.
> ☒ **A, B,** and **D** are incorrect. **A** and **B** are incorrect because collocated teams are not dispersed. **D** is incorrect because a collocated team does not ensure that costs are reduced. In some situations, costs may be increased due to the travel expenses of bringing all the team members together to complete the project.

Chapter 10

Introducing Project Communications Management

CERTIFICATION OBJECTIVES

10.01	Planning Communications	10.04	Reporting Project Performance
10.02	Managing Project Communications	✓	Two-Minute Drill
10.03	Monitoring Project Communications	Q&A	Self Test

What's a project manager's most important skill?

Communication.

Project managers spend about 90 percent of their time communicating. Think about it: meetings, phone calls, memos, e-mails, reports, presentations—the list goes on and on. Project managers spend the bulk of their day communicating news, ideas, and knowledge. They are communicators.

Project communication management centers on determining who needs what information and when, and then producing a plan to provide that needed information. It includes generating, collecting, disseminating, and storing communication. Successful projects require successful communication, and communication is the key link between people, ideas, and information.

Project communication management includes three processes that may overlap one another and other knowledge areas. There are only three communications processes, but these processes affect the entire project and are time intensive for the project manager:

■ **Plan communications management**   The project manager needs to identify the communication needs of the project based on the type of project, the stakeholders, and the tools available.

■ **Manage communications**   The project manager analyzes the project's conditions and then determines who'll need the information, how to communicate the information, and how urgent the communication must be. Communications management also handles the disposal or storage of the information in the project.

■ **Monitor communications**   The larger the project, the greater the need for the project manager to communicate. This process covers how the project manager will determine the effectiveness of the project communication.

Communicating in Projects

Communication is so vital to successful projects that it's something you'll do right from the start of the project. All project documents communicate something. Meetings communicate something. Even your body language is communication, albeit non-verbal. Communication is about exchanging information:

■ **Written communications**   Memos, reports, project web site, and e-mails

■ **Spoken communications**   Phone calls and face-to-face chats

■ **Formal and informal communications**   Formal presentations, reports, and ad hoc meetings

■ **Body language and tone**   Your gestures, facial expressions, and how you say something

■ **Media**   Charts, graphs, pictures, word choice, and the modality

■ **Choice of words**   The words you choose to communicate affect the message

As a project manager you've likely experienced good communications and miscommunications. What you think you heard and what was said can be two different things. What stakeholders hear is often interpreted by them to mean what they want it to mean, unless there is clear, concise communications. It's not always what is said, but what isn't said, that can affect the message. Good project managers are good communicators.

Consider Communication Activities

Communication in project management is about getting out the right message, at the right time, to the right people, and in the right modality. If any of those factors are missing, the entire message can be lost or misconstrued. Communication demands accuracy, planning, monitoring, and thought. Consider all the different aspects of project management communication:

- **Internal**   Speaking with the project stakeholders
- **External**   Communicating with customers, vendors, organizations, government agencies, and even the public about your project
- **Formal**   The organization's required tone of reports and presentations and expectations of the stakeholder the project manager must abide by
- **Informal**   Hallway meetings, sometimes called ad hoc meetings, and casual conversations you have with stakeholders
- **Hierarchical focus**   The chain of command in communication—who speaks to whom—and your role as you speak upward with senior management, downward to the project team, and horizontally to other project managers or colleagues
- **Official**   Organizational communications such as annual reports
- **Unofficial**   Project profile and recognition in the organization to foster relationship and create excitement about the project
- **Written and oral**   Your verbal communication and written communications

Communication happens when information transferred from the source becomes knowledge and understanding to the intended recipient. Communication requires a strategy to determine what needs to be communicated to whom, who will do the communicating, and what will be the best way to communicate. A huge risk that's going to wreck your project probably deserves more than a text message to the intended recipient. What's being communicated affects how you'll communicate the information. Communications also requires the five Cs:

- **Correct grammar and spelling**   Poor grammar and spelling can affect the message and understanding of what you want to say.
- **Concise expression and excessive words**   Less is often more when it comes to writing reports and presentations. Get to the point.

- **Clear purpose**   Communicate exactly and clearly what the audience needs to hear.
- **Coherent and logical flow of ideas**   Create a logical flow of ideas, and use markers such as section headings and bullet points in reports to communicate quickly and effectively.
- **Controlled flow of ideas**   Ensure that ideas are communicated among the project team and stakeholders in an organized way.

These five points support the most common communications skills you'll need as a project manager:

- **Listen actively**   Stay in the conversation, and summarize back what you've heard to ensure understanding.
- **Understand cultural and personal differences**   By understanding the difference in culture and personal traits between you and the other people in the conversation, you've more insight into what's being truly said in the conversation.
- **Manage conflict**   Conflicts are natural, but conflict management is needed to keep conflicts from disrupting the project.
- **Manage meetings**   Prepare the meeting agenda, stick to the start and stop times for the meeting, keep attendees on point, manage meeting expectations, and record all actions and assigned responsibilities in the meeting.

Tailoring Communications in Project Management

Every project and every organization is unique, so it's no surprise that you'll tailor the communication processes to fit your organization. High-profile projects will require a different communication approach than low-level, simple projects. You'll adapt your communications strategy to fit what the project needs. Consider why you'll tailor communications in any project:

- **Stakeholder expectations**   What information do the stakeholders need? Are you communicating with internal and external stakeholders?
- **Physical locations**   Where are the stakeholders located? How will that affect how you speak with the stakeholders?
- **Technology**   Are you using only written reports? Or will you use e-mail, videoconferences, texting, social media, and other communication technologies.
- **Languages**   Do all stakeholders speak the same language? If not, how will you address the complexity of communicating in different languages effectively?
- **Knowledge management**   How will you store and access communication artifacts? Is there a knowledge management system in place in the organization?

Communicating in Agile Environments

If you're managing an agile project you'll have communication considerations that predictive life cycles don't have. For example, documentation is not considered an added value in agile projects. That's right. All those reports and stuffy forms? Not used in agile projects—which can be a blessing and a curse. Agile projects also have rules and approaches to meeting with teams, communicating with stakeholders, and protecting the team from interruptions during iterations.

Agile projects do have meetings—sometimes daily meetings—and end-of-iteration reviews and retrospectives to ensure that everyone has the same message and the same opportunities to speak and contribute. Communication in agile environment is often more face-to-face and informal, but it's still important to keeping the project moving forward. Agile communication must be fast, accurate, and transparent.

CERTIFICATION OBJECTIVE 10.01

Planning Communications

Because project managers spend so much of their time communicating, it's essential for them to provide adequate planning for communication. Such planning focuses on who needs what information and when they need it. A project manager must identify the stakeholders' requirements for communication, determine what information is actually needed, and then plan to deliver the needed information on a preset schedule or based on project conditions. The project manager considers all aspects of the communication in this planning activity:

- Who needs the information
- When the information will be needed
- The expected modality of the information
- How the communications will be archived and, if necessary, retrieved
- Communication influences (time zones, languages, working hours, technology, and cultural considerations)

Communication planning is typically completed early in the project, but will happen throughout the project as needed. As part of this planning, the modality of the communications is documented. Some stakeholders may prefer hard-copy documents rather than e-mails. Later in the project, these needs can change. Throughout the project, the needs of the stakeholders, the type of information requested, and the modality of the information should be reviewed for accuracy—and updated if needed.

In the communications management plan, the project manager must consider and document how communications will be stored and retrieved. E-mails are a popular, logical choice but not always the best choice based on the urgency of the message or the stakeholders. Whatever modality is selected—verbal, electronic, or paper-based—there should be some acknowledgement and documentation of the message. Throughout the project, the project manager and the project team may need to retrieve past communications to make current project decisions.

Considering the Project Management Plan and Charter

The project charter is an input to planning communication, because it identifies the key stakeholders and their expected roles and responsibilities. The charter will also offer an indication to the profile of the project and expectations for what constitutes project success.

The project management plan is a key input to communication management planning because it defines the intent of each of the knowledge areas in the project. Consider the related communication triggers that may be needed for schedule, cost, scope, quality, resources, risk, procurement, and, of course, the project stakeholders. Through project integration management, each area of the project affects all other areas of the project—and this is why communication is so important. Without proper communication planning (and execution), the interactions and coordination of the project will likely suffer.

Though project managers do consider all of the project plans, they must also examine the constraints and assumptions that will affect decisions, activities, and stakeholders. Every project has constraints and assumptions. Recall that constraints are any force that limits the project's options. A project constraint, such as contractual obligations, may require extensive communications. The requirements of the contract should be evaluated against the demands of the project staff to determine whether extra resources will be needed to handle the communications. Constraints the project manager should consider when it comes to communications include the following:

- The project team members' geographical locales
- The compatibility of communications software
- Technical capabilities
- Language barriers
- Telephone and videoconferencing abilities

Within the project management plan, you'll rely on the resource management plan to reference categories of resources, management of resources, and how you'll release the resources as needed throughout the project. You'll also reference the stakeholder engagement plan, something I'll address in Chapter 13—but for now, know that it will help guide you on keeping stakeholders engaged in the project.

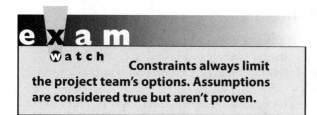

Constraints always limit the project team's options. Assumptions are considered true but aren't proven.

Assumptions will no doubt vary from project to project. Thus, the project manager and the project team should attempt to identify the assumptions made in the project that may hinder successful project communications.

Consider a project operating under the assumption that communication with management can happen only through e-mail. Management, however, expects the project manager to provide formal status reports and daily updates via memos and also needs staffing updates from each of the project team members. These assumptions can impose schedule demands that the project manager doesn't expect.

Though they are not necessarily part of the project management plan, two project documents are also required in your planning: the requirements documentation and the stakeholder register. The requirements documentation may include the requirements for stakeholder communications. The stakeholder register is the directory of who you'll be communicating with.

Leveraging Enterprise Environmental Factors

When planning project communications, project managers should also consider enterprise environmental factors. As a reminder, the following are the basic enterprise environmental factors that need to be considered for communications planning:

- Organizational culture and structure
- Relevant standards and regulations
- Risk thresholds
- Personnel administration policies for your organization
- Organizational communication channels, tools, and systems
- Geographical makeup of the organization

These factors can help the project management team determine what needs to be communicated and to whom. The project manager can also rely on organizational process assets (covered in Chapter 4). The project manager can use proven information from the past to make decisions about the present project. Organizational process assets can also include policies for social media, ethics, security of information, risk, and change management procedures. Your organization may also have a methodology for accessing and storing project communications.

Identifying Communication Requirements

Stakeholders will need different types of information, depending on their interest in the project and the priority of the project. The project manager will need to complete an analysis of the identified stakeholders to determine what information they actually need and how often the information is needed.

There is no value in expending resources on generating information, reports, and analyses for stakeholders who have no interest in the information. An accurate assessment of stakeholders' needs for information is required early in the project planning processes. As a rule of thumb, you should provide information when its presence contributes to success or when a lack of information can contribute to failure.

See the video "Communications Model."

The project manager and the project team can identify the demand for communications using the following:

- Communication requirements from the stakeholder register and stakeholder engagement plan
- Project development approach
- Organization charts
- Communication channels
- Logistics for remote stakeholders
- Project structure within the performing organization
- Stakeholder responsibility relationships
- Departments and disciplines involved with the project work
- Number of individuals involved in the project and their locales
- Internal and external information needs
- Legal requirements for communication
- Stakeholder information

On the PMP exam, and in the real world, the project manager will need to identify the number of communication channels within a project. Here's a magic formula to calculate the number of communication channels:

$$N (N - 1) / 2$$

where N represents the number of identified stakeholders. For example, if a project has 10 stakeholders, the formula would read 10 (10 − 1) / 2 for a total of 45 communication channels. Figure 10-1 illustrates the formula.

Know this formula:
N (N − 1) / 2, where N represents the number of stakeholders. It's easy to remember, and you'll probably encounter it on the PMP exam.

FIGURE 10-1

Communication channels must be identified.

Step 1
Know the formula.

$$\frac{N(N-1)}{2}$$

Step 2
Enter the values.

$$\frac{10(9)}{2}$$

Step 3
Get your answer.

$$\frac{90}{2} = 45$$

Exploring Communication Technologies

Let's face it: A project manager and a project team can take many different avenues to communicate. Project teams can effectively communicate via hallway meetings or formal project status meetings. Information can be transferred from stakeholder to stakeholder through written notes or by using complex online databases and tracking systems.

As part of communication planning, the project manager should identify all of the required and approved methods of communicating during the project. Some sensitive projects may involve classified information that not all stakeholders are privy to, while other projects may involve information that's available for anyone to explore. Whatever the case, the project manager should identify what requirements exist, if any, for the communication modalities.

Communication modalities can also include meetings, reports, memos, e-mails, and so on. The project manager should identify the preferred methods of communicating based on the conditions of the message to be communicated. Consider the following, which may have an effect on the communication plan:

- **Urgency of the information**   When the information is communicated can often be as important as what's being communicated. For some projects, information should be readily available, while for other projects, information needs are less demanding.

- **Technology**   Because of the demands of the project, technology changes may be needed to fulfill the project request. For example, the project may require an internal web site that details project progress. If such a web site does not exist, time and monies will need to be invested into this communication requirement. Also consider the availability of the project stakeholders to access the technology used to communicate.

- **Ease of use**   The project manager should evaluate the abilities of the project team to determine whether appropriate levels of competency exist to fulfill the communication requirements or whether training will be required for the project team.

- **Project environment**   The length of the project can influence the project technology. Advances in technology may replace a long-term project's communication model. A short-term project may not have the same technology requirements as a long-term project but could nevertheless benefit from the successful model a larger project uses. Also consider collocated teams versus virtual teams, languages, and culture.

- **Sensitivity and confidentiality**   The nature of the message may affect how the message is communicated. Consider resource issues, news about vendors, and major disruptions in the project execution, costs, schedule, or risks. Some news is more sensitive than others, so the project manager must determine the most appropriate way to communicate and guard sensitive information.

Examining Communication Skills

Here's a news flash: communication skills are used to send and receive information. Sounds easy, right? If communication is so easy, why are there so many problems on projects stemming from misunderstandings, miscommunications, failures to communicate, and similar communication failings?

Figure 10-2 demonstrates a few different communication models. All models, regardless of the technology involved, include a sender, a message, and a recipient. Depending on the communication model, several additional elements can be included. Here's a summary of all the different parts of communication models:

- **Sender**   The person or group sending the message to the receiver.
- **Encoder**   The device or technology that encodes the message to travel over the medium. For example, a telephone encodes the sender's voice to travel over telephone wires.
- **Medium**   The path the message takes from the sender to the receiver. This is the modality in which the communication travels and typically refers to an electronic model, such as e-mail or telephone.

FIGURE 10-2

Sender models can vary based on the modality of the message.

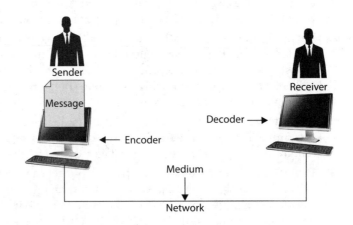

■ **Decoder** The inverse of the encoder. If a message is encoded, a decoder translates it into a usable format. For example, the sender's e-mail message is encoded to travel across the network, and the receiver's computer translates the message back to a usable format.

■ **Receiver** This is, of course, the recipient of the message.

■ **Noise** Includes anything that disrupts the transfer of the message.

■ **Acknowledgement** Verbal and/or nonverbal signs that the message has been received. Just because a message has been received doesn't mean the receiver necessarily agrees with the message.

■ **Possible feedback** The recipient of the message could offer a response or feedback depending on the message and the modality. For example, a face-to-face conversation may offer feedback, while a web site may not.

Creating Successful Communications

The most common type of communication between a sender and a receiver is verbal communication. When verbal communication is involved, the project manager should remember that half of every communication is listening. This means the project manager must confirm that the receiver understands the message being sent. The confirmation of the sent message can be expressed in the recipients' body language, feedback, and verbal confirmation of the sent message. Five terms are used to describe the process of communicating:

■ **Paralingual** The pitch, tone, and inflections in the sender's voice affect the message being sent.

■ **Feedback** The sender confirms that the receiver understands the message by directly asking for a response, questions for clarification, or other confirmation of the sent message.

■ **Active listening** The receiver confirms the message is being received through feedback, questions, prompts for clarity, and other signs of confirmation.

■ **Effective listening** The receiver is involved in the listening experience by paying attention to visual clues from the speaker and paralingual characteristics, and by asking relevant questions.

■ **Nonverbal** Nonverbal clues affect the message being communicated. Facial expressions, hand gestures, and body language contribute to the message.

PMP Coach In interactive communications, such as a meeting, two or more people are communicating at one time. In push communications, such as a group e-mail, the message is pushed out to the recipients. In pull communications, such as information on a web site, the recipients retrieve the information from a central source.

The medium in communication can help or hinder the message. For example, when a project manager talks to a stakeholder in person, the stakeholder has the advantage not only of hearing the message and tone but also of seeing the communicator's body language. Remove body language from a conversation, and the message is interpreted by just the words and tonality. Always be aware of the downsides of various nondirect communication modalities: e-mail, reports, memos, and letters.

Electronic communications are more prevalent now than ever before: e-mail, texting, chats, collaborative software, and web meetings. All of these forms of communications are evolving daily, and the rules of how you communicate with these tools change just as quickly. It's important for the project manager and the project team to establish ground rules for communication when it comes to electronic communication. The project type may dictate what type of communication is appropriate or official and when to use electronic communication versus face-to-face communication.

Depending on the project and the message, different methods can be used to communicate:

- **Interpersonal communication**   Individuals communicating, often face-to-face
- **Small group communication**   Three to six people communicating
- **Public communication**   Sometimes called a one-to-many approach, in which one person is communicating out to many people
- **Mass communication**   No real connection between the sender and receiver, such as a press release or web site
- **Network and social computing communications**   Social media–like presence for communicating project information with and among stakeholders

Creating the Communications Management Plan

Based on stakeholder analysis, the project manager and the project team can determine what communications are needed, to whom communications are to be sent, and who will be responsible for the communication. There's no advantage to supplying stakeholders with information that isn't needed or desired, and the time spent creating and delivering such information is a waste of resources.

A communications management plan can organize and document the processes, types, and expectations of communications. It provides the following:

- The stakeholder communications requirements to communicate the appropriate information as demanded by the stakeholders.
- Information on what is to be communicated, including the expected format, content, and detail—think project reports versus quick e-mail updates.

■ Details on how needed information flows through the project to the appropriate individuals. The communication structure documents where the information will originate, to whom the information will be sent, and in what modality the information is acceptable. This is especially important when dealing with the public, the media, or with sensitive information.

■ Methods for communicating including e-mails, memos, reports, and even press releases.

■ Schedules of when the various types of communication should occur. Some communication, such as status meetings, should happen on a regular schedule, while other communications may be prompted by conditions within the project.

■ Escalation processes and time frames for moving issues upward in the organization when they can't be solved at lower levels.

■ Methods of retrieving information as needed.

■ Instructions on how the communication management plan can be updated as the project progresses.

■ Flowchart of how the communication should flow in the project.

■ Communication constraints based on organization policies, regulations, or technology.

■ Project glossary.

Because communication planning can happen throughout the project, the communications management plan may need to be updated throughout the project. Changes to the project management plan, including the communication management plan, will follow the project's change control process (this can also include changes to the stakeholder engagement plan). There might also be updates to the project schedule for planned communication events and updates to the stakeholder register as stakeholders enter and leave the project.

CERTIFICATION OBJECTIVE 10.02

Managing Project Communications

The process of managing project communications includes gathering project information, distributing project information, and archiving project communications for later retrieval if needed. At the heart of this process, however, is the actual distribution of the information to the appropriate parties. Information distribution ensures that the proper stakeholders get the appropriate information when and how they need it. Essentially, it's the implementation of the communication management plan. The communication management plan details how the information is to be created and dispersed—and also how the dispersed information is archived.

Five elements serve as inputs to managing the project communications:

- **Project management plan**   This plan serves as the guide for communicating project issues within the performing organization. You'll rely on the resource management plan, communication management plan, and the stakeholder engagement plan from the overall project management plan.

- **Project documents**   Project documents will help you determine what information needs to be communicated based on what's happening in the project. Specifically, the change log, issue log, lessons learned register, quality report, risk report, and the stakeholder register will help manage communication.

- **Work performance reports**   The work performance reports document how the project is performing on cost, schedule, quality, and other key performance indicators. Work results, good or bad, serve as inputs to communication because they show progress (or lack of progress), quality issues, and other relevant information.

- **Enterprise environmental factors**   The organization's internal requirements may affect how the project manager and the project team are allowed to communicate and with whom. Regulatory and government requirements will also likely affect how and with whom the project manager can communicate.

- **Organizational process assets**   The organization may have forms, procedures, templates, and electronic workflows established for the project manager and the project team to follow in communications. These elements are all part of organizational process assets that can assist and structure the communications.

Exploring Communication Technology and Methods

As I've already discussed, many different technologies are available to communicate and manage communications. There must be clarification as to which communication modality will be used and in what scenario. How you communicate should be in alignment with the communication message, the technology must be available and reliable, and the stakeholders need to know in what technology they can expect communications from you. Consider e-mail, paper documents, and texting: Which method is acceptable, preferred, and required?

The PMIS can help organize and automate communications. Web sites for the project can help distribute and collect information, information portals can enable searches and sharing of information, and collaborative tools can help the project team communicate with one another. But what good is information if no one can find it? An information retrieval system allows for fast and accurate access to project information. It can be a simple manual filing system, an advanced database repository, or a robust project management software suite. Whatever the approach, the information must be accessible, organized, and secure.

The project team, the project manager, the customer, and other stakeholders may need access to design specs, blueprints, plans, and other project information. A good information retrieval system is reliable and easy to navigate, and it is updated as new information becomes available.

The *PMBOK Guide* lists seven tools and techniques for managing communications:

- **Communication technology**   Using the agreed-upon technology to communicate
- **Communication methods**   Meeting communications expectations as set forth in the communication management plan
- **Communication skills**   Communication competence, feedback, nonverbal communication, and presentations
- **Project management information system**   The automation, provisioning, and collection of information handled through the PMIS (e-mail, fax, voice, social media, and so on)
- **Project reporting**   Meeting the reporting requirements and expectations of the stakeholders
- **Interpersonal and team skills**   Includes active listening, conflict management, cultural awareness, meeting management, networking, and political awareness
- **Meeting management**   Important to successful project management, you'll meet often with the project team and stakeholders

Distributing Information

Throughout the project, the project manager, the project sponsor, the project team, and other stakeholders are going to need information from and to supply information to one another. The methods used for distributing information can vary, but the best modality is the one that's most appropriate to the information being conveyed. In other words, an e-mail may not be the appropriate format in which to share variance information regarding project costs.

Information can be distributed through some of the following methods, given project demands and available technology:

- Project meetings
- Hard-copy documentation
- Databases
- Faxes
- E-mails
- Telephone calls
- Videoconferences
- Project web site

Examining the Results of Communication Management

Communications management results in the following:

- **Project communications** All of the project communications are part of the organizational process assets. These include e-mails, memos, letters, and faxes. In some instances, the project team can also contribute by keeping their records in a project notebook.

- **Project management plan updates** Changes to the project management plan will follow the integrated change control process for the project. Specifically, you may need to update the communication plan and the stakeholder engagement plan.

- **Project document updates** Project documents that can be updated as a result of communications management include the issue log, schedule, risk register, stakeholder register, and lessons learned register. When lessons learned sessions are completed, they're available to be used and applied in the current project. They are now part of the organization's process assets.

- **Organizational process assets updates** Reports are formal communications on project activities, their status, and conditions. Management, customers, and policies within the performing organization may have differing requirements regarding when reports are needed. Presentations are useful in providing information to customers, management, the project team, and other stakeholders. The delivery and degree of formality of the presentation should be appropriate for the conditions and information being delivered within the project.

CERTIFICATION OBJECTIVE 10.03

Monitoring Project Communications

The project manager must know the quality being communicated among the project team, the project customers, the vendors, and even among the public. Good communication skills are a key asset for the project manager and her team, but this involves more than just being able to speak with stakeholders. Monitoring the project communications is an integral part of the project manager's daily role. The project manager needs to examine, on a regular basis, the effectiveness of what's being communicated in the project, who needs to be informed of the project events, and how the information is packaged, delivered, and protected.

Monitoring the project communications doesn't mean that only the project manager reads every communication about the project. It means that the project manager is responsible for the effectiveness of communications—she ensures that actions are taken so that the appropriate project stakeholders communicate with one another. Of course, the project manager will issue the most communications regarding the project, but she must also coordinate bringing stakeholders together so that the parties can contribute to the project information. A good project manager is a good communicator, but also a good facilitator.

Preparing for Communications Monitoring

It takes some foresight to monitor how project communications take place, and part of this comes from project planning. By thinking through the strengths and weaknesses of project communications, the project manager and the project team can identify appropriate strategies for ensuring that the correct stakeholders get the correct information at the correct time. Following are the inputs for communication monitoring:

- **Project management plan** The project management plan ensures that the project information will be communicated to meet the stakeholder expectations for communication in all areas of the project. This includes the frequency of the communications, the parties that need to be involved in the communications, and the modality of the communications. You'll need the resource management plan, the communication management plan, and the stakeholder engagement plan from the project management plan.

- **Project documents** The project's issue log documents known issues, their effect on the project, issue owners, dates for resolution, and the outcome of known issues. The issue log is needed in the monitor communications process because the known issues will need to be discussed and monitored until they are resolved. You'll also rely on the lessons learned register and the existing project communications. Existing communications, such as performance reports, status reports, schedule updates, costs, and risks, affect how the project manager communicates, how the news is communicated, and the sensitivity of the communication.

- **Work performance date** The health of the project will affect the project communications. Consider any variance in costs, schedule, and scope and how the project manager must react to, communicate, and monitor this information.

- **Enterprise environmental factors** The organizational culture and politics, communications channels, technologies, geographical location, and the communication trends and habits all are inputs to monitoring communications.

- **Organizational process assets** The organization may rely on templates, forms, and standardized approaches to communicate and monitor the communications in the project. Consider archival practices, through the PMIS, security of the documentation, policies, media relations, and approved modalities for project communications.

Reviewing the Monitoring Communications Tools and Techniques

There are five tools and technique for monitoring communications in a project:

- **Expert judgment** You'll use experts to monitor communications internally and externally.
- **PMIS** The PMIS can help you capture and store communications within the project, and to make certain communications are read, distributed, and properly accessed within the project.
- **Data representation** You can use a stakeholder engagement matrix (which I'll discuss in Chapter 13) to gauge how engaged stakeholders are now and create goals for future engagements.
- **Interpersonal and team skills** Discussion with the project team, requests from stakeholders, observation, and conflict resolution are all parts of monitoring communications.
- **Meetings** Of course there will be meetings with the project team, customers, management, and other relevant stakeholders.

CERTIFICATION OBJECTIVE 10.04

Reporting Project Performance

Throughout the project, customers and other stakeholders will need updates on the project performance. The work performance information, the status of what's been completed and what's left to do, is always at the heart of performance reporting. Stakeholders want to be kept abreast of how the project is performing.

Performance reporting is the process of collecting, organizing, and disseminating information on how project resources are being used to complete the project objectives. In other words, the people footing the bill and affected by the outcome of the project need some confirmation that things are going the way the project manager has promised.

Performance reporting covers more than just cost and schedule, though these are the most common concerns. Another huge issue is the influence of risks on the project's success. The project manager and the project team must continue to monitor and evaluate risks, including pending risks and their impacts on the project's success.

Another major concern with reporting is the level of quality. No one will praise the project manager and the project team for completing the project on schedule and on budget if the quality of the work is unacceptable. In fact, the project could be declared a failure and cancelled as a result of poor quality, or the project team may be forced to redo the work, business could be lost, or individuals could even be harmed as a result of the poor quality of the project work.

Reviewing Project Performance

The project manager will host performance review meetings to ascertain the progress and level of success the project team is having with the project work. Performance review meetings focus on the work that has been completed and how the work results measure up to the schedule and cost estimates. In addition, the project manager and the project team will evaluate the project scope to protect it from change and creep. The project manager and the project team will also examine quality and its effect on the project as a whole. Finally, the project manager must lead a discussion on pending or past risks and then determine any new risks, as well as the overall risk likelihood and its potential impact on the project's success.

Completing Trend Analysis

Picture this: You're a project manager for a long-term project. You'd like to examine the project's performance for the past few years to predict what the upcoming performance will be like. You're doing trend analysis, an approach that studies trends in past performances in order to predict what upcoming experiences might resemble. It is great for long projects, analysis of team performance, and predicting future activities.

Examining the Results of Performance Reporting

The goal of performance reporting is to share information regarding the project performance with the appropriate stakeholders. Of course, performance reporting is not something that occurs only at the end of the project or after a project phase. Instead, it is done according to a regular schedule, as detailed in the communication plan or as project conditions warrant. Outputs of performance reporting include such things as the following:

- **Performance reports**   These are the results and summation of the project performance analysis. The communication management plan will detail the type of report needed based on the conditions within the project, the timing of the communication, and the demands of the project stakeholders.

- **Forecasting**   Will the project end on schedule? Will the project be on budget? How much longer will it take to complete the project? And how much more money will this project need to finish?

- **Change requests**   Performance results may prompt change requests to some area or areas of the project. The change requests should flow into the change control system for consideration and then be approved or denied.

- **Recommended corrective actions**   Corrective actions bring future project performance back in alignment with the project plan.

e**x**am

Forecasting project performance can use a time series method, such as earned value management, linear prediction, or the growth curve of the project. Forecasting can also use causal **and econometric approaches to predict project performance. The Delphi Technique, scenarios, and forecasts by analogy are all examples of judgmental methods.**

INSIDE THE EXAM

Communication is a project manager's most important skill. Project managers spend the majority of their time communicating. Because the project manager is expected to spend so much time communicating, you can bet she needs a plan to determine what needs to be communicated, to whom, and when. The communications management plan is the comprehensive plan that the project manager and the project team rely on for guidance to all communication.

The organizational structure affects the level of communications the project manager can expect. Matrix structures must include the functional managers of the project team from the different units within the organization, whereas a functional organization doesn't require the same level of complexity in reporting.

The basic communication model consists of a sender, a message, a medium, and a receiver. When technology is involved, the project can become more complex: encoders, the medium, and decoders are included. Consider sending an e-mail: You are the sender, Jane is the recipient, and the message is the information on the page to be sent via the e-mail system. The encoder is your outgoing e-mail server and software, and Jane's incoming e-mail server and software on her computer is the decoder. The network between the e-mail servers, computers, and e-mail software are all the medium. Any interference affecting the medium is noise and could possibly disrupt the message during transmission.

Management, customers, and other concerned stakeholders will be interested in the project performance. The project manager will need to meet their expectations on an established schedule or based on conditions within the project. One of the most common methods for showing performance is through earned value analysis.

Stakeholder management is vital to a project's success. Stakeholders expect the project manager to lead stakeholder management and to include them in the project. Issue management is paramount. If a project manager fails to resolve project issues that are important to the stakeholder, the project is likely to be riddled with delays, conflict, and stakeholder anxiety.

CERTIFICATION SUMMARY

Communication is a project manager's most important skill. Project managers must communicate with management, customers, the project team members, and the rest of the stakeholders involved with the project. The project manager's foundation is communication. Without effective communication, how will the right work get completed, progress reported, and information dispersed?

Communications planning centers on two questions: "Who needs what information, and when do they need it?" Consider all the different channels for communication on any project. That's many different possibilities for information to be lost, messages to be skewed, and progress to be hindered.

The formula for calculating the communication channels is $N (N - 1) / 2$, where N represents the number of stakeholders. As a general rule, larger projects require more detail—and detail means more planning for communications.

The communications management plan organizes and documents the communication processes, acceptable modalities for types of communication, and the stakeholder expectations for communication. The plan should detail how information is gathered, organized, accessed, and dispersed. The plan should also provide a schedule of expected communication, such as project status meetings, based on a calendar schedule. Some communications are prompted by conditions within the project, such as cost variances, schedule variances, or other performance-related issues.

The communication model illustrates the flow of communication from the sender to the receiver. The sender sends the message. The message is then encoded by the encoder and travels over the medium. Once it arrives at its destination, a decoder decodes the message for the receiver. This model is easy to remember if you apply the processes to a telephone call.

Within a communication, four characteristics affect the message:

- **Paralingual** Pitch, tone, and voice inflections
- **Feedback** Sender confirmation of the message by asking questions, requesting a response, or other confirmation signals
- **Active listening** Receiver confirms message receipt, is involved in the conversation, summarizes the message back to confirm understanding
- **Nonverbal** Facial expressions, hand gestures, and body language

KEY TERMS

To pass the PMP exam, you will need to memorize the following terms and their definitions. For maximum value, create your own flashcards based on these definitions and review them daily. Further explanation can also be found in both this chapter and the Glossary.

active listening   Occurs when the receiver confirms the message is being received by offering feedback, questions, prompts for clarity, and other signs of having received the message.

communications formula   The formula N (N – 1) / 2 shows the number of communication channels in a project. N represents the total number of stakeholders.

communications management plan   A plan that documents and organizes the stakeholder needs for communication. This plan covers the communications system, its documentation, the flow of communication, modalities of communication, schedules for communications, information retrieval, and any other stakeholder requirements for communications.

decoder   Part of the communications model; it is the inverse of the encoder. If a message is encoded, a decoder translates it back to usable format.

encoder   Part of the communications model; the device or technology that packages the message to travel via the medium.

feedback   Sender confirmation of the message by asking questions, requesting a response, or other confirmation signals.

forecasting   An educated estimate of how long the project will take to complete; can also refer to how much the project may cost to complete.

interactive communication   Communication between two or more parties, usually through active communications such as meetings, phone calls, and videoconferencing.

issue   Any point of contention, debate, or unmade decision in the project that may affect the project's success.

issue log   A log documenting all identified issues affecting the project. Each issue is assigned an issue owner and an ideal date for resolution, and its status is maintained through the issue log.

medium   Part of the communications model: the path the message takes from the sender to the receiver; the modality in which the communication travels. Typically refers to an electronic model, such as e-mail or the telephone.

monitor communications   Project management process that ensures that communication happens according to the project's communications management plan.

nonverbal   Approximately 55 percent of oral communication is nonverbal. Facial expressions, hand gestures, and body language contribute to the message.

paralingual   The pitch, tone, and inflections in the sender's voice affect the message being sent.

progress reports   Provide current information on the project work completed to date.

pull communications   Information is pulled from a repository, such as a database or web site.

push communications   Information is pushed to the recipients, such as an e-mail or a text message.

receiver   Part of the communications model: the recipient of the message.

sender   Part of the communications model: the person or group delivering the message to the receiver.

stakeholder registry   A document that defines each stakeholder, their project requirements, their influence on the project, phases of interest, details on the stakeholders contributions, and their contact information for the project.

status reports   Provide current information on the project cost, budget, scope, and other relevant information.

TWO-MINUTE DRILL

Communications Planning

- ❏ Communication centers on who needs what information, when the information is needed, and how the information is delivered.
- ❏ Communication requirements are set by stakeholders.
- ❏ Communication planning is accomplished early in the planning process.
- ❏ Communications are linked to the organizational structure of the performing organization.
- ❏ Constraints and assumptions can affect the communications planning.
- ❏ Acknowledgment of a message can be positive or negative. Just because a receiver got the message, it doesn't mean she has to agree with it.
- ❏ The communication plan provides instructions on the communication methods, such as hard copies, reports, and e-mail.

Managing Project Communications

- ❏ The choice of media is dictated by the urgency and importance of the message to be communicated.
- ❏ The project manager should be versed in meeting management techniques to run a meeting effectively. Agendas, minutes, and a timetable should be enforced at most meetings.
- ❏ The project manager should identify a method to access needed information between regularly scheduled communications for the project stakeholders.

Monitoring Project Communications

- ❏ The project manager is responsible for managing project communication.
- ❏ Face-to-face meetings are best for resolving issues with stakeholders.
- ❏ Issue logs document issues with the stakeholders or the project. When issues are resolved, the issue log should be updated to reflect the resolution.
- ❏ Communications can bring about project change requests depending on the information communicated to the stakeholders.

Reporting Project Performance

- ❑ Status reporting provides current information on the project.
- ❑ Progress reporting provides information on what the team has accomplished and may include information on what is yet to be accomplished.
- ❑ Forecasting provides information on how the remainder of the project or phase is expected to proceed.
- ❑ Variance analysis examines the reasons why cost, schedule, scope, quality, and other factors may vary from what was planned.
- ❑ Trend analysis is the study of trends over time to reveal patterns and expectations of future results.
- ❑ Earned value analysis is a series of formulas that reveal and predict project performance.

SELF TEST

1. In the project communication model, many elements must be present to allow communication to occur. One element, noise, can prevent the effectiveness of the communication message. Of the following, which one is an example of noise?
   A. E-mail servers
   B. Ad hoc conversations
   C. Contractual agreements
   D. Distance

2. You are the project manager of a large technical project. You believe that Jose has received an important message but does not agree with it based on his body language. This is known as what?
   A. Acknowledgement
   B. Transmission
   C. Negotiation
   D. Decoder

3. You are the project manager for the LKH Project. Management has requested that you create a document detailing what information will be expected from stakeholders and to whom that information will be disseminated. Management is asking for which one of the following?

   A. The roles and responsibilities matrix
   B. The scope management plan
   C. The communications management plan
   D. The communications worksheet

4. You are the project manager of the HBQ Project in your organization. This project will last for six months, and you must communicate with 35 stakeholders throughout the project. You and the project team will create a communication management plan as part of project planning. Which of the following will help you, the project manager, complete the needed communication management plan by identifying the stakeholders' communication needs?

   A. Identification of all communication channels
   B. Formal documentation of all communication channels
   C. Formal documentation of all stakeholders
   D. Lessons learned from previous similar projects

5. You are the project manager for the JGI Project, which has 32 stakeholders involved. How many communication channels do you have?

   A. Depends on the number of project team members
   B. 496
   C. 32
   D. 1

6. You are the project manager for the KLN Project. You had 19 stakeholders on this project and have added 3 team members. How many more communication channels do you have now compared to before?

   A. 171
   B. 231
   C. 60
   D. 1

7. You are the project manager of the HQS Project for your organization. Your project will utilize both push and pull communications on a daily basis. A memo has been sent to you and project team members and the project customers from the project sponsor. In this instance, who is the encoder?

   A. Project sponsor
   B. Project manager
   C. Project team members
   D. Project customers

8. Mary is a project manager of the JQL Project for her company. This project is a multinational project with stakeholders in three countries: the United States, Belgium, and Germany. In this project, Mary will need to plan for project assumptions and constraints that affect how she and the other project stakeholders will communicate. Which one of the following is an example of a project communication constraint?

   A. Ad hoc conversations through web conferencing software
   B. Demands for formal reports
   C. Stakeholder management
   D. The geographical locales of the project team

9. Project managers can present project information in many different ways. Which one of the following is *not* a method a project manager can use to present project performance?

   A. Histograms
   B. S-curves
   C. Bar charts
   D. RACI charts

10. How the message is communicated affects the meaning of the message. Of the following, which term describes the pitch and tone of an individual's voice?

   A. Paralingual
   B. Feedback
   C. Effective listening
   D. Active listening

11. You are the project manager of the KMH Project. This project is slated to last eight years. You have just calculated EVM and have a CV of −$3500, which is outside of the acceptable thresholds for your project. What type of report is needed for management?

   A. Progress report
   B. Forecast report
   C. Exception report
   D. Trends report

12. You are presenting your project performance to your key stakeholders. Several of the stakeholders receive phone calls during your presentation, and this is distracting from your message. This is an example of what?

   A. Noise
   B. Negative feedback
   C. Outside communications
   D. Message distracter

13. You are the project manager for the OOK Project. You will be hosting project meetings every week. Of the following, which one is *not* a valid rule for project meetings?

   A. Schedule recurring meetings as soon as possible.
   B. Allow project meetings to last as long as needed.
   C. Distribute meeting agendas prior to the meeting start.
   D. Allow the project team to have input to the agenda.

14. As a PMP candidate, you must be familiar with the communication model and the structure of communication in a project. The three basic elements needed for communication in project management include which of the following?

   A. Words, sentences, paragraphs
   B. Proper grammar, spelling, ideas
   C. Verbal, nonverbal, action
   D. Sender, receiver, message

15. Your project is slated to last three years and will include stakeholders from four countries. In this project, you'll rely on teleconferencing and web collaboration software to reduce the travel costs throughout the project life cycle. Based on this information, which one of the following is a project factor that may affect project communication?

   A. Communications management
   B. Management by walking around
   C. The project length
   D. Variance analysis reporting

16. Your project team relies on telephone calls and e-mails to communicate information on a daily basis. As the project manager, you'd like to see more interactive, face-to-face meetings for project team members that are located in the same geographical area. A team member asks why, and you say it's because of the advantages offered by nonverbal language. What percentage of a message is sent through nonverbal communications, such as facial expressions, hand gestures, and body language?

   A. More than 50 percent
   B. 30 to 40 percent
   C. 20 to 30 percent
   D. 10 to 20 percent

17. One of the organizational process assets that your project communications management plan must address is the concept of lessons learned documentation. When does lessons learned identification take place?

    A. At the end of the project

    B. At the end of each project phase

    C. Throughout the project life cycle

    D. Whenever a lesson has been learned

18. Why should a project team complete lessons learned documentation?

    A. To ensure project closure

    B. To show management what they've accomplished in the project

    C. To show the project stakeholders what they've accomplished in the project

    D. To help future project teams complete their projects more efficiently

19. Often as a project manager you will have to negotiate. Negotiations work best in which environment?

    A. Caution and yielding

    B. Sincerity, honesty, and extreme caution

    C. Mutual respect and admiration

    D. Mutual respect and cooperation

20. You are the project manager for the PMU Project. Your project team has 13 members. You have been informed that next week your project will receive the 7 additional members you requested. How many channels of communication will you have next week?

    A. 1

    B. 78

    C. 190

    D. 201

21. You are the project manager of the NH Project for your company, and you're required to use earned value management in the project. The outcomes of earned value management contribute to the requirements and targets for performance reporting. Performance reporting should generally provide information on all of the following except for which one?

    A. Scope

    B. Schedule

    C. Labor issues

    D. Quality

22. Sam is the project manager of the AZA Project for your company, and he is required to use earned value management in the project. Management has created performance targets for CPI and SPI based on the project team's overall performance in the project. Sam must follow the enterprise environmental factors for reporting all components of EVM. Which one of the following is an output from performance reporting?

    A. Trend analysis
    B. EVM
    C. Variance analysis
    D. Change request

23. As a PMP candidate, you must be familiar with the project communication processes, the communications model, and the terminology associated with communications. For instance, the process of sending information from the project manager to the project team is called what?

    A. Functioning
    B. Matrixing
    C. Blended communications
    D. Transmitting

24. George is the project manager of the 7YH Project. In this project, George considers the relationship between himself and the customer to be of utmost importance. Which one of the following is a valid reason for George's belief in this?

    A. The customer will complete George's performance evaluation. A poor communication model between George and the customer will affect his project bonus.
    B. The customer is not familiar with project management. George must educate the customer about the process.
    C. The customer is always right.
    D. The communication between the customer and George can convey the project objectives more clearly than can the language in the project contract.

25. Betty is the project manager for her organization and she's currently managing the HGF Project. Her project has 45 stakeholders in two different time zones. According to the communications model, which one of the following means that communications occur when Betty communicates with the project team?

    A. The transfer of knowledge
    B. The outputting of knowledge
    C. The presence of knowledge
    D. The transmission of knowledge

A

SELF TEST ANSWERS

1. In the project communication model, many elements must be present to allow communication to occur. One element, noise, can prevent the effectiveness of the communication message. Of the following, which one is an example of noise?
    A. E-mail servers
    B. Ad hoc conversations
    C. Contractual agreements
    D. Distance

    ☑ **D.** Noise is anything that interferes with the transmission and understanding of the message. Distance is an example of noise.
    ☒ **A, B,** and **C** are incorrect. **A,** e-mail servers, is incorrect because it is an example of a decoder. **B** is incorrect; ad hoc conversations are informal conversations. **C,** contractual agreements, are a type of formal communication.

2. You are the project manager of a large technical project. You believe that Jose has received an important message but does not agree with it based on his body language. This is known as what?
    A. Acknowledgement
    B. Transmission
    C. Negotiation
    D. Decoder

    ☑ **A.** Acknowledgement means that Jose has received the message but may not agree with it.
    ☒ **B, C,** and **D** are incorrect. A transmission is the output of the message, negotiation is not relevant to this scenario, and a decoder is the mechanism for decoding the message.

3. You are the project manager for the LKH Project. Management has requested that you create a document detailing what information will be expected from stakeholders and to whom that information will be disseminated. Management is asking for which one of the following?
    A. The roles and responsibilities matrix
    B. The scope management plan
    C. The communications management plan
    D. The communications worksheet

> ☑ **C.** Management is requesting a communication management plan, which details the requirements and expectations for communicating information among the project stakeholders.
> ☒ **A, B,** and **D** are incorrect. A is incorrect because a roles and responsibilities matrix depicts who does what and who makes which decisions. **B,** the scope management plan, is also incorrect because this plan explains how changes to the scope may be allowed depending on the circumstances. **D** is not a valid answer for this question.

4. You are the project manager of the HBQ Project in your organization. This project will last for six months, and you must communicate with 35 stakeholders throughout the project. You and the project team will create a communication management plan as part of project planning. Which of the following will help you, the project manager, complete the needed communication management plan by identifying the stakeholders' communication needs?
    A. Identification of all communication channels
    B. Formal documentation of all communication channels
    C. Formal documentation of all stakeholders
    D. Lessons learned from previous similar projects

> ☑ **D.** Lessons learned and historical information from a previous project are ideal inputs to communications planning.
> ☒ **A, B,** and **C** are incorrect. These answers do not fully answer the question. Lessons learned from previous similar projects is the best tool for identifying stakeholders' requirements for communication.

5. You are the project manager for the JGI Project, which has 32 stakeholders involved. How many communication channels do you have?
    A. Depends on the number of project team members
    B. 496
    C. 32
    D. 1

☑ **B.** Using the formula N (N − 1) / 2, where N represents the number of stakeholders, you have 496 communication channels.

☒ **A, C,** and **D** are incorrect. These values do not reflect the number of communication channels on the project.

6. You are the project manager for the KLN Project. You had 19 stakeholders on this project and have added 3 team members. How many more communication channels do you have now compared to before?

   A. 171
   B. 231
   C. 60
   D. 1

☑ **C.** This is a tough question, but it's typical of the PMP exam. The question asks how many more communication channels exist. You'll have to calculate the new value, which is 231, and then subtract the original value, which is 171, for a total of 60 new channels.

☒ **A, B,** and **D** are incorrect. **A** is incorrect because 171 is the original number of communication channels. **B** is incorrect because this value reflects the new number of communication channels. **D** is not a valid answer.

7. You are the project manager of the HQS Project for your organization. Your project will utilize both push and pull communications on a daily basis. A memo has been sent to you and project team members and the project customers from the project sponsor. In this instance, who is the encoder?

   A. Project sponsor
   B. Project manager
   C. Project team members
   D. Project customers

☑ **A.** The project sponsor is the source, or encoder, of the memo because this is the sender of the memo.

☒ **B, C,** and **D** are incorrect. They are all recipients of the memo, not the sender, so they cannot be the source of the message.

8.   Mary is a project manager of the JQL Project for her company. This project is a multinational project with stakeholders in three countries: the United States, Belgium, and Germany. In this project, Mary will need to plan for project assumptions and constraints that affect how she and the other project stakeholders will communicate. Which one of the following is an example of a project communication constraint?
   A.   Ad hoc conversations through web conferencing software
   B.   Demands for formal reports
   C.   Stakeholder management
   D.   The geographical locales of the project team

   ☑   **D.** Team members who are located physically close together can be a communications constraint, because it's tougher to communicate when distance between team members exists.
   ☒   **A, B,** and **C** are incorrect. These are not project communications constraints.

9.   Project managers can present project information in many different ways. Which one of the following is *not* a method a project manager can use to present project performance?
   A.   Histograms
   B.   S-curves
   C.   Bar charts
   D.   RACI charts

   ☑   **D.** RACI charts do not show project performance, but the relationship between roles on various tasks of the resources involved in the project.
   ☒   **A, B,** and **C** are incorrect. These answers do present project performance.

10.   How the message is communicated affects the meaning of the message. Of the following, which term describes the pitch and tone of an individual's voice?
   A.   Paralingual
   B.   Feedback
   C.   Effective listening
   D.   Active listening

   ☑   **A.** Paralingual is a term used to describe the pitch and tone of one's voice.
   ☒   **B, C,** and **D** are incorrect. **B,** feedback, is a request to confirm the information sent in the conversation. **C,** effective listening, is the ability to understand the message through what is said, facial expressions, gestures, tone and pitch, and so on. **D,** active listening, is the process of confirming what is understood and asking for clarification when needed.

11. You are the project manager of the KMH Project. This project is slated to last eight years. You have just calculated EVM and have a CV of –$3500, which is outside of the acceptable thresholds for your project. What type of report is needed for management?
    A. Progress report
    B. Forecast report
    C. Exception report
    D. Trends report

    > ☑ **C.** An exception report is typically completed when variances exceed a given limit.
    > ☒ **A, B,** and **D** are incorrect. **A** is incorrect because a progress report describes the progress of the project or phase. **B** is incorrect because this is not a valid answer. **D,** a trends report, is an analysis of project trends over time.

12. You are presenting your project performance to your key stakeholders. Several of the stakeholders receive phone calls during your presentation, and this is distracting from your message. This is an example of what?
    A. Noise
    B. Negative feedback
    C. Outside communications
    D. Message distracter

    > ☑ **A.** Noise is the correct answer because their phone calls are distracting from your message.
    > ☒ **B, C,** and **D** are incorrect. They do not answer the question.

13. You are the project manager for the OOK Project. You will be hosting project meetings every week. Of the following, which one is *not* a valid rule for project meetings?
    A. Schedule recurring meetings as soon as possible.
    B. Allow project meetings to last as long as needed.
    C. Distribute meeting agendas prior to the meeting start.
    D. Allow the project team to have input to the agenda.

    > ☑ **B.** Project meetings should have a set time limit.
    > ☒ **A, C,** and **D** are incorrect. These are good attributes of project team meetings.

14. As a PMP candidate, you must be familiar with the communication model and the structure of communication in a project. The three basic elements needed for communication in project management include which of the following?

A. Words, sentences, paragraphs

B. Proper grammar, spelling, ideas

C. Verbal, nonverbal, action

D. Sender, receiver, message

> ☑   **D.** The three parts of communication are sender, receiver, and message.
> ☒   **A, B,** and **C** are incorrect.

15. Your project is slated to last three years and will include stakeholders from four countries. In this project, you'll rely on teleconferencing and web collaboration software to reduce the travel costs throughout the project life cycle. Based on this information, which one of the following is a factor that may affect project communication?

A. Communications management

B. Management by walking around

C. The project length

D. Variance analysis reporting

> ☑   **C.** The project duration is the only factor that may affect project communication. Project communication is always needed, but longer, larger projects will require more communications than shorter, smaller scoped projects.
> ☒   **A, B,** and **D** are incorrect. **A** is incorrect because communication management focuses on managing communication, not performance. **B,** management by walking around, is an effective management style, but it does not reflect project performance. **D,** variance analysis, is incorrect because it focuses on the root causes of variances within the project, but not solely on the project performance.

16. Your project team relies on telephone calls and e-mails to communicate information on a daily basis. As the project manager, you'd like to see more interactive, face-to-face meetings for project team members that are located in the same geographical area. A team member asks why, and you say it's because of the advantages offered by nonverbal language. What percentage of a message is sent through nonverbal communications, such as facial expressions, hand gestures, and body language?

A. More than 50 percent

B. 30 to 40 percent

C. 20 to 30 percent

D. 10 to 20 percent

   ☑ **A.** More than 50 percent of a message is conveyed through nonverbal communications.
   ☒ **B, C,** and **D** are incorrect.

17. One of the organizational process assets that your project communications management plan must address is the concept of lessons learned documentation. When does lessons learned identification take place?
  A. At the end of the project
  B. At the end of each project phase
  C. Throughout the project life cycle
  D. Whenever a lesson has been learned

   ☑ **C.** Lessons learned takes place throughout the project life cycle, not just at the end of the project or its phases.
   ☒ **A, B,** and **D** are incorrect. Lessons are learned throughout the project life cycle.

18. Why should a project team complete lessons learned documentation?
  A. To ensure project closure
  B. To show management what they've accomplished in the project
  C. To show the project stakeholders what they've accomplished in the project
  D. To help future project teams complete their projects more efficiently

   ☑ **D.** Lessons learned documentation helps future project teams complete their projects with more efficiency and effectiveness.
   ☒ **A, B,** and **C** are incorrect. Each statement does not reflect the intent of lessons learned documentation: to help future project teams.

19. Often as a project manager you will have to negotiate. Negotiations work best in which environment?
  A. Caution and yielding
  B. Sincerity, honesty, and extreme caution
  C. Mutual respect and admiration
  D. Mutual respect and cooperation

   ☑ **D.** Mutual respect and cooperation is the environment needed for fair and balanced negotiations.
   ☒ **A, B,** and **C** are incorrect. **A,** caution and yielding, is not a good environment for negotiations. **B,** although tempting, is not the best answer. **C** is incorrect because the people involved in negotiations don't necessarily need to admire one another.

20. You are the project manager for the PMU Project. Your project team has 13 members. You have been informed that next week your project will receive the 7 additional members you requested. How many channels of communication will you have next week?

A. 1

B. 78

C. 190

D. 201

> ☑ **C.** The project currently has 13 team members, and next week 7 additional team members will come aboard, thus making a total of 20 team members. Using the formula N (N − 1) / 2, where N is the number of identified stakeholders, the communication channels equal 190.
> ☒ **A, B,** and **D** are incorrect.

21. You are the project manager of the NH Project for your company, and you're required to use earned value management in the project. The outcomes of earned value management contribute to the requirements and targets for performance reporting. Performance reporting should generally provide information on all of the following except for which one?

A. Scope

B. Schedule

C. Labor issues

D. Quality

> ☑ **C.** Labor issues are not part of performance reporting.
> ☒ **A, B,** and **D** are incorrect. They are all part of performance reporting.

22. Sam is the project manager of the AZA Project for your company, and he is required to use earned value management in the project. Management has created performance targets for CPI and SPI based on the project team's overall performance in the project. Sam must follow the enterprise environmental factors for reporting all components of EVM. Which one of the following is an output from performance reporting?

A. Trend analysis

B. EVM

C. Variance analysis

D. Change request

☑ **D.** Of all the answers, a change request is the only acceptable answer. Incidentally, there are two outputs of performance reporting: change requests and performance reports.

☒ **A, B,** and **C** are incorrect. **A,** trend analysis, is the study of project performance results to determine whether the project is improving or failing. It is a tool used as part of performance reporting, but it is not an output of performance reporting. **B** and **C** are also tools used in performance reporting, but they are not an output of the process.

23. As a PMP candidate, you must be familiar with the project communication processes, the communications model, and the terminology associated with communications. For instance, the process of sending information from the project manager to the project team is called what?
    A. Functioning
    B. Matrixing
    C. Blended communications
    D. Transmitting

☑ **D.** When information is sent, it is considered to be transmitted.

☒ **A, B,** and **C** are incorrect. Functioning, matrix, and blended communications are not valid communication models.

24. George is the project manager of the 7YH Project. In this project, George considers the relationship between himself and the customer to be of utmost importance. Which one of the following is a valid reason for George's belief in this?
    A. The customer will complete George's performance evaluation. A poor communication model between George and the customer will affect his project bonus.
    B. The customer is not familiar with project management. George must educate the customer about the process.
    C. The customer is always right.
    D. The communication between the customer and George can convey the project objectives more clearly than can the language in the project contract.

☑ **D.** George and the customer's relationship can allow clearer communication on the project objectives than what may be expressed in the project contract. The contract should take precedence on any issues, but direct contact is often the best way to achieve clear and concise communication.

☒ **A, B,** and **C** are incorrect. **A** is incorrect because the focus is on personal gain rather than the good of the project. **B** is incorrect because the customer does not necessarily need to be educated about the project management process. **C** is incorrect because the customer is not always right—the contract will take precedence in any disagreements.

25. Betty is the project manager for her organization and she's currently managing the HGF Project. Her project has 45 stakeholders in two different time zones. According to the communications model, which one of the following means that communications occur when Betty communicates with the project team?

A. The transfer of knowledge
B. The outputting of knowledge
C. The presence of knowledge
D. The transmission of knowledge

☑ **A.** The transfer of knowledge is evidence that communication has occurred.

☒ **B, C,** and **D** are incorrect. B and C do not necessarily mean that knowledge has originated from the source and that it has been transferred to the recipient. **D** is incorrect because messages are transmitted, but knowledge is transferred.

Chapter 11

Introducing Project Risk Management

CERTIFICATION OBJECTIVES

11.01	Planning for Risk Management	11.06	Implementing Risk Responses
11.02	Identifying Risks	11.07	Monitoring Risks
11.03	Using Qualitative Risk Analysis	✓	Two-Minute Drill
11.04	Preparing for Quantitative Risk Analysis	Q&A	Self Test
11.05	Planning for Risk Responses		

Risk is everywhere. It's inherent in the activities we choose—from driving a car to parachuting. Within a project, risks are unplanned events or conditions that can have positive or negative effects on a project's success. Not all risks are bad, but almost all are seen as a threat. Even launching a project represents risk, because the project could succeed or fail—there's uncertainty in the endeavor.

The risks that activities bring are an exchange for the benefits we get from accepting the risks. If a person chooses to jump out of a perfectly good airplane for the thrill of the fall, the exhilaration of the parachute opening, and the view of Earth rushing up, there is still a risk that the chute may not open—a risk that thrill-seekers are willing to accept.

Project managers, to some extent, are like thrill-seekers. Parachutists complete training, pack their chutes, check and double-check their equipment, and make certain there's an emergency chute for those "just-in-case" scenarios. Project managers—good project managers—take a similar approach.

Risks in a project, should they come to fruition, can mean total project failure, increased costs, and extended project duration, among other things. Risk often has a negative connotation, but as it does for the parachutist, the acceptance of the risk can also offer a reward. For the parachutist, the risk is certain death—but the reward is the thrill of the activity. For project managers, risk can mean failure, but the reward can mean a time or cost savings as well as other benefits. After a risk event happens, it's known as an issue. This chapter focuses on managing risks before they become issues.

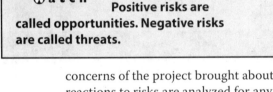

Positive risks are called opportunities. Negative risks are called threats.

Risk management is the process by which the project manager and project team identify project risks, analyze and rank them, and determine what actions, if any, need to be taken to avert these threats. Associated with this process are the costs, schedule, and quality concerns of the project brought about by the solutions to those risks. In addition, the reactions to risks are analyzed for any secondary risks that the solutions may have created.

In this chapter, we'll discuss risk management planning, risk identification and analysis, response planning and implementation, and monitoring the identified risks. For the PMP exam, you'll need to have a firm grasp of these concepts. You'll be taking a *real* risk if you don't know them well.

Building a Strong Risk Understanding

Risks in project management are either threats, which are negative risk events, or opportunities, which are positive risk events. Negative risk events are easy to see: loss of data, potential for injury, late resource delivery from a vendor. Positive risk events are sometimes cloudier to see, but they do exist. Consider investing in a faster piece of equipment, hiring a vendor to do a portion of the project work, or saving costs by paying in advance for a service the project needs. Positive risks are opportunities to save time, money, or effort, or to increase productivity. Some risks, positive or negative, are negligible and are documented and accepted, while other risk events need to be quantified, planned for, and closely monitored throughout the project.

There are two levels of risks in a project to consider:

- **Individual project risks**   The risk events that can hinder or help the project reach its objectives
- **Overall project risk**   The combination of all risk events that will reveal the project's risk exposure and determine just how risky the project is for the organization

Generally, the higher the project priority, the more willing the organization is to spend time or money to address risk events. You'll also consider business risks and pure risks in a project. Business risks can have an upside and a downside, such as investing in that new piece of equipment. Pure risks have only a downside, such as someone getting injured on the job site because they took a shortcut in the work process. Of course, we want to address negative risks at all costs because we don't want people to be injured in the project.

Reviewing Project Risk Considerations

Stakeholder tolerance for risk is one of the first things you'll need to know when you start a project. Risk tolerance, sometimes called the risk appetite, refers to the stakeholders' willingness to take on risk events. The risk tolerance describes how much risk is acceptable in relation to the cost of addressing the risk event. Some projects and organizations have a high tolerance for risk—they readily take on risks, but their tolerance is in relation to the perceived reward the risk will bring them. It's just like investing in the stock market—you could earn money or lose money. Do you buy all safe and solid stocks? Or do you invest in only startup companies and penny stocks? Or, more likely, is there a distribution of low-risk and high-risk investments? From a project portfolio management perspective, a distribution of risk in projects is a safer bet than one or the other.

Within the project, you'll consider both event-based risks and non–event-based risks. Event-based risks are the risks project managers most often consider—events that will help or hinder the project objectives. Non–event-based risks are risks that are more nebulous and uncertain. There are two types of non–event-based risks:

- **Variability risks**   Uncertainty surrounding a project activity or decision. Fluctuations in productivity, number or errors and defects, or even the weather affecting the project are all examples of variability risks. You can't really predict with certainty productivity, errors, or weather, so these risks vary within the project.

- **Ambiguity risks**   Uncertainty about what the future holds. These risks are impossible to predict accurately: certainty of a new technical solution, future laws or regulations, or even complexity in the project approach.

Another risk factor to consider is the project resilience. You won't be able to identify some risks until they happen; these are called the unknown-unknowns. Project resilience is the project's ability to weather these risks through resilience in the form of

- Budget and schedule contingency
- Flexible project processes to identify and address risks as they are discovered
- Strong change management policies and procedures
- Empowered project team that's trusted to take actions to complete the project work
- Ongoing risk identification activities throughout the project
- Input from stakeholders to address emergent risks in the scope or project strategy

Integrated risk management is part of the organization's approach to risk. It's the distribution of risk events and how the risks are managed. Some risks may be assigned to the project manager to manage, and some risks may need to be escalated to management to address and manage. The integrated nature of risk management is beyond the boundaries of project management; the risk should be given to the party who's most appropriate to manage the risk event for the organization, not just the project or even the program.

For agile projects, uncertainty is part of the approach. Because of the nature of uncertainty and the expectation of change in an agile project, there are iteration reviews, knowledge sharing, and risk management involved at each iteration. The project team, the product manager, and the project manager all work together at the beginning of an iteration to address potential risks and at the end of the iteration to review what did, or didn't, work in the iteration. While the iteration is in motion, the project team and project manager work to monitor and address risks as they may be pending or have happened. The team is empowered to address the risk events to achieve the project's objectives in the current iteration.

Tailoring Risk Management in Projects

Like all knowledge areas, you can also tailor risk management to fit your organization and processes. Risk management should always be adjusted to fit the project you're managing—there is no blanket approach to risk management that will fit every project. For risk management in your projects you'll have to consider the following:

- **Size of the project**   Larger projects generally require a more formal risk management approach than smaller, low-priority projects.
- **Complexity of the project**   Simple is always better when it comes to project management, but that's not always feasible. A complex project, based on the technology involved, the endeavor's work, and external dependencies, can include many uncertainties that have to be addressed in risk management.

- **Importance of the project**   A high-profile project that the organization considers important for opportunities, investment, reputation, and other considerations will warrant a well-thought-out project management risk approach.
- **Development of the project**   A waterfall or predictive project calls for risk planning upfront, as opposed to an agile project, where risks are addressed at the start of each iteration. Both project types call for risk management, but the approach is different with each type.

CERTIFICATION OBJECTIVE 11.01

Planning for Risk Management

Risk management planning is about making decisions. The project manager, the project team, and other key stakeholders are involved to determine the risk management processes.

These processes are related to the scope of the project, the priority of the project within the performing organization, and the impact of the project deliverables. In other words, a simple, low-impact project won't have the same level of risk planning as a high-priority, complex project. It's important to complete risk management planning to manage, plan for, analyze, and react to identified risks successfully.

Examining Stakeholder Tolerance

Depending on the project, the conditions, and the potential for loss or reward, stakeholders will have differing tolerances for risk. Stakeholders' risk tolerance may be known at the launch of the project through written policy statements or by their actions during the project. *Risk tolerance* describes the amount of risk exposure an organization is willing to tolerate in a project. A large project in a construction company, for example, might have a low tolerance for risk, even though the nature of the work involves many risks. The low tolerance and high risk exposure would generally mean the company would look to alleviate the high risks as much as possible—such as safety approaches and the like. *Risk appetite* is similar, but it describes the amount of risk an organization will allow in hopes of the reward the risk will bring. Risk appetite describes the general attitude toward risk—how hungry a company is to accept risk in relation to the reward. An investment company, for example, may have a larger risk appetite than a government agency.

exam
ⓦatch
Risk appetite describes an organization's willingness to take on risks in anticipation of the reward the risks will bring. Some organizations are risk adverse— they have a low appetite for risks. Others look for risk because of the potential big rewards the risk gamble may bring. Risk threshold defines the Go/No Go decision for taking on the risk or avoiding the risk for a project.

Consider a project to install new medical equipment in a hospital. There's little room for acceptance of errors because life and death are on the line. No shortcuts or quick fixes are allowed. Now consider a project to create a community garden. Not only are life and death not on the line in the garden project, but the acceptance of risk is different as well. The nature of the project and the organization determines the type of risks and the approach to manage the risk events.

A person's willingness to accept risk is known as the *utility function.* The time and money costs required to eliminate the chance of failure is in proportion to the stakeholders' tolerance of risk on the project. The cost of assuring there are no threats must be balanced with the confidence that the project can be completed without extraordinary costs. Figure 11-1 demonstrates the utility function.

FIGURE 11-1

The higher the project priority, the lower the risk tolerance.

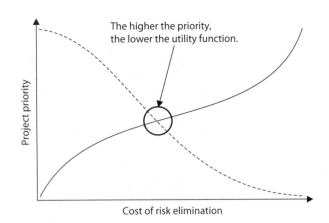

The higher the priority, the lower the utility function.

Project priority

Cost of risk elimination

Budgeting

Based on the size, impact, and priority of the project, a budget may need to be established for the project's risk management activities. A project with high priority and no budget allotment for risk management activities may face uncertain times ahead. A realistic dollar amount is needed for risk management activities if the project is to be successful.

Scheduling

The risk management process needs a schedule to determine how often and when risk management activities should occur throughout the project. If risk management happens too late in the project, the project could be delayed because of the time needed to identify, assess, and respond to the risks. A realistic schedule should be developed early in the project to accommodate risks, risk analysis, and risk reaction.

Risk Analysis Scoring

Prior to beginning quantitative and qualitative analysis, the project manager and the project team must have a clearly defined scoring system and an interpretation of it. Altering the scoring process during risk analysis—or from analysis to analysis—can skew the seriousness of a risk, its impact, and the effect of the risk on the project. The project manager and the project team must have clearly defined scores that will be applied to the analysis to ensure consistency throughout the project.

Risk Categories

Based on the nature of the work, there should be identified categories of risks within the project. Figure 11-2 shows one approach to identifying risk categories by using a risk breakdown structure (RBS). Throughout the project, the risk categories should be revisited to update and reflect the current status of the project. If a previous, similar project's risk management plan is available, the project team may elect to use this plan as a template and tailor the risk categories to the specific project.

FIGURE 11-2

A risk breakdown structure categorizes project risks.

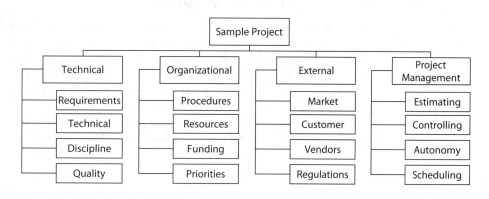

Creating Risk Categories

Risk categories should be identified before risk identification begins, and they should include common risks that are typical in the industry in which the project is occurring. Risk categories help organize, rank, and isolate risks within the project. Risks can be categorized according to these four areas:

- **Technical risks**   Technical risks are associated with new, unproven, or complex technologies being used on the project. Changes to the technology during the project implementation can also be a risk. Quality risks are the levels set for expectations of impractical quality and performance. Changes to industry standards during the project can also be lumped into this category of risks. Performance risks can be tied to how solutions perform, such as hardware, software, or vendors. Be careful, because risks in established technologies are not common and often overlooked.

- **Management risks**   These risks deal with faults in the management of the project: the unsuccessful allocation of time, resources, and scheduling; unacceptable work results (low-quality work); and lousy project management. This category can also address any risks within the program, portfolio, operations, organization, resourcing, and communications.

- **Commercial risks**   When working with vendors, new risks are introduced to the project specific to the contractual relationship. Risk categories can include the contract terms, internal procurement procedures, suppliers, subcontracts, client and customer stability, and any partnerships or joint ventures.

- **External risks**   These risks are outside of the project but directly affect it: legal issues, labor issues, a shift in project priorities, and weather. *Force majeure* risks can be scary and usually call for disaster recovery rather than project management. These are risks caused by earthquakes, tornados, floods, civil unrest, and other disasters. External risks can also include exchange rates, facilities, competition, and pending regulations.

Using a Risk Management Plan Template

The performing organization may rely on templates for the risk management plan. The template can guide the project manager and the project team through the planning processes, the risk identification, and the values that may trigger additional planning. Hopefully, the organization allows the template to be modified or appended based on the nature of the project. Because most projects resemble other historical projects, an existing template may need only minor changes to be adapted to the current project.

A risk management plan may grant the project manager decision-making abilities on risks below a certain threshold. Risks above a preset threshold may need to be escalated to a risk management board or a project steering committee for a determination of their cost and impact on the project's success.

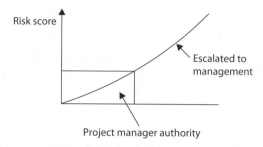

CERTIFICATION OBJECTIVE 11.02

Identifying Risks

After completing the risk management plan, you'll need to get to work identifying risks that can hinder the project's success. Risk identification is the process of identifying the risks and then documenting how their presence can affect the project. Risk identification is an iterative process and can be completed by the project manager, the project team, a risk management team, and even SMEs. In some instances, stakeholders and even people outside of the project can complete additional waves of risk identification. Risk identification addresses both individual risks and the overall project risks.

Preparing for Risk Identification

The risk management plan, a subsidiary plan to the overall project management plan, is one of the key inputs to the risk identification process. It describes how the risks will be identified, the requirements for risk analysis, and the overall management of the risk response process. The risk management plan does not include the actual responses to the risks, but rather the approach to the management of the process. In addition to the risk management plan are several other inputs to the risk identification process. The following risk management plan components are referenced here:

- The roles and responsibilities for risk management activities
- The budget for risk management activities
- The schedule for risk management activities
- Categories of risk

Other subsidiary plans from the project management plan can also be utilized in risk identification:

- **Requirements management plan** Identify objectives that are prone to risks
- **Schedule management plan** Review parts of the schedule that are risk laden
- **Cost management plan** Address any cost ambiguity activities or cost uncertainties
- **Resource management plan** Identify resources, physical or human, that have ambiguity or assumptions made
- **Quality management plan** Address assumptions about quality that could introduce risk
- **Scope baseline** Review the qualifications for acceptance for the deliverables and use the WBS as a guide for the risk breakdown structure
- **Schedule baseline** Review milestones and due dates that may be susceptible to risk events or introduce risk into the project
- **Cost baseline** Review the cost thresholds, limits, range of variances, and other aspects of costs that may introduce risk to the project success

Project documents are also reviewed as an input to risk identification throughout the project. You'll need to review all the following for assumptions and potential risks:

- Assumption log
- Cost estimates
- Duration estimates
- Issue log
- Lessons learned register
- Requirements
- Resource requirements
- Stakeholder register

Identifying the Project Risks

Armed with the inputs to risk identification, the project manager, the project team, and experts are prepared to begin identifying risks. Risk identification should be a methodical, planned approach. Should risk identification move in several different directions at once, some risks may be overlooked. A systematic, scientific approach is best.

Reviewing Project Documents

One of the first steps the project team can take is to review the project documentation. The project plan, scope, and other project files should be reviewed. Constraints and assumptions should be reviewed, considered, and analyzed for risks. This structured review takes a broad look at the project plan, the scope, and the activities defined within the project.

Testing the Assumptions

All projects have assumptions. Assumption analysis is the process of examining assumptions to see what risks may stem from false assumptions. Examining assumptions is about finding their validity. For example, consider a project to install a new piece of software on every computer within an organization. The project team has assumed that all the computers within the organization meet the minimum requirements to install the software. If this assumption were wrong, cost increases and schedule delays would occur.

This examination also requires a review of assumptions across the whole project for consistency. For example, consider a project with an assumption that a senior employee will be needed throughout the entire project; the cost estimate, however, has been billed at the rate of a junior employee. All assumptions and their conditions should be recorded in the assumptions log. You'll update this log based on the accuracy of the assumptions and the outcome of assumptions testing.

False assumptions can ruin a project. They can wreck schedule, cost, and even the quality of a project deliverable. For this reason, assumptions are treated as risks and must be tested and weighed to truncate the possibility of an assumption turning against the project. Assumptions are weighed using two factors:

- **Assumption stability**   How reliable is the information that led to this assumption?
- **Assumption consequence**   What is the effect on the project if this assumption is false?

The answers to these two questions will help the project team deliver the project with more confidence. Should an assumption prove to be false, the weight of the assumption consequence may be low to high—depending on the nature of the assumption.

Brainstorming the Project

Brainstorming is likely the most common approach to risk identification. It's usually completed by the entire project team to identify the risks within the project. The risks are identified in broad terms and posted, and then the risks' characteristics are detailed. The identified risks are categorized and will later pass through qualitative and quantitative risk analyses.

A multidisciplinary team, hosted by a project facilitator, can also complete brainstorming. This approach can include subject matter experts, project team members, customers, and other stakeholders who contribute to the risk identification process.

Using Checklists

Checklists can serve as a good reminder of what to review for risk events, specific steps to follow, and project points to be considered for risk events. A checklist can evolve over time and is part of organizational process assets. A project manager can rely on a checklist for prompts during risk identification meetings, where the checklist could provide a series of questions, confirmations, or reminders. However, the checklist can't, and won't, cover every feasible risk event, so it's important not to treat the checklist as a comprehensive list that addresses every possible risk in the project.

PMP
Coach

The Delphi Technique is an anonymous method used to query experts about foreseeable risks within a project, phase, or component of a project. The results of the survey are analyzed by a third party, organized, and then circulated to the experts. There can be several rounds of anonymous discussion with the Delphi Technique—without fear of backlash or offending other participants in the process. The Delphi Technique's goal is to gain consensus on risks within the project. The anonymous nature of the process ensures that no one expert's advice overtly influences the opinion of another participant. The Delphi Technique can also take out the fear of retribution some people may have about showing a risk that could make a colleague or supervisor look bad in front of other team members.

Identifying Risks Through Interviews

Interviewing subject matter experts and project stakeholders is an excellent approach to identifying risks on the current project based on the interviewees' experience. The people responsible for risk identifications understand the overall purpose of the project and the project's work breakdown structure (WBS), and they likely have made the same assumptions as the interviewee.

The interviewee, through questions and discussion, shares his insight on what risks he perceives within the project. The goal of the process is to learn from the expert what risks may be hidden within the project, what risks this person has encountered on similar work, and what insight he has into the project work. Part of the interview process is also to examine, even challenge, the assumptions the stakeholders may have as part of the project.

Analyzing SWOT

SWOT stands for strengths, weaknesses, opportunities, and threats. SWOT analysis is the process of examining the project from the perspective of each characteristic. For example, a technology project may identify SWOT as follows:

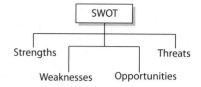

- ▧ **Strengths** The technology to be installed in the project has been installed by other large companies in our industry.
- ▧ **Weaknesses** We have never installed this technology before.
- ▧ **Opportunities** The new technology will allow us to reduce our cycle time for time-to-market on new products. Opportunities are things, conditions, or events that allow an organization to differentiate itself from competitors and improve its standing in the marketplace.
- ▧ **Threats** The time to complete the training and simulation may overlap with product updates, new versions, and external changes to our technology portfolio.

PMP
Coach   **You can use SWOT analysis as you prepare to pass your PMP exam. Review your end-of-chapter exam scores to see which chapters contain information you're strong or weak in and which chapters represent your opportunities and threats.**

Utilizing Diagramming Techniques

The project team can utilize several diagramming techniques to identify risks:

- ▧ **Ishikawa** These cause-and-effect diagrams, as shown, are also called fishbone diagrams. They are great for the root-cause analysis of factors that are causing risks within the project. The goal is to identify and treat the root of the problem, not the symptom.

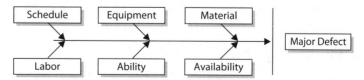

- ▧ **Flowcharts** System or process flowcharts show the relationship between components and how the overall process works. These are useful for identifying risks between system components.

■ **Influence diagrams**   An influence diagram, shown next, charts out a decision problem. It identifies all the elements, variables, decisions, and objectives—and how each factor may influence another.

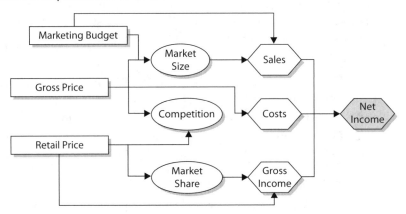

Using Prompt Lists

If you're doing the same types of projects over and over, such as IT projects or construction projects, you might use a prompt list to help the project team better identify project risks. Prompt lists are risk categories that were identified in the risk management plan. For example, your prompt list might ask, "What type of risks are lurking in hardware for this project?" or "Are there any new materials that could have risks we should consider?" The prompt list prompt risk identification participants to think about individual risks based on the prompts you include.

Overall project risks subscribe to one of three common types of prompt lists:

■ **VUCA**   volatility, uncertainty, complexity, and ambiguity
■ **TECOP**   technical, environmental, commercial, operational, and political
■ **PESTLE**   political, economic, social, technological, legal, and environmental

Creating a Risk Register

The risk register is a project document that contains all the information related to the risk management activities. It's updated as risk management activities are conducted to reflect the status, progress, and nature of the project risks. The risk register includes the following:

■ **Risks**   Of course, the most obvious output of risk identification is the risk that has been successfully identified. Recall that a risk is an uncertain event or condition that could potentially have a positive or negative effect on the project's success.

■ **Potential responses**   During the initial risk identification process, there may be solutions and responses to identified risks. This is fine as long as the responses are documented in the register. Along with the risk responses, the identification of risk triggers may occur. Triggers are warning signs or symptoms that a risk has occurred or is about to occur. For example, should a vendor fail to complete her portion of the project as scheduled, the project completion may be delayed.

■ **Potential risk owners**   If you've identified a person or role on the project team or in the organization who will own the risk, you'll include that information in the risk register. The ownership of the risk will be confirmed in the qualitative risk analysis process.

■ **Possible additional data**   Risk identification may include additional information, such as risk category, current risk status, root cause(s) of an identified risk, risk triggers, WBS references, risk timing, and deadlines.

Creating a Risk Report

Another output of risk identification is a risk report. The risk report explains the overall project risks and provides summaries about the individual project risks. You'll update the risk report through the project as more information becomes available through analysis and experience in the project. The report will be updated with risk responses and the response outcomes, and any additional details as a result of monitoring risks in the project. Your risk report, depending on what's required in the organization, may include sources of overall project risk exposure, trends among the individual risks, number of threats and opportunities, and other related information.

CERTIFICATION OBJECTIVE 11.03

Using Qualitative Risk Analysis

Qualitative risk analysis "qualifies" the risks that have been identified in the project. Specifically, qualitative risk analysis examines and prioritizes the risks based on their probability of their occurrence and the impact on the project if they did occur. Qualitative risk analysis is a broad approach to ranking risks by priority, which then guides the risk reaction process. The facilitator of the qualitative risk analysis process, whether an expert or the project manager, must be aware of perception and bias of how and why risks are rated by the participants.

The end result of qualitative risk analysis (once risks have been identified and prioritized) can lead to more in-depth quantitative risk analysis, or it can move directly into risk response planning. Qualitative is subjective, because it's really a fast human judgment based on experience, a gut feeling, or a best guess about the risk's impact and probability.

Preparing for Qualitative Risk Analysis

The risk management plan is the key input to qualitative risk analysis. The plan will dictate the process, the methodologies to be used, and the scoring model for identified risks. In addition to the risk management plan, the identified risks from the risk register, obviously, will be needed to perform an analysis. These are the risks that will be scored and ranked based on their probability and impact.

The status of the project will also affect the process of qualitative risk analysis. Early in the project, there may be several risks that have not yet surfaced. Later in the project, new risks may become evident and need to pass through qualitative analysis. The status of the project is linked to the available time needed to analyze and study the risks. More time may be available early in the project, while a looming deadline near the project's end may create a sense of urgency to find solutions for the newly identified risks.

The project type also has some bearing on the process. As in the following illustration, a project that has never been done before, such as the installation of a new technology, has more uncertainty than a project that has been undertaken repeatedly within an organization. Recurring projects have historical information that you can rely on, while first-time projects have limited resources upon which to build a risk hypothesis.

All risks are based upon some belief, proof, and data. The accuracy and source of the data must be evaluated to determine the level of confidence in the identified risks. A hunch that an element is a risk is not as reliable as measured statistics, historical information, or expert knowledge that an element is a risk. The data precision needed is in proportion to the reality of the risk.

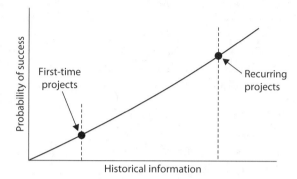

Prior to the risk analysis, a predetermined scale of probability and impact must be in place. A project manager can elect to use a number of scales, but generally they should be in alignment with the risk management plan. If the performing organization has a risk management model, the scale identified by the performing organization should be used. (I'll discuss the scale values in the next section.)

The assumptions used in the project must be revisited, so you'll also rely on the assumptions log. Throughout the project, assumptions are accrued in the assumption log, which was initially generated as part of building the project charter. These assumptions will be evaluated as risks to the project's success if they prove false. Finally, the project's stakeholder register serves as an input, too, because certain stakeholders may be identified as risk owners.

Completing Qualitative Analysis

Not all risks are worth responding to, but some demand attention. Qualitative analysis is a subjective approach to organizing and prioritizing risks. The risk data quality assessment helps to determine the reliability of the data about the identified risks and their rankings. Using good, reliable, proven data along with a methodical and logical approach, the identified risks can be rated according to probability and potential impact.

The project manager needs to determine the quality of the data used to understand the accuracy and reliability of the risk scoring; low-quality data is little more than opinion and not a good foundation for qualitative risk analysis. One of the toughest parts of qualitative risk analysis is the biased, subjective nature of the process. A project manager and the project team must question the reliability and reality of the data that led to the ranking of the risks. For example, Susan may have great confidence in herself when it comes to working with new, unproven technologies. Based on this opinion, she petitions for the risk probability of the work to be a very low score.

However, because she has no experience with the technology because of its newness, the probability of the risk of failure is actually very high. The biased opinion that Susan can complete the work with zero defects and problems is slightly skewed, because she has never worked with the technology before. Obviously, a low-ranked score on a risk that should be ranked high can have detrimental effects on the project's success.

Data precision ranking takes into consideration the biased nature of the ranking, the accuracy of the data submitted, and the reliability of the biased ranking submitted to examine the risk scores. Data precision ranking is concerned with the following:

- The level of understanding of the project risk
- The available data and information about the identified risk
- The quality of the data and information about the identified risk
- The reliability of the data about the identified risk

Imminent risks are usually considered of higher urgency than distant risks. Consider the risk ranking, the time needed for the risk response, and the conditions that indicate the risk is coming to fruition.

The outcome of the ranking determines four certain things:

- It identifies the risks that require additional analysis through quantitative risk analysis.
- It identifies the risks that may proceed directly to risk response planning.
- It identifies risks that are not critical, project-stopping risks, but that still must be documented.
- It prioritizes risks.

Qualitative risk analysis also takes a cursory look at and documentation of the following:

- **Urgency of the risk**   How long before the risk may happen in the project?
- **Proximity**   How long before the risk will affect a project objective?
- **Dormancy**   How long after the risk has occurred before its impact is noticed?
- **Manageability**   How easily can the risk be managed?
- **Controllability**   How easily can the outcome of the risk event be controlled?
- **Detectability**   How easily can the evidence of a risk's occurrence be detected?
- **Connectivity**   How connected is a risk to other risks within the project?

- **Strategic impact**   What size of impact will the risk event have on the organization's strategic goals?
- **Propinquity**   What is the risk perception by key stakeholders?

Applying Probability and Impact

The project risks are rated according to their probability and impact. Risk probability is the likelihood that a risk event may happen, while risk impact is the consequence that the result of the event will have on the project objectives. Each risk is measured based on its likelihood and its impact. Two approaches exist to ranking risks:

- **Cardinal scales**   Identify the probability and impact on a numeric value from 0.01 (very low) to 1.00 (certain).
- **Ordinal scales**   Identify and rank the risks with common terms, such as very high to very unlikely, or using an RAG (red, amber, green) rating to signify the risk score.

Creating a Probability-Impact Matrix

Each identified risk is fed into a probability-impact matrix, as shown in Figure 11-3. The matrix maps out the risk, its probability, and its possible impact. The risks with higher probability and impact are a more serious threat to the project objectives than the risks with lower impact and consequences. The risks that are threats to the project require quantitative analysis to determine the root of the risks, the methods to monitor the risks, and effective risk management. We'll discuss quantitative risk management later in this chapter.

FIGURE 11-3

A probability-impact matrix measures the identified risks within the project.

Odds and Impact

Risk	Probability	Impact	Risk Score
Data Loss	Low	High	Moderate
Network Speed	Moderate	Moderate	Moderate
Server Downtime	High	Low	Moderate
E-mail Service Down	Low	Low	Low

Each identified risk

Subjective score

The project is best served when the probability scale and the impact scale are predefined prior to qualitative analysis, as was done when creating the risk management plan. For example, the probability scale rates the likelihood of an individual risk happening and can be on a cardinal scale (0.1, 0.3, 0.5, 0.7, 0.9) or on an ordinal scale (low, medium, high). The scale, however, should be defined and agreed upon in the risk management plan. The impact scale, which measures the severity of the risk on the project's objectives, can also be on an ordinal or a cardinal scale.

The value of identifying and assigning the scales to use prior to the process of qualitative analysis enables all risks to be ranked by the system and allows for future identified risks to be measured and ranked by the same system. A shift in risk rating methodologies midproject can cause disagreements regarding the method for handling the project risks.

A probability-impact matrix multiplies the value for the risk probability by the risk impact for a total risk score. The risk's scores can be cardinal, as shown in Figure 11-4, and then preset values can qualify the risk for a risk response. For example, an identified risk in a project is the possibility that the vendor may be late in delivering the hardware. The probability is rated at 0.9, but the impact of the risk on the project is rated at 0.1. The risk score is calculated by multiplying the probability times the impact—in this case, resulting in a score of 0.09.

The scores within the probability-impact matrix can be referenced against the performing organization's policies for risk reaction. Based on the risk score, the performing organization can place the risk in differing categories to guide risk reaction. There are three common categories based on risk score:

- **Red condition**   These high risk scores are high in impact and probability.
- **Amber condition (aka yellow condition)**   These risks are somewhat high in impact and probability.
- **Green condition**   These risks are generally fairly low in impact, probability, or both.

FIGURE 11-4

The results of a probability-impact matrix create a risk score.

Risk Scores					
Probability					
0.9	0.05	0.09	0.18	0.36	0.72
0.7	0.04	0.07	0.14	0.28	0.56
0.5	0.03	0.05	0.10	0.20	0.40
0.3	0.02	0.03	0.06	0.12	0.24
0.1	0.01	0.01	0.02	0.04	0.08
	0.05	0.10	0.20	0.40	0.80
Impact					

Legend □ Low
□ Moderate
□ High

o n t h e
job **Your organization may not use a classification of risks based on red, amber, and green—called RAG rating. Your project risks should map to the methodology your organization uses to identify and classify project risks. If there is no classification of risks, take the initiative and create one for your project. Be certain to document your classification for historical information and include this information in your lessons learned documentation.**

Building a Hierarchical Chart

It's tempting, and often convenient, to rate risks based only on probability and impact. However, you can rate risks based on several factors, such urgency, proximity, and impact, to create a more robust chart. By scoring any number of factors, you can create histograms, pie charts, or bubble charts. In a bubble chart, shown next, you'll plot out the factors from low to high and add the variable of the size of the bubble to show the bubble impact value. The larger the bubble, the larger the impact of the risk. Where the bubbles land in the chart, based on the factors selected, will help determine which risks need additional analysis, aren't acceptable, or have low factors and might be acceptable in the project.

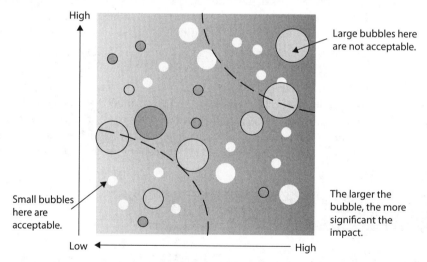

Examining the Results of Qualitative Risk Analysis

Qualitative risk analysis happens throughout the project. As new risks become evident and identified, the project manager should route the risks through the qualitative risk analysis process. The end results of qualitative risk analysis include the following:

- **Assumption log**   Assumptions can be updated and new assumptions are added to log.
- **Issue log**   Any new issues discovered are added to the log, and issues that have changed are updated to reflect their new status.

■ **Risk register** New risks that have been identified are added to the register, while existing risks will have their attributes updated to reflect the qualitative risk analysis findings.

■ **Risk report** The risk report is updated with any changes to the summary on the individual risks and the overall risk ranking of the project. This enables the project manager, management, customers, and other interested stakeholders to comprehend the risk, the nature of the risk, and the condition between the risk score and the likelihood of success for a project. The risk score can be compared to other projects to determine project selection, the placement of talent in a project, prioritization, the creation of a benefit/cost ratio, or even the cancellation of a project because it is deemed too risky.

■ **Risk categories** Within the risk register, categories of risks should be created. The idea is that not only will related risks be lumped together, but there may also be some trend identification and root-cause analysis of identified risks. Having risks categorized should also make it easier to create risk responses.

■ **Near-term risks** Qualitative analysis should also help the project team identify which risks require immediate or near-term risk responses. Risks that are likely to happen later in the project can be acknowledged, enabling imminent risks to be managed first. Urgent risks can go right to quantitative analysis and risk response planning.

■ **Low-priority risk watch list** Let's face it: not all risks need additional analysis. However, these low-priority risks should be identified and assigned to a watch list for periodic monitoring.

■ **Trends in qualitative analysis** As the project progresses and risk analysis is repeated, trends in the ranking and analysis of the risk may become apparent. These trends can enable the project manager and other risk experts to respond to the root cause, predict trends to eliminate, or respond to the risks within the project.

CERTIFICATION OBJECTIVE 11.04

Preparing for Quantitative Risk Analysis

Quantitative risk analysis attempts to assess the probability and impact of the identified risks numerically. It also creates an overall risk score for the project. This method is more in-depth than qualitative risk analysis and relies on several different tools to accomplish its goal. You don't have to do quantitative analysis on every project and certainly not for every identified risk. You'll only do quantitative analysis on projects that demand the process, usually high-profile projects, and on risk events that are deemed significant through qualitative risk analysis.

Qualitative risk analysis typically precedes quantitative analysis. All or a portion of the identified risks in qualitative risk analysis can be examined in the quantitative analysis. The performing organization may have policies on the risk scores in qualitative analysis that require the risks to advance to quantitative analysis. Schedule and budget constraints may also be factors in the determination of which risks should pass through quantitative analysis. Quantitative analysis is a more time-consuming process and is, therefore, also more expensive. Following are the goals of quantitative risk analysis:

- To ascertain the likelihood of reaching project success
- To ascertain the likelihood of reaching a project objective
- To determine the risk exposure for the project
- To determine the likely amount of the contingency reserve needed for the project
- To determine the risks with the largest impact on the project
- To determine realistic schedule, cost, and scope targets

Considering the Inputs for Quantitative Analysis

Based on the time and budget allotments for quantitative analysis, as defined in the risk management plan, the project manager can move into quantitative analysis. The project manager should rely on the following 16 inputs to quantitative risk analysis:

- **Risk management plan** The risk management plan identifies the risk management methodology, the allotted budget for risk analysis, the schedule, and the risk scoring mechanics—among other attributes.
- **Scope baseline** You'll utilize the scope baseline to see what's being affected in scope by the identified risk events.
- **Schedule baseline** Risks don't affect just the scope; they can also affect the project's schedule.
- **Costs baseline** Risks can also affect the costs of the project, so the cost baseline also serves as an input to quantitative risk analysis.
- **Assumptions log** Assumptions are uncertain and their uncertainty can serve as an input to quantitative risk analysis. Constraints are also examined in this process.
- **Basis of estimates** How the cost and activity duration estimates were modeled and formulated are subject to quantitative risk analysis.
- **Cost estimates** Cost estimates are examined because there may be a range of variance in the cost estimates that could introduce risks to the project.
- **Cost forecasts** Through earned value management, you may have created an estimate to complete, estimate at completion, budget at completion, and a to-complete performance index that have introduced risks into the project, or they may be at risk of being false assumptions about the costs to complete the project work.

■ **Duration estimates** Duration estimates, and their supporting detail, may be subject to risk, because there's uncertainty in predicting how long an activity will take to complete. You don't know how long something will truly take to do, usually, until you do the activity.

■ **Milestone list** The target dates for achieving milestones can pass through quantitative risk analysis because there may be a level of uncertainty for reaching the target dates.

■ **Resource requirements** Resources, human and physical, may have variations for their performance, availability, and completion of the project work.

■ **Risk register** The risks that have been identified and promoted to quantitative analysis are needed. The project team will also need their ranking and risk categories—all of which are documented in the risk register.

■ **Risk report** The current individual risks and the overall project risks are defined.

■ **Schedule forecasts** The predicted timeline of the project can introduce risks and may need to pass through quantitative risk analysis to determine a level of confidence of actually achieving the project schedule as planned and predicted.

■ **Enterprise environmental factors** The organization may require the project manager to utilize risk databases from similar projects within the organization or from industry sources. The enterprise environmental factors may also include reports, checklists, and business cases from similar projects within your industry.

■ **Organizational process assets** Historical information is one of the best inputs for risk analysis, as it is proven information for the project. An examination of the project risks from past experiences can help the project team complete quantitative risk analysis activities.

Interviewing Stakeholders and Experts

Interviews with stakeholders and SMEs can be among the first tasks involved in quantifying the identified risks. These interviews can focus on worst-case, best-case, and most-likely scenarios if the goal of the quantitative analysis is to create a triangular distribution; most quantitative analysis, however, uses continuous probability distributions. Figure 11-5 shows five sample distributions: normal, lognormal, beta, triangular, and uniform.

FIGURE 11-5   Risk distributions illustrate the likelihood and impact of an event within a project.

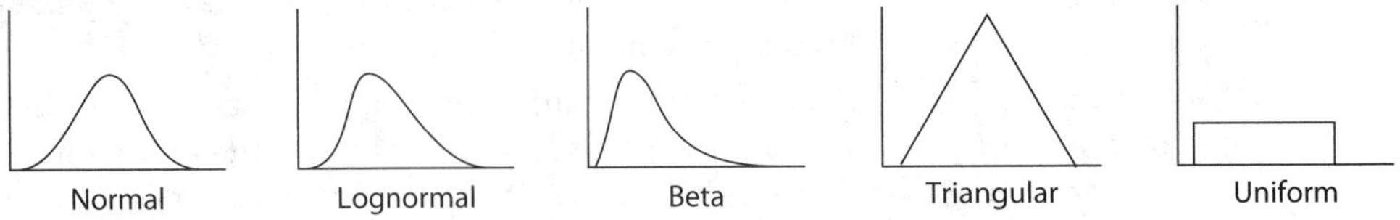

Normal   Lognormal   Beta   Triangular   Uniform

Continuous probability distribution is an examination of the probability of all possibilities within a given range. For each variable, the probability of a risk event and the corresponding consequence for the event may vary. In other words, depending on whether the risk event occurs and how it happens, a reaction to the event may also occur. Here are the distributions of the probabilities and impacts, sometimes called "representations of uncertainty":

- Uniform
- Normal
- Triangular
- Beta
- Lognormal

watch It's doubtful that you'll be tested on these risk distributions for the exam. The *PMBOK Guide* mentions them only briefly, so you'll need to be topically aware of them. Don't invest hours memorizing the subject.

Applying Sensitivity Analysis

Sensitivity analysis examines each project risk on its own merit. It is an analysis process to determine which risks could affect the project the most. All other risks in the project are set at a baseline value. The individual risk is then examined to see how it may affect the success of the project. The goal of sensitivity analysis is to determine which individual risks have the greatest impact on the project's success and then escalate the risk management processes on these risk events. Sensitivity analysis is often associated with a tornado diagram.

Finding the Expected Monetary Value

The expected monetary value of a project or event is based on the probability of outcomes that are uncertain. For example, one risk may cost the project an additional $10,000 if it occurs, but there's only a 20 percent chance of the event occurring. In the simplest form, the expected monetary value of this individual risk is thus $2000. Project managers can also find the expected monetary value of a decision by creating a decision tree.

See the video "Risk Reserve."

Using a Decision Tree

A decision tree is a method used to determine which of two or more decisions is the best to make. For example, it can be used to determine buy-versus-build scenarios, lease-or-purchase equations, or whether to use in-house resources rather than outsourcing project work. The decision tree model examines the cost and benefits of each decision's outcomes and weighs the probability of success for each of the decisions.

The purpose of the decision tree is to make a decision, calculate the value of that decision, or determine which decision costs the least. Follow Figure 11-6 through the various steps of the decision tree process.

Completing a Decision Tree

Let's look at a scenario. As the project manager of the new GFB Project, you have to decide whether to create a new web application in-house or send the project out to a developer. The developer you would use if you were to outsource the work quotes the project cost at $175,000. Based on previous work with this company, you are 85 percent certain they will finish the work on time.

Your in-house development team quotes the cost of the work as $165,000. Again, based on previous experience with your in-house developers, you are 75 percent certain they can complete the work on time. Now let's apply what you know to a decision tree:

- Buy or build is simply the decision name.
- The cost of the decision if you buy the work outside of your company is $175,000. If you build the software in-house, the cost of the decision is $165,000.

FIGURE 11-6

Decision trees analyze the probability of events and calculate decision values.

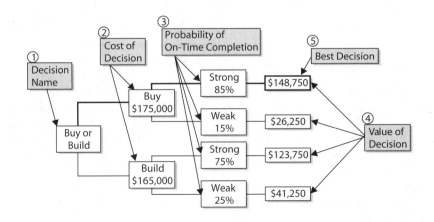

- Based on your probability of completion by a given date, you apply the 85 percent certainty to the "strong" finish for the buy branch of the tree. Because you're 85 percent certain, you're also 15 percent uncertain; this value is assigned to the "weak" value on the buy branch. You complete the same process for the build branch of the tree.

- The value of the decision is the percentage of strong and weak applied to each branch of the tree.

- The best decision is based solely on the largest value of all possible decisions identified in the decision tree.

Using a Project Simulation

Project simulations enable the project team to play "what-if" games without affecting any areas of production. The Monte Carlo analysis technique, discussed in earlier chapters, is the most common simulation. Monte Carlo, typically completed using a software program, completely simulates a project with values for all possible variables to predict the most likely model. Monte Carlo simulations can create a probability distribution, called an S-curve, to show the likelihood of a desired outcome, or loss, in the project.

Examining the Results of Quantitative Risk Analysis

Quantitative risk analysis is completed throughout the project as risks are identified and passed through qualitative analysis, as project conditions change, or on a preset schedule. The result of quantitative risk analysis should be reflected in the risk report and should include the following:

- **Overall project risk exposure**   The overall project risk exposure is documented in the project's chances of success, which indicates how likely the project is to reach its key objectives. The degree of inherent remaining variability in the project is assessed. This means how much risk the project is carrying based on how the variations of possible project outcomes.

- **Probabilistic analysis**   The risks within the project enable the project manager or other experts to predict the likelihood of the project's success. The project may be altered by the response to certain risks; this response can increase cost and push back the project's completion date. The results of quantitative analysis can be shown through tornado diagrams and S-curves to plot out the project's risks. The analysis also can identify the major risk events, contingency reserve needed, and which risks have the most uncertainty and most probability of happening.

- **Prioritized list of individual project risks**   The risk events are prioritized by their likelihood of occurring and the impact on the project if the risk events do occur.

- **Trends in quantitative analysis**   As the project moves toward completion, quantitative risk analysis may be repeated. In each round of analysis, trends in the identified risks may become visible. The trends in the risk can help the project team eliminate the root causes of the risk, reduce their probability, or address their impact.
- **Recommended risk responses**   Risk response planning is covered in detail in the next section, but the risk report may also include the recommended risk responses. These recommendations will serve as an input to planning the risk responses formally.

CERTIFICATION OBJECTIVE 11.05

Planning for Risk Responses

Risk response planning is all about options and actions. It focuses on how to decrease the possibility of risks adversely affecting the project's objectives and how to increase the likelihood of positive risks that can aid the project. Risk response planning assigns responsibilities to people and groups close to the risk event. Risks will increase or decrease based on the effectiveness of risk response planning.

The responses to identified risks must be in balance with the risks themselves. The cost and time invested in reducing a risk's impact and probability must be compared with the expected gains. In other words, a million-dollar solution for a hundred-dollar problem is unacceptable. The people or individuals who are assigned to the risk must have the authority to react to the project risk as planned. In most cases, several risk responses may be viable for the risk—the best choice for the identified risk must be documented, agreed upon, and then followed through should the risk occur.

Preparing for Risk Response

To prepare successfully for risk response, the project manager, project team, and appropriate stakeholders rely on just two inputs: the risk management plan and the risk register. The inputs for planning the risk responses include the following:

- **Project management plan**   Resource management plan, risk management plan, and cost baseline
- **Project documents**   Lessons learned register, schedule, team assignments, resource calendars, risk register, risk report, and stakeholder register

- **Enterprise environmental factors**   Risk appetite and risk thresholds of the key stakeholders
- **Organizational process assets**   Templates for the risk management plan, risk register, risk report, any historical databases, and lessons learned from similar projects

Creating Risk Responses

The project team can employ several tools and techniques to respond to risks. Each risk should be evaluated to determine which category of risk response is most appropriate. When a category of risk response has been selected, the response must then be developed, refined, documented, and readied for use, if needed. In addition, secondary responses may be selected for each risk. The purpose of risk response planning is to bring the overall risk of the project down to an acceptable level, while leveraging any positive risks. In addition, risk response planning must address any risks that have unacceptably high scores.

Expert judgment, interviews, and facilitation techniques are three of the nine tools and techniques used for creating risk responses. These three tools deal with discussing the risk responses, getting stakeholders involved in the planning, and ensuring that the best decisions for the risk responses are made. These are the other six tools and techniques:

- Strategies for threats
- Strategies for opportunities
- Contingent response strategies
- Strategies for overall project risk
- Data analysis
- Decision-making

I'll discuss each of these in detail in this section.

Escalating the Risk Event

Not all risks should be managed at the project level. Some risks that are outside of the boundary of the project should be escalated when the project team, project sponsor, or project manager believes the risk management would exceed the authority the project manager has over the risk event. In these instances, the risk is escalated to management, a program manager, or the portfolio manager in the organization. The escalated threat should be communicated to the new owner of the risk event to explain why it's beyond the project boundaries, and the new owner must also agree to accept the risk as part of her responsibility. Like negative risk events, threats and opportunities can be escalated.

Avoiding the Negative Risk and Threats

Avoidance is simply avoiding the risk. This can be accomplished in many different ways and generally happens early in the project, when any change will result in fewer consequences than it would later in the project plan. Here are some examples of avoidance:

- Changing the project plan to eliminate the risk
- Clarifying project requirements to avoid discrepancies
- Hiring additional project team members who have experience with the technology involved in the project
- Using a proven methodology rather than a new approach

Transferring the Negative Risk

Transference is the process of transferring the risk (and the ownership of the risk) to a third party. The risk doesn't disappear; it's just someone else's problem. Transference of a risk usually costs a premium for the third party to own and manage that risk. Here are common examples of risk transference:

- Insurance
- Performance bonds
- Warrantees
- Guarantees
- Fixed-price contracts

Mitigating the Negative Risk

Mitigating risks is an effort to reduce the probability and/or impact of an identified risk in the project. Mitigation occurs before the risk event happens. The cost and time to reduce or eliminate the risk is more cost effective than repairing the damage caused by the risk. The risk event may still happen, but hopefully the cost and impact will be low.

Mitigation plans can be created so that they are implemented should an identified risk cross a given threshold. For example, a manufacturing project may have a mitigation plan to reduce the number of units created per hour should the equipment's temperature exceed a given threshold. The reduction is the number of units per hour that implementing the plan may cost the project in time. In addition, the cost of extra labor to run the equipment longer because the machine is now operating at a slower pace may be attributed to the project. However, should the equipment fail, the project would have to replace the equipment and could be delayed for weeks while awaiting repairs.

Here are some examples of mitigation:

- Adding activities to the project to reduce the risk probability or impact
- Simplifying the processes within the project
- Completing more tests on the project work before implementation
- Developing prototypes, simulations, and limited releases

INSIDE THE EXAM

Risk management planning is the process of determining how risk management should be handled. The stakeholder analysis will reveal the stakeholders' willingness to tolerate risk—which is also known as their utility function. The performing organization may have standard practices for risk management, risk management templates, or guidance from historical information.

There are two types of risk: business risk, which is a gain or loss from a financial point of view, and pure risk, which has only a downside. Both types of risk must be assessed and managed. Remember that not all risks are bad. The risk impact may have a negative effect on the project, but a risk may often have a positive impact.

Risk identification happens early in the project to allow time for risk response planning. It also happens throughout the project. The project manager, the project team, customers, and other stakeholders should be involved in the process. There are several methods to risk identification—interviews and the Delphi Technique are two of the most common approaches.

Qualitative analysis qualifies the list of risks in a matrix based on impact and probability.

This subjective approach can use common grading similar to very low, low, moderate, high, and very high rankings. The risks can be prioritized based on their score.

After qualitative analysis, some risks may be sent through quantitative analysis. This approach attempts to quantify the risks with hard numbers, values, and data. Quantification of the risk can lead to schedule and cost contingencies for the project, a prioritization of the risks, and an overall risk score. Monte Carlo simulations are typically associated with quantitative risk analysis.

There are five risk responses for negative risks:

- **Avoidance**   The project plan is altered to avoid the identified risk.
- **Mitigation**   An effort is made to reduce the probability, impact, or both of an identified risk in the project before the risk event occurs.
- **Transference**   The risk is assigned to a third party, usually for a fee. The risk still exists, but the responsibility is deflected to the third party.

(Continued)

INSIDE THE EXAM

■ **Escalation**   The risk is escalated when the risk is outside of the project scope or when the response would exceed the project manager's authority in the project.

■ **Acceptance**   The risk is accepted by the project manager as is.

Here are the five risk responses for positive risks:

■ **Exploitation**   The organization wants to ensure that the identified risk does happen to realize the positive impact associated with the risk event.

■ **Sharing**   Sharing is nice. When sharing, the risk ownership is transferred to the organization that can capitalize most on the risk opportunity.

■ **Enhancement**   To enhance a risk is to attempt to modify its probability of occurrence and/or its impacts on the project to realize the most gains from the identified risk.

Following are the two responses for both positive and negative risks:

■ **Accepting**   The risks are nominal, so they are accepted. Risks, regardless of size, that have no other recourse may also be accepted.

■ **Escalation**   Opportunities and threats can both be escalated to a more appropriate party if the risk event is beyond the boundaries of the project.

As the project progresses, risk monitoring is implemented. Risks are monitored for risk triggers—signs that the risks may be coming to fruition. The project team and the project manager execute the risk response plan and document the results. Earned value analysis, which is typically used to measure project performance, can also be used to signal impending project risks.

Managing the Positive Risks and Opportunities

Although most risks have a negative connotation, not all risks are bad. There are instances when a risk may create an opportunity that can help the project, other projects, or the organization. The type of risk and the organization's willingness to accept the risks will dictate the appropriate response.

Exploiting the Positive Risk or Opportunity

When an organization wants to ensure that a positive risk definitely happens, it can exploit the risk. Exploiting a risk means that the project team works to ensure a 100 percent probability of the risk event. Positive risk exploitation can be realized by adding the most-qualified resources to an activity, using a faster piece of equipment, or employing another method to make the likelihood of a positive risk event definite.

Sharing the Positive Risk

The idea of sharing a positive risk really means sharing a mutually beneficial opportunity between two organizations or projects, or creating a risk-sharing partnership. When a project team can share the positive risk, ownership of the risk is given to the organization that can best capture the benefits from the identified risk. Teaming agreements and joint ventures are examples of sharing a positive risk.

Enhancing a Positive Risk

This risk response seeks to modify the size of the identified opportunity. The goal is to strengthen the cause of the opportunity to ensure that the risk event does happen. Enhancing a project risk looks for solutions, triggers, or other drivers to ensure that the risk does come to fruition so that the rewards of the risk can be realized by the performing organization. Crashing a project to receive an award, for example, is an example of enhancing a positive risk.

Escalate a Positive Risk

When a risk, even a positive risk, is outside of the project manager's authority or outside the scope of the project, the risk is escalated. Once an opportunity is escalated, it's no longer monitored by the project manager or team; it's owned by some other entity in the organization, and the project manager and team return to focus on the project scope.

Accepting a Risk

Risk acceptance is the process of accepting a risk because no other action is feasible, or the risk is deemed to be of small probability, impact, or both, and a formal response is not warranted. Passive acceptance requires no action; the project team deals with the risk when it happens. Active acceptance entails developing a contingency plan should the risk occur. Acceptance may be used for both positive and negative risks.

Creating a Project Contingency Response

A contingency response is a predefined set of actions the project team will take should certain events occur. Contingency plans are sometimes called worst-case scenario plans or fallback plans. Events that trigger the contingency plan should be tracked. A fallback plan is a reaction to a risk that has occurred when the primary response proves to be inadequate.

Most risk acceptance policies rely on a contingency allowance for the project. A project contingency allowance is the amount of money the project will likely need in the contingency reserve based on the impact, probability, and expected monetary value of a risk event.

For example, Risk A has a 25 percent chance of happening and has a cost impact of –$20,000. The probability of 25 percent times the impact of –$20,000 equates to a –$5000 expected monetary value (Ex$V). Another risk, Risk B, has a 45 percent chance of happening and has a positive benefit value of $3000. The Ex$V for Risk B is positive, $1350. If these were the only risks in the project, an ideal contingency reserve would be $3650. This is calculated by adding the positive and negative risk values to predict the amount by which the project is likely to be underfunded if the risks happen. Table 11-1 shows several risks and their Ex$Vs.

Examining the Results of Risk Response Planning

The major output of risk response planning is the risk register updates, though change requests, project management plan updates, and project documents might also be outputs depending on the risk responses created. These risk responses are documented in the risk register and guide the reaction to each identified risk. They include the following:

- A description of the risk, what area of the project it may affect, the causes of the risk, and its impact on project objectives
- Risk response strategies
- Contingency plans and fallback plans
- The identities of the risk owners and their assigned responsibilities
- The outputs of qualitative and quantitative analyses
- Risk strategies and the specific actions necessary to implement those strategies
- Symptoms and warning signs, sometimes called triggers, of each risk event

TABLE 11-1

Contingency Reserve Calculations

Risk	Probability	Impact: Cost Is Negative; Benefits Are Positive	Ex$V
A	25%	–$20,000	–$5000
B	45%	$3000	$1350
C	10%	$2100	$210
D	65%	–$25,000	–$16,250
		Project Contingency Reserve Fund	$19,690

- A description of the response to each risk, such as avoidance, transference, mitigation, or acceptance
- The actions necessary to implement the responses
- The budget and schedule for risk responses
- The contingency and fallback plans
- Change requests

Working with Residual Risks

The risk response plan also acknowledges any residual risks that may remain after planning, avoidance, transfer, or mitigation. Residual risks are typically minor and have been acknowledged and accepted. Management may elect to add both contingency costs and schedule to account for the residual risks within the project.

Accounting for Secondary Risks

Secondary risks stem from risk responses. For example, the response of transference may call for a third party to manage an identified risk. As you can see in the following illustration, a secondary risk caused by the solution is the failure of the third party to complete their assignment as scheduled. Secondary risks must be identified, analyzed, and planned for, just as any another identified risk.

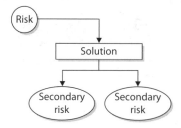

Creating Contracts for Risk Response

When multiple entities are involved in a project, contractual agreements may be necessary to identify the responsible parties for identified risks. The contract may be needed for insurance purposes, customer acceptance, or the acknowledgement of responsibilities between the entities completing the project. Transference is an example of contractual agreements to transfer the responsibility for risks within a project.

Justifying Risk Reduction

To reduce risk, additional time or monies are typically needed. The process and logic behind the strategies to reduce a risk should be evaluated to determine whether the solution is worth the tradeoffs. For example, a risk may be eliminated by adding $7500 to a project's budget. However, the likelihood of the risk occurring is relatively low. Should the risk happen, it would cost, at a minimum, $8000 to correct, and the project would be delayed by at least two weeks. The cost of preventing the risk versus the cost of responding to it must be weighed and justified. If the risk is not eliminated with the $7500 cost and the project moves forward as planned, it has, theoretically, saved $15,500 because the risk did not happen and the response to the risk did not need to happen. However, if the risk does happen, the project will lose at least $8000 and will be delayed at least two weeks. The cost inherent in the project delay may be more expensive than the solution to the risk. The judgment of solving the risk to reduce the likelihood of delaying the project may be wiser than ignoring the risk, hoping the risk won't happen, and saving the costs incurred. In other words, sometimes it's better to purchase a solution than to gamble that the risk won't happen.

Updating the Project Plan

The risk reactions, contingency plans, and fallback plans should all be documented and incorporated into the project plan—for example, updating the schedule, budget, and WBS to accommodate additional time, money, and activities for risk responses. The responses to the risks may change the original implementation of the project and should be updated to reflect the project plan and intent of the project team, management, and other stakeholders. A failure to update the project plan and the risk register may cause risk reactions to be missed and may skew performance measurements. The following specific project management plan components may need a change request to be updated:

- Schedule management plan
- Cost management plan
- Resource management plan
- Procurement management plan
- Scope, schedule, and cost baselines

CERTIFICATION OBJECTIVE 11.06

Implementing Risk Responses

Once the risk responses have been identified, documented, and agreed upon, the project manager will also need to make certain that the responses are carried out as planned. It's too easy to assume that the risk owners will attend to the risk responses—that assumption is a risk. Implementing risk responses creates the mechanisms to ensure that the response has been taken.

Preparing to Implement Risk Responses

To complete this process you'll need three inputs:

- **Risk management plan**   The roles and responsibilities of the risk management plan are needed to make certain the right people are carrying out the right responses. You'll also need the risk management plan to identify and communicate the risk thresholds, which will signal when the risk response is needed.
- **Project documents**   The lessons learned register, risk register, and risk report are inputs to this process.
- **Organizational process assets**   Historical information from similar projects can help the project manager and the project team implement the risk responses.

Reviewing the Tools and Techniques for Implementing Risk Responses

You should be familiar with three tools and techniques for implementing risk responses:

- **Expert judgment**   Expert judgment, a common tool and technique, is also used in implementing risk responses. Experts can help to implement the risk response or even modify the risk response based on conditions within the project.
- **Interpersonal and team skills**   The project manager may need to influence the risk owner to act on the risk that needs the response. The risk owner could be outside of the project team, so influencing is the interpersonal skill that's needed: influence that person to act to keep the project moving.
- **Project Management Information System**   The PMIS can help to ensure that the risk response activities are integrated into the schedule, resource planning, and cost of the project.

Examining the Results of Implementing Risk Responses

There are just two results of implementing risk responses:

- **Change requests**   As you might expect, change requests could be generated because the risk response may cause a change to the project's cost or schedule baseline. The change request must be documented and must flow through the integrated change control process.

- **Project document updates**   Lots of project documents could be updated because of the risk response. Documents that might need updating include the issue log, lessons learned register, project team assignments, risk register, and the risk report.

CERTIFICATION OBJECTIVE 11.07

Monitoring Risks

Risks must be actively monitored, and new risks must be responded to as they are discovered. Risk monitoring is the process of monitoring identified risks for signs that they may be occurring, addressing identified risks with the agreed-upon responses, looking for new risks that may creep into the project, and then following the outcomes of the risk responses to track their effectiveness. Risk monitoring also is concerned with the documentation of the success or failure of risk response plans and keeping records of metrics that signal risks are occurring, fading, or disappearing from the project.

Risk monitoring is an active process that requires participation from the project manager, the project team, key stakeholders, and, in particular, risk owners within the project. As the project progresses, risk conditions may change and require new responses, additional planning, or the implementation of a contingency plan.

There are several goals to risk monitoring:

- To confirm that risk responses are implemented as planned
- To determine whether risk responses are effective or whether new responses are needed
- To determine the validity of the project assumptions
- To determine whether risk exposure has changed, evolved, or declined due to trends in the project progression
- To monitor risk triggers
- To confirm that policies and procedures happen as planned
- To monitor the project for new risks

■ To confirm the continued validity of the risk management approach

■ To determine whether the project contingency reserves (cost and schedule) are adequate

Preparing for Risk Monitoring

Risk monitoring is an active process. The project team and the project manager must rely on several inputs to monitor and address risks effectively:

■ **The risk management plan**   Defines the organization's approach to risk management. It is not the strategy for specific risks within a project, but the overall strategy for risk analysis and planning.

■ **Project documents**   The central repository for all project risk information, the risk register, is the primary document you'll need. The risk register includes the identified risks, the potential responses, the root causes of risks, and any identified categories of risk. You may also reference the lessons learned register, the issue log, and the risk report.

■ **Work performance data and work performance reports**   The results of project work can inform the project manager and the project team of new and pending risks. In addition, project team members may create reports to monitor or document risks. Project performance focuses on the balance of the project schedule, costs, and scope. Should the performance of time, cost, or scope suffer, new risks are likely to enter the project.

Completing Risk Monitoring

Risk monitoring happens throughout the project—it is not a solitary activity that is completed once and never revisited. The project manager and the project team must actively monitor risks, respond with the agreed-upon actions, and scan the horizon for risks that have not been addressed. Risk monitoring is a recurring activity that requires input from all project participants. Several tools are available for implementing risk monitoring, and they are discussed in the following sections.

Completing Risk Response Audits

A risk response audit examines the planned risk response, how well the planned actions work, and the effectiveness of the risk owner in implementing the risk response. The project manager is responsible to ensure that audits happen throughout the project to measure the effectiveness of mitigating, transferring, and avoiding risks. The risk response audit should measure the effectiveness of the decision and its impact on schedule and cost.

Completing Periodic Risk Reviews

Project risk should be on the agenda at every project team meeting. The periodic risk review is a risk reassessment scheduled regularly throughout the project to ascertain the level of foreseeable risks and the success of risk responses in the project to date, and to review pending risks. Based on circumstances within the project, risk rankings and prioritization may fluctuate. Changes to the project scope, team, or conditions may require qualitative and quantitative analyses.

Using Earned Value Analysis

Earned value analysis measures project performance. When project performance is waning, the project is likely missing targeted costs and schedule goals. The results of earned value analysis can signal that risks are happening within the project or that new risks may be developing.

For example, a schedule performance index (SPI) of 0.93 means the project is off schedule by 7 percent. A risk based on this value could mean that the project team is having difficulty completing the project work as planned. Additional work will continue to be late, the project will finish late, and quality may suffer as the team attempts to rush to complete assigned tasks.

Measuring Technical Performance

Throughout the project, the project team's technical competence with the technology being used in the project should increase. The level of technical achievement should be in proportion to the expected level of technical performance within the project. If the project team is not performing at a level of expected technical expertise, the project may suffer additional risks resulting from the discrepancy. Technical performance can be measured by the successful completion of activities throughout the project or project phases.

Completing Additional Risk Planning

Most likely, new risks will become evident during the project implementation. The project team, project manager, and key stakeholders who discover the risks should communicate them. The risks must then be acknowledged, documented, analyzed, and planned for. The project team must be encouraged to communicate the discovery of new risks.

on the job

Often, project team members don't want to share discovered risks with the project manager because the presence of a risk can be seen as bad news. The project manager must stress to the project team members that identified risks should be communicated so that the risks can be planned for through escalation, avoidance, mitigation, transference, or even acceptance.

When a risk event occurs and the project manager uses a portion of the risk reserve, it's necessary to examine the balance of the contingency reserve in relation to the risks still in the project. In other words, you'll want to see how much the risk event has cost the project and determine whether enough funds remain in the contingency reserve to cover the remaining risk events should any of these events happen. Reserve analysis is a necessary practice throughout the project.

Examining the Results of Risk Monitoring

Risk monitoring helps the project become more successful. It measures the planned responses to risks and creates reactions to unplanned risks. The outputs of risk monitoring also aim to help the project reach its objectives. The process has several outputs:

- **Work performance information**   What happens in the project because of monitoring risks and risk responses will create work performance information. This information affects what needs to be communicated and what actions the project manager and team may take next, and it helps with project decisions.

- **Change requests**   Risk monitoring may cause the project's cost or schedule baseline to need to be updated. The update of a baseline will need a change request that follows the integrated change control process. Project management plan updates could also be an output of this process, and these updates will also require a change request. Corrective actions are taken to bring the project back into compliance with the project plan. Preventive actions are taken to bring the project back into alignment with the project management plan.

- **Project document updates**   As the project moves along and the project manager and the project team complete the risk assessments, audits, and risk reviews, they'll need to record their findings in the risk register, risk report, or both. This update may include the reevaluation of the risk's impact, probability, and expected monetary value. For those risks that have passed in the project, the risk register should record what happened with the risk event and its impact on the project. The project's assumption log, issue log, lessons learned register, risk register, and risk report can all be updated because of this process.

- **Organizational process assets updates**   The risks from the current project can help other project managers in the future. Therefore, the project manager must work to ensure that the current risks, their anticipated impact, and their actual impact are recorded. The current risk matrix, for example, can become a risk template for other projects in the future. This is true for just about any risk document—from risk responses, to the risk breakdown structure, lessons learned, and checklists.

■ **Project management plan updates** All component plans are potentially updated as some risk responses will require change requests that require that the project management plan to be updated. As risks occur, the responses to those risks should be documented and updated in the risk response plan. Should risk rankings change during the project, the change in ranking, the logic behind the change, and the results of the risk rank change should be documented in the individual risk response plans. For the risks that do not occur, the risks should be documented and considered closed in the risk response plan. Issue and assumption logs as well as the lessons learned may also need to be updated.

CERTIFICATION SUMMARY

PMP candidates must have a firm grasp on how to plan for, monitor, and respond to projects' risks. To handle risks effectively, the project manager needs to begin with risk management planning. A large, complex project will likely have more risks than a smaller project. In any situation, however, risks must be identified and planned for. The performing organization will often have risk management policies that dictate how the risk planning sessions are to be performed and what level of risks call for additional planning.

Some stakeholders—and organizations—will be more tolerant than others of accepting risks.

Qualitative risk analysis qualifies identified risks and creates a prioritization of each. Every risk is considered for its impact and likelihood of occurring. Once the risks have passed through qualitative risk analysis, quantitative risk analysis can be done if appropriate for the project. Quantitative risk analysis assesses the probability and impact of the risks, and it determines a risk score based on further analysis, discussion, expert judgment, simulations, and interviews with stakeholders.

Risk responses are created and risk owners are assigned. Thresholds and triggers are identified for the risks, and these are then monitored throughout the project. Risk responses are then implemented. Risk monitoring tracks the risk response effectiveness and the conditions of the risk events, and periodically reviews the status of risks, including the low-level risk watch list, to see if the probability and/or impact of the risks have changed.

KEY TERMS

If you're serious about passing the PMP exam, memorize the following terms and their definitions. For maximum value, create your own flashcards based on these definitions and review them daily. You can find additional information on these terms in the project glossary.

acceptance   A response to a risk event, generally made when the probability of the event and/or its impact is small. No proactive action is taken on the risk. It is used when escalation, mitigation, transference, and avoidance are not selected.

ambiguity risks   These risks are impossible to predict accurately: certainty of a new technical solution, future laws or regulations, or even complexity in the project approach.

avoidance   One response to a risk event. The risk is avoided by removing the risk from the project.

brainstorming   The most common approach to risk identification; it is performed by a project team to identify the risks within the project. A multidisciplinary team, hosted by a project facilitator, can also perform brainstorming.

bubble chart   A hierarchical chart that uses three parameters for mapping the axes of the risks and the magnitude of the third parameter. The larger the bubble the more significant parameter.

cause-and-effect diagrams   Used for root-cause analysis of what factors are creating the risks within the project. The goal is to identify and treat the root of the problem, not the symptom.

commercial risks   When working with vendors, new risks are introduced to the project specific to the contractual relationship. Risk categories can include the contract terms, internal procurement procedures, suppliers, subcontracts, client and customer stability, and any partnerships or joint ventures.

contingency reserve   A time or dollar amount allotted as a response to risk events that may occur within a project.

decision tree analysis   A type of analysis that determines which of two decisions is the best. The decision tree assists in calculating the value of the decision and determining which decision costs the least.

Delphi Technique   A method to survey experts anonymously on foreseeable risks within the project, phase, or component of the project. The results of the survey are analyzed and organized, and then circulated to the experts. There can be several rounds of anonymous discussions when using the Delphi Technique. The goal is to gain consensus on project risks, and the anonymous nature of the process ensures that no one expert's advice overtly influences the opinions of other participants.

enhance To enhance a risk is to attempt to modify its probability and/or its impacts to realize the most gains from it. Enhance applies only to positive risks (opportunities).

escalate risk response Some risks that are outside of the boundary of the project should be escalated when the project team, project sponsor, or project manager believes the risk management would exceed the authority the project manager has over the risk event.

exploit The organization wants to ensure that the identified risk does happen to realize the positive impact associated with the risk event.

individual project risks An individual risk that hinders or helps realize the project objectives.

influence diagram A diagram that charts out a decision problem. It identifies all of the elements, variables, decisions, and objectives—and how each factor may influence another.

mitigation A process of reducing the probability or impact of a risk.

overall project risk A combination of all risk events that will reveal the project's risk exposure and determine just how risky the project is for the organization.

PESTLE Analysis of overall project risks by determining political, economic, social, technological, legal, and environmental uncertainty.

qualitative risk analysis An examination and prioritization of the risks based on their probability of occurring and the impact on the project if they do occur. Qualitative risk analysis guides the risk reaction process.

quantitative risk analysis A numerical assessment of the probability and impact of the identified risks. Quantitative risk analysis also creates an overall risk score for the project.

residual risks Risks that are left over after mitigation, transference, and avoidance. These are generally accepted risks. Management may elect to add contingency costs and time to account for the residual risks within the project.

risk   An uncertain event that can have a positive or negative influence on the project's success.

risk categories   These help organize, rank, and identify risks within the project.

risk management plan   A subsidiary project management plan for determining how risks will be identified, how quantitative and qualitative analyses will be completed, how risk response planning will happen, how risks will be monitored, and how ongoing risk management activities will occur throughout the project life cycle.

risk owners   The individuals or groups responsible for a risk response.

risk register   Documentation of all risk events and their conditions, impact, probability, and overall risk score.

risk report   A document that explains the overall project risks and provides a summary about the individual project risks. You'll update the risk report through the project as more information becomes available through analysis and experience in the project.

scales of probability and impact   Used in a risk matrix in both qualitative risk analysis and quantitative risk analysis to score each risk's probability and impact.

secondary risks   Risks that stem from risk responses. For example, the response of transference may call for hiring a third party to manage an identified risk. A secondary risk caused by the solution is the failure of the third party to complete its assignment as scheduled. Secondary risks must be identified, analyzed, and planned for, just like any other identified risk.

sensitivity analysis   Examines each project's risk on its own merit to assess the impact on the project. All other risks in the project are set at a baseline value.

share   Sharing is nice. When sharing, the risk ownership is transferred to the organization that can most capitalize on the risk opportunity.

simulation   Allows the project team to do "what-if" analysis without affecting any areas of production.

system or process flowcharts   Show the relationship between components and how the overall process works. They are useful for identifying risks between system components.

TECOP   Analysis of overall project risks by determining technical, environmental, commercial, operational, and political uncertainty.

transference   A response to risks in which the responsibility and ownership of the risk are transferred to another party (for example, through insurance).

triggers   Warning signs or symptoms that a risk has occurred or is about to occur (for example, a vendor failing to complete their portion of the project as scheduled).

utility function   A person's willingness to accept risk. The higher the utility function, the more likely the person or organization is willing to accept risk.

variability risks   Uncertainty surrounding a project activity or decision. Fluctuations in productivity, number or errors and defects, or even the weather affecting the project are all examples of variability risks.

VUCA   Analysis of overall project risks by determining volatility, uncertainty, complexity, and ambiguity.

workarounds   Unplanned responses to risks that were not identified or expected.

 # TWO-MINUTE DRILL

Planning for Risk Management

- ❑ Risk management planning involves determining how the risk management activities within the project will take place. It is not the response or identification of risks, but the determination of how to manage project risks.
- ❑ Risk management planning is accomplished through planning meetings with the project team, management, customers, and other key stakeholders.
- ❑ A utility function, also called risk tolerance, is a stakeholder's willingness to accept or tolerate risks.
- ❑ Risks are uncertain events that can affect a project's objectives for good or bad.
- ❑ Risks can be placed into four different categories: technical, management, commercial, and external risks.
- ❑ The risk management plan defines the process to identify, analyze, respond to, and monitor all project risk events.

Identifying Risks

❑ Project records from published information and previous projects can serve as input to risk identification.

❑ Assumptions are things that are believed to be true but that haven't been proven to be true. Assumptions can become risks based on the assumption stability and consequence if the assumption is false.

❑ Triggers are warning signs that a risk is about to happen or has happened.

Using Qualitative Risk Analysis

❑ Qualitative risk analysis is a high-level, fast analysis of the identified project risks.

❑ Risks are evaluated for their impact and likelihood.

❑ Risks can be ranked in an ordinal fashion by using indicators such as very low, low, moderate, high, and very high.

❑ Risks can also be analyzed using a cardinal ranking system of numeric values that are assigned to each risk based on its impact and probability.

❑ An overall project risk ranking can be used to compare the current projects with other projects in the organization.

❑ Risks that have a high score from qualitative analysis can be moved into quantitative analysis for further study.

Preparing for Quantitative Risk Analysis

❑ Risks are assigned an expected monetary value—for example, there is a 50 percent likelihood that the risk will occur, causing a $10,000 cost.

❑ Quantitative analysis is an in-depth study of the risk's probability and impact.

❑ Risks and their impacts, status, responses, and updates are all recorded in the risk register.

Planning for Risk Responses

❑ Risk response planning focuses on reducing threats and increasing opportunities as a result of risks.

❑ Risk tolerance or appetite, documented in risk management planning, describes the acceptable level of risk within a company.

❑ Risk owners are the individuals or groups that are responsible for a risk response and that should participate in the risk response planning.

❑ Enhancing a positive risk requires that the organization take steps to increase the probability and/or impact of the risk.

Implementing Risk Responses

❑ Risk avoidance changes the project plan to avoid the risk (as well as conditions that promote the risk).

❑ Risk transference moves the risk consequence to a third party. The risk doesn't go away, but the responsibility for it is shifted. However, the performing organization still retains the ultimate accountability and results of the risk event.

❑ Risk mitigation involves actions designed to reduce the likelihood of a risk occurring, the impact of a risk on the project objectives, or both.

❑ Risk acceptance acknowledges that the risk exists but deems it unworthy of a more in-depth response, or a more in-depth response isn't available for the risk.

❑ Residual risks remain after avoidance, transference, mitigation, and acceptance.

❑ Secondary risks are new risks that arise from a risk response.

❑ To exploit a positive risk requires that an organization implement measures to ensure that the risk happens.

❑ Sharing a risk assigns ownership of the positive risk to an organization that is most likely to utilize the positive risks for the benefit of the project.

Monitoring Risks

❑ Identified risks must be tracked, monitored for warning signs, and documented. The responses to the risks are monitored and documented as successful or less successful than expected.

❑ Risk response audits measure the success of the responses and the effectiveness of the cost, scope, and quality values gained or lost by the risk responses.

❑ Earned value analysis can measure project performance, but it can also predict and signal pending risks within the project.

❑ As unexpected risks arise, the project team may elect to use workarounds to diminish the impact and probability of those risks. Workarounds, however, should be documented and incorporated into the project plan and risk response plan as they occur.

SELF TEST

1. Beth is the project manager for her company, and Marty, her supervisor, is concerned with the possibility of Beth accepting one of the project risks. Beth explains that this risk should be accepted within the project. When is it appropriate to accept a project risk?

   A. It is never appropriate to accept a project risk.

   B. All risks must be mitigated or transferred.

   C. It is appropriate to accept a risk if the project team has never completed this type of project work before.

   D. It is appropriate to accept a risk if the risk is in balance with the reward.

2. Frances is the project manager of the LKJ Project. Which of the following techniques will she use to create the risk management plan?

   A. Risk tolerance

   B. Status meetings

   C. Planning meetings

   D. Variance meetings

3. You are the project manager of the HQQ Project, and part of your requirement in this role is to create a risk management plan. Which of the following is *not* part of a risk management plan?

   A. Roles and responsibilities

   B. Methodology

   C. Technical assessment board compliance

   D. Risk categories

4. You are the project manager of the GHK Project. You and the manufacturer have agreed to substitute the type of plastic used in the product to a slightly thicker grade should there be more than a 7 percent error in production. The thicker plastic will cost more and require a production slowdown, but the errors should diminish. This is an example of which of the following?

   A. Threshold

   B. Tracking

   C. Budgeting

   D. JIT manufacturing

5. Hans is a project manager for his organization, and he's working with his sponsor to identify the organization's risk tolerance. Understanding the risk tolerance and any associated enterprise environmental factors will help Hans and the project team plan for risk responses. An organization's risk tolerance is also known as what?

   A. The utility function
   B. Herzberg's Theory of Motivation
   C. Risk acceptance
   D. The risk–reward ratio

6. As a project manager, you must understand the components of an identified risk, a risk response, a risk trigger, risk thresholds, and issues. A risk trigger is also called which of the following?

   A. A warning sign
   B. A delay
   C. A cost increase
   D. An incremental advancement of risk

7. The customers of the project have requested additions to the project scope. The project manager brings notice that additional risk planning will need to be added to the project schedule. Why?

   A. The risk planning should always take the same amount of time as the activities required by the scope change.
   B. Risk planning should always occur whenever the scope is adjusted.
   C. Risk planning should occur only at the project manager's discretion.
   D. The project manager is incorrect. Risk planning does not need to happen at every change in the project.

8. You are the project manager of your organization, and you're working with your project team and the project stakeholders to identify the risks within the project. Some of the risks have not yet happened, and some of the risks are already issues. You tell the project team that all risks must be documented in the risk register, but they are not familiar with this document. Which one of the following best describes the risk register?

   A. It documents the individual risks.
   B. It's a document that contains the initial risk identification entries.
   C. It's a system that tracks all negative risks within a project.
   D. It's part of the project's PMIS for integrated change control.

9. An understanding of the different types of risk events can help the project manager work better with the enterprise environmental factors and the organizational process assets that affect the risk management in a project. Based on this information, a _____ include(s) fire, theft, or injury, and offer(s) no chance for gain.
    A. Business risks
    B. Pure risks
    C. Risk acceptance
    D. Life risks

10. Complete this sentence: A project risk is a(n) _____ occurrence that can affect the project for good or bad.
    A. Known
    B. Dangerous
    C. Uncertain
    D. Known-unknown

11. Risk identification is an iterative process in the project and requires participation from the project manager, the project team, and other key stakeholders. Because of the nature of risk, when should risk identification happen?
    A. As early as possible in the initiation process
    B. As early as possible in the planning process
    C. Throughout the product management life cycle
    D. Throughout the project life cycle

12. You are the project manager of the KLJH Project. This project will last two years and has 30 stakeholders. How often should risk identification take place?
    A. Once at the beginning of the project
    B. Throughout the execution processes
    C. Throughout the project
    D. Once per project phase

13. You are the project manager of the HNN Project and you're working with the project stakeholders, including the project team and the project sponsor, to identify risks within the project. You have identified an opportunity that the organization could take advantage of as an additional revenue stream. As the project manager, what's the best risk response to choose for this risk?
    A. Exploit
    B. Enhance
    C. Escalate
    D. Share

14. You are the project manager for a project that will create a new and improved web site for your company. Currently, your company has more than 8 million users around the globe. You would like to poll experts within your organization with a simple, anonymous form asking about any foreseeable risks in the design, structure, and intent of the web site. With the collected information, subsequent anonymous polls will be submitted to the group of experts. This is an example of _____.
    A. Risk identification
    B. A trigger
    C. An anonymous trigger
    D. The Delphi Technique

15. As a PMP candidate, you must be familiar with the different approaches to risk identification. One approach is called SWOT. Which of the following describes SWOT?
    A. An analysis of strengths, weakness, options, and timing
    B. An analysis of strengths, weakness, opportunities, and threats
    C. An elite project team that comes in and fixes project risks and threats
    D. Ratings of 1 to 100

16. You are the project manager of the GLI Project for your organization. Your project sponsor has asked that you use an approach to measure the probability and impact of the risk events and then to rank the events accordingly. Which risk analysis provides the project manager with a risk ranking?
    A. Quantifiable
    B. Qualitative
    C. The utility function
    D. SWOT analysis

17. A table of risks, their probability, their impact, and a number representing the overall risk score is called a _____.
    A. Risk table
    B. Probability and impact matrix
    C. Quantitative matrix
    D. Qualitative matrix

18. You are presented with the following table:

Risk Event	Probability	Impact Cost/Benefit	EMV
1	.20	−4000	
2	.50	5000	
3	.45	−300	
4	.22	500	
5	.35	−4500	

What is the EMV for Risk Event 3?

A. $135

B. −$300

C. $45

D. −$135

19. You are presented with the following table:

Risk Event	Probability	Impact Cost/Benefit	Ex$V
1	.35	−$4000	
2	.40	$50,000	
3	.45	−$300,000	
4	.30	$50,000	
5	.35	−$45,000	

Based on the preceding numbers, what is the amount needed for the contingency fund?

A. Unknown with this information

B. $249,000

C. $117,150

D. $15,750

20. The water sanitation project manager has determined that the risks associated with handling certain chemicals are too high. He has decided to allow someone else to complete this portion of the project, so he has outsourced the handling and installation of the chemicals and filter equipment to an experienced contractor. This is an example of which of the following?

A. Avoidance

B. Acceptance

C. Mitigation

D. Transference

21. A project manager and the project team are actively monitoring the pressure gauge on a piece of equipment. Sarah, the engineer, recommends a series of steps to be implemented should the pressure rise above 80 percent. The 80 percent mark represents what?

A. An upper control limit

B. The threshold

C. Mitigation

D. A workaround

22. You are presented with the following table:

Risk Event	Probability	Impact Cost/Benefit	Ex$V
1	.20	−4000	
2	.50	5000	
3	.45	−300	
4	.22	500	
5	.35	−4500	
6			

What would Risk 6 be based on the following information: Marty is 60 percent certain that he can get the facility needed for $45,000, which is $7000 less than what was planned for?

A. .60, 45,000, 27,000

B. .60, 52,000, 31,200

C. .60, 7000, 4200

D. .60, −7000, −4200

23. What can a project manager use to determine whether it is better to make or buy a product?

A. A decision tree analysis

B. A fishbone model

C. An Ishikawa diagram

D. An ROI analysis

24. Which of the following can determine multiple scenarios, given various risks and the probability of their impact?

A. Decision trees

B. Monte Carlo simulations

C. Pareto charts

D. Gantt charts

25. Gary is a project manager for his organization and he's evaluating the risks within his project. Some of the risk events have a high impact, while other risk events have a low probability. In this project, many risks have high-risk impact scores but an overall low-risk score. How is this possible?

A. The risk scores are graded on a bell curve.

B. The probability of each risk is low.

C. The impact of each risk is not accounted for until it comes to fruition.

D. The risks are rated high, medium, or low.

SELF TEST ANSWERS

1. Beth is the project manager for her company, and Marty, her supervisor, is concerned with the possibility of Beth accepting one of the project risks. Beth explains that this risk should be accepted within the project. When is it appropriate to accept a project risk?
   A. It is never appropriate to accept a project risk.
   B. All risks must be mitigated or transferred.
   C. It is appropriate to accept a risk if the project team has never completed this type of project work before.
   D. It is appropriate to accept a risk if the risk is in balance with the reward.

   ☑ **D.** Risks that are in balance with the reward are appropriate for acceptance.
   ☒ **A, B,** and **C** are incorrect. These solutions are all false responses to risk management. It certainly is appropriate to accept a project risk in some instances. Consider the weather or the dangerous nature of project work such as construction. You don't have to mitigate or transfer all risks because some are worth accepting, escalating, exploiting, enhancing, or even sharing.

2. Frances is the project manager of the LKJ Project. Which of the following techniques will she use to create the risk management plan?
   A. Risk tolerance
   B. Status meetings
   C. Planning meetings
   D. Variance meetings

   ☑ **C.** Planning meetings are used to create the risk management plan. The project manager, project team leaders, key stakeholders, and other individuals with the power to make decisions regarding risk management attend the meetings.
   ☒ **A, B,** and **D** are incorrect. These choices do not fully answer the question.

3. You are the project manager of the HQQ Project, and part of your requirement in this role is to create a risk management plan. Which of the following is *not* part of a risk management plan?
   A. Roles and responsibilities
   B. Methodology
   C. Technical assessment board compliance
   D. Risk categories

   ☑ **C.** The technical assessment board may be used as part of the change control system. It is not relevant to risk management planning.
   ☒ **A, B,** and **D** are incorrect. **A** is incorrect because roles and responsibilities are a part of the risk management plan. **B,** methodology, is part of the risk management plan because it identifies the approaches, tools, and data sources for risk management. **D,** risk categories, is part of the risk management plan.

4. You are the project manager of the GHK Project. You and the manufacturer have agreed to substitute the type of plastic used in the product to a slightly thicker grade should there be more than a 7 percent error in production. The thicker plastic will cost more and require a production slowdown, but the errors should diminish. This is an example of which of the following?
   A. Threshold
   B. Tracking
   C. Budgeting
   D. JIT manufacturing

   ☑ **A.** An error value of 7 percent represents the threshold under which the project can operate. Should the number of errors increase beyond 7 percent, the current plastic will be substituted.
   ☒ **B, C,** and **D** are incorrect. **B** is incorrect because tracking is the documentation of a process through a system or workflow, or the documentation of events through the process. **C,** budgeting, is also incorrect, because the scenario deals with identifying the risk threshold, not the cost associated with the risk event. **D,** JIT manufacturing, is a scheduling approach to ordering the materials only when they are needed to keep inventory costs down.

5. Hans is a project manager for his organization, and he's working with his sponsor to identify the organization's risk tolerance. Understanding the risk tolerance and any associated enterprise environmental factors will help Hans and the project team plan for risk responses. An organization's risk tolerance is also known as what?
   A. The utility function
   B. Herzberg's Theory of Motivation
   C. Risk acceptance
   D. The risk–reward ratio

☑   **A.** The utility function describes a person's willingness to tolerate risk.

☒   **B, C,** and **D** are incorrect. **B** is incorrect because Herzberg's Theory of Motivation is an HR theory that describes motivating agents for workers. **C** is incorrect because risk acceptance describes the action of allowing a risk to exist because it is deemed low in impact, low in probability, or both. **D,** the risk–reward ratio, describes the potential reward for taking a risk in the project.

6. As a project manager, you must understand the components of an identified risk, a risk response, a risk trigger, risk thresholds, and issues. A risk trigger is also called which of the following?

A. A warning sign

B. A delay

C. A cost increase

D. An incremental advancement of risk

☑   **A.** Risk triggers can also be known as warning signs. Triggers signal that a risk is about to happen or has happened.

☒   **B, C,** and **D** are incorrect. These answers do not properly describe a risk trigger.

7. The customers of the project have requested additions to the project scope. The project manager brings notice that additional risk planning will need to be added to the project schedule. Why?

A. The risk planning should always take the same amount of time as the activities required by the scope change.

B. Risk planning should always occur whenever the scope is adjusted.

C. Risk planning should occur only at the project manager's discretion.

D. The project manager is incorrect. Risk planning does not need to happen at every change in the project.

☑   **B.** When the scope has been changed, the project manager should require risk planning to analyze the additions for risks to the project's success.

☒   **A, C,** and **D** are incorrect. **A** is incorrect because the scope changes may not require the same amount of time as the activities needed to complete the project changes. **C** is incorrect because risk planning should not occur at the project manager's discretion. Instead, it should be based on evidence within the project and the policies adopted in the risk management plan. **D** is incorrect because when changes are added to the project scope, risk planning should occur.

8. You are the project manager of your organization, and you're working with your project team and the project stakeholders to identify the risks within the project. Some of the risks have not yet happened, and some of the risks are already issues. You tell the project team that all risks must be documented in the risk register, but they are not familiar with this document. Which one of the following best describes the risk register?
   A. It documents the individual risks.
   B. It's a document that contains the initial risk identification entries.
   C. It's a system that tracks all negative risks within a project.
   D. It's part of the project's PMIS for integrated change control.

   ☑ **A.** The risk register documents the individual risks.
   ☒ **B, C,** and **D** are incorrect. These are not definitions of the risk register.

9. An understanding of the different types of risk events can help the project manager work better with the enterprise environmental factors and the organizational process assets that affect the risk management in a project. Based on this information, a _____ include(s) fire, theft, or injury and offer(s) no chance for gain.
   A. Business risks
   B. Pure risks
   C. Risk acceptance
   D. Life risks

   ☑ **B.** Pure risks are the risks that could threaten the safety of the individuals on the project.
   ☒ **A, C,** and **D** are incorrect. **A** is incorrect because business risks affect the financial gains or loss of a project. **C** and **D** are incorrect because these terms are not relevant.

10. Complete this sentence: A project risk is a(n) _____ occurrence that can affect the project for good or bad.
    A. Known
    B. Dangerous
    C. Uncertain
    D. Known-unknown

☑ **C.** Risks are not planned—they are left to chance. The accommodation and the reaction to a risk can be planned, but the event itself is not planned. If risks could be planned, Las Vegas would be out of business.

☒ **A, B,** and **D** are incorrect. These terms do not accurately complete the sentence. Not all risks are known and certainly not all risks are unknown. In addition, not all risks are dangerous, but all risks are uncertain.

11. Risk identification is an iterative process in the project and it requires participation from the project manager, the project team, and other key stakeholders. Because of the nature of risk, when should risk identification happen?

   A. As early as possible in the initiation process

   B. As early as possible in the planning process

   C. Throughout the product management life cycle

   D. Throughout the project life cycle

☑ **D.** Risk identification is an iterative process that happens throughout the project life cycle.

☒ **A, B,** and **C** are incorrect. **A** and **B** are both incorrect because risk identification is not limited to any one process group. **C** is incorrect because risk identification technically happens throughout the project management life cycle, which is unique to each project, not the product management life cycle.

12. You are the project manager of the KLJH Project. This project will last two years and has 30 stakeholders. How often should risk identification take place?

   A. Once at the beginning of the project

   B. Throughout the execution processes

   C. Throughout the project

   D. Once per project phase

☑ **C.** Risk identification happens throughout the project. Recall that planning is iterative—as the project moves toward completion, new risks may surface that call for identification and planned responses.

☒ **A, B,** and **D** are incorrect. **A** is incorrect because risk identification should happen throughout the project, not just at the beginning. **B** is incorrect because risk identification is part of planning. **D** is incorrect because the nature of the project phase may require and reveal more than one opportunity for risk identification.

13.   You are the project manager of the HNN Project and you're working with the project stakeholders, including the project team and the project sponsor, to identify risks within the project. You have identified an opportunity that the organization could take advantage of as an additional revenue stream. As the project manager, what's the best risk response to choose for this risk?

A.   Exploit

B.   Enhance

C.   Escalate

D.   Share

☑   **C.** The best response for this positive risk event is to escalate the risk/opportunity. This risk is beyond the boundaries of the project because it may generate an additional revenue stream for the organization, not the project.

☒   **A, B,** and **D** are incorrect. A is incorrect because exploiting would be to make certain the opportunity happens. **B** is incorrect because enhancing would aim to attempt to make the probability increase. **D** is incorrect because sharing happens when there's a teaming agreement or joint venture to seize the opportunity.

14.   You are the project manager for a project that will create a new and improved web site for your company. Currently, your company has more than 8 million users around the globe. You would like to poll experts within your organization with a simple, anonymous form asking about any foreseeable risks in the design, structure, and intent of the web site. With the collected information, subsequent anonymous polls will be submitted to the group of experts. This is an example of _____.

A.   Risk identification

B.   A trigger

C.   An anonymous trigger

D.   The Delphi Technique

☑   **D.** An anonymous poll allowing experts to submit their opinion freely without fear of backlash is an example of the Delphi Technique.

☒   **A, B,** and **C** are incorrect. They do not accurately answer the question.

15.   As a PMP candidate, you must be familiar with the different approaches to risk identification. One approach is called SWOT. Which of the following describes SWOT?

A.   An analysis of strengths, weakness, options, and timing

B.   An analysis of strengths, weakness, opportunities, and threats

C.   An elite project team that comes in and fixes project risks and threats

D.   Ratings of 1 to 100

☑ **B.** SWOT analysis is part of risk identification and examines the strengths, weakness, opportunities, and threats of the project to make certain all possibilities for risk identification are covered.

☒ **A, C,** and **D** are incorrect. **A** is incorrect because SWOT does not examine options and timing. **C** and **D** are incorrect because these ratings are part of quantitative/qualitative risk analysis.

16. You are the project manager of the GLI Project for your organization. Your project sponsor has asked that you use an approach to measure the probability and impact of the risk events and then to rank the events accordingly. Which risk analysis provides the project manager with a risk ranking?
    A. Quantifiable
    B. Qualitative
    C. The utility function
    D. SWOT analysis

☑ **B.** The risk ranking is based on the qualitative values of very high, high, medium, low, and very low attributes of the identified risks.

☒ **A, C,** and **D** are incorrect. **A** is incorrect because it is not relevant to the question. Look again—**A** is quantifiable, not quantitative. **C** is incorrect because utility function describes an organization's tolerance for risk. **D,** SWOT analysis, is part of risk identification.

17. A table of risks, their probability, their impact, and a number representing the overall risk score is called a _____.
    A. Risk table
    B. Probability and impact matrix
    C. Quantitative matrix
    D. Qualitative matrix

☑ **B.** A table of risks, their probability, and their impact equate to a risk score in a risk probability and impact matrix.

☒ **A, C,** and **D** are incorrect. **A** is incorrect because it does not fully answer the question. **C** and **D** are incorrect because a risk matrix can be used in both quantitative and qualitative risk analyses.

18. You are presented with the following table:

Risk Event	Probability	Impact Cost/Benefit	Ex$V
1	.20	−$4000	
2	.50	$5000	
3	.45	−$300	
4	.22	$500	
5	.35	−$4500	

What is the Ex$V for Risk Event 3?

A. $135

B. −$300

C. $45

D. −$135

> ☑ **D.** Risk Event 3 has a probability of 45 percent and an impact cost of −$300, which equates to −$135.
>
> ☒ **A, B,** and **C** are incorrect. The formula probability × impact is used to find the Ex$V for each risk event.

19. You are presented with the following table:

Risk Event	Probability	Impact Cost/Benefit	Ex$V
1	.35	−$4000	
2	.40	$50,000	
3	.45	−$300,000	
4	.30	$50,000	
5	.35	−45,000	

Based on the preceding numbers, what is the amount needed for the contingency fund?

A. Unknown with this information

B. $249,000

C. $117,150

D. $15,750

☑ **C.** Probability × impact determines the Ex$V. The sum of the Ex$V column reveals the risk exposure; the inverse is the ideal contingency reserve. The calculated amount for each of the risk events is shown in the following table:

Risk Event	Probability	Impact Cost/Benefit	Ex$V
1	0.35	−$4,000	−$1400
2	0.4	$50,000	$20,000
3	0.45	−$300,000	−$135,000
4	0.3	$50,000	$15,000
5	0.35	−$45,000	−$15,750
			−$117,150

☒ **A, B,** and **D** are incorrect. They do not reflect the contingency amount needed for the project based on the preceding table.

20. The water sanitation project manager has determined that the risks associated with handling certain chemicals are too high. He has decided to allow someone else to complete this portion of the project, so he has outsourced the handling and installation of the chemicals and filter equipment to an experienced contractor. This is an example of which of the following?

A. Avoidance

B. Acceptance

C. Mitigation

D. Transference

☑ **D.** Because the risk is not eliminated but transferred to someone else or another entity, it is considered transference.

☒ **A, B,** and **C** are incorrect. **A** is incorrect because the risk still exists, but it is handled by another entity. **B** is incorrect because the project manager has not accepted the risk, deciding instead to allow another entity to deal with it. **C** is incorrect because the risk has not been mitigated in the project.

21. A project manager and the project team are actively monitoring the pressure gauge on a piece of equipment. Sarah, the engineer, recommends a series of steps to be implemented should the pressure rise above 80 percent. The 80 percent mark represents what?
     A. An upper control limit
     B. The threshold
     C. Mitigation
     D. A workaround

     ☑   **B.** The 80 percent mark is a threshold.
     ☒   **A, C,** and **D** are incorrect. **A** is incorrect because an upper control limit is a boundary for quality in a control chart. **C** is incorrect because mitigation is a planned response should a risk event happen. **D** is incorrect because a workaround is an action to bypass the risk event.

22. You are presented with the following table:

Risk Event	Probability	Impact Cost/Benefit	Ex$V
1	.20	−$4000	
2	.50	$5000	
3	.45	−$300	
4	.22	$500	
5	.35	−$4500	
6			

     What would Risk 6 be based on the following information: Marty is 60 percent certain that he can get the facility needed for $45,000, which is $7000 less than what was planned for?
     A. .60, $45,000, $27,000
     B. .60, $52,000, $31,200
     C. .60, $7000, $4200
     D. .60, −$7000, −$4200

     ☑   **C.** Marty is 60 percent certain he can save the project $7000. The $4200 represents the 60 percent certainty of the savings.
     ☒   **A, B,** and **D** are incorrect. These values do not reflect the potential savings of the project.

23. What can a project manager use to determine whether it is better to make or buy a product?
    A. A decision tree analysis
    B. A fishbone model
    C. An Ishikawa diagram
    D. An ROI analysis

    ☑ **A.** A decision tree analysis can separate the pros and cons of buying versus building.
    ☒ **B, C,** and **D** are incorrect. **B** and **C** are incorrect because a fishbone diagram and an Ishikawa diagram show cause and effect. **D** is incorrect because an ROI analysis does not answer the question as well as decision tree analysis.

24. Which of the following can determine multiple scenarios, given various risks and the probability of their impact?
    A. Decision trees
    B. Monte Carlo simulations
    C. Pareto charts
    D. Gantt charts

    ☑ **B.** Monte Carlo simulations can reveal multiple scenarios and examine the risks and probability of impact.
    ☒ **A, C,** and **D** are incorrect. **A,** decision trees, help guide the decision-making process. **C,** a Pareto chart, helps identify the leading problems in a situation. **D,** Gantt charts, compare the lengths of activities against a calendar in a bar chart format.

25. Gary is a project manager for his organization and he's evaluating the risks within his project. Some of the risk events have a high impact, while other risk events have a low probability. In this project, many risks have high-risk impact scores but an overall low-risk score. How is this possible?
    A. The risk scores are graded on a bell curve.
    B. The probability of each risk is low.
    C. The impact of each risk is not accounted for until it comes to fruition.
    D. The risks are rated high, medium, or low.

    ☑ **B.** A risk can have a very high impact on the project but inversely have an extremely low probability score. For example, the possibility of a tornado wrecking the project's construction site would have a high impact if it happened, but the probability of it happening is relatively low.
    ☒ **A, C,** and **D** are incorrect. **A** is incorrect and not relevant to the scenario. **C** is not a true statement. **D** is incorrect because a model using high, medium, and low versus a numbering system would not alter the overall high- or low-risk score of the project.

Chapter 12

Introducing Project Procurement Management

CERTIFICATION OBJECTIVES

12.01   Planning for Purchases

12.02   Conducting Procurements

12.03   Controlling Procurements

✓   Two-Minute Drill

Q&A   Self Test

Projects routinely require procurements. They need materials, equipment, consultants, training, and many other goods and services. Project procurement management is the process of purchasing the products necessary for meeting the needs of the project scope. It involves planning, sourcing and acquiring the products or services administering the contract, and closing out the contract. Procurement management, as far as the PMP exam is concerned, can include the practices from the point of view of the buyer or the seller (for example, contractor, subcontractor, vendor, or supplier). In some instances, you'll have to answer the question from the perspective of the buyer, and in others you'll look at the scenario from the seller's point of view.

Your organization may have a specific method established for procuring goods or services from a vendor. For example, you may need to create a purchase order, a memoranda of agreements (MOA), or a service level agreement (SLA) through the project organization channels. For all of these instances, when you organization is buying anything from a vendor, the buyer needs a contract, which becomes a key input to many of the processes that occur within the project. The contract, more than anything else, specifies the rules and agreements for the project.

Here's a neat twist: When the seller is completing their obligations to supply a product, PMI treats those obligations as a project itself. In other words, if ABC Electricians were wiring a building for your company, ABC Electricians would be the performing organization completing its own project. Your company becomes the customer of their project—and your company is, of course, a stakeholder in their project. When the vendor is completing work for a portion of your project, the contract-closing activities don't wait until the end of the project—they happen as needed.

In the scenarios described in this chapter, the seller will be outside of the performing organization. The buyer will be managing a project and procuring resources from a vendor. However, all of the details in this chapter can be applied to internal work orders, internal service level agreements, formal agreements, and contracts between organizational units within a single entity.

For the PMI examination, you'll need to be familiar with three processes dealing with project procurement management. First, like all of the project management knowledge areas, is the associated planning. Once the procurement management plan has been created, you'll actually do the procurement. You'll control the procurement process to ensure that all parties are meeting the terms of the agreement.

Building the Project Procurement Foundation

Procurement is a special project management knowledge area for many reasons, but a key principle is that procurement may not be actually managed by the project manager, but by a procurement office or centralized contracting. Procurement is also unique from the other knowledge areas because your organization, through your project, is entering into a legal agreement with another entity. The contract, which is key to procurement decisions, holds both parties accountable for what's being delivered by the seller and what's being paid for by the buyer.

Contracts define the obligations of both parties: the buyer and the seller. Contracts should be written to define clearly what everyone in the relationship is required to do: services and/or materials provided and in consideration of the payment. Contracts can stipulate timelines, payment conditions, how disputes and claims are managed, the court that will be utilized should the relationship go sour, and many other considerations. Contracts must be signed by someone who has the authority to represent the organization in the contract—this may be called the delegation of authority. In your organization, this person may or may not be you, the project manager. More likely, a contracting officer or an attorney for your organization will write the contract and someone higher in the organization will sign the contract.

Considering Procurement Practices for Projects

One of the predominant changes over the past few years for project procurement management has been the availability of online tools for managing the procurement process. Some organizations, such as universities or government agencies, are required to advertise projects that are open for bids. This can be much work for the organization to write and post the ad in newspapers, online, and in magazines. Now software can streamline the process, communicate with bidders, and provide a holistic view of the entire process. Organizations are also adapting the construction industry's building information model (BIM) to help cut claims in construction projects, save time, and improve performance on costs and schedule.

Contracts can also address risks, as you saw in Chapter 11 on risk transference, so that organizations that specialize in managing certain types of risks manage the risk for the client. The contract can specify the risk and set the risk management process entirely upon the seller or management. Contracts can also be used for positive risk agreements, as in sharing, by creating teaming agreements and joint partnerships for specific projects.

Multibillion-dollar projects, sometimes called megaprojects, can span countries and introduce threats and opportunities for buyers and sellers. Contracts can be written to address the span of the project, currency exchange rates, and pricing for bulk purchasing. If the project does span multiple countries, however, the complexity of the contracting increases; considerations are given for international legalities, management of work in different countries, regulations, and even holidays, language, and culture.

Large construction projects also address logistics and supply chain management through contracting. Procurement lead times, lead time to produce the materials needed, and then delivery of materials to job sites can become complex and will likely require expert judgment to help guide the process, planning, and execution of the contracted work. Logistics can include one- or two-year lead times for materials; the procurement processes could start even before the entire design of the product is complete based entirely on the early requirements in the project. Delays in delivery of the material can cost a project millions, so there are often backup vendors and suppliers to alleviate the risk of missed opportunities. In addition, some countries' regulations require that the organization purchase materials from suppliers in the country where the project work is occurring rather than importing goods from suppliers outside the country.

A popular trend in public projects is transparency—regarding not only the projected cost of the project, but also the actual cost of the project work. Right now, you can search the web to view live webcams of construction projects, to access job reports, and to view web sites dedicated to information about public projects. Webcams can serve not only as good public relations by the seller for communities and taxpayers, but they can also alleviate claims, because there's video evidence of what has actually happened on the job site.

Organizations are also contracting with sellers on a trial basis, rather than committing to a long contract on their first engagement. During the trial period, each party can learn how the other works. Sellers would contribute to a portion of the project and, based on their performance, could then go on to be awarded additional project work if their work is acceptable to the buyer.

Agile projects have considerations for procurement, too. Often in agile projects, the project team consists of both internal developers and contract-based developers. All members of the project team, regardless of whether they are in-house or from the outside, should be treated as part of the team and not succumb to an "us-against-them" mentality. Agile projects might also be treated as a part of a master service agreement, where the agile project is an addendum or supplement to the contract—this allows the change-driven approach to agile while still abiding by the terms of the contract.

Procurement, more than any other knowledge area, generates the most questions when I teach my PMP boot camps. I've designed this chapter to address exactly what you should know for your PMP exam, and for your role as a project manager.

Tailoring the Procurement Processes

Of course, you can tailor the three procurement processes, because every organization is different, and every project is different. You tailor the process to fit your organization, not the other way around. There are four considerations for tailoring procurement:

- **Complexity**   As the number of suppliers involved in a project increase, so, too, will the complexity. Consider a general contractor in a house construction project: this involves scheduling with the foundation company, framers, plumbers, electricians, finishers, roofers, and more.

- **Physical location**   Where the project work takes place can affect the procurement process, as can the locale of the supplier(s). Currency exchange rates, language barriers, time zones, and other considerations come into play with this facet of the contract and project.

- **Regulations**   There may local, national, and international regulations and laws that affect the procurement process and auditing process. Consider government-based contracts, for example.

- **Contractor schedule**   The availability of the contractors may, or may not, mesh with your plans, and that needs to be addressed. A delay within your organization can also affect the vendor, who may have scheduled the work or delivery according to your plan for your current project and with consideration for their other customers.

CERTIFICATION OBJECTIVE 12.01

Planning for Purchases

Procurement planning is the process of identifying which part of the project should be procured from resources outside of the organization. Generally, procurement decisions are made early on in the planning processes. Procurement planning centers on four elements:

- Whether procurement is needed
- What to procure
- How much to procure
- When to procure

When the project manager begins the procurement process, she'll rely on more enterprise environmental factors and organizational process assets than she needs for any other process. For example, the project manager has to consider the marketplace conditions, the availability of the needed items or services in the marketplace, and how the procurement process works within the performing organization. If the project manager's organization has forms, policies, and management guidelines that direct the procurement process, she must follow those established processes.

Sellers are also known as contractors, subcontractors, vendors, suppliers, and service providers. Buyers are also known as clients, customers, prime contractors, contractors, acquiring organizations, government agencies, service requestors, or purchasers. When faced with procurement questions, you'll need to identify who is buying and who is selling, and then address the questions.

Often, an organization will have resources for managing the procurement process, including contracting and negotiating on behalf of the project. If, however, the performing organization has no such resources for the project manager to rely upon, it is up to the project manager to supply the procurement management resources, including capabilities for negotiating and for obtaining, in a fiscally responsible way, the right products or services for a fair price on behalf of the performing organization.

There are six inputs to procurement planning:

- Project charter
- Business documents (business case and benefits management plan)
- Project management plan (scope management plan, quality management plan, resource management plan, and the scope document)
- Project documents (milestone list, project team assignments, requirements documentation, requirements traceability matrix, resource requirements, risk register, and stakeholder register)
- Enterprise environmental factors
- Organizational process assets

Evaluating the Market Conditions

Part of procurement management involves determining what sources are available to provide the required products or services for the project. An evaluation of the marketplace is needed to determine what products and services are available and from whom and on what terms and conditions they are available.

Although in most free-market enterprise societies, multiple vendors offer comparable products, there may be times when your choices of vendors are limited. The following are three specific terms to know for the PMP exam that you may encounter:

- **Sole source**   Only one qualified seller exists in the marketplace.
- **Single source**   The performing organization prefers to contract with a specific seller.
- **Oligopoly**   There are very few sellers, and the actions of one seller will have a direct effect on the other sellers' prices and the overall market condition.

Referring to the Scope Baseline

The project's scope statement, work breakdown structure (WBS), and WBS dictionary all serve as input in making procurement decisions, although the *PMBOK Guide* lumps these into the project management plan. Because the project scope baseline defines the project work, and only the required work, to complete the project, it also defines the limitations of the project work. Knowing the limits of what the project includes can help the project manager, the contract specialists, and other procurement professionals determine what needs to be purchased and what does not.

The WBS and the WBS dictionary define the details and requirements for acceptance of the project. This information also serves as valuable input regarding what needs to be procured and what does not. The WBS defines what the end result of the project will be. When dealing with vendors to procure a portion of the project, you must ensure that the work to be procured supports the requirements of the project customer.

A statement of work (SOW) or terms of reference (TOR) may define the work to be accomplished within the project, but it generally does not define the product description as a whole. However, when an entire project is to be procured from a vendor, the SOW and the product description become one and the same. Along with the SOW, you may need to reference the requirements documentation to ensure that the procurement planning process defines exactly what's needed and adheres to any relevant laws, regulations, and standards.

Relying on the Project Management Plan

The project management plan is also needed during the procurement planning processes, because it will guide how the project should progress, and each subsidiary plan may need to be referenced for procurement guidelines. For example, the resource management plan, the scope management plan, the quality management plan, and the staffing management plan may all be needed for effective procurement planning.

One of the biggest things you'll need to consider during procurement management is the reliance on the risk response transference. Recall that transference is the assignment of a risk to a third party—typically with a fee involved. Insurance and contractors for dangerous work are two common examples of transference. The risk register will help identify the costs associated with the identified risks, and the contractual agreements for transference will be referenced as part of the project costs.

The project documents also include the project schedule and milestone list—and the project manager needs to consider procurement leads, fulfillment time for vendors, and when resources are needed to keep the project moving along. Couple the project schedule with the activity cost estimate and the cost performance baseline, and the project manager can do cash flow forecasting, communicate with management about upcoming expenses, and ensure that vendors are paid on time.

Teaming with Other Organizations

If your organization and another organization agree to partner on an opportunity, it's called a teaming agreement. It's a legally binding venture between two or more organizations that plan to complete a defined set of work or to seize an opportunity or some other venture that the parties involved couldn't necessarily complete on their own. Teaming agreements end when the venture ends. You might have heard these agreements loosely defined as "coopetition"—a fun way to describe cooperating with the competition, although teaming doesn't have to be just a partnership with the competition.

Teaming agreements should define in a contract the roles, buyer-and-seller relationships, and how the teaming agreement ends. The parties must all be in agreement with one another as to who does what, how communication occurs, and how decisions in the partnership will be made.

Planning for the Project Requirements

When it comes to project procurements, you'll specifically need the project requirements to determine what you'll purchase from vendors. The requirements are also needed to determine whether any aspects may affect the contracting process, such as licenses, permits, intellectual property rights, nondisclosure agreements, and insurance. Basically, anything that affects the project's performance, the project environment, or the people involved in the project should be considered when it comes to project procurement and the project requirements.

You'll also need to consider the risks within the project, the project schedule, the costs of the activities within the project, and the overall project budget. The project schedule must be considered because the vendor can affect the project schedule if they don't complete their contractual obligations on time. The project budget is needed because you'll need to determine how much you can afford to spend on the vendor—and whether your internal project estimates are accurate or way, way off base.

Completing Procurement Planning

Procurement planning should occur early in the planning processes, with certain exceptions. As needs arise, as project conditions change, or as other circumstances demand, procurement planning may be required throughout the project. Whenever procurement planning happens early in the project, as preferred, or later in the project, as needed, a logical approach to securing the proper resources is necessary.

Determining to Make or Buy

The decision to make or buy a product is a fundamental aspect of management. Under some conditions, it is more cost-effective to buy; in other cases, it makes more sense to create an in-house solution. The make-or-buy analysis should occur in the initial scope definition to determine whether the entire project should be completed in-house or procured. As the project evolves, additional make-or-buy decisions may be needed.

The initial costs of the solution for the in-house or procured product must be considered, but so, too, must the ongoing expenses of the solutions. For example, a company may elect to lease a piece of equipment. The ongoing expenses of leasing the piece of equipment should be weighed against the expected ongoing expenses of purchasing the equipment and the monthly costs to maintain, insure, and manage the equipment.

Here's an example: Figure 12-1 shows the mathematical approach for determining whether it is better to create a software program in-house or buy one from a software company. The in-house solution will cost your company $25,000 to create your own software package and (based on historical information) another $2500 per month to maintain the software.

FIGURE 12-1

Make-or-buy
formulas are
common exam
questions.

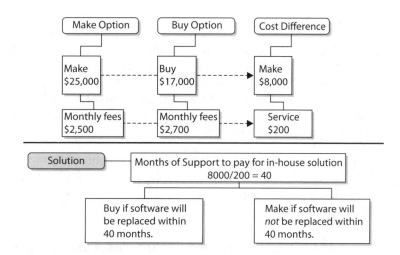

The development company has a solution that will cost your company $17,000 to purchase, but the development company requires a maintenance plan for each software program installed, which will cost your company $2700 per month. The initial difference between making the software and buying the software is $8000. The difference between supporting the software the organization has made and allowing the external company to support their software is only $200 per month.

The $200 per month is divided into the difference between creating the software internally and buying the software—which is $8000 divided by $200—which equates to 40 months. If the software is to be replaced within 40 months, the company should buy the software. If the software will not be replaced within 40 months, it should build the software.

An organization may choose to make or buy for multiple reasons. The following table shows some common examples or reasons for making and buying.

Reasons to Make	Reasons to Buy
Less costly	Less costly
Use in-house skills	In-house skills aren't available or don't exist
Control of work	Small volume of work
Control of intellectual property	More efficient
Learn new skills	Transfer risks
Available staff	Available vendor
Focus on core project work	Enables project team to focus on other work items

Using Expert Judgment

Procurement planning can rely on expert judgment. Roles and responsibilities for procurement should happen during procurement management planning to ensure that you've the right experts to make the best decisions for procurement. Yes, it may be beneficial to rely on the wisdom of others—those in the performing organization or subject matter experts—to determine the need for procurement. Expert judgment for procurement management planning can come from the following:

- Units or individuals within the performing organization
- Consultants and subject matter experts
- Professional, trade, or technical associations
- Industry groups

PMP Coach **You're at the second-to-the-last knowledge area. Congrats! In my experience teaching PMP boot camps, most candidates are worn out by this topic. And they rationalize that because they personally don't handle much of the procurement, they can ease off in this chapter. Wrong! You can expect plenty of questions on procurement on your PMP exam—don't take it easy. You're almost there, but you're not there yet. Keep going—think of how good you'll feel when you're done with this exam.**

Determining the Contract Type

There are multiple types of contracts when it comes to procurement. The project work, the market, and the nature of the purchase determine the contract type. The following are some general rules that PMP exam candidates, and project managers, should know:

- A contract is a formal agreement between the buyer and the seller. Contracts can be oral or written—though written is preferred.
- The United States and most developed countries back all contracts through the court system.
- Contracts should clearly state all requirements for product acceptance.
- Any changes to the contract must be formally approved, controlled, and documented.
- A contract is not fulfilled until all of the requirements of the contract are met.
- Contracts can be used as a risk mitigation tool, as in transferring the risk. All contracts have some level of risk; depending on the contract type, the risk can be transferred to the seller. If a risk response strategy is to transfer, risks associated with procurement are considered secondary risks and must go through the risk management process.

- Legal requirements govern contracts. In order for a contract to be valid, it must
  - Contain an offer
  - Have been accepted
  - Provide for a consideration (payment)
  - Be for a legal purpose
  - Be executed by someone with capacity and authority
- The terms and conditions of the contract should define breaches, copyrights, intellectual rights, and *force majeure. Force majeure* is French for superior force—sometimes called "acts of God." You might know these as tornados, earthquakes, and hurricanes.

See the video "Contracts."

Fixed-Price Contracts

Fixed-price contracts (also known as firm fixed-price and lump-sum contracts) are agreements that define a total price for the product the seller is to provide. These contracts must clearly define the requirements the vendor is to provide. These contracts may also provide incentives for meeting or exceeding contract requirements—such as meeting deadlines—and require the seller to assume the risk of cost overruns, as Figure 12-2 demonstrates.

FIGURE 12-2

Fixed-price contracts transfer the risk to the seller.

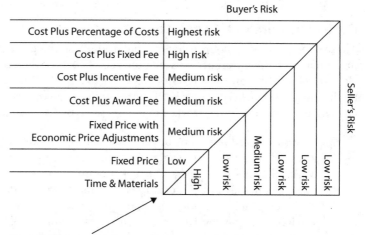

T&M can be a high risk for buyer if the contract does not include a "total not-to-exceed" clause. Also called an NTE clause.

You should know three types of fixed-priced contracts:

■ **Firm fixed-price contract** This contract type defines the exact amount for the goods or services provided by the vendor. It's the most common and most preferred contract type for organizations, as the risk for the buyer is relatively low. For the seller, however, the risk is that if their cost of materials, doing business, or completing the work defined in the contract increases, they cannot pass on that cost to the customer. A firm fixed-price contract is also known as a lump-sum contract.

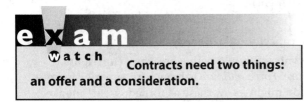

Contracts need two things: an offer and a consideration.

■ **Fixed-price incentive fee contract** This contract type is similar to the firm fixed-price contract in that a lump sum amount is agreed upon between the buyer and the seller for the work to be performed. However, this contract type allows the contract to include incentives for the project, such as a bonus for completing the project work early, saving costs in the project, or meeting other performance objectives. This contract can also have penalties for the vendor if they're late on the project work or their performance is less than it should be.

■ **Fixed-price with economic price adjustment** This contract type is for long-term projects that may span years to complete the project work. The contract does define a fixed price, with caveats for special categories of price fluctuation over the life of the project, including inflation, electricity, shipping, labor costs, cost of materials, or other resources that could affect the feasibility of the vendor completing the work. The contract must define the financial indexes that will be used to determine the fluctuation in the identified cost categories.

Cost-Reimbursable Contracts

These contract types pay the seller for the product. In the payment to the seller, there is a profit margin—the difference between the actual costs of the product and the sales amount. Cost-reimbursable contracts require the buyer to assume the risk of cost overruns. You might use a cost-plus type contract if there are many unknowns in the project or many changes are expected in the work. There are four types of cost-reimbursable contracts:

■ **Cost plus fixed fee** The buyer is responsible for all costs the contracted work incurs plus a predetermined fee for the vendor to manage and complete the contracted work. The fee for the work is usually tied to a percentage of the estimated project costs, but not always. For example, I'll remodel your condo, but you have to pay for all the materials and labor I'll need, which should be close to $80,000. In addition, you'll have to pay me 15 percent of the costs, which will be $12,000. You'll pay the costs as the project progresses and pay my fee based on milestones completed in the project. If I don't finish the project, you don't finish paying me. You do have some risks, though—if I waste materials, you have to buy more and you'll still have to pay my fee for the work.

■ **Cost plus incentive fee**   This contract type requires that the buyer pay for all the preapproved costs for materials and labor in the project plus an incentive fee for completing the project early, saving on project costs, managing certain risks, or meeting other performance objectives. The contract will define how the incentives are determined. One popular method attaches dollar amounts to completed milestones and dates. If the vendor delivers the milestones ahead of the promised dates on a consistent basis, the value of the work increases and so will the incentive fee for the vendor. If the contract is based on cost savings for the project and early completions are cost savings, the contract must define how the cost savings are split between the buyer and the seller. Usually, the seller receives 20 percent of the cost savings in what's called an "80/20 split."

■ **Cost plus award fee**   This contract requires the buyer to pay for all the project costs and gives the seller an award fee based on the project performance, certain project criteria, or other goals established by the buyer. The award fee can be tied to any factor the buyer determines, and the factor doesn't have to be exact. For example, the buyer can set an award fee of up to $100,000 for a $1 million project based on the technical ingenuity of the project solution, the quality of the work, or the actual cost savings the solution creates for the organization.

■ **Cost plus percentage of costs**   This contract type is the absolute pits for the buyer, and most organizations won't participate in these contracts. In this case, the buyer has to pay for all of the costs of the materials plus a predetermined percentage for the cost of the materials. The obvious risk is that the vendor can waste materials and the buyer will have to buy new materials and pay the percentage of costs for the materials again. It's easy for the vendor to run up the total project costs just by wasting materials.

on the **Job**

The only time it might be appropriate, and I stress the word _might_, to use a cost plus percentage of costs contract is when the vendor is working with a highly specialized material and type of work. For example, imagine an artist who's sculpting a marble statue for the lobby of a building or a scientist who's working with a highly complex chemical. The nature of this type of work is so specialized that the artist and the scientist are unlikely to waste materials on purpose just to crank up their project costs. Having said that, I doubt you will see this on the PMP exam. As a general rule, avoid the cost plus percentage of costs contract.

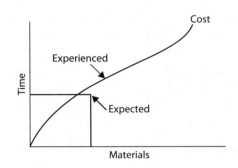

FIGURE 12-3

Time and
materials
contracts must
be kept in check,
or costs can
skyrocket.

Time and Materials Contracts

Time and materials (T&M) contracts are sometimes called time and means contracts. Time and materials contracts are considered a hybrid contract because they require the buyer to pay for the costs and a fixed fee. They are ideal when an organization contracts out a small project when smaller amounts of work within a larger project are to be completed by a vendor. T&M contracts, however, can grow dangerously out of control as more work is assigned to the seller. T&M contracts should have a not-to-exceed clause (NTE clause) to put a ceiling on the procured work. Figure 12-3 shows an example of how T&M contracts can pose a risk for the buyer.

Summary of Contract Types

On the PMP examination, you can expect a few questions on contract types. Familiarize yourself with the information in Table 12-1.

Using the Statement of Work

In the contract SOW, the seller fully describes the work to be completed and/or the product to be supplied. The contract SOW becomes part of the contract between the buyer and the seller. The contract SOW is typically created as part of the procurement planning process, and it allows the seller to determine whether they can meet the written requirements of the SOW. You might also see the SOW called a TOR, for terms of reference.

Particular industries have different assumptions about what constitutes an SOW. What one industry calls an SOW may be a statement of objectives (SOO) in another. An SOO is a document describing a problem to be solved by the seller. The SOW, what you'll most likely see on the PMP exam, defines the project specifications, requirements for vendor qualification, and details about the project work, location, expected time frame, and similar conditions.

TABLE 12-1   Project Contracts Advantages and Risks for Buyer and Seller

Contract type	Acronym	Attribute	Risk issues
Cost plus fixed fee	CPFF	Actual costs plus profit margin for seller	Cost overruns represent risk to the buyer.
Cost plus percentage of cost	CPPC	Actual costs plus profit margin for seller	Cost overruns represent risk to the buyer. This is the most dangerous contract type for the buyer.
Cost plus award fee	CPAF	Actual costs plus an award based on seller-defined objectives for the project	Buyer carries the risk, as the seller is the judge of the contract work and performance.
Cost plus incentive fee	CPIF	Actual costs plus a profit margin for seller	Cost overruns represent risk to the buyer.
Fixed-price	FP	Agreed-upon price for contracted product; can include incentives for the seller	Seller assumes the risk.
Fixed-price with economic price adjustment	FP-EPA	Agreed-upon price for contracted product; can include cost adjustments based on predefined categories of cost	Seller assumes the risk.
Firm fixed-price	FFP	Agreed-upon price for contracted product	Seller assumes the risk.
Fixed-price incentive fee	FPIF	Agreed-upon price for contracted product; can include incentives for the seller	Seller assumes the risk.
Time and materials, or time and means	T&M	Price assigned for the time and materials provided by the seller	Contracts without "not-to-exceed" clauses can lead to cost overruns.
Unit price		Price assigned for a measurable unit of product or time (for example, $130 for engineer's time on the project)	Risk varies with the product. Time represents the biggest risk if the amount needed is not specified in the contract.

Determining the Source Selection Criteria

Another output of contracting planning is the evaluation criteria to determine which source the organization will purchase from. The evaluation criteria is used to rate and score proposals from the sellers. In some instances, such as a bid or quote, the evaluation criterion is focused just on the price the seller offers. In other instances, such as a proposal, the evaluation criteria can be multiple values: experience, references, certifications, and more.

It's essential for the project manager and the project team to create selection criteria that will guide their decision-making later in the project. Common questions that should be considered prior to vendor selection include the following:

- Does the vendor understand the project need?
- What is the overall project and/or life-cycle cost?
- What is the vendor's technical capability?
- What is the vendor's management and technical approach to the project work?
- What is the vendor's financial capacity to complete the project work?
- What risk is associated with the work and how will the vendor manage the risk?
- Does the vendor qualify in areas that may help in rewarding the contract (such as a small business, veteran-owned business, or minority-owned business)?
- What are the proprietary rights and intellectual property rights associated with the project work?
- Will the vendor provide a warranty for the work they complete?

The source selection analysis is a review of the selection methods you'll use when choosing a seller for the project. Selection methods include the following:

- **Least cost** The lowest bid is awarded the contract.
- **Qualifications only** Based on a short list of sellers, the buyer chooses the vendor with the best qualifications for the contract.
- **Quality-based/highest technical proposal score** Seller submits proposal for the work and a proposed cost to do the work. If the buyer likes the technical proposal, the seller and the buyer will negotiate the pricing.
- **Quality and cost-based** Cost and quality are considered important, though in projects that are likely to have many risks and uncertainties, quality can take a higher priority than cost in source selection.
- **Sole source** A specific seller is asked to do the work. This could be based on the marketplace conditions or past experience with the vendor.
- **Fixed budget** The buyer shares the budget for the project work with the seller. The seller then prepares a proposal based on the predefined budget—or declines to participate as the fixed budget may not be realistic. In addition, the SOW must be well-defined and little changes to the project are expected so the seller can work with the expectation of exactly what's needed to satisfy the contract requirement within the fixed budget.

Reviewing the Procurement Management Plan

Procurement planning should happen early in the planning processes. The outputs of procurement planning enable the project manager and the project team to proceed with confidence in the procuring of products and services needed to complete the project successfully. If it is determined early in the project that there is no need for procurements, then, obviously, the balance of the procurement processes is not necessary for the project.

This subsidiary project plan documents the decisions made in the procurement planning processes. It specifies how the remaining procurement activities will be managed. The procurement plan details the following:

- The coordination between sellers and the project team and among project activities, project reporting, scheduling, business operations, and other project concerns
- How vendors will be selected
- The types of contracts to be used
- The process of independent estimating (also known as should-cost estimates)
- The relationship between the project team and the procurement office within the performing organization (if one exists)
- Planning for the timetable and lead time requirements between the vendor and the organizational purchasing processes
- Requirements for performance bonds and insurance requirements for the vendors
- The procurement forms, such as contracts, that the project team is required to use
- How multiple vendors will be managed to supply their contracted product
- Metrics to be used to determine which vendors qualify for project work and to complete vendor selection

- Requirements for vendors' proof-of-insurance certificates, bonds, licenses, or other risk-mitigation qualifications
- Enterprise environmental factors that affect which vendors may participate in the bidding process, vendor selection, and other internal rules and processes you're required to follow as the project manager
- Roles and responsibilities for procurement, including the project manager, project team, and procurement office
- Definition of the legal jurisdiction and how the vendor will be paid and in what currency
- Constraints, assumptions, risk management, and prequalified sellers, if applicable

Creating the Procurement Documents

These documents guide the relationship between the buyer and the seller. Communication between the buyer and the seller should always be specific as to the requirements and expectations of the buyer and seller. In initial communications, especially when requesting a price or proposal, the buyer should include the SOW, relevant specifications, and, if necessary, any nondisclosure agreements (NDAs). A project may also include independent cost estimates and source selection criteria, if applicable to the organization. Requests from buyers to sellers should be specific enough to give the seller a clear idea of what the buyer is requesting, but general enough to allow the seller to provide viable alternatives.

Following are some specific terms the project manager—and the PMP candidate—should be familiar with:

Document	Purpose
Bid	From seller to buyer. Price is the determining factor in the decision-making process.
Quotation	From seller to buyer. Price is the determining factor in the decision-making process.
Proposal	From seller to buyer. Other factors—such as skill sets, reputation, and ideas for the project solution—may be used in the decision-making process.
Invitation for bid (IFB)	From buyer to seller. Requests the seller to provide a price for the procured product or service.
Request for quote (RFQ)	From buyer to seller. Requests the seller to provide a price for the procured product or service.
Request for proposal (RFP)	From buyer to seller. Requests the seller to provide a proposal to complete the procured work or to provide the procured product.
Request for Information (RFI)	From buyer to seller. Asks for additional information about the seller's products and/or services.

CERTIFICATION OBJECTIVE 12.02

Conducting Procurements

Once the contracting planning has been completed, the actual process of contracting can
begin. Fortunately, the sellers, not the buyers, perform most of the activity in solicitations—
usually at no additional cost to the project. The sellers are busy trying to win the business.
The process of conducting procurements has six inputs:

- Project management plan (scope management plan, requirements management
  plan, communications management plan, risk management plan, procurement
  management plan, configuration management plan, and cost baseline)
- Project documentation (lessons learned register, project schedule, requirements
  documentation, risk register, and stakeholder register)
- Procurement documents
- Proposals from sellers
- Enterprise environmental factors
- Organizational process assets

Procuring Goods and Services

There are five tools and techniques used to conduct procurement within an organization:

■ **Expert judgment**   A consultant or expert from your organization can often help you make the best decision as to which seller you should select. Reviewing bids and proposals can be a cumbersome task as you'll often need to compare and contrast proposals, delivery dates, pricing, experience, and other factors that will affect your decision.

■ **Advertising**   In many circumstances, advertisements inviting bidders are expected. These advertisements can run in newspapers or trade journals specific to the industry of the organization. Some government agencies require advertisements inviting sellers to acquire the project work, attend a bidder conference, or present a proposal for the described work.

■ **Bidder conferences**   A bidder conference, also called a contractor conference, pre-bid conference, or vendor conference, is a meeting with prospective sellers to ensure that all sellers have a clear and common understanding of the product or service to be procured and are on equal footing. Bidder conferences enable sellers to query the buyer on the details of the product to help ensure that the seller's proposal is adequate and appropriate for the proposed agreement. At this point of the process, all sellers are considered equal.

■ **Data analysis**   When you create an invitation for bid, request for quote, or request for proposal and send that out to sellers, you'll likely receive lots of information back from the sellers. Data analysis is the sorting, comparing, and contrasting of the information to help you make the best decision. This is really proposal evaluation and may be done with the tool and technique of expert judgment to help you make the best decision.

■ **Interpersonal and team skills**   The big category of interpersonal and team skills is really, for this process, negotiation. Negotiation is the act of seeking a fair agreement for both parties in the contract. Negotiation is more than just finding a price; it can include negotiation materials, resources, access to the site, the schedule, and any other condition for the contracted work. Negotiation should be led by someone within the organization who has the authority to sign the contract.

on the **Job**   **A standard of procurement is that bids and quotes are looking for sellers to provide a price. Proposals are asking the sellers to provide solutions.**

Examining the Results of Contracting

The end result of contracting, as expected, is a collection of proposals, bids, and quotations. These documents indicate the sellers' ability and preparedness to complete the project work. The proposals should be in alignment with the buyer's stated expectations, and they may be presented orally, electronically, or in hard-copy format. Of course, the relationship between the buyer and the seller—and the type of information being shared—will determine which modality is the best choice for communication.

Selecting the Seller

Once the sellers have presented their proposals, bids, or quotes (depending on what the buyer requested of them), their documents are examined so that the project manager or the organization's decision-maker can select which sellers are the best choice for the project work. In many instances, price may be the predominant factor for choosing a particular seller—but not always. Factors other than price may also be taken into consideration:

- The cost of an item may not reflect the true cost to the performing organization if the item cannot be delivered in a timely manner. If a seller promises to have a product on site by a specific date and fails to do so, the project can be delayed, costing the organization thousands—or more—in losses.
- Proposals can be separated into two categories: technical and commercial. The technical category describes the approach and methodology to complete the project work, and the commercial category delves into the price to complete the project work. An evaluation takes into consideration both categories to determine the best choice for the project.
- Critical, high-priority projects may rely on multiple sellers to complete the project work. This redundancy can balance risk, cost, and opportunity among multiple vendors.

Preparing for Source Selection

Source selection weighs and evaluates the proposals, bids, and quotes for the procured portions of the project and then makes a determination as to which seller is the best for the project work. The source selection decision-making process involves three inputs:

- **Proposals**   The proposals, bids, and quotations provided by the sellers are key inputs. These are the documents the performing organization will evaluate to determine which seller is the best provider for the project.
- **Evaluation criteria**   The evaluation criteria, such as referrals, samples of previous work, and references, are considered. The evaluation criteria are evidence of the quality, depth, and experience of work the seller has performed in the past and, hopefully, is capable of performing on the current project. Evaluation criteria are developed in contracting planning and are applied in source selection.

■ **Organizational policies**   The performing organization likely has procurement policies and procedures that the project manager is expected to follow in regard to source selection. The organizational policies should be known before starting the source selection process to avoid any discrepancies, conflicts of interest, or other breaches of policies. For example, some organizations' procurement policies do not allow project managers to accept any gifts worth more than $25 in value.

Completing the Seller Selection Process

For the performing organization to finalize the process of seller selection, there must first be eligible sellers. Assuming more than one seller can satisfy the demands of the project, the project manager can rely on several tools and techniques when making a selection:

■ **Weighting system**   A weighting system takes out the personal preferences of the decision-maker in the organization to ensure that the best seller is awarded the contract. A weighting system creates a matrix, as shown in Figure 12-4. Weights are assigned to the values of the proposals, and each proposal is scored. Because the weights are determined before the decision-maker reviews the proposals, the process is guaranteed to be free of personal preferences and bias. The seller with the highest score is awarded the contract.

■ **Independent estimates**   These estimates are often referred to as "should-cost" estimates. They are created by the performing organization or by outside experts to predict what the cost of the procured product should be. If there is a significant difference between what the organization has predicted and what the sellers have proposed, the statement of work was inadequate, the sellers misunderstood the requirements, or the price provided by the sellers is too high.

■ **Screening system**   A screening system can remove sellers from consideration if they do not meet given conditions. For example, screening could require that sellers be certified by a specific organization, have prior experience with the project technology, or meet other values. Sellers that don't meet the requirements are removed from the selection process and their proposals are not considered.

FIGURE 12-4   Weighting systems remove personal preference from the selection process.

Possible Score	20	20	15	10	10	5	20	100
Value	Experience	Certifications	Level IV Engineers	Security Clearance	Start Date	Waste Removal	Price	Total Score
ABC Constructions	15	20	7	10	10	5	12	79
Allen Builders	12	20	12	10	10	0	10	74
FRJ Construction	18	20	11	0	10	5	18	82
Howe & Who Construction	18	15	5	0	5	5	15	73
Martin & Martin	9	20	13	10	5	0	18	65
Ralph Engineers	15	8	8	0	10	5	17	73

- **Contract negotiation** The performing organization creates an offer, and the seller considers it. The contract negotiation process is an activity to create a fair price for the work the seller is to complete. The performing organization and the seller must be in agreement on the expectations, requirements, authorities, terms, technical and business management approaches, price, and any other pertinent factors covered within, and by, the contract prior to signing it.

- **Seller rating systems** How the vendor has performed in the past may guide current and future project procurement decisions. Consider a vendor that has offered poor performance in quality, delivery, and contractual compliance versus a vendor that has scored high marks in quality, delivery, and contract compliance; which should the project manager choose? That's the goal of the seller rating system: to collect and disseminate information on the performance of sellers in order to guide project decisions.

- **Expert judgment** Often, the project manager and the project team may not be knowledgeable in the discipline the vendor is offering and that the project requires. In these instances, the project manager can rely on expert judgment to help make the best decisions regarding the project's welfare.

- **Proposal evaluation techniques** There are many different approaches to evaluating vendors' proposals—from weighting systems to screening systems—but all will rely on expert judgment and some sort of evaluation criteria.

e x a m

ⓦ a t c h A letter of intent is a letter from the buyer to the seller indicating that the seller will be awarded the contract. In other words, it states that the buyer intends to do business with the seller.

Examining the Results of Conducting Procurement

The primary output of conducting procurement is a contract between the buyer and the seller. A contract is a legally binding agreement between the buyer and the seller in which the seller provides the described product and the seller pays for the product. Contracts are known by many names:

- Agreement
- Subcontract
- Purchase order
- Memorandum of understanding

Contracts have to be signed by a person with the power to authorize the requirements and payment specified in the contract. This role is called the delegation of procurement authority. Whether or not this person is the project manager depends on the procurement policies of the performing organization.

In some organizations, all contracts flow through centralized contracting. Centralized contracting requires all contracts for all projects to be approved through a central unit within the performing organization. Other organizations use a decentralized contracting approach, which assigns a contract administrator or contract officer to the project. Agreements will include the following:

- Procurement SOW
- Schedule and milestones for the seller
- How performance is reported and tracked
- Pricing and payment agreements
- Inspection of the work and what constitutes success
- Warranty
- Incentives and penalties
- Insurance and performance bonds
- Subcontractor permissions and approvals for subcontractors
- General terms and conditions
- How change requests will be managed
- Termination and alternative dispute resolution terms

Should there be any changes to the project manager plan, the schedule, or the project documents, the changes should flow through the project's integrated change control process. For example, a contract could be created for services in the project, but the date the vendor can do the work is a week later than what was planned in the project. Through negotiations, the organization has agreed to this date and will need to change its project management plan and schedule to accommodate this contracted agreement.

Updates to project documents can include updating the lessons learned register, but also, more importantly, the requirements documentation. Through the contracting process, technical and legal requirements could be added to the requirements documentation and requirements traceability matrix. You might also need to update the resource calendars to reflect any new resources brought onto the project through the contract, update the risk register for any newly identified risks, and update the stakeholder register by adding the selected seller.

CERTIFICATION OBJECTIVE 12.03

Controlling Procurements

Controlling procurement is the process of ensuring that the seller and the buyer live up to the agreements in the contract. The project manager and the contract administrator must work together to make certain the seller meets their obligations. If the seller does not fulfill their contractual requirements, legal remedies may ultimately be pursued. This process is based on the terms of the contract—the contract overrides everything else between the buyer and the seller.

Another aspect of controlling procurement, especially on larger projects with multiple sellers providing various products, is the coordination between the contractors. The project manager or contract officer schedules and confirms the performance of the sellers so that the deliverables, schedule, and performance of a contractor do not infringe or adversely affect the performance of another contractor.

There are eight inputs to control procurements:

- Project management plan
- Project documents
- Agreements
- Procurement documentation
- Approved change requests
- Work performance data
- Enterprise environmental factors
- Organizational process assets

Perhaps the most important consideration is the contract. The contract must also include the terms of payment. Typically, the performance and progress of the seller is directly linked to payments they receive. The project manager must track performance and quality to approve or decline payment as needed. The contract should define the metrics for acceptance to avoid disagreements on performance and to ensure that vendors get paid on time.

Preparing for Contract Administration

The contract and the procurement management plan are needed to guide effective contract administration. The contract dictates the requirements and expectations of the seller and the buyer. The obligations of both parties should be in alignment with the contract—if they are not, disagreements, delays, and even work stoppage can ensue. Contract administration includes the following:

- **Performance reports**   Within the contract, the terms for acceptance are defined. Reports on the seller's performance are needed to compare with the requirements of the contracted work.
- **Records management**   Date of the work performed, quality of the work, financial records, performance, and other procurement data is gathered and documented.
- **Invoice payment**   According to the terms of the contract, the vendor will submit an invoice and the buyer will pay the invoice.
- **Change requests**   Change requests can complicate contract administration. The performing organization's change control system must somehow mesh with the seller's change control system. Changes to the project that affect the contracted work require changes to the contract, addendums to the contract, or a new contract for the additional or changed work. In some instances, the seller and the buyer may disagree about the cost of the changes. These differences may be labeled as claims, disputes, or appeals, and may ultimately slow the project's progress if not remedied.

on the **J**ob   **If the seller's performance is unacceptable and a resolution to the problem cannot be found, the performing organization may elect to cancel the contract. This termination of the contract is also handled as a change request within the change control system. The contract should include the terms for how cancellation can occur and alternative dispute resolution methods, such as a mediator, may happen.**

INSIDE THE EXAM

Project procurement management first begins by determining which facets of the project can best be served through procurement. This decision often focuses on a make-or-buy analysis that asks the following questions:

- Is it more cost-effective to make or buy the product or service?

- Is it more time-efficient to make or buy the product or service?
- Are the resources available within the organization to make the product or service?

If the decision has been made to buy the product or service, a SOW is needed to detail

(Continued)

INSIDE THE EXAM

exactly what product or service the organization is buying. The SOW will be given to potential sellers so that they can prepare their offers in alignment with what is needed by the performing organization.

To find potential sellers, the performing organization issues an SOW to the sellers with the appropriate procurement documents. Sellers can be found through a preferred vendor list, advertisements, industry directories, trade organizations, or other methods. The initial communication from the buyer to the seller is a request. Specifically, the seller issues one of the following documents:

- **Request for proposal** This is used when there are multiple factors in addition to price to determine which seller is awarded the contract. The buyer is looking for a solution to a need.

- **Request for quotation** This is used when the deciding factor is price.

- **Invitation for bid** This is used when the deciding factor is price.

The seller can host a bidder conference to ensure that all sellers have equal opportunity to gain information about the procured work or service and that the information they do get is the same. After the seller conference, the selection process is based on several things:

- Procurement documents from the sellers

- Company policies and procedures

- Screening systems to sift out sellers that do not qualify for the work

- Weighting system to make an unbiased selection of a seller

Once the seller has been selected, the contract is created between the buyer and the seller. This formal, preferably written, agreement between the buyer and the seller defines all requirements of both the buyer and the seller. The seller's requirements specify how and when the work will be completed. The buyer's requirements, on the other hand, specify the terms and conditions that the seller is expected to maintain. The contract may also include information on resolving claims, how changes to the contract are to be made, and who are the authorities within the buyer's organization and the seller's organization.

Contract administration is the process of ensuring that the seller meets the obligations and requirements specified in the contract. If changes arise in the project that affect the contract, there may be additional negotiation for payments based on the added or removed components of the procured work.

At the completion of the contract, the seller and the buyer complete product verification, which is much like administrative closure, to confirm that the seller has met their obligations. Documentation of the procurement experience is created so that the information can be applied to other procurement activities on the current projects and to other projects within the organization.

Completing Contract Administration

The actual process of completing contract administration relies heavily on communication among the project manager, the contract officer, and the seller. The communications plan may have considerations for how and when the communication between the buyer and the seller should take place and what the purpose of the communication should be. There are six primary concerns, in addition to communication, within contract administration:

- **Integrated change control** Changes to the contract will follow the terms of the contract as this defines the procedures for how the contract may be changed. The process for changing the contract includes the forms; documented communications; tracking; conditions within the project, business, or marketplace that justify the needed changes; dispute resolution procedures; and the procedures for getting the changes approved within the performing organization.

- **Performance reviews and audits** As the vendor completes the contracted work, the seller will need to inspect the work for progress, compliance with contract requirements, and adherence to agreed-to schedule, cost, and quality constraints.

- **Performance reporting** Performance reporting is the communication between the project manager and management on how the seller is performing with regard to the guidelines in the contract. This is part of communications and should be documented within the communications management plan. Earned value analysis and trend analysis can be used to monitor performance of the seller.

- **Payment system** Sellers like to be paid when they have completed their obligations. How the sellers are paid is controlled by the payment system, which includes interactions between the project manager and the accounts payable department. The performing organization may have strict guidelines for how payment requests are submitted and approved, and how payments are completed. On larger projects, the project management team may have specific procedures for submitting the payment requests.

- **Claims administration** This is not fun. Claims result from contested changes, such as disagreements about a change that has occurred and who should pay for that change. Although these go by various names—claims, disputes, and appeals—they all mean the same thing: The buyer and the seller are in disagreement over who should pay for the changes to the project work. Resolution may come through negotiation, mediation, or arbitration, as defined by the contract.

- **Records management system** This is part of the project management information system that is designed to track all contracting documentation. This is essential, since it assists the project manager in managing procurement documents and records, and serves as a point of reference regarding communications and procurement paperwork.

Inspecting and Auditing the Procurement Process

Like controlling quality and scope validation, inspection is also needed for the goods and services the seller provides to the buyer. An inspection, depending on the size of the procured work and services, might be a walk-through or an in-depth inspection of the work and its quality. In some projects, a government official may act on behalf of the customer and inspect the work, such as electrical and plumbing work in construction.

The successes and failures within the procurement process of the project are reviewed from the procurement planning stage through contract administration. The intent of the audit is to learn what worked and what didn't during the procurement processes. This knowledge can then be applied to other areas within the current project and to other projects within the performing organization. The documentation of the procurement process should become part of the records management system, which in turn will become part of organizational process assets.

Audits examine the entire procurement process to ensure that all parties are abiding by the terms of the contract. From the buyer's perspective, they want to make certain that all is delivered according to the terms of the contract prior to payment terms. On large, complex projects and contracts an audit may examine the billing and the deliverables by the seller, and identify any variances that exist. A reconciliation happens to ensure that what was purchased was actually delivered. The terms of the contract define up front the audit process and sets expectations for both parties.

Reviewing the Results of Procurement Control

Once the deliverables have been accepted and the contract has been closed, it's essential to collect all of the contract information and record it in the contract file. A contract file is a complete indexed set of records of the procurement process and is incorporated into the administrative closure process. These records include financial information as well as information on the performance and acceptance of the procured work.

Assuming the procured work is acceptable and meets the requirements of the contract, the contract can be closed. The formal closure of a project comes in a written notice from the contract officer to the seller. The notice informs the seller that its work is acceptable and that the contract is considered closed. The formal closure process may vary according to the size of the project. The requirements for contract closeout should be documented within the contract. Closing procurement is an enterprise process and is an output of the control procurement process.

Within the contract, the terms for payment are specified. The terms for payment may stipulate under what conditions the seller will provide an invoice for the work completed. In addition, the buyer may specify when and how the invoices are paid (for example, "Net 30 days from receipt of the invoice"). If the project is using an external payment system, there will be communication between the buyer and the seller, and between the buyer and the external payment system. If the performing organization is handling its own payment processing, this output would simply be payments.

Termination of the contract may not always be caused by something the vendor did wrong. The buyer may no longer need the goods or services being provided, but the buyer may still be contractually obligated to pay the vendor. The contract overrides everything. When there is a dispute, technically a claim, the contract even directs the claims administration process.

Should the buyer and the seller not be able to work out their differences themselves, things are escalated. This means the buyer and the seller will participate in alternative dispute resolution—a nice way of not having to say, "Here come the attorneys!" Alternative dispute resolution includes mediation, arbitration, and aims to avoid litigation.

Both approved and declined changes are documented as to their cost, time, and effect on the project and the procured work. Changes that are approved require updates to the project plan, subsidiary plans, and possibly to other project documentation. Remember that all changes must flow through the project's integrated control system. Changes to the project management plan can include updates to the following:

- Risk management plan
- Procurement management plan
- Schedule baseline
- Cost baseline
- Project documents

The performance of the contracted work, the contract obligations, and the procedures of the performing organization generate correspondence between the buyer and the seller. The correspondence often takes the form of warnings, letters of discontent, and project performance reviews from the buyer to the seller. This correspondence can serve as documentation for legal action if disputes arise between the buyer and the seller. All of the invoices, seller performance information, and lessons learned are updated and become part of the organizational process assets updates. You'll also include a procurement file that includes all contract documentation as part the final project files for archiving.

CERTIFICATION SUMMARY

Project procurement management enables a project to obtain resources, materials, equipment, services, and other components needed to complete the project successfully. It is the process of finding sellers that can supply the needed products or services at a fair rate and that meet the quality, schedule, and cost expectations of the project. The product description will help the project manager and the vendor determine the best solution for the procurement need.

One of the first activities the project manager and the project team complete together before procuring products is to decide the need to buy versus the ability to make the product in-house. A decision tree can help the project manager determine which decision is most cost-effective, reliable, and best for the project. A make-or-buy analysis can compare the benefits of buying versus creating in-house—including attributes other than just price and time.

Bidder conferences allow the bidders to meet with the project managers and other officials representing the seller to confirm the details of the contract statement of work. Recall that the statement of work (SOW) is provided to all vendors that may be creating bids or proposals for the seller. The bidder conference enables the bidders to obtain any additional information they may need to create a full and complete bid, quote, or proposal and for all bidders to hear the same information. It is part of the contracting process and proceeds to source selection.

PMP candidates—and project managers—must be familiar with the different contract types and when to use each one. Here's a recap of the most common contract types:

- **Cost plus fixed fee** Details the fixed cost of the contract, which includes a profit margin for the seller.
- **Cost plus percentage of cost** Has a price for the contracted product or service, but cost overruns are assigned to the buyer.
- **Cost plus award fee** Requires the buyer to pay for all the project costs and give the seller an award fee based on the project performance, including meeting certain project criteria or other goals established by the buyer. The award fee can be tied to any factor the buyer determines, and the factor doesn't have to be exact.
- **Cost plus incentive fee** The seller determines a price for the product or service but includes an incentive reward for completing the procured work on time or ahead of schedule.
- **Fixed-price** A simple fixed price for the contract. This can also include incentives for the seller to complete the project early or ahead of schedule, or for other savings shared between the buyer and the seller.
- **Fixed-price with economic price adjustment** Ideal for long-term projects that may span years to complete the project work. The contract defines a fixed price, with caveats for special categories of price fluctuation.
- **Time and materials** A price is assigned for the time and materials provided by the seller.

KEY TERMS

To pass the PMP exam, you will need to memorize the following terms and their definitions. For maximum value, create flashcards based on these definitions and review them daily. The definitions can be found within this chapter and in the glossary.

bid   A document presented by the seller to the buyer. Used when price is the determining factor in the decision-making process.

bidder conference   A meeting with prospective sellers to ensure that they all have a clear and common understanding of the product or service to be procured. Bidder conferences enable sellers to query the buyer on the details of the product to help ensure that the proposal the seller creates is adequate and appropriate for the proposed agreement.

centralized contracting   All contracts for all projects need to be approved through a central contracting unit within the performing organization.

contract   A legal, binding agreement, preferably written, between a buyer and the seller, detailing the requirements and obligations of both parties. Must include an offer, an acceptance, and a consideration.

contract administration   The process of ensuring that the buyer and the seller both perform to the specifications within the contract.

contract change control system   Defines the procedures for how contracts may be changed. Includes the paperwork, tracking, conditions, dispute resolution procedures, and procedures for getting the changes approved within the performing organization.

contract closeout   A process for confirming that the obligations of the contract were met as expected. The project manager, the customer, the key stakeholders, and, in some instances, the seller complete the product verification together to confirm that the contract has been completed.

contract file   A complete indexed set of records of the procurement process incorporated into the administrative closure process. These records include financial information as well as information on the performance and acceptance of the procured work. This is also known as the procurement file and it becomes part of organizational process assets.

cost plus award fee contract   A contract that requires the buyer to pay for all the project costs and gives the seller an award fee based on the project performance, meeting certain project criteria, or meeting other goals established by the buyer. The award fee can be tied to any factor the buyer determines, and the factor doesn't have to be exact.

cost-reimbursable contracts   A contract that pays the seller for the product. In the payment to the seller is a profit margin of the difference between the actual costs of the product and the sales amount.

direct costs   Costs incurred by the project in order for it to exist. Examples include equipment needed to complete the project work, salaries of the project team, and other expenses tied directly to the project's existence.

evaluation criteria   Used to rate and score proposals from sellers. In some instances, such as a bid or quote, the evaluation criterion is focused just on the price the seller offers. In other instances, such as a proposal, the evaluation criteria can be multiple values: experience, references, certifications, and more.

fixed-price contracts   Fixed-price contracts are also known as firm fixed-price and lump-sum contracts. These contracts have a preset price for which the vendor is obligated to perform the work or to provide materials for the agreed-upon price.

fixed-price with economic price adjustment contract   A contract for long-term projects that may span years to complete the project work. The contract does define a fixed price, with caveats for special categories of price fluctuation.

force majeure   A powerful and unexpected event, including "acts of God," such as a hurricane or another disaster.

invitation for bid   A document from the buyer to the seller that asks the seller to provide a price for the procured product or service.

letter of intent   A document that expresses the intent of the buyer to procure products or services from the seller. Not equivalent to a contract.

make-or-buy analysis   Used in determining what part of the project scope to make and what part to purchase.

oligopoly   A market condition in which the actions of one competitor affect the actions of all the other competitors.

procurement   The process of a seller soliciting, selecting, and paying for products or services from a buyer.

procurement audit   Reviews what worked and what did not work during the procurement processes. The successes and failures within the procurement process are reviewed from procurement planning through contract administration.

procurement management plan   A subsidiary project management plan that documents the decisions made in the procurement planning processes. It specifies how the remaining procurement activities will be managed.

proposal   A document from the seller to the buyer responding to a request for proposal or other procurement document.

qualified sellers list   A list that generally includes contact information, history of past experience with the seller, and other pertinent information. The performing organization may have lists of qualified sellers, preferred sellers, or approved sellers.

quote   A document from the seller to the buyer; used when price is the determining factor in the decision-making process.

request for proposal   A document from the buyer to the seller that asks the seller to provide a proposal for completing the procured work or for providing the procured product.

request for quote   A document from the buyer to the seller asking the seller to provide a price for the procured product or service.

should-cost estimates   Estimates created by the performing organization to predict what the cost of the procured product should be. If there is a significant difference between what the organization has predicted and what the seller has proposed, the statement of work was inadequate, the seller has misunderstood the requirements, or the price is too high.

single source   A specific seller that the performing organization prefers to contract with.

sole source   The only qualified seller that exists in the marketplace.

statement of work   A document that fully describes the work to be completed, the product to be supplied, or both. The SOW becomes part of the contract between the buyer and the seller. It is typically created as part of the procurement planning process and is used by the seller to determine whether they can meet the project's requirements. This is also known as a TOR, terms of reference.

time and materials   A contract type whereby the seller charges the buyer for the time and materials for the work completed. T&M contracts should have a not-to-exceed (NTE) clause to contain costs. These contracts are also called time and means contracts. They are considered a hybrid contract because they require the buyer to pay a fixed fee for the time and a variable fee for the materials purchased.

TWO-MINUTE DRILL

Planning for Purchases

☐ Procurement planning involves determining which aspects of the project can best be fulfilled by procuring the specified products or services.

☐ A clearly defined product description is needed to procure the product successfully.

☐ A make-or-buy analysis calculates and predicts which is better: for the performing organization to make the product in-house or to hire an entity outside of the organization to make the product.

☐ Some contracts can transfer the risk to the seller, while other contract types require the buyer to retain the risk of cost overruns.

☐ The procurement management plan describes the procedures for procuring work or products.

☐ Bids and quotes are needed when the decision will be made based on price. Proposals are needed when decisions are based on other factors, such as experience, qualifications, and approaches to the project work.

☐ The buyer should provide the seller with an SOW; details on the type of response needed such as a proposal, quote, or bid; and any information on contractual provisions, such as nondisclosure agreements or a copy of the model contract that the buyer intends to use.

☐ Contracting is requesting the potential sellers to provide bids, proposals, or quotes to complete the project work or supply the described product.

☐ An organization may retain a qualified sellers list from which the project team is forced to select a vendor. In other instances, the project team can rely on trade associations, industry directories, and other resources to locate qualified sellers.

☐ Advertisements for the procurement needs in newspapers and trade publications can increase the list of sellers from which the buyer can choose. Many government entities must publish procurement opportunities.

☐ Bidder conferences enable sellers to meet with the buyer to query the buyer on details of the procurement process. The goal of the bidder conference is to ensure that all prospective sellers have the same information and all the needed information to complete an accurate bid or proposal.

Conducting Procurements

☐ Samples of the sellers' previous related products or services can serve as evaluation criteria.

☐ Contract negotiation focuses on finding a fair and reasonable price for both the buyer and the seller.

❑ Weighting systems are unbiased approaches to determine which seller has the best offer to complete the procured product or service.

❑ Screening systems enable an organization to screen out sellers that do not qualify for the procured product or service.

❑ "Should-cost" estimates are completed by the performing organization to determine whether sellers completely understand the requirements of the project work.

Controlling Procurements

❑ Controlling the contract ensures that the sellers are meeting their contractual obligations.

❑ Change requests may require updates to the contract between the buyer and the seller. Contract change requests are part of the integrated change control system.

❑ The project manager must document and report to the seller and management on how the seller is meeting its contract obligations.

❑ Procurement audits are intended to review, document, and share the successes and failures of the current project's procurement process. The information can be applied to other projects within the organization.

❑ A contract procurement file is created and is included with the project records as part of the historical information of the current project.

SELF TEST

1. You are the project manager of the GHY Project for your organization. A portion of this project includes dangerous work; although members of the project team could likely complete the work, your sponsor doesn't want to accept the risk. In this situation, which of the following may be used as a risk mitigation tool?

   A. A vendor proposal

   B. A contract

   C. A quotation

   D. Project requirements

2. As a PMP candidate, you must understand the provisions of project procurement even if your typical projects do not include procurements. Based on the information in this chapter, a contract cannot have provisions for which one of the following?

   A. A deadline for the completion of the work
   B. Illegal activities
   C. Subcontracting the work
   D. Penalties and fines for disclosure of intellectual rights

3. You are the project manager for the 89A Project. You have created a contract for your customer. The contract must have which two things?

   A. An offer and consideration
   B. Signatures and the stamp of a notary public
   C. The value and worth of the procured item
   D. A start date and an acceptance of the start date

4. The WBS and the WBS dictionary can help a project manager plan for purchases and acquisitions. Which one of the following best describes this process?

   A. The WBS defines the specific contracted work.
   B. The WBS defines the requirements for the specific contracted work.
   C. The WBS defines the specific contracted work, which must support the requirements of the project customer.
   D. Both parties must have and retain their own copy of the WBS.

5. Yolanda has outsourced a portion of the project to a vendor. The vendor has discovered some issues that will influence the cost and schedule of its portion of the project. How must the vendor and Yolanda update the agreement?

   A. As a new contract signed by Yolanda and the vendor
   B. By submitting the change request to the contract change control system
   C. As a memo and SOW signed by Yolanda and the vendor
   D. By submitting the change request to the cost change control system

6. You are the project manager of the HHQ Project for your company. You have hired a vendor to complete a portion of the project, but the vendor doesn't seem to have met the project requirements as defined in the contract. You have tried alternative dispute resolutions to no avail, and you think the claims administration may have to be escalated. The United States backs all contracts through which of the following?

   A. Federal law
   B. State law
   C. Court system
   D. Lawyers

7. Terry is the project manager of the MVB Project. She needs to purchase a piece of equipment for her project. The accounting department has informed Terry that she needs a unilateral form of contract. Accounting is referring to which of the following?

A. The SOW

B. A legally binding contract

C. A purchase order

D. An invoice from the vendor

8. Bonnie is the project manager for the HGH Construction Project. She has contracted a portion of the project to the ABC Construction Company and has offered a bonus to ABC if they complete their portion of the work by August 30. This is an example of which one of the following?

A. A project requirement

B. A project incentive

C. A project goal

D. A fixed-price contract

9. You are a project manager for your organization and are progressing through the procurement management processes. Who should receive the procurement document package?

A. Your client

B. Your project sponsor

C. Your accounting/finance department

D. Each seller that will participate in the bidding

10. You are the project manager for a company that completes the installation of electrical fixtures in manufacturing environments. Part of your typical contractual agreement included coverage of intellectual rights and privity. Privity is what?

A. The relationship between the project manager and a known vendor

B. The relationship between the project manager and an unknown vendor

C. The contractual, confidential information between the customer and vendor

D. The professional information regarding the sale between the customer and vendor

11. Sammy is the project manager of the DSA Project. He is considering proposals and contracts presented by vendors for a portion of the project work. Of the following, which contract is least dangerous to the DSA Project?

A. Cost plus fixed fee

B. Cost plus percentage of cost

C. Cost plus incentive fee

D. Fixed-price

12. Bennie is the project manager for his company and he's working with his project stakeholder to determine the pros and cons of the different contract types for a portion of his project. Of the following contract types, which one requires the seller to assume the risk of cost overruns?
   A. Cost plus fixed fee
   B. Cost plus incentive fee
   C. Lump sum
   D. Time and materials

13. Benji is the project manager of the PLP Project. He has hired an independent contractor for a portion of the project work. The contractor is billing the project $120 per hour, plus materials. This is an example of which one of the following?
   A. Cost plus fixed fee
   B. Time and materials
   C. Unit price
   D. Lump sum

14. Mary is the project manager of the JHG Project. She has created a contract statement of work (SOW) for a vendor. All of the following should be included in the contract SOW except for which one?
   A. The items being purchased
   B. The signatures of both parties agreeing to the SOW
   C. The expected quality levels
   D. A description of the collateral services required

15. You are the project manager for a software development project for an accounting system that will operate over the Internet. Based on your research, you have discovered it will cost you $25,000 to write your own code. Once the code is written, you estimate you'll spend $3000 per month updating the software with client information, government regulations, and maintenance. A vendor has proposed to write the code for your company and charge a fee based on the number of clients using the program every month. The vendor will charge you $5 per month per user of the web-based accounting system. You will have roughly 1200 clients using the system each month. However, you'll need an in-house accountant to manage the time and billing of the system, so this will cost you an extra $1200 per month. How many months can you use the system before it's better to write your own code rather than hire the vendor?
   A. 3 months
   B. 4 months
   C. 6 months
   D. 15 months

16. You are the project manager of a project that will span six years in Columbus, Ohio. You are negotiating with your project customer for considerations for inflation, cost of utilities, and other cost factors that will likely fluctuate over the course of the project. What type of contract should your project have?
A. Cost plus award fee
B. Fixed-price with economic price adjustments
C. Lump sum
D. Fixed-price incentive fee

17. A contract between an organization and a vendor may include a clause that penalizes the vendor if the project is late. The lateness of a project has a monetary penalty. Thus, the penalty should be enforced or waived based on which one of the following?
A. Whether the project manager could have anticipated the delay
B. Whether the project manager knew the delay was likely
C. Whether the delay was because of an unseen risk
D. Who caused the delay and the reason why

18. A project manager is considering the marketplace and how it may affect the pricing on the procured portion of her project. She determines that in her market, there is only a single-source seller. A single-source seller means what?
A. There is only one qualified seller.
B. There is only one seller the company wants to do business with.
C. There is a seller that can provide all aspects of the project procurement needs.
D. There is only one seller in the market.

19. Thomas is the project manager for his organization, and he is preparing the procurement process for his project. Several enterprise environmental factors and organizational process assets assist Thomas in making the vendor selection. In the enterprise environmental factors are several evaluation criteria that Thomas must consider when he chooses a vendor for the project. Which one of the following is *not* a valid evaluation criterion for source selection?
A. The age of the contact person at the seller
B. The technical capability of the seller
C. Financial capacity
D. Price

20. Henry has sent the ABN Contracting Company a letter of intent. This means which one of the following?
A. Henry intends to sue the ABN Contracting Company.
B. Henry intends to buy from the ABN Contracting Company.
C. Henry intends to bid on a job from the ABN Contracting Company.
D. Henry intends to fire the ABN Contracting Company.

21. Martha is the project manager of the MNB Project. She wants a vendor to offer her one price to do all of the detailed work. Martha needs to prepare which type of document?

    A. A request for proposal

    B. A request for information

    C. A proposal

    D. An invitation for bid

22. In your organization, all project procurement must pass through a centralized contracting office. All correspondence between you and the vendors must be recorded and stored as part of the procurement records management system. These rules also provide instructions for the project's procurement document packages from procurement planning through contract closure. Which one of the following is true about procurement document packages?

    A. They offer no room for bidders to suggest changes.

    B. They ensure the receipt of complete proposals.

    C. They inform the performing organization why the bid is being created.

    D. The project manager creates and selects the bid.

23. A key component of the project procurement management knowledge area is the actual seller selection. Seller selection is based on many inputs and enterprise environmental factors by which the project manager must abide. From a PMP candidate's perspective, in what process group does source selection happen?

    A. Initiating

    B. Planning

    C. Executing

    D. Closing

24. Within your organization, all project managers are required to document the performance quality ratings, delivery performance, and contractual compliance of each vendor with which they interact. This is known as what?

    A. A requirement

    B. A seller rating system

    C. Procurement selection

    D. An incentive contract

25. You are the project manager for a seller, but you are managing another company's project as well. Things have gone well on the project, and the work is nearly complete. There is still a significant amount of funds in the project budget. The buyer's representative approaches you and asks that you complete some optional requirements to use up the remaining budget. You should do which one of the following?

    A. Negotiate a change in the contract to take on the additional work.

    B. Complete a contract change for the additional work.

    C. Submit the proposed change through the integrated change control system.

    D. Deny the change because it was not in the original contract.

SELF TEST ANSWERS

1. You are the project manager of the GHY Project for your organization. A portion of this project includes dangerous work; although members of the project team could likely complete the work, your sponsor doesn't want to accept the risk. In this situation, which of the following may be used as a risk mitigation tool?
    A. A vendor proposal
    B. A contract
    C. A quotation
    D. Project requirements

    ☑ **B.** A contract can be used as a risk mitigation tool. Procurement of risky activities is known as transference—the risk does not disappear, but the responsibility for the risk is transferred to the vendor.
    ☒ **A, C,** and **D** are incorrect. A vendor proposal, a quotation, and project requirements do nothing to serve as risk mitigation tools.

2. As a PMP candidate, you must understand the provisions of project procurement even if your typical projects do not include procurements. Based on the information in this chapter, a contract cannot have provisions for which one of the following?
    A. A deadline for the completion of the work
    B. Illegal activities
    C. Subcontracting the work
    D. Penalties and fines for disclosure of intellectual rights

    ☑ **B.** A contract cannot include provisions for illegal activities.
    ☒ **A, C,** and **D** are incorrect. **A** is incorrect because a contract can stipulate a deadline for the project work. **C** is incorrect because contracts can specify rules for subcontracting the work. **D** is incorrect because a contract can assess penalties and fines for disclosing intellectual rights and secret information.

3. You are the project manager for the 89A Project. You have created a contract for your customer. The contract must have what two things?
    A. An offer and consideration
    B. Signatures and the stamp of a notary public
    C. The value and worth of the procured item
    D. A start date and an acceptance of the start date

☑ **A.** Of all the answers presented, **A** is the best. Contracts have an offer and a consideration.

☒ **B, C,** and **D** are incorrect. **B** is incorrect because not all contracts demand signatures and notary public involvement. **C** is incorrect because a contract may not explicitly determine what the value and worth of the procured product or service is. **D** is incorrect because a contract may specify a start date, but the acceptance of the start date is vague and not needed for all contracts.

4. The WBS and the WBS dictionary can help a project manager plan for purchases and acquisitions. Which one of the following best describes this process?

   A.   The WBS defines the specific contracted work.

   B.   The WBS defines the requirements for the specific contracted work.

   C.   The WBS defines the specific contracted work, which must support the requirements of the project customer.

   D.   Both parties must have and retain their own copy of the WBS.

☑ **C.** The WBS defines the details and requirements for acceptance of the project. This information also serves as valuable input to the process of determining what needs to be procured. The WBS defines the end result of the project. In dealing with vendors to procure a portion of the project, the work to be procured must support the requirements of the project customer.

☒ **A, B,** and **D** are incorrect. **A** is incorrect because the WBS defines the project scope as a whole, not just the contracted work, which may be just a portion of the project. **B** is incorrect because the WBS does not define the requirements for the contract work. **D** is incorrect because the vendor likely will not have a copy of the WBS.

5. Yolanda has outsourced a portion of the project to a vendor. The vendor has discovered some issues that will influence the cost and schedule of its portion of the project. How must the vendor and Yolanda update the agreement?

   A.   As a new contract signed by Yolanda and the vendor

   B.   By submitting the change request to the contract change control system

   C.   As a memo and SOW signed by Yolanda and the vendor

   D.   By submitting the change request to the cost change control system

☑ **B.** This is the best answer because the question is asking for the vendor to update the agreement; the change should follow the details of the contract change control system.

☒ **A, C,** and **D** are incorrect. **A,** although feasible, is not the best answer to the question. A new contract does not update the original agreement and may cause delays, because the contract may have to be resubmitted, reapproved, and so on. **C** and **D** are not viable answers.

6. You are the project manager of the HHQ Project for your company. You have hired a vendor to complete a portion of the project, but the vendor doesn't seem to have met the project requirements as defined in the contract. You have tried alternative dispute resolutions to no avail, and you think the claims administration may have to be escalated. The United States backs all contracts through which of the following?

A. Federal law
B. State law
C. Court system
D. Lawyers

☑ **C.** All contracts in the United States are backed by the U.S. court system.
☒ **A, B,** and **D** are incorrect. Often the county and state court systems will make determinations of contract disputes if the need arises. The best answer is simply the court system, not federal law, state law, or lawyers.

7. Terry is the project manager of the MVB Project. She needs to purchase a piece of equipment for her project. The accounting department has informed Terry that she needs a unilateral form of contract. Accounting is referring to which of the following?

A. The SOW
B. A legally binding contract
C. A purchase order
D. An invoice from the vendor

☑ **C.** A unilateral form of a contract is simply a purchase order.
☒ **A, B,** and **D** are incorrect. **A** is incorrect because an SOW is a statement of work. **B** is incorrect because a legally binding contract does not fully answer the question. **D,** an invoice from the vendor, is not what the purchasing department is requesting.

8. Bonnie is the project manager for the HGH Construction Project. She has contracted a portion of the project to the ABC Construction Company and has offered a bonus to ABC if they complete their portion of the work by August 30. This is an example of which one of the following?

A. A project requirement
B. A project incentive
C. A project goal
D. A fixed-price contract

☑ **B.** A bonus to complete the work by August 30 is an incentive.
☒ **A, C,** and **D** are incorrect. **A** is incorrect because the question does not indicate that August 30 is a required deadline. **C** is incorrect because it does not fully answer the question. **D** is incorrect because the contract-type details are not disclosed in this question.

9. You are a project manager for your organization and are progressing through the procurement management processes. Who should receive the procurement document package?

A. Your client

B. Your project sponsor

C. Your accounting/finance department

D. Each seller that will participate in the bidding

☑ **D.** Each vendor that participates in the bidding will need to receive the procurement document package.

☒ **A, B,** and **C** are incorrect. These parties do not need the procurement document package.

10. You are the project manager for a company that completes the installation of electrical fixtures in manufacturing environments. Part of your typical contractual agreement included coverage of intellectual rights and privity. Privity is what?

A. The relationship between the project manager and a known vendor

B. The relationship between the project manager and an unknown vendor

C. The contractual, confidential information between the customer and the vendor

D. The professional information regarding the sale between the customer and the vendor

☑ **C.** Privity is a confidential agreement between the buyer and the seller.

☒ **A, B,** and **D** are incorrect. They do not fully answer the question.

11. Sammy is the project manager of the DSA Project. He is considering proposals and contracts presented by vendors for a portion of the project work. Of the following, which contract is least dangerous to the DSA Project?

A. Cost plus fixed fee

B. Cost plus percentage of cost

C. Cost plus incentive fee

D. Fixed-price

☑ **D.** A fixed-price contract contains the least amount of risk for a project. The seller assumes all of the risk because cost overruns are the seller's responsibility.

☒ **A, B,** and **C** are incorrect. These contract types carry the risk of cost overruns being assumed by the buyer.

12. Bennie is the project manager for his company and he's working with his project stakeholder to determine the pros and cons of the different contract types for a portion of his project. Of the following contract types, which one requires the seller to assume the risk of cost overruns?

   A. Cost plus fixed fee
   B. Cost plus incentive fee
   C. Lump sum
   D. Time and materials

> ☑   **C.** A lump sum is a fixed fee to complete the contract; the seller absorbs any cost overruns.
> ☒   **A, B,** and **D** are incorrect. **A** and **B** are incorrect because these contracts require the seller to carry the risk of cost overruns. **D** is incorrect because time and materials contracts require the buyer to pay for cost overruns on the materials and the time invested in the project work.

13. Benji is the project manager of the PLP Project. He has hired an independent contractor for a portion of the project work. The contractor is billing the project $120 per hour, plus materials. This is an example of which one of the following?

   A. Cost plus fixed fee
   B. Time and materials
   C. Unit price
   D. Lump sum

> ☑   **B.** The contractor's rate of $120 per hour plus the cost of the materials is an example of a time and materials contract.
> ☒   **A, C,** and **D** are incorrect. **A** is incorrect because a cost plus fixed fee charges the cost of the materials, plus a fixed fee, for the installation or work to complete the contract. **C** is incorrect because a unit price has a set price for each unit installed on the project. **D** is incorrect because a lump sum does not break down the time and materials.

14. Mary is the project manager of the JHG Project. She has created a contract statement of work (SOW) for a vendor. All of the following should be included in the contract SOW except for which one?

   A. The items being purchased
   B. The signatures of both parties agreeing to the SOW
   C. The expected quality levels
   D. A description of the collateral services required

> ☑   **B.** Signatures of both parties agreeing to the SOW are not required. That stipulation will be included in the contract.
> ☒   **A, C,** and **D** are incorrect. These things are generally included in the SOW.

15. You are the project manager for a software development project for an accounting system that will operate over the Internet. Based on your research, you have discovered it will cost you $25,000 to write your own code. Once the code is written, you estimate you'll spend $3000 per month updating the software with client information, government regulations, and maintenance. A vendor has proposed to write the code for your company and charge a fee based on the number of clients using the program every month. The vendor will charge you $5 per month per user of the web-based accounting system. You will have roughly 1200 clients using the system each month. However, you'll need an in-house accountant to manage the time and billing of the system, so this will cost you an extra $1,200 per month. How many months can you use the system before it's better to write your own code rather than hire the vendor?

   A. 3 months
   B. 4 months
   C. 6 months
   D. 15 months

   ☑ **C.** The monies invested in the vendor's solution would have paid for your own code in 6 months. This is calculated by finding your cash outlay for the two solutions: $25,000 for your own code creation and zero cash outlay for the vendor's solution. The monthly cost to maintain your own code is $3000. The monthly cost of the vendor's solution is $7200. Subtract your cost of $3000 from the vendor's cost of $7200, which equals $4200. Divide this number into the cash outlay of $25,000 to create your own code, and you'll come up with 5.95 months.
   ☒ **A, B,** and **D** are incorrect. They do not correctly answer the question.

16. You are the project manager of a project that will span six years in Columbus, Ohio. You are negotiating with your project customer for considerations for inflation, cost of utilities, and other cost factors that will likely fluctuate over the course of the project. What type of contract should your project have?

   A. Cost plus award fee
   B. Fixed-price with economic price adjustments
   C. Lump sum
   D. Fixed-price incentive fee

   ☑ **B.** Projects that last for several years often use a fixed price with economic price adjustment contracts for cost categories that are likely to increase over the project duration.
   ☒ **A, C,** and **D** are incorrect. These contract types do not accommodate fluctuations in the price for economic variables such as inflation.

17. A contract between an organization and a vendor may include a clause that penalizes the vendor if the project is late. The lateness of a project has a monetary penalty. Thus, the penalty should be enforced or waived based on which one of the following?

  A. Whether the project manager could have anticipated the delay
  B. Whether the project manager knew the delay was likely
  C. Whether the delay was because of an unseen risk
  D. Who caused the delay and the reason why

> ☑   **D.** This is the best answer because the party that caused the delay is typically the party responsible for it. It would not be acceptable for the project manager to cause a delay willingly and then penalize the contractor because the project was late.
>
> ☒   **A, B,** and **C** are incorrect. Although these choices may be valid reasons for why a project is late, the best, all-inclusive answer is to determine who caused the delay and why. Choosing any of the other answers eliminates all other possible reasons for delaying the project and the assigned accountability for the lateness.

18. A project manager is considering the marketplace and how it may affect the pricing on the procured portion of her project. She determines that in her market, there is only a single-source seller. A single-source seller means what?

  A. There is only one qualified seller.
  B. There is only one seller the company wants to do business with.
  C. There is a seller that can provide all aspects of the project procurement needs.
  D. There is only one seller in the market.

> ☑   **B.** A single-source seller means there is only one seller the company wants to do business with.
>
> ☒   **A, C,** and **D** are incorrect. **A** describes a sole-source seller. **C** is incorrect because multiple sellers may be able to satisfy the project needs, but only one can be used. **D** is also incorrect. Just because there is only one seller in the market does not mean the seller can adequately and fully fill the project needs.

19. Thomas is the project manager for his organization, and he is preparing the procurement process for his project. Several enterprise environmental factors and organizational process assets assist Thomas in making the vendor selection. In the enterprise environmental factors are several evaluation criteria that Thomas must consider when he chooses a vendor for the project. Which one of the following is *not* a valid evaluation criterion for source selection?

  A. The age of the contact person at the seller
  B. The technical capability of the seller
  C. Financial capacity
  D. Price

  ☑ **A.** The age of the contact person at the seller should not influence the source selection. The experience of the person doing the work, however, may influence selection.
  ☒ **B, C,** and **D** are incorrect. Technical capability, financial capacity, and price can be valid evaluation criteria.

20. Henry has sent the ABN Contracting Company a letter of intent. This means which one of the following?

  A. Henry intends to sue the ABN Contracting Company.
  B. Henry intends to buy from the ABN Contracting Company.
  C. Henry intends to bid on a job from the ABN Contracting Company.
  D. Henry intends to fire the ABN Contracting Company.

  ☑ **B.** Henry intends to buy from the ABN Contracting Company.
  ☒ **A, C,** and **D** are incorrect. They do not describe the purpose of the letter of intent.

21. Martha is the project manager of the MNB Project. She wants a vendor to offer her one price to do all of the detailed work. Martha is looking for which type of document?

  A. A request for proposal
  B. A request for information
  C. A proposal
  D. An invitation for bid

  ☑ **D.** An IFB is typically a request for a sealed document that lists the seller's firm price to complete the detailed work.
  ☒ **A, B,** and **C** are incorrect. A and B are incorrect because both are documents from the buyer to the seller requesting information about completing the work. **C** does not list the price to complete the work, but instead offers solutions to the buyer for completing the project needs.

22. In your organization, all project procurement must pass through a centralized contracting office. All correspondence between you and the vendors must be recorded and stored as part of the procurement records management system. These rules also provide instructions for the project's procurement document packages from procurement planning through contract closure. Which one of the following is true about procurement document packages?
    A. They offer no room for bidders to suggest changes.
    B. They ensure the receipt of complete proposals.
    C. They inform the performing organization why the bid is being created.
    D. The project manager creates and selects the bid.

    ☑ **B.** Procurement document packages detail the requirements for the work to help ensure complete proposals from sellers.
    ☒ **A, C,** and **D** are incorrect. **A** is incorrect because procurement documents allow input from the seller to suggest alternative ways to complete the project work. **C** is incorrect because informing the performing organization on why the bid is being created is not the purpose of the procurement documents. **D** is not realistic.

23. A key component of the project procurement management knowledge area is the actual seller selection. Seller selection is based on many inputs and enterprise environmental factors by which the project manager must abide. From a PMP candidate's perspective, in what process group does source selection happen?
    A. Initiating
    B. Planning
    C. Executing
    D. Closing

    ☑ **C.** Source selection happens during the executing process group.
    ☒ **A, B,** and **D** are incorrect. These process groups do not include source selection.

24. Within your organization, all project managers are required to document the performance quality ratings, delivery performance, and contractual compliance of each vendor with which they interact. This is known as what?
    A. A requirement
    B. A seller rating system
    C. Procurement selection
    D. An incentive contract

☑ **B.** This scenario describes the seller rating system, which can help future project managers choose the best vendor based on past performance.

☒ **A, C,** and **D** are incorrect. **A** is incorrect because requirements describe the scope of the project or the procured items. **C** is incorrect because this term is not valid. **D** is incorrect because an incentive contract would define the reward or penalties for adhering to or failing to adhere to the contract requirements.

25. You are the project manager for a seller, but you are managing another company's project as well. Things have gone well on the project, and the work is nearly complete. There is still a significant amount of funds in the project budget. The buyer's representative approaches you and asks that you complete some optional requirements to use up the remaining budget. You should do which one of the following?

    A. Negotiate a change in the contract to take on the additional work.
    B. Complete a contract change for the additional work.
    C. Submit the proposed change through the integrated change control system.
    D. Deny the change because it was not in the original contract.

☑ **C.** Any additional work is a change in the project scope. Changes to the project scope should be approved by the mechanisms in the integrated change control system. The stakeholders need to approve the changes to the project scope.

☒ **A, B,** and **D** are incorrect. These are not realistic expectations of the project. This question could fall into the realm of the PMP Code of Ethics and Professional Conduct. Typically, when a project scope has been fulfilled, the project work is done. The difference in this situation is that the additional tasks are optional requirements for the project scope.

Chapter 13

Introducing Project Stakeholder Management

CERTIFICATION OBJECTIVES

13.01	Identifying the Project Stakeholders	13.04	Monitoring Stakeholder Engagement
13.02	Planning for Stakeholder Management	✓	Two-Minute Drill
13.03	Managing Stakeholder Engagement	**Q&A**	Self Test

S ome project managers believe that if it weren't for the project stakeholders, their projects would go smoothly. But that's like saying swimming would be easy if it weren't for all the water. Project management—your job—wouldn't exist if there were no stakeholders. And although stakeholder management can be a challenge, which is a nice way of saying a pain in the neck, the truth is that you need stakeholders in order to have a project. Stakeholders include anyone, including you, who has a vested interest in the project's outcome.

Stakeholders are usually the key individuals on the project: the project customer, the project manager, the program manager, the project team, vendors, and decision-makers for the project. These key stakeholders can influence the project and shift the project in a certain direction, and they have political power to help overcome obstacles that may otherwise stall the project's advancement. Stakeholders can also object to project decisions, challenge other key stakeholders, argue about the project work, and stall the project's advancement.

Other stakeholders you'll also have to manage don't usually have as much power to exert over the project as the key stakeholders do. These are people and groups that include end users, the media, customers, and your target audience for the project deliverables. Sure, sometimes these groups and people can really dislike your project and cause havoc, but most of the time, these stakeholders are more passive and simply accept the existence of your project. You'll have positive stakeholders, negative stakeholders, and neutral stakeholders in most of your projects.

Positive stakeholders, as you might guess, are the cheerleaders. Negative stakeholders are opposed to your project. Neutral stakeholders don't care if your project succeeds or not, but they're still involved with the project work. A neutral stakeholder could be an employee in your company's procurement department who is involved with your project, but who doesn't really care about your project's success or failure.

Building a Strong Stakeholder Management Foundation

Stakeholder management is a project management knowledge area that focuses on four activities: identifying the project stakeholders, planning for stakeholder engagement, managing the stakeholder engagement, and monitoring the stakeholder engagement. Stakeholder management is an important, ongoing activity in any project. For your PMP examination, you'll need to answer questions on how you'll complete the four stakeholder management processes. The ultimate goal of stakeholder management is to keep stakeholders involved, interested, and supportive of the agreed-upon project scope.

The success of the project begins by identifying what constitutes project success. Much of what constitutes success will be easy to see: requirements, cost, quality, and schedule. But also included will be the stakeholder satisfaction—and that's often a perception of how the project manager communicates, manages the project, and makes the stakeholders feel valued and welcome in the project. Stakeholder engagement is about meeting needs and expectations, so it's no surprise that an important part of stakeholder management is understanding the stakeholders' needs and expectations of the project manager. If you know what someone wants, it's easier to satisfy that need in the project.

Leading Stakeholder Management

Leading stakeholder management begins by identifying the project stakeholders—all of the stakeholders, not just the people closely connected to the project. This broader set of stakeholders can include inspectors, regulatory bodies, lobby groups, environmentalists, your community, and even the media. Identification of stakeholders is the first step—and one of the most important steps—to leading stakeholders. If you overlook people who should be involved in your project, you're likely going to have some people who aren't very happy with you, and that's a tough situation to overcome.

Stakeholder management is more than just identifying the stakeholders; it's also about engaging people and keeping people engaged throughout the project. Stakeholder management includes the following:

- Keeping the project team involved with stakeholder engagement
- Periodically reviewing stakeholders to ensure that new stakeholders have come into the project
- Meeting with stakeholders to discuss how the project may affect them, which includes the concept of co-creation—meaning stakeholders become partners in the project, rather than just recipients of the project

Consider the positive and negative values of stakeholder engagement. Positive value describes the pros of keeping stakeholders engaged, while negative value describes the cons of not keeping stakeholders engaged. The negatives can include more than just financial consequences, and can also impact political capital, reputation, and customers satisfaction.

Agile projects promote the team, project manager, and stakeholder interactions. Often the developers and the stakeholder can communicate directly about the requirements, issues within the project, and goals of the current iteration. Transparency is important in agile, and that requires open communication among all the stakeholders. Change is expected, so access to the project team isn't as guarded as you might find a predictive life cycle project. Stakeholders can attend project meetings, review project artifacts, and participate in reviews in agile projects.

Tailoring the Stakeholder Management Processes

I'll bet you know this concept by now: You can tailor the stakeholder management processes for your organization. Every organization, every project, and every stakeholder is different, so you can certainly tailor the project to meet the concerns and expectations of project stakeholders. When you go about tailoring stakeholder management processes, there are three primary considerations:

- **Diversity of the stakeholders** The number of stakeholders, the organization culture, and even the social consideration of the organization and the project can influence how the processes are tailored.

- **Complexity of stakeholder relationships** The larger the project, the more complex the parts of the project will be. When stakeholders are considered parts of many different groups, miscommunications can happen, conflicts can erupt among the groups, and poor information can trickle out to the different types or categories of stakeholders.
- **Communication technology** Stakeholder engagement aligns with the project's communications management plan. The communication technology needs to be considered because it can affect how you'll communicate and who can receive communications based on the technical modalities you've selected for the project.

CERTIFICATION OBJECTIVE 13.01

Identifying the Project Stakeholders

All the project's stakeholders should be identified before the project planning gets too far underway. One of the first project management processes a project manager should do, stakeholder identification ensures that all the stakeholders are identified and represented, and their needs, expectations, and concerns are addressed. Stakeholder identification helps the project manager communicate with the appropriate people throughout the project.

Before the project manager can begin project management communications, she needs someone to communicate with. This is where project stakeholders come into play. Stakeholders, as you know, are the people and organizations that are affected by the project. It's essential for planning and for communications to identify the project stakeholders as early as possible in the project. Things can get ugly quickly when the project manager realizes that she may have overlooked any stakeholders who need to contribute to the project.

Stakeholder identification helps the project manager and the project team plan for the project's activities, resources, and deliverables. The project manager and the project team may lead the stakeholder identification process, or a business analyst may help identify the stakeholders. In either case, it's ideal to group stakeholders by their overall influence over project decisions, their involvement in the project work, and their interest in the project outcome. This categorization can help streamline communication.

Contracts are the most formal of all communications, because they are legally binding agreements between two or more parties. If the project is a result of a contract, everyone mentioned in the contract is considered a key stakeholder in the project. The organization's procurement management processes, part of enterprise environmental factors, may affect how stakeholder identification and management happen when contracts are involved.

Preparing for Stakeholder Identification

Imagine that you've just landed a new project for a client you've never worked with. You'd be challenged to identify all the stakeholders in the project—after all, you might have a general idea of who should be involved in the project, but you don't know who's who at this new client. You'll need some documents and some help to prepare stakeholder identification. This is the approach you should take in all your projects: always be thorough and pretend you don't know who should be involved in the project. You don't want an assumption to cause an oversight in stakeholder identification.

To prepare for the stakeholder identification process, you'll need seven inputs:

- **Project charter**   The charter identifies the people and groups that the project is for. It's a great place to start collecting names and requirements of people the project affects.

- **Business documents**   The business case will provide an initial list of the project stakeholders. The benefits management plan may also provide stakeholders who will benefit from the project.

- **Project management plan**   You'll specifically reference the communication managements plan and the stakeholder engagement plan.

- **Project documents**   The change log is an input to this process, as changes to the project may introduce new stakeholders. The issue log can also identify stakeholders based on the issues. Requirements documentation can also help identify stakeholders.

- **Agreements**   If you're completing the project for another entity, the project's contracts will help you identify some of the stakeholders you'll need to manage. If your project procures goods and services, the vendors you'll buy from are also stakeholders you'll need to manage.

- **Enterprise environmental factors**   The culture of an organization, regulations that affect the project, global stakeholder considerations, the physical location of the work and resources, and organizational trends and practices are all enterprise environmental factors that can affect stakeholder identification.

- **Organizational process assets**   If you're completing a current project that's similar to a past project, you can use historical information to help you assess stakeholders, groups, and vendors. You can also use the stakeholder register from the past project as a template, and use lessons learned and plans from past projects to help identify the stakeholders in the current project.

Performing Stakeholder Identification

One of the best approaches to stakeholder identification is to meet with the project stakeholders you do know and ask who else should be involved in the project. These meetings, sometimes called profile analysis meetings, help the project manager learn about the project stakeholders and confirm that appropriate stakeholders are involved, are accounted for, and are contributing to the project's success. A profile analysis meeting examines each of the roles in the project and documents each role's interests, concerns, influence, knowledge about the project, and attitude toward the project.

PMP
Coach   **Stakeholder identification tools and techniques includes data gathering through the traditional brainstorming approach. Another approach is called brain writing, in which participants review the questions or topics prior to the brainstorming session so they're prepared to share their thoughts with the group.**

Stakeholder analysis is a process that considers and ranks project stakeholders based on their influence, interests, and expectations of the project. This process uses a systematic approach to identify all the project stakeholders, ranking the stakeholders by varying factors, and then addressing stakeholders' needs, requirements, and expectations. Stakeholder analysis follows three logical steps:

1. Identify the project stakeholders and their interest, influence, project contributions, contact information, and expectations of the project. You can complete this through interviews to determine who are the project decision-makers and champions of the project's objectives.

2. Prioritize the identified stakeholders based on their power, influence, or impact on project decisions. Project managers can use a grid system to rank stakeholder attributes from low to high.

3. Anticipate and plan how stakeholders will respond in different project scenarios. This anticipation helps the project manager influence the stakeholders and prepare them for project news, actions, and risk management.

Stakeholder analysis aims to identify stakeholders and what their stakes in the project may be. Stakes in the project are defined as follows:

- **Interest**   The stakeholder is affected by the project.
- **Rights (legal or moral rights)**   The stakeholder may have legal rights, such as physical safety, or moral rights, such as environmental concerns about where the project work is taking place.
- **Ownership**   The stakeholder has ownership of an asset.

- **Knowledge**   The stakeholder has knowledge that can help the project.
- **Contribution**   The stakeholder is contributing to the project through funds, resources, or support of the project.

Visualizing Stakeholder Influence

Sometimes it's best to visualize how the stakeholders can influence the project. You don't want to spend hours and hours meeting with stakeholders who have little power over and little influence on your project. This doesn't mean you ignore stakeholders with little power and little influence; you simply manage them differently than you would the CIO or the primary project customer. Classification models can help you rate the stakeholders who have the most power and influence over the project. One of the most common models, shown in Figure 13-1, is a power-interest grid. Instead of listing stakeholders' names, you'd use letters or numbers to plot their power-interest on the grid.

Each type of classification model demonstrates the amount of power, influence, interest, and impact a stakeholder can have on a project. Although all the models are similar, they each rate differing factors of the stakeholders:

- **Power/interest grid**   This grid shows the relationship between the stakeholders' power and interest over the project objectives.
- **Power/influence grid**   This chart maps the amount of power and influence the stakeholders have over the project objectives.
- **Influence/impact grid**   Similar to the other models, this chart plots out stakeholders' influence in the project in relation to the impact of their power over the project decisions and objectives.

FIGURE 13-1

A power-interest grid depicts the stakeholders' power and interest over the project.

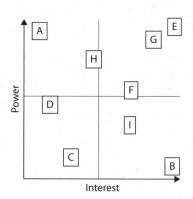

- **Salience model** This model typically uses three circles to show stakeholders' power, urgency, and legitimacy over the project work, decisions, and influence on project objectives. Power, in this model, means the stakeholder's level of authority and influence over decision-making. Urgency refers to the stakeholder's need for attention regarding a project topic. Legitimacy means that the stakeholder should be involved in the project or decision. In some models, legitimacy can be substituted with proximity to rank stakeholder involvement with the project.

- **Stakeholder cube** This model is a three-dimensional cube that combines the power, influence, and impact grids.

- **Direction of influence** This illustrates a stakeholder's influence on the project in one of five ways:

  - **Upward** Senior management, customer, or steering committee
  - **Downward** Project team, subject matter expert, or consultant
  - **Outward** Suppliers, vendors, government agencies, customers, or the public
  - **Sideward** Peers of the project manager or middle management who may need the same resources the project manager needs in the project
  - **Prioritization** Priority levels of stakeholders in a large project; some stakeholders have greater priority than others

watch A salience model is a stakeholder classification that ranks stakeholders based on their power, urgency, and legitimacy in the project.

Reviewing the Results of Stakeholder Identification

The primary output of stakeholder identification is the stakeholder register. This document defines the stakeholders for the project and their contact information. The stakeholder register is a directory of all the stakeholders and should include the following:

- Stakeholder name and classification
- Geographic location
- Project role and contribution
- Project requirements and expectations
- Project influence

- Phase of the project the stakeholder is most concerned with
- Details on the stakeholder's role—for example, internal or external, supporter of the project, negative stakeholder, or neutral

The stakeholder registry can help the project manager create a stakeholder management strategy. This strategy is an effort to manage stakeholder expectations and create synergy and buy-in. A stakeholder analysis matrix can help define the stakeholders' interest, assessments of project impact, and any potential responses to the anticipated stakeholder results.

See the video "Stakeholders."

This process also creates three additional outputs:

- **Change requests**   Stakeholder identification could result in change requests to the requirements, project documents, or project management plan. Changes flow through the project's integrated change control system.
- **Project management plan updates**   The project management plan may need to be updated as a result of the stakeholder identification process. The requirements management plan, risk management plan, communications management plan, and stakeholder engagement plan can all be updated as a result of stakeholder identification.
- **Project documents**   Project documents that may be updated as a result of the stakeholder identification process are the assumptions log, issue log, and risk register.

CERTIFICATION OBJECTIVE 13.02

Planning for Stakeholder Management

Stakeholder management planning is the process of creating a strategy to manage the stakeholders in the project. It's the analysis of what the stakeholders want the project to do, how a stakeholder's requirements align with those of other stakeholders, and how the stakeholders are prioritized within the project. In other words, it involves balancing the most important stakeholders in the project with the stakeholders who have less interest and influence over the project requirements.

That's right—some stakeholders are more important than others. Some project managers bristle at the concept that not all stakeholders are considered equal. Sorry, but they aren't equal. If you're paying a company to build a house for you—a house that you've visualized and designed—do you really care that the landscaper in the project thinks your bedroom should go in the basement? No, you probably don't; you've already created the house, you know where you want the rooms, and, besides, you're paying for the new home, not the guy planting shrubs in the backyard. Now this doesn't mean you tell the landscaper to buzz off; you should still manage the landscaper because he is a stakeholder in the project—he's just not the most important stakeholder.

Stakeholder management is about managing how the project will affect all the stakeholders during the project execution and after the project is done. A software development project, for example, might include stakeholders' input at the design stage, but you'll also need to address the post-project support for the end users. The end users may fear what the project will create and how they'll use the deliverables in their day-to-day lives. Stakeholder management is about communicating and addressing the needs, wants, threats, and even the perceived threats regarding the project, and this requires a plan.

Organizing the Planning

Because you're creating a strategy for managing the project stakeholders, you'll need to gather several documents and project components to craft your approach effectively. You'll use these to help you understand the stakeholders—to see the project and deliverables from their perspectives—and to guide your strategy. The stakeholder management plan will go through versioning as the project progress. You may have to update the plan at the start of each phase or when changes occur within the organization. Less obvious times to update the plan include when people are no longer considered stakeholders because they leave the department, group, or project—and when new stakeholders come into the project. Changes within the project, such as risk or scope changes, can introduce or remove stakeholders, too.

You'll need the following input to create the stakeholder management plan:

- **Project charter**   The charter will have the base layer of stakeholder information and what's important to these stakeholders.

- **Project management plan**   The project management plan, as much as it may be created, will define the project's life cycle and how the work is to be executed. The subsidiary plans you'll review are the resource management plan, communications management plan, and the risk management plan.

- **Project documents**   The assumption log, issue log risk register, and the change log will help you evaluate the stakeholders introduced to the project, and how the assumptions, issues, and risk management may affect them and your need to communicate and engage the stakeholders. You'll also review the project schedule to communicate and engage stakeholders for upcoming work and the risk register for risks that may affect the stakeholders. The recently created stakeholder register will help you identify the stakeholders and formulize a strategy for stakeholder management.

- **Agreements**   Contracts and internal agreements can help you plan for managing engagement with suppliers, sellers, and other entities within your organization.

- **Enterprise environmental factors**   The culture of an organization, regulations that affect the project, and organizational policies will help with stakeholder management planning. You'll also consider personnel administration policies, risk appetites, communication channels, global and regional trends and culture, and the physical location of project resources.

- **Organizational process assets**   Lessons learned and historical information, especially from projects with the same or similar stakeholders, can provide insight on how best to manage the project stakeholders. Other organizational process assets can include corporate policies and procedures for social media, ethics, and security. You'll also reference policies on risk, change, and data management and guidelines for the collection, storage, and retrieval of data. Your organization might also have software to help with stakeholder management.

Analyzing Stakeholder Engagement

At the launch of a project, it's not unusual for the stakeholders to be excited about what you're about to create. They'll envision the better future state, the problem solved, the new opportunities seized. Stakeholders will want to come to your status meetings, they'll gladly respond to project-related e-mails, and you can always get answers to your questions. But then the bloom begins to fade—especially on longer projects. Stakeholders get busy with other projects and other more pressing demands, and their interest in the project wanes.

Stakeholder engagement is the process of keeping stakeholders interested, involved, and supportive of the project. You need to help maintain the stakeholders' energy for the project and keep them contributing and excited about what the project is creating. Stakeholder analysis is an approach that measures who's interested in the project work and whose interest is fading. Stakeholder analysis helps you create a strategy to keep stakeholders engaged in the project.

Constraint and assumption analysis is needed to consider how the identified constraints and assumptions may affect your stakeholder engagement approach. You'll use root cause analysis to determine why stakeholders may not be supportive of your project, and SWOT analysis to help you create a stakeholder strategy to improve upon current engagement of stakeholders.

You'll perform stakeholder analysis not just at the beginning of a project, but throughout the project. Subject matter experts can help with this process, of course. You'll monitor the status of the stakeholders and determine whether any attitudes toward the project success have changed; you'll rank the current stakeholder engagement and set a goal for the desired level of stakeholder engagement. After analysis, you can categorize stakeholders into five groups in a stakeholder engagement matrix:

- **Unaware**   The stakeholder doesn't know about the project or the effect the project may have on him.
- **Resistant**   The stakeholder is aware of your project but isn't keen on the changes your project will create.
- **Neutral**   The stakeholder is aware of your project and doesn't care if the project succeeds or fails.
- **Supportive**   The stakeholder is aware of your project, is happy about the project, and hopes your project is successful.
- **Leading**   The stakeholder is aware of your project, wants the project to succeed, and is helping to lead the charge to make certain the project outcome is positive.

PMP Coach   **Your interactions and meetings with the stakeholders will help you determine who's excited about the project, who's unaware of the project changes, and who just doesn't want your project to succeed. You can chart out the results of stakeholder analysis in a simple table, but keep this chart away from prying eyes. You don't want a negative stakeholder to see the analysis and become more agitated and aggressive about the project. This analysis helps you and the project team create a plan for stakeholder engagement; it's not a plan for political battles in the office.**

Building the Stakeholder Management Plan

The stakeholder management plan helps the project manager and the project team define a strategy for managing the project stakeholders. It helps to establish stakeholder engagement at the launch of the project and throughout the project life cycle, and it shows how to improve upon the level of engagement identified. Stakeholder management doesn't necessarily aim to win over all the stakeholders to the project's vision, but it can help you manage the stakeholders' attitudes toward the project. For example, the CEO of a company can say that the organization will be migrating to a new type of software. The end users may not be happy about the choice—in fact, they could be angry about the choice. The organizational power, the CEO, however, has defined the project and mandate so the project manager must complete the project accordingly.

Just because you have a negative stakeholder—or even many negative stakeholders—doesn't mean that your project will fail. Negative stakeholders who are able to influence project decisions, or even hold up the project due to indecisions, must still be managed. The power influence of each stakeholder directly affects how the project manager manages the stakeholders in the project. These are the types of conditions that need to be documented and strategized in the stakeholder management plan. It's an honest assessment of who the stakeholders are and how the stakeholders can help or hinder the project.

The stakeholder management plan defines the following:

- Current stakeholder engagement levels and goals for improvement
- How the project will affect the stakeholders
- Relationships among stakeholders
- Communication requirements for the project stakeholders
- Plan and schedule for updating the stakeholder management plan as needed based on conditions within the project

The stakeholder management plan can be adapted from organizational process assets—specifically, older and similar projects. The stakeholder management plan is tightly linked to the project's communications management plan, especially regarding information distribution. Both plans define who needs what information, when the information is needed, and the expected modality of the information. The stakeholder management plan, however, predicts and documents how the stakeholders will react to the information that the project manager distributes. It shouldn't take a mind-reader to know that bad news won't be accepted gently from the stakeholders.

w a t c h **Never present a problem without also presenting a solution. Be proactive with your stakeholders by helping them make the decisions you want them to make.**

CERTIFICATION OBJECTIVE 13.03

Managing Stakeholder Engagement

Early in the project, it's obvious that stakeholders need to be involved, but as the project moves forward, stakeholder engagement often tends to wane. Stakeholder engagement simply means that you're keeping the stakeholders involved in the project, you're communicating with the project stakeholders, and you're addressing their needs, fears, and perceptions about the project work. In some instances, stakeholder engagement means that you're working with negative stakeholders through negotiations to overcome their opposition to the project.

Stakeholder engagement is linked closely to project communications. Recall in Chapter 10 the purpose of the project communications management plan: to get the right message to the right audience at the right time. Stakeholder engagement relies heavily on the project communications management plan as part of its approach. The project communications must be accurate, timely, and precise, or the project manager could damage the relationship between the project and the stakeholders. You don't want to create new problems for the project—and new stakeholder management challenges—by simply failing to communicate. Communication of good or bad news is something that the project manager should always do.

You'll need four total inputs in the manage stakeholder engagement process:

- **Project management plan**   Within the project management plan, you'll need the communication management plan, the risk management plan, the stakeholder management plan, and the change management plan.

- **Project documents**   Several project documents will help you manage stakeholder engagements: the change log, issue log, lessons learned register, and stakeholder register.

- **Enterprise environmental factors**   Enterprise environmental factors to consider include the organizational culture, politics, governance, personnel administration, risk thresholds, communication channels, global and regional trends and practices, and geographical location of project resources.

- **Organizational process assets**   Historical information, change control procedures, the approach for issue management, data management, and your organization's communication methodology are all organizational process assets that are used as part of stakeholder engagement inputs.

Engaging Stakeholders

As soon as people and groups get involved in the project, you're starting the process of stakeholder engagement. Ideally, you've had time to plan and ponder how to engage stakeholders, but often your interactions with stakeholders are early in the project. This is where your years of experience as a project manager and professionalism come into play: you instinctively know how to deal with people and how to respect people, and you understand their needs and wants for the project. These are the interpersonal skills that you develop and refine over time—the softer skills of project management that you'll finesse with practice, through trial and error, and through maturity. You'll need the following interpersonal skills to engage stakeholders:

- Conflict management
- Cultural awareness
- Negotiation
- Observation and conversation
- Political awareness

Your interpersonal skills must be balanced with your management skills. As likeable and charming as you may be, you must have some management skills to help move the project and stakeholders along. Management is about getting things done—organizing and directing people to work together, rather than independently, to get the project done. As a project manager, you need the organization, vision, and authority to guide and direct the project team, vendors, organizations, and other stakeholders to dig in and get the work done. You'll need the following management skills to engage stakeholders:

- Ability to present project information
- Ability to negotiate with stakeholders
- Ability to write and communicate
- Ability to speak in public

Notice that these management skills are linked in some way to communication. Communication is the underlying principle to engaging stakeholders effectively. When you communicate with stakeholders, you're interacting with them, you're providing information, and you're taking in information—that's the engagement of stakeholders. Communication is so important for a project manager that if you fail to communicate well, your project is likely doomed.

Three types of communications are linked to effective stakeholder engagement:

- **Interactive communications** Information is flowing among stakeholders in a forum. Meetings, videoconferences, phone conferences, and even ad hoc conversations are all examples of interactive communications in which the participants are actively communicating with one another to ensure that all participants receive the correct messages and conclusions.
- **Push communications** In push communications, the sender pushes the same message to multiple people. Think of memos, faxes, press releases, broadcast e-mails: these are all pushed from one source to multiple recipients.
- **Pull communications** Often projects use web sites to present project information, reports, status updates, and documents for project stakeholders to peruse. Such a central repository of information enables stakeholders to pull the information from the central source when they want it. In pull communication, the stakeholders retrieve the information as they desire rather than the information being sent, or pushed, to them.

e x a m

ⓦatch **Inspecting the project report and documents helps to ensure that everyone is adhering to the stakeholder management plan. You'll also establish ground rules in the team charter for the team, and the project manager, to agree to support the stakeholder engagement strategy and treat stakeholders with respect.**

Examining Results of Stakeholder Engagement

Stakeholder engagement provides many benefits for the project manager, but chief among them is feedback from the project stakeholders. The whole point of stakeholder engagement is to keep stakeholders involved in the project, to foster communications, and to safeguard the project from delays, wasted time, and miscommunications. Although stakeholder involvement creates feedback for the project manager and the project team, you should be familiar with the following outputs of the process for your PMP exam:

- **Change requests** Ah, yes.... Change requests are a likely output of stakeholder engagement. Although changes can be the bane of a project manager's job, they are expected and need to be managed. Remember, too, that just because someone asks for a change doesn't necessarily mean the change is going to happen in the project.

- **Updates to the project management plan** The project management plan is a fluid document that will evolve throughout the project life cycle. Stakeholder engagement can cause the project management plan to be updated through change requests, risk identification, quality concerns, changes to communication needs, and more. As you engage stakeholders, they become more involved with the project, and their involvement should help you refine the project management plan.

- **Updates to the project documents** The issue log, change log, lessons learned register, and the stakeholder register can all be updated.

exam

watch Stakeholder engagement is about getting stakeholders involved and maintaining their involvement in the project. Feedback from stakeholders helps you, the project manager, better manage the project. This is critical process, so expect several questions on managing stakeholder engagement.

CERTIFICATION OBJECTIVE 13.04

Monitoring Stakeholder Engagement

Although it would be nice and dreamy for stakeholder engagement to run itself, it doesn't work that way. You, the project manager, must be involved in the process, adjusting your actions, fostering relationships, and keeping an eye on stakeholders and their wants, needs, fears, and perceived threats. Projects will evolve, change, and fall prey to gossip, politics, and other nasty elements, but you'll have to keep stakeholders involved to solve problems, be readily available to communicate, and take on challenges as they pop up. Projects are created by and for people, so it makes sense that you'll have to control the depth of stakeholder engagement as the project moves toward its happy conclusion.

Monitoring stakeholder engagement isn't a stand-alone process. Like all project management processes, it's integrated with the other knowledge areas. Consider the decisions you'll make in any area of the project and how those decisions will affect your stakeholders. Stakeholders usually put their trust and confidence in you to lead the project, but times will occur when a decision or action won't keep all the stakeholders satisfied and content with the project. These are the moments you'll need to act, to communicate with stakeholders and help them see why your actions, decisions, and good judgment are best for the overall project.

Taking Action for Stakeholder Engagement

Monitoring stakeholder engagement means that you, the project team, and the key stakeholders are communicating with one another on a consistent basis. If, for example, your project team is conveying information to stakeholders that differs from what you're telling stakeholders, trouble will abound. When stakeholders hear conflicting information about the project, they'll be confused and concerned, and often they may choose to listen to the message that suits them best. The foundation for stakeholder engagement, and monitoring stakeholder engagement, begins with a solid foundation of communications.

To monitor stakeholder engagement, you'll need several components to help with the process:

- **Project management plan** The project management plan helps you monitor stakeholder engagement because it establishes the project governance and project framework. You'll utilize the resource management plan, communications management plan, and the stakeholder engagement plan.
- **Project documents** Specifically, you'll need the issue log, lessons learned register, project communications, risk register, and stakeholder register.
- **Work performance data** Key performance metrics are measured, analyzed, and reported. This includes such objectives as time, cost, percentage of work completed, quality control measurements, and any other factors that need to be measured in your project. These elements will help you communicate the project's health and manage the stakeholder expectations of the project's success. You'll typically measure work performance at predesignated points in the project, such as at milestones or key project deliverables.

■ **Enterprise environmental factors** The usual business in the enterprise environmental factors will help you monitor stakeholder engagement. This usual business includes the culture, politics, personnel administration, risk thresholds, communication channels, global aspects of the project, and the geographical location of resources.

■ **Organizational process assets** Organizational process assets are also used to monitor stakeholder engagements. The policies and procedures for social media, ethics, security, and risk, change, and data management are included in organizational process assets. You might also reference guidelines on information management and historical information from past, similar projects.

INSIDE THE EXAM

Stakeholder engagement is crucial for successful projects, and that means that you, the project manager, must get the project stakeholders involved. It's a huge mistake for a project manager to get the project stakeholders to sign off on the project scope and then go about the project work with few communications with the stakeholders. The project manager and the project stakeholders must work together throughout the project, not just at the launch and the project's closure. This is a key exam point: communication with the stakeholders is the crux of stakeholder engagement.

The first process of stakeholder engagement management is to identify the project stakeholders. Ideally, you'll identify the project stakeholders as early as possible in the project. One of the key methods used for identifying the stakeholders is to ask current stakeholders who else should be involved in the project. Analysis of the project, its impact on the organization, and the people and groups the project affects are mandatory considerations as you identify the stakeholders. Each stakeholder should be recorded in the stakeholder register.

For your exam, be familiar with these five tools and techniques for identifying stakeholders:

■ Expert judgment
■ Data gathering
■ Data analysis
■ Data representation
■ Meetings

As with all knowledge areas in project management, you'll need a plan. The stakeholder management plan defines the stakeholders, the strategy for managing stakeholders, and your approach to keeping stakeholders involved in the project. This process is tightly linked to the project's communications management plan, so it may be ideal to create these two plans in tandem or, at a minimum, document how the contents of one plan affect the contents of the other. Six tools and techniques are used for planning for stakeholder engagement:

■ Expert judgment
■ Data gathering
■ Data analysis
■ Decision-making

(Continued)

INSIDE THE EXAM

- Data representation
- Meetings

Once you have created a stakeholder management plan, you'll continue the process of managing stakeholder engagement. I say "continue the process of stakeholder engagement" because you can start this process even before the stakeholder management plan exists. Stakeholders are involved from the project launch, before the stakeholder management plan is completed.

Your experience as a project manager and a leader will help you keep the stakeholders engaged. Issue management is a key part of stakeholder engagement, and the issue log will need to be updated to reflect the identified issues and their outcomes. Six tools and techniques are required for managing stakeholder engagement:

- Expert judgment
- Inspection
- Communication skills

- Interpersonal and team skills
- Ground rules
- Meetings

Finally, you'll monitor the stakeholder engagement by working with your project team to communicate effectively, manage project issues, control changes within the project, and provide accurate project information to the stakeholders throughout the project. The project management plan, the issue log, work performance data, and project documents all contribute to the process of monitoring stakeholder engagement. You'll also use these six tools and techniques for monitoring stakeholder engagement:

- Data analysis
- Decision-making
- Data representation
- Communication skills
- Interpersonal and team skills
- Meetings

on the job **When in doubt, communicate. The largest problem I've experienced as a project management consultant is that project managers don't communicate with their stakeholders. Communication is the number one strategy for improving your project.**

Completing Stakeholder Engagement Monitoring

The actual act of monitoring stakeholder engagement requires, of course, communication among the project manager, project team, and other key stakeholders, but some tools and techniques can also assist the process. One of the primary tools is simply to meet with stakeholders. That's right: face-to-face meetings are one of the best communication methods, because you gain insight via nonverbal communications and you and the stakeholders can quickly hash out any differences, find resolutions, and then get back to the project.

You can also use a reporting system tool, which is usually a software program that can capture, store, and provide data analysis on the project. A good reporting tool enables the project manager to take project information, such as percentage of work complete, run the data through some earned value analyses, and then create reports to share with the stakeholders. This is also a good example of a tool that could be a push communicator—you'd push the reports out to the stakeholders—and a tool that would also serve as a pull communicator—stakeholders could retrieve the information as they see fit. In either case, the central repository of project data enables the project manager to create reports, make presentations, and perform data analysis.

Remember data representation in the stakeholder engagement matrix? That matrix can help you monitor the current stakeholder engagement levels and confirm that stakeholder statuses are moving toward or remaining engaged. Your interpersonal skills and team skills, along with communication skills, can be leveraged here as well. The goal is get and keep a satisfactory level of stakeholder engagement.

The final tool and technique you'll use to monitor stakeholder engagement is to rely on expert judgment. Experts, such as senior management, organizational units, functional managers, other project managers, consultants, and key stakeholders, can help the project manager identify new stakeholders, resolve issues among stakeholders, and provide assessment of current stakeholders. This tool also provides an approach to remove management of stakeholders who may no longer be involved in the project.

Reviewing the Results of Monitoring Stakeholder Engagement

You'll never really stop monitoring stakeholder engagement until your project moves into closure. Throughout the project, you'll have different levels of stakeholder engagement, which in turn will require different levels of effort. As a rule, the larger the project, the more stakeholders will be involved, and this means you'll have to provide more stakeholder engagement monitoring. Actively monitoring stakeholders helps you keep an eye on the project progress, keep stakeholders from losing interest and support in the project, and keep accountable to key stakeholders who are sponsoring and paying for the project.

There are four outputs of monitoring stakeholder engagement:

■ **Work performance information** The data that has been collected throughout the project is assimilated and analyzed, and the resulting information is used by the project manager to make project decisions. Examples include the project schedule status, percentage of work completed, and forecasts for project schedule and costs.

■ **Change requests** Work performance information, stakeholder communications, and the results of the project work can all lead to change requests in the project. Change requests also include recommended corrective and preventive actions.

■ **Project management plan updates** Changes to the project management plan go through integrated change control. Three primary plans are likely to be updated by monitoring stakeholder engagement: resource management plan, communications management plan, and the stakeholder engagement plan.

■ **Project document updates** Documents, the stakeholder register and the issue log, will likely be updated as a result of monitoring stakeholder engagement. These documents will become part of organizational process assets once the project is closed. The risk register and the lessons learned register may also be updated.

CERTIFICATION SUMMARY

Stakeholders are the people and groups involved in the project and the people who are affected by the project. If you, as the project manager, will be speaking with someone about the project, chances are that person is a stakeholder. Stakeholders can influence the success or failure of the project. Positive stakeholders are the people who are cheering your project onward and want your project to succeed. Negative stakeholders are the humbugs who don't want your project to exist at all. Finally, neutral stakeholders, such as inspectors and procurement people, don't care one way or the other about your project's success.

Stakeholders need to be identified as early as possible in the project—and new stakeholders will be identified throughout the project life cycle. This process ensures that the appropriate stakeholders are involved in the project; if you overlook a stakeholder or a group of stakeholders in the project, this person or group won't be keen on cheering your project forward. Meeting with existing stakeholders can help you identify other stakeholders. Consultants, management, and other project managers in the organization can also help you identify who should be involved in the project. A stakeholder register is a log of all the stakeholders you've identified along with their attitudes, interests, and concerns about the project.

A stakeholder management plan is a tool to help you create a strategy for managing stakeholder concerns, interests, and level of engagement in the project. The stakeholder management plan is tied to the project's communications management plan, because so much of stakeholder management is about communicating with stakeholders. You need to know who needs what information, when the information is needed, and what the best approach is to deliver the project information. Stakeholders have expectations about project communication, and it's up to the project manager to identify those expectations and meet them throughout the project.

Stakeholder engagement is a process of keeping stakeholders involved, interested, and contributing to the project. If the stakeholders lose interest in the project, especially stakeholders with lots of influence on the project decisions, the project can succumb to politics, negativity, and lack of organizational interest—not something any project manager wants to happen. Stakeholder engagement helps the project manager keep the stakeholders engaged and informed in the project through communications, interpersonal skills, and management skills. You must meet, talk with, and encourage stakeholders to contribute to the project to keep their interest and involvement.

Key Terms

To pass the PMP exam, you will need to memorize the following terms and their definitions. For maximum value, create flashcards based on these definitions and review them daily. The definitions can be found within this chapter and in the glossary.

interactive communications   A flow of information among stakeholders in which participants are actively communicating with one another to ensure that all participants receive the correct message and conclusions. Meetings, videoconferences, phone conferences, and even ad hoc conversations are examples of interactive communications.

leading stakeholders   Stakeholders who are aware of your project, want the project to succeed, and are leading the charge to make certain the project outcome is positive.

negative stakeholders   Stakeholders who are opposed to the project's existence; they do not want the project to succeed, because they do not see or agree with the benefits the project may bring about for the organization.

neutral stakeholders   Stakeholders who are not concerned about the project's success or failure, such as inspectors, procurement officers, and some end users.

positive stakeholders   Stakeholders who want the project to succeed; these are often the people who have the most to gain from the project's success and/or the most to lose if the project fails.

pull communications   The central repository of information enables stakeholders to pull the information from the central source when they want it. In pull communications, the audience retrieves the information as they desire rather than the information being sent, or pushed, to them.

push communications   The sender pushes the same message to multiple people via memos, faxes, press releases, broadcast e-mails, and other forms of group communication.

reporting system   Often a software program that can capture, store, and provide data analysis regarding the project. A good reporting system tool enables the project manager to gather project information, such as percentage of work complete; run the data through some earned value analyses; and then create reports to share with stakeholders.

resistant stakeholders   Stakeholders who are aware of your project, but aren't keen on the changes your project will create.

stakeholder analysis   A process that considers and ranks project stakeholders based on their influence, interests, and project expectations. This process uses a systematic approach to identify all of the project stakeholders, ranking the stakeholders by varying factors, and then addressing stakeholders' needs, requirements, and expectations.

stakeholder classification models   Grids that rank stakeholders' influence in relation to their interest in the project. Several types of these models are used as part of stakeholder analysis. The most common models are the power/interest grid, the power/influence grid, the influence/impact grid, and the salience model.

stakeholder cube   A three-dimensional cube model that combines the power, influence, and impact grids.

stakeholder engagement   The process of keeping stakeholders interested, involved, and supportive of the project. The project manager needs to maintain the energy of the stakeholders and keep them contributing to and excited about the project.

stakeholder identification   The process of ensuring that all the stakeholders have been identified as early as possible in the project: all the stakeholders are identified and represented, and their needs, expectations, and concerns are addressed.

stakeholder management   A project management knowledge area that focuses on four activities: identifying the project stakeholders, planning on how to manage the stakeholders, managing the stakeholders, and monitoring the stakeholders' engagement.

stakeholder management plan   A plan that helps the project manager and the project team define a strategy for managing the project stakeholders. It helps to establish stakeholder engagement at the launch of the project and throughout the project life cycle, and it offers information about how to improve the level of engagement identified.

stakeholder management planning   The process of creating a strategy to manage the stakeholders in the project. It's the analysis of what the stakeholders want the project to do, how a stakeholder's expectations align with those of other stakeholders, and the prioritization of the stakeholders within the project.

stakeholder register   A register that documents all the stakeholders' information, position, concerns, interests, and attitude toward the project. The stakeholder register should be updated as new stakeholders are identified or as stakeholders leave the project.

supportive stakeholders   Stakeholders who are aware of your project, are happy about the project, and hope your project is successful.

unaware stakeholders   Stakeholders who don't know about the project and the effect the project may have on them.

TWO-MINUTE DRILL

Identifying the Project Stakeholders

- ❑ Stakeholders are all the people, groups, and organizations that can affect the project or that are affected by the project.
- ❑ Stakeholder identification should begin as early as possible in the project and should continue throughout the project.
- ❑ Stakeholder analysis helps the project manager rate the stakeholders' influence, power, interest, and impact on the project. This analysis can be charted into a classification model.
- ❑ All identified stakeholders are documented in the stakeholder register. The stakeholder register includes the stakeholders' identification, assessment of the project, and classification of stakeholder type.
- ❑ The stakeholder register should be updated as new stakeholders are identified in the project, when stakeholders leave the project, or when stakeholder information changes during the course of the project.

Planning for Stakeholder Management

- ❑ The stakeholder management plan helps the project manager determine the required level of engagement for the identified stakeholders throughout the project life cycle.

❑ Stakeholder engagement is needed to keep stakeholders interested, involved, and informed about the overall project status.

❑ Stakeholders are categorized based on their project engagement levels as unaware, resistant, neutral, supportive, and leading. These rankings can change over the project life cycle, and they help the project manager determine the level of needed engagement and communication with the stakeholders.

❑ Planning for stakeholder management is linked closely to the project's communications management plan. Stakeholders require varying levels of communication based on their needs, wants, concerns, and fears about the project.

Managing Stakeholder Engagement

❑ The process of managing stakeholder engagement aims to meet stakeholders' needs and expectations. Communicating with stakeholders and following the project's stakeholder management plan and the project's communications management plan accomplish much of this process.

❑ Stakeholder engagement aims to reinforce the concept that stakeholders share the ownership of the project.

❑ Communications with stakeholders are pushed to the stakeholder through a distribution system, pulled by the stakeholder from a central source, or are interactive among the stakeholders through multidirectional communications, such as meetings and conferences.

❑ Stakeholder engagement is also achieved through the project manager's interpersonal skills, such as building trust, resolving conflicts among the stakeholders, and overcoming stakeholders' resistance to the changes the project may bring about. Other management skills are also needed: presenting ideas and project status, facilitating negotiations, and communicating through writing and public speaking.

Monitoring Stakeholder Engagement

❑ Stakeholder engagement, like many project management processes, must be monitored throughout the project. There's a balance between planning, executing, and monitoring this knowledge area.

❑ A reporting system can help the project manager collect and distribute project information through reports, analysis, push and pull communications.

❑ Stakeholder identification must also be monitored in the sense that new stakeholders must be identified as they become involved with the project. All stakeholders must be documented in the stakeholder register.

❏ Monitoring stakeholder engagement may result in change requests, including corrective and preventive actions. Stakeholder engagement is reliant on project communications, so it's natural that stakeholders may readily communicate desired changes or flaws they've identified in the project.

❏ Organizational process assets are updated as part of monitoring the stakeholder engagement. This includes stakeholder notifications, reports, presentations, performance records, feedback, and lessons learned.

SELF TEST

1. You are the project manager of the Server Update Project for your organization. This project has 543 stakeholders, many of which are end users. Some of the end users are critical of the server update because they're concerned about where the data is stored, how they'll access the data in the future, and their mapped drives. You've communicated with all the users that the server update will change how the users will access their files and home folders in the future. Now some of the end users have been complaining to their functional managers about the change. In this scenario, what type of stakeholders are the end users?
   A. Uninformed
   B. Negative
   C. Unresponsive
   D. Low influence/low interest

2. Beth is the project manager of a new construction project for her organization's client. This project will construct a new bridge in a major thoroughfare in her city. Beth is preparing for stakeholder identification because she wants to capture all the internal and external stakeholders who may influence and be influenced by this project. In her preparations, Beth will need all the following documents as inputs except for which one?
   A. Project charter
   B. Enterprise environmental factors
   C. Organizational process assets
   D. Risk management plan

3. You are the project manager for a software development project for your company. This project will create a web-based application that will enable users to create maps for different hiking trails in North America. You'll be working with developers who are employees of your company and developers who are contract-based. Your project will also include information from the National Parks Service, local communities, and hikers from around the United States. You and the project team will first complete stakeholder analysis to make certain that you've captured all the project stakeholders. What are the three logical steps to stakeholder analysis for this project?

   A. Identify the stakeholders, prioritize the stakeholders, anticipate stakeholder responses

   B. Identify the stakeholders, confirm the project scope, communicate the project plan

   C. Identify the stakeholders, anticipate stakeholder responses, create a response strategy

   D. Identify the stakeholders, meet with the stakeholders to address concerns, create a stakeholder response plan

4. You have been working on a new project that will affect your entire organization of 1233 people. You and the project team know that you should create a stakeholder register for the stakeholders, but is it necessary to create 1233 entries in this register?

   A. Yes; all stakeholders should be identified.

   B. Yes, but it is appropriate to group the stakeholders for easier management.

   C. No; only the key stakeholders need to be identified in the stakeholder register.

   D. No; only negative stakeholders and key stakeholders must be documented in the stakeholder register.

5. Mike is the project manager of a new software deployment project that will affect 3235 people in his organization. He's communicated the deployment and explained the effect the software will have on the organization, and his plan includes training for the end users. Some of the stakeholders, especially the functional managers, are worried about the deployment and how it will affect the organization's productivity. Anna, the project sponsor, asks Mike to create a visual diagram showing which stakeholders can affect the project the most based on their power in the organization. What chart should Mike create?

   A. Power/influence diagram

   B. Pareto diagram

   C. Tornado diagram

   D. Ishikawa diagram

6. Harold is the project manager for a large construction project his company is completing for a client. This project has internal and external stakeholders, including members of the community who are opposed to the project, although it has been approved by the city. Harold is preparing to create a stakeholder management plan and he's gathering several inputs for the plan's creation. Which one of the following inputs will most help Harold create a strategy for stakeholder management and engagement?

   A. Project management plan

   B. Stakeholder register

   C. Enterprise environmental factors

   D. Communications management plan

7. You are the project manager of a large software deployment project for your organization. This project will replace the operating systems on the computers of all employees. Many of the employees are in favor of this change in operating systems, while others are not. As part of your plan, you complete an analysis of the stakeholders. In this analysis, you and the project team have discovered that some of the project stakeholders didn't know about the change in the company's approved computer operating system. How would you classify these stakeholders?

   A. Unaware
   B. Uninformed
   C. Lacking
   D. Target for positive

8. You are the project manager of a large software deployment project for your organization. This project will replace the operating systems on the computers of all employees. Many of the employees are in favor of this change in operating systems, while others are not. As part of your plan, you complete an analysis of the stakeholders. In this analysis, you and the project team have also learned that the functional managers are not in favor of the change of the operating system for their employees' laptops. How would you classify these stakeholders?

   A. Neutral
   B. Resistant
   C. Leading
   D. Hesitant

9. What is the purpose of the stakeholder management plan?

   A. To convert all stakeholders to positive, supportive stakeholders
   B. To identify the stakeholders who are opposed to the project
   C. To manage the stakeholders' attitudes toward the project
   D. To communicate with the stakeholders about the project status

10. Morgan is the project manager of a web site creation project for a client. Some employees at the client's site are excited about the change and they are helpful with Morgan's plan for the new web site design. In the stakeholder management plan, Morgan has identified the tactics for managing the stakeholders, and she has identified the positive stakeholders with which categorization?

    A. Happy
    B. Leading
    C. Supportive
    D. Informed

11. You are a project manager for your company and you've just created the project's stakeholder management plan. This plan is based on organizational process assets and enterprise environmental factors that you're required to use in the project. The stakeholder management plan includes all the following components except for which one?

    A. The relationships among the stakeholders
    B. The relationships among the project team
    C. The schedule of stakeholder information distribution
    D. Communication requirements for stakeholders

12. Sam is the project manager of the GHQ Project for his company, and he's recently discovered a scheduling conflict with two of the vendors on the project. Sam knows that the conflict will likely cause a two-week delay in the completion of the project. What should Sam do?

    A. Report the problem to management.
    B. Report the problem to the stakeholders.
    C. Say nothing unless the delay becomes greater than two weeks.
    D. Propose a solution to management.

13. You are the project manager of a large project in your company. Your project has been in motion for three months, and you're about to move into the first phase of project execution. Your sponsor calls to report that you've apparently overlooked some stakeholders during the project's planning phase. What should you do now?

    A. Immediately contact the stakeholders, apologize, and analyze the stakeholders.
    B. Begin the project execution but contact the stakeholders for a meeting.
    C. Determine whether the oversight has damaged the project's objectives.
    D. Schedule a meeting with the stakeholders to catch them up on the project.

14. Steve is the project manager of a new project that will affect 4534 people in his organization. Some of the stakeholders are not happy about the project, but they understand the need for the project work. How should Steve manage these unhappy but compliant stakeholders?

    A. Ignore their complaints.
    B. Explain the benefits of the project.
    C. Categorize them as resistant.
    D. Some stakeholders may just be unhappy.

15. Marvin is the project manager of a new project for his company. He's been working with the project team and the project sponsor to keep the stakeholders engaged. As part of this process, Marvin will need four inputs to stakeholder engagement. Which one of the following is *not* one of the inputs for stakeholder engagement?

    A. Change log
    B. Organizational process assets
    C. Communications management plan
    D. Quality management plan

16. You are the project manager of a large project that will affect how your organization accepts and processes orders from customers. Many of the stakeholders have strong opinions about the project and how it should proceed. Thomas, the manufacturing manager, and Jane, the sales manager, have been in conflict with each other over some of the project's requirements. You've met with these two stakeholders to identify their differences, negotiate a resolution, and come to an agreement about the requirements in the project. What stakeholder engagement tool and technique have you used effectively in this scenario? Choose the best answer.

    A. Active listening
    B. Stakeholder resolution
    C. Management skills
    D. Interpersonal skills

17. One of the tools you'll have to use as a project manager in the stakeholder management knowledge area is management skill. Management skills help you organize stakeholder concerns and keep the project moving forward. All the following are examples of management skills except for which one?

    A. Presenting project information
    B. Negotiating with stakeholders
    C. Public speaking
    D. Analyzing work performance information

18. You are the project manager of the JNH Project for your company. This project is scheduled to last 18 months and will affect 435 stakeholders in your organization. The project has sensitive information that only certain stakeholders should have access to, so you've created a plan for communicating the information to the correct parties throughout the project through special e-mail bulletins. What type of communication is secured e-mail considered to be?

    A. Push
    B. Interactive
    C. Sensitive
    D. Passive

19. You are the project manager for your organization, and you've contracted two organizations to complete parts of the project. The project requires that these two different companies work together on parts of the project. One of the vendors will need to install network cables throughout a building, while the other company is responsible for connecting the networking cables to a central patch panel and to the individual networking receptacles. The vendors disagree about how the work should take place. What's the best approach to manage this scenario?

    A. The vendors are not stakeholders and must live up to the terms of their contract.
    B. The vendors are stakeholders, and you should determine who'll do what activities in the project.
    C. The vendors are not stakeholders, but you should use conflict resolution to find the best solution for the contracted work.
    D. The vendors are project stakeholders, and you should utilize conflict resolution to find the best solution for the project.

20. You are the project manager for your company. Your project sponsor has asked you to include interactive communications as part of your stakeholder management plan. Which one of the following best illustrates the concept of interactive communications in stakeholder management?

    A. Sending e-mail messages to select project stakeholders

    B. Creating a report on the project status

    C. Hosting a project status meeting

    D. Creating a secured project repository that only allowed stakeholders can access

21. You are the project manager for your organization and you're serving as a coach for several junior project managers. You're currently reviewing the inputs for monitoring stakeholder engagement with your project team. The team members are confused about some of the inputs needed for monitoring stakeholder engagement. One of the inputs to monitoring stakeholder engagement is the issue log. How does the issue log help you prepare to monitor stakeholder engagement?

    A. This is false; this issue log is not an input to monitor stakeholder engagement.

    B. This issue log will help you determine which stakeholders are causing the project issues.

    C. The issue log is needed only when issues are defined by stakeholders.

    D. The issue log will help you track and respond to issues and communicate issue status.

22. Your project sponsor has requested that you find a software package to serve as a central repository for all project information. They'd like for the software to capture, store, and provide data analysis on key performance metrics. The software should be able to help complete reports, analyze data, and track overall project performance. What is the project sponsor requesting?

    A. Reporting system

    B. Earned value management system

    C. Project management information system

    D. Integrated change control system

23. As a project manager, you must use multiple types of communication with stakeholders to keep them engaged with the project work. All the following are types of communications that are related to stakeholder engagement except for which one?

    A. Pull communications

    B. Push communications

    C. Interactive communications

    D. Ad hoc communications

24. Stakeholder engagement is key to a successful project, so you and the project team have created a stakeholder management plan that includes many different methods for engaging stakeholders. As part of your plan, you should also reference what other project management plan component?

    A. Project communications management plan

    B. Project procurement contracts

    C. Project scope statement

    D. Milestone charts for the project schedule

25. You are the project manager of a new software development project in your company. Your company operates in a matrix environment and utilizes a project management office to structure projects. This current project has 78 stakeholders and will last for 18 months. Sam, one of the project stakeholders, informs you that two of his employees will be leaving the organization and will no longer be available as resources on your project. In addition to the project staffing management plan, what other document should you update?
    A. Stakeholder register
    B. Risk register
    C. Change log
    D. Project schedule

SELF TEST ANSWERS

1. You are the project manager of the Server Update Project for your organization. This project has 543 stakeholders, many of which are end users. Some of the end users are critical of the server update because they're concerned about where the data is stored, how they'll access the data in the future, and their mapped drives. You've communicated with all the users that the server update will change how the users will access their files and home folders in the future. Now some of the end users have been complaining to their functional managers about the change. In this scenario, what type of stakeholders are the end users?
    A. Uninformed
    B. Negative
    C. Unresponsive
    D. Low influence/low interest

   ☑ **B.** Negative stakeholders are people who do not want your project to succeed or even exist in the organization.

   ☒ **A, C,** and **D** are incorrect. **A** is incorrect because uninformed describes a stakeholder who doesn't know about your project; you'll need to inform them about the project and how the project may affect them. **C** and **D** are incorrect because unresponsive and low influence/low interest are not correct descriptions of project stakeholders for your PMP examination. Although these answers may seem fitting, they are not the terminology used to describe stakeholder attitudes toward your project.

2. Beth is the project manager of a new construction project for her organization's client. This project will construct a new bridge in a major thoroughfare in her city. Beth is preparing for stakeholder identification because she wants to capture all the internal and external stakeholders who may influence and be influenced by this project. In her preparations, Beth will need all the following documents as inputs except for which one?
A. Project charter
B. Enterprise environmental factors
C. Organizational process assets
D. Risk management plan

☑ **D.** Beth will not need the risk management plan as part of the stakeholder identification process.
☒ **A, B,** and **C** are incorrect. These are the correct inputs for stakeholder identification. Note that the question asked which one is *not* an input to the process. Beth will need the project charter, business documents, communications management plan, stakeholder engagement plan, change log, issue log, requirements documentation, agreements, enterprise environmental factors, and organizational process assets.

3. You are the project manager for a software development project for your company. This project will create a web-based application that will enable users to create maps for different hiking trails in North America. You'll be working with developers who are employees of your company and developers who are contract-based. Your project will also include information from the National Parks Service, local communities, and hikers from around the United States. You and the project team will first complete stakeholder analysis to make certain that you've captured all the project stakeholders. What are the three logical steps to stakeholder analysis for this project?
A. Identify the stakeholders, prioritize the stakeholders, anticipate stakeholder responses
B. Identify the stakeholders, confirm the project scope, communicate the project plan
C. Identify the stakeholders, anticipate stakeholder responses, create a response strategy
D. Identify the stakeholders, meet with the stakeholders to address concerns, create a stakeholder response plan

☑ **A.** There are three logical steps to stakeholder analysis: First you need to identify the project stakeholders. Next, you'll prioritize the stakeholders based on their role and influence in the project. Finally, you'll anticipate stakeholder responses to issues, concerns, and requirements in the project.
☒ **B, C,** and **D** are incorrect. These answers do not reflect the correct order of activities in stakeholder analysis. Although they begin with the correct answer of stakeholder identification, they do not follow the correct order of first identifying the stakeholders, prioritizing the stakeholders, and finally anticipating stakeholder responses.

4. You have been working on a new project that will affect your entire organization of 1233 people. You and the project team know that you should create a stakeholder register for the stakeholders, but is it necessary to create 1233 entries in this register?
   A. Yes, all stakeholders should be identified.
   B. Yes, but it is appropriate to group the stakeholders for easier management.
   C. No; only the key stakeholders need to be identified in the stakeholder register.
   D. No; only negative stakeholders and key stakeholders must be documented in the stakeholder register.

   ☑ **B.** A project that has this many stakeholders is likely to create groups of stakeholders to manage. For example, the stakeholders could be grouped by departments, roles in the organization, or even interests in the project. Grouping stakeholders helps the project manager address a large group with a common message rather than manage multiple messages to many stakeholders individually.
   ☒ **A, C,** and **D** are incorrect. It's not practical or necessary to identify each individual stakeholder when grouping the stakeholders would suffice. Although the key stakeholders should be identified in the stakeholder register, the project manager should also identify and record the grouping of stakeholders in the register. Both positive and negative stakeholders are recorded in the stakeholder register, not just negative stakeholders.

5. Mike is the project manager of a new software deployment project that will affect 3235 people in his organization. He's communicated the deployment and explained the effect the software will have on the organization, and his plan includes training for the end users. Some of the stakeholders, especially the functional managers, are worried about the deployment and how it will affect the organization's productivity. Anna, the project sponsor, asks Mike to create a visual diagram showing which stakeholders can affect the project the most based on their power in the organization. What chart should Mike create?
   A. Power/influence diagram
   B. Pareto diagram
   C. Tornado diagram
   D. Ishikawa diagram

   ☑ **A.** Mike should create a power/influence diagram, which shows the correlation between power over the project and the influence over the project for each key stakeholder. Stakeholders with high power and high influence need to be managed more closely than stakeholders with low power and low influence, for example. This chart helps the project team create a better defined stakeholder management strategy and prioritization of stakeholders in the project.
   ☒ **B, C,** and **D** are incorrect. **B,** Pareto diagram, shows the ordered distribution of defects as a result of quality control. **C,** tornado diagram, shows the forces for and against a decision. **D,** Ishikawa diagram, is also called a fishbone diagram or cause-and-effect diagram and is used to determine casual factors that are contributing to an effect in the project. Ishikawa diagrams are most often used in quality control.

6. Harold is the project manager for a large construction project his company is completing for a client. This project has internal and external stakeholders, including members of the community who are opposed to the project, although it has been approved by the city. Harold is preparing to create a stakeholder management plan and he's gathering several inputs for the plan's creation. Which one of the following inputs will most help Harold create a strategy for stakeholder management and engagement?

   A. Project management plan
   B. Stakeholder register
   C. Enterprise environmental factors
   D. Communications management plan

   ☑ **B.** Harold needs the stakeholder register to create a strategy for stakeholder management and engagement. The stakeholder register defines the role, interests, contact information, and attitudes of the stakeholders toward the project objectives.

   ☒ **A, C,** and **D** are incorrect. Although Harold will rely on the project management plan, specifically the communications management plan, the most influential element for stakeholder management and engagement is the stakeholder register. This document defines the stakeholders, their interests and concerns, and the stakeholders' attitudes toward the project objectives. **C,** enterprise environmental factors, are an input to stakeholder management planning as they define the organizational rules and policies for the stakeholder management and the structure of the organization.

7. You are the project manager of a large software deployment project for your organization. This project will replace the operating systems on the computers of all employees. Many of the employees are in favor of this change in operating systems, while others are not. As part of your plan, you complete an analysis of the stakeholders. In this analysis, you and the project team have discovered that some of the project stakeholders didn't know about the change in the company's approved computer operating system. How would you classify these stakeholders?

   A. Unaware
   B. Uninformed
   C. Lacking
   D. Target for positive

   ☑ **A.** Stakeholders who don't know about your project are classified as unaware. Unaware stakeholders have been overlooked in the planning of the project and they may be offended, have requirements that the project must add, or become resistant to the project's existence because they have not been consulted and included in the project planning.

   ☒ **B, C,** and **D** are incorrect. Uninformed, lacking, and target for positive are not stakeholder classifications.

8. You are the project manager of a large software deployment project for your organization. This project will replace the operating systems on the computers of all employees. Many of the employees are in favor of this change in operating systems, while others are not. As part of your plan, you complete an analysis of the stakeholders. In this analysis, you and the project team have also learned that the functional managers are not in favor of the change of the operating system for their employees' laptops. How would you classify these stakeholders?

A. Neutral

B. Resistant

C. Leading

D. Hesitant

☑ **B.** These negative stakeholders can be accurately classified as resistant to the project goals. These functional managers and employees are resistant to the goals of the project, and it's part of stakeholder management to determine the stakeholder objections and then create a strategy to overcome the resistance to change.

☒ **A, C,** and **D** are incorrect. **A** is incorrect because neutral describes a stakeholder who is neither for nor against the project. **C** is incorrect because leading describes the stakeholders who are working to ensure that the project is successful. **D,** hesitant, is not a categorization of stakeholders, so this is incorrect.

9. What is the purpose of the stakeholder management plan?

A. To convert all stakeholders to positive, supportive stakeholders

B. To identify the stakeholders who are opposed to the project

C. To manage the stakeholders' attitudes toward the project

D. To communicate with the stakeholders about the project status

☑ **C.** The stakeholder management plan essentially creates a strategy to manage the stakeholders' attitudes toward the project.

☒ **A, B,** and **D** are incorrect. These answers do not describe the purpose of the stakeholder management plan. It is not the intent of the stakeholder management plan to convert all stakeholders to positive stakeholders, though that would be nice. Stakeholder identification, a process, identifies all stakeholders, positive or negative, and records their information in the stakeholder register. The communications management plan defines how the project manager and project team will communicate with the project stakeholders.

10. Morgan is the project manager of a web site creation project for a client. Some employees at the client's site are excited about the change and they are helpful with Morgan's plan for the new web site design. In the stakeholder management plan, Morgan has identified the tactics for managing the stakeholders, and she has identified the positive stakeholders with which categorization?
   A. Happy
   B. Leading
   C. Supportive
   D. Informed

    ☑ **C.** Supportive stakeholders, as in this example, are aware of the project and the changes the project will bring, and are supportive of the project.
    ☒ **A, B,** and **D** are incorrect. Happy isn't a classification of stakeholders. Leading stakeholders are the people who are cheering the project on, are working toward the project success, and are active in promoting the project and its success. Informed isn't a classification for stakeholders, so this is incorrect.

11. You are a project manager for your company and you've just created the project's stakeholder management plan. This plan is based on organizational process assets and enterprise environmental factors that you're required to use in the project. The stakeholder management plan includes all the following components except for which one?
   A. The relationships among the stakeholders
   B. The relationships among the project team
   C. The schedule of stakeholder information distribution
   D. Communication requirements for stakeholders

    ☑ **B.** The stakeholder management plan doesn't address the relationships among the project team. The staffing management plan, part of resources planning, may address team development and how the team interacts.
    ☒ **A, C,** and **D** are incorrect. They are all part of the stakeholder management plan, which addresses several things: desired and current stakeholder engagement levels, relationships among stakeholders, communication requirements, information to be distributed, reasoning for communications and anticipated stakeholder responses, time frame and frequency of stakeholder communications, and method of updating the stakeholder management plan.

12. Sam is the project manager of the GHQ Project for his company, and he's recently discovered a scheduling conflict with two of the vendors on the project. Sam knows that the conflict will likely cause a two-week delay in the completion of the project. What should Sam do?
    A. Report the problem to management.
    B. Report the problem to the stakeholders.
    C. Say nothing unless the delay becomes greater than two weeks.
    D. Propose a solution to management.

    ☑ **D.** Problems will happen throughout a project, but the project manager should always present the bad news to the appropriate stakeholders and be prepared with a possible solution.
    ☒ **A, B,** and **C** are incorrect. **A** isn't the best choice, because this reports the problem only to management. A solution to the problem is also needed. **B,** report the problem to stakeholders, isn't the best choice, because all stakeholders may not need to know about the problem. In addition, the problem should also have a proposed solution. **C** is incorrect because saying nothing is ignoring the problem and may cause more issues within the project.

13. You are the project manager of a large project in your company. Your project has been in motion for three months and you're about to move into the first phase of project execution. Your sponsor calls to report that you've apparently overlooked some stakeholders during the project's planning phase. What should you do now?
    A. Immediately contact the stakeholders, apologize, and analyze the stakeholders.
    B. Begin the project execution but contact the stakeholders for a meeting.
    C. Determine whether the oversight has damaged the project's objectives.
    D. Schedule a meeting with the stakeholders to catch them up on the project.

    ☑ **A.** Although it's imperative to identify all the project stakeholders as early in the project as possible, it's not uncommon for a project manager to overlook some of the stakeholders. When this happens, the project manager should immediately deal with the problem and look for a solution. In this case, contacting the stakeholders, apologizing for the oversight, and then analyzing the stakeholders' attitudes toward the project will be most helpful.
    ☒ **B, C,** and **D** are incorrect. **B** isn't the best answer, because executing the project work may not be appropriate without the stakeholders' input. **C** isn't the best answer, because it doesn't include the stakeholders in the analysis of the project. Stakeholders need to be notified and communicated with about the project and how the project may affect them. Although **D** suggests contacting the stakeholders to schedule a meeting, it does not empathize with the stakeholders by apologizing for the mistake the project manager made in the project.

14. Steve is the project manager of a new project that will affect 4534 people in his organization. Some of the stakeholders are not happy about the project, but they understand the need for the project work. How should Steve manage these unhappy but compliant stakeholders?
    A. Ignore their complaints.
    B. Explain the benefits of the project.
    C. Categorize them as resistant.
    D. Some stakeholders may just be unhappy.

    ☑ **B.** Steve should explain the benefits of the project and how the project will help the organization and the individuals affected by the project.
    ☒ **A, C,** and **D** are incorrect. It's never a wise idea to ignore the complaints of the stakeholders, even if the complaints are invalid. Clear communications from the launch of the project can stem many complaints. To categorize the stakeholders as resistant may be appropriate, but simply categorizing the stakeholders doesn't address their complaints or engage the stakeholders. Although it's true that some stakeholders may just be unhappy, this answer doesn't attempt to address the stakeholders' needs or concerns.

15. Marvin is the project manager of a new project for his company. He's been working with the project team and the project sponsor to keep the stakeholders engaged. As part of this process, Marvin will need four inputs to stakeholder engagement. Which one of the following is *not* one of the inputs for stakeholder engagement?
    A. Change log
    B. Organizational process assets
    C. Communications management plan
    D. Quality management plan

    ☑ **D.** The quality management plan is not an input to stakeholder engagement.
    ☒ **A, B,** and **C** are incorrect. To manage stakeholder engagement, the project manager will need four inputs: stakeholder management plan, communications management plan, organizational process assets, and the change log. The quality management plan is not needed for this process.

16. You are the project manager of a large project that will affect how your organization accepts and processes orders from customers. Many of the stakeholders have strong opinions about the project and how it should proceed. Thomas, the manufacturing manager, and Jane, the sales manager, have been in conflict with each other over some of the project's requirements. You've met with these two stakeholders to identify their differences, negotiate a resolution, and come to an agreement about the requirements in the project. What stakeholder engagement tool and technique have you used effectively in this scenario? Choose the best answer.
   A. Active listening
   B. Stakeholder resolution
   C. Management skills
   D. Interpersonal skills

   ☑ **D.** Interpersonal skills include building trust, resolving conflict, active listening, and overcoming resistance to change.
   ☒ **A, B,** and **C** are incorrect. **A,** active listening, is an interpersonal skill, but in this example, you've used conflict resolution. **B,** stakeholder resolution, is not a valid interpersonal skill or managerial skill. **C** is incorrect because management skills include presentations, negotiations, writing skills, and public speaking.

17. One of the tools you'll have to use as a project manager in the stakeholder management knowledge area is management skill. Management skills help you organize stakeholder concerns and keep the project moving forward. All the following are examples of management skills except for which one?
   A. Presenting project information
   B. Negotiating with stakeholders
   C. Public speaking
   D. Analyzing work performance information

   ☑ **D.** Analyzing work performance information is not a management skill, but it is a facet of data analysis and preparing for stakeholder engagement.
   ☒ **A, B,** and **C** are incorrect. These answers are examples of management skills you'll use as a project manager.

18. You are the project manager of the JNH Project for your company. This project is scheduled to last 18 months and will affect 435 stakeholders in your organization. The project has sensitive information that only certain stakeholders should have access to, so you've created a plan for communicating the information to the correct parties throughout the project through special e-mail bulletins. What type of communication is secured e-mail considered to be?

A. Push

B. Interactive

C. Sensitive

D. Passive

☑ **A.** Push communication describes information that is sent out to an audience or stakeholders via e-mail, memos, letters, or reports.

☒ **B, C,** and **D** are incorrect. **B,** interactive communications, describe events, such as meetings or conferences, where information is exchanged among participants. **C,** sensitive, is not a valid communication type, so this choice is incorrect. **D,** passive communication, also isn't a valid choice. The three types of communication are push, pull, and interactive.

19. You are the project manager for your organization, and you've contracted two organizations to complete parts of the project. The project requires that these two different companies work together on parts of the project. One of the vendors will need to install network cables throughout a building, while the other company is responsible for connecting the networking cables to a central patch panel and to the individual networking receptacles. The vendors disagree about how the work should take place. What's the best approach to manage this scenario?

A. The vendors are not stakeholders and must live up to the terms of their contract.

B. The vendors are stakeholders, and you should determine who'll do what activities in the project.

C. The vendors are not stakeholders, but you should use conflict resolution to find the best solution for the contracted work.

D. The vendors are project stakeholders, and you should utilize conflict resolution to find the best solution for the project

☑ **D.** Vendors are stakeholders in the project, and the project manager must utilize conflict resolution to find the best solution for the project. Although the project contracts may already define the order of the work and the terms of the agreement, the project manager should meet with the vendors to come to an agreeable approach for all parties to work together and for the project to move forward smoothly.

☒ **A, B,** and **C** are incorrect. The vendors are stakeholders because they are affected by the project and can affect the project's success. The contract should, in ideal conditions, define all aspects of the work and the requirements for the vendors to work together, but that's not always the case. Should the issue escalate, there may be a need for alternative dispute resolution.

20. You are the project manager for your company. Your project sponsor has asked you to include interactive communications as part of your stakeholder management plan. Which one of the following best illustrates the concept of interactive communications in stakeholder management?

    A. Sending e-mail messages to select project stakeholders
    B. Creating a report on the project status
    C. Hosting a project status meeting
    D. Creating a secured project repository that only allowed stakeholders can access

    ☑   **C.** Interactive communications means that the stakeholders can communicate with one another. Meetings, video conferences, and teleconferences are good examples of interactive communications.
    ☒   **A, B,** and **D** are incorrect. **A,** e-mail, is an example of a push communication. **B,** creating a report, doesn't actually communicate with the stakeholders. **D** is an example of a pull communication as a central repository, such as a reporting system, which requires the stakeholders to query the central site to pull information from it.

21. You are the project manager for your organization and you're serving as a coach for several junior project managers. You're currently reviewing the inputs for monitoring stakeholder engagement with your project team. The team members are confused about some of the inputs needed for monitoring stakeholder engagement. One of the inputs to monitoring stakeholder engagement is the issue log. How does the issue log help you prepare to monitor stakeholder engagement?

    A. This is false; this issue log is not an input to monitor stakeholder engagement.
    B. This issue log will help you determine which stakeholders are causing the project issues.
    C. The issue log is needed only when issues are defined by stakeholders.
    D. The issue log will help you track and respond to issues and communicate issue status.

    ☑   **D.** Issues are risks that have come into fruition. Once the issue exists, you'll need to document it in the issue log and then work to resolve it. Because issues will always affect stakeholders, you'll use the issue log as part of your stakeholder engagement to resolve conflicts and issues and communicate with the stakeholders.
    ☒   **A, B,** and **C** are incorrect. The issue log is an input to stakeholder engagement (**A**), but it's not necessarily used to identify stakeholders that are causing issues (**B**). Issues could happen by no fault of the stakeholders—consider a tornado or hurricane and how it may affect a project and the stakeholders. Stakeholders won't prompt for the issue log (**C**); it is the project manager's responsibility to bring the issue log into stakeholder engagement and issue resolution.

22. Your project sponsor has requested that you find a software package to serve as a central repository for all project information. They'd like for the software to capture, store, and provide data analysis on key performance metrics. The software should be able to help complete reports, analyze data, and track overall project performance. What is the project sponsor requesting?
    A. Reporting system
    B. Earned value management system
    C. Project management information system
    D. Integrated change control system

    ☑   **A.** The project sponsor is asking for a reporting system. These help the project manager create reports but can also allow stakeholders to use pull communications to check in on the project's progress.
    ☒   **B, C,** and **D** are incorrect. A is incorrect because earned value management can help predict and measure project performance, a nice addition to reporting, but it's not a requirement of the reporting system. **C** is incorrect because the project management information system is a software tool that helps the project manager manage, not just create reports. **D** is incorrect because the integrated change control system is part of change control; it examines a change's effect on the entire project.

23. As a project manager, you must use multiple types of communication with stakeholders to keep them engaged with the project work. All the following are types of communications that are related to stakeholder engagement except for which one?
    A. Pull communications
    B. Push communications
    C. Interactive communications
    D. Ad hoc communications

    ☑   **D.** Ad hoc communications is the best answer because it's not a structured stakeholder management communication type. You will, as a project manager, use ad hoc communications to facilitate quick, informal communications, but it's not a structured, planned approach to managing communication to and from the project stakeholders.
    ☒   **A, B,** and **C** are incorrect. A is incorrect because pull communications, such as information from a project web site, is a form of structured communications. **B** is incorrect because push communications, such as an e-mail or memo you'd send to the stakeholders, is a structured stakeholder management communication approach. **C,** interactive communications, is a structured and planned communication approach you'll use to communicate with and among the project stakeholders.

24. Stakeholder engagement is key to a successful project, so you and the project team have created a stakeholder management plan that includes many different methods for engaging stakeholders. As part of your plan, you should also reference what other project management plan component?
    A. Project communications management plan
    B. Project procurement contracts
    C. Project scope statement
    D. Milestone charts for the project schedule

    ☑ **A.** Stakeholder management and project communications are tightly linked together. You'll need the project's communications management plan to help you communicate properly with the correct stakeholders, at the correct time, with the correct message, and in the expected communication format.
    ☒ **B, C,** and **D** are incorrect. B is incorrect because the project's procurement contract isn't part of the project management plan. **C** is incorrect because the project scope is not needed for stakeholder engagement. **D** is incorrect because milestone charts are not an input to stakeholder engagement.

25. You are the project manager of a new software development project in your company. Your company operates in a matrix environment and utilizes a project management office to structure projects. This current project has 78 stakeholders and will last for 18 months. Sam, one of the project stakeholders, informs you that two of his employees will be leaving the organization and will no longer be available as resources on your project. In addition to the project staffing management plan, what other document should you update?
    A. Stakeholder register
    B. Risk register
    C. Change log
    D. Project schedule

    ☑ **A.** The stakeholder register is the best answer, because it contains information about the stakeholders that are currently involved in the project. When a stakeholder leaves the project, you should update the stakeholder register so that you don't include non-stakeholders in project communications and engagement.
    ☒ **B, C,** and **D** are incorrect. When a stakeholder leaves the project, you won't necessarily update the risk register or the project schedule, because some stakeholders leaving the project won't always affect these two elements of the project. There is no need to update the project's change log simply because people leave the project.

Chapter 14

The PMI Code of Ethics and Professional Conduct

CERTIFICATION OBJECTIVES

14.01   Responsibilities to the Profession

14.02   Responsibilities to the Customer and to the Public

✓   Two-Minute Drill

Q&A   Self Test

The PMI Code of Ethics and Professional Conduct is the authoritative guide on how all PMI members should behave. In regard to the PMP exam, this PMI document defines how the Project Management Professional (PMP) should act as a professional and how the PMP should behave with customers and the public in general. Thus, as a PMP exam candidate, you will be tested on your knowledge of the PMI Code of Ethics and Professional Conduct, which is really about ethics, fair business dealing, and doing what's fundamentally correct as a project manager.

The code, eight pages in length, covers a broad array of do's and don'ts for PMI members. Essentially, the PMP should always take the high road. There should be no room for misconceptions, errors in judgment, or actions that could be interpreted as conflicts of interest, shady, or just plain wrong.

Whenever you are considering doing something that might be seen as unethical, remember this: "When in doubt, don't do it." The full PMI Code of Ethics and Professional Conduct is available through PMI's web site at www.pmi.org, and you'll have to agree to abide by it when you complete and submit your exam application.

The PMP exam covers more than just the PMI Code of Ethics and Professional Conduct in regard to professional responsibility. Many of these topics have been covered in communications and human resources. The PMI Code of Ethics and Professional Conduct is not a stand-alone exam topic, but it's integrated into all of the process groups. You'll be tested on ethics and professional conduct throughout the PMP examination, not just in one big chunk.

The four areas of professional responsibility consist of the following:

- Responsibility
- Respect
- Fairness
- Honesty

CERTIFICATION OBJECTIVE 14.01

Responsibilities to the Profession

The PMP must adhere to a high set of principles, rules, and policies. This includes the organizational rules and policies, the certification process, and the advancement of the profession. As you're taking the PMP exam, always choose the answer that best supports the PMP profession and the higher set of principles the PMP is expected to adhere to. PMPs are to accept and manage only projects that they're qualified to manage. And, as a PMP, you're to aspire to follow the core of ethics not only in business but also in the project decisions that affect society, public safety, and the environment.

Complying with Rules and Policies

Honesty is expected in all areas regarding the PMP examination process, including the following:

- Exam applications must be honest and reflect actual education and work experience.
- You don't provide false information for other PMP candidates, and you don't ask others to do the same for you.

■ Test items, questions, answers, and scenarios are not to be shared with other PMP candidates.

■ PMP renewal information must reflect an honest assessment of education and experience.

■ Continuing education information must be honest and accurate and reflect actual courses completed.

The PMP should report violations of the PMI Code of Ethics and Professional Conduct when clear and factual evidence of this exists. Based on the scenario, the information may be presented to PMI, to the performing organization's management, or to the proper law enforcement authorities.

The PMP must disclose to clients and customers scenarios in which the PMP may be perceived as having an unfair advantage or a conflict of interest, or if she may profit from conditions within the project. Any appearances of impropriety must be avoided and disclosed.

PMP
Coach
Be wary of the Internet. It's tempting to scour the Web looking for more insight on the PMP exam, but PMP candidates are not to share exam question specifics with anyone. Furthermore, just because some clown in Boise says it's a real-live test question doesn't make it a real-live test question. Although practice questions are nice, I think you'll be better off studying the facts that this book and the *PMBOK Guide* offer. Study what you know is accurate, not what might be accurate.

Applying Honesty to the Profession

The PMP candidate is expected, at all times, to provide honesty in experience documentation, the advertisement of skills, and the performance of services. The PMP must, of course, adhere to and abide by all applicable laws governing the project work. In addition, the PMP should adhere to the ethical standards within the trade or industry.

on the
Job
Industry standards are recommendations for how the work and practice should be completed. Regulations are requirements for how the work and practice must be completed. A PMP must know the difference.

Advancing the Profession

The PMP must respect and recognize the intellectual work and property of others. The PMP can't claim others' work as his own. He must give credit where credit is due. Work, research, and development sources must be documented and acknowledged by the PMP when he is relying on others' work.

on the
Job
You can advance the PMP profession by distributing the PMI Code of Ethics and Professional Conduct to PMP candidates. You can get your copy for free at www .pmi.org.

CERTIFICATION OBJECTIVE 14.02

Responsibilities to the Customer and to the Public

The PMP has a responsibility to the customer of the project and to the public. Projects that affect internal customers are expected to meet requirements and standards and fulfill the business need of the performing organization. Essentially, as a PMP, you have a duty of loyalty based on the type of work you are doing, whether you are employed by the organization or not. You may be working for your employer, or you may be a volunteer. Similar to a person performing a public service, the PMP is also accountable for the work completed for the public—and for the transactions, quality of work, and ethics enforced in the project.

INSIDE THE EXAM

The PMI Code of Ethics and Professional Conduct imparts many messages to the PMP. The responsibility of the PMP includes responsibility, respect, honesty, and ethics. The PMP may often find herself in scenarios in which she can personally profit through the information available within a project. For example, a PMP may discover a project is finishing ahead of schedule—but by finishing early, the PMP's contract will be closed and she'll lose income. The PMP must do what's ethically correct and best for the good of the project and project customer. This means finishing the project work according to the project plan and circumstances in the project. No stalling, adding unneeded activities, or running up the billable hours just because there's an opportunity to do so.

On the PMP exam, you will face many questions on professional conduct. Always, even if you disagree in theory with the outcome of the scenario, choose the moral high ground. The questions you'll face on the exam are extreme circumstances, but they still test your knowledge of this code of ethics.

Part of the PMI Code of Ethics and Professional Conduct deals with customs and laws of foreign countries. The PMP must recognize these laws and customs and understand how to operate within them. The Sapir–Whorf hypothesis holds that an understanding of the local language, its implied meaning, and colloquialisms enables individuals to have a deeper understanding of the people, their values, and their actions. Simply put, the theory suggests a link between the language spoken and how the language speaker operates.

The PMP, when operating in countries other than his home country, should consider the practices and customs of the local country before reacting to conditions and scenarios. What may be considered a conflict of interest in one country may be a common practice in another. Culture shock is the initial disorientation a person first experiences when visiting a country other than his own. Ethnocentrism is judging another culture solely by the values and standards of one's own country, especially with concern to language, behavior, customs, and religion. Many people tend to believe that their culture is superior to other cultures.

Enforcing Project Management Truth and Honesty

PMPs must represent themselves and their projects truthfully to the general public. This includes statements made in advertising, press releases, and public forums. When project managers are involved in the creation of estimates, truth is also expected. The PMP must provide accurate estimates on time, cost, services to be provided, and realistic outcomes of the project work.

When a project is assigned to the PMP, the project manager is responsible for meeting the project scope as expected by the customer. PMPs work for the customer and must strive for customer satisfaction while fulfilling the project objectives. As part of the project implementation, the PMP must keep confidential information confidential. There is an obligation to the customer to maintain privacy, confidentiality, and the nondisclosure of sensitive information.

Project managers should play fair. This means that the project manager should remain impartial, make decisions for the good of the project, provide access to information, and treat stakeholders fairly. In procurement, the project manager should make fair decisions and make opportunities equally available to all qualified providers. The project manager doesn't use favoritism in any area of the project and avoids any kind of prejudice, discrimination, or nepotism.

Eliminating Inappropriate Actions

A PMP must avoid conflicts of interest and scenarios in which conflicts of interest could seem apparent, opportunistic, or questionable to the customer or other stakeholders. In addition, the PMP must not accept any inappropriate gifts, inappropriate payments, or any other compensation for favors, project management work, or influence of a project. The exception to this rule is when the laws or customs of the country where the project is being performed call for gifts to the project manager. However, the PMP should be aware of what gifts are acceptable and appropriate within the country where the project is taking place. Lavish gifts outside of the norm should be refused.

See the video "Ethics."

Respecting Others

Project managers are to respect the stakeholders and people with which they work. This means that the project manager listens to other people and tries to understand what they are trying to convey. If the project manager doesn't understand, she should ask questions to encourage understanding. Part of respecting others is educating ourselves and understanding how other cultures operate to avoid offending someone in that culture.

There's little doubt that in project management conflicts with others will occur. When conflicts are happening, it's up to the project manager to approach those involved to seek a resolution to the conflict. Conflict resolution should always be in the best interest of the project, not the project manager. The project manager should always negotiate in good faith, treat others professionally, and respect the property rights of others—even if other people don't treat the project manager this way.

CERTIFICATION SUMMARY

The PMI Code of Ethics and Professional Conduct and the professional conduct of a project manager is included in the 200 questions on the PMP exam, but these ethical questions are not a separate category of questions. They are interwoven into the PMP exam domains. To answer these questions correctly, you should always take the "ethical high road." The questions concerning ethics, conflict of interest, and personal gain are representative of the types of situations project managers can find themselves in on a regular basis. For the PMP exam—and in daily practice—follow the PMI Code of Ethics and Professional Conduct, and you'll do fine.

A project manager must adhere to the laws by which he is governed. This means knowing the difference between optional standards and the required regulations. Next, the project manager must follow the policies of the organization by which he is employed. This means if the project manager's company has a policy against a certain condition—no matter how small or innocent it may seem—the policy must be followed first. Finally, the project manager must avoid and disclose conflicts of interest and any appearance of impropriety.

When a project manager is completing projects in another country, the project manager must be respectful of the laws, people, culture, and values of the country in which the work is taking place. Project managers must not succumb to ethnocentrism—the act of believing their own culture is better than everyone else's culture. The project manager must work to understand the culture, traditions, and expectations of the people in the country in which he is working while still complying with the policies of her organization.

KEY TERMS

To pass the PMP exam, you will need to memorize the following terms and their definitions. For maximum value, create your own flashcards based on these definitions and review them daily. The definitions can be found within this chapter and in the glossary.

confidentiality   A project manager should keep certain aspects of a project confidential, such as contract negotiations, human resource issues, and trade secrets of the organization.

conflict of interest   A situation in which the project manager could influence a decision for personal gain.

culture shock   The initial disorientation a person experiences when in a foreign environment.

ethics   The personal, cultural, and organizational interpretation of right and wrong; project managers are to operate ethically and fairly.

ethnocentrism   A belief that one's own culture is superior to other cultures; can occur when individuals measure and compare a foreigner's actions against their own local culture.

inappropriate compensation   Compensation, such as bribes of other unethical acts, that must be avoided. The project manager is to act in the best interest of the project and the organization.

PMI Code of Ethics and Professional Conduct   A PMI document that defines the expectations of its members to act responsibly, respectfully, fairly, and honestly in their leadership of projects and programs.

Sapir–Whorf hypothesis   A theory that suggest that a link exists between the language a person (or culture) speaks and how that person (or culture) behaves in the world.

TWO-MINUTE DRILL

Responsibilities to the Profession

- ❏ PMP candidates and certificate holders must provide accurate and truthful information in all aspects of PMP certification.
- ❏ PMP exam questions and scenarios should not be shared with other PMP candidates.
- ❏ Violations of the PMI Code of Ethics and Professional Conduct should be reported to the proper parties.
- ❏ PMPs must acknowledge and recognize others' work, intellectual property, and development.

Responsibilities to the Customer and to the Public

- ❑ PMPs must comply with all laws, regulations, and ethics in regard to project management practices.
- ❑ PMPs must provide accurate and truthful information when estimating costs, services, and the realistic outcomes of project work.
- ❑ PMPs must keep confidential information confidential.
- ❑ PMPs must avoid conflicts of interest and disclose any perceivable incidences.
- ❑ PMPs must not accept inappropriate compensation or gifts for their project management work.

SELF TEST

1. You are the project manager of the JKN Project. The project customer has requested that you inflate your cost estimates by 25 percent. He reports that his management always reduces the cost of the estimates, so this is the only way to get the monies needed to complete the project. Which of the following is the best response to this situation?
   A. Do as the customer asked to ensure the project requirements can be met by adding the increase as a contingency reserve.
   B. Do as the customer asked to ensure the project requirements can be met by adding the increase across each task.
   C. Do as the customer asked by creating an estimate for the customer's management and another for the actual project implementation.
   D. Complete an accurate estimate of the project. In addition, create a risk assessment on why the project budget would be inadequate.

2. You are the project manager for the BNH Project. This project takes place in a country different from yours. The project leader from this country presents a team of workers who are all from his family. You should do which one of the following?
   A. Reject the team leader's recommendations and assemble your own project team.
   B. Review the résumé and qualifications of the project team leader before approving the team.
   C. Determine whether the country's traditions include hiring from the immediate family before hiring from outside the family.
   D. Replace the project leader with an impartial project leader.

3. You are about to begin negotiations on a new project that is to take place in another country. Which of the following should be your guide on what business practices are allowed and discouraged?

    A. The project charter

    B. The project plan

    C. Company policies and procedures

    D. The PMI Code of Ethics and Professional Conduct

4. One of your project team members reports that he sold pieces of equipment because he needed the money to pay for his daughter's school tuition. He says he has paid back the money by working overtime without reporting the hours worked so that his theft remains private. What should you do?

    A. Fire the project team member.

    B. Report the team member to his manager.

    C. Suggest that the team member report his action to human resources.

    D. Tell the team member you're disappointed in what he did, and advise him not to do something like this again.

5. You are the project manager of the SUN Project. Your organization is a functional environment, and you do not get along well with the functional manager leading the project. You are in disagreement with the manager about how the project should proceed, the timings of the activities, the suggested schedule, and the expected quality of the work. The manager has requested that you get to work on several of the activities on the critical path even though you and she have not solved the issues concerning the project. Which of the following should you do?

    A. Go to senior management and voice your concerns.

    B. Complete the activities as requested.

    C. Ask to be taken off the project.

    D. Refuse to begin activities on the project until the issues are resolved.

6. PMI has contacted you regarding an ethics violation of a PMP candidate. The question is in regard to a friend who said he worked as project manager under your guidance. You know this is not true, but to save a friendship, you avoid talking with PMI. This is a violation of which of the following?

    A. The PMI Code to cooperate on ethics violations investigations

    B. The PMI Code to report accurate information

    C. The PMI Code to report any PMP violations

    D. The law concerning ethical practices

7. You are the project manager for the Log Cabin Project. One of your vendors is completing a large portion of the project. You have heard a rumor that the vendor is losing many of its workers because of labor issues. In light of this information, what should you do?

A. Stop work with the vendor until the labor issues are resolved.

B. Communicate with the vendor in regard to the rumor.

C. Look to secure another vendor to replace the current vendor.

D. Negotiate with the labor union to secure the workers on your project.

8. You are the project manager for the PMH Project. Three vendors have submitted cost estimates for the project. One of the estimates is significantly higher than similar project work in the past. In this scenario, you should do which of the following?

A. Ask the other vendors about the higher estimate from the third vendor.

B. Use the cost estimates from the historical information.

C. Take the high cost to the vendor to discuss the discrepancy before reviewing the issue with the other vendors.

D. Ask the vendor that supplied the high estimate for information about how the estimate was prepared.

9. You are the project manager of the LKH Project. This project must be completed within six months, but after two months, the schedule has begun to slip. As of now, the project is one week behind schedule. Based on your findings, you believe you can make some corrective actions and recover the lost time over the next month to get the project back on schedule for its completion date. Management, however, requires weekly status reports on cost and schedule. Which of the following should you do?

A. Report that the project is one week behind schedule but will finish on schedule based on cited corrective actions.

B. Report that the project is on schedule and will finish on schedule.

C. Report that the project is off schedule by a few days but will finish on schedule.

D. Report that the project is running late.

10. As a contracted project manager, you have been assigned a project with a budget of U.S. $1.5 million. The project is scheduled to last seven months, but your most recent EVM report shows that the project will finish ahead of schedule by nearly six weeks. If this happens, you will lose $175,000 in billable time. What should you do?

A. Bill for the entire $1.5 million since this was the approved budget.

B. Bill for the $1.5 million by adding more work at the end of the project.

C. Report to the customer the project status and completion date.

D. Report to the customer the project status and completion date, and ask if they'd like to add any features to account for the monies not spent.

11. You are the project manager of the PMH Project. You have been contracted to design the placement of several pieces of manufacturing equipment. You have completed the project scope and are ready to pass the work over to the installer. The installer begins to schedule you to help with the installation of the manufacturing equipment. Which of the following should you do?

    A. Help the installer place the equipment according to the design documents.

    B. Help the installer place the equipment as the customer sees fit.

    C. Refuse to help the installer since the project scope has been completed.

    D. Help the installer place the equipment, but insist that the quality control be governed by your design specifications.

12. You are the project manager of the 12BA Project. You have completed the project according to the design documents and have met the project scope. The customer agrees that the design document requirements have been met; however, the customer is not pleased with the project deliverables and is demanding additional adjustments be made to complete the project. What is the best way to continue?

    A. Complete the work as the customer has requested.

    B. Complete the work at 1.5 times the billable rate.

    C. Do nothing. The project scope is completed.

    D. Do nothing. Management from the performing organization and the customer's organization will need to determine why the project failed before adding work.

13. You are the project manager of the AAA Project. Due to the nature of the project, much of the work will require overtime between Christmas and New Year's Day. Many of the project team members, however, have requested vacation during that week. What is the best way to continue?

    A. Refuse all vacation requests and require all team members to work.

    B. Allow vacation requests only for those team members who are not needed during that week.

    C. Divide tasks equally among the team members so each works the same amount of time.

    D. Allow team members to volunteer for the overtime work.

14. You are a project manager for your organization. Your project is to install several devices for one of your company's clients. The client has requested that you complete a few small tasks that are not in the project scope. To maintain the relationship with the client, you oblige her request and complete the work without informing your company. This is an example of which of the following?

    A. Effective expert judgment

    B. A violation of ethics

    C. Contract change control

    D. Integrated change control

15. You are completing a project for a customer in another country. One of the customs in this country is to honor the project manager of a successful project with a gift. Your company, however, does not allow project managers to accept gifts worth more than $50 from any entity. At the completion of the project, the customer presents you with a new car in a public ceremony. Which of the following should you do?
    A. Accept the car since it is a custom of the country. To refuse it would be an insult to your hosts.
    B. Refuse to accept the car because it would result in a conflict with your organization to accept it.
    C. Accept the car and then return it to the customer in private.
    D. Accept the car and then donate the car to a charity in the customer's name.

16. A project team member is sabotaging your project because he does not agree with it. Which of the following should you do?
    A. Fire the project team member.
    B. Present the problem to management.
    C. Present the problem to management with a solution to remove the team member from the project.
    D. Present the problem to management with a demand to fire the project team member.

17. You are the project manager of a project in Asia. You discover that the project leader has hired family members for several lucrative contracts on the project. What should you consider?
    A. Cultural issues
    B. Ethical issues
    C. Organizational issues
    D. Political issues

18. Of the following, which one best achieves customer satisfaction?
    A. Completing the project requirements
    B. Maintaining the project cost
    C. Maintaining the project schedule
    D. Completing the project with the defined quality metrics

19. A PMP has been assigned to manage a project in a foreign country. Which of the following describes the disorientation the PMP will likely experience as he gets acclimated to the country?
    A. The Sapir–Whorf hypothesis
    B. Time dimension
    C. Ethnocentrism
    D. Culture shock

20. You are the project manager for an information technology project. It has come to your attention that a technical problem has stopped the project work. How should you proceed?
    A. Measure the project performance to date and account for the cost of the technical problem.
    B. Rebaseline the project performance to account for the technical problem.
    C. Work with the project team to develop alternative solutions to the technical problem.
    D. Outsource the technical problem to a vendor.

21. A PMP has been assigned to manage a project in a foreign country. What should be done to ensure that the project's success is not hindered by the fact that the project manager is working in a foreign country?

   A. Teach the project manager about the customs and laws of the foreign country.
   B. Find a project manager who is from that country.
   C. Assign the project manager a guide to the foreign country.
   D. Allow the project manager to travel home on weekends.

22. Your company does not allow project managers to accept gifts of any kind from vendors. A friend who you have known for years now works for a vendor that your company may be doing business with. Your friend from the vendor asks you to lunch to discuss an upcoming project, and you accept. When the check arrives at the lunch table, your friend insists on paying. You should do which of the following?

   A. Allow the friend to buy because you've been friends for years.
   B. Allow the friend to buy because lunch isn't really a gift.
   C. Don't allow the friend to buy, because your company does not allow any gifts from vendors.
   D. Insist that you purchase your friend's lunch and your friend buys yours.

23. You are a project manager on a construction project. Your project needs an experienced mason to repair and restore an old chimney that the customer wants to keep as part of the project. Your brother, as it happens, is an expert at restoring historical chimneys, and you award the work to him. This is an example of what?

   A. Networking
   B. A conflict of interest
   C. Poor procurement
   D. Acceptable practice, because your brother is an expert

24. While studying for your PMP exam, you are invited to participate in a study group. At your first meeting, another attendee announces that he has "real, live questions" from the PMP exam. What should you do?

   A. Examine the questions.
   B. Report the study group to PMI.
   C. Leave the study group.
   D. Ask where the person got the questions so you can report the testing center to PMI.

25. You are a project manager within an organization that completes technical projects for other entities. You have plans to leave your company within the next month to launch your own consulting business, which will compete with your current employer. Your company is currently working on a large proposal for a government contract that your new company could also benefit from. What should you do?

   A. Resign from your current job and bid against your employer to get the contract.
   B. Decline to participate due to a conflict of interest.
   C. Help your employer prepare the proposal.
   D. Inform your employer that you will be leaving the company within a month and it would be inappropriate for you to work on the current proposal.

SELF TEST ANSWERS

1. You are the project manager of the JKN Project. The project customer has requested that you inflate your cost estimates by 25 percent. He reports that his management always reduces the cost of the estimates, so this is the only way to get the monies needed to complete the project. Which of the following is the best response to this situation?
   A. Do as the customer asked to ensure the project requirements can be met by adding the increase as a contingency reserve.
   B. Do as the customer asked to ensure the project requirements can be met by adding the increase across each task.
   C. Do as the customer asked by creating an estimate for the customer's management and another for the actual project implementation.
   D. Complete an accurate estimate of the project. In addition, create a risk assessment on why the project budget would be inadequate.

   ☑ **D.** It would be inappropriate to bloat the project costs by 25 percent. A risk assessment describing how the project may fail if the budget is not accurate is most appropriate.
   ☒ **A, B,** and **C** are incorrect. They are ethically wrong. The PMP should always provide honest estimates of the project work.

2. You are the project manager for the BNH Project. This project takes place in a country different from yours. The project leader from this country presents a team of workers who are all from his family. You should do which one of the following?
   A. Reject the team leader's recommendations and assemble your own project team.
   B. Review the résumé and qualifications of the project team leader before approving the team.
   C. Determine whether the country's traditions include hiring from the immediate family before hiring from outside the family.
   D. Replace the project leader with an impartial project leader.

   ☑ **C.** You should first confirm what the local practices and customs call for in regard to hiring family members before others.
   ☒ **A, B,** and **D** are incorrect. A and D are incorrect because they do not consider the qualifications of the project team leader and the project team. In addition, they do not take into account local customs. B is incorrect as well; although the qualifications of the project team leader are an important aspect, this choice does not consider the local customs. In addition, the project team leader's ability is not called into question; the family members are the issue.

3. You are about to begin negotiations on a new project that is to take place in another country. Which of the following should be your guide on what business practices are allowed and discouraged?
   A. The project charter
   B. The project plan
   C. Company policies and procedures
   D. The PMI Code of Ethics and Professional Conduct

   ☑ **C.** The company policies and procedures should guide you regarding the decisions you make in the foreign country.
   ☒ **A, B,** and **D** are incorrect. **A** and **B** are incorrect because these documents are essential but usually do not reference allowed business practices. **D** is also incorrect. Although the PMP Code of Ethics and Professional Conduct harbors crucial information, the company's policies and procedures are more specific to the project work and requirements.

4. One of your project team members reports that he sold pieces of equipment because he needed the money to pay for his daughter's school tuition. He says he has paid back the money by working overtime without reporting the hours worked so that his theft remains private. What should you do?
   A. Fire the project team member.
   B. Report the team member to his manager.
   C. Suggest that the team member report his action to human resources.
   D. Tell the team member you're disappointed in what he did, and advise him not to do something like this again.

   ☑ **B.** This situation calls for the project team member to be reported to his manager for disciplinary action.
   ☒ **A, C,** and **D** are incorrect. **A** is inappropriate because the project manager may not have the authority to fire the project team member. **C** is inappropriate because the project manager must take action to bring the situation to management's attention. **D** is inappropriate because no formal discipline actions are taken to address the problem.

5. You are the project manager of the SUN Project. Your organization is a functional environment, and you do not get along well with the functional manager leading the project. You are in disagreement with the manager about how the project should proceed, the timings of the activities, the suggested schedule, and the expected quality of the work. The manager has requested that you get to work on several of the activities on the critical path even though you and she have not solved the issues concerning the project. Which of the following should you do?

   A. Go to senior management and voice your concerns.

   B. Complete the activities as requested.

   C. Ask to be taken off the project.

   D. Refuse to begin activities on the project until the issues are resolved.

   ☑ **B.** The project manager must respect the authority of the functional manager.
   ☒ **A, C,** and **D** are incorrect. These are inappropriate actions because they do not complete the assigned work the functional manager has delegated to the project manager.

6. PMI has contacted you regarding an ethics violation of a PMP candidate. The question is in regard to a friend who said he worked as project manager under your guidance. You know this is not true, but to save a friendship, you avoid talking with PMI. This is a violation of which of the following?

   A. The PMI Code to cooperate on ethics violations investigations

   B. The PMI Code to report accurate information

   C. The PMI Code to report any PMP violations

   D. The law concerning ethical practices

   ☑ **A.** By avoiding the conversation with PMI in regard to the ethics violation of a friend, you are, yourself, violating the PMI Code of Ethics and Professional Conduct.
   ☒ **B, C,** and **D** are incorrect. They do not fully answer the question. The situation requires you, a PMP, to work with PMI on its investigations. You're not reporting accurate information or a PMP violation, so these choices aren't appropriate for the question. In this instance, PMI isn't concerned about laws, but about a PMP candidate who happens to be your friend.

7. You are the project manager for the Log Cabin Project. One of your vendors is completing a large portion of the project. You have heard a rumor that the vendor is losing many of its workers because of labor issues. In light of this information, what should you do?

   A. Stop work with the vendor until the labor issues are resolved.

   B. Communicate with the vendor in regard to the rumor.

   C. Look to secure another vendor to replace the current vendor.

   D. Negotiate with the labor union to secure the workers on your project.

☑ **B.** The project manager should confront the problem by talking with the vendor about the rumor.

☒ **A, C,** and **D** are incorrect. **A,** stopping work, would delay the project and possibly cause future problems. **C,** trying to secure another vendor, may violate the contract between the buyer and the seller. **D** is also incorrect—the agreement is between the vendor and the performing organization, not the labor union.

8. You are the project manager for the PMH Project. Three vendors have submitted cost estimates for the project. One of the estimates is significantly higher than similar project work in the past. In this scenario, you should do which of the following?

   A. Ask the other vendors about the higher estimate from the third vendor.
   B. Use the cost estimates from the historical information.
   C. Take the high cost to the vendor to discuss the discrepancy before reviewing the issue with the other vendors.
   D. Ask the vendor that supplied the high estimate for information about how the estimate was prepared.

☑ **D.** Most likely, the vendor did not understand the project work to be procured, so the estimate is skewed. A clear statement of work is needed for the vendors to provide accurate estimates.

☒ **A, B,** and **C** are incorrect. These are inappropriate actions because they reveal other vendors' estimates. This information should be kept confidential between the buyer and the sellers. In some government projects, however, release of the winning bid information may be required.

9. You are the project manager of the LKH Project. This project must be completed within six months, but after two months, the schedule has begun to slip. As of now, the project is one week behind schedule. Based on your findings, you believe you can make some corrective actions and recover the lost time over the next month to get the project back on schedule for its completion date. Management, however, requires weekly status reports on cost and schedule. Which of the following should you do?

   A. Report that the project is one week behind schedule but will finish on schedule based on cited corrective actions.
   B. Report that the project is on schedule and will finish on schedule.
   C. Report that the project is off schedule by a few days but will finish on schedule.
   D. Report that the project is running late.

☑ **A.** You should report an honest assessment of the project with actions on how you plan to correct the problem.

☒ **B, C,** and **D** are incorrect. **B** and **C** are incorrect because they do not provide honest answers to management. **D** is incorrect because it does not provide a solution to the problem.

10. As a contracted project manager, you have been assigned a project with a budget of U.S. $1.5 million. The project is scheduled to last seven months, but your most recent EVM report shows that the project will finish ahead of schedule by nearly six weeks. If this happens, you will lose $175,000 in billable time. What should you do?

 A. Bill for the entire $1.5 million since this was the approved budget.

 B. Bill for the $1.5 million by adding more work at the end of the project.

 C. Report to the customer the project status and completion date.

 D. Report to the customer the project status and completion date, and ask if they'd like to add any features to account for the monies not spent.

☑   **C.** An honest and accurate assessment of the project work is always required.

☒   **A, B,** and **D** are incorrect. **A** and **B** are incorrect because these actions do not reflect an honest assessment of the work. **D** is incorrect because it offers gold plating and recommends additional changes that were not part of the original project scope. In addition, because this is a contractual relationship, the additional work may not be covered within the original project contract and may result in legal issues.

11. You are the project manager of the PMH Project. You have been contracted to design the placement of several pieces of manufacturing equipment. You have completed the project scope and are ready to pass the work over to the installer. The installer begins to schedule you to help with the installation of the manufacturing equipment. Which of the following should you do?

 A. Help the installer place the equipment according to the design documents.

 B. Help the installer place the equipment as the customer sees fit.

 C. Refuse to help the installer since the project scope has been completed.

 D. Help the installer place the equipment, but insist that the quality control be governed by your design specifications.

☑   **C.** When the project scope is completed, the contract is fulfilled and the project is done. Any new work items should be sent through the proper channels within an organization to create a new project or work order. In this instance, the contract change control system should be used or a new contract should be created.

☒   **A, B,** and **D** are incorrect. These choices are outside of the scope and have not been covered in the contract.

12. You are the project manager of the 12BA Project. You have completed the project according to the design documents and have met the project scope. The customer agrees that the design document requirements have been met; however, the customer is not pleased with the project deliverables and is demanding additional adjustments be made to complete the project. What is the best way to continue?

A. Complete the work as the customer has requested.
B. Complete the work at 1.5 times the billable rate.
C. Do nothing. The project scope is completed.
D. Do nothing. Management from the performing organization and the customer's organization will need to determine why the project failed before adding work.

☑ **C.** When the project scope has been completed, the project is completed. Any additional work, without a contract change or new contract, would be dishonest and would betray the customer or the project manager's company.

☒ **A, B,** and **D** are incorrect. **A** and **B** are incorrect because additional work is not covered in the current contract. **D** is incorrect because the project did not fail—the deliverables met the requirements of the project scope and the design document.

13. You are the project manager of the AAA Project. Due to the nature of the project, much of the work will require overtime between Christmas and New Year's Day. Many of the project team members, however, have requested vacation during that week. What is the best way to continue?
A. Refuse all vacation requests and require all team members to work.
B. Allow vacation requests only for those team members who are not needed during that week.
C. Divide tasks equally among the team members so each works the same amount of time.
D. Allow team members to volunteer for the overtime work.

☑ **D.** This is the best choice for this scenario because it allows the project team to be self-led and is sensitive to the needs of the project team.

☒ **A, B,** and **C** are incorrect. There are all autocratic responses to the problem, and although the results may seem fair, **D** is the best choice.

14. You are a project manager for your organization. Your project is to install several devices for one of your company's clients. The client has requested that you complete a few small tasks that are not in the project scope. To maintain the relationship with the client, you oblige her request and complete the work without informing your company. This is an example of which of the following?
A. Effective expert judgment
B. A violation of ethics
C. Contract change control
D. Integrated change control

☑ **B.** When the project manager completes activities outside of the contract and does not inform the performing organization, it is essentially the same as stealing. The PMP must be held accountable for all the time invested in a project.

☒ **A, C,** and **D** are incorrect. **A** is incorrect because this is not expert judgment. **C** is incorrect because the contract has not been changed or attempted to be changed. **D** is incorrect because the changes the project manager completed for the customer were not sent through any change control system, but were completed without documentation or reporting.

15. You are completing a project for a customer in another country. One of the customs in this country is to honor the project manager of a successful project with a gift. Your company, however, does not allow project managers to accept gifts worth more than $50 from any entity. At the completion of the project, the customer presents you with a new car in a public ceremony. Which of the following should you do?
    A. Accept the car since it is a custom of the country. To refuse it would be an insult to your hosts.
    B. Refuse to accept the car because it would result in a conflict with your organization to accept it.
    C. Accept the car and then return it to the customer in private.
    D. Accept the car and then donate the car to a charity in the customer's name.

    ☑ **B.** Although this solution may seem extreme, **B** is the best answer because to accept the car in public would give the impression that the project manager has defied company policy. In addition, accepting the car would appear to be a conflict of interest for the project manager.
    ☒ **A, C,** and **D** are incorrect. Accepting the car, even with the intention of returning it or donating it to charity, would be in conflict with the company's policies regarding the acceptance of gifts.

16. A project team member is sabotaging your project because he does not agree with it. Which of the following should you do?
    A. Fire the project team member.
    B. Present the problem to management.
    C. Present the problem to management with a solution to remove the team member from the project.
    D. Present the problem to management with a demand to fire the project team member.

    ☑ **C.** The project team member who is causing the problems should be discussed with management along with a solution to remove the team member from the project. Remember that whenever the project manager must present a problem to management, she should also present a solution to the problem.
    ☒ **A, B,** and **D** are incorrect. **A** is incorrect because it likely is not the project manager's role to fire the project team member. **B** is incorrect because it does not address a solution to the problem. Never go to management with a problem unless a proposed solution is also presented. **D** is incorrect because the project manager's focus should be on the success of the project. By recommending that the project team member be removed from the project, the problem is solved from the project manager's point of view. Management, however, may come to the decision on their own accord to dismiss the individual from the company altogether. In addition, a recommendation from the project manager to fire someone may be outside the boundary of the human resource procedure for employee termination.

17. You are the project manager of a project in Asia. You discover that the project leader has hired family members for several lucrative contracts on the project. What should you consider?
  A. Cultural issues
  B. Ethical issues
  C. Organizational issues
  D. Political issues

  ☑ **A.** The project manager should first determine what the country's customs and culture call for when hiring relatives. It may be a preferred practice in the country to work with qualified relatives first before hiring other individuals to complete the project work.
  ☒ **B, C,** and **D** are incorrect. These are not the best choices in this scenario. They may be considered, however, after first examining the cultural issues within the country.

18. Of the following, which one best achieves customer satisfaction?
  A. Completing the project requirements
  B. Maintaining the project cost
  C. Maintaining the project schedule
  D. Completing the project with the defined quality metrics

  ☑ **A.** The largest factor when it comes to customer satisfaction is the ability to complete the project requirements.
  ☒ **B, C,** and **D** are incorrect. Achieving these factors, while satisfying to the customer, is not as complete as achieving the project requirements, which may include the cost, schedule, and quality expectations.

19. A PMP has been assigned to manage a project in a foreign country. Which of the following describes the disorientation the PMP will likely experience as he gets acclimated to the country?
  A. The Sapir–Whorf hypothesis
  B. Time dimension
  C. Ethnocentrism
  D. Culture shock

  ☑ **D.** Culture shock is the typical disorientation a person feels when visiting a foreign country.
  ☒ **A, B,** and **C** are incorrect. **A,** the Sapir–Whorf hypothesis, states that an individual can understand a culture by understanding its language. **B,** time dimension, is the local culture's general practice for respecting time and punctuality. **C,** ethnocentrism, is the belief by individuals that their own culture is the best and that all other cultures should be measured against it.

20. You are the project manager for an information technology project. It has come to your attention that a technical problem has stopped the project work. How should you proceed?

   A. Measure the project performance to date and account for the cost of the technical problem.
   B. Rebaseline the project performance to account for the technical problem.
   C. Work with the project team to develop alternative solutions to the technical problem.
   D. Outsource the technical problem to a vendor.

   ☑ **C.** When problems arise that stop project tasks, the project manager should work with the team to uncover viable alternative solutions.
   ☒ **A, B,** and **D** are incorrect. **A** and **B** do nothing to find a solution to the problem, so they are incorrect. **D** is incorrect because the solution for the problem has not necessarily been addressed. The end result of **C,** to find an alternative solution, may involve outsourcing the problem to a vendor, but answer **D** should not be the first choice in this scenario.

21. A PMP has been assigned to manage a project in a foreign country. What should be done to ensure that the project's success is not hindered by the fact that the project manager is working in a foreign country?

   A. Teach the project manager about the customs and laws of the foreign country.
   B. Find a project manager who is from that country.
   C. Assign the project manager a guide to the foreign country.
   D. Allow the project manager to travel home on weekends.

   ☑ **A.** Training the project manager on the laws and customs of the foreign country is the best choice to ensure the project's success is not jeopardized.
   ☒ **B, C,** and **D** are incorrect These may all work, but they are not the best options, considering that the project manager has already been selected and needs to be educated about the foreign country's customs. **D** is incorrect because the travel option does not take into consideration the customs of the foreign country.

22. Your company does not allow project managers to accept gifts of any kind from vendors. A friend who you have known for years now works for a vendor that your company may be doing business with. Your friend from the vendor asks you to lunch to discuss an upcoming project, and you accept. When the check arrives at the lunch table, your friend insists on paying. You should do which of the following?

   A. Allow the friend to buy because you've been friends for years.
   B. Allow the friend to buy because lunch isn't really a gift.
   C. Don't allow the friend to buy, because your company does not allow any gifts from vendors.
   D. Insist that you purchase your friend's lunch and your friend buys yours.

    ☑   **C.** Although you have been friends for years, your friend is now working with a vendor, and it would be inappropriate for your friend to buy your lunch. This would clearly be a violation of your company's policies because you and your friend are discussing an upcoming project.

    ☒   **A, B,** and **D** are incorrect. By allowing your friend to purchase your lunch, you would be going against company policies.

23. You are a project manager on a construction project. Your project needs an experienced mason to repair and restore an old chimney that the customer wants to keep as part of the project. Your brother, as it happens, is an expert at restoring historical chimneys, and you award the work to him. This is an example of what?

    A. Networking

    B. A conflict of interest

    C. Poor procurement

    D. Acceptable practice, because your brother is an expert

    ☑   **B.** This is a conflict of interest—or it may appear to be a conflict of interest to others on the project. The project manager can do several things in this scenario: excuse himself from the decision because of the relationship with the brother, create a weighted scoring model, allow several vendors to participate, and so on.

    ☒   **A, C,** and **D** are incorrect. These choices do not address the potential for the conflict of interest.

24. While studying for your PMP exam, you are invited to participate in a study group. At your first meeting, another attendee announces that he has "real, live questions" from the PMP exam. What should you do?

    A. Examine the questions.

    B. Report the study group to PMI.

    C. Leave the study group.

    D. Ask where the person got the questions so you can report the testing center to PMI.

    ☑   **C.** You should not participate in the study group.

    ☒   **A, B,** and **D** are incorrect. **A** is incorrect because it clearly violates the PMI Code of Ethics and Professional Conduct. **B** and **D** are not good choices because there is no clear evidence that the questions are genuine. The questions may have been purchased through a web site or other entity—not necessarily through a testing center.

25. You are a project manager within an organization that completes technical projects for other entities. You have plans to leave your company within the next month to launch your own consulting business, which will compete with your current employer. Your company is currently working on a large proposal for a government contract that your new company could also benefit from. What should you do?

   A. Resign from your current job and bid against your employer to get the contract.

   B. Decline to participate due to a conflict of interest.

   C. Help your employer prepare the proposal.

   D. Inform your employer that you will be leaving the company within a month and it would be inappropriate for you to work on the current proposal.

   ☑ **D.** Of the choices presented, this is the best answer. You should inform your employer of your intent to leave the organization and work on similar projects to avoid a conflict of interest.
   ☒ **A, B,** and **C** are incorrect. **A** is incorrect because you would have a conflict of interest, information gained about your current employer's proposal (such as price and methods), and other advantages that would be ethically wrong. **B** is incorrect because there is no rationale behind what the conflict of interest may be. **C** is incorrect because a conflict of interest exists by preparing the proposal for your future competition.

Part III

Appendices

APPENDICES

A   Critical Exam Information

B   About the CD-ROM

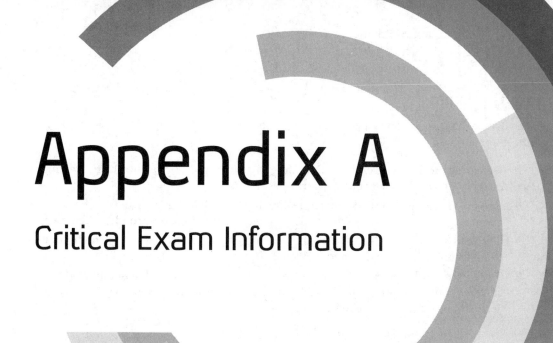

Appendix A
Critical Exam Information

Exam candidates want to pass their PMP exam on the first attempt. Why bother sitting for an exam if you know you're not prepared? In this appendix, you'll find the details that you must know to pass the exam. These facts won't be everything you need to know to pass the PMP exam—but you can bet you won't pass if you do not know the critical information in this appendix.

Exam Test-Passing Tips

For starters, don't think of this process as preparing to take an exam; think of it as preparing to *pass* an exam. Anyone can prepare to take an exam: just show up. Preparing to pass the PMP exam requires project management experience, diligence, and a commitment to study.

Days Before the Exam

In the days leading up to your scheduled exam, here are some basics you should do to prepare yourself for success:

- **Get some moderate exercise** Find time to go for a jog, lift weights, take a swim, or do whatever workout routine works best for you.
- **Eat smart and healthy** If you eat healthy food, you'll feel good—and feel better about yourself. Be certain to drink plenty of water, and don't overdo the caffeine.
- **Get your sleep** A well-rested brain is a sharp brain. You don't want to sit for your exam feeling tired, sluggish, and worn out.
- **Time your study sessions** Don't overdo your study sessions—long cram study sessions aren't that profitable. In addition, try to study at the same time every day at the time your exam is scheduled.

Practice the Testing Process

If you could take one page of notes into the exam, what information would you like on this one-page document? Of course, you absolutely cannot take any notes or reference materials into the exam area. However, if you can create and memorize one sheet of notes, you absolutely may re-create this once you're seated in the exam area.

Practice creating a reference sheet so you can immediately, and legally, re-create this document once your exam has begun. You'll be supplied with several sheets of blank paper and a couple of pencils. Once your exam process begins, re-create your reference sheet. You cannot begin creating your reference sheet until you've started the exam. The following are key pieces of information you'd be wise to include on your reference sheet (you'll find all of this key information in this appendix):

- Activities within each process group
- Estimating formulas
- Communication formula
- Normal distribution values
- Earned value management formulas
- Project management theories

Testing Tips

The questions on the PMP exam are fairly direct and not too verbose, but they may offer a few red herrings. For example, you may face questions that state, "All of the following are correct options expect for which one?" The question wants you to find the incorrect option, or the option that would not be appropriate for the scenario described. Be sure to understand what the question is asking for. It's easy to focus on the scenario presented in a question and then see a suitable option for that scenario in the answer. The trouble is that if the question is asking you to identify an option that is *not* suitable, you just missed the question. Carefully read the question to understand what is expected for an answer.

Here's a tip that can work with many of the questions: Identify what the question wants for an answer and then look for an option that doesn't belong with the other possible answers. In other words, find the answer that doesn't fit with the other three options. Find the "odd man out." Here's an example: EVM is used during the _____.

    A. Controlling phase

    B. Executing phase

    C. Closing phase

    D. Entire project

Notice how options A, B, and C are exclusive? If you choose A, the controlling phase, it implies that EVM is not used anywhere else in the project. The odd man out here is D, the entire project; it's considered the "odd" choice because it, by itself, is not an actual process group. Of course, this tip won't work with every question—but it's handy to keep in mind.

For some answer choices, it may seem like two of the four options are both possible correct answers. However, because you may only choose one answer, you must discern which answer is the best choice. Within the question, there will usually be some hint describing the progress of the project, the requirements of the stakeholders, or some other clue that can help you determine which answer is the best for the question.

Answer Every Question—Once

The PMP exam has 200 questions—of which 175 are "real questions." You don't have to answer every question correctly; just answer enough correctly to pass. In other words, don't waste three of your four hours laboring over one question—the easy questions are worth just as much as the hard ones. And you know, I'm sure, that you never leave any question blank—even if you don't know the answer. A blank question is the same as a wrong answer. As you move through the exam and you find questions that stump you, use the "mark question" option in the exam software, choose an answer you suspect may be correct, and then move on. When you have answered all of the questions, you are given the option to review your marked answers.

Some questions in the exam may prompt your memory to come up with answers to questions you have marked for review. However, resist the temptation to review those questions you've already answered with confidence and haven't marked. More often than not, your first instinct is the correct choice. When you completed the exams at the end of each chapter, did you change correct answers to wrong answers? If you did it in practice, you'll do it on the actual exam.

Use the Process of Elimination

When you're stumped on a question, use the process of elimination. For each question, there'll be four choices. On your scratch paper, write down "ABCD." If you can safely rule out "A," cross it out of the ABCD you've written on your paper. Now focus on which of the other answers won't work. If you determine that "C" won't work, cross it off your list. Now you've got a 50-50 chance of finding the correct choice. If you prefer, the exam testing software also includes the ability to "mark out" answers from the selection choices, but I prefer to do this process on the scratch paper to add any notes and references to the specific question should I need to come back to it later in the exam.

If you cannot determine which answer is best, "B" or "D" in this instance, here's the best approach:

1. Choose an answer in the exam (no blank answers, remember?).
2. Mark the question in the exam software for later review.
3. Circle the "ABCD" on your scratch paper, jot any relevant notes, and then record the question number next to the notes.
4. During the review, or from a later question, you may realize which choice is the better of the two answers. Return to the question and confirm that the best answer is selected.

Everything You Must Know

As promised, this section covers all of the information you must know going into the exam. It's highly recommended that you create a method to recall this information. Here goes.

The 49 Project Management Processes

Table A-1 lists the 49 project management processes you should be familiar with. I've ordered them here according to knowledge area and the corresponding chapter in this book.

TABLE A-1	Project Management Processes *(Continued)*		
Knowledge Area	**Number of Processes**	**Processes**	**Chapter**
Project Integration Management	7	Develop project charter Develop project management plan Direct and manage project work Manage project knowledge Monitor and control the project work Perform integrated change control Close project or phase	4

TABLE A-1   Project Management Processes

Knowledge Area	Number of Processes	Processes	Chapter
Project Scope Management	6	Plan scope management Collect requirements Define scope Create WBS Validate scope Control scope	5
Project Schedule Management	6	Plan schedule management Define activities Sequence activities Estimate activity durations Develop schedule Control schedule	6
Project Cost Management	4	Plan cost management Estimate costs Determine budget Control costs	7
Project Quality Management	3	Plan quality management Manage quality Control quality	8
Project Resource Management	6	Plan resource management Estimate activity resources Acquire resources Develop team Manage project team Control resources	9
Project Communications Management	3	Plan communications management Manage communications Control communications	10
Project Risk Management	7	Plan risk management Identify risks Perform qualitative risk analysis Perform quantitative risk analysis Plan risk responses Implement risk responses Monitor risks	11
Project Procurement Management	3	Plan procurement management Conduct procurements Control procurements	12
Project Stakeholder Management	4	Identify project stakeholders Plan stakeholder engagement Manage stakeholder engagement Monitor stakeholder engagement	13

Magic PMP Formulas

The following shows the major formulas you should know for the exam.

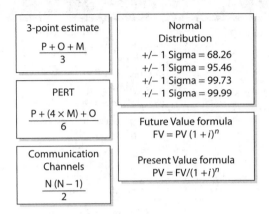

3-point estimate

$$\frac{P + O + M}{3}$$

Normal Distribution

+/− 1 Sigma = 68.26
+/− 1 Sigma = 95.46
+/− 1 Sigma = 99.73
+/− 1 Sigma = 99.99

PERT

$$\frac{P + (4 \times M) + O}{6}$$

Future Value formula
$FV = PV \, (1 + i)^n$

Present Value formula
$PV = FV/(1 + i)^n$

Communication Channels

$$\frac{N \, (N - 1)}{2}$$

Earned Value Management Formulas

Table A-2 shows the EVM formulas you should know for the exam.

Quick PMP Facts

This section has some quick facts you should know at a glance. Hold on—this moves pretty fast.

Organizational Structures

Organizational structures are relevant to the project manager's authority.

- **Organic or simple**   People work along one another regardless of their roles in the organization and the project manager may have little to no authority over the project resources.
- **Functional (centralized)**   Project managers in functional organizations have little authority, little autonomy, report directly to a functional manager, and may be known as project coordinators or team leaders.
- **Multidivisional**   This structure involves replication of functions for each division; similar to the functional organization within each division. The project manager will have little authority and could be called a project coordinator rather than a project manager.

TABLE A-2   Project Management Earned Value Management Formulas

Name	Formula
Planned Value	PV = % complete where the project should be
Earned Value	EV = % complete × BAC
Cost Variance	CV = EV – AC
Schedule Variance	SV = EV – PV
Cost Performance Index	CPI = EV / AC
Schedule Performance Index	SPI = EV / PV
Estimate at Completion Standard formula	EAC = BAC / CPI
Estimate at Completion Future work at planned costs	AC + BAC – EV
Estimate at Completion Initial cost estimates flawed	AC + Estimate for remainder of project
Estimate at Completion SPI and CPI affect remainder of work	AC + [BAC – EV/(CPI × SPI)]
Estimate to Complete	ETC = EAC – AC
To-complete performance index (BAC)	(BAC – EV) / (BAC – AC)
To-complete performance index (EAC)	(BAC – EV) / (EAC – AC)
Variance at Completion	VAC = BAC – EAC

- **Weak matrix**   Weak matrix structures map closely to a functional organization. The project team may come from different departments, but the project manager reports directly to a specific functional manager. The project manager has little authority or autonomy; the project manager and the team work part-time on the project. The functional manager controls the budget.

- **Balanced matrix**   A balanced matrix structure has many of the same attributes as a weak matrix, but the project manager has more time and power regarding the project. The project team and the project manager work part-time on the project. The project manager and the functional manager share the management of the project budget.

- **Strong matrix**   A strong matrix equates to a strong project manager. In a strong matrix organization, many of the same attributes for the project team exist, but the project manager gains power and time when it comes to project work. The project manager is a full-time project manager and the project manager manages the project budget.

- **Project-oriented**   A project-oriented organizational structure groups employees, collocated or not, by activities on a project. The project manager in a project-oriented structure may have complete, or very close to complete, power over the project team. Project managers in a project-oriented structure enjoy a high level of autonomy over their projects, but they also have a higher level of responsibility regarding the project's success.

- **Virtual**   A virtual organization utilizes a network structure within the organization. Points of contact represent the different departments or lines of business within the organization. Communication can be a challenge in a virtual organization as messages are filtered through the point of contact for each department or stakeholder group. The project manager has low authority over the project team and shares authority over the project budget with the functional manager.

- **Hybrid**   Because hybrid structures are unique to each organization, it's impossible to define the level or authority and the project manager's role in a project. In some organizations using a hybrid model the project manager may have total control over the team and the project budget, while other organizations may allocate the project manager authority over the team, but keep the budget management for the functional manager.

- **PMO**   A project management office (PMO) organizes and manages control over all projects within an organization. A PMO is also known as a program management office, project office, or sometimes, the program office.

WBS Facts

The work breakdown structure is the big picture of the project deliverables: It is not the activities that will create the project, but the components the project will create. The WBS helps the project team and the project manager create accurate cost and time estimates. The WBS also helps the project team and the project manager create an accurate activity list. The WBS is part of the scope baseline, which also includes the scope statement, the WBS dictionary, the work packages, and the planning packages.

Project Scope Facts

Projects are temporary endeavors to create a unique product. They are selected by one of two methods:

- **Benefit measurement methods**   These include scoring models, cost-benefit ratios, and economic models.

- **Constrained optimization**   These include mathematical models based on linear, integer, and dynamic programming. (This probably won't be on the PMP exam as a viable answer.)

The project scope defines all the required work, and only the required work, to complete the project. Scope management is the process of ensuring that the project work is within scope and protecting the project from scope creep. The scope statement, along with the WBS and WBS dictionary, is the baseline for all future project decisions. There are two types of scope:

- **Product scope**   Defines the attributes of the product or service the project is creating
- **Project scope**   Defines the required work of the project to create the product

Scope validation is the process completed at the end of each phase and of each project to confirm that the project has met the requirements. It leads to formal acceptance of the project deliverable.

Project Schedule Facts

Time can be a project constraint. Effective time management is the scheduling and sequencing of activities in the best order to ensure that the project completes successfully and in a reasonable amount of time. These are some key terms for time management:

- **Lag**   Waiting between activities.
- **Lead**   Activities come closer together and even overlap.
- **Free float**   The amount of time an activity can be delayed without delaying the next scheduled activity's start date.
- **Total float**   The amount of time an activity can be delayed without delaying the project's finish date.
- **Float**   Sometimes called *slack*—a perfectly acceptable synonym.
- **Duration**   May be abbreviated as "du." For example, du = 8d means the duration is eight days.

There are three types of dependencies between activities:

- **Mandatory**   This hard logic requires a specific sequence between activities.
- **Discretionary**   This soft logic prefers a sequence between activities.
- **External**   Due to conditions outside of the project, such as those created by vendors, the sequence must happen in a given order.

Project Cost Facts

The following are methods of providing project estimates:

- **Bottom-up**   Project costs start at zero, each component in the WBS is estimated for costs, and then the "grand total" is calculated. This is the longest method to complete, but it provides the most accurate estimate.
- **Analogous**   Project costs are based on a similar project. This is a form of expert judgment, but it is also a top-down estimating approach, so it is less accurate than a bottom-up estimate.
- **Parametric modeling**   Using historical data, price is based on cost per unit; examples include cost per metric ton, cost per yard, and cost per hour.

Four types of costs are attributed to a project:

- **Variable costs**   The costs are dependent on other variables. For example, the cost of a food-catered event depends on how many people register to attend the event.
- **Fixed costs**   The cost remains constant throughout the project. For example, a rented piece of equipment requires the same fee each month, even if it is used more in some months than in others.
- **Direct costs**   The cost is directly attributed to an individual project and cannot be shared with other projects (for example, airfare to attend project meetings, hotel expenses, and leased equipment that is used only on the current project).
- **Indirect costs**   These are the costs of doing business; examples include rent, phone, and utilities.

Quality Management Facts

The cost of quality is the money spent investing in training, in meeting requirements for safety and other laws and regulations, and in taking steps to ensure quality acceptance. The cost of nonconformance is the cost associated with rework, downtime, lost sales, and waste of materials.

Some common quality management charts and methods include the following:

- *Ishikawa diagrams* (also called *fishbone diagrams* and *why-why charts*) are used to find causes and effects that contribute to a problem.
- *Flow charts* show the relationship between components and the flow of a process through a system.
- *Pareto diagrams* identify project problems and their frequencies. These are based on the 80/20 rule: 80 percent of project problems stem from 20 percent of the work.

- *Control charts* plot out the result of samplings to determine whether projects are "in control/specification" or "out of control/specification."
- *Kaizen technologies* comprise approaches to make small improvements in an effort to reduce costs and achieve consistency.
- *Just-in-time* ordering reduces the cost of inventory, but requires additional quality because materials would not be readily available if mistakes occur.

Project Resource Facts

The PMP candidate should be familiar with the following human resource theories that may appear on the PMP exam:

- **Maslow's Hierarchy of Needs**   There are five layers of needs for all humans: physiological, safety, social (such as love and friendship), self-esteem, and the crowning jewel, self-actualization.
- **McClelland's Theory of Needs**   Needs are developed by the person's life experiences and may shift over time. Of the three needs that drive people—power, affiliation, and achievement—one of these is the most prominent in the individual. McClelland developed the Thematic Apperception Test to determine what needs are driving individuals.
- **Herzberg's Theory of Motivation**   There are two catalysts for workers: hygiene agents and motivating agents.
  - *Hygiene agents* do nothing to motivate, but their absence demotivates workers. Hygiene agents are the expectations all workers have: job security, a paycheck, clean and safe working conditions, a sense of belonging, civil working relationships, and other basic attributes associated with employment.
  - *Motivating agents* are the elements that motivate people to excel. They include responsibility, appreciation of work, recognition, opportunity to excel, education, and other opportunities associated with work other than just financial rewards.
- **McGregor's Theory of X and Y**   This theory states that "X" people are lazy, don't want to work, and need to be micromanaged and "Y" people are self-led, motivated, and can accomplish things on their own.
- **Ouchi's Theory Z**   This theory holds that workers are motivated by a sense of commitment, opportunity, and advancement. Workers will work if they are challenged and motivated. Think participative management.
- **Expectancy Theory**   People will behave based on what they expect as a result of their behavior. In other words, people will work in relation to the expected reward of the work.

Communication Facts

Communicating is the most important skill for the project manager. With that in mind, here are some key facts on communication:

- Communication channels formula: $N(N-1)/2$. N represents the number of stakeholders. For example, if you have 10 stakeholders, the formula would read $10(10-1)/2$ for 45 communication channels. Pay special attention to questions wanting to know how many additional communication channels you have based on added stakeholders. For example, if you have 25 stakeholders on your project and have recently added 5 team members, how many additional communication channels do you now have? You'll have to calculate the original number of communication channels, $25(25-1)/2 = 300$; then calculate the new number with the added team members, $30(30-1)/2 = 435$; and finally, subtract the difference between the two: $435 - 300 = 135$, the number of additional communication channels.

- Fifty-five percent of communication is nonverbal.

- Effective listening is the ability to watch the speaker's body language, interpret paralingual clues, and decipher facial expressions. Following the message, effective listening has the listener asking questions to achieve clarity and offering feedback.

- Active listening requires receivers of the message to offer clues, such as nodding to indicate they are listening. It also requires receivers to repeat the message, ask questions, and continue the discussion if clarification is needed.

- Communication can be hindered by trendy phrases, jargon, and extremely pessimistic comments. In addition, other communication barriers include noise, hostility, cultural differences, and technical interruptions.

Risk Management Facts

Risks are uncertain events that can have positive or negative effects on a project. Most risks are seen as threats to the project's success—but not all risks are bad. For example, there is a 20 percent probability that the project will realize a discount in shipping, which will save the project $15,000. If this risk happens, the project will save money; if the risk doesn't happen, the project will have to spend the $15,000. Risks should be identified as early as possible in the planning process. A person's willingness to accept risk is the utility function (also called the utility theory).

The only output of risk planning is the risk management plan. There are two broad types of risks:

- **Business risk**   The loss of time and finances (where a downside and upside exist)
- **Pure risk**   The loss of life, injury, and theft (where only a downside exists)

Risks can be responded to via one of seven methods:

- **Escalate** The threat or opportunity may exceed the project boundaries or the project manager's authority, so the risk is escalated to program manager, portfolio manager, or management.
- **Avoidance** Avoid the risk by planning a different technique to remove the risk from the project.
- **Transference** The risk is not eliminated, but the responsibility and ownership of the risk are transferred to another party (for example, through insurance).
- **Mitigation** Reduce the probability or impact of the risk.
- **Acceptance** The risk's probability or impact may be small enough that the risk can be accepted.
- **Exploit** The organization wants to ensure that the identified risk does happen so that the positive impact associated with the risk event is realized.
- **Share** Sharing is nice. When sharing, the risk ownership is transferred to the organization that can most capitalize on the risk opportunity.
- **Enhance** To enhance a risk is to attempt to modify its probability and/or its impacts to realize the most gains from the identified risk.

Risk management also includes the monitoring and controlling of risk characteristics, new risks, and the results of risk responses. Following are terms that are unique to risk management:

- **Risk Contingency funds** Monies reserved for risk events.
- **Secondary risks** A risk that comes into a project as a direct result of another risk response.
- **Risk triggers** A condition, event, or warning signs of a risk event that causes a risk reaction.
- **Residual risks** Risks that remain after a risk response. These are usually small and are accepted by the project team.

Procurement Facts

A contract statement of work (SOW) is provided to the potential sellers so they can create accurate bids, quotes, and proposals for the buyer. A bidders' conference may be held so sellers can query the buyer on the product or service to be procured.

A contract is a formal agreement, preferably written, between a buyer and a seller. On the PMP exam, procurement questions are usually from the buyer's point of view. All requirements the seller is to complete should be clearly written in the contract. Requirements of both parties must be met, or legal proceedings may follow. Table A-3 sums up all the contract types you should know for your exam.

　　You should also know that *a purchase order* is a unilateral form of contract and that a *letter of intent* is not a contract, but shows the intent of the buyer to purchase from a specific seller.

TABLE A-3　　Project Management Contract Types

Contract Type	Acronym	Attribute	Risk Issues
Cost Plus Fixed Fee	CPFF	Actual costs plus profit margin for seller	Cost overruns represent risk to the buyer.
Cost Plus Percentage of Cost	CPPC	Actual costs plus profit margin for seller	Cost overruns represent risk to the buyer. This is the most dangerous contract type for the buyer.
Cost Plus Award Fee	CPAF	Actual costs plus an award based on seller-defined objectives for the project	Buyer carries the risk, as the seller is the judge of the contract work and performance.
Cost Plus Incentive Fee	CPIF	Actual costs plus profit margin for seller	Cost overruns represent risk to the buyer.
Fixed-Price	FP	Agreed-upon price for contracted product; can include incentives for the seller	Seller assumes risk.
Fixed-Price with Economic Price Adjustment Contracts	FP-EPA	Agreed-upon price for contracted product; can include cost adjustments based on predefined categories of cost	Seller assumes risk.
Firm Fixed-Price	FFP	Agreed-upon price for contracted product	Seller assumes risk.
Fixed-Price Incentive Fee	FPIF	Agreed-upon price for contracted product; can include incentives for the seller	Seller assumes risk.
Time and Materials	T&M	Price assigned for the time and materials provided by the seller	Contracts without "not-to-exceed" clauses can lead to cost overruns.
Unit Price		Price assigned for a measurable unit of product or time (for example, $130/hr for engineer's time on the project)	Risk varies with the product. Time represents the biggest risk if the amount needed is not specified in the contract.

Stakeholder Engagement Facts

You must manage and engage the project stakeholders to create buy-in and ownership of the project—and this keeps the project moving forward. Stakeholder management means that you, the project manager, communicate with the project stakeholders, but you also work to keep them involved and informed of the project work.

Here are some facts you'll need to know about stakeholder management for your PMP exam:

- Stakeholder identification and documentation should happen as early as possible in the project. This process is part of project initiation.

- You'll need a stakeholder management plan to define the direction and strategy for engaging the stakeholders. This plan works along with the project's communications management plan.

- Stakeholder engagements mean that you'll work with the stakeholders to maintain their interest and support of the project. You'll address their needs, concerns, perceived threats, and even their pet requirements. The goal is to maintain stakeholder buy-in of the project.

- Everything in a project is iterative, including the planning and controlling of stakeholder engagement. If a stakeholder management strategy isn't working, revisit planning and find a new way to communicate and engage the project stakeholders.

- Stakeholders aren't just the recipients of the project work. You must also work to engage the project team, vendors, and stakeholders that have little interest or influence over your project. Yes, you'll prioritize based on power and influence, but don't forget to keep all of the stakeholders engaged.

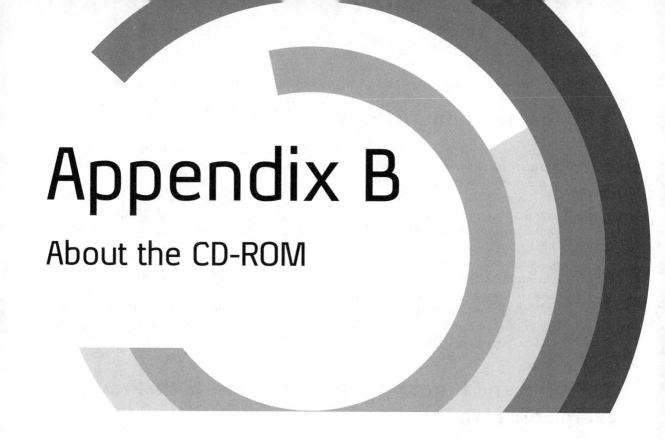

Appendix B

About the CD-ROM

The CD-ROM included with this book comes complete with Total Tester customizable practice exam software, including hundreds of PMP practice exam questions and a process review quiz; video training from the author; worksheets for Time Value of Money, Earned Value, and a Float Exercise; as well as a PDF copy of the book for studying on the go.

System Requirements

The software requires Windows Vista or later and 30MB of hard disk space for full installation, in addition to a current or prior major release of Chrome, Firefox, Internet Explorer, or Safari. To run, the screen resolution must be set to 1024×768 or higher. The PDF files require Adobe Acrobat, Adobe Reader, or Adobe Digital Editions to view.

Total Tester Premium Practice Exam Software

Total Tester provides you with a simulation of the live exam. You can also create custom exams from selected certification objectives or chapters. You can further customize the number of questions and time allowed.

The exams can be taken in either Practice Mode or Exam Mode. Practice Mode provides an assistance window with hints, references to the book, explanations of the correct and incorrect answers, and the option to check your answer as you take the test. Exam Mode provides a simulation of the actual exam. The number of questions, the types of questions, and the time allowed are intended to be an accurate representation of the exam environment. Both Practice Mode and Exam Mode provide an overall grade and a grade broken down by certification objectives.

To take a test, launch the program and select the exam suite from the Installed Question Packs list. You can then select Practice Mode, Exam Mode, or Custom Mode. After making your selection, click Start Exam to begin.

Installing and Running Total Tester Premium Practice Exam Software

From the main screen, you may install the Total Tester by clicking the Total Tester Practice Exams button. This will begin the installation process and place an icon on your desktop and in your Start menu. To run Total Tester, navigate to Start | (All) Programs | Total Seminars, or double-click the icon on your desktop.

To uninstall the Total Tester software, go to Start | Settings | Control Panel | Programs And Features (Vista/7/8), and then select the Total Tester program. Select Remove and Windows will completely uninstall the software.

Note: If you do not have a CD-ROM drive you may download the Total Tester by simply clicking the link below:

http://www.totalsem.com/125986197Xd

Also, to access the other downloads available on the CD-ROM, visit McGraw-Hill Professional's Media Center by clicking the link below and entering the 13-digit ISBN 978-1-259-86197-0 **and your e-mail address. You will then receive an e-mail message with a download link for the additional content.**

https://www.mhprofessionalresources.com/mediacenter/

Video Training from the Author

Video MP4 clips provide detailed examples of key certification topics in audio-video format direct from the author of the book. You can access the videos directly from the Video table of contents by clicking the Videos link on the main page.

Secure PDF Copy of the Book

The entire contents of the print book are provided as a PDF on the CD-ROM. This file is viewable on your computer and many portable devices.

- **To view the PDF on a computer**   Adobe Acrobat, Adobe Reader, or Adobe Digital Editions is required. A link to Adobe's web site, where you can download and install Adobe Reader, has been included on the CD-ROM.

  Note: For more information on Adobe Reader and to check for the most recent version of the software, visit Adobe's web site at www.adobe.com and search for the free Adobe Reader or look for Adobe Reader on the product page. Adobe Digital Editions can also be downloaded from the Adobe web site.

- **To view the PDF on a portable device**   Copy the PDF file to your computer from the CD-ROM, and then copy the file to your portable device using a USB or other connection. Adobe offers a mobile version of Adobe Reader, the Adobe Reader mobile app, which currently supports iOS and Android. For customers using Adobe Digital Editions and an iPad, you may have to download and install a separate reader program on your device. The Adobe web site has a list of recommended applications, and McGraw-Hill Education recommends the Bluefire Reader.

Technical Support

Technical Support information is provided as follows, by feature.

Total Seminars Technical Support

For questions regarding the Total Tester software or operation of the CD-ROM, visit **www.totalsem.com** or e-mail **support@totalsem.com**.

McGraw-Hill Education Content Support

For questions regarding the video content, worksheets, or any of the PDF content, e-mail **techsolutions@mhedu.com** or visit **http://mhp.softwareassist.com**.

For questions regarding book content, e-mail **hep_customer-service@mheducation.com**.

For customers outside the United States, e-mail **international_cs@mheducation.com**.

Glossary

360-degree appraisal   A performance review completed by a person's peers, managers, and subordinates. It's called a 360-degree appraisal because it's a circle of reviews by people at different levels of an organization.

acceptance   A response to a risk event, generally made when the probability of the event and/or its impact is small. It is used when mitigation, transference, and avoidance are not selected.

active listening   Occurs when the receiver confirms the message is being received by feedback, questions, prompts for clarity, and other signs of having received the message. The message receiver paraphrases what's been said to fully understand and confirm the message, providing an opportunity for the sender to clarify the message if needed.

active problem-solving   Active problem-solving begins with problem definition. Problem definition is the ability to discern between the cause and effect of the problem. Root-cause analysis looks beyond the immediate symptoms to the cause of the symptoms, which then affords opportunities for solutions.

activity attributes Activities that have special conditions, requirements, risks, and other conditions should be documented. Activity attributes include information on duration, effort, successors and predecessors, and resources.

activity list A listing of all the project activities required to complete each project phase or the entire project.

activity-on-node (AON) A network diagramming approach that places the activities on a node in the project network diagram.

activity sequencing The process of mapping the project activities in the order in which the work should be completed.

actual costs (AC) The amount of funds the project has spent to date. The difference between actual costs and the earned value will reveal the cost variance.

adaptive life cycle Life cycles can be either iterative or incremental. Change is highly probable, and the project team will be working closely with the project stakeholders. You might also know this approach as *agile* or *change-driven*.

adjourning The final stage of team development; once the project is done, the team moves on to other assignments as a unit, or the project team is disbanded and individual team members go on to other work.

affinity diagram A diagram that clusters similar ideas together and allows for decomposition of ideas to compare and contrast project requirements.

alternative analysis Data analysis technique used to consider the corrective and preventive actions to take in the project. You are analyzing the different options available.

ambiguity risks These risks are impossible to predict accurately—for example, certainty of a new technical solution, future laws or regulations, even complexity in the project approach.

analogous estimating A form of estimating that relies on historical information to predict estimates for current projects. Analogous estimating is also known as *top-down estimating* and is a form of expert judgment.

application areas The areas of discipline that a project may center upon. Consider technology, law, sales, marketing, and construction, among many others.

appraisal costs   The costs of measuring, testing, auditing, and evaluating the project's product to confirm that quality has been achieved in the work results.

assumption log   A document that clearly identifies and tracks assumptions that are made in the project. All assumptions need to be tested for their validity, and the outcome of the test should be recorded.

autocratic   The project manager, sponsor, or other authority makes all of the project decisions.

avoidance   One response to a risk event. The risk is avoided by removing the risk from the project.

avoiding power   The project manager or other decision-maker refuses to act, get involved, or make decisions.

basis of estimates   Explanation of how the activity duration and cost estimates were created.

benchmarking   The process of using prior projects internal or external to the performing organization to compare and set quality standards for processes and results.

benefit/cost analysis   The process of determining the pros and cons of any project, process, product, or activity.

benefit/cost ratio (BCR)   Shows the proportion of benefits to costs; for example, 4:1 would equate to four benefits to one cost.

benefit measurement methods   Project selection methods that compare the benefits of projects to determine into which project the organization should invest its funds.

benefits management   The management and control of when the benefits of the project will become available. Some projects have benefits only once the project is complete; other projects will have intermittent benefits for the organization.

bid   A document presented by the seller to the buyer. Used when price is the determining factor in the decision-making process.

bidder conference   A meeting with a group of prospective sellers and buyer representatives that ensures that all sellers have a clear understanding of the product or service to be procured. Bidder conferences enable sellers to query the buyer on the details of the project and product to help ensure that the proposal a seller creates is adequate and appropriate for the proposed agreement.

bottom-up estimating   A technique by which an estimate for each component in the WBS is developed and then totaled for an overall project budget. This is the most time-consuming method to complete, but it provides the most accurate estimate.

brainstorming   A process performed by a project team to identify the risks within the project. A multidisciplinary team, hosted by a project facilitator, can also perform brainstorming. It is the most common approach to many processes within a project, such as estimating costs and predicting duration.

bubble chart   A hierarchical chart that uses three parameters for mapping the axes of the risks and the magnitude of the third parameter. The larger the bubble, the more significant the parameter.

budget at completion (BAC)   The predicted budget for the project; what the project should cost when it is completed. Budget at completion represents 100 percent of the planned value for the project's completion.

burndown chart   A graph that tracks the project's completeness, including scope changes, in a downward curve against the project timeline.

burnup chart   A graph that tracks the project's completeness in an upward curve against the project timeline.

business analyst   Organizational role that is responsible for eliciting requirements from stakeholders and analyzing the requirements to predict feasibility, likelihood of project success, and estimated time and costs to create the requirements.

business requirements   Why the project has been initiated and what the high-level expectations are for the project deliverables and performance. As the project scope is developed, more detailed business requirements may emerge.

business value   The total value of the tangible and intangible elements of an organization. Consider liquid assets, real estate, equipment, reputation, brand recognition, and trademarks.

causal analysis The analysis of why a problem exists to develop an understanding of why the problem is happening. Root-cause analysis defines the problem, or the effect you're trying to resolve, and then identifies all of the causal factors that may be independently or collaboratively contributing to the defect.

cause-and-effect diagrams Used for root-cause analysis to determine what factors are creating problems within a project. The goal is to identify and treat the root of the problem, not the symptom.

centralized contracting All contracts for all projects need to be approved through a central contracting unit within the performing organization.

change control board (CCB) A group of decision-makers that reviews proposed project changes.

change control system (CCS) A predefined set of activities, forms, and procedures that establishes how project change requests may proceed.

change log As changes to any part of the project emerge during the project, they should be recorded in the change log for future reference.

charismatic leadership The leader is motivating, has high-energy, and inspires the team through strong convictions about what's possible and what the team can achieve. Positive thinking and a can-do mentality are characteristics of a charismatic leader.

chart of accounts A coding system used by the performing organization's accounting system to account for the project work.

checklist A listing of activities that workers check to ensure that the work has been completed consistently; used in quality control.

checksheet Also called a *tally sheet*. Used to count errors and defects in different categories of failure in the project, but can be used with any checklist, even those not related to defects.

Code of Ethics and Professional Conduct The PMI code that addresses the values project managers should possess, including responsibility, respect, fairness, and honesty.

coercive power The project manager or other person with authority in the organization uses fear and threats to manage the project team.

collective bargaining agreements   Contractual agreements initiated by employee groups, unions, or other labor organizations; they may act as a constraint on the project.

commercial risks   When working with vendors, new risks are introduced to the project specific to the contractual relationship. Risk categories can include the contract terms, internal procurement procedures, suppliers, subcontracts, client and customer stability, and any partnerships or joint ventures.

communication management plan   A plan that documents and organizes the stakeholder needs for communication. This plan covers the communications system, its documentation, the flow of communication, modalities of communication, schedules for communications, information retrieval, and any other stakeholder requirements for communications.

communications formula   The formula $N(N-1)/2$ shows the number of communication channels in a project. N represents the total number of stakeholders.

composite structure   An organizational structure that uses a blend of the functional, matrix, and project-oriented structures to operate and manage projects.

compromising   A conflict resolution approach that requires both parties to give up something. The ultimate decision is a blend of both sides of the argument. Because neither party completely wins, it occasionally results in a lose-lose solution.

confidentiality   A project manager should keep certain aspects of a project confidential, such as contract negotiations, human resource issues, and trade secrets of the organization.

configuration management   The control and documentation of the project's product features and functions.

conflict of interest   A situation in which the project manager could influence a decision for personal gain. This is a core item in the PMI Code of Ethics and Professional Conduct that all PMI members and PMI certificate holders and candidates must adhere to.

constraints   Anything that limits the project manager's options: time, cost, and scope are always project constraints.

context diagram   A diagram that illustrates all of the components, called "actors," that interact with a project's solutions, such as systems, software, hardware, and people.

contingency reserve   A time or dollar amount allotted as a response to risk events that may occur within a project.

contract   A legal, binding agreement, preferably written, between a buyer and seller detailing the requirements and obligations of both parties. Must include an offer, an acceptance, and a consideration.

contract administration   The process of ensuring that the buyer and the seller both perform to the specifications within the contract.

contract change control system   Defines the procedures for how contracts may be changed. Includes the paperwork, tracking, conditions, dispute resolution procedures, and procedures for getting the changes approved within the performing organization.

contract closeout   A confirmation that the obligations of the contract were met as expected. The project manager, the customer, the key stakeholders, and, in some instances, the seller complete the product verification together to confirm the contract has been completed.

contract file   A complete indexed set of records of the procurement process incorporated into the administrative closure process. These records include financial information as well as information on the performance and acceptance of the procured work. This is also known as the *procurement file* and it becomes part of organizational process assets.

control chart   Illustrates the performance of a project over time. It maps the results of inspections against a chart. Control charts are typically used in projects or operations that have repetitive activities, such as manufacturing, testing series, or help desk functions. Chart trending and upper and lower control and specification limits indicate whether values are in control or out of control.

controlling PMO   Defines project governance through project management frameworks, templates, forms, project management activities, and communications. The project management office (PMO) control is considered moderate.

corrective actions   Actions taken to correct problems and to ensure that the project work is in alignment with plans.

cost baseline   Usually shown in an S-curve, the cost baseline indicates what the project is expected to spend. It enables the project manager and management to predict when the project will be spending monies and over what duration. The purpose of the cost baseline is to measure and predict project performance.

cost–benefits analysis   Data analysis technique used to examine of the cost of the proposed corrective actions you may take and the consideration of the benefits these actions may bring to the project.

cost budgeting   A process of assigning a cost to individual work packages. This process shows costs over time. The cost budget results in an S-curve that becomes the cost baseline for the project.

cost change control   This is part of the integrated change control system and documents the procedures to request, approve, and incorporate changes to project costs.

cost control   An active process to control causes of cost change, to document cost changes, and to monitor cost fluctuations within the project. When changes occur, the cost baseline must be updated.

cost estimating   The process of calculating the costs, by category, of the identified resources to complete the project work.

cost management plan   A subsidiary plan of the overall project management plan that defines how costs will be estimated, budgeted, and controlled. The plan may be based on a range of acceptable variances and the expected response to variances over a given threshold.

cost performance index (CPI)   The process of calculating the costs, by category, of the identified resources to complete the project work.

cost plus award fee contract   A contract that requires the buyer to pay for all the project costs and give the seller an award fee based on the project performance, meeting certain project criteria, or meeting other goals established by the buyer. The award fee can be tied to any factor the buyer determines, and the factor doesn't have to be exact.

cost-reimbursable contracts   A contract that pays the seller for the product. In the payment to the seller is a profit margin of the difference between the actual costs of the product and the sales amount.

cost variance (CV)   The difference between the earned value and the actual costs.

crashing   A duration-compression technique that adds project resources to the project in an effort to reduce the amount of time allotted for effort-driven activities.

critical path method (CPM) A network diagramming approach that identifies the project activities that cannot be delayed or the project completion date will be late.

cultural norm The accepted practices, culture, ideas, vision, and nature of an organization.

culture shock The initial disorientation a person experiences when in a foreign environment.

decision tree analysis A type of analysis that determines which of two decisions is the best. The decision tree assists in calculating the value of the decision and determining which decision costs the least.

decoder Part of the communications model; it is the inverse of the encoder. If a message is encoded, a decoder translates it back to usable format.

decomposition The process of breaking down the major project deliverables into smaller, manageable components. The smallest item of the project's decomposition into the WBS is the work package.

dedicated project team A project team that works full time on the project for the duration of the project.

defect repair Actions taken to fix defects within the project. Defect repair will also require validation that the defects were corrected properly.

deliverable A thing that a project creates; projects generally create many deliverables as part of the project work.

Delphi Technique A method to query experts anonymously on foreseeable risks within the project, phase, or component of the project. The results of the survey are analyzed and organized, and then circulated to the experts. There can be several rounds of anonymous discussions with the Delphi Technique. The goal is to gain consensus on project risks, and the anonymous nature of the process ensures that no one expert's advice overtly influences the opinions of other participants.

Design for X (DfX) A philosophy in product design where the X can mean, excellence, or, more often, a specific characteristic of a solution. The X is usually a variable that the project is trying to address, such as cost, uptime, return on investment, or another facet the organization is pursuing.

design of experiments approach   Relies on statistical "what-if" scenarios to determine which variables within a project will result in the best outcome; can also be used to eliminate a defect. This approach is most often used on the product of the project, rather than on the project itself.

development life cycle   Defines how the project will happen. The life cycle is typically a predictive or adaptive life cycle, depending on the project and the enterprise environmental factors.

direct costs   Costs incurred by the project in order for it to exist. Examples include equipment needed to complete the project work, salaries of the project team, and other expenses tied directly to the project's existence.

directive PMO   A project management office that manages and controls all projects within the organization. The PMO control is considered high.

discretionary dependencies   Project activities do not have to be completed in a particular order; instead, these tasks can be completed in the order determined by the project manager or at the project manager's or project team's discretion.

duration estimates   The prediction of how long the project activities will take to complete in work units.

earned value   The value of the work that has been completed and the budget for that work: EV = % Complete × BAC.

earned value management (EVM)   Integrates scope, schedule, and cost to provide an objective, scalable, point-in-time assessment of the project. EVM calculates the performance of the project and compares current performance against the plan. EVM can also be a harbinger of things to come. Results early in the project can predict the likelihood of the project's success or failure.

emotional intelligence   A person's awareness of their inbound and outbound emotions; by becoming emotionally intelligent, the person can better control their emotions and understand the emotions of others.

encoder   Part of the communications model; the device or technology that packages the message to travel over the medium.

enhance To attempt to modify the probability of a risk and/or its impacts to realize the most gains from it.

enterprise environmental factors Elements that create the boundaries for the project manager. These may help or hinder the project manager's ability to navigate within the project. Examples include rules, regulations, industry standards, and organizational procedures the project manager is obliged to follow.

escalate risk response Some risks that are outside of the boundary of the project should be escalated when the project team, project sponsor, or project manager believes the risk management would exceed the authority the project manager has over the risk event.

estimate at completion (EAC) A hypothesis of what the total cost of the project will be. Before the project begins, the project manager completes an estimate for the project deliverables based on the WBS. As the project progresses, there will likely be some variance between the cost estimate and the actual cost. The EAC is calculated to predict what the new estimate at completion will be.

estimate to complete (ETC) Represents how much more money is needed to complete the project work: ETC = EAC − AC.

estimating publications Typically, a commercial reference to help the project estimator create, confirm, and predict the accuracy of estimates. If a project manager elects to use one of these commercial databases, the estimate should include a pointer to this document for future reference and verification.

ethics The personal, cultural, and organizational interpretation of right and wrong; project managers are to operate ethically and fairly per the PMI Code of Ethics and Professional Conduct.

ethnocentrism Happens when individuals measure and compare a foreigner's actions against their own local culture. Ethnocentric people typically believe their own culture is superior to the foreigner's culture.

evaluation criteria Used to rate and score proposals from sellers. In some instances, such as a bid or quote, the evaluation criterion is focused just on the price the seller offers. In other instances, such as a proposal, the evaluation criteria can be multiple values: experience, references, certifications, and more.

exit criteria   Defines the criteria that must be present for the project to move from one phase to the next.

Expected Monetary Value (Ex$V)   The amount of funds that represents the risk exposure in a quantitative risk analysis risk matrix. It's found by multiplying the risk probability by the dollar amount of the risk impact.

expert power   The project manager has deep skills and experience in a discipline (for example, years of working in IT helps an IT project manager better manage IT projects).

explicit knowledge   Knowledge that can be quickly expressed through documentation, conversations, facts, and figures.

exploit   The organization wants to ensure that the identified positive risk does happen so that the positive impact associated with the risk event is realized.

external enterprise environmental factors   Factors that are outside of the organization's control but that confine the decision for the project manager and the project. For example, laws and regulations are external enterprise environmental factors that directly affect the project manager.

facilitated workshop   A collection of stakeholders from around the organization that come together to analyze, discuss, and determine the project requirements.

failure costs   The cost of completing the project with unacceptable quality, including wasted time for corrective actions, rework, and wasted materials. Failure costs include internal failure costs, which is the cost of corrective actions and defect repair incurred by doing the work twice. External failure costs describe the loss of sales and opportunities, and damage to the organization's reputation due to poor quality.

failure mode and effect analysis (FMEA)   An analytical technique used to identify the severity of something that has failed within the project and the likelihood that the failure will occur again.

fast-tracking   A duration-compression technique that allows activities or entire phases of a project to overlap other phases.

fault tree analysis   Deductive reason to start very broad with the identified fault and then narrow the likely causes into most likely causes.

feedback   Sender confirmation of a message by asking questions, requesting a response, or other confirmation signals.

finish no earlier than (FNET)   A project constraint that requires an activity to finish no earlier than a specific date.

finish-to-finish   A relationship between project activities whereby the predecessor activities must finish before successor activities may finish.

finish-to-start   A relationship between project activities whereby the predecessor activities must finish before the successor activities may start; this is the most common network diagramming relationship type.

fist-to-five voting   A process by which team members vote using their hands. For instance, a team may rate the accuracy of an activity duration estimate by showing their fists, which represent low confidence, or up to five fingers, which shows higher confidence. Votes of three fingers or less are discussed to gain consensus.

fixed costs   Costs that remain the same throughout the project.

fixed-price contracts   Fixed-price contracts are also known as *firm fixed-price* and *lump-sum* contracts. These contracts have a preset price for which the vendor is obligated to perform the work or to provide materials for the agreed-upon price.

fixed-price with economic price adjustment contract   A contract for long-term projects that may span years to complete the project work. The contract does define a fixed price, with caveats for special categories of price fluctuation.

float   A generic term that describes the amount of time an activity may be delayed without delaying any successor activities' start dates.

flowchart   A chart that illustrates how the parts of a system occur in sequence.

focus groups   A meeting for stakeholders to have a conversation about the project goals, concerns, requirements, and other project information.

force majeure   A powerful and unexpected event, such as a hurricane or other disaster.

forcing   A conflict resolution method whereby one person dominates, or forces, his point of view or solution to a conflict. This is also known as *directing*.

forecast   Throughout the project, the project manager will create forecasts about the expected project completion date and projected project costs.

formal power   The project manager has been assigned by senior management to be in charge of the project.

forming   Part of the Tuckman model for team formation. The initial stage of team development, in which the project team members meet and learn about their roles and responsibilities on the project.

fragnet   Repetitive actions within a network diagram that can be reused. It is sometimes a portion of the project that is usually contracted to a vendor to complete, yet the project work is still represented in the project network diagram.

functional managers   The managers of the permanent staff in each organizational department, line of business, or function such as sales, finance, and technology. Project managers and functional managers interact for project decisions that affect functions, projects, and operations.

functional organizations   Entities that have a clear division regarding business units and their associated responsibilities. Project managers in functional organizations have little power and report to the functional managers, and the project team exists within one department. This is an organization that groups staff according to their expertise—for example, sales, marketing, finance, and information technology.

future value   A formula to predict the current amount of funds into a future amount of funds. The formula is Future Value = Present Value $(1 + i)^n$, where i is the interest rate and n is the number of time periods.

Gantt chart   A bar chart against a calendar to show the duration of activities and the sequence of activities in a project.

guilt-based power   The project manager or other person makes the team and stakeholders feel guilty in order to gain compliance in the project.

halo effect   When one attribute of a person influences a decision that is often based solely on the single attribute.

hard logic   The project activities must be completed in a particular order; this is also known as *mandatory dependencies*.

Herzberg's Theory of Motivation   Posits that there are two catalysts for workers: hygiene agents and motivating agents. Hygiene agents do nothing to motivate, but their absence demotivates workers. Hygiene agents are the expectations all workers have: job security, paychecks, clean and safe working conditions, a sense of belonging, civil working relationships, and other basic attributes associated with employment. Motivating agents are components such as reward, recognition, promotion, and other values that encourage individuals to succeed.

histogram   A bar chart, such as a Pareto diagram.

historical information   Any information created in the past that can help the current project succeed.

hybrid life cycle   A combination of predictive and adaptive life cycles. Parts of the project can follow the predictive life cycle, such as project requirements and the budget, yet still utilize the flexibility and iterations that the adaptive life cycle offers.

hybrid organizational structure   The organization utilizes a mix of other project structures to create a project structure for a specific project. For example, an organization could be a weak matrix, but for one high-priority project, it shifts to create a project-centric environment.

inappropriate compensation   An inappropriate compensation, such as a bribe, that the project manager is expected to avoid. The project manager is to act in the best interest of the project and the organization. This is part of PMI's Code of Ethics and Professional Conduct.

incremental life cycle   Creates the final product deliverable through a series of iterations. Each iteration of the project will add more and more functionality. Iterations are a predetermined set amount of time, such as two or four weeks, for example.

indirect costs   Costs that can be shared across multiple projects or operations that use the same resources—such as costs to rent a training room or a piece of equipment.

individual project risk   An individual risk that hinders or helps obtain the project objectives, as opposed to overall project risk.

influence diagram   A diagram that charts out a decision problem by identifying all of the elements, variables, decisions, and objectives, and how each factor may influence others.

informational power   The individual has power and control of the data gathering and distribution of information.

ingratiating power   The project manager aims to gain favor with the project team and stakeholders through flattery.

integrated change control   The analysis of a change's effect on all components of the project. It examines the proposed change and how it may impact scope, schedule, costs, quality, resources, communications, risk, procurement, and stakeholder management.

interactional leadership   The leader is a hybrid of transactional, transformational, and charismatic leaders. The interactional leader wants the team to take action, is excited and inspired about the project work, yet still holds the team accountable for their results.

interactive communications   Communication methods that involve interactions with other stakeholders via meetings, phone calls, and videoconferencing.

internal dependencies   Dependencies that are internal to the project and are often related to the nature of the work that's being completed.

internal enterprise environmental factors   Factors unique to the organization that confine the project decisions.

internal rate of return   A benefit measurement formula to calculate when the present value of the cash inflow equals the project's original investment.

interview   One-on-one discussion used in project integration management as part of the data-gathering technique to create the project charter.

invitation for bid   A document from the buyer to the seller that asks the seller to provide a price for the procured product or service.

Iron Triangle   A term used to describe the three constraints of every project: time, cost, and scope. The sides of the Iron Triangle must be kept in balance or the quality of the project will suffer.

ISO 9000   An international standard that helps organizations follow their own quality procedures. ISO 9000 is not a quality system, but a method of following procedures created by an organization.

issue   Any point of contention or debate, or a decision that has not yet been made in the project that may affect the project's success. Issues are also risk events that have occurred.

issue log   Issues, such as risk events or points of contention, are recorded in the issue log, along with an issue owner designation, an issue date for resolution, and the eventual outcome of the issue. Each issue is assigned an issue owner and an ideal date for resolution, and its status is maintained through the issue log.

iterative life cycle   An approach that requires that the project scope be defined at a high level at the beginning of the project, but the costs and schedules are developed through iterations of planning as the project deliverable is more fully understood. The project moves through iterations of planning and definition based on discoveries during the project execution.

just-in-time (JIT) manufacturing   Material is received and resources are placed on the project as late as possible in the schedule. This approach reduces waste, keeps inventory at a minimum, and helps the project manager forecast resource utilization more accurately.

kaizen   A Japanese business philosophy that suggests that implementing small changes to the organization and project team over time will result in large changes overall. Kaizen posits that small changes in processes are easier to accept and incorporate than large, sweeping changes for the organization or project.

Kanban   A sign board to show work in progress as requirements move through the predefined stages of a project. Most often used in lean and agile environments.

knowledge management   A systematic way of collecting, distributing, and storing useable knowledge in the project.

lag   Time added to a project activity to delay its start time; lag time is considered positive time and is sometimes called *waiting time.*

laissez-faire leadership The leader takes a hands-off approach to the project. This means the project team makes decisions, takes initiative in the actions, and creates goals. Although this approach can provide autonomy, it can make the leader appear absent when it comes to project decisions.

lead The time in which a task can be started earlier than scheduled; lead time is negative time, as it moves the activities closer to the project's start date.

leadership Aligning, motivating, and inspiring the project team members to do the right thing, build trust, think creatively, and challenge the status quo.

leading stakeholders Stakeholders who are aware of your project, want the project to succeed, and are leading the charge to make certain the project outcome is positive.

lessons learned register An ongoing collection of documentation about what has and has not worked in this and other projects; the project manager and the project team participate in lessons learned creation.

letter of intent Expresses the intent of the buyer to procure products or services from the seller. Not equivalent to a contract.

majority decision A group decision process by which a vote is offered and the majority wins.

make-or-buy analysis Used in determining what part of the project scope or where a project's deliverable should be made or purchased.

management A group that utilizes positional power to maintain, administrate, control, and focus on getting things done without challenging the status quo of the project and organization.

managing project knowledge Project management process to manage all knowledge within the project. This includes refining the knowledge, documenting what was learned, making the information available to others, and archiving the documentation to be part of organizational process assets.

mandatory dependencies Project activities must happen in a particular order due to the nature of the work; also known as *hard logic*.

Maslow's Hierarchy of Needs   A theory that states that all humans have five layers of needs: physiological, safety, social, esteem, and the crowning jewel, self-actualization.

matrix structure   An organization that groups staff by function but openly shares resources on project teams throughout the organization. Project managers in a matrix structure share the power with functional management. Three types of matrix structures—weak, balanced, and strong—describe the amount of authority for the project manager.

McClelland's Theory of Needs   A theory that states that all humans have three needs: achievement, affiliation, and power. One of the needs drives a person's actions.

McGregor's Theory of X and Y   A theory that states that "X" people are not motivated to work, don't want to work, and need to be micromanaged. "Y" people are self-led, motivated, and strive to accomplish.

media selection   The process of choosing the right media for a message. The choice is based on the audience and the message being sent.

medium   Part of the communications model; this is the path the message takes from the sender to the receiver. It is the modality in which the communication travels and typically refers to an electronic model, such as e-mail or the telephone.

meeting management   How the meeting is led, managed, and controlled to influence the message being delivered. Agendas, minutes, and order are mandatory for effective communication within a meeting.

milestone chart   Shows when milestones are expected to be reached in the project schedule and when the milestone was actually achieved.

mind mapping   A visual representation of like and opposing ideas, thoughts, and project requirements.

mitigation   Reducing the probability or impact of a risk.

monitor communications   Project management process that ensures that communication happens according to the project's communication management plan.

Monte Carlo analysis   A "what-if" scenario tool to determine how scenarios may work out, given any number of variables. The process doesn't create a specific answer, but a range of possible answers. When Monte Carlo is applied to a schedule, it can present, for example, the optimistic completion date, the pessimistic completion date, and the most likely completion date for each activity in the project.

multicriteria decision analysis tools   Also called *multiple-criteria decision-making tools*, these help the project manager evaluate multiple facets of decision when it comes to quality. The tools can help determine tradeoffs for achieving quality expectations, but also keep the project's costs, schedule, and flow of work all in balance.

multidivisional structure   An organizational structure in which functions are replicated for each division. This structure is similar to the functional organization within each division. The project manager will have little authority and could be called a project coordinator rather than a project manager.

negative float   A project task is running late on its deadline so the schedule is compacted in order to meet the deadline, or, more likely, the task will miss its deadline and will be late.

negative stakeholders   Stakeholders who are opposed to the project's existence; they do not want the project to succeed, because they do not see or agree with the benefits the project may bring about for the organization.

negative total float   When the activities on the critical path don't have enough time to meet the defined late finish date for the project. Experienced when a project is running late on its implementation or if there's a predefined deadline for the project.

net present value (NPV)   A benefit measurement formula that provides a precise measurement of the present value of each year the project generates a return on investment. This could be the project, its deliverables, or its equipment or resources.

network template   A network diagram based on previous similar projects that is adapted for the current project work.

neutral stakeholders   Stakeholders who are not affected by the project's success or failure. Examples include inspectors, procurement officers, and some end users.

nominal group technique   A group creativity technique that follows the brainstorming model but scores each brainstorm idea.

nonverbal   Approximately 55 percent of oral communication involves facial expressions, hand gestures, and body language that contribute to the message.

norming   Part of the Tuckman model for team formation, where project team members go about getting the project work, begin to rely on one another, and generally complete their project assignments.

observation   A requirements elicitation process whereby the observer shadows a person to understand how she completes a process. An observer may be a participant observer or an invisible observer.

oligopoly   A market condition in which the actions of one competitor affect the actions of all the other competitors.

operations   The ongoing work of the business; a generic term used to describe the activities that support the core functions of a business entity.

operations manager   Managers who deal directly with the income-generating products or services the company provides. Projects often affect the core business, so these managers are stakeholders in the project.

organic organization structure   Sometimes called a *simple organization structure,* an organic structure means that the work groups within the organization are flexible. People work alongside one another regardless of their roles in the organization, and the project manager may have little to no authority over the project resources.

organizational breakdown structures   Though these charts are similar to the WBS, the breakdown is by department, unit, or team.

organizational chart   Shows how an organization, such as a company or large project team, is ordered, its reporting structures, and the flow of information.

organizational governance framework   The structure and approach to managing a project within your organization. Governance framework describes how you operate within a system: the cultural norms, relationships, and organizational processes to get things done.

organizational process assets   Resources that have been created to assist the project manager in managing the project better. Examples include historical information, forms, project approaches, defined procedures, and templates.

organizational project management (OPM)   An organizational approach to coordinate, manage, and control projects, programs, and portfolio management in a uniform, consistent effort.

organizational systems   Provide structure and governance for how the project manager leads the project team and manages the work of project management.

organization knowledge repositories   Databases of past project files, historical information, lessons learned, issue and defect databases, financial databases, and other knowledge that can be quickly accessed for the current project.

Ouchi's Theory Z   A theory that posits that workers are motivated by a sense of commitment, opportunity, and advancement. Workers will work if they are challenged and motivated.

overall project risk   A combination of all risk events that will reveal the project's risk exposure and determine just how risky the project is for the organization.

paralingual   The pitch, tone, and inflections in the sender's voice that affect the message being sent.

parametric modeling   Also called *parametric estimating*. A mathematical model based on known parameters to predict the cost of a project. The parameters in the model can vary based on the type of work being done. A parameter can be cost per cubic yard, cost per unit, and so on. Ideal for projects with repetitive work where a parameter, such as five hours per unit, is used to estimate the project duration.

Pareto diagram   A diagram related to Pareto's Law: 80 percent of the problems come from 20 percent of the issues (this is also known as the 80/20 rule). A Pareto diagram illustrates problems by assigned cause, from smallest to largest.

Parkinson's Law   Work expands to fill the amount of time allotted to it.

part-time project team   The project team works on the project for a percentage of their scheduled work time. The project team may work on core operations and other projects in addition to the current project.

payback period   The duration of time it takes a project to earn back the original investment.

performance reports   Formal reports that define how the project is performing with regard to time, cost, scope, quality, and other relevant information.

performing   Part of the Tuckman model for team formation. If a project team can reach the performing stage of team development, they trust one another, they work well together, and issues and problems get resolved quickly and effectively.

personal or charismatic power   The project manager has a warm personality that others like.

persuasive power   Power gained by persuading people to move toward a specific outcome or decision.

PESTLE   A categorization model or the analysis of overall project risks by determining political, economic, social, technological, legal, and environmental uncertainty

planned value   The worth of the work that should be completed by a specific time in the project schedule.

plurality decision   A group decision process approach that allows the biggest section of a group to win even if a majority doesn't exist.

PMBOK Guide   The abbreviated definition for PMI's *A Guide to the Project Management Body of Knowledge.*

PMI Code of Ethics and Professional Conduct   A PMI document that defines the expectations of its members to act responsibly, respectfully, fairly, and honestly in their leadership of projects and programs.

PMI Talent Triangle   Defines three areas of professional development units (PDUs) for PMI certified professionals to maintain their certification. The PMI Talent Triangle includes technical project management, leadership, and strategic and business management.

PMP   Your goal. A PMP is certified by the Project Management Institute as a Project Management Professional.

portfolio   A collection of projects and programs that have been selected by the organization based on factors such as risk, profitability, business value, business need, market demand, and other components.

portfolio management review board A collection of organizational decision-makers, usually executives, who review proposed projects and programs for their value and return on investment for the organization.

positional power The project manager's power is a result of the position she has as the project manager. This is also known as formal, authoritative, and legitimate power.

positive stakeholders Stakeholders who want the project to succeed; these are often the people who have the most to gain from the project's success and/or the most to lose if the project fails.

precedence diagramming method (PDM) The most common method of arranging the project work visually. The PDM puts the activities in boxes, called nodes, and connects the boxes with arrows. The arrows represent the relationship and the dependencies of the work packages.

predictive life cycle The predictive approach requires the project scope, the project schedule, and project costs to be defined early in the project timeline. Predictive life cycles have predefined phases, where each phase completes a specific type of work and usually overlaps other phases in the project.

presentation The delivery of information, usually face-to-face, to a group. In formal presentations, the presenter's oral and body language, visual aids, and handouts all influence the message being delivered.

present value A benefit measurement formula to determine what a future amount of funds is worth today. The formula is Present Value = Future Value / $(1 + i)^n$, where i is the interest rate and n is the number of time periods.

pressure-based power The project manager restricts choices to get the project team to perform the project work.

prevention costs Defines the costs of preventing poor quality in the project. The cost of completing the project work to satisfy the project scope and the expected level of quality. Examples include training, safety measures, and having the correct tools to do the project work.

preventive actions Actions taken to ensure that potential problems don't enter the project and that future project work is in alignment with the project management plan.

prioritization matrix   Evaluates and prioritizes the elements of an issue. Each element is prioritized, weighed, and then plotted in the matrix to achieve a score that will determine the activities the project manager and project team should take.

problem-solving   The ability to determine the best solution for a problem in a quick and efficient manner.

process adjustments   When quality is lacking, process adjustments are needed for immediate corrective actions or for future preventive actions to ensure that quality improves. Process adjustments may qualify for a change request and be funneled through the change control system as part of integration management.

process decision program chart   A chart that helps the project team identify all of the needed steps that are required to achieve the project goal.

procurement   The process of a seller soliciting, selecting, and paying for products or services from a buyer.

procurement audits   The successes and failures within the procurement process are reviewed from procurement planning through contract administration. The intent of the audit is to learn from what worked and what did not work during the procurement processes.

procurement documents   All of the documents for purchasing, such as request for quotes, invitation to bid, request for proposal, and the responses, are included in the project documents.

procurement management plan   A subsidiary project management plan that documents the procurement processes and tools to use. It specifies how the remaining procurement activities will be managed.

product life cycle   The unique life, duration, and support of the thing a project creates. A product life cycle is separate from the project life cycle.

product scope   The attributes and characteristics of the deliverables the project is creating.

professional development units (PDUs)   Training or performance credits that are earned to maintain the PMP certification. PMPs are required to earn 60 PDUs per three-year certification cycle. Of the 60 PDUs, a minimum of 35 hours must come from educational opportunities.

program manager   Coordinates the efforts of multiple projects working together in the program. Programs are made up of projects, so it makes sense that the program manager would be a stakeholder in each of the projects within the program.

programs   A collection of related projects managed in unison to realize benefits that could not be achieved by managing each project independently of the others.

progress reports   Provide current information on the project work completed to date.

progressive elaboration   The process of starting with a large idea and, through incremental analysis, actions, and planning, making the idea more and more specific. Progressive elaboration is the generally accepted planning process for project management, wherein the project management team starts with a broad scope and works toward a specific, detailed plan.

project   A temporary endeavor to create a unique product, service, or result.

project baselines   Three baselines in a project are used to measure project performance: cost, schedule, and scope.

project calendar   A calendar that defines the working times for the project. For example, a project may require the project team to work nights and weekends so as not to disturb the ongoing operations of the organization during working hours. In addition, the project calendar accounts for holidays, working hours, and work shifts the project will cover.

project charter   A document that authorizes the project, defines the high-level requirements, identifies the project manager and the project sponsor, and provides initial information about the project.

project communication management   One of the ten project management knowledge areas, this is the planning and management of communication among project stakeholders.

project cost management   One of the ten project management knowledge areas, this is the estimating, budgeting, and controlling of the project expenses.

project feasibility study   A study that examines a potential project to determine if it is feasible to do the project work.

project funding requirements   In larger projects, this document identifies the timeline of when capital is required for the project to move forward. It defines the amount of funds a project needs and when the project funds are needed in order to reach its objectives.

project governance   Defines the rules for a project; it's up to the project manager to enforce the project governance to ensure the project's ability to reach its objectives. The project management plan defines the project governance and how the project manager, the project team, and the organization will follow the rules and policies within the project.

project integration management   The art and science of ensuring that your project moves forward and that your plan is fully developed and properly implemented. Ten knowledge areas (project integration management, scope, schedule, cost, quality, resources, communications, risk, procurement, and stakeholder management) have processes that contribute to the comprehensive project management plan.

project knowledge management   The project management process of managing all knowledge within the project. This includes refining the knowledge, documenting what was learned, making the information available to others, and archiving the documentation to be part of organizational process assets.

project life cycle   The phases of a project as it moves from its launch to completion. Project life cycles are unique to each project and are not universal.

project management   The management of the projects within an organization. It is the initiation, planning, executing, monitoring and controlling, and closing of the temporary endeavor of the project.

project management information system (PMIS)   Typically a software system, such as Microsoft Project, used to assist the project manager in managing the project.

project management life cycle   Universal to all projects, this life cycle comprises the project management process groups of initiating, planning, executing, monitoring and controlling, and closing. The process groups are not phases, but collections of processes.

project management office (PMO)   A stakeholder of the project that supports the project manager and is responsible for the project's success. PMOs typically provide administrative support, training for project managers, resource management for the project team, project staffing, and centralized communication.

project management plan   A comprehensive document comprising several subsidiary plans that communicates the intent and direction of the project.

project management team   People on the project team who are involved with managing the project.

project manager   The person accountable for managing the project and guiding the team through the project phases to completion.

project-oriented structure   Grouping employees, collocated or not, by activities on a particular project. The project manager in a project-oriented structure may have complete, or very close to complete, power over the project team.

project portfolio management   A management process to select the projects that should be invested in. Specifically, it is the selection process based on the need, profitability, and affordability of the proposed projects.

project procurement management   One of the ten project management knowledge areas; this knowledge area oversees the purchasing and contract administration for a project.

project quality management   One of the ten project management knowledge areas; this knowledge area defines quality assurance, quality control, and the quality policy for the project.

project resource management   One of the ten project management knowledge areas, in which projects are completed by people, and the project manager generally oversees the management of the resources on the project team.

project risk management   One of the ten project management knowledge areas; project risk management defines the risk identification, analysis, responses, and control of risk events.

project schedule management   One of the ten project management knowledge areas; this knowledge area defines the approach to duration estimating, scheduling, and control of the project activities.

project scope management   One of the ten project management knowledge areas; this knowledge area defines the project requirements, scope creation, and control.

project scope statement   The definition of what the project will create for the project stakeholders. It includes the product scope description, product acceptance criteria, project deliverables, project exclusions, project assumptions, and project constraints.

project sponsor   The entity that authorizes the project. This person or group within the performing organization authorizes the project and ensures that the project manager has the necessary resources, including monies, to get the work done. The project sponsor has the power to authorize and sanction the project work and is ultimately accountable for the project's success.

project team   The collection of individuals who will work together to ensure the success of the project. The project manager works with the project team to guide, schedule, and oversee the project work. The project team completes the project work.

proposal   A document that contains ideas, suggestions, recommendations, and solutions to an opportunity provided by a vendor for a seller. Proposals include a price for the work and record how the vendor would provide the service to the buyer.

prototype   A mockup of the project deliverable to confirm, adapt, or develop the project requirements.

pull communications   The information is pulled from a repository, such as a database or web site. Stakeholders pull the information from the source when they want it. In pull communications, the audience retrieves the information as they desire rather than the information being sent, or pushed, to them.

punitive or coercive power   The project manager can punish the project team.

push communications   The sender pushes the same message to people via memos, faxes, press releases, broadcast e-mails, and other forms of group communication.

qualified sellers list   The performing organization may have lists of qualified sellers, preferred sellers, or approved sellers. The qualified sellers list generally includes contact information, history of past experiences with the sellers, and other pertinent information.

qualitative risk analysis   An examination and prioritization of risks that establishes their probability of occurring and the impact on the project if they do occur. Qualitative risk analysis guides the risk reaction process.

quality assurance (QA)   A process to ensure that the project is adhering to the quality expectations of the customer and organization. QA is a prevention-driven process to perform the project work with quality to avoid errors, waste, and delays.

quality control (QC)   A function in which the work results are monitored to see if they meet relevant quality standards. The *PMBOK Guide* refers to this as "control quality."

quality management plan   A document that describes how the project manager and the project team will fulfill the quality policy. In an ISO 9000 environment, the quality management plan is referred to as the "project quality system."

quality policy   The formal policy an organization follows to achieve a preset standard of quality. The project team should either adapt the quality policy of the organization to guide the project implementation or create its own policy if one does not exist within the performing organization.

quality requirements   Any condition, metric, performance objective, or condition the project must meet in order to be considered of quality.

quantitative risk analysis   A numerical assessment of the probability and impact of the identified risks. Quantitative risk analysis also creates an overall risk score for the project.

quote   A document from the seller to the buyer that is used when price is the determining factor in the decision-making process.

RACI chart   A chart that designates each team member against each project activity as Responsible, Accountable, Consult, or Inform (RACI). It is technically a type of responsibility assignment matrix (RAM) chart.

receiver   Part of the communications model: the recipient of the message.

referent power   Power that is present when the project team is attracted to or wants to work on the project or with the project manager. Referent power also exists when the project manager references another, more powerful person, such as the CEO.

regression analysis   A forecasting tool used to measure and predict the link between two variables within a project.

relational power   Power gained by networking, making connections, and creating alliances with others.

reporting system   Often a software program that can capture, store, and provide data analysis regarding the project. A good reporting system tool enables the project manager to gather project information such as percentage of work complete, run the data through some earned value analysis, and then create reports to share with stakeholders.

request for proposal (RFP)   A document from the buyer to the seller that asks the seller to provide a proposal for completing procured work or for providing a procured product.

request for quote (RFQ)   A document from the buyer to the seller asking the seller to provide a price for the procured product or service.

requirements documentation   A clearly defined explanation of the project requirements. The requirements must be measurable, complete, accurate, and approved by the project stakeholders.

requirements management plan   Defines how requirements will be managed throughout the phases of the project. This plan also defines how any changes to the requirements will be allowed, documented, and tracked through project execution.

requirements traceability matrix (RTM)   A table that identifies all the project requirements, when the requirements are due, when the requirements are created, and any other pertinent information about the requirements.

reserve analysis   A contingency reserve for risk events should be periodically reviewed to ensure that the amount of funds in the contingency reserve is adequate for the remaining risks and their probabilities in the project.

residual risks   Risks that remain after mitigation, transference, and avoidance. These are generally accepted risks. Management may elect to add contingency costs and time to account for the residual risks within the project.

resistant stakeholders   Stakeholders who are aware of your project, but they aren't keen on the changes your project will create.

resource breakdown structure (RBS)　A type of chart that breaks down the project by types of resources utilized on the project no matter where the resources are being used in the project.

resource calendar　Shows when resources, such as project team members, consultants, and subject matter experts (SMEs), are available to work on the project. It considers vacations, other commitments within the organization, restrictions on contracted work, overtime issues, and so on.

resource histogram　A bar chart reflecting when physical resources, individual employees, groups, or communities are involved in a project. It's often used by management to see when resources are most or least active in a project.

resource leveling　A method to flatten the schedule when resources are overallocated or allocated unevenly. Resource leveling can be applied in different methods to accomplish different goals. One of the most common methods is to ensure that workers are not overextended on activities.

resource management plan　A subsidiary plan that documents how project team members and physical resources will be included in the project and excused from the project. This plan is included in the project management plan.

resource requirements　A document that identifies what resources are needed to complete the project work. This includes people, materials, equipment, facilities, and services.

resource smoothing　A technique that enables the project manager to do resource leveling, but only on noncritical path activities. This approach levels resource utilization by taking advantage of activities that have available float. For those activities with no float, the resource utilization will not be edited.

resources plan　Details on how the project team members and other physical resources will be brought onto and released from the project.

reverse shadowing　An expert follows someone learning to perform a skill to offer coaching or feedback at the end of the session. This is a type of work shadowing.

responsibility　The person who decides what will happen in a project regarding a particular area.

responsibility assignment matrix chart   A chart type designating the roles and responsibilities of the project team.

reward power   The project manager's authority to reward the project team.

risk   An uncertain event that can have a positive or negative influence on the project's success. It can affect any aspect of a project. All risks and their statuses should be recorded in the risk register.

risk breakdown structure   A visual decomposition of the project risks. This structure helps to visualize where the risks are within the different portions of the project.

risk management plan   A subsidiary project management plan for determining how risks will be identified, how quantitative and qualitative analyses will be completed, how risk response planning will happen, how risks will be monitored, and how ongoing risk management activities will occur throughout the project life cycle.

risk owners   The individuals or groups responsible for a risk response.

risk register   All risks, regardless of their probability or impact, are recorded in the risk register, and their status is kept current in the issue log.

risk report   A report that explains the overall project risks and provides a summary about each individual project risk. You'll update the risk report through the project as more information becomes available through analysis and experience in the project.

role   Designates the type of activities a person on the project team performs in a project.

roles and responsibilities   Maps project roles to responsibilities within the project; roles are positions on the project team, and responsibilities are project activities.

run chart   Similar to a control chart, a run chart tracks trends over time and displays those trends in a graph with the plotted data mapped to a specific date.

Sapir–Whorf hypothesis   A theory that suggest a link exists between the language a person speaks or the culture they operate within that affects how the person thinks.

scales of probability and impact   Used in a risk matrix in both qualitative and quantitative risk analyses to score each risk's probability and impact.

scatter diagram   Tracks the relationship between two or more variables to determine whether one variable affects the other. It enables the project team, quality control team, or project manager to make adjustments to improve the overall results of the project.

schedule change control   Part of integrated change management, schedule change control is concerned with three things: the project manager confirms that any schedule changes are agreed upon, the project manager examines the work results and conditions to know if the schedule has changed, and the project manager manages the actual change in the schedule.

schedule management plan   A subsidiary plan of the project management plan, used to control changes to the schedule. A formal schedule management plan has procedures that control how changes to the project plan can be proposed, accounted for, and then implemented.

schedule performance index (SPI)   This reveals the efficiency of work. The closer the quotient is to 1, the better: $SPI = EV / PV$.

schedule variance (SV)   The difference between the earned value and the planned value.

scope baseline   Comprises the project scope statement, the work breakdown structure (WBS), and the WBS dictionary.

scope management plan   Explains how the project scope will be identified and managed and how scope changes will be factored into the project plan. Based on the conditions of the project, the project work, and the confidence of the project scope, the scope management plan should also define the likelihood of changes to the scope, how often the scope may change, and how much the scope can change.

scope validation   An inspection-driven process led by the project customer to determine the exactness of the project deliverables. Scope validation is a process that leads to customer acceptance of the project deliverables.

scoring model   A project selection method that assigns categories and corresponding values to measure a project's worthiness of investment.

secondary risks   Risks that stem from risk responses. For example, the response of transference may call for hiring a third party to manage an identified risk. A secondary risk caused by the solution is the failure of the third party to complete its assignment as scheduled. Secondary risks must be identified, analyzed, and planned for, just like any other identified risk.

sellers list   A list of the vendors with which an organization does business. Also called *preferred vendors list*.

sender   Part of the communications model: the person or group delivering the message to the receiver.

sender-receiver model   Communication requires a sender and a receiver. Within this model may be multiple avenues to complete the flow of communication, but barriers to effective communication may be present as well.

sensitivity analysis   Examines each project's risk on its own merit to assess the impact on the project. All other risks in the project are set at a baseline value.

servant leadership   The leader puts others first and focuses on the needs of the people he serves. Servant leaders provide opportunity for growth, education, autonomy within the project, and the well-being of others. The primary focus of servant leadership is service to others.

share   Sharing is nice. When sharing, the risk ownership is transferred to the organization that can most capitalize on the risk opportunity.

should-cost estimates   Estimates created by the performing organization to predict what the cost of the procured product should be. If there is a significant difference between what the organization has predicted and what the sellers have proposed, the statement of work (SOW) was inadequate, the sellers have misunderstood the requirements, or the price is too high.

simulation   A tool that enables the project team to play "what-if" games without affecting any areas of production.

single source   A specific seller that the performing organization prefers to contract with.

situational power   The project manager has power because of certain situations in the organization.

smoothing   A conflict resolution method that smooths out the conflict by minimizing the perceived size of the problem. It is a temporary solution, but it can calm team relations and reduce boisterousness of discussions. Smoothing may be acceptable when time is of the essence or when any of the proposed solutions would work.

soft logic   The preferred order of activities. Project managers should use these relationships at their discretion and document the logic behind making soft logic decisions. Also known as *discretionary dependencies*. Discretionary dependencies allow activities to happen in a preferred order because of best practices, conditions unique to the project work, or external events.

sole source   The only qualified seller that exists in the marketplace.

source selection criteria   A predefined listing of the criteria to determine how a vendor will be selected—for example, cost, experience, certifications, and the like.

sprint   Time-boxed duration, typically two-to-four weeks, of project execution in an agile environment. Sprints are iterations of executing the prioritized list of product backlog requirements.

stage gates   Project phase completions that allow a project to continue after a performance and deliverable review against a set of predefined metrics. If the deliverables of the phase, or stage, meet the predefined metrics, the project is allowed to continue.

stakeholder analysis   A process that considers and ranks project stakeholders based on their influence, interests, and project expectations. This process uses a systematic approach to identify all of the project stakeholders, ranking the stakeholders by varying factors, and then addressing stakeholders' needs, requirements, and expectations.

stakeholder classification models   Grids that rank stakeholders' influence in relation to their interest in the project. Several types of these models are used in stakeholder analysis. The most common models are the power/interest grid, the power/influence grid, the influence/impact grid, and the salience model.

stakeholder cube   A three-dimensional cube model that combines the power, influence, and impact grids.

stakeholder engagement   The process of keeping stakeholders interested, involved, and supportive of the project. The project manager needs to maintain the energy of the stakeholders and keep them contributing to and excited about the project.

stakeholder identification　The process of ensuring that all the stakeholders have been identified as early as possible in the project. All the stakeholders are identified and represented, and their needs, expectations, and concerns are addressed.

stakeholder management　A project management knowledge area that focuses on four activities: identifying the project stakeholders, planning on how to manage the stakeholders, managing the stakeholders, and controlling the stakeholders' engagement.

stakeholder management plan　A plan that helps the project manager and the project team define a strategy for managing the project stakeholders. It helps to establish stakeholder engagement at the launch of the project and throughout the project life cycle, and it offers information about how to improve the level of engagement identified.

stakeholder management planning　The process of creating a strategy to identify and monitor the stakeholders in the project. It's the analysis of what the stakeholders want the project to do, how the stakeholders' expectations align with those of other stakeholders, and the prioritization of the stakeholders within the project.

stakeholder register　A register that documents all the stakeholders' information, positions, concerns, interests, and attitudes toward the project. The stakeholder register should be updated as new stakeholders are identified or as stakeholders leave the project.

stakeholder requirements　The individual stakeholder and stakeholder group requirements for the project.

start no earlier than (SNET)　A project constraint that demands that a project activity start no earlier than a specific date.

start-to-finish　A relationship structure that requires an activity to start so that a successor activity may finish; it is unusual and is rarely used.

start-to-start　A relationship structure that requires a task to start before a successor task activity may start. This relationship allows both activities to happen in tandem.

statement of work (SOW)　Fully describes the work to be completed, the product to be supplied, or both. The SOW becomes part of the contract between the buyer and the seller. It is typically created as part of the procurement planning process and is used by the seller to determine whether they can meet the project's requirements. This is also known as *terms of reference (TOR)*.

statistical sampling   A process of choosing a percentage of results at random for inspection. Statistical sampling can reduce the costs of inspection.

status reports   Provide current information on the project cost, budget, scope, and other relevant information.

storming   The second stage of the Tuckman team development; the project team struggles for project positions, leadership, and project direction.

storytelling   Tacit knowledge sharing approach; by telling stories, team members can better understand tacit knowledge and interact with one another.

style   The tone, structure, and formality of a message being sent should be in alignment with the audience and the content of the message.

subprojects   Projects that exist under a parent project, but that follow their own schedules to completion. Subprojects may be outsourced, assigned to other project managers, or managed by the parent project manager but with a different project team.

supporting detail for estimates   The project manager should document how time and cost estimates were created.

supportive PMO   A project management office that acts as a consultative role by offering advice, best practices, lessons learned, forms and software, and project information from similar projects. The PMO control is low.

supportive stakeholders   Stakeholders who are aware of your project, are happy about the project, and hope your project is successful.

SWOT   An analysis, problem-solving, and risk identification approach that aims to identify Strengths, Weaknesses, Opportunities, and Threats.

system or process flowcharts   Show the sequential relationship between components and how the overall process works. They are useful for identifying risks between system components.

systems engineering   Focuses on satisfying the customers' needs, cost requirements, and quality demands through the design and creation of the product. An entire science is devoted to systems engineering in various industries.

tacit knowledge   Knowledge that's more difficult to express because it's personal beliefs, values, knowledge gained from experience, and "know-how" when doing a task.

TECOP   Analysis of overall project risks by determining technical, environmental, commercial, operational, and political uncertainty

theory of constraints   A theory that posits that a management system is limited by its weakest components, the constraint. Adapts the phrase "a chain is only as strong as its weakest link."

The Standard for Project Management   A foundational publication, included in the *PMBOK Guide*, sixth edition, that describes, not prescribes, the most common best practices of project management.

three-point estimate   An estimate that uses optimistic, most likely, and pessimistic values to determine the cost or duration of a project component. Also called *triangular distribution*.

to-complete performance index   An earned value management (EVM) formula that can forecast the likelihood of a project to achieve its goals based on what's currently happening in the project.

top-down estimating   A technique that bases the current project's estimate on the total of a similar project. A percentage of the similar project's total cost may be added to or subtracted from the total, depending on the size of the current project.

transactional leadership   The leader emphasizes the goals of the project and offers rewards and disincentives for the project team. This is sometimes called *management by exception* because it's the exception that is rewarded or punished.

transference   A response to a risk in which the responsibility and ownership of the risk are transferred to another party (for example, through insurance).

transformational leadership   The leader inspires and motivates the project team to achieve the project goals. Transformational leaders aim to empower the project team to take action, be innovative in the project work, and accomplish through ambition.

transition requirements   Describe the needed elements to move from the current state to the desired future state.

tree diagram   Any diagram that represents a tree in a parent–child relationship. The work breakdown structure (WBS) is an example of a tree diagram, as are a risk breakdown structure (RBS) and an organizational chart.

trend analysis   Examines recurring problems, threats, and even opportunities so you can react to the situation based on the trends you've identified.

triggers   Warning signs or symptoms that a risk has occurred or is about to occur (for example, a vendor failing to complete their portion of the project as scheduled).

Triple Constraints of Project Management   Describes the required balance of time, cost, and scope constraints for a project. The Triple Constraints of Project Management is also defined by the Iron Triangle of Project Management.

unanimity decision   A group decision process whereby all participants are in agreement.

unaware stakeholders   Stakeholders who don't know about the project and the effect the project may have on them.

user stories   A backlog of prioritized requirements. User stories are prioritized by value with the product owner and project team in an agile environment. User stories are assigned story points to predict the difficulty of creating the requirement. Only so many story points are allowed per iteration.

utility function   A person's willingness to accept risk. The higher the utility function, the more likely the person or organization is willing to accept risk.

value analysis   Like value engineering, this focuses on the cost/quality ratio of the product. Value analysis focuses on the expected quality against the acceptable cost.

value engineering   Deals with reducing costs and increasing profits, all while improving quality. Its focus is on solving problems, realizing opportunities, and maintaining quality improvement.

variability risks   Uncertainty surrounding a project activity or decision. Fluctuations in productivity, number or errors and defects, or even the weather affecting the project are all examples of variability risks.

variable costs   Costs that vary, depending on the conditions within the project.

variance at completion (VAC)   The time or cost difference between what was planned and what was actually experienced.

virtual organizational structure   The organization uses a network structure with points of contact for each group represented in the project. The project manager may have low to moderate authority over the project resources and may share authority over the project budget with the functional manager.

virtual teams   Project teams that are not collocated and that may rarely, if ever, meet face-to-face with other project team members. The virtual team relies on e-mail, video, and teleconferences to communicate on the project.

voice of the customer (VOC)   The initial collection of customer requirements that serves as part of quality function deployment in a facilitated workshop.

Vroom's Expectancy Theory   People will behave based on what they expect because of their behavior. In other words, people will work in relation to the expected reward of the work.

VUCA   Analysis of overall project risks by determining volatility, uncertainty, complexity, and ambiguity.

war room   A centralized office or locale for the project manager and the project team to work on the project. It can house information on the project, including documentation and support materials. It allows the project team to work in close proximity.

withdrawal   A conflict resolution method that is used when the issue is not important or the project manager is outranked. The project manager pushes the issue aside for later resolution. It can also be used as a method for cooling down. The conflict is not resolved, and it is considered a yield-lose solution.

workarounds   Responses to an issue or mitigation for a risk that are reduce their impact.
work breakdown structure (WBS)   A decomposition of the project scope statement into work packages.

work breakdown structure dictionary   A companion to the WBS, the WBS dictionary defines all of the characteristics of each element of the WBS.

work breakdown structure template   Based on historical information, this is a WBS from a past project that has been adapted to the current project.

work performance data   Raw data about the project work. This can be data on activities completed, costs, schedule, and other items measured for analysis.

work performance information   Work performance information is useable information based on the work performance data. Work performance data is analyzed and becomes work performance information.

work performance reports   The communication devices used to share the work performance information with the appropriate stakeholders as defined in the project's communication management plan.

work shadowing   A person follows, or shadows, an expert in their work to learn how to do the job. Reverse shadowing reverses roles.

INDEX

A

AC (actual cost)
    to-complete performance index, 380
    cost performance index, 378
    cost variance, 377
    earned value management, 377
    estimate at completion, 379–380
    measuring project performance, 393
acceptance criteria, product, 243
acceptance, risk
    defined, 588
    exam facts, 757
    overview of, 589
    self test, 611
accommodation, in conflict resolution, 486, 488
accuracy level, schedule management plan, 284
acknowledgement, of communication, 525, 545
acquisition, of project resources, 475–479
active listening
    communicating project information, 105, 135,
        142–143
    communication exam facts, 756
    project manager communication skills, 518
    in successful communications, 525
activities
    building project team by creating, 481
    project management communication about,
        517–518
    tying constraints to individual project, 312
activity attributes
    documenting, 289–290
    estimating activity durations, 299
    estimating activity resources, 474
    project documents and files, 170

    project schedule development, 313
    sequencing activities, 292, 298
activity definition
    activity attributes documentation, 289–290
    activity dependencies, 294–295
    activity list compilation, 288–289
    activity list creation, 286–287
    decomposing project work packages, 287
    finalizing, 290–291
    planning components, 288
    in project schedule management, 285–286
    rolling wave planning, 287–288
    using templates, 287
activity duration estimates
    activity list update for, 303
    analogous estimating, 304
    bottom-up estimates, 306
    calculating float in PND, 315
    calendar considerations, 302–303
    cost estimates using project schedule, 361
    creating project schedule with, 311
    creating resource breakdown structure for, 302
    Delphi technique, 306–307
    evaluating result of, 308–309
    expert judgment for, 303–304
    factoring in reserve time for, 307–308
    fist-to-five approach, 307
    inputs for, 298–300
    inside PMP exam, 309
    overview of, 298
    parametric estimates, 304–305
    project schedule management, 298
    project work considerations, 300–301
    resource availability, 301–302
    self test, 347, 349
    three-point estimate, 305–306

activity list
  creating, 286–291
  estimating activity durations using, 299, 303
  in project management plan, 170
  sequencing activities using, 292, 298
activity resources, 299, 473–475
activity sequencing
  activity dependencies, 294–295
  creating network diagrams, 292
  inputs, 292
  leads and lags, 295–296
  network templates used in, 296
  outputs, 296
  precedence programming method of, 292–294
  project network diagram used in, 297
  project schedule management, 291
  updating project documents, 297–298
actual cost. *See* AC (actual cost)
adaptive life cycle
  in hybrid life cycle, 29
  overview of, 28–29
  product scope, 226–227
  project scheduling, 281–282
  tailoring project scope, 227–228
adjourning, project team development phase, 482
advancement, project, 33–35
advertising, procuring goods and services via, 642
affinity diagrams, 236, 424
agile environments
  adaptive life cycles in, 28–29
  communicating in, 519
  cost management approach in, 356
  estimating project work in, 301
  integration management in, 152
  planning schedule in, 324
  procurement practices in, 626
  product scope in, 226–228
  project integration management in, 152
  project scheduling in, 281–282
  quality in, 413–414
  stakeholder management in, 677
agreements
  controlling resources, 489
  cost budgeting, 372

documenting in project charter, 156
monitoring/controlling, 184–185
resource planning, 464
schedule development, 310
stakeholder identification, 679
stakeholder management plan, 685
alternatives analysis
  cost estimating, 368
  deciding on project changes, 193
  managing project quality, 423
  monitoring/controlling project work, 186
alternatives identification, 243, 271, 276
ambiguity risks, 557
analogous estimating
  estimating activity durations, 304
  estimating activity resources, 474
  estimating project cost, 365
  exam facts, 754
  self test, 346, 400
anomalies, estimate to complete, 381
answers. *See* self test answers
appraisal costs, 420
assignable cause, control charts, 432, 457
assumption consequence, testing assumptions, 567
assumption log
  controlling resources, 490
  creating project charter, 155
  estimating activity durations, 299
  estimating activity resources, 474
  project management plan, 170
  project scope statement, 244
  qualitative risk analysis, 577
  quantitative risk analysis, 579
  sequencing project work, 298
assumptions
  benefits management plan, 40
  communication planning, 520–521
  cost estimates, 370
  creating project schedule, 313
  identify risks by testing, 567
  qualitative risk analysis, 573
  testing, 573
attribute sampling, quality management, 412
audioconferencing, and team locale, 481

audits
    contract administration, 650
    procurement, 651
    quality, 424–425
    risk response, 595
authority
    project management team, 463
    resource planning assignments, 466
    self test, 505, 734
authorization, collaborative PMIS packages for
    work, 176
autocratic decisions, project requirements, 238
automation, integration management trends, 150
avoidance
    as approach to conflict resolution, 486
    of power, 117, 124
avoidance of risk, 586, 587, 757

B

balanced matrix organizational structure
    exam facts, 751
    overview of, 76
    pros and cons of, 80
bar chart, presenting project schedule as, 323
baselines
    performance measurement. *See* performance
        measurement baseline
    project. *See* project baseline
    project cost. *See* cost baseline
    project schedule. *See* schedule baseline
    project scope. *See* scope baseline
basis of estimates, 170, 579
benchmarking, 240, 418
benefit/cost analysis, quality management
    planning, 419
benefit/cost ratio (BCR), benefit measurement method,
    159–160
benefit measurement method
    benefit/cost ratio models, 159–160
    calculating net present value, 161–162
    discounted cash flow, 160–161
    payback period estimation, 160
    project scope exam facts, 752

project selection criteria in project charter, 157
    scoring models, 159
benefits management plan, 40, 372
benefits management, project integration, 152
bidder conferences, 642
bids
    examining results of contracting, 642–643
    procurement documents, 640
    procurement practices for projects, 625
blended approach, sequencing activities, 291
body language and tone, communicating via,
    516, 526
bottom-up estimates
    activity durations, 306
    activity resources, 474
    exam facts, 754
    project cost, 367
    self test, 401, 403
brain writing, 680
brainstorming
    data for project charter, 155
    group decisions on project requirements, 236
    quality management planning, 419
    risk identification, 567–568
    stakeholder identification, 680
bubble charts, rating risk, 577
budget
    creating project, 371–374
    estimates, 370
    project charter defining, 154
    risk management plan, 563
    self test, 219
budget at completion (BAC)
    budget variances, 377
    to-complete performance index, 380
    estimate at completion, 379–380
    estimate to complete, 382
    self test, 406
    variance at completion, 382
budget constraints, 217, 272–273, 579
budget variance (VAR), 377
burndown charts, 188, 327
burnup charts, 188
business analyst, project scope, 227

business case
  cost budgeting, 372
  developing project charter, 153, 156
  eliciting project requirements, 232
  reviewing, 39
  self test, 61
business documents, 628, 679
business risks, 557, 587, 756
business value, 13, 25, 54
buyers
  creating procurement documents, 640–641
  other names used for, 627
  source selection criteria, 638

C

calendar
  project. *See* project calendar
  resource. *See* resource calendar
cardinal scales, ranking risks, 575–577
categories
  risk. *See* risk categories
  risk score, 576–577
causal analysis, monitoring/controlling project work, 186
cause-and-effect diagrams. *See* Ishikawa diagrams
centralized structure. *See* functional (centralized)
  organizational structure
change
  in adaptive life cycle, 28–29
  driven by projects, 12
  in project life cycle, 30
  updating project documents after, 179
change control board (CCB)
  within CCS, 192
  reviewing change requests, 188
  self test, 276
change control system (CCS). *See also* integrated change
  control
  relying on, 190–192
  reviewing change requests, 188
  self test, 274, 736
change log
  communications management, 528
  defined, 201

integrated change control, 194
  project management plan, 170
  stakeholder engagement, 688
  stakeholder management plan, 679
change management
  cost changes, 375
  in project integration management, 152
  in project management plan, 167
  scope change control, 254
change requests
  activity definition and, 291
  contract terminations handled as, 648
  contracts and, 648
  cost estimating and, 369–370, 384
  integrated change control for, 188–194
  performance reporting and, 533–534
  project plan execution and, 178–179
  project work and, 174–175, 187
  quality control and, 427
  risk monitoring and, 597
  risk responses and, 594
  schedule control, 325
  scope control and, 254–256
  self test, 216–217, 231, 275, 552–553, 665
  stakeholder engagement and, 690, 695
  stakeholder identification and, 683
  updating project documents after, 179
charismatic leadership
  defined, 119
  in interactional leadership, 119
  of project manager, 117, 128
charts
  bar, 323
  bubble, 577
  burndown. *See* burndown charts
  burnup. *See* burnup charts
  control. *See* control charts
  Gantt. *See* Gantt charts
  hierarchical, 577
  milestone, 323, 325
  of project resources, 465
  why-why. *See* Ishikawa diagrams
chats, dealing with team locales, 481
checklists, 456, 568

choice of words, in communications, 516

claims administration, contracts, 650

classification models, of stakeholder influence, 681–682

closing project or phase
    experience needed to pass PMP exam, 9
    project integration management, 194–197
    project management process, 16

Code of Ethics and Professional Conduct. *See* PMI Code of Ethics and Professional Conduct

coding structure, project schedule, 322

coercive power
    defined, 492
    as punitive, 117
    self test, 512

cognitive-level project integration, 122

collaboration, in conflict resolution, 486

collaborative PMIS packages, work authorization, 176

collocated teams, 481

commercial databases, 66

commercial duration estimating databases, 300, 348

commercial risk, 564

communication channels
    formula for identifying number of, 522–523
    formula to know for exam, 750, 756
    self test, 547, 552

communication planning
    communication requirements, 522–523
    communication skills, 524–525
    communications management plan, 526–527
    enterprise environmental factors, 521
    overview of, 519–520
    self test, 546
    successful, 525–526
    technology for, 523–524
    using project management plan/charter, 520–521

communications
    avenues of, 106
    communicating project information, 105–106
    developing project team, 482
    five Cs of, 517–518
    influencing organization, 136
    influencing project, 110
    project management plan development, 164, 171
    self test, 60, 142, 717

stakeholder engagement and, 687–689
    and team locales, 481

communications management
    communicating in projects, 516–519
    exam information on, 534, 749, 756
    as knowledge area, 17
    managing, 527–530
    monitoring, 530–532
    overview of, 515–516
    planning. *See* communications management plan
    reporting project performance, 532–534
    review drill, 538–539
    review key terms, 536–537
    review summary, 535
    self test, 539–544
    self test answers, 545–554
    three processes of, 516

communications management plan
    aligning stakeholder engagement, 678
    creating, 526–527
    developing. *See* communication planning
    dispersing/archiving information, 527–530
    project management plan development, 168–169
    self test, 718
    updating throughout project, 527

communities of practice, project knowledge, 181

compensation, inappropriate, 723, 740

competency
    assignments in resource planning, 466
    project management team, 463
    project manager, 113–116, 136, 144

completion of project, 154, 187–188

complexity
    of procurement, 626
    of stakeholder relationships, 678

compromise, in conflict resolution, 486, 513

computers
    activity sequencing driven by, 291
    cost estimating software, 369
    performance measurement via, 384

confidence, in cost estimate, 371

confidentiality
    communication technology planning, 524
    of PMP, 722

configuration management
    integrated change control, 192–193
    plan, 167, 253
    self test, 221, 223
conflict of interest
    PMP avoids, 723
    PMP must disclose, 721
    self test, 738, 741, 742
conflict resolution
    managing in project team, 485–487
    project manager communication skills for, 518
    self test, 715
confronting problems, 483, 498, 509
constrained optimization method
    examining, 162–163
    project scope exam facts, 752
    project selection criteria, 157
constraints
    budget, 217, 272–273, 579
    cost, 37, 200
    milestone, 312
    project. *See* project constraints
    scope, 37, 200
    theory of, 462, 508
    time, 37, 199, 312
context diagram, 238–239
context-level project integration, 123
contingency reserve
    activity duration estimates, 308
    allotted to risk events, 589–590
    calculating project risk, 590–591
    cost estimating using risk register, 362
    risk management exam facts, 757
    risk monitoring and, 597
    self test, 349, 618–620
Continuing Certification Requirements handbook,
    PMI, 113
continuous improvement, project quality, 413
contractor schedule, procurement, 626
contracts
    administration of, 647–648, 650
    building foundation for procurement, 624–626
    conducting procurement with, 645–646
    documenting in project charter, 156

exam facts to know, 757–758
inspecting/auditing procurement and, 651
monitoring/controlling project work with, 184–185
project charters vs., 154
in resource planning, 464
self test, 664–672, 736, 737
seller selection and, 645
termination of, 648, 652
contracts, types of
    cost-reimbursable, 634–635
    determining source selection criteria, 638–639
    examining results of, 642–643
    fixed-price contracts, 633–634
    overview of, 636–637
    procurement documents, 640–641
    rules for, 632–633
    statement of work (SOW), 636–637
    time and materials (T&M) contracts, 635
control
    cost. *See* cost control
    procurement. *See* procurements, controlling
    project schedule, 325–328
    project scope, 252–254
    project work. *See* project work, monitoring/
        controlling
    quality. *See* QC (quality control)
    resources, 488–491
control charts
    creating for quality control, 430–432
    exam facts, 754
    self test, 449, 457
control thresholds, 284, 359
controlling PMO, 79
"coopetition," procurement planning, 629
corrective actions
    performance measurement, 385
    performance reporting, 533–534
    project work, 174, 187
    schedule control, 328
    scope control, 254–256, 275
cost. *See also* cost management
    benefit/cost analysis, 419
    change requests in project plan execution, 178–179
    project baseline document, 170

project life cycle, 29
self test, 351
cost aggregation, project budget, 372
cost baseline
    cost control, 375
    preparing for quality, 416
    project budget, 373
    quantitative risk analysis, 579
    updating as result of controlling resources, 490
    updating for approved changes, 189
cost-benefit analysis, 186, 193
cost budgeting, 371–374, 404
cost constraints, 37, 200
cost control
    implementing, 374–375
    lessons learned, 385
    measuring project performance, 393
    monitoring cost variances, 384
cost estimates, 370
cost estimating
    analogous estimating, 365
    analyzing data, 368
    analyzing results, 369–370
    bottom-up estimating, 367
    computer software for, 369
    decomposing project deliverables, 248
    exam facts, 754
    inputs, 360–364
    making decisions, 369
    overview of, 359
    parametric estimating, 365–366
    project management plan, 170
    for projects, 364–365
    quantitative risk analysis and, 579
    refining, 370
    self test, 402, 732, 735
    supporting detail for, 370–371
    three-point estimates, 367–368
    updating as project progresses, 384–385
cost forecasts
    monitoring/controlling project work, 183, 188
    project management plan, 171
    quantitative risk analysis, 579

cost management. *See also* cost estimating
    creating project budget, 371–374
    exam facts to know, 754
    exam information for processes in, 749
    implementing cost control, 374–375
    inside PMP exam, 390
    as knowledge area, 17
    measuring project performance. *See* performance measurement
    overview of, 355–356
    planning project costs, 357–359
    review drill, 391–393
    review key terms, 387–389
    review summary, 386
    self test, 394–399
    self test answers, 400–408
    tailoring approach to, 356–357
cost management plan
    cost control input, 375
    creating, 358–359
    inputs, 358
    overview of, 358
    project management plan development, 168
    self test, 402
cost performance index. *See* CPI (cost performance index)
cost plus award fee (CPAF) contracts, 635, 637
cost plus fixed fee (CPFF) contracts, 634–635, 637
cost plus incentive fee (CPIF) contracts, 635, 637
cost plus percentage of costs (CPPC) contracts, 635, 637
cost-reimbursable contracts, 634–635
cost variance (CV), finding, 377
costs of quality, 368, 419, 455
CPAF (cost plus award fee) contracts, 635, 637
CPFF (cost plus fixed fee) contracts, 634–635, 637
CPI (cost performance index)
    calculating, 378
    estimate at completion, 379–380
    estimate to complete, 382
    measuring project performance, 393
    self test, 407
    trend analysis monitoring, 435
CPIF (cost plus incentive fee) contracts, 635, 637

CPM (critical path method)
    calculating float in PND, 315
    calculating minimum project duration, 314
    examining schedule variance, 327
    project scheduling using, 281–282
    resource leveling using, 319–320
    self test, 345, 351–352
CPPC (cost plus percentage of costs) contracts, 635, 637
crashing project
    as duration compression, 320–321
    self test, 346, 350, 351
creativity management techniques, managing
    knowledge, 181
critical path method. *See* CPM (critical path method)
cultural norm, 72
culture influences/issues
    as external enterprise environmental factors, 66
    PMP responsibility to learn, 722
    project manager and, 112, 518
    self test, 732–733, 738–740
culture of quality, 413
culture shock, 722, 739
customers
    control chart and, 430
    as most important stakeholder in project, 61
    PMP responsibility to, 722–724
    project management plan development, 166
    projects created for, 24
    quality management and, 412
    self test, 54, 510, 739
CV (cost variance), finding, 377

D

data
    gathering project charter, 155
    presenting project schedule as, 323
    project management information and, 38–40
    work performance. *See* work performance data
data analysis
    controlling resources with, 489
    cost estimating with, 368
    eliciting project requirements with, 235
    estimating activity resources using, 474

    measuring project schedule performance with, 327
    monitoring project work, 185–186
    procuring goods and services with, 642
    project simulation using, 321
    qualitative risk analysis, 573–574
    schedule management plan using, 284
    scope management plan using, 231
data representation tools
    monitoring communications, 529
    monitoring stakeholder engagement, 694
    quality control, 428–429
    quality management planning, 421
decision-making
    cost estimating with, 369
    eliciting project requirements using group,
        235–238
    for making vs. buying product, 630–631
    for project changes, 193
    in project life cycle, 30
decision tree analysis, 582–583, 621
decoder, communication, 525
decomposition
    affinity diagram allows for, 236
    managing schedule with project work packages,
        287
    parametric estimating of activity durations,
        304–305
    of project deliverables in WBS, 248–249, 262
defect repairs, 174, 188
definition, project scope, 241–245
definitive estimates, cost estimates, 370
deliverables
    decomposing in WBS, 248–249
    in knowledge management, 180
    may/may not be temporary, 12
    product vs. project scope, 229–230
    project phase, 33–36
    project scope statement, 243
    quality control, 427
    reliance of operations/projects for, 24
    scope management plan, 231
    scope validation by formally accepting, 251
    self test, 448
    subproject, 22–23

Delphi technique
    consensus on project risks, 568
    estimating activity durations, 306–307
    group decisions on project requirements,
        236–237
    self test, 616
demands, activity duration estimates and, 307
dependencies between activities, 294–295, 753
description, high-level project, 154
Design for X approach, quality management, 425
development life cycle, 151
diagramming techniques, risk identification, 569–570
dictionary. *See* WBS dictionary
direct costs, 361, 754
directing, in conflict resolution, 486
direction of influence, stakeholders, 682
directive PMO, 79, 99
disagreements, team, 485–486
discounted cash flow, benefit measurement, 160–161
discretionary dependencies, 294–295, 753
discussion forums, project knowledge, 181
dispute resolution, procurement, 652, 666
diversity, stakeholder management and, 677
document analysis, quality management, 423
documentation
    activity attributes, 289–290
    activity duration estimates, 308
    honesty of PMPs about their, 721
    project plan, 164
    project scope, 240
    scope change control, 254
documents
    procurement, 196, 640–641
    project charter, 156
    project management, 37–38, 170–172
    updating project changes in, 179
domains, passing PMP exam, 7–9
duration
    compression, for project schedule, 320–321
    critical path calculates minimum project, 314
    effort vs., 300, 305
    project schedule exam facts, 753
    resource leveling likely extends project, 319
    self test, 550

duration estimates. *See also* activity duration estimates
    project management plan, 171
    quantitative risk analysis input, 580
duty of loyalty, project manager, 723

E

e-mail, dealing with team locales, 481
EAC (estimate at completion)
    to-complete performance index, 380
    measuring project performance, 393
    measuring variance at completion, 382
    preparing for, 378–380
early finish (EF), calculating float, 315–316
early start (ES), calculating float, 315–316
earned value. *See* EV (earned value)
earned value management. *See* EVM (earned value
  management)
ease of use, communication technologies, 523
economic conditions, project manager influencing, 112
education
    PMI Talent Triangle and, 114–116
    PMP exam requirements, 7
    project manager continuing, 112
EF (early finish), calculating float, 315–316
effective listening, communications and, 525, 756
effort, duration vs., 300, 305
electronic communications, 526
employees, as internal enterprise environmental
  factors, 65
encoder communication model, 524, 547
end dates, of projects, 23–24, 53
end users, project manager influencing, 109
engineering review board (ERB), 192
enhancement of risk, 588–589, 757
enterprise environmental factors
    acquiring project resources, 476
    in communication planning, 521
    communications management, 527
    cost budgeting input, 372
    as cost estimating input, 363
    cost planning input, 358
    creating activity list, 286
    developing project team, 480

enterprise environmental factors *(cont.)*
    estimating activity durations, 300
    estimating activity resources, 474
    identifying in project charter, 156–157
    as input for schedule management plan, 283
    as input to activity sequencing, 292
    as input to scope definition, 242
    managing project team, 485
    monitoring communications, 531
    preparing for quality control, 427
    procurement planning, 628
    in project management, 64–66
    project management plan development, 164
    quality management planning input, 417
    quantitative risk analysis input, 580
    resource planning input, 464
    reviewing final inputs for monitoring/
        controlling, 185
    risk response planning input, 585
    self test, 93–94, 96
enterprise environmental factors input
    conducting procurements, 641
    managing stakeholder engagement, 688
    monitoring stakeholder engagement, 692
    preparing for stakeholder identification, 679
    schedule development, 310
    scope management plan, 230
    stakeholder management plan, 685
environments
    agile. *See* agile environments
    project manager influence on, 112
    projects changing things and, 12
ERB (engineering review board), 192
ES (early start), calculating float, 315–316
escalate risk response
    overview of, 585
    for positive/negative risks, 588–589
    risk management exam facts, 757
    self test, 616
estimate at completion. *See* EAC (estimate at
    completion)
estimating project costs. *See* cost estimating
ETC (estimate to complete), 380–382, 393
ethics. *See* PMI Code of Ethics and Professional Conduct

ethics violations
    reporting, 721
    self test, 733–734, 737, 741
ethnocentrism, 722
EV (earned value)
    to-complete performance index, 380
    cost performance index, 378
    cost variance, 376
    estimate to complete, 382
    management. *See* EVM (earned value management)
    measuring project performance, 393
    monitoring/controlling project work, 186
    risk monitoring, 596
    schedule performance index, 378
    schedule variance, 377
    self test, 403, 407
evaluation criteria, source selection, 643–644
evaluation documents, 172, 427
event-based risks, 557
EVM (earned value management)
    formulas, 356, 382–383, 750–751
    measuring project performance, 376–377
    monitoring/controlling project work, 185, 208
    scope change control, 253
    self test, 224
exam. *See* PMP exam
execution of project
    directing/managing. *See* project work, directing/
        managing
    passing PMP exam on, 9
    project management processes for, 15
    work performance data from, 184
exit criteria
    closing project or phase, 195, 197
    project charter, 154
Expectancy Theory. *See* Vroom's Expectancy Theory
expected monetary value (Ex$V)
    contingency reserve for project risk, 590–591
    quantitative risk analysis, 581
    self test, 618–619
experience, PMP exam requirements, 7–9
expert judgment
    analogous estimating and. *See* analogous estimating
    defining project scope, 242

developing project budget, 372

developing schedule management plan, 284

estimating activity durations, 303–304

estimating activity resources, 474

hosting meetings, 187

implementing risk responses, 593

managing project knowledge, 181

monitoring communications, 532

monitoring/controlling project work, 185

monitoring stakeholder engagement, 694

procurement planning relying on, 632

procuring goods and services, 642

project execution, 175

resource planning, 464

scope management plan, 231

seller selection process, 645

expert power, project manager and, 117

explicit knowledge, 180

exploitation of risk, 588–589, 757

external dependencies

activity sequencing, 295

project schedule exam facts, 753

self test, 344

external enterprise environmental factors

change requests due to, 275

common, 65–66

self test, 94, 100

external risks, 564

F

facilitated workshop, 238

facilitation

flow of communication, 106

project management plan development, 165–166

facilities, as internal enterprise environmental factors, 65

failure costs, 420, 450–451, 454–455

fair agreement, in negotiation, 107, 135

fairness, of PMP, 722

fast tracking, 320–321, 350–351

feasibility. *See* project feasibility study

feedback, 483–484, 525

FF (finish-to-finish), 293

FFP (firm fixed-price) contracts, 634, 637

files, project management plan, 170–172

final build, project life cycle, 32

finalizing, activity definition, 290–291

financial, as external enterprise environmental
      factor, 66

financing, project budget and, 373

finish, calculating project, 314

first build, project life cycle, 32

fishbone diagrams. *See* Ishikawa diagrams

fist-to-five voting, estimating activity durations, 307

fixed costs

cost estimating, 361

project cost exam facts, 754

self test, 406

fixed-price (FP) contracts, 633, 637, 667

fixed-price incentive fee (FPIF) contracts, 634, 637

fixed-price with economic price adjustment (FP-EPA)
      contracts, 634, 637, 669

flawed estimates, finding estimate to complete, 381

float

calculating in project network diagram, 315–317

critical path calculating activities with least, 314

examining schedule variance, 327

project schedule exam facts, 753

types of, 315

flowcharts

identifying risk, 569

implementing quality control, 429, 434

managing project quality, 424

quality management exam facts, 754

FNET (finish no earlier than), schedule time
      constraint, 312

FNLT (finish no later than), schedule time constraint, 312

focus groups

eliciting project requirements via, 233

project charter, 155

project knowledge management, 181

project management plan, 166

force-field analysis, quality management planning, 420

forcing

conflict resolution method, 486

self test, 509, 513

forecasts
    cost, 171, 183
    cost management plan for cash-flow, 168
    future project performance/outcomes, 185
    performance reporting results, 533–534
    schedule, 172, 184
formal acceptance
    defined, 273
    scope management plan, 231
    as scope validation result, 262
formal communications, 516
formats, project schedule, 323
forming, in naturally developed project teams, 482
formulas, PMP exam
    EVM, 750–751
    practicing test processes, 746
    summary of, 750
four sigma values, control charts, 430–432
FP-EPA (fixed-price with economic price adjustment)
    contracts, 634, 637, 669
FP (fixed-price) contracts, 633, 637, 667
FPIF (fixed-price incentive fee) contracts, 634, 637
frameworks, understanding, 69
free float, 315, 753
FS (finish-to-start), 293, 344
functional (centralized) organizational structure
    exam facts, 750
    managing projects in, 74–75
    pros and cons of, 80
    self test, 101
functional managers
    project manager vs., 79
    self test, 100, 505, 734
functional requirements, project scope, 233
funding limit reconciliation, project budget, 372–373
FV (future value)
    cost estimating using project schedule, 361
    in discounted cash flow, 160–161
    formula for predicting, 188
    formula to know for exam, 750

G

Gantt charts, 325, 350–351
general management skills, project management, 482–483

gifts, PMP cannot ethically accept, 723
gold plating, project quality management and, 414
governance
    controlling PMO defines project, 79
    integration management, 152
    as internal enterprise environmental factor, 86
    organizational governance frameworks, 69
    organizational systems provide, 69
    project, 70, 85
    project manager influence on, 109
    scope management, 228
    self test, 97
government standards, 66
grade vs. quality, 411
group decisions, on project requirements, 235–238
guilt-based power, project manager and, 117

H

halo effect, 464, 508–509
hammock (summary) activities, project network
    diagrams, 297
hard logic
    defined, 329
    duration compression and, 320
    evaluating, 311
    mandatory dependencies as, 294
Herzberg's Theory of Motivation, 468–469, 755
hidden time, activity duration estimates and, 307
hierarchical chart, risk rating, 577
Hierarchy of Needs, Maslow, 468, 754
histograms, for quality control, 424, 432–433
historical information
    analogous estimating of activity duration, 304
    developing project budget, 372
    in organizational process assets. *See* organizational
        process assets
    in process charter, 157–158
    self test, 408
honesty
    PMP responsibility for, 720–721, 723
    self test, 732–733, 735–737
human resources. *See* resource management
human resources, acquiring, 478
hybrid approaches, project management, 151

hybrid life cycle, 29
hybrid organizational structure, 78, 100, 752
hygiene agents, 468–469, 755

I

ideas management techniques, 181
IFB (invitation for bid)
    inside PMP exam, 649
    procurement documents, 640
    self test, 671
illegal activities, contracts cannot include, 664
impact
    in qualitative risk analysis, 574
    in quantitative risk analysis, 581
    ranking risks on, 575
incentives
    cost plus incentive fee contracts, 635, 637
    fixed-price contracts with, 633, 637
    fixed-price incentive fee contracts, 634, 637
    self test, 666
incremental life cycle, 28
independent estimates, seller selection process, 644
indirect costs, 361, 754
individual project risk, 557
industry
    project manager influence on, 112
    standards, 66
influence diagrams, identifying risk, 570
influence, project manager
    levels of, 108–110
    skills in, 483
    success/failure of project and, 110
influence, visualizing stakeholder, 681–682
informal communications, 516
information. *See also* communications management
    distributing, 529
    exchanging. *See* communications
    managing communication, 105–106
    managing project knowledge, 182
    project management data and, 38–40
    work performance. *See* work performance
        information

informational power, of project manager, 116
infrastructure, as internal enterprise environmental
    factor, 65
ingratiating power, 117
initiation of project
    context of, 13
    experience needed to pass PMP exam, 8
    project management processes for, 14
inputs
    activity definition, 288
    activity list creation, 286–287
    activity sequencing, 292
    communication monitoring, 531
    communications management, 527
    cost budgeting, 371–372
    cost control, 374
    cost estimating, 360–364
    cost planning, 358
    estimating activity durations, 298–299
    estimating activity resources, 474
    final monitoring and controlling, 184–185
    knowledge management, 180
    procurement planning, 628
    procurements, 641
    project team management, 485
    quality control, 427
    quality management planning, 417–418
    quantitative risk analysis input, 579–580
    resources, acquiring project, 476
    resources, controlling, 489
    resources, planning, 464
    risk monitoring, 595
    risk response, 584–585, 593
    schedule control, 326
    schedule development, 310
    schedule management plan, 283
    scope change control, 253–254
    scope definition, 242
    scope management plan, 230
    scope validation, 251
    stakeholder engagement, 688
    stakeholder management plan. *See* work
        performance data

inspections
   procurement process, 651
   quality control, 427–428
   quality management, 413, 421
inspiration, leading project team, 105
Instructing.com, 7
integrated change control
   approving changes to project scope, 673
   configuration management for, 192–193
   contract administration and, 650
   deciding on project changes, 193
   evaluating outputs of, 194
   overview of, 188–189
   review summary, 198, 200
   revisiting planning processes, 193
   self test, 216, 220, 222
   tools and techniques, 190–192
integration management
   activity resource estimates, 473–475
   in agile environments, 152
   benefit measurement methods, 158–162
   closing project or phase, 194–197
   cognitive-level integration, 122
   context-level integration, 123
   directing/managing project work, 173–179
   emerging trends, 150–151
   exam information for processes, 748
   exploring, 149–150
   integrated change control, 188–194
   as knowledge area, 17
   managing project knowledge, 179–183
   monitoring/controlling project work, 183–188
   overview of, 147–149
   performing project integration, 121–123
   project charter. *See* project charter; project
      management plan
   project manager leading, 149
   review drill, 207–209
   review key terms, 200–207
   review summary, 198–200
   of risk, 558
   self test, 55, 59, 140, 209–214
   self test answers, 215–224
   tailoring, 151–152

interactional leadership, 119, 124
interactive communications, 525, 689, 716
interest in project, stakeholder analysis, 680
internal dependencies, activity sequencing, 295
internal enterprise environmental factors, 64–65, 93
internal rate of return (IRR), benefit measurement
   method, 162
international influences, project manager, 112
interpersonal and team skills
   communications management, 529
   procuring goods and services, 642
   risk responses, 593
   successful communications, 526
interpersonal skills, stakeholder engagement, 688
interviews
   eliciting project requirements, 234
   gathering data for project charter, 155
   managing project knowledge, 181
   quality management planning, 419
   quantitative risk analysis, 580–581
   risk identification via, 568
   stakeholder. *See* scope management,
      requirements
invitation for bid (IFB)
   inside PMP exam, 649
   procurement documents, 640
   self test, 671
invoice payment, contract administration, 648
Iron Triangle
   preparing for quality, 416
   project management, 37
   self test, 55
IRR (internal rate of return), benefit measurement
   method, 162
Ishikawa diagrams
   identifying risks, 569
   quality control implementation, 428–429
   quality management, 424, 754
   self test, 453, 456
ISO 9000 standards, 412, 415, 452
issue log
   project management plan, 171
   project plan execution, 177–178
   qualitative risk analysis results in, 577

self test, 716
updating as result of controlling resources, 490
IT software, as internal enterprise environmental
factor, 65
iterations
estimating work in agile project, 301
planning schedule in agile project, 324
schedule management plan for length of, 284
iterative life cycles, 28
iterative, process groups as, 16–17
iterative scheduling, 281–282

JAD (joint application design) workshop, 238
just-in-time (JIT) ordering
exam facts, 755
self test, 451, 504
trends in managing resources, 462

K

Kaizen technologies
quality management, 412, 755
self test, 452–453
trends in managing resources, 462
Kanban, on-demand scheduling, 281–282
knowledge
fairs and cafes, 182
managing project, 179–183
in stakeholder analysis, 681
tailoring project scope management, 227–228
knowledge areas, PMP exam
project communications management. *See*
communications management
project cost. *See* cost management
project integration. *See* integration management
project procurement management. *See*
procurement management
project quality. *See* quality management
project resources. *See* resource management
project risk management. *See* risk management
project schedule. *See* schedule management

project scope. *See* scope management
project stakeholder management. *See* stakeholder
management
types of, 17–18
knowledge management
communications management, 518
integration management, 152

labor costs, project cost management, 356
lag
documenting activity attributes, 290
project schedule exam facts, 753
self test, 344, 351
sequencing activities in project schedule, 295–296
laissez-faire leadership, 119
languages, tailoring communications for different, 518
late finish (LF), calculating float, 316–317
late start (LS), calculating float, 316–317
laws, as external enterprise environmental factors, 66
LCLs (lower control limits), control charts, 430–432
leadership
aligning/motivating to achieve goals in, 118
charismatic, 119
exploring styles of, 118–119
interactional, 119
interrelated with management, 105
laissez-faire, 119
personality traits of, 119–120
in project manager, 115–116
project manager skills in, 482
of project team, 105
self test, 137, 139
servant, 115–116, 119
transactional, 119
transformational, 119
leading, stakeholder engagement matrix, 686
leads
documenting activity attributes, 290
exam facts, 753
project schedule, 309
sequencing activities in project schedule, 295–296

Lean Six Sigma, 412, 415
learning curve
    as parametric estimating, 366
    self test, 401, 408
legal requirements, contracts, 633
lessons learned register
    closing project, 197
    cost control, 375, 385
    cost estimating, 364
    estimating activity durations, 299
    estimating activity resources, 474
    integration management, 152
    knowledge management, 179, 180, 182–183
    monitoring/controlling project work, 184, 188
    project management plan, 171
    project team development, 480
    quality control, 427
    quality management, 423
    resources control, 490
    schedule control, 328
    self test, 215, 222–223, 546, 551
letter of intent, 645, 671
level of precision, cost management plan, 358
LF (late finish), calculating float, 316–317
life-cycle costs, 402
locales
    dealing with team, 481, 514
    tailoring communications for physical, 518
logistics, procurement, 625
lose-lose situation, conflict resolution, 513, 514
low-priority risk watch list, qualitative risk
    analysis, 578
lower control limits (LCLs), control charts, 430–432
loyalty, project manager, 723
LS (late start), calculating float, 316–317
lump sum contracts, 633–634, 668

M

MACD (move, add, change, delete), mapping projects
    to, 12
maintenance, resource, 462
majority decision, project requirements, 237

management
    Ouchi's Theory Z on worker involvement in, 510–511
    project communications, 527–530
    reserves, 308, 362
    risks, 564
    tailoring integration, 151
    team process, 484–488
management skills. *See also* project work,
    directing/managing
    about getting things done, 118
    leadership interrelated with, 105
    project management plan, 166
    scope requirements, 240–241
    self test, 139, 142, 714
    stakeholder engagement, 689
mandatory dependencies, 294, 753
manual activity sequencing, 291
marketplace conditions
    create temporary projects for window in, 12
    evaluating in procurement planning, 628
    as external enterprise environmental factors, 66
    self test, 100, 670
Maslow's Hierarchy of Needs, 468, 755
mass communication, 526
matrix diagrams, managing project quality, 424
matrix structures
    management in, 76–77
    schedule management for, 281
    self test, 94
McClelland's Theory of Needs, 470, 755
McGregor's Theory of X and Y, 469, 507
McGregor's Theory of X and Y, 755
media communications, 516
media selection, flow of communication, 106
mediation, 107, 143
medium communication model, 524
meeting management
    communication, 106, 518, 529
    defined, 125
    facilitating, 243
    project charter, 155
    project knowledge, 181
    project plan, 166

meetings
 in agile environments, 519
 estimating activity resources, 474
 executing project work, 176
 monitoring/controlling project work, 186–187
 monitoring stakeholder engagement, 694
 profile analysis, 680
 risk management, 561
 schedule management plan, 284
 scope management plan, 231
 self test, 549
methods
 communications management, 529
 risk management plan, 562
metrics
 benefits management plan, 40
 identifying quality, 422
 project performance measurement baseline, 184
 quality control, 427
 quality input, 423
micromanagement, Theory of X and Y, 469, 507
milestone chart, project schedule as, 323, 325
milestone constraints, project schedule, 312
milestone list
 activity sequencing, 292, 298
 estimating activity durations, 299
 finalizing activity definition, 290
 project management plan, 171
 quantitative risk analysis, 580
milestone schedule, project charter defining, 154
mind mapping, project requirements, 236–237
mitigation of risk
 exam facts, 757
 response to negative risk, 586–587
 using contract for, 632
models
 communication, 524–525
 schedule development, 284
monitoring
 communications, 530–532
 risk, 594–598
 stakeholder engagement, 690–695
 work. *See* project work, monitoring/controlling

Monte Carlo analysis, 321, 621
most likely cost estimate, PERT formula, 367–368
motivating agents, 755
motivation, leading project team, 105
multicriteria decision analysis
 group decisions on project requirements, 236
 project changes, 193
 project quality, 424
 quality management planning, 420
multidivisional organizational structure
 exam facts, 750
 managing projects in, 75
 pros and cons of, 80
 self test, 98, 100

N

NASA program management, 20
naturally developing project teams, 482
NDAs (nondisclosure agreements), procurement documents, 640
near-term risks, qualitative risk analysis, 578
negative risks
 avoiding, 586
 five responses to, 587–588
 mitigating, 586
 as threats, 556
 transferring, 586
negative stakeholders
 building stakeholder management plan, 686–687
 overview of, 676
 results of stakeholder identification, 683
 self test, 706, 710
negative total float, 315
negotiation
 acquiring project resources, 477
 procuring goods and services, 642
 project manager skills in, 107, 483
 self test, 135, 551
 seller selection process, 645
net present value (NPV), benefit measurement, 161–162
network communication, 526
network diagrams, 292

network templates, sequencing activities, 296
networking, managing project knowledge, 181
neutral stakeholders
    overview of, 676
    stakeholder engagement matrix, 686
    stakeholder identification, 683
nodes, precedence programming method (PDM), 292–294
noise, 525, 545, 549
nominal group technique, 236, 269
non-event based risks, 557
nondirect communication modalities, 526
nondisclosure agreements (NDAs), procurement documents, 640
nonfunctional requirements, scope requirements, 233
nonverbal communications, 525, 550–551, 756
normal distribution values
    formula to know for exam, 750
    four sigma values for, 430
    practicing test processes for, 746
norming, naturally developed project teams, 482
NPV (net present value), benefit measurement, 161–162

O

observation, in requirements elicitation, 239
on-demand scheduling, 281–282
on schedule, activity duration estimates, 308
100-percent rule, WBS, 249
operations
    portfolios containing, 20–22
    project life cycle transfers, 32
    project reliance on, 23–24
    projects vs., 23–24, 54
    self test, 59
OPM (organizational project management), 22
opportunities, positive risks as, 445, 556
opportunity costs, 386–387, 405
optimistic cost, PERT formula, 367–368
ordinal scales, ranking risks, 575–577
organic (simple) organizational structure
    exam facts, 750
    overview of, 74

pros and cons, 80
    self test, 99
organization, project manager influences, 111
organizational breakdown structure, charting project resources, 465
organizational charts, resources, 465
organizational culture, 65, 72
organizational governance frameworks, 65, 69
organizational knowledge repository, 96, 102
organizational managers, 108
organizational planning, 465
organizational procedure links, cost management plan, 359
organizational procedures links, schedule management plan, 284
organizational process assets
    acquiring resources, 476
    activity duration estimates, 300
    activity list, 286
    activity resources estimates, 474
    activity sequencing, 292
    communications management, 527, 530
    communications monitoring, 531
    controlling resources, 489
    cost planning, 286, 358, 372, 375
    knowledge management, 183
    leveraging, 66–67
    procurement planning, 628
    procurements, 641
    project charter identifying, 157–158
    project management plan development, 164
    project team development, 481
    project team management, 485
    project work monitoring, 185
    quality control, 427
    quality management, 417, 423
    quantitative risk analysis, 580
    recognizing common, 67
    risk monitoring, 597
    risk response implementation, 593
    risk response plan, 585
    schedule development, 310
    schedule management, 283
    scope definition, 242

scope management plan, 230–232
self test, 95, 101, 269
stakeholder engagement, 688, 692
stakeholder identification, 679
stakeholder management plan, 685
organizational project management (OPM), 22
organizational structures
    completing projects. *See* project completion in
        different organizational structures
    exam facts to know, 750–752
    internal enterprise environmental factors, 65
    project completion and. *See* project completion in
        different organizational structures
    project schedule management and, 281
    self test, 99–100
organizational systems
    general management skills, 70–71
    organizational culture, 72
    organizational governance frameworks, 69
    portfolio, program, and project governance, 70
    self test, 96, 137
    working with, 68–69
organizational theories
    Herzberg's Theory of Motivation, 468–469
    Maslow's Hierarchy of Needs, 468
    McClelland's Theory of Needs, 470
    McGregor's Theory of X and Y, 469
    Ouchi's Theory Z, 470
    using in resource planning, 467–470
    Vroom's Expectancy Theory, 470
organizations, teaming agreements with other, 629
Ouchi's Theory Z
    resource exam facts, 755
    resource planning, 470
    self test, 510–511
overall project risk
    creating risk report, 571
    creating risk responses, 585
    defined, 557
    exposure, quantitative risk analysis, 583
ownership
    benefits management plan, 40
    in stakeholder analysis, 680
    transferring risk, 586

P

paralingual, 525, 548
parametric estimating
    of activity durations, 304–305
    estimating project cost, 365–366, 754
    self test, 400
Pareto diagrams
    quality control, 432
    quality management exam facts, 754
    self test, 457
Parkinson's Law, 307–308, 348–349
part-time project team, managing in matrix structure, 76
passing score, PMP exam, 7
payback period, benefit measurement method, 160
payment system, contract administration, 650
PDM (precedence diagramming method), 292–294
PDUs (professional development units), 112–116
performance
    appraisals of project team, 483–484
    assessments, 485
    creating information on work, 184
    managing work, 38–39
    PMP honesty about their, 721
    reporting project, 532–534
    risk monitoring by measuring technical, 596
    work performance reports, 187
performance measurement
    additional planning, 383–384
    to-complete performance index (TCPI), 380
    cost control results, 384
    cost management plan, 359
    cost performance index (CPI), 378
    creating change requests, 384–385
    earned value management (EVM), 376–377
    earned value management (EVM) rules, 382–383
    estimate at completion (EAC), 378–380
    estimate to complete (ETC), 380–382
    project schedule control, 327
    schedule management plan, 284
    schedule performance index (SPI), 378
    updating lessons learned, 385
    using computers, 384
    variance at completion (VAC), 382
    variances, 377

performance measurement baseline
    cost control input, 375
    creating work performance information, 184
    scope change control, 253
performance reporting
    contract administration, 648, 650
    examining work results, 177
    self test, 552–553
performance reviews
    contract administration, 650
    controlling resources, 489
performing, in naturally developed project teams, 482
periodic risk reviews, risk monitoring, 596
personal or charismatic power, 117
personality traits, leadership, 119–120
persuasive power, 117
PERT (program evaluation and review technique),
    averaging project costs, 367
    formula to know for exam, 750
    as three-point estimate, 305
pessimistic cost estimate, PERT formula, 367–368
PESTLE, risk analysis, 570
phases
    project deliverables in, 33
    project life cycle, 29–33
physical enterprise environmental factors, 66, 96
physical location
    dealing with team locales, 481
    managing resources, 462
    of resources/facilities, 65
    stakeholder identification, 679
    tailoring procurement, 626
physical resource assignments
    controlling resources, 491
    project management plan, 171
    schedule management, 281
plan-do-check-act, project quality management, 412
planned value. See PV (planned value)
planning
    communication. See communication planning
    experience needed to pass PMP exam, 8–9
    integrated change control in, 193
    project costs, 357–359
    project management. See project management plan

project scope management, 228–232
quality management, 417–422
resource. See resource planning
risk management. See risk management plan
risk response. See risk response planning
schedule in agile project, 324
stakeholder management, 683–687
planning components, activity definition, 288
planning packages, WBS, 249, 288
plurality decision, project requirements, 238
PMBOK Guide
    all about, 4–5
    course of action for processes/procedures in, 53
    as focus of this book, 5–6
    overview of, 4
    project management best practices, 18
PMI Code of Ethics and Professional Conduct
    negotiating for resources, 477
    overview of, 719–720
    PMP exam and, 10
    responsibilities to customer/public, 722–724
    responsibilities to profession, 720–721
    review drill, 725–726
    review key terms, 724–725
    review summary, 724
    self test, 726–731
    self test answers, 732–742
PMI Talent Triangle, 114–116, 137
pmi.org, exam details at, 10
PMIS (Project Management Information System)
    activity sequencing for project schedules, 296
    communications management, 529
    communications monitoring, 529
    estimating activity resources, 474
    implementing risk responses, 593
    project execution, 175–176
    project integration management trends, 150
    project management plan development, 166
    self test, 220, 224
    as work authorization system, 176
PMO (project management office)
    exam facts, 752
    operating under, 78–79
    project manager influence on, 108

pros and cons of, 80
self test, 98, 99, 102
PMP exam
all about, 6–10
communications management, 534
cost management, 390
integration management, 191
knowledge areas. *See* knowledge areas,
PMP exam
PMI Code of Ethics and Professional Conduct, 721
procurement management, 632, 636–637,
648–649
project management, 37, 81
quality management, 435–436
resource management, 487
risk management, 587–588
schedule management, 309, 318
scope management, 245
serving as project manager, 120
stakeholder management, 692–693
PMP exam, critical information
49 management processes, 748–749
communications facts, 756
EVM formulas, 750–751
major formulas, 750
organizational structures, 750–752
procurement facts, 757–758
project cost facts, 754
project resource facts, 755
project schedule facts, 753
project scope facts, 752–753
quality management facts, 754–755
risk management facts, 756–757
stakeholder facts, 759
WBS facts, 752
PMP exam, test-passing tips
days before exam, 746
how to answer questions, 747
practice the testing process, 746
testing tips, 746–747
using process of elimination, 748
PMP Handbook, 10
PMP (Project Management Professional), continuing
certification requirements, 112, 113, 143

PND (project network diagram)
calculating float, 315–317
creating schedule, 310–311
creating schedule with project coding structure, 322
presenting project schedule as, 323, 325
visualizing flow of project work, 297
policies
PMP compliance with, 720
preparing for source selection, 644
quality, 413, 415
risk management plan, 561
self test, 733, 738, 740
politics, project management and, 116
portfolio management
overview of, 20–22
review board, 70
self test, 57, 61
portfolios, programs vs., 57
positional power, 116, 138
positive attitude, 110, 136
positive risks
managing, 588–589
as opportunities, 445, 556
responses to, 588
positive stakeholders, 676, 683
power
avoiding, 117
guilt-based, 117
informational, 116
ingratiating, 117
persuasive, 117
pressure-based, 117
project manager, 486
punitive or coercive, 117
referent. *See* referent power
relational, 117
reward, 117
self test, 138–139, 140–141, 512
situational, 117
types of project manager, 116–117
power/influence diagram, 708
power-interest grid, stakeholder influence, 681
preassigned staff, 478
precedence programming method (PDM), 292–294

predictive life cycle
    in hybrid life cycles, 29
    overview of, 28
    product scope in, 226–227
    self test, 58
    tailoring project scope management, 227–228
preferential logic. *See* soft logic
preferred logic. *See* soft logic
presentation, flow of communication, 106
pressure-based power, 117
prevention-driven, quality as, 420, 454
prevention, project quality management, 412
preventive actions, project work, 174, 187
pricing, cost estimating vs., 359
prioritizing likelihood of risks, quantitative risk
    analysis, 583
privity, 650, 667
probability
    quantitative risk analysis, 581, 583
    ranking risk on, 575
    self test, 621
probability-impact matrix, 575–577, 617
problem-solving
    managing project quality, 425
    project manager skills in, 107–108, 483
    self test, 140, 509
process analysis, managing project quality, 423
process description, schedule management plan, 284
process documentation, conducting procurements, 641
process group interactions, project management, 16–18
process-level project integration, 121–122
procrastination, activity duration estimates with reserve
    for, 307
procurement documents
    closing project or phase, 196
    conducting procurements, 641
    creating, 640–641
    self test, 667, 672
procurement management
    building foundation for, 624–626
    conducting procurements. *See* procurements,
      conducting
    controlling procurements. *See* procurements,
      controlling

    exam information, 649, 749, 757–758
    as knowledge area, 18
    overview of, 623–624
    planning. *See* procurement planning
    review drill, 657–658
    review key terms, 653–656
    review summary, 652–653
    self test, 658–663
    self test answers, 664–673
procurement planning
    completing, 630
    contract types for, 632–637
    creating procurement documents, 640–641
    determining source selection criteria, 638
    expert judgment in, 632
    make or buy decisions, 630–631
    market conditions for, 628
    overview of, 627–628
    project management plan development, 169
    for project requirements, 630
    relying on project management plan, 629
    reviewing, 639–640
    reviewing procurement management plan,
      639–640
    scope baseline in, 628–629
    statement of work (SOW), 636
    teaming with other organizations, 629
procurements, conducting
    completing seller selection process, 644–645
    goods and services, 642
    overview of, 641
    preparing for source selection, 643–644
    results of, 645–646
    results of contracting, 642–643
    selecting seller, 643
procurements, controlling
    completing contract administration, 650
    contract administration, 647–648
    inspecting/auditing procurement process, 651
    overview of, 647
    results of, 651–652
product analysis, project scope, 243
product backlog, estimating project work in
    agile, 301

product breakdown, product analysis, 243
product documents, project work, 188
product life cycle, vs. project, 31
product scope
    project scope exam facts, 753
    project scope vs., 226, 229–230
    specific to deliverable of project, 229
product vision, planning schedule in agile project, 324
products, projects create, 11
professional development units (PDUs), 112–116
professional responsibility
    advancing PMP profession, 721
    areas of, 720
    compliance with rules/policies, 720–721
    to customers and public, 722–724
    honesty, 721
    PMI Code of Ethics and Professional Conduct, 719–720
profile analysis meetings, stakeholder identification, 680
program evaluation and review technique. *See* PERT (program evaluation and review technique),
program management
    implementing subprojects vs., 22–23
    overview of, 19–20
    self test, 56
programs
    portfolios can contain, 20
    portfolios vs., 21, 57
    self test, 57
project
    eliciting project requirements, 233
    have end dates, 23–24
    project manager influence on success of, 110
    project manager influencing, 110
    vs. operations, 23–24, 54
project baseline
    defining scope, 249–250
    project documents for, 170
    project plan providing, 164
    project schedules presented as, 323
    self test, 218–220
    updating when changes are approved, 189
project budget. *See* budget

project calendar
    estimating activity durations, 302
    project management plan, 171
    project schedule development, 325
project characteristics
    changes things/environments, 12
    creates business value, 13
    creates unique products, services, or results, 11
    overview of, 10
    reasons for project initiation, 13
    as temporary, 11–12
project charter
    benefit measurement methods, 158–162
    in communication planning, 520–521
    constrained optimization methods, 162–163
    contract vs., 154
    cost planning input, 358
    creating, 154–156
    documenting project agreements/contracts, 156
    enterprise environmental factors, 156–157
    organizational process assets, 157
    overview of, 153–154
    procurement planning, 628
    project management plan development, 164
    project selection criteria, 157–158
    quality management planning, 417
    reliance on business documents, 156
    resource planning, 464
    review summary, 198
    schedule management plan, 283
    scope definition, 242
    scope management plan, 230
    self test, 55
    stakeholder identification, 679
    stakeholder management plan, 684
project communications management. *See* communications management
project completion in different organizational structures
    functional organizations, 74–75
    hybrid organizations, 78
    inside PMP exam, 81
    matrix structures, 76–77
    multidivisional structures, 75

project completion in different organizational
structures *(cont.)*)
    organic (or simple) structures, 74
    overview of, 73–74
    project management offices, 78–79
    pros and cons of various organizational types, 80
    virtual organizations, 77
project constraints
    communications management, 548
    cost estimates, 370
    evaluating, 311–312
    project management, 16
    project management plan/charter, 520
    review summary, 199–200
    schedule management plan, 283–284
    schedule network analysis, 314
project documents
    activity duration estimates, 309
    communication planning, 521
    communications management, 527, 530
    communications monitoring, 531
    controlling resources, 489
    cost budgeting, 371
    estimating activity resources, 474
    managing project team, 485
    managing stakeholder engagement, 688
    monitoring stakeholder engagement, 691
    preparing for risk monitoring, 595
    preparing for stakeholder identification, 679
    procurement planning, 628
    project resources, 476
    project scope statement, 243
    quality management planning, 417
    resource planning, 464
    results of monitoring stakeholder
      engagement, 695
    risk identification, 567
    risk monitoring results, 597
    risk response planning, 584
    risk responses, 593–594
    schedule development, 310
    scope change control, 253
    scope control, 256
    scope definition, 242

    sequencing project work, 297–298
    stakeholder identification, 683
    stakeholder management plan, 684–685
project exclusions, scope statement, 243
project feasibility study
    examining project life cycle, 27–28
    exploring different life cycles, 28–29
    overview of, 27
    project life cycle in action, 31–32
    project life cycle vs. product life cycle, 31
    working through project life cycle, 29–31
project files, in cost estimating, 364
project float, defined, 315
project funding requirements, 373, 375
project governance, 70, 79
project initiation
    feasibility studies, 27
    processes to know for, 14
    reasons for, 13
    self test, 55
project knowledge management. *See* knowledge
   management
project launch, 154
project life cycle
    in action, 31–32
    adaptive life cycles, 28–29
    arranging WBS by, 249
    examining, 27
    hybrid life cycles, 29
    incremental life cycles, 28
    iterative life cycles, 28
    overview of, 25–26
    predictive life cycles, 28
    product life cycle vs., 31
    project feasibility study, 27
    project phase deliverables, 33–36
    self test, 56, 58
    tailoring integration management, 151
    walking through, 29–31
    working through, 26
project management
    closing, 16
    execution, 15
    initiation, 14

integration management trends, 151
monitoring and controlling, 15–16
overview of, 13–14
planning, 14–15
process group interactions, 16–18
software for creating project schedule, 322
tailoring project process, 18–19
project management in different environments
enterprise environmental factors, 64–66
leveraging organizational process assets, 66–67
organizational structures. *See* project completion in different organizational structures
organizational systems, 68–73
overview of, 63–64
review drill, 86–87
review summary, 82
review terms, 82–85
self test, 88–93
self test answers, 93–102
Project Management Information System. *See* PMIS (Project Management Information System)
project management, introduction
about PMP exam, 6–10
about this book, 5–6
Code of Ethics and Professional Conduct, 10
defining data/information for, 38–40
defining project management, 13–18
exploring related areas, 18–25
inside PMP exam, 37
PMBOK Guide, 4–5
project life cycle. *See* project life cycle
review drill, 45–48
review key terms, 41–45
review summary, 40–41
self test, 48–52
self test answers, 53–61
what projects are/are not, 10–13
project management office. *See* PMO (project management office)
project management plan
accounting for changes in, 189
acquiring project resources, 476
change management plan, 167

communication planning, 520–521
communications management, 527, 530
communications management plan, 168–169
communications monitoring, 531
conducting procurements, 641
configuration management plan, 167
controlling resources, 489, 490
cost budgeting, 371
cost estimating, 360–361
cost management plan, 168
cost planning, 358
estimating activity resources, 474
finalizing activity definition, 291
knowledge management results, 183
managing stakeholder engagement, 688
monitoring stakeholder engagement, 691
overview of, 163
PMIS, 166
preparing for stakeholder identification, 679
preparing to develop, 164–165
preparing to manage knowledge, 180
procurement management plan, 169
procurement planning, 628, 629
project baseline document, 170
project documents and files, 170–172
project team development, 480
project team management, 485
project work results, 188
purpose of, 164
quality management plan, 168, 417
requirements management plan, 167
resource management plan, 168
resource planning, 464
results of monitoring stakeholder engagement, 695
review summary, 199
risk management plan, 169
risk monitoring results, 598
risk response planning, 584
schedule development, 310
schedule management plan, 167–168, 283
scope control, 253, 256
scope definition, 242

project management plan *(cont.)*
scope management plan, 167, 230
scope validation, 251
self test, 94–95, 218–219, 223
stakeholder engagement plan, 169
stakeholder identification, 683
stakeholder management plan, 684
tools and techniques for developing, 165–166
Project Management Professional (PMP). *See* PMI Code of Ethics and Professional Conduct
project management, related areas
business value, 25
exploring, 19
portfolio management, 20–22
program management, 19–20
projects vs. operations, 23–24
subprojects, 22–23
project manager
cultural norm and, 72
estimating risk in project activity duration, 300
functional managers vs., 79
managing schedule changes, 326
organizational structures /authority of, 750–752
project charter defines, 155
project integration management led by, 149–150
project management plan development, 164, 166
self test, 39, 94–102
project manager, serving as
active problem-solving, 107–108
building competencies, 113–117
communicating project information, 105–106
cultural and industry influences, 112
inside PMP exam, 120
international influences, 112
leading project team, 105
learning/managing project, 118–121
levels of influence, 108–112
negotiating project terms/conditions, 107
organizational influences, 111
overview of, 103–104
performing project integration, 121–123
project outcome influences, 110
review answers, 135–144

review drill, 127–129
review key terms, 124–126
review summary, 123
role of, 104–105
self test, 129–134
social/economic/environmental influences, 111–112
project network diagram. *See* PND (project network diagram)
project-oriented organizational structure
exam facts, 752
overview of, 77
pros and cons of, 80
self test, 98–99, 101
project performance measurement. *See* performance measurement
project procurement management. *See* procurement management
project quality management. *See* quality management
project resilience, as risk factor, 558
project resource management. *See* resource management
project risk management. *See* risk management
project schedule management. *See* schedule management
project scope. *See* scope
project scope management. *See* scope management
project selection criteria, in project charter, 157–158
project sponsor, defined in project charter, 155
project stakeholder management. *See* stakeholder management
project team
charter, 172, 472–473, 480
cost estimating using members of, 364
developing, 480–484
estimating risk in project activity duration, 300
managing, 484–488
naturally developing, 482
preassigned, 478
preparing to manage knowledge, 180
project management plan development, 166
project manager influence on, 108
project manager leading, 105
recruiting members of, 477
resource plan defines roles of, 463
self test, 101, 141, 737, 740
virtual, 478–479

project team assignment
    developing project team, 480
    estimating activity durations, 299
    resource, 172
project timeline, creating project schedule, 313–314
project work, directing/managing
    change requests, 174–175
    corrective action, 174
    defect repair, 174
    executing project plan, 173–174
    outputs of project plan execution, 176–179
    preventive actions, 174
    review summary, 198
    tools/techniques for, 175–176
project work, monitoring/controlling
    creating work performance information, 184
    examining results of project work, 187–188
    experience needed to pass PMP exam, 9
    overview of, 183
    preparing for, 183–184
    project management processes for, 15–16
    reviewing final inputs for, 184–185
    tools and techniques, 185–187
project work, performance management, 38–39
prompt lists, risk identification, 570
proof-of-concept, project life-cycle, 31–32
proposals
    conducting procurements, 641
    contracting, 642–643
    procurement documents, 640
    procuring goods and services, 642
    selecting seller, 643–644
    seller selection process, 645
prototype
    project life cycle, 32
    requirements elicitation, 239
public communication, 526
public, PMP responsibility to, 722–724
pull-based scheduling approach, 281–282
pull communications, 525, 689
punitive or coercive power, 117
purchase orders (or unilateral contracts), 641, 666

pure risks
    defined, 557
    in PMP exam, 587, 756
    self test, 614
push communications, 525, 689, 715
PV (planned value)
    earned value management, 376
    finding schedule performance index, 378
    finding schedule variance, 377
    measuring project performance, 393
PV (present value)
    cost estimating using schedule, 361
    in discounted cash flow, 160–161
    formula for exam, 750
    self test, 403

Q

Q & A. *See* self test; self test answers
QA (quality assurance)
    managing quality, 422–426
    programs for quality management, 413
    quality management plan, 422
    self test, 449, 451
QC (quality control)
    applying trend analysis, 434–435
    completing statistical sampling, 434
    creating control chart, 430–432
    creating histogram, 432–433
    creating Pareto diagrams, 432
    creating run chart, 433
    creating scatter diagram, 434
    data representation tools, 428–430
    flowcharting, 434
    inspecting results, 427–428
    looking at big picture, 410–414
    managing project quality. *See* quality management
    overview of, 426
    preparing for, 427
    preparing to manage quality, 423
    project management plan, 171
    quality management plan, 421
    recommended defect repair, 188
    results of, 435–436
    self test, 451, 455

qualified seller lists, 641
qualitative, quantitative vs., 570
qualitative risk analysis
    adding probability and impact, 575
    building hierarchical chart, 577
    completing, 573–575
    creating probability-impact matrix, 575–577
    examining results of, 577–578
    overview of, 572
    preparing for, 572–573
quality
    defined, 416
    requirements elicitation process, 233
    vs. grade, 411
quality assurance. *See* QA (quality assurance)
quality control. *See* QC (quality control)
quality management
    accepting approach to, 410–411
    in agile environments, 413–414
    exam facts, 754
    exam facts to know, 754–755
    exam information for processes in, 749
    grade vs. quality, 411
    implementing, 412–413
    implementing quality control.
      See QC (quality control)
    as knowledge area, 17
    managing quality, 422–426
    overview of, 409–410
    planning for, 417–422
    preparing for, 414–417
    quality improvement, 412
    review drill, 440–441
    review key terms, 437–439
    review summary, 436–437
    self test, 442–447
    self test answers, 447–457
    tailoring quality, 413
quality management plan
    benchmarking practices, 418
    benefit/cost analysis, 419
    brainstorming and interviews, 419
    cost of quality, 420
    creating, 421–422

data representation tools, 421
identifying quality metrics, 422
inputs, 417–418
multicriteria decision analysis tools, 420
preparing for quality control, 427
preparing to manage quality, 423
in project management plan development, 168
quality improvement, 422
testing and inspection, 421
quality metrics, project management plan, 171
quality policies, 413, 415
quality report, project management plan, 171
quantitative, qualitative vs., 570
quantitative risk analysis
    examining results of, 583–584
    finding expected monetary value, 581
    inputs for, 579–580
    interviewing stakeholders/experts, 580–581
    overview of, 578–579
    preparing for, 578–579
    using decision tree, 582–583
    using project simulation, 583
    using sensitivity analysis, 581
questions. *See* self test
quotations
    examining results of contracting, 642–643
    procurement documents, 640

R

RACI charts, 465–466, 511, 547
RAG (red, amber, green) rating, risk score, 576–577
RAM (responsibility assignment matrix) chart, 465, 466–467
ranking, project stakeholders, 680
ranking risk
    building hierarchical chart, 577
    creating probability-impact matrix, 575–577
    for probability and impact, 575
    qualitative risk analysis, 573–575
    self test, 617
rating systems, seller selection process, 645, 672–673
RBS (risk breakdown structure), 563
readiness requirements, project scope requirements, 233

receiver, communication, 525

reconciliation, conflict resolution method, 486

records management, contract administration, 648, 650

recruitment, project team members, 477–478

referent power, 116, 138, 512

regression analysis, 196, 366

regulations

    as external enterprise environmental factors, 66

    planning for quality management, 417

    tailoring procurement, 626

relational power, 117

release, in schedule management plan, 284

reports

    communications management, 529

    monitoring stakeholder engagement, 694

    performance, 532–534, 648

    project management work performance, 39

    risk, 571, 578

    schedule management plan, 284

    self test, 717

representations of uncertainty, quantitative risk analysis, 581

request for information (RFI), 640

request for proposal (RFP), 640, 649

request for quote (RFQ), 640, 649

requirements

    communication planning by identifying, 522–523

    documentation, 172

    PMP exam, 7

    procurement documents, 640

    procurement planning using project, 630

    product scope based on, 227

    project charter identifying, 154

    project scope. *See also* scope management, requirements, 227–228

    traceability matrix, 172

requirements documentation

    in communication planning, 521

    as input to scope definition, 242

    as input to scope validation, 251

    updating for project scope statement, 244

requirements management plan

    in project management plan development, 167

    scope change control, 254

    scope management plan, 231

requirements traceability matrix (RTM)

    as input to scope validation, 251

    project management plan, 172

    project scope management, 240–241

    self test, 272

    updating for project scope statement, 244

research

    as external enterprise environmental factor, 66

    PMP acknowledges intellectual property of others, 721

    projects driven by, 11

reserve analysis, 368, 372

residual risks, 591, 757

resistant stakeholders, 686, 710

resource assignments, 172

resource breakdown structure

    charting project resources, 465

    estimating activity durations, 299

    estimating activity durations by creating, 302

    estimating activity resources by creating, 474

    project management plan, 172

resource calendar

    estimating activity durations, 299, 302

    project management plan, 172

    project schedule development, 325

    project team development, 480

    self test, 343

resource histograms, 471

resource leveling, 318–320, 351

resource management

    acquiring project resources, 475–479

    controlling resources, 487–491

    developing project team, 480–484

    estimating project activity resources, 473–475

    exam facts to know, 755

    exam information for processes in, 749

    exploring, 460–461

    inside PMP exam, 487

    as knowledge area, 17

    managing project team, 484–488

    overview of, 459–460

    resource planning. *See* resource planning

    review drill, 496–498

    review key terms, 492–495

    review summary, 491–492

resource management *(cont.)*
   self test, 498–503
   self test answers, 504–514
   trends in, 462
resource management plan
   as cost estimating input, 361
   creating, 471–472
   preparing. *See* resource planning
   in project management plan development, 168
   updating as result of controlling resources, 490
resource planning
   applying resource practices, 467
   charting project resources, 465–466
   completing organizational planning, 465
   creating resource management plan, 471–472
   creating team charter, 472–473
   identify requirements, 464
   preparing for, 463–464
   relating to organizational theories, 467
   relying on templates, 466–467
   role and responsibility assignments, 466
resource requirements
   creating project schedule by updating, 324
   estimating activity resources results in, 474
   identifying for resource planning, 464
   project management plan, 172
   quantitative risk analysis input, 580
   self test, 348, 504–505
resource smoothing, 320
resources
   estimating activity duration, 301–302, 306
   as internal enterprise environmental
     factors, 65
   leveraging organizational process assets, 66–67
   managing. *See* resource management
   managing knowledge, 180
   schedule management, 281
   working through project life cycle, 29
respect, 724
responsibility
   project management team, 463
   resource planning assignments, 466
responsibility assignment matrix (RAM) chart, 465,
  466–467

results
   communications management, 530
   conducting procurement, 645–646
   controlling resources, 490–491
   cost estimating, 369–370
   developing project schedule, 324–325
   examining contracting, 642–643
   examining team development, 484
   implementing risk responses, 594
   monitoring stakeholder engagement, 694–695
   performance reporting, 533
   procurement control, 651
   projects creating, 11
   qualitative risk analysis, 577–578
   quality control, 435–436
   quality management, 425–426
   quantitative risk analysis, 583–584
   risk monitoring, 597–598
   risk response planning, 590–591
   scope change control, 255–256
   stakeholder engagement, 690
   stakeholder identification, 682–683
return on investment (ROI), 359, 404
reverse resource allocation scheduling, 319
reverse shadowing, 181, 218
reward power, 117, 139
rewards
   project team, 483
   Vroom's Expectancy Theory on, 510–511
RFI (request for information), 640
RFP (request for proposal), 640, 649
RFQ (request for quote), 640, 649
rights, in stakeholder analysis, 680
risk analysis scoring, 563
risk appetite, risk tolerance vs., 559–560
risk breakdown structure (RBS), 563
risk categories, 563, 578
risk exposure, quantitative risk analysis, 583
risk identification
   brainstorming project, 567–568
   creating risk register, 570–571
   creating risk report, 571
   diagramming techniques for, 569–570
   overview of, 565

preparing for, 565–566
prompt lists for, 570
reviewing project documents, 567
self test, 615, 616
SWOT analysis, 569
testing assumptions, 567
through interviews, 568
using checklists, 568
risk management
exam facts to know, 587, 756–757
exam information for processes in, 749
identifying risks, 565–571
implementing risk responses, 593–594
as knowledge area, 17
monitoring risks, 594–598
overview of, 555–556
planning. *See* risk management plan;
    risk response planning
project risk considerations, 557–558
review drill, 602–604
review key terms, 598–602
review summary, 598
self test, 605–610
self test answers, 611–621
tailoring in projects, 558–559
understanding risk, 556–559
using qualitative risk analysis, 572–578
using quantitative risk analysis, 578–584
risk management plan
creating, 561, 611–612
examining, 562–563
implementing risk responses, 593
policies, 561
preparing for qualitative risk analysis, 572
preparing for risk monitoring, 595
in project management plan development, 169
quantitative risk analysis input, 579
risk categories, 564
risk monitoring by adding to, 596
stakeholder tolerance, 559–560
using template, 564–565
risk register
cost estimating, 363
creating, 570–571

creating schedule, 313
estimating activity durations, 300
project management plan, 172
qualitative risk analysis, 578
quantitative risk analysis, 580
self test, 614
risk report
creating, 571
project management plan, 172
qualitative risk analysis, 578
quantitative risk analysis, 580
risk response audits, 595
risk response, implementing, 593–594
risk response planning
accepting risk, 589
accounting for secondary risks, 591
avoiding negative risk and threats, 586
contracts for, 591–592
creating project contingency response, 589–590
justifying risk reduction, 592
managing positive risks/opportunities, 588–589
mitigating negative risk, 586–587
overview of, 584
preparing for, 584–585
residual risks, 591
results of, 590–591
risk management exam facts, 757
secondary risks, 591
self test, 613
transferring negative risk, 586
updating project plan, 592
using quantitative risk analysis results for, 584
risk score, probability-impact matrix, 576–577
risk tolerance, risk appetite vs., 559–560
risk triggers
risk management facts, 757
as warning signs, 571, 590, 613
risks
abundance of lead time and, 296
benefits management plan, 40
cost estimating, 369–370
estimating activity durations, 300
fast tracking increasing, 320–321
managing quality, 423

risks *(cont.)*
    mitigating with three-point duration estimates, 305–306
    product life cycle and, 30
    project assumptions as, 155
    project charter states known, 154
    self test, 55, 351
    as supporting detail for cost estimates, 371
ROI (return on investment), 359, 404
roles and responsibilities
    assignments in resource planning, 466
    change control system, 192
    mapping, 206
    project management team, 463
    project manager, 104–105
    resource management, 466
    risk management plan, 562
roles and responsibilities matrix, 507
rolling wave planning, 287–288
ROM (rough order of magnitude), cost estimates, 370
root cause analysis
    managing project quality, 423
    monitoring/controlling project work, 186
    project manager skill in problem solving, 107–108
    self test, 456
rough order of magnitude (ROM), cost estimates, 370
Rule of Seven, 432, 457
rules, PMP responsibility for, 720
run charts, quality control, 432

S

salience model, stakeholder influence, 682
Sapir-Whorf hypothesis, 722
scale of probability and impact, qualitative risk analysis, 573
scatter diagrams, project quality, 424, 433
schedule
    constraints, 271
    project management planning, 171–172
    project plan execution creating, 178–179
    risk management planning, 563

schedule baseline
    preparing for quality, 416
    project schedule control using, 325, 326
    project schedule development, 324–325
    as project schedule format, 323
    in quantitative risk analysis, 579
    showing project performance, 170
    updating as result of controlling resources, 490
    updating for approved changes, 189
schedule development
    in agile environments, 324
    applying duration compression, 320–321
    calculating float in PND, 315–317
    defining project timeline, 313–314
    evaluating project constraints, 311–312
    evaluating risk management register, 313
    examining activity attributes, 313
    examining project schedule, 323
    optimizing resource utilization, 318–320
    overview of, 310
    performing schedule network analysis, 314
    PMP exam and, 318
    project schedule as output of, 324
    reevaluating assumptions, 313
    relying on activity duration estimates, 311
    relying on project coding structure, 322
    reviewing results of, 324–325
    updating resource requirements, 324
    using project management software, 322
    using project network diagram, 310–311
    using project simulation, 321
    using schedule management plan, 324
schedule forecasts
    monitoring/controlling project work, 183, 188
    project management planning, 172
    in quantitative risk analysis, 580
schedule management
    activity duration estimates. *See* activity duration estimates
    activity sequencing. *See* activity sequencing
    in agile/adaptive environments, 281–282
    cost estimating using, 362–363
    creating schedule management plan, 283–285
    defining activities. *See* activity definition

exam facts to know, 309, 753
exam information for processes in, 749
as knowledge area, 17
overview of, 279–280
project schedule control, 325–328
review drill, 334–337
review key terms, 330–333
review summary, 329
schedule development process.
　　See schedule development
self test, 338–343
self test answers, 343–353
six processes of, 280
tailoring, 281
schedule management plan
　　in activity sequencing, 292
　　creating, 283–285
　　creating activity list, 286
　　creating project schedule via, 324
　　estimating activity durations, 299
　　in project management plan development,
　　　　167–168
schedule network analysis, 314
schedule network diagram, 171
schedule performance index. *See* SPI
　　(schedule performance index)
schedule resources, only when needed, 472
schedule variance. *See* SV (schedule variance)
scope
　　change requests in project plan execution, 178–179
　　constraints, 37, 200
　　exam facts, 753
　　product scope vs. project, 229–230
　　programs vs. portfolios, 57
　　project baseline document, 170
　　risk planning after changes to, 613
　　self test, 673, 736, 737
　　size of program vs. project, 20
　　as supporting detail for cost estimates, 370
　　updating baseline for approved changes, 189
scope baseline
　　in activity sequencing, 292
　　creating activity list, 286
　　defining in WBS, 249–250

estimating activity durations, 299
preparing for quality, 415–416
in procurement planning, 628
in quantitative risk analysis, 579
scope change control, 253
in scope validation, 251
scope control, 252–254, 275
scope management
　　controlling scope, 252–256
　　creating work breakdown structure, 246–250
　　definition of project scope, 241–245
　　exam facts to know, 752–753
　　exam information for processes in, 749
　　as knowledge area, 17
　　overview of, 225–227
　　planning, 228–232
　　review drill, 261–262
　　review key terms, 257–260
　　review summary, 257
　　self test, 263–268
　　self test answers, 269–278
　　self test for quality and, 453
　　tailoring, 227–228
　　validating scope, 250–252
scope management plan
　　creating, 230
　　overview of, 228–230
　　in project management plan, 167
　　in project scope management, 228–232
　　in schedule management plan, 283
　　in scope change control, 253–254
　　self test, 272
　　templates, 270
scope management, requirements
　　benchmarking requirements, 240
　　creating prototypes, 239
　　data analysis, 235
　　hosting requirements workshop, 238
　　interviewing stakeholders, 234
　　leading focus group, 234
　　making group decisions, 235–237
　　managing requirements, 240–241
　　observing stakeholders, 239–240
　　overview of, 232–233

scope management, requirements *(cont.)*
    surveys, 234–235
    using group decisions, 237–238
    utilizing context diagram, 238–239
scope statement, project
    defined, 171, 229
    defining project scope, 244–245
    exam facts, 753
    examining, 244
    preparing for quality, 415
    scope management plan, 231
    self test, 271, 277–278
scope validation
    overview of, 250–252
    in PMP exam, 245
    project scope exam facts, 753
    in project scope management, 228
    self test, 273, 276, 278
scoring models, benefit measurement, 159
scoring, risk analysis, 563
screening system, seller selection process, 644
secondary risks, 591, 757
self test
    procurement management, 658–663
    project communications management, 539–544
    project cost management, 394–399
    project management in different environments,
      88–93
    project management overview, 48–52
    project quality management, 442–447
    project resource management, 498–503
    project schedule management, 338–343
    project scope management, 263–268
    risk management, 605–610
    serving as project manager, 129–134
    stakeholder management, 700–706
    in this book, 6
self test answers
    procurement management, 664–673
    project communications management, 545–554
    project cost management, 400–408
    project management in different environments,
      93–102

project management overview, 53–61
project quality management, 447–457
project resource management, 504–514
project schedule management, 343–353
project scope management, 269–278
risk management, 611–621
serving as project manager, 135–144
stakeholder management, 706–718
sellers
    creating procurement documents, 640–641
    examining results of contracting, 642–643
    finding with qualified seller lists, 641
    fixed-price contracts transfer risk to, 633
    other names used for, 627
    selecting, 643
    selection criteria, 638
sender-receiver models, communication, 106, 524, 550
sensitivity
    planning communication technologies, 524
    in quantitative risk analysis, 581
servant leadership, 115–116, 119
SF (start-to-finish), PDM, 294
shared portal, dealing with team locales, 481
sharing risk, 588–589, 757
should-cost estimates, 639, 644
sigma values, control charts, 430–432
simple organizational structure. *See* organic (simple)
   organizational structure
simulation
    project schedule, 321
    quantitative risk analysis, 582–583
    self test, 621
situational power, 117, 141
Six Sigma, 412, 415
skills
    building project manager competencies, 113–116
    communication, 524–525, 529
    PMP honesty about their, 721
    project manager, 482–483
small group communication, 526
SMEs (subject matter experts), quantitative risk
   analysis, 580–581
smoothing, in conflict resolution, 486

SNET (start no earlier than), schedule time constraint, 312
SNLT (start no later than), schedule time constraint, 312
social influences, on projects, 111–112
social media, 526
soft logic
    defined, 329
    discretionary dependencies as, 295
    duration compression and, 320
    evaluating in project network diagram, 311
    self test, 347
software, scheduling, 321
solutions, project requirements, 233
source selection criteria
    completing seller selection process, 644–645
    conducting procurements, 643–645
    preparing for source selection, 643–644
    preparing to manage knowledge, 180
    purchase planning, 638
    selecting seller, 643
    self test, 669, 671–672
    using qualified seller lists, 641
SOW (statement of work) contract
    finding potential sellers, 649
    procurement documents, 640
    procurement exam facts, 757
    in procurement planning, 629
    self test, 668
    using, 636
SPI (schedule performance index)
    estimate at completion (EAC), 379–380
    finding, 378
    measuring performance, 393
    trend analysis monitoring, 435
spoken communications, 516
sponsors, project manager influencing, 109
sprints, in agile projects, 301, 324
SS (start-to-start), PDM, 293
stage gates, project phase completions, 35–36
stakeholder analysis
    defined, 697
    self test, 707
    for stakeholder engagement, 685–686

stakeholder identification, 680–681, 683, 707
    visualizing stakeholder influence, 681–682
stakeholder cube, 682
stakeholder engagement
    exam facts, 759
    managing, 687–690
    monitoring, 690–695
    self test, 712, 713, 714
    stakeholder analysis for, 685–686
stakeholder engagement matrix, 694
stakeholder management
    building strong foundation for, 676–678
    exam information for processes in, 749
    identifying project stakeholders, 678–683
    as knowledge area, 18
    managing stakeholder engagement, 687–690
    monitoring stakeholder engagement, 690–695
    overview of, 675–676
    planning, 683–687
    review drill, 698–700
    review key terms, 696–698
    review summary, 695–696
    self test, 700–706
    self test answers, 706–718
    tailoring processes for, 677–678
stakeholder management plan
    analyzing stakeholder engagement, 685–686
    building, 686–687
    organizing, 684–685
    overview of, 683–684
    in project management plan development, 169
    self test, 710, 711
stakeholder register
    in communication planning, 521
    overview of, 682–683
    in project management plan, 172
    self test, 709, 718
    updating for project scope statement, 244
stakeholder tolerance, 557, 559–560
stakeholders
    eliciting project requirements, 232, 234, 239–240
    in knowledge management, 180
    project charter listing, 154

stakeholders *(cont.)*
  project management plan development, 164
  project manager influence on, 108–109
  in quantitative risk analysis, 580–581
  resource planning using, 463
  self test, 61, 506
  tailoring communications for, 518
  tailoring project quality in organization, 412
Standard for Project Management, *PMBOK Guide*
  based on, 5
standards
  ISO 9000 project quality, 410–411
  PMP adherence to ethical, 721
  quality management, 417
start no earlier than (SNET), schedule time
  constraint, 312
start no later than (SNLT), schedule time constraint, 312
start-to-finish (SF), PDM, 294
start-to-start (SS), PDM, 293
statement of work. *See* SOW (statement of work) contract
statistical sampling, quality control, 434
steering committee, project manager influence on, 109
sticky notes, sequencing activities, 291
storming, in naturally developed project teams, 482
story points, agile projects, 324, 333, 347
storytelling, managing knowledge, 181
straight-line depreciation, 362, 406
strategic alignment, benefits management plan, 40
strong matrix organizational structure, 76–77, 80, 751
styles
  communication, 106
  leadership, 118–119
subject matter experts (SMEs), quantitative risk
  analysis, 580–581
subprojects, 22–23, 58
summary (hammock) activities, project network
  diagrams, 297
sunk costs
  evaluating if project should continue, 381
  project advancement and, 34
  self test, 60, 404
suppliers, project manager influence on, 109
supply chain management, procurement practices
  for projects, 625

supporting detail for cost estimates, 370–371
supportive PMO, 79
supportive stakeholders, 686, 710
surveys, project requirements, 234–237
SV (schedule variance)
  defined, 325
  examining, 327
  finding at end of project, 377
  measuring performance, 393
SWOT analysis, 569, 616–617
system dynamics, 69, 97
systems engineering, product analysis, 243

T

T&M (time and materials) contracts, 635, 637, 668
TAB (technical assessment board), 192
tacit knowledge, 180
tailoring project integration management, 151–152
Talent Triangle, PMI, 114–116
target benefits, benefits management plan, 40
TCPI (to-complete performance index), 380, 393
team. *See* project team
teaming agreements, procurement planning, 629
technical assessment board (TAB), 192
technical performance, 435, 596
technical review board (TRB), 192
technical risks, risk category, 564
techniques
  controlling resources, 489–490
  creating schedule management plan, 284
  implementing risk responses, 593
  integrated change control, 190–192
  managing project knowledge, 181–182
  monitoring communications, 532
  monitoring/controlling project work, 185
  project plan development, 165–166
  risk response, 585
  scope management plan, 230–231
technology, communication
  aligning stakeholder engagement with, 678
  management of, 528–529
  planning, 523–524
  tailoring, 518

TECOP, risk analysis, 570
templates
    activity definition for schedule management, 287
    asset. *See* organizational process assets
    network, 296
    resource planning, 466
    risk management plan, 564–565
    self test, 270
    standard project cost management plan, 357
    work breakdown structure, 247–248
temporary, projects as, 11–12, 54
termination of contracts, 648, 652
terms of reference (TOR), procurement planning, 629
test answers. *See* self test answers
test questions. *See* self test
The Standard for Project Management, 5
theory of constraints, 462, 508
Theory of Motivation, Herzberg, 468–469, 755
Theory of Needs, McClelland, 470, 755
Theory of X and Y, McGregor, 469, 507
third-party estimates, procured work, 639
this book, all about, 5–6
threats
    avoiding, 586
    negative risks as, 556
three-point estimates
    averaging project costs, 367–368
    estimating activity durations, 305–306
    formula to know for exam, 750
    PERT calculations similar to, 305
threshold, risk
    enterprise environmental factors, 585
    implementing risk responses, 593
    mitigating negative risk, 586
    risk appetite and, 560
    self test, 612, 620
    using risk management plan template, 564–565
time
    activity duration estimates with added reserve,
        307–308
    managing. *See* project schedule management
    quality and, 416
time and materials (T&M) contracts, 635, 637, 668
time and means contracts, 636

time-boxed iterations, agile projects, 324
time constraints
    all projects bound by, 37
    creating project schedule, 312
    project integration management, 199
time estimates, project deliverables in WBS, 248
timeline, benefits management plan, 40
to-complete performance index (TCPI), 380, 393
tolerances, quality management, 412
tools
    controlling resources, 489–490
    creating schedule management plan, 284
    developing project budget, 372–373
    implementing risk responses, 593
    integrated change control, 190–192
    managing project knowledge, 181–182
    monitoring communications, 532
    monitoring/controlling project work, 185
    procurement practices, 625–626
    procurement practices for projects, 625
    project management plan development, 165
    resource leveling using more efficient, 319
    risk response, 585
    scope management plan, 230–231
TOR (terms of reference), procurement planning, 629
total float, 315, 753
total productive maintenance, managing
    resources, 462
total quality management (TQM), 412, 415, 454
training
    managing project knowledge, 181
    project manager competencies, 113–116
    project team, 483
transactional leadership, 119, 141
transference of risk
    exam facts, 757
    negative risk, 586, 587
    during procurement management, 629
    procurement practices, 625
    self test, 619
transformational leadership, 119
transition requirements, scope requirements, 233
transparency, procurement practices, 625–626
TRB (technical review board), 192

trend analysis
 controlling resources, 489
 implementing quality control, 434
 monitoring/controlling project work, 186
 in qualitative risk analysis, 578
 reporting project performance, 533
trends
 managing resources, 462
 quantitative risk analysis, 584
Triple Constraints of Project Management, 37
truthfulness, of PMP, 722, 732

U

UCLs (upper control limits), control charts, 430–432
unanimity decision, project requirements, 237
unaware stakeholders, 686, 709
unilateral contracts (purchase orders), 641, 666
unit price contracts, 637
units of measure
 cost management plan, 358
 schedule management plan, 285
unknown-unknowns risks, project resilience, 558
upper control limits (UCLs), control charts, 430–432
upper-level management, portfolios, 20
urgency of information, planning communication, 523
user stories, agile projects
 estimating project work, 301
 planning schedule, 324
 requirements workshop, 238
 self test, 347
utility function
 defined, 560
 exam facts, 756
 self test, 612

V

VAC (variance at completion), 382
validation. *See* scope validation
value analysis, of products, 243

value engineering
 defined, 361
 product analysis, 243
 self test, 401
VAR (budget variance), 377
variability risks, as non-event based risks, 557
variable costs
 cost estimating, 361
 project cost exam facts, 754
 self test, 405
variance
 cost estimates, 371
 cost management plan, 358
 estimate to complete and, 381
 monitoring/controlling project work, 186
 project baseline documents, 170
 project budget, 377, 407
variance at completion (VAC), 382
vendors
 monitoring/controlling, 184–185
 outsourcing subprojects to, 22–23
 self test, 715
verification, project deliverables in WBS, 249
vertical communications, 106, 143
videoconferencing, and team locales, 481
virtual organizational structure
 exam facts, 752
 overview of, 77
 pros and cons, 80
virtual teams, 478–479
visual management tools, integration management, 150
VOC (voice of the customer), requirements, 238
voting
 estimating activity durations with fist-to-five, 307
 monitoring/controlling project work, 186
 on project changes, 193
Vroom's Expectancy Theory
 project resource exam facts, 755
 resource planning, 470
 self test, 511
VUCA, risk analysis, 570

W

warning signs, risk triggers as, 571, 590, 613
WBS dictionary
    contents of, 246–247
    preparing for quality, 415–416
    in procurement planning, 628
    scope baseline comprised of, 249–250
    scope control using, 253
    self test, 274
WBS (work breakdown structure)
    charting project resources, 465
    compiling activity list, 288–289
    decomposing project work packages, 287
    estimating activity durations, 303
    exam facts to know, 752
    exam questions and, 199
    planning components, 288
    procurement planning, 628
    quality planning, 415–416
    scope baseline document, 170
    scope management, 17, 246–250
    scope management plan, 231
    self test, 278, 400, 665
    templates, 247–248
weak matrix organizational structure
    exam facts, 751
    overview of, 76
    pros and cons, 80
webcams, procurement practices for projects, 625–626
weighted average, using PERT, 305
weighted scoring models, benefit measurement, 159
weighting system, seller selection process, 644
what-if analysis, project simulation, 321, 583
why-why charts. *See* Ishikawa diagrams
win-lose situation, conflict resolution, 514
withdrawal, in conflict resolution, 486
work breakdown structure. *See* WBS
    (work breakdown structure)
work performance data
    controlling resources, 489
    cost control input, 375
    examining project work, 177

    monitoring communications, 531
    monitoring stakeholder engagement, 691
    preparing for quality control, 427
    quality control, 427
    risk monitoring, 595
    self test, 60
    understanding, 38–39
    work performance information from, 184
    work performance reports from, 187
work performance information
    creating, 184
    creating work performance reports from, 187
    defined, 375
    examining project work, 177
    monitoring stakeholder engagement, 694
    risk monitoring, 597
    understanding, 39
work performance reports
    burnup/burndown charts for, 188
    communications management, 527
    creating from work performance information, 177
    managing project team, 485
    preparing for risk monitoring, 595
    project work results, 187
    understanding, 39
work, project
    acknowledging intellectual property of others, 721
    building quality into, 413
    estimating, 300–301
    inspecting, 251
    project plan execution, 177
    schedule control, 326
work shadowing, 181
workarounds, risk, 604
workshops
    defining project scope, 243
    hosting requirements, 238
written communications, 516

Y

yield-lose situation, withdrawing/avoiding as, 510